A Teacher's Guide
to **Including**
Students with
Disabilities in
General Physical Education
THIRD EDITION

A Teacher's Guide to **Including Students** with **Disabilities** in General Physical Education

THIRD EDITION

by

Martin E. Block, Ph.D.
University of Virginia
Charlottesville

with invited contributors

·P A U L·H·
BROOKES
PUBLISHING Co®

Baltimore • London • Sydney

Paul H. Brookes Publishing Co.
Post Office Box 10624
Baltimore, Maryland 21285-0624

www.brookespublishing.com

Typeset by Integrated Publishing Solutions, Grand Rapids, Michigan.
Manufactured in the United States of America by
Victor Graphics, Inc., Baltimore, Maryland.

The case studies in this book are fictionalized composites that are based on the authors' experience and do not represent the lives of specific individuals, and no implications should be inferred.

Library of Congress Cataloging-in-Publication Data

Block, Martin E., 1958–
A teacher's guide to including students with disabilities in general physical
education / by Martin E. Block.—3rd ed.
    p.   cm.
Includes bibliographical references and index.
ISBN-13: 978-1-55766-835-6 (pbk.)
ISBN-10: 1-55766-835-3 (pbk.)
1. Physical education for people with disabilities.   2. Mainstreaming in education.
I. Title.

GV445.B56 2006
371.9'04486—dc22   2006035051

British Library Cataloguing in Publication data are available from the British
Library.

Contents

About the Author

Martin E. Block, Ph.D., Associate Professor, Kinesiology Program, University of Virginia, 210 Emmet Street South, Box 400407, Charlottesville, Virginia 22904

Dr. Block has been the director of the master's program in adapted physical education (APE) at the University of Virginia since 1993. During that time he has supervised and graduated more than 60 master's students. Dr. Block has served as an APE specialist in Virginia, working with children with severe disabilities and learning and behavioral problems. Dr. Block has been a consultant to Special Olympics, Inc., helping to create the Motor Activities Training Program, a sports program for athletes with severe disabilities. He has authored or coauthored four books and more than 50 refereed articles, and he has conducted more than 100 international and national presentations on various topics in APE. Dr. Block has served as Chair of the Adapted Physical Activity Council and of the Motor Development Academy. He was named the Virginia College Professor of the Year in 2004.

About the Contributors

Phillip Conatser, Ph.D., CAPE, Assistant Professor, University of Texas at Brownsville, 80 Fort Brown, Brownsville, Texas 78520

For more than 20 years, Dr. Conatser has dedicated his work to the advancement of adapted aquatics through coaching, teaching, publications, presentations, research, and an international web site. His undergraduate, master's, and doctoral studies have focused on improving the health and wellness of individuals with disabilities. He is the 2006 recipient of the John Williams Jr. International Adapted Aquatics Award.

Steven Elliott, Ph.D., M.Ed., Assistant Professor, Department of Health and Applied Human Sciences, University of North Carolina Wilmington (UNCW), 601 South College Road, Wilmington, North Carolina 28403

Dr. Elliott is an Assistant Professor at the University of North Carolina at Wilmington. He taught elementary physical education for 3 years before completing his graduate studies in physical education pedagogy at the University of Virginia. Dr. Elliott was named the University of Virginia Curry School of Education Outstanding Doctoral Student in 2003 and received the Georgia Southern University Award for Teaching Excellence in 2005. Dr. Elliott enjoys most sports and is involved with the men's soccer team at UNCW as a volunteer assistant coach.

Ron French, Ed.D., Professor, Department of Kinesiology, Texas Woman's University (TWU), Post Office Box 425647, Denton, Texas 76204

Dr. French has spent the last 22 years at TWU and is Professor in the Department of Kinesiology. In 2005, he was recognized by TWU with the Cornaro Award for excellence in teaching, scholarship, and dedication to the University. This is also the most prestigious award TWU bestows upon faculty. He has also been honored as the Adapted Physical Activity Council Scholar. Dr. French is the Director of a U.S. Department of Education, Office of Special Education and Rehabilitative Services, training grant supporting the TWU master's degree program in adapted physical education. He has held this grant for the past 18 years. The current grant is for $1.3 million over a 5-year period.

Mel L. Horton, Ed.D., Unit Assessment Coordinator, Winthrop University, 111 Tillman, Rock Hill, South Carolina 29733

Dr. Horton completed her doctoral degree in adapted physical education at the University of Virginia in 2000. She is the Unit Assessment Coordinator for the Richard W. Riley College of Education at Winthrop University in Rock Hill, South Carolina. She also teaches part time in the Department of Health and Physical Education at Winthrop University.

Iva Obrusnikova, Ph.D., Assistant Professor, University of Delaware, Department of Health, Nutrition, and Exercise Sciences, 26 North College Avenue, Newark, Delaware 19716

Dr. Obrusnikova teaches adapted physical education and related courses to health and physical education teacher preparation majors. She received her doctoral and master's degrees in adapted physical activity from Palacky University, Olomouc, Czech Republic. Her current research interests include psychosocial variables in inclusive physical education.

Ana Palla-Kane, M.S., Faculty, Department of Kinesiology, California State University, Northridge, 18111 Nordhoff Street, Northridge, California 91330

Ms. Palla-Kane did her undergraduate studies at and received her master's degree in physical education from the State University of Sao Paulo in Brazil. She is currently completing her doctoral work in adapted physical education at the University of Virginia. Ms. Palla-Kane is also a lecturer in the Department of Kinesiology at California State University, Northridge. She teaches courses to graduate and undergraduate students in adapted physical education. Ms. Palla-Kane's research is directed at multicultural education and diversity issues in adapted physical education.

Lisa Silliman-French, Ph.D., CAPE, Assistant Professor, Texas Woman's University, Post Office Box 425647, Denton, Texas 76204

Dr. Silliman-French has taught adapted physical education (APE) for 17 years in the public schools in Texas and is an assistant professor at Texas Woman's University. She has authored chapters in two different APE texts: this book and *Adapted Physical Activity, Recreation, and Sport: Crossdisciplinary and Lifespan, Sixth Edition* (Sherrill, McGraw-Hill, 2004). She is the Texas State Adapted Physical Activity Committee Chair for the Texas Association for Health, Physical Education, Recreation, and Dance (TAHPERD), and received the TAHPERD Scholar award in December 2005. She was also the recipient of the International Federation of Adapted Physical Activity Elly D. Friedmann Young Professional Award in 2003. She enjoys traveling and protecting the environment and animals.

Amanda D. Stewart Stanec, Ph.D., Assistant Professor, St. Francis Xavier University, Department of Education, Post Office Box 5000, Antagonish, Nova Scotia, Canada B26 2W5

Dr. Stewart Stanec is Assistant Professor of Physical Education at St. Francis Xavier University and a recent graduate of The University of Virginia. Recently, Dr. Stewart Stanec was elected to represent Nova Scotia on the Board of Directors of the Canadian Association for Health, Physical Education, Recreation and Dance. A lover of the outdoors, she models an active lifestyle through triathlons, snowboarding, kayaking, running, and hiking with her husband, Jim.

Foreword

For more than 35 years, Special Olympics has been engaged in the work of promoting the skill and competitive spirit of people with intellectual disabilities. Started in 1968 with just more than 1,000 athletes in one event, it now spans 168 countries, and includes more than 2 million athletes competing in some 25,000 events annually. It has expanded in its impact, too, on all those who support the athletes—parents, coaches and volunteers—all those who come to believe that through these simple games, human acceptance can become the norm and fear of difference can be overcome.

At its simplest level, Special Olympics is an example of a movement dedicated to allowing people with intellectual disabilities to learn through the use of their bodies, to master physical skills, to develop relationships through physical activities, and to find the joy of competition and teamwork through physical competition. In each of these respects, Special Olympics subscribes to the rarely articulated belief that the body itself is a source of learning and that what one does with one's body can be a source of growth and development, joy and achievement. To see a Special Olympics athlete improve his or her time in an athletic sprint or score a goal in a team sport is to almost always see the body stretched, the body developed, the body joyful.

But in a larger sense, the activities that constitute physical education and sport develop more than the body; they promote opportunities for people who may not ordinarily meet to come together. They promote opportunities for people who might ordinarily not get the chance to learn from each other, to enter into a shared relationship of growth and joy. They create the opportunity through sport for whole communities to come together in celebration of the joy of achievement. For many of us, we can remember a moment in sport when we scored, when we won, when we achieved. But we can also remember who was around us, who cheered, who supported us, and the community which made it possible for us to wear the winner's ribbon.

For all of these reasons, it is clear that Dr. Martin E. Block's book is crucial for today's educators. At a very basic level, this book teaches methods for promoting opportunities for people with disabilities to learn and play in the classroom and on the playing fields with those who may not have such a diagnosis. But more importantly, it reminds us of a lesson too frequently overlooked—that people with intellectual disabilities are still too frequently left out. They are still too frequently the last ones picked. They are still too frequently the victims of name-calling. In recent years we have seen stronger and stronger data that point to the pain behind this picture: The fact that more than 60% of Americans do not want a child with intellectual disabilities educated in their child's school remains a stunning finding in part because it suggests so much ignorance and in part because it suggests so much sadness. The pain of exclusion and separation has been ignored for too long, and this book is an important step in reversing it.

At a practical level, the text serves to illustrate Dr. Block's passion for the basic premise that children, no matter what their disability, can be provided with the opportunity to be educated in an inclusive environment. In this new edition, every chapter in the book has been updated, but the focus remains the same as in previous editions—it offers a practical model for creating and implementing a program for children with physical and intellectual disabilities, and a general physical education program as well. While the first edition of the book was the first of its kind and focused solely on inclusion, the current edition helps the reader to understand not only why inclusion has become popular, but how to create a plan to use assessment data to make decisions regarding inclusion and then, in very practical ways, how to include students in the physical education program.

These practical solutions cover a range of ready-to-use strategies such as modifications to games and sports that are popular in general physical education, modifications to how material is presented to children with different types of disabilities, and finally very specific suggestions based on the exact diagnosis or disability type. In this book you will find guidelines on how to include a child in a wheelchair in basketball and how to include a child who is blind in golf. The book is always about making the teacher's life easy, practical, and successful.

New to Dr. Block's current edition are two key elements, both of which are particularly important today. First, there is a chapter devoted to multicultural issues in the physical education setting. This chapter (Chapter 14) focuses on issues such as dealing with parents and children who come from diverse religious cultural and ethnic backgrounds. It also offers an in-depth discussion of the issues raised by teaching children in poverty and children with limited English proficiency. Second, there is a new chapter (Chapter 13) on community-based instruction and recreation in which the focus is on assisting students in the transition from school-based physical education to community recreation. All too frequently children who develop their physical skills in school and develop relationships through sporting activities in school lose all of them when leaving the structure of an educational institution. Dr. Block has made it a priority to help teachers and school assist with step-by-step procedures for creating and implementing a transition plan to community-based recreation, including sports programs like Special Olympics.

It is clear from the research done by Special Olympics and other scholars that through sport, attitudes can change between people with and without intellectual disabilities. By having students with and without disabilities learning together, the right environment for attitude change is created. Special Olympics Unified Sports—a program that includes people with and without intellectual disabilities on the same team—has demonstrated that the best way to effect attitude change is through direct activities and direct experiences between young people. In 2003, we learned that through Unified Sports, 93% of Unified partners—those without intellectual disabilities—reported better understanding of individuals with intellectual disabilities, and nearly 100% reported getting along with their teammates, enjoying being with their teammates, and being willing to recommend Unified Sports to friends. By far, the social benefits derived through Unified Sports were more valuable than the physical or athletic outcomes.

As practical as this book is, it is also important—important not just for teachers and just for children, but also for whole communities and in fact for our country. To think beyond our limits and beyond our current practices is the challenge each of us faces as we try to find the way to make an impact in our communities and amongst our friends. Dr. Block invites us not just to think about how to exceed past expectations, but also how to abandon the fear of special education programs, how to abandon the concern about behavioral problems, and how to abandon the ignorance that so frequently creates a barrier between people who have not yet had a chance to understand one another.

Most important, this book is about abandoning the idea of disability as most people conceive it. Dr. Block in effect has written a book about ability, about the ability of each child to play, to learn to use his or her body for exercise, for recreation, for competition, and for joy. In this book there are many designations, many specific recommendations, and many types of disabling conditions discussed. But in reading it, the great joy is to realize that there are no real disabilities, but only different abilities. There are no conditions that limit possibility for any child. The limits of our capacity to include children with all forms of "difabilities" are only in the extent to which we can imagine a more inclusive and more accepting world.

Timothy P. Shriver, Ph.D.
Chairman of the Board
Special Olympics

Acknowledgments

I would like to thank several people for their assistance in the development and completion of this third edition. First, I would like to thank my family—my wife Vickie and my two daughters, Samantha and Jessica. Playing tennis, going for a walk, or catching a movie with Vickie; watching Sam play volleyball or watching a football or basketball game with her; and coaching Jessie in soccer or volleyball are more special to me than you will ever know.

I would like to give a special thanks to all of my coauthors. This third edition has more coauthored chapters than any of the previous editions, and it is a much stronger book because of your contributions. Ron French and Lisa Silliman-French from Texas Woman's University again did a wonderful job with the chapter on dealing with children with behavior challenges. Even more gratifying to me is that all of the other coauthors of this third edition are former doctoral students who are emerging into the next generation of leaders in pedagogy and adapted physical education.

I would like to thank the staff at Paul H. Brookes Publishing Co. for guiding me through the process of completing this third edition. Acquisitions Editor Rebecca Lazo assisted and encouraged me through the first phase of this project, including reviewing my outline and giving me feedback on proposed additions and the first drafts of several chapters. Associate Editor Steve Peterson guided me through the middle part of this project by making sure I received feedback on each chapter. And, finally, Editorial Supervisor Mika Smith did a wonderful job of carefully checking to make sure I addressed the final details in the proofs, tables, and permissions needed to complete the book. Thank you all for your time and effort.

I would like to thank all my master's degree students who provided physical education to students with disabilities during their internships while attending the University of Virginia. Observing you teach children with disabilities led to many of the suggestions provided in this book. While you may have thought I was teaching you when I came to supervise you, in many cases you were teaching me by demonstrating unique teaching techniques, motivating lesson plans, and how to get along with others in the school. I am so pleased that most of you continue to teach general or adapted physical education in public schools across the United States.

Finally, thanks to all of the children with and without disabilities, physical education teachers, special education teachers, therapists, and parents whom I have interacted with over the past several years. I have learned so much from these interactions, and you have truly been my best teachers. I look forward to more interactions and conversations in the future.

Previous editions of my book were dedicated to my mother who worked with children who were blind for many, many years. She passed away in 1992, but I still think of her and am inspired by her every day. This edition of my book is dedicated to my father, who recently celebrated his 90th birthday. His continued love of learning, his wonderful sense of humor, and his unconditional support for me throughout my life has in large part made me the person I am today.

CHAPTER 1

What Is Physical Education?

by Martin E. Block, Steven Elliot, and Amanda D. Stewart Stanec

Jade is a bouncy 9-year-old third grader who loves her school, loves her friends, and loves her teacher! She cannot wait to go to school every day. But unlike her classmates, getting to school is not easy for Jade. Jade has spina bifida, which requires her to use a walker for mobility. Jade attends Ray Charles Elementary School where she participates in general physical education twice a week with Mr. Newman, a general physical education teacher; there is no adapted physical education specialist in this school district.

Jade and all of the other children at Ray Charles Elementary love physical education with Mr. Newman for a number of reasons. First, Jade and her classmates always know ahead of time what they will be doing because Mr. Newman sends home a monthly list of units or themes as well as an outline of how each day's activities fit into the theme. Some themes revolve around learning multiple skills and concepts related to a specific topic such as dancing, gymnastics, physical fitness, or a sport. Other themes focus on learning one specific skill such as the overhand throw or jumping rope. Each theme lasts 2–4 weeks depending on the number of skills within a theme and the skill level of the children. Several themes are revisited two and even three times during the year; these include physical fitness (which is a districtwide priority) and themes with skills that are difficult to master (e.g., overhand throw). Students are encouraged to practice skills at home as well. This thematic approach to teaching allows Mr. Newman to help his students—regardless of their individual ability level—focus on, improve, and eventually master specific skills within a theme.

Second, Mr. Newman makes sure each child knows exactly what to work on and how to work on it. Rather than holding all children to the same standard, Mr. Newman gives each child individual goals within each skill or concept based on his or her ability. For example, in an underhand toss unit, some children worked on their follow-through, some worked on fully extending their arm back, and others who had mastered all of the components of the underhand toss worked on tossing for distance and accuracy. Jade concentrated on performing the underhand toss while standing in her walker, using a special throwing pattern that she and Mr. Newman created especially for her.

Third, Mr. Newman provides a lot of choices of activities and equipment during practice and games. For example, in his volleyball serve unit for fifth graders, students can choose to serve into a suspended parachute, over a large refrigerator box, into a curtain on the stage, and against the wall. In addition, children are allowed to choose what type of ball to serve (e.g., regulation volleyball, volleyball trainer, beach ball) as well as how far away to stand from the target. This gives each student a chance to be successful and challenged at his or her own level.

Fourth, Mr. Newman always finds a way to make sure all of his students are active and engaged in fun activities. You would never see students in Mr. Newman's class standing around and waiting for their turn. Rather, each student has his or her own piece of equipment (unless involved in partner or group work), and the gymnasium is set up so that there is lots of space for everyone to move at the same time in a safe manner. Also, Mr. Newman plays games that reinforce a particular skill theme. He never plays traditional sports following regulation rules, which result in a lot of students standing around and not getting many turns. He also does not play elimination games in which students have to sit out for extended periods. Instead, students play tag games while practicing dribbling, keep-away games to reinforce passing and trapping, and a two-person relay race to practice dribbling and shooting towards a goal in a third-grade soccer unit. Jade often got tagged during the dribble tag games, but all she had to do was reach down and touch her toes three times to get back into the game. She never had to sit out.

Fifth, Mr. Newman uses a variety of teaching styles to keep the students interested, to encourage active learning and cognitive development, and to promote interaction with peers. For example, during a fitness theme Mr. Newman had students do cooperative sit-ups. Students were placed into groups of four and were told to determine how many sit-ups they could do as a team. Some students did regular, bent-knee sit-ups;

others did simple curl-ups. (Jade actually has very strong abdominal muscles, so she did regular sit-ups.) Each group earned a total score, and cooperative teams worked to beat their previous day's scores. Mr. Newman often uses cooperative learning as well as reciprocal teaching (i.e., peer tutoring), child-designed activities, task sheets, and guided discovery.

What type of physical education program do you conduct? Is it like Mr. Newman's: a carefully planned, comprehensive program that is designed to meet each student's needs? Do you make an effort to teach your students skills and concepts? Do your students receive lots of practice opportunities in activities in which they can be successful, regardless of individual ability levels?

Before you can provide an appropriate program for students with disabilities who are included in your general physical education class, you must develop a quality general physical education program. The purpose of this chapter is to review the basics of quality physical education. This chapter also provides information about the legal basis for physical education services as outlined in the Individuals with Disabilities Education Act (IDEA) and the most recent reauthorization of this act—the Individuals with Disabilities Education Improvement Act of 2004 (PL 108-446). Finally, a discussion of developmentally appropriate practices in physical education and a definition of adapted physical education are provided.

WHAT IS QUALITY PHYSICAL EDUCATION?

A careful examination of Mr. Newman's program reveals that he has structured his curriculum and teaching practices around the national standards for physical education provided by the National Association for Sport and Physical Education (NASPE; 2004). In 1986, NASPE's first attempt to answer the question, "What should physically educated students know and be able to do?" culminated in a definition of a physically educated person that included five major focus areas. The Council on Physical Education for Children, an entity within NASPE, updated this definition as follows. A physically educated student

1. HAS learned the skills necessary to perform a variety of physical activities

2. DOES participate regularly in physical activity

3. IS physically fit

4. KNOWS the implications of and the benefits from involvement in physical activities

5. VALUES physical activity and its contributions to a healthful lifestyle (NASPE, 1992, p. 3)

This definition was applied to selected grade levels through 20 outcome statements with sample benchmarks and published in the *Outcomes of Quality Physical Education Programs* document (NASPE, 1992). This was followed by the release of the landmark document *Moving into the Future: National Standards for Physical Education* (NASPE, 1995), which included assessment guidelines designed to complement the 1992 outcome statements and benchmarks. A second edition of *Moving into the Future: National Standards for Physical Education* was released in 2004 and has been recognized as an essential tool for developing, implementing, and evaluating kindergarten through twelfth-grade school physical education programs. The national standards clearly identify what students should know and be able to do as a result of a quality physical education program (see Table 1.1). The six national content standards are as follows (NASPE, 2004):

1. Demonstrates competency in motor skills and movement patterns needed to perform a variety of physical activities

2. Demonstrates understanding of movement concepts, principles, strategies, and tactics as they apply to the learning and performance of physical activities

3. Participates regularly in physical activity

4. Achieves and maintains a health-enhancing level of physical fitness

5. Exhibits responsible personal and social behavior that respects self and others in physical activity settings

6. Values physical activity for health, enjoyment, challenge, self-expressions and/or social interaction

The revised standards group grade levels into ranges (i.e., K–2, 3–5, 6–8, 9–12). For each of the six standards, student expectations are stated along with sample performance outcomes. The student expectations statements reflect what students should know and be able to do at the end of each range. The sample performance outcomes provide examples of student behavior that demonstrates progress toward achieving the standard (NASPE, 2004).

According to NASPE, the overall goal of physical education is to "develop physically educated individuals who have the knowledge, skills, and confidence to enjoy a lifetime of healthful physical activity" (2004, p. 11). Mr. Newman and other effective physical educators are meeting this goal by

Table 1.1. National Association for Sport and Physical Education (NASPE) definition of a physically educated person

The Physically Educated Person:

HAS learned the skills necessary to perform a variety of physical activities

1. . . . moves using concepts of body awareness, space awareness, effort and relationship.
2. . . . demonstrates competence in a variety of manipulative, locomotor and non-locomotor skills.
3. . . . demonstrates competence in combinations of manipulative, locomotor and non-locomotor skills performed individually and with others.
4. . . . demonstrates competence in many different forms of physical activity.
5. . . . demonstrates proficiency in a few forms of physical activity.
6. . . . has learned how to learn new skills.

IS physically fit

7. . . . assesses, achieves and maintains physical fitness.
8. . . . designs safe, personal fitness programs in accordance with principles of training and conditioning.

DOES participate regularly in physical activity

9. . . . participates in health enhancing physical activity at least three times a week.
10. . . . selects and regularly participates in lifetime physical activities.

KNOWS the implications of and the benefits from involvement in physical activities

11. . . . identifies the benefits, costs and obligations associated with regular participation in physical activity.
12. . . . recognizes the risk and safety factors associated with regular participation in physical activity.
13. . . . applies concepts and principles to the development of motor skills.
14. . . . understands that wellness involves more than being physically fit.
15. . . . knows the rules, strategies and appropriate behaviors for selected physical activities.
16. . . . recognizes that participation in physical activity can lead to multi-cultural and international understanding.
17. . . . understands that physical activity provides the opportunity for enjoyment, self-expression and communication.

VALUES physical activity and its contributions to a healthful lifestyle

18. . . . appreciates the relationships with others that result from participation in physical activity.
19. . . . respects the role that regular physical activity plays in the pursuit of life-long health and well-being.
20. . . . cherishes the feelings that result from regular participation in physical activity.

Reprinted from *Moving into the Future: National Standards for Physical Education*, Second Edition (2004), with permission from the National Association for Sport and Physical Education (NASPE), 1900 Association Drive, Reston, VA 20191, USA.

employing various teaching strategies to promote student learning in physical education, including

1. Providing all students with the opportunity to learn by ensuring that all students are kept active

2. Teaching meaningful content aligned with state/national standards for physical education

3. Delivering appropriate instruction and providing students with a variety of activities that can be individualized to each student's ability level

Pangrazi identified and described eight components of a quality physical education program (2007):

1. A quality physical education program is organized around content standards that offer direction and continuity to instruction and evaluation.

2. A quality program is centered on the developmental urges, characteristics, and interests of students.

3. Quality physical education makes physical activity and motor-skill development the core of the program.

4. Physical education programs teach management skills and self-discipline.

5. Quality programs emphasize inclusion of all students.

6. In a quality physical education setting, instruction is focused on the process of learning skills rather than on the product or outcome of the skill performance.

7. A quality physical education program teaches lifetime activities that students can use to promote their health and personal wellness.

8. Quality physical education teaches cooperation and responsibility and helps students develop sensitivity to diversity and gender issues.

Benefits of Quality Physical Education

Quality physical education leads to a physically educated person. In turn, a physically educated person derives the following benefits as noted by the Surgeon General's Report (U.S. Department of Health and Human Services, 1996):

- Significant health benefits can be obtained by including a moderate amount of physical activity (e.g., 30 minutes of brisk walking or raking leaves, 15 minutes of running, 45 minutes of volleyball) on most, if not all, days of the week. Through a modest increase in daily activity, most Americans can improve their health and quality of life. (p. 4)

- Additional health benefits can be gained through greater amounts of physical activity. People who can maintain a regular regimen of activity that is of longer duration or more vigorous intensity are likely to derive greater benefit. (p. 4)

- Physical activity reduces the risk of premature mortality in general, and of coronary heart disease, hypertension, colon cancer, and diabetes mellitus in particular. Physical activity also improves mental health and is important for the health of muscles, bones, and joints. (p. 4)

- Consistent influences on physical activity patterns among adults and young people include confidence in one's ability to engage in regular physical activity (e.g., self-efficacy), enjoyment of physical activity, support from others, positive beliefs concerning the benefits of physical activity, and lack of perceived barriers to physical activity. (p. 249)

- Physical activity appears to improve health-related quality of life by enhancing psychological well-being and by improving physical functioning in persons compromised by poor health. (p. 8)

Additional benefits of *quality* physical education programs include the development of a variety of motor skills and abilities related to lifetime leisure skills; improved understanding of the importance of maintaining a healthy lifestyle throughout life; improved understanding and appreciation of the human body and how it can move; improved knowledge of rules, strategies, and behaviors of particular games and sports; and improved self-confidence and self-worth as they relate to physical education and recre-

ation activities (Graham, Holt-Hale, & Parker, 2004; NASPE, 2004; Sherrill, 2004).

These benefits of physical education are just as important for students with disabilities. Most individuals with disabilities have limited recreation skills, which greatly restrict their abilities to participate in community activities and interact with peers who do not have disabilities. Extra free time coupled with limited recreation skills often leads to a sedentary lifestyle, which in turn can lead to health and social problems (Schleien, Ray, & Green, 1997). Quality physical education programs can help students with disabilities acquire critical lifetime leisure skills, including an appreciation for continued participation in active recreational pursuits.

Legal Definition of Physical Education

The amount of physical education that a child without special needs receives varies between states, school districts, and sometimes schools within the same school district. There are no federal laws that mandate that physical education should be taught in public schools to children without disabilities (Siedentop, 2004). Typically, minimal standards for physical education requirements are set at the state level ("Latest Shape of the Nation," 2001), with each school district given the opportunity to interpret the state standards for their schools. State and school districts, however, are responsible for providing physical education to students with special needs.

In fact, physical education services, specially designed if necessary, must be made available to *every* child with a disability receiving a free appropriate public education (Block & Burke, 1999). Physical education has been required since the enactment of the Education for Handicapped Children Act of 1975 (PL 94-142). It has remained an essential part of special education services through its many reauthorizations (see Table 1.2 for a brief chronology). In fact, physical education is the only curricular area that lawmakers placed in the definition of special education:

(25) The term *special education* means specially designed instruction, at no cost to parents, to meet unique needs of a child with a disability including —
(A) instruction conducted in the classroom, in the home, in hospitals and institutions, and in other settings; and
(B) instruction in *physical education* [emphasis added]. (IDEA Amendments of 1997, PL 105-17, 20 U.S.C. §1401[25])

Unfortunately, many parents, professionals, and administrators are unfamiliar with the physical education requirements in the law, and students with disabilities continue to be excluded from physical education or to receive inappropriate physical education services (Chandler & Greene, 1995; Jansma & Decker, 1992). This is exactly what lawmakers feared would happen when they placed the following comments into the rules and regulations of the original law:

> Special education as set forth in the Committee bill includes instruction in physical education, which is provided as a matter of course to all non-handicapped children enrolled in public elementary and secondary schools. The Committee is concerned that although these services are available to and required of all children in our school systems, they are often viewed as a luxury for handicapped children. . . . The Committee . . . specifically included physical education in the definition of special education to make clear that the Committee expects such services, specially designed where necessary, to be provided as an integral part of the education program of every handicapped child. (Federal Register, August 23, 1977, p. 42489)

The regulations for IDEA and its reauthorizations define physical education services as follows:

> (a) *General.* Physical education services, specifically designed if necessary, must be made available to every child with a disability receiving FAPE ("Assistance to States," 2006, §300.307 [a]).

This statement reinforces the notion that all children with disabilities must receive some form of physical education. Many school districts have placed physical education on their individualized education program (IEP) forms (basically a place to check general or adapted physical education) to make it clear that each child must receive some form of physical education services. IDEA regulations state,

> (b) *Regular physical education.* Each child with a disability must be afforded the opportunity to participate in the regular physical education program available to typically-developing children unless:
> (1) the child is enrolled full time in a separate facility; or
> (2) the child needs specially designed physical education, as prescribed in the child's individualized education program. ("Assistance to States," 2006, §300.307 [b])

This statement suggests that many children with disabilities can receive a safe, successful, and meaningful physical education experience in general and do not need any special goals or objectives on their IEP (Bateman, 1998–2000). However, some children might need some modifications to the curriculum, equipment, and/or instruction to be successful in general physical education. These subtle modifications might include an interpreter for a child who is deaf, a beep ball for a child who is blind, a peer tutor for a child with an intellectual disability, or a teacher assistant for a child who has autism. These individually determined accommodations need to be noted

Table 1.2. Chronology of the Individuals with Disabilities Education Act (IDEA)

Act/year	Description
Education for All Handicapped Children Act (EHC) of 1975 (PL 94-142)	Landmark legislation that provided free appropriate public education, including physical education, for all eligible children ages 3–21. EHC was reauthorized by PL 101-476 and PL 105-17.
Education of the Handicapped Act (EHA) Amendments of 1983 (PL 98-189)	Increased funding and provided *incentives* for states to develop and implement an early intervention system to serve children with disabilities from birth to 5. States were not mandated to provide services to children birth to age 3 at this point.
EHA Amendments of 1986 (PL 99-457)	*Required* states to provide services to eligible preschoolers ages 3–5 years or lose some federal funding. Part H of PL 99-457 (now referred to Part C of IDEA) commissioned funds to states to develop and implement a comprehensive, multidisciplinary, interagency program of early intervention services for infants and toddlers with disabilities (birth to age 3) and their families.
Individuals with Disabilities Education Act (IDEA) of 1990 (PL 101-476)	All references to *handicapped* are replaced with the term *disability*. Major changes include new definitions of attention-deficit/hyperactivity disorder and traumatic brain injury and the creation of an eligibility category for autism. Emphasized the least restrictive environment (LRE), with a focus on training general education personnel and the use of assistive technology. Added the term *transition services,* which emphasized a coordinated effort to help students ages 16 and older (14 for students with severe disabilities) acquire the skills needed to move from school to postschool activities, including social services, recreation therapy, and rehabilitation counseling.
IDEA Amendments of 1997 (PL 105-17)	Greater focus on parental rights and participation in planning process, on LRE, and on justification of placement in settings other than general education. Required general educator to participate in all IEP meetings
Individuals with Disabilities Education Improvement Act (IDEA) of 2004 (PL 108-446)	Aligned with the No Child Left Behind Act of 2001 (PL 107-110), reinforcing the need for highly qualified special education teachers and inclusion of children with disabilities in statewide assessment

on the child's IEP (Bateman, 1998–2000; Block & Burke, 1999).[1]

(c) *Special physical education.* If specially designed physical education is prescribed in a child's individualized education program, the public agency responsible for the education of that child shall provide the services directly, or make arrangements for it to be provided through other public or private programs. ("Assistance to States," 2006, §300.307 [c])

If through assessment it is determined that a child with a disability needs special physical education, then individual goals and objectives for physical education should be created by the child's IEP team and placed in the child's IEP (Bateman, 1998–2000; Block & Burke, 1999). For example, a 10-year-old child with cerebral palsy needs to learn how to walk using a special gait trainer. Because this is a unique goal for this child (i.e., does not match what other 10-year-olds are doing in physical education), this goal and incremental short-term objectives should be written into this child's IEP.

It is important to note that qualifying for special physical education and having IEP objectives for physical education does not necessarily mean that the child will be pulled out into a separate adapted physical education program. Many children with disabilities can work on their unique IEP goals and objectives within the general physical education setting. For example, a 10-year-old with cerebral palsy can practice walking in his gait trainer while the other children are running laps during warm-up, playing tagging and fleeing games, and playing games that require running such as basketball and soccer. The child might need a peer or an assistant for safety, but he should be able to work on his unique goals while having an opportunity to interact with peers without disabilities.

(d) *Education in separate facilities.* The public agency responsible for the education of a handicapped child who is enrolled in a separate facility shall insure that the child receives appropriate physical education services in compliance with paragraphs (a) and (c) of this section. (Federal Register, August 23, 1977, p. 42489)

This means that a child with a disability who is educated in a separate facility such as a school for the deaf must still receive physical education services, specially designed if necessary (Bateman, 1998–2000). Clearly, lawmakers define physical education as an important, *direct service* that should be a part of every student's educational program.

All students should receive physical education services, whereas only those students who need extra support to benefit require related services (including physical, occupational, or recreation therapy). Related services *cannot* be considered a substitute for the physical education requirement, nor can recess, unstructured free time, or training in sedentary recreation activities (e.g., board games, card games) (Block & Burke, 1999; Sherrill, 2004).

Components of Physical Education

Although it is clear that physical education should be viewed as an important part of a student's overall education program, what exactly is physical education? Physical education is further defined in PL 94-142 and IDEA and its amendments as

The development of physical and motor fitness, fundamental motor skills and patterns, and skills in aquatics, dance, and individual and group games and sports (including intramural and lifetime sports). The term includes special physical education, adapted physical education, movement education, and motor development. (Federal Register, August 23, 1977, p. 42480)

The following sections provide a detailed examination of each component contained within this definition.

Physical and Motor Fitness

Physical and motor fitness refers to development of both health- and skill-related fitness. Health-related fitness focuses on factors pertaining to a healthy lifestyle and the prevention of disease related to a sedentary lifestyle (Graham, Holt-Hale, & Parker, 2004; Pangrazi, 2007). Pangrazi (2007) and Winnick (2000a) provided the following definitions of the specific components of health-related fitness:

- *Cardiovascular endurance* (aerobic endurance): ability of the heart, blood vessels, and the respiratory system to deliver oxygen efficiently over an extended period of time. Moving (e.g., riding a bike, walking, jogging) without stopping for extended periods of time retains or increases cardiovascular efficiency.

- *Body composition:* the division of total body weight into two components: fat weight and lean weight. It basically is a measure of the amount of body fat a person carries. A fit person has a relatively low percentage of body fat. Performing aerobic and strength activities as well as following a reasonable diet will help retain or decrease percentage of body fat.

- *Flexibility:* the ability to move the musculature (i.e., muscles, tendons, and ligaments) through their full range of motion. Flexibility is joint spe-

---

[1]In this book, the terms *accommodations* and *modifications* are used interchangeably.

cific, so it must be measured and stretched at several joints. Stretching activities help musculature retain or increase elasticity.

- *Muscular strength:* the ability of muscles to exert force (e.g., to lift heavy objects). Lifting weights or other objects that are heavier than what one lifts in activities of daily living increases muscular strength.

- *Muscular endurance:* the ability of muscles to exert force over an extended period of time. Lifting weight or heavy objects repeatedly retains or increases muscular endurance.

Skill-Related Fitness

Skill-related fitness refers to specific fitness components associated with successful performance in specific motor activities and sports (Graham et al., 2004; Pangrazi, 2007). Hastad and Lacky (1998) and Pangrazi (2007) provided the following definitions of the specific components of skill-related fitness:

- *Agility:* ability to rapidly and accurately change the position of the body in space. Quickly changing positions in wrestling or avoiding a tackler in football are examples of agility.

- *Balance:* the maintenance of equilibrium while stationary (static balance) or moving (dynamic balance). Performing a head stand or maintaining balance while swinging a golf club are examples of static balance, and walking a balance beam or running in a football game without falling are examples of dynamic balance.

- *Coordination:* the ability to simultaneously perform multiple motor tasks smoothly and accurately. Hitting a tennis ball, using a smooth throwing pattern when pitching a ball, or dribbling a soccer ball are examples of athletic skills that require coordination.

- *Power:* the ability to transfer energy explosively into force. Examples of skills that require power include the standing long jump, the shot put, and kicking a soccer ball.

- *Speed:* the ability to perform a movement in a short period of time. A batter running to first base or a basketball player dribbling a ball quickly down the court are examples of activities that require speed.

- *Reaction time:* difference between the stimulation (seeing, hearing, feeling something) and the response (moving) to the stimulation. A sprinter's response to the starting gun or a racquetball player's reaction to a hard-hit ball are examples of activities that require short reaction time.

Fundamental Motor Skills and Patterns

Fundamental motor skills and patterns refer to the development of basic motor skills that form the foundation for more advanced, specific movements used in individual and team sports and activities (Gabbard, 2004; Gallahue & Ozmun, 2006; Graham et al., 2004; Pangrazi, 2007). Each fundamental motor skill has a distinct pattern or structure that defines the movement. Fundamental movement patterns are usually divided into locomotor and manipulative patterns. Locomotor patterns are movements used by individuals to travel from one place to another; manipulative patterns are used to propel balls away from the body or receive balls. Table 1.3 provides more detailed description of the most common fundamental locomotor and manipulative patterns as described by Graham et al. (2004) and Gallahue and Ozmun (2006).

Aquatics

Aquatics refers to activities conducted in the water, including swimming, which involves moving independently in the water using various strokes; water exercises, which work on the development of health-related fitness; and hydrotherapy, which involves using the water environment to work on specific therapeutic goals such as walking, relaxing, and maintaining/increasing range of motion (Lepore, 2000; Lepore, Gayle, & Stevens, 1998).

Rhythm and Dance

Rhythm and dance refer to the ability to repeat an action or movement with regularity and in time to a particular pattern (Kirchner & Fishburne, 1998). Rhythm involves three major components: tempo (speed), pattern (even or uneven beats), and accent (emphasis) (Kirchner & Fishburne, 1998). Dance is a combination of movement and rhythm in which movement qualities, movement components, and rhythmic movements are purposefully integrated into a progression with a beginning, middle, and end (Kowalski, 2000). Dance can include anything from basic rhythmic activities and action songs for young children to traditional dances (e.g., ballroom, folk, square), aerobic dances, and modern dances (creative dance) for older children and adults (Graham et al., 2004; Kowalski, 2000).

Individual Sports

Individual sports include culturally popular sports that involve one player or teams of no more than two players. Popular individual sports in the United States are listed in Table 1.4. Activities within each sport can include working on skills, playing lead-up (simpler or modified forms of traditional sports that help children acquire game skills and concepts),

Table 1.3. Description of fundamental locomotor and manipulative patterns

Walking	Standing upright with eyes forward, swing one leg forward while swinging the opposite arm forward. Then swing the other leg forward and the other arm forward.
Running	Standing upright with eyes forward, bend arms at elbow. Push off and swing one leg forward while swinging opposite arm forward. Then swing the other leg forward and the other arm forward.
Jumping	Stand upright with eyes forward and feet shoulder width apart. Bend legs at knee and bring both arms behind body. Simultaneously, lean forward, swing arm forward, and forcefully straighten out legs.
Galloping	Standing upright with eyes forward, start with one leg forward of the other. Slide the back leg toward the front leg, and then step forward with the front leg. Pump arms either together or alternating.
Hopping	Stand upright with one leg bent so that the foot is off the ground. Bend the support leg at the knee while bringing both arms back behind the body. Simultaneously, lean forward, swing arms forward, and forcefully straighten out support leg.
Skipping	Alternate hopping on one foot, then stepping onto the other foot and then hopping with that foot. Hop-step on one foot, followed by hop-step on opposite foot.

Description of fundamental manipulative patterns

Throwing	Propelling a small ball away from the body using one hand. Skillful throwing is initiated by a forward step with opposite leg, followed by hip and trunk rotation, and concluded with a whipping arm action.
Catching	Receiving and controlling a ball that is tossed or kicked to student. Skillful catching is noted by extending arms to meet the ball, retracting hands upon contact with the ball, and using hands to catch the ball rather than trapping the ball against body.
Striking (bat)	Propelling a ball away from body by hitting ball with a long-handled implement. Skillful, two-handed striking consists of stepping forward, followed by quick hip, trunk, and arm rotation; swinging horizontally; and whipping arms forward in a forceful follow-through.
Striking (racket)	Propelling ball away from body by hitting ball with a racket. Skillful, one-handed striking consists of stepping forward, followed by quick hip, trunk, and arm rotation; swinging horizontally; and whipping arm forward in a forceful follow-through.
Kicking	Propelling ball away from body by using foot to impart force on ball. Skillful kicking consists of planting support leg next to ball, bringing leg back by flexing knee, forcefully swinging leg forward to contact ball, then continuing to swing leg forward in forceful follow-through.
Punting	Propelling ball away from body using foot to impart force on ball. Punting is different than kicking in that the ball is held and then dropped by the punter, and the ball is punted before ball touches the ground.

Locomotor patterns can also include pushing a manual wheelchair or controlling an electric wheelchair.

Table 1.4. Popular individual sports

Archery	Ice skating
Badminton	Martial arts
Bocce	Racquetball
Bowling	Roller skating
Cycling	Scuba diving
Croquet	Shooting
Fencing	Skiing
Darts	Swimming
Golf	Table tennis
Gymnastics	Tennis
Hiking	Track and field
Horseback riding	Water skiing
Horseshoes	Weight training
Hunting	

playing recreational games, or playing competitive games. In addition, many of these sports are considered lifetime leisure activities because they can be played across the life span.

Team Sports

Team sports include culturally popular sports that involve three or more players per side. Popular team sports in the United States are listed in Table 1.5. As is the case with individual sports, activities in each team sport can include working on skills, playing lead-up or modified games, playing recreational games, or playing competitive games. It is interesting to note that some team sports (e.g., football, baseball) are not considered lifetime leisure activities because most individuals do not participate in these activities after middle age. Team sports such as volleyball and softball are played by older adults and could be considered lifetime leisure activities.

Objectives of Physical Education

The purpose of a quality physical education program is to guide children in the process of becoming physically active for a lifetime. This is achieved by helping children to become physically educated individuals. The Healthy People 2010 Report released by the U.S. Department of Health and Human Services in 2000 clearly states objectives for health and physical education. The overall goal of Healthy People 2010 is to identify the most significant preventable

Table 1.5. Popular team sports

Basketball	Rugby
Baseball	Soccer
Field hockey	Softball
Floor hockey	Team handball
Football	Volleyball
Lacrosse	Ultimate Frisbee

threats to health and to establish national goals to reduce these threats. The following objectives identify how physical education in public schools can help in this effort (USDHHS, 2000):

1. Increase the proportion of the nation's public and private schools that require daily physical education.

2. Increase the proportion of adolescents who participate in daily school physical education.

3. Increase the proportion of adolescents who spend at least 50% of school physical education class being physically active.

The components of physical education help define the types of activities that should be included in a comprehensive physical education program. However, presenting activities without purpose or focus is not effective physical education. Good physical education programs use these activities to promote more global physical education objectives that facilitate psychomotor (motor and fitness performance) cognitive (intellectual skills), and affective development (feelings, opinions, attitudes, beliefs, values, interests, and desires) (Sherrill, 2004).

DEVELOPMENTALLY APPROPRIATE PROGRAMMING IN PHYSICAL EDUCATION

COPEC, part of NASPE, recommended that quality, daily physical education be available to all children. Quality physical education is both instructionally appropriate and developmentally appropriate for all children being taught. COPEC has published guidelines for quality physical education at the elementary (COPEC, 2000), middle school (COPEC, 2001), and high school level (COPEC, 2004). These booklets describe physical education practices that are in the best interest of children (appropriate) and those that are not in the best interests of children (inappropriate). The booklets include guidelines for curriculum design, learning experience, fitness activities, fitness testing, assessment, use of technology, forming groups, competition, and many others. These booklets have proved to be an excellent resource for parents, school administrators, and teachers who are responsible for providing physical education (COPEC, 2000). Sample components from the appropriate practices for elementary physical education document (Table 1.6) and the appropriate practices for high school physical education document (Table 1.7) are presented.

Physical education is composed of several different components designed to promote certain global objectives (i.e., to be physically educated), and it is important that all students receive training in all of these components if these objectives are to be achieved. Yet, should young children learn how to play either team sports or participate in intricate dances? Should older students and young adults participate solely in simple rhythms activities or activities that promote fundamental motor skill development? The answer is no. Students should be exposed to all physical education components, but these should be presented across the life span of the student. The term *developmentally appropriate* refers

Table 1.6. Sample components from the appropriate practices for elementary physical education document

Component	Forming groups/partners
Appropriate practice	Groups/partners are formed in a way that preserves the dignity and self-respect of every child. For example, a teacher privately forms groups or teams by using knowledge of children's skills abilities in ways that will facilitate learning. Groups or teams may also be formed by grouping clothing colors, birthdays, and favorite activities.
Inappropriate practice	Groups or teams are formed by student "captains" publicly selecting one child at a time, exposing the less skilled students to peer ridicule or embarrassment. Groups or teams are formed by pitting boys against girls, emphasizing gender differences rather than cooperation.

Reprinted from *Appropriate Practices for Elementary School Physical Education* (2000), with permission from the National Association for Sport and Physical Education (NASPE), 1900 Association Drive, Reston, VA 20191, USA.

Table 1.7. Sample components from the appropriate practices for high school physical education document

Component	Warm-up activities
Appropriate practice	Teachers design warm-up activities that are instructionally sound. They use warm-up activities to reinforce/practice skills from previous lessons as well as to lead into the day's lesson. Warm-up activities are safe, appropriate exercises that accommodate different fitness levels and produce perspiration as a sign of internal body heat. Stretching occurs after an appropriate general warm-up activity. Teachers consider warm-up in relation to the total lesson and ensure that students understand why and how to warm-up appropriately.
Inappropriate practice	Teachers have students warm up on their own, possibly without supervision. A single warm-up routine is used regardless of the lesson, ignores individual fitness levels, and/or is potentially unsafe. Mass exercise sessions are conducted without instructional focus. Stretching occurs without general warm-up.

Reprinted from *Appropriate Practices for High School Physical Education* (2004), with permission from the National Association for Sport and Physical Education (NASPE), 1900 Association Drive, Reston, VA 20191, USA.

to presenting activities that are geared to a student's developmental status, previous movement experiences, fitness and skill level, body size, and age (COPEC, 1992). Developmentally appropriate practices suggest that programming as well as instruction should be different for preschool-age children, compared with that for elementary-age students, compared with that for secondary-age students.

Wessel and Kelly (1986) outlined major content areas for general physical education activities broken down by grade level (see Table 1.8). Note that younger children are learning activities that promote development of motor skills and movement competencies, while older students are learning to apply these skills and competencies to culturally popular sports and lifetime leisure/fitness activities.

Most physical educators understand what is appropriate for younger students and what is appropriate for older students. However, this understanding is often lost when it comes to students with disabilities. Oftentimes, physical educators present activities based on a student's *mental* rather *chronological age.* Unfortunately, such an approach may result in students with disabilities graduating from school with a smattering of developmental skills but no real ability to participate in lifetime leisure activities. It is critical that students with disabilities, including students with severe disabilities, be exposed to chronological-age–appropriate activities that will lead to the development of functional skills that they can use when they graduate from school (see Block, 1992, and Krebs & Block, 1992, for in-depth discussions of helping students acquire lifetime leisure skills).

CURRICULAR MODELS IN PHYSICAL EDUCATION

Numerous curricular models have been adopted by school districts and individual schools. Specific curricular models have included movement education,

Table 1.8.   Major content areas for general physical education by grade level

Lower elementary school (K–3rd grade)	Upper elementary/middle school (4th–7th grade)	High school (8th–12th grade)
Locomotor patterns • Run • Skip • Jump • Slide • Gallop • Leap • Hop • Climb	*Locomotor patterns for sports* • Locomotor patterns used in sports • Combine two or more locomotor patterns • Locomotor patterns used in dance • Locomotor patterns used in leisure activities	*Locomotor sports* • Track events • Special sports applications
Manipulative patterns • Throw • Catch • Kick • Strike	*Manipulative patterns for sports* • Throw • Volley • Catch • Dribble • Kick • Punt • Strike	*Ball sports* • Basketball, soccer, softball, volleyball, bowling, golf, tennis, racquetball, etc.
Body management • Body awareness • Body control • Space awareness • Effort concepts	*Body management for sports* • Gymnastics • Body management skills applied to sports	*Body management for sports* • Body management skills applied to sports
Health and fitness • Endurance • Strength • Flexibility to perform locomotor and manipulative skills skills	*Health and fitness* • Cardiorespiratory endurance • Muscular strength and endurance • Flexibility	*Health and fitness* • Personal conditioning • Lifetime leisure exercises • Introduction to body composition concepts
Rhythms and dance • Moving to a beat • Expressing self through movement • Singing games • Applying effort concepts	*Dance* • Folk • Modern • Interpretive • Aerobic	*Dance* • Folk • Modern • Interpretive • Aerobic and social
Low organized games • Relays and tag games • Games with partners • Games with a small group	*Lead-up games to sports* • Lead-up games to team sports	*Modified and regulation sports* • Modified sport activities • Regulation sports

From Wessel, J.A., & Kelly, L. (1986). *Achievement-based curriculum development in physical education.* Philadelphia: Lea & Febiger; reprinted by permission.

health-related physical education, the academic integration model, the social development model, and the adventure education model (Siedentop, 2004). One of the more popular curricular models has been the sport education model. This model acknowledges that sport is the content of physical education at the secondary level and provides students with an authentic sport experience within physical education classes. Table 1.9 highlights the key characteristics of the sport education model.

There is a movement in many school districts to implement a curriculum commonly referred to as the "new physical education," which involves creating more engaging and developmentally appropriate programs for children. There is no room in the new physical education for games such as dodge ball, Red Rover, and relay races, all of which have been placed into the physical education hall of shame, games characterized by elimination of participants, low activity time, lack of a meaningful learning objective, lack of content progression, safety issues, or an overemphasis on fun rather than skill acquisition (Hastie & Martin, 2006; Williams, 1992, 1994, 1996). The new physical education stresses the importance of lifetime fitness over team sports, and competition and curricula typically involve instruction about heart rate zones, problem solving, and cooperation. Many schools that have implemented the new physical education have taken advantage of grant opportunities such as the Carol M. White Physical Education for Progress Grant (PEP) to raise money to buy equipment such as pedometers, heart rate monitors, climbing walls, in-line skates, dance pads, and exercise bikes with video game consoles (McCollum, Elliott, Burke, Civalier, & Pruitt, 2005).

Status of Physical Education

The prevalence of physical education is inconsistent throughout the country, as physical education requirements differ among grade level and states. Generally speaking, approximately 40% of kindergarten classes across the country have some sort of physical education requirement (Burgeson, Wechsler, Brener, Young, & Spain, 2001). At the first- through fifth-grade levels (i.e., elementary level), this increases to approximately 50% (Burgeson et al., 2001). States requiring physical education at the elementary level differ in the amount of time required (i.e., duration). For example, 30 minutes of physical education per week is the requirement in some states, while others require 150 minutes per week (NASPE, 2004). Unfortunately, as students grow older, the required time allocated for physical education decreases (Burgeson et al., 2001). In fact, only about 6.9% of high

Table 1.9. Defining characteristics of the sport education curricular model

The academic year is separated into seasons, rather than instructional units.

Students are placed on teams and remain on those teams until the end of the sport season. Teams are changed after each season/sport.

Similar to a "real sport" experience, the season is broken down into a training camp/preseason, regular season, and post-season.

The season ends in a culminating event.

Students (players) on each team assume different roles and responsibilities when they are playing and not playing. Roles include team manager, coach, statistician, publicist, equipment manager, and referee. The teacher serves as a league commissioner.

Source: Siedentop, Hastie, and van der Mars (2004).

schools provide at least 3 days per week of physical education for the duration of 1 school year. These high schools, like elementary schools, vary in the time required in physical education. For example, some schools require 80 minutes per week, while others require 275 minutes per week (NASPE, 2004).

Fortunately, Burgeson and colleagues (2001) reported that more than 70% of states have a person who is in charge of physical education programs throughout the state. This means that the majority of states have placed an individual in a position to lead campaigns to increase the physical education requirements (both frequency and duration).

WHAT IS ADAPTED PHYSICAL EDUCATION?

As noted previously, the legislators who created PL 94-142 believed that students with disabilities could benefit from physical education and that physical education services, modified when necessary, should be a part of all students' educational programs. Although legislators realized that many students with disabilities could participate in general physical education without the need for modifications to the general program, they also realized that some students with disabilities would have difficulty safely and successfully participating in and benefiting from general physical education without modifications or support. Thus, various adaptations would be necessary for these students to truly benefit from physical education. When students with disabilities need extra support to benefit from general physical education or when these students need a special physical education program, they qualify for "specially designed physical education" or *adapted physical education* (Auxter, Pyfer, & Huettig, 2005; Sherrill, 2004).

Definition of Adapted Physical Education

Adapted physical education is a subdiscipline of physical education with an emphasis on physical education for students with disabilities. The term *adapted physical education* generally refers to school-based programs for students ages 3–21; the more global term *adapted physical activity* refers to programs across the life span, including postschool programs (Sherrill, 2004). Because this book focuses on school-age students, the term *adapted physical education* is used throughout.

Various definitions of adapted physical education have been developed over the past 20 years (e.g., Auxter Pyfer, & Huettig, 2005; Sherrill, 2004; Winnick, 2000a). However, the definition by Dunn seems to be most appropriate: "Adapted physical education programs are those that have the same objectives as the regular physical education program, but in which adjustments are made in the regular offerings to meet the needs and abilities of exceptional students" (1997, p. 3). Note that both general and adapted physical education share the same objectives. In addition, the components of physical education as defined in IDEA 2004 should be included in a comprehensive adapted physical education program. The major difference between general and adapted physical education is that in the latter, "adjustments" or adaptations are made to the regular offerings to ensure safe, successful, and beneficial participation (Dunn, 1997; Sherrill, 2004). Simple adaptations such as asking a peer to provide assistance, modifying the equipment and rules of games, or providing alternative activities under the guidance of a trained adapted physical education specialist do little to disrupt the learning environment and create a productive and enjoyable physical education experience for all students.

Many adaptations can be implemented within the general physical education setting. For example, a high school–age student who uses a wheelchair can work on special stretching exercises during general physical education while his peers perform their warm-up activities. Similarly, this student can work on individual goals such as pushing his wheelchair forward and developing the ability to play cerebral palsy soccer (an official sport of the National Disability Sport Alliance) while his peers practice their running and soccer skills. This student may require special equipment such as a wheelchair and a larger ball as well as extra assistance in the form of a peer tutor, volunteer, or paraprofessional. However, the student can easily be accommodated in the general program and still receive an appropriate, individualized physical education program designed to meet his unique needs.

Objectives of adapted and general physical education are the same, and how objectives are prioritized vary from individual to individual in both. Therefore, while individualization is one of the hallmarks of adapted physical education programs, the wide range of skill level in general physical education classes requires careful planning for children without disabilities as well. However, meeting specific objectives with children with disabilities is crucial. For example, maintenance of low levels of health-related physical fitness might be a priority for a student with muscular dystrophy or cystic fibrosis but not for a physically fit student without disabilities. Because activities that promote physical fitness, motor skill development, and social development are offered to some extent or another in general physical education, it is relatively easy to accommodate students with disabilities who have these goals as priorities.

Finally, it is important to note that adapted physical education should not be viewed as a place a child goes to receive special physical education or as a person who provides these special services. Rather, adapted physical education is a service that can be provided in a variety of settings (including general physical education) and by a variety of qualified people (including, in many states, a general physical education specialist). Thus, a child with a disability could receive adapted physical education services (individual goals and objectives for physical education) within a general physical education setting provided by a general physical education teacher. Decisions regarding what services will be provided, where they will be provided, and who will provide them vary from state to state but generally are left up to each child's IEP team.

Who Is Qualified to Provide Physical Education Services?

Legislators wanted to make sure that only "qualified" individuals would provide physical education services to children with disabilities. However, legislators felt strongly that determining who was qualified to provide services to students with disabilities (including physical education services) should be left up to each state: "Qualified means that a person has met State educational agency approved or recognized certification, licensing, registration, or other comparable requirements which apply to the area in which he or she is providing special education or related services" (Federal Register, August 23, 1977, p. 42479). This has not changed with any of the reauthorizations of IDEA. Legislators intended for states to establish requirements for physical education specialists who work with children who have disabilities (Kelly, 1991; National Consortium on Physical Education and Recreation for Individuals with Disabilities [NCPERID], 1995). Unfortunately, nearly 30 years after the original passage of the law, only 17 have developed specific requirements and/or licensure for professionals who provide physical education services to students with disabilities (Kelly & Gansneder, 1998). However, states that do not require any special training/licensure often certify many professionals as "qualified" to provide physical education services to students with disabilities. In many states these professionals include general physical education teachers, special education teachers, and general classroom teachers. Unfortunately, many of these "qualified" professionals do not have any training, knowledge, or experience to provide physical education to children with disabilities (Block & Rizzo, 1995; Chandler & Greene, 1995; National Association of State Directors of Special Education, 1991).

Since the mid-1990s a national examination known as the Adapted Physical Education National Standards (APENS; NCPERID, 1995, 2006) examination has been offered. Individuals who have a baccalaureate degree in physical education, a minimum of 200 hours of practicum experiences in adapted physical education, at least one 3-credit course in adapted physical education, and a valid teaching license can sit for the exam. Those who pass the exam become Certified Adapted Physical Educators (CAPE) (Kelly, 1998). It is hoped that more professionals will become CAPEs and that more states will recognize the need to hire more CAPEs to provide physical education to children with disabilities. There are no requirements for local school districts to hire CAPEs (NCPERID, 1995).

SUMMARY

The purpose of this chapter is to define physical education and introduce the concepts that comprise a quality physical education program. Physical education is considered a direct service in IDEA and its amendments, which means that all children, including children with disabilities, are required to receive physical education. In addition, specialized physical education services, which can be provided in integrated or separate settings, should be provided to any child with disabilities who requires them.

Physical education consists of a diverse program of activities, including motor skills, physical fitness, and individual and team sports. These activities should be presented in such a way that they facilitate the achievement of global physical education objectives, including motor skill competency, social and cognitive development, and healthy self-concept. How much time and emphasis a particular student spends working on a particular component (as well as how these skills are presented) vary based on several factors such as a student's age, abilities, and interests.

What Is Inclusion?

by Martin E. Block and Iva Obrusnikova

 Andre has been a proud member of Rocky Crest Elementary School since kindergarten. As a rising fifth grader, he is one of the elite students at school—the oldest and biggest group (and if you ask Andre, the smartest group, too!) that will be moving on to middle school next year. But Andre is not worried about sixth grade. He is excited about starting his last year at Rocky Crest. Outsiders might find Andre's attitude somewhat surprising, given that Andre has Down syndrome. He clearly is smaller than all of his peers, has very little speech, wears glasses and hearing aids, and does academic work on par more with kindergartners and first graders rather than fifth graders. His latest evaluation found that his IQ is in the range of 40–50, and the school district has given him the special education label of MOID (moderate intellectual disability).

Although some might argue that Andre would be better served in a special education class for children with intellectual disabilities, Andre has been in general education classes (including general physical education) since kindergarten. Not only has he been enrolled in general education classes, but also his peers and his teachers have always treated Andre as a true member of the class, and he has been making excellent progress toward his individualized education program (IEP) goals and objectives. This often requires team meetings with all of the students in the class, the classroom teacher, and the special education teacher. But once everyone learned about Andre, his abilities and interests, his unique needs, and how important it is to make Andre truly a member of the class, the students and the teachers did a wonderful job of accepting Andre. The special education teacher also explained to his general education teachers and to his classmates that Andre usually needs to work on different skills from other students but that Andre could work on these different skills in the general education environment with support from his peers and from his special education teacher. For example, when Andre was in fourth grade, his classmates worked on fractions and decimals. During this time, Andre worked on reading the price tags on clothing and food labels and simple addition using pretend dollar bills. A peer sitting next to him often helped Andre,

checking his work and guiding him to the next activity in his packet.

Physical education was a fun time for Andre when he was in kindergarten, first, and second grade. However, starting in third grade, physical education became a little more of a struggle for Andre. He was clearly falling further behind his peers in general physical education. Andre could see how much better his peers were than he was in physical fitness, ball skills, and games. This started to frustrate Andre, and he began to act out or just sit in the corner. Fortunately, Mrs. Hobbs (his general physical educator) had worked with Andre since he was a kindergartner. She knew that she also had the support of the special education teacher and a traveling adapted physical education specialist who came to work with Andre one-to-one on locomotor patterns and ball skills. Adaptations to help Andre were not that difficult to create and implement, and before long Andre was back to his old self, doing the best he could with that ear-to-ear smile.

First, Mrs. Hobbs talked to Andre about his abilities and all of the things he could do. For example, Andre was really good at kicking balls and performing log rolls. She also reminded Andre that every year, he had the best score on the "sit-and-reach" test of flexibility. That made Andre smile. She then reminded Andre that physical education at Rocky Crest was a time for everyone to improve. It did not matter how good you were; it only mattered how hard you tried and whether you achieved the goals you created for yourself for each skill.

Andre soon began to participate again. During the mile run, Andre knew that his goal was to walk the long straight part and run the shorter straight part. (Mrs. Hobbs laid out a rectangular-shaped grid around the soccer field.) Andre knew that if he could just do this run–walk–run–walk that Mrs. Hobbs would be proud of him. It also helped that Andre's peers would encourage him every time they ran past him. During a throwing unit, Andre knew that he could stand closer to the target. In fact, Mrs. Hobbs encouraged all of the students to choose a distance and a target that allowed them to throw using the correct overhand pattern. Andre was surprised to see some of his classmates standing at the same distance that he did and aiming at the same target. And as with the encouragement during the mile run, it was fun to have Andre's classmates remind him of the correct throwing pattern and then tell him he was doing a good job. Andre liked trying to say the words: "side-orientation" and "step with opposite foot." And when the class played tagging and fleeing games for warm-ups, Andre was as successful as his peers at avoiding being tagged and tagging. Andre was pretty sure he remembered his classmates being faster, but he was surprised at his own speed and ability to catch his friends. (It was nice that his classmates helped Andre by running a little slower when he was "it.")

Although this scenario may seem too good to be true, such programs are being implemented in many schools. When done right, inclusion demonstrates that students with disabilities can receive an appropriate and challenging education within the general physical education setting (Block & Obrusnikova, in press). But what exactly does *inclusion* mean? This chapter reviews the concepts of the least restrictive environment (LRE), mainstreaming, the regular (general) education initiative, and inclusion. Included are a rationale for inclusion programs as well as a review of research that has demonstrated the potential success of inclusive physical education programs.

EVOLUTION OF INCLUSION

The Early Years: Limited Access to Education

Inclusion has grown out of a long history of how individuals with disabilities are viewed. The biggest hurdle for children with disabilities in the first part of the 20th century was simply to receive any special education. Children with mild disabilities were placed in general education classes without any special support. As long as they kept up with the other students in the class and did not cause any problems, the teacher and their classmates accepted them. There were no special services and no trained specialists to help the child with disabilities or the general education teacher (Lewis & Doorlag, 1991). If the child was falling behind, causing problems, or was perceived as having disabilities that were too severe for the child to benefit from education, then the child was simply sent home and excluded from the public schools (Beirne-Smith, Patton, & Ittenbach, 1994; Karagiannis, Stainback, & Stainback, 1996; Sigmon, 1983). As noted by Sigmon, "Almost all children who were wheelchair-bound, not toilet trained, or considered uneducable were excluded because of

the problems that schooling would entail" (1983, p. 3). The one exception was special schools for children who were deaf or blind.

Special Schools/Special Classes

From 1950 to the early 1970s, educating children with disabilities was done primarily in special schools. Initially, parents who were frustrated with the lack of special education for their children with disabilities within the public schools privately developed many of these special schools. Many of these schools were in the basements of churches, with parents serving as teachers. These parents also formed groups such as The Association for Retarded Citizens (now known as The Arc) to advocate for more educational opportunities for their children (Beirne-Smith et al., 1994; Karagiannis et al., 1996). This advocacy as well as a new awareness of the needs and capabilities of children with disabilities led to the public schools developing special schools or special classes for children with disabilities. For example, the New York City Board of Education established "600" schools for children who were "disturbed" and "maladjusted" (Kauffman, 1993). In other places, one school within a district was dedicated to all children with a particular type of disability. If there were several special classes, then a wing or annex of the school housed these special classes.

Special schools and classes were developed based on the reasoning that children with disabilities needed a highly structured, very intense, and unique teaching environment conducted by a trained specialist (Lewis & Doorlag, 1991). It was also understood that children with disabilities were not wanted in general schools or classrooms, and their removal would inevitably benefit children without disabilities (Chaves, 1977). Even when special classes were housed in general school buildings, rarely did students with disabilities (or, for that matter, the staff who served these students) become true members of the school. And children with more severe disabilities were still excluded from education in many states (Stainback, Stainback, & Bunch, 1989).

The most popular model for educating children with disabilities was special schools that had special education teachers and therapists with special training and who used special materials, equipment, and teaching methodologies. While such special training was certainly warranted, the end result was a rather elaborate dual system of education with general education on the one hand and special education on the other (Stainback et al., 1989). Programs for children with specific types of disabilities became so specialized that different day and residential facilities were created for children with learning disabilities, children with hearing impairments, visual impairments, intellectual disabilities, emotional disturbances, and physical disabilities. (Many of these special schools are still in existence today.)

While the special school/special class model proliferated in the 1960s and early 1970s, many were beginning to find fault with the system. First, it was becoming clear that students with disabilities were viewed as different, and different meant excluding them from education with children without disabilities (DuBow, 1989; Stainback et al., 1989). Reports to Congress in the early 1970s suggested that labeling and separating children with disabilities from their peers without disabilities led to stigma, ridicule, and poor self-image (Lewis & Doorlag, 1991; Turnbull, 1990).

Second, there was a concern that many children with disabilities were placed in special programs without first determining whether the student could benefit from general education placement (a practice that continues today despite the LRE mandate) (Brown, 1994; Stainback et al., 1989). There was no effort to determine if individually prescribed curricular and instructional adaptations could occur within the general setting (Block, 1994; Snell & Drake, 1994; Snell & Eichner, 1989). Furthermore, it was becoming clear that many children with disabilities were able to participate at least in some of the activities of the general class, and almost all could benefit from contact with their typically developing peers (Lewis & Doorlag, 1991).

Third, following the *Brown v. Board of Education* (1954) ruling, there was evidence suggesting that separate but equal self-contained classrooms tended to be unequal (Karagiannis et al., 1996; Stainback et al., 1989; Taylor, 1988). Special class placement in the 1960s and early 1970s often meant having the "worst" teacher, the most inferior facilities, and limited educational materials (Lewis & Doorlag, 1991). Stories about being placed in a small room in the basement of the school next to the boiler or having untrained teachers were not uncommon at the time. In addition, children with disabilities who were in special classes in general schools were inexplicably excluded from assemblies and other schoolwide activities (Lewis & Doorlag, 1991).

Fourth, there was growing concern over the "terminal aspects of special education" (Turnbull, 1990, p. 150). At the time (and still evident today), children with disabilities were placed in separate special education programs; many of these children would spend the rest of their education in these separate programs (Taylor, 1988). Tracking students with disabilities into special classes without any op-

portunity to move out of these classes was common (Karagiannis et al., 1996).

In addition to the problems associated with special schools and special classes, there was a growing awareness of civil rights. The *Brown v. Board of Education* decision as well as the Civil Rights Act of 1964 (PL 88-352) led to examination of the practice of separating children with disabilities from the mainstream of public education (Beirne-Smith et al., 1994; Stainback et al., 1989). There was also increasing advocacy for children with disabilities to learn in a more normalized school environment with their peers without disabilities (Karagiannis et al., 1996; Nirje, 1969; Wolfensberger, 1972). And lawsuits in Pennsylvania (*Pennsylvania Association for Retarded Children v. Commonwealth of Pennsylvania*, 1971) and the District of Columbia (*Mills v. D.C. Board of Education*, 1972) established the rights of children with disabilities within these jurisdictions to a free and appropriate public education.

Federal Intervention: IDEA and Least Restrictive Environment

Out of this dissatisfaction with special education and a realization that children with disabilities could benefit from more interactions with children without disabilities, the federal government enacted the Education for All Handicapped Children Act in 1975 (PL 94-142). Now known as the Individuals with Disabilities Education Act (IDEA), this landmark legislation guaranteed the rights of individuals with disabilities to a free appropriate public education. Included in this legislation was a provision designed to ensure that children with disabilities would have greater opportunities to be placed in general education programs and to interact with peers without disabilities. Termed the *least restrictive environment (LRE)* in IDEA, the provision directs public agencies

(1) To the maximum extent appropriate, children with disabilities, including children in public or private institutions or other care facilities, are educated with children who are not disabled; and

(2) That special classes, separate schooling, or other removal of children with disabilities from the regular educational environment occurs only when the nature or severity of the disability is such that education in regular classes with the use of supplementary aids and services cannot be achieved satisfactorily. (20 U.S.C. 1412 [5][B])

This passage suggests that the LRE for students with disabilities was, whenever possible, the same environment in which students without disabilities received their education. Clearly, lawmakers advocated placing students with disabilities in general schools and general classrooms (including general physical education) whenever possible (Aufsesser, 1991; Taylor, 1988; Turnbull, 1990). This passage also suggested that *appropriate* placement of students with disabilities into general settings may necessitate the use of supplementary aids, support, and services. Without such support, the student may fail in the general setting. In other words, it might not be the setting that is inappropriate but rather the support that is given to a student within that setting (Block & Krebs, 1992). The LRE provision is still contained in the most recent reauthorization, IDEA 2004 (PL 108-446).

Although segregated placement was not prohibited under the law, school districts were required to clearly demonstrate that a child with a disability placed in a separate setting could not be satisfactorily educated within the general setting, even with supplementary aids and services (Arnold & Dodge, 1994; Hollis & Gallegos, 1993; Lipton, 1994; Maloney, 1994; Osborne, 1990). Lawmakers wanted to prevent the unnecessary placement of children with disabilities in separate programs while ensuring that students with and without disabilities were educated together whenever possible. The practice of simply placing students in separate programs based on a label or pre-placement evaluation was considered a violation of the intent of the act (Bateman & Chard, 1995; Lipton, 1994; Maloney, 1994; Osborne, 1996).

However, placement options other than the general education classroom for children with disabilities were still required under the law. Lawmakers made this clear when they added a statement regarding a "continuum of alternative placements":

(a) Each public agency shall ensure that a continuum of alternative placements is available to meet the needs of children with disabilities for special education and related services.
(b) The continuum . . . must —
  (1) Include the alternative placements listed in the definition of special education (instruction in regular classes, special classes, special schools, home instruction, and instruction in hospitals and institutions); and
  (2) Make provisions for supplementary services (such as resource room or itinerant instruction) to be provided in conjunction with regular class placement. (Federal Register, September 29, 1992, p. 44823)

An example of a continuum of placement options for physical education can be found in Table 2.1. Note that, by strict definition of the law, school districts should offer these or similar options for physical education placement because not all children with disabilities within a district can be accommo-

Table 2.1.   Sample of continuum of placement options for physical education

- Full-time general physical education (GPE), no support needed
- Full-time GPE, accommodations needed (e.g., interpreter, adapted equipment, special instructions)
- Adapted physical education (APE) provided within the GPE setting (child has unique goals and objectives and needs special accommodations, but accommodations can be carried out within the GPE setting)
- APE provided within GPE setting, direct support from APE specialist (APE specialist comes into GPE to help child work on his or her unique goals and objectives and with special accommodations)
- APE provided part time within GPE and part time in a special APE class
- APE provided full time in special APE class in general school building
- APE provided full time in special APE class in special school
- APE provided full time in special APE class, either at home, in a hospital, or in a treatment facility

dated within only one or two of these options. For example, a child with cerebral palsy who is hospitalized could not receive physical education within the general setting.

Although the continuum of placement provision is important and continues to be a part of IDEA, it should be read within context. Data presented to Congress in the 1970s showed that more than half of the students with disabilities in the United States were in educational programs that were deemed inappropriate for their needs, and an estimated 1 million children with disabilities were excluded entirely from the public school system. Prior to 1975, many children with disabilities resided at home, in residential facilities, or in hospitals. The few day programs that were available for students with disabilities usually were separate from public school buildings (e.g., in churches, in rented office spaces). In most cases, these residential facilities, hospitals, and day programs did not provide any systematic educational programs (Brown, 1994; Stainback et al., 1989). Rather, these children were more or less "warehoused"; their basic needs were taken care of but not their educational and social needs. As noted by Turnbull (1990), the dual system of education prior to 1975 had a variety of effects, one of which was the denial of educational opportunities for children with disabilities.

In light of the exclusion of educational opportunities, lawmakers made a clear statement that, regardless of where a child with a disability resides or level of severity of disability, he or she still must receive education commensurate with individual abilities and needs. Thus, even children who were not in traditional school programs were guaranteed free appropriate public education under the law (Turnbull, 1990). It was never the intent of lawmakers to have these separate placements become an option for placing students with disabilities unless "the IEP of a child with a disability requires some other arrangement" (Federal Register, September 29, 1992, p. 44823). Lawmakers appeared to favor having students with disabilities educated alongside peers without disabilities whenever appropriate. It seems unlikely that they meant for the continuum statement to serve as a justification for placement in these separate settings (Taylor, 1988; Turnbull, 1990).

In summary, Congress created the educational setting and LRE statements in the federal laws as a reaction to inappropriate special education practices at the time. These statements showed Congress's strong preference that children with and without disabilities should be educated together to the maximum extent possible. In addition, LRE brought attention to the notion that most children with disabilities could receive an appropriate education within the general setting if given supplementary services and aids. A continuum was presented to ensure that students already placed in these more restrictive environments would receive appropriate educational programs. Finally, the law clearly noted that all placement decisions needed to be made on an individual basis.

Mainstreaming

Administrators and educators in 1975 were faced with the dilemma of implementing the provisions and mandates of PL 94-142. It was clear that lawmakers wanted as many children with disabilities as appropriate to be educated alongside children without disabilities. But how to provide special education within the general setting was never really made clear. Slowly, students with disabilities were moved from special schools to special classes within general schools and more efforts were made to integrate children with disabilities into general education classes and general school activities when it was deemed appropriate. However, determining when to place children with disabilities into general education programs and how to support these children within special programs was confusing to many professionals. In an effort to provide some direction as to how to implement the law, the Council for Exceptional Children (CEC; 1975) coined the term *mainstreaming* to describe the process of placing students with disabilities in general education classes with appropriate support services as determined by the student's IEP. CEC suggested that mainstreaming was

providing the most appropriate education for each student in the least restrictive setting,

placing students based on assessed educational needs rather than clinical labels,

providing support services to general educators so they may effectively serve children with disabilities in the general setting

uniting general and special education to help students with disabilities have equal educational opportunities.

CEC noted that mainstreaming was not

wholesale return of all exceptional children to general classes

permitting children with special needs to remain in general classes without the support services they needed

ignoring the need of some children for a more specialized program that could be provided in the general education program.

Despite this definition, mainstreaming became associated with unsuccessful dumping of students with disabilities into general education classes without support (DePaepe, 1984; Grosse, 1991; Lavay & DePaepe, 1987). In contrast to what CEC suggested, children with disabilities who were mainstreamed into general education classes (including general physical education classes) were asked to follow the same curricular content, using the same materials and instruction, and following the same pace as the other students in the class. Not surprising, many children with disabilities failed in such settings. The term *mainstreaming* has been misused so much that it is no longer recommended by CEC.

Regular Education Initiative

Despite the setback with mainstreaming, more and more children with disabilities were receiving some or all of their education in general education settings. In addition, research in the 1970s and 1980s began to show that special class placements were rather ineffective in educating students with disabilities (e.g., Madden & Slavin; 1983; Schnorr, 1990; Semmel, Gottlieb, & Robinson, 1979; Wang & Baker, 1986). For example, Wang, Reynolds, and Walberg (1987) suggested that traditional "pull-out" programs were limited for a variety of reasons, including that the system for classifying students with disabilities was not educationally sound, there was virtually no evidence to suggest that students with disabilities were making any educational gains simply based on special education placement, and special class placement promoted isolation and stigmatization.

In 1986, Madeleine Will (then Assistant Secretary for the Office of Special Education and Rehabilitative Services, U.S. Department of Education) called for a regular education initiative (REI). In her article *"Educating Students with Learning Problems: A Shared Responsibility,"* Will (1986) argued that the dual system of separate special and general education was not effective for students with mild disabilities. Will suggested several changes to the dual system, all of which where designed to appropriately serve students with disabilities in general education. She proposed increased instructional time, empowerment of principals to control all programs and resources at the building level, provision of support systems for general education teachers, and the use of new approaches such as curriculum-based assessment, cooperative learning, and personalized curricula (Will, 1986). Proponents of REI encouraged the scaling back of traditional special education classrooms in favor of a new merger between special and general education.

Some advocates noted that students with severe disabilities could learn important life skills in the general setting without interfering with the program for students without disabilities (Snell, 1988; Snell & Eichner, 1989; Stainback & Stainback, 1990; Taylor, 1988). In addition, heterogeneous grouping actually enriched all students (Stainback & Stainback, 1990). Although REI was initially argued from a philosophical/moral point of view, research began to support including students with severe disabilities in general education (e.g., Chadsey-Rusch, 1990; Condon, York, Heal, & Fortschneider, 1986; Peck, Donaldson, & Pezzoli, 1990; York, Vandercook, Macdonald, Heise-Neff, & Caughey, 1992).

WHAT IS INCLUSION?

Inclusion is an outgrowth of the regular education initiative of the 1980s and is used to describe the philosophy of merging special and general education (Lipsky & Gartner, 1987; O'Brien, Forest, Snow, & Hasburg, 1989; Stainback & Stainback, 1987; Stainback et al., 1989; Taylor, 1988). The term reflects a philosophy in which all children, regardless of abilities or disabilities, are educated within the same environment, an environment where each child's individual needs are met (Downing, 1996; Karagiannis, Stainback, & Stainback, 1996; Stainback & Stainback, 1990; Stainback et al., 1989). The philosophy of inclusion is perhaps best summed up by the following statement: "Although some children, especially those with severe and multiple disabilities, may have unique ways of learning, separating them from others who learn in a different way is unnecessary and could prevent them from achieving their full potential" (Downing, 1996, p. xii). It also is important to note that an inclusion philosophy goes be-

yond simply physically placing a child in a general education classroom (Block, 1999; Bricker, 1995; Brown et al., 1989; Downing, 1996; Ferguson, 1995; Snell, 1991; Stainback & Stainback, 1990). As noted by Stainback and Stainback, "An inclusive school is a place where everyone belongs, is accepted, supports, and is supported by his/her peers and other members of the school community in the course of having his/her educational needs met" (1990, p. 3).

Embedded within this definition was the understanding that children with disabilities would receive an individually determined, appropriate program with supplementary services and supports to meet their unique needs (Block, 1994; Stainback & Stainback, 1990, 1991). However, these services would be provided to the child with a disability within the general education environment (Downing, 1996). In terms of physical education services, this meant that individually determined goals, objectives, and accommodations would be provided within the general physical education setting by an adapted physical education specialist, trained general physical education specialist, trained teacher assistant, or trained peer tutor (Block, 1999). This notion of bringing services to the general education setting provided continual opportunities for the child with disabilities to interact with, learn from, and form friendships with peers while ensuring that the child received an appropriate, individualized program (Downing, 1996; Stainback & Stainback, 1990, 1991).

Another critical tenet of the inclusion philosophy was that children with disabilities were the responsibility of both general and special education staff (Downing, 1996; Giangreco, 1997; Givner & Haager, 1995; Sailor, Gee, & Karasoff, 1993; Stainback & Stainback, 1990). Unlike traditional self-contained programs in which the special education teacher (with the support of related services personnel) was solely responsible for a child's education, in inclusive programs it was the responsibility of all the school staff to make sure that each child's educational program was carried out appropriately (Downing, 1996; Sailor et al., 1993; Stainback & Stainback, 1990, 1991). However, it was unreasonable to expect the resources, knowledge base, and personnel available in general education to serve the needs of both children with and without disabilities (Stainback & Stainback, 1991). Yet, it also was becoming clear that special education resources and personnel could not serve all of the needs of children with disabilities. The inclusion philosophy suggested that only through the merger of resources, knowledge, and talents of general and special education could both children with and without disabilities receive a comprehensive, appropriate education (Lipsky & Gartner, 1998; Sailor et al., 1993; Stainback & Stainback, 1991). Continual support and training for the general education teacher was certainly required to make such a merged system work. In addition, the use of various co-teaching arrangements (the general and special education teacher dividing and sharing class instruction) might be an effective way to facilitate inclusive programs (Lipsky & Gartner, 1998). For example, Block and Zeman (1996) noted the effectiveness of having the adapted physical education specialist work with students with and without disabilities and co-teach various aspects of the general physical education lesson. Co-teaching arrangements also have been advocated by Sherrill (2004) and Lipsky and Gartner (1998).

Providing services within general education did not necessarily mean that all services for a particular child would always take place within the general education setting (Block, 1994; Brown et al., 1991; Lipsky & Gartner, 1998; Sailor et al., 1993). For limited periods of time during the school day, a child with a disability (as well as any other child in the class) could receive specialized instruction using specialized equipment in specialized environments outside the general education classroom. For example, a high school student with severe intellectual disabilities may need extra time in the locker room with the support of a teacher assistant getting dressed to go back to class. This student may leave general physical education 10 minutes early so he can work on these functional dressing skills. However, this student is still perceived as a member of the general physical education class (Block, 1994; Lipsky & Gartner, 1998).

Rationale for Inclusion

Students with disabilities have traditionally been viewed as fundamentally different from students without disabilities. Lipsky and Gartner (1998), Rainforth, York, and MacDonald (1992), Snell and Eichner (1989), Stainback and Stainback (1991), Stainback et al. (1989), and Will (1986), to name a few, have argued that a dual system of education is not necessary to provide appropriate educational services to students with disabilities. For example, Stainback et al. (1989) outlined a rationale for one educational system for all students that included the following key points:

1. *Instructional needs of all students vary from individual to individual.* A student with disabilities should be viewed as just another student whose instructional needs should be individualized to optimize learning. Individualization can be implemented in an integrated setting as easily as in a segregated setting. For example, most physical education classes

are composed of students with varying motor abilities, physical fitness, and knowledge of the rules and strategies of games. Good physical educators present activities in such a way that individual students' needs are accommodated. A student with disabilities is just another student who requires activities to be individualized to accommodate his or her unique abilities.

2. *A dual system is inefficient because there is inevitably competition and duplication of services.* The majority of activities presented in general physical education programs are the exact same activities that are presented in specialized adapted physical education programs. For example, most elementary-age students in general physical education work on the development of fundamental motor patterns, perceptual motor skills, physical fitness, and simple rhythms and games. These same activities are appropriate for elementary-age students with disabilities. Similarly, high school students work on individual and team sports, including lifetime leisure sports and physical fitness. Again, adapted physical education programs designed for high school students with disabilities work on the exact same activities. With a dual system, two professionals are teaching the same activities at the same time. A more logical and cost-effective model would be to include students with disabilities into the general program with modifications as needed to ensure their success.

3. *Dual systems foster inappropriate attitudes.* Students with disabilities, especially students who spend most of their time separated from their peers without disabilities, are viewed as different by general education teachers and peers (e.g., Voeltz, 1980, 1982). Teachers assume that educational programs that take place in special education must be extraordinary. That is, special education staff often are viewed as exceptional people who have different

skills and abilities from general education staff and who use different equipment and materials with their students. Similarly, students with disabilities often are viewed as more different from than similar to students without disabilities. In fact, most students with disabilities are more similar than different to their peers without disabilities. They probably enjoy watching the same TV shows and listening to the same music, cheer for the same sports teams, enjoy the same recreational activities, and hate cleaning their room and doing their homework. Unfortunately, teachers and peers who are not exposed to students with disabilities may view them as people who should be pitied, teased, or feared. By combining students with and without disabilities, teachers learn that teaching students with disabilities is not that different from teaching typical students. Similarly, peers without disabilities quickly learn that students with disabilities are more similar than different (Forest & Lusthaus, 1989; Stainback et al., 1989).

BENEFITS OF INCLUSION

In addition to the rationale for merging general and special education, there are benefits available in inclusion programs that are not available in segregated settings. Downing (2002), Snell and Eichner (1989), and Stainback and Stainback (1985, 1990) outlined several benefits of including students with disabilities into general education programs (see Tables 2.2 and 2.3).

Table 2.2.   Benefits of inclusion for students with disabilities

- Opportunity to learn social skills in integrated, more natural environments with natural cues and consequences; no need to generalize to integrated environments later in life
- More stimulating, motivating environment (e.g., hallways, the cafeteria, the recess yard, the bus loading area); dress, conversations, and social exchanges are characteristic of their age and location
- Opportunity to learn appropriate social skills (e.g., refrain from stigmatizing behavior, use appropriate greetings, wear age-appropriate clothes)
- Availability of age-appropriate role models without disabilities
- Participation in a variety of school activities suited to chronological age and neighborhood (e.g., assemblies, music, art, athletic events)
- Potential for new friendships with peers without disabilities
- Includes parents, special education teachers, and other special education staff into general schools, giving them new experiences and relationships and, thus, less isolation

Sources: Downing (2002); Snell & Eichner (1989); and Stainback & Stainback (1985, 1990).

Table 2.3.   Benefits of inclusion for staff members and students without disabilities

- Special education teachers (as well as adapted physical educators) tend to have higher expectations for students with disabilities in inclusive environments than for those in self-contained environments.
- Special education teachers learn what is appropriate for children without disabilities.
- With guidance from adults, students' attitudes toward students with disabilities improve.
- With guidance from adults, students without disabilities learn to appreciate individual differences.
- Students without disabilities gain perspective. For example, having acne or getting a C on a test seems less devastating when the person next to you is working as hard as he or she can to keep his or her head up and eyes focused.
- Everyone learns to face individuals with disabilities with greater personal knowledge and optimism and less prejudice.

Sources: Downing (2002); Snell & Eichner (1989); and Stainback & Stainback (1985, 1990).

No Child Left Behind Act of 2001

In 2001, Congress amended the Elementary and Secondary Education Act of 1965 (PL 89-10) as the No Child Left Behind Act (NCLB). NCLB is essentially a national extension of the standards-based education reform movement based on the Improving America's Schools Act of 1994 (PL 103-382). The major focus of NCLB is "to ensure that all children have a fair, equal, and significant opportunity to obtain a high-quality education and reach, at a minimum, proficiency on challenging State academic achievement standards and State academic assessments" (20 U.S.C. 6301). It encourages states and school districts to keep up with standards-based reforms. Two key aspects of the law include new requirements designed to close the achievement gap that exists between students who are economically disadvantaged, are from racial or ethnic minority groups, have disabilities, or have limited English proficiency, and to give assurances that there is a highly qualified teacher in each classroom for each subject being taught. Goals or benchmarks of the law are raised each year, with the expectation that all students and all subgroups of students will perform at grade level by the 2013–2014 school year (Wright, Wright, & Heath, 2004). The act covers all states, school districts, and schools that accept federal Title I grants. (Title I grants provide funding for remedial education programs for poor and disadvantaged children in public and even some private schools [Wright et al., 2004].)

One important concept in NCLB is the provision for "highly qualified teachers." Too often teachers without specific training in their subject area are teaching in the public schools. For example, a teacher without certification in mathematics might be asked to teach an introductory geometry class. Obviously, this teacher—regardless of her best intentions—could not teach geometry as well as someone with a strong foundation in mathematics. This is particularly problematic for students in lower income school districts who are more likely than their peers in wealthier districts to have teachers who were not "highly qualified" in the subject matter they are teaching (Wright & Wright, 2004). As directly stated in the law, physical educators should be trained in all aspects of health and physical education in order to be considered highly qualified. It is important to note that IDEA 2004 also requires school districts to hire special education teachers who are "highly qualified." This new provision has been somewhat controversial for special education teachers who teach multiple content areas. For example, some special education teachers may teach all content areas (mathematics, language arts, science, social studies). Should these teachers be certified in all of these content areas? Also, although not specifically mentioned in IDEA 2004, a physical education teacher who works with students with disabilities should have training in adapted physical education in order to become highly qualified.

An important concept within the law is the concept of *adequate yearly progress* (AYP). Schools are expected to make AYP toward meeting state standards in reading, mathematics, and science and to measure this progress for each student in order to receive federal funds (Paige, 2003). For example, in Virginia the AYP for 2005 was that 65% of all students throughout the state pass the reading test (read at grade level). The AYP calculations permit a school and school district to incorporate a percentage adjustment for children with disabilities who are receiving services under IDEA 2004 and have an IEP. This way, the school will not be adversely affected as the result of providing educational services to children with disabilities (Wright et al., 2004). In most cases, the percentage of student scores that can be exempt from AYP is 1% of the overall school-age population (representing those students with the most severe disabilities). However, this means that the scores of most students with disabilities in the school district will be counted toward AYP. The law recognizes that most students have disabilities that are not related to their cognitive ability and allow them to keep up with their peers academically and take standardized assessments successfully. For example, a student with a visual impairment might need a version of the test in braille. These students with disabilities may require modifications or accommodations in order to take the general assessment; however, they must perform just like other students in their class.

As noted by Wright and Wright (2004),

Since a large number of students with disabilities would have to fail in order for this failure to have an impact on the district's AYP status, and since a great many students with disabilities can succeed on standardized tests, a finding of "needs improvement" achieves the primary goal of this law—it shines a light on those groups of students for whom the American dream of a quality public school education has not always been a reality. If we allow this light to dim—by exempting the scores of more students from AYP—students with disabilities will recede back into the shadowy backrooms they inhabited for all those years before laws were passed to protect their civil rights.

SPECIFIC PHILOSOPHIES THAT SUPPORT INCLUSION

Inclusion should not be confused with early attempts at mainstreaming. Mainstreaming tended to place students with disabilities into general education without support. In addition, students often were expected to follow the general curriculum. In contrast inclusion philosophies suggest that each student's unique educational needs be met through adaptations to the curriculum and with the provision of supports. The following, adapted from Stainback and Stainback (1990), outlines key philosophies regarding inclusion.

Adapt the Curriculum

One of the greatest misconceptions of inclusion is that all students must somehow fit into the existing curriculum. In many cases, the curriculum used in the general class is not appropriate for students with disabilities. In such cases, the curriculum must somehow be adapted to meet the unique educational objectives and learning needs of the student. For example, an elementary student with cerebral palsy may have difficulty performing activities in a typical tumbling/gymnastics unit. This student could work on balance skills, rolls, and movement concepts, but he or she will work on these skills differently. This child might, for example, work on simple sitting balance while his peers work on more complex sitting balances such as a v-sit. While other students work on forward and backward rolls, this student might work on independently rolling from the stomach to the back and then getting to a standing position. Note how all students work on the same basic physical education educational objective (movement control) and learn together within the same general physical education activities (tumbling unit), but some students are evaluated using different curriculum objectives.

In some cases, the curriculum may not seem to match the needs of a particular student at all. In such cases, different parts of the curriculum might be presented at different times for different students. For example, a middle school student who is blind may not need to work on lacrosse, an activity found in many physical education curricula in the mid-Atlantic and northeast United States. This student might be given opportunities to feel the equipment and learn the rules of lacrosse, but during most of the lacrosse unit, this student may work on the softball/beep baseball skills of throwing, striking with a bat, and retrieving beep balls. Still, the basic skills of lacrosse are catching with a lacrosse stick, tossing with a lacrosse stick, and advancing the ball by tossing or running. Softball is part of the middle school curriculum and also includes skills of catching (with hands), tossing (throwing), and advancing the ball (striking). Thus, this student works on similar educational objectives (catching, tossing, and advancing a ball) but in a way that is more beneficial to him. In addition, this student can work on these skills within the general physical education class (see Chapter 6, 7, and 8 for more information on adaptations).

Integrate Personnel and Resources

Another misconception of inclusion is that students with disabilities will be dumped into general programs without support. As noted, the inclusion philosophy directs that students be supported in general education classes. Supports include specialized equipment; special instruction; and personnel such as volunteers, teacher assistants, and education specialists—many of the same supports that would have been given to a student in a segregated program. Students might have special equipment such as walkers, gait trainers, mats, or bolsters that should be brought to general physical education.

Utilize Natural Proportions

One of the reasons why early attempts at mainstreaming in physical education often failed was that entire special education classes (up to 10 students) were placed in one general physical education class. Such a situation was doomed because no physical educator could adequately meet the needs of all of these students plus those of a class full of children without disabilities. Inclusion philosophy suggests that students with disabilities be placed following the principle of *natural proportions*, meaning that the normal distribution of individuals with and without disabilities be maintained when placing students in general classes. Data suggest that perhaps 10%–15% of the school-age population has some type of disability, with more who have high-incidence disabilities such as learning disabilities, emotional disabilities, and intellectual disabilities and fewer who have low-incidence disabilities such as cerebral palsy, hearing impairments, and visual impairments. Such numbers translate to two or three students with disabilities (usually mild disabilities) in each class. Such a situation is much more manageable for the general physical educator.

RESEARCH ON INCLUSION IN PHYSICAL EDUCATION

There have been several significant studies from 1995 to 2005 examining issues and questions surrounding inclusion in general physical education (GPE). These studies have begun to shed some light onto the realities of inclusion in GPE. The following, modified from Block and Obrusnikova (in press), provides a brief review of these studies. This review is organized into four themes: 1) support, 2) attitudes of students without disabilities, 3) lack of training and negative attitudes of GPE teachers, and 4) social isolation of students with disabilities.

Support

Under certain circumstances, including students with disabilities in GPE (and even community sports programs) can be a positive experience for students with and without disabilities as well as general physical educators. One of these circumstances is support either in the form of peer tutors, teacher assistants, or an adapted physical education (APE) specialist. Peer tutoring in particular seems to be the most popular and effective support mechanism. Planned and appropriately implemented peer-tutoring programs have been found to be effective. Peer tutors provide a very cost-effective and simple way for GPE teachers to accommodate the individual needs of students with disabilities. Research has indicated that utilizing trained peer tutors could result in improved skill development and opportunities to respond (Houston-Wilson, Dunn, van der Mars, & McCubbin, 1997), physical activity levels (Lieberman, Dunn, van der Mars, & McCubbin, 2000), motor-appropriate engagement (Lieberman, Newcomer, McCubbin, & Dalrymple, 1997), and time on task (DePaepe, 1985; Webster, 1987) of students with disabilities.

For students with more severe disabilities, support from teacher assistants seems to be necessary to facilitate successful inclusion. For example, Murata and Jansma (1997) found that a combination of support from trained peer tutors with trained teacher assistants resulted in higher participation of students with severe disabilities in both physical and cognitive activities. This form of support not only aided students with disabilities but also prevented students with disabilities from disrupting the learning of peers without disabilities. Similar results were found in studies by Block and Zeman (1996) and Vogler, Koranda, and Romance (2000). These researchers confirmed that teacher assistants and trained APE specialists do not result in negative outcomes for students without disabilities in GPE as noted by no difference in motor skill acquisition (Block & Zeman, 1996) and motor-appropriate engagement (Vogler et al., 2000).

In addition, research has shown that GPE teachers with only limited consultative support can successfully include a student with a disability in GPE without negatively affecting the learning of peers without disabilities. For example, Obrusnikova, Block, and Válková (2003) found that the inclusion of a student with muscular dystrophy and indirect consultative support by an APE specialist and untrained peer tutors did not negatively affect the skill or cognitive acquisition of upper elementary students without disabilities. Intensive level of indirect consultative support from an APE specialist was also found to be effective in a study by Heikinaro-Johansson and her colleagues (1995).

Although it would be desirable to have teacher assistants and an APE teacher available, most school programs do not have this level of support. So, can we successfully include students with disabilities in GPE with virtually no support? The results of research are contradictory. Vogler, van der Mars, Cusimano, and Darst (1998) found that students with mild disabilities could maintain a high level of academic learning time–physical education (ALT-PE) when included in middle school GPE with peers without disabilities without any support. In addition, the inclusion did not seem to negatively affect the learning of students without disabilities or the ability of the GPE teacher to conduct an effective class. In contrast, Temple and Walkley (1999) found that elementary or middle school students with mild disabilities may under certain circumstances experience limited ALT-PE. The authors mentioned that there was no effort made by the GPE teacher to provide any accommodations for these students (e.g., curricular, equipment, or instructional adaptations)

to ensure their success. Perhaps the GPE teachers in this study felt that if the students were included in GPE, then the expectations for participation and success should be the same as peers without disabilities. Perhaps GPE teachers would make more accommodations for students who had very visible disabilities, such as visual or physical disabilities.

Some research suggests that students with disabilities might view such help negatively. For example, Goodwin (2001) found that 12 elementary school students with physical disabilities perceived peer interactions as either self-supporting or self-threatening. Self-supporting feelings were positive in nature and reflected peer interactions that were instrumental, caring, and consensual. Self-threatening feelings were negative in nature and reflected a loss of independence, a threat to self-image, help that was reckless, or in some cases interfering. It was not surprising that participant responses to the helping behaviors became more complex with age. Creating a long-term state of dependency is not good and may lead to a state of helplessness. It is important to remove any help that interferes with the independent completion of tasks, that is imposed rather than offered, or that implies personal inadequacy (Goodwin, 2001). Too much support can cause students with disabilities to feel helpless or dependent, or be limited from natural peer interactions.

Attitudes of Students without Disabilities

Attitudes toward individuals with disabilities have been the focus of much research. Researchers have found that students without disabilities tend to have positive attitudes toward having peers with disabilities in their GPE. For example, Block (1995b) found that middle school students had favorable attitudes toward inclusion of students with physical disabilities in GPE and were willing to allow for modifications for these students so that they could successfully participate in GPE activities. Verderber, Rizzo, and Sherrill (2003) found similar results with middle school students, even toward peers with severe disabilities. In addition, Verderber et al. (2003) found that peer pressure did not influence the attitude responses. Rather, students responded in a way that implied that they generally do what parents and teachers think they should do. This means that GPE teachers, parents, and maybe even support staff play a crucial role in successful inclusion of students with disabilities in GPE programs, at least in middle schools. Thus, identifying or affecting teacher attitudes can also influence the attitudes of students both with and without disabilities.

Evidence also exists that various attributes in inclusive GPE settings can affect students' attitudes. Favorable attitudes have been associated with gender (females more positive than males; Hazzard, 1983; Loovis & Loovis, 1997; Slininger, Sherrill, & Jankowski, 2000; Tripp, French, & Sherrill, 1995; Verderber et al., 2003; Voeltz, 1980, 1982) and experience with a family member or a close friend with a disability (Block, 1995b). In contrast, negative attitudes have been associated with being competitive (Block, 1995b) or with a disability type (Tripp, French, & Sherrill, 1995). Students in inclusive GPE programs were found to have different attitudes toward certain disability categories. For example, Tripp et al. (1995) found that students had less favorable attitudes toward including peers with physical disabilities than toward peers with behavioral disabilities. Lack of knowledge of and experience with disability can lead to unfavorable attitudes toward students with disabilities.

Tripp et al. (1995) found that unstructured contact with students with disabilities did not positively affect attitudes of elementary school students without disabilities. Even structured contact in Slininger et al. (2000), which occurred in cooperative games and rhythms and lasted for 4 weeks, did not result in positive effects on the attitudes of students without disabilities toward students with disabilities. Slininger et al. (2000) determined three major reasons why expected changes in attitudes were not found. First, similarly to Tripp et al. (1995), large class sizes may have limited the intensity of contact needed to cause changes in student attitudes. Second, the instruction in how to interact, play, and assist the students with disabilities may have been too limited. Third, the authors noted students had initially positive attitudes toward peers with disabilities, so improvement in attitudes would have to be considerable to show a statistically significant effect.

Murata, Hodge, and Little (2000) reported that contact did have a positive effect on the attitudes of 12 high school students without disabilities. These students were interviewed, and their responses showed initial skepticism and even fear; these feelings changed over time due to frequent, positive interactions with peers with disabilities. In addition, students reported that over time they began to appreciate and accept individual differences. Murata et al. noted several variables that contributed to the positive attitudes of high school students including that

> There were equal status contacts between and among peers with and without disabilities, social interactions among all students was encouraged by the GPE teacher, contacts were pleasant and rewarding, the contact situations involved common noncompetitive goals, and these individuals had occasion to develop meaningful relationships. (2000, p. 63)

In other words, the key to the positive attitude change is not simply placing students with disabilities into any GPE setting. Rather, the GPE teacher and teacher assistants need to facilitate equal status environment, positive peer interactions, and noncompetitive play.

Finally, Loovis and Loovis (1997) and Lockhart, French, and Gench (1998) attempted to determine the effect of specific, planned disability awareness training on attitudes of students without disabilities. The findings from these two studies resulted in different outcomes. Loovis and Loovis (1997) examined the effects of disability simulations (orientation and mobility when blindfolded, moving in a wheelchair, communicating with sign language) on second- through sixth-grade students from two different elementary schools. Results showed that only females were positively affected in their attitudes after the program. In contrast, Lockhart et al. (1998) did not find any significant effect on attitudes among students without disabilities following either cognitive or affective empathy training (10 days, 30 minutes each day). This evidence has proven that a planned disability awareness program through simulations or empathy training does not always work.

Lack of Training and Negative Attitudes of GPE Teachers

These research findings indicate that some GPE teachers can successfully accommodate students with disabilities in their GPE classes with, or even without, support. Nevertheless, inclusion will most likely fail if general educators, including GPE teachers, are left on their own or lack sufficient training to include students with disabilities. In fact, studies (Chandler & Greene, 1995; Janney, Snell, Beers, & Raynes, 1995; LaMaster, Gall, Kinchin, & Siedentop, 1998; Lieberman, Houston-Wilson, & Kozub, 2002; Lienert, Sherrill, & Myers, 2001) indicate that most GPE teachers do not feel competent to adequately meet the needs of students with disabilities who are included in their GPE programs. Teacher concerns focus on lack of knowledge, prior experience, perceived adequacy of professional preparation, need for more in-service training, and lack of equipment or programming. Still, some GPE teachers do an excellent job with including students with disabilities, even though they may feel that they need more training or support. On a positive note, Janney et al. (1995) found that such perceptions can change over time. By getting to know the students, the GPE teachers in this study gained knowledge and understanding of the students and in turn gained a new perspective on inclusion.

Teachers in these two studies were clearly dedicated and motivated to do what was best for all of their students, but would they have felt more successful with more preservice training? To answer that question, Block and Rizzo (1995) surveyed K–12 suburban teachers from a Midwestern state and found that attitudes were positively associated with coursework in APE or special education. Similarly, Maeda, Murata, and Hodge (1998) surveyed elementary and high school GPE teachers from Hawaii and found the same effect with graduate coursework in APE.

Again, the findings in this section support the belief that many GPE teachers do not feel prepared to include students with disabilities into their GPE program. More in-service training is needed as is ongoing training by IEP team members (e.g., special education teacher, APE specialist, therapists). GPE teachers who are willing to accept students with disabilities will be more successful and more satisfied with inclusion. It is perfectly normal for GPE teachers to feel a bit apprehensive and nervous about having students with disabilities in their GPE program. No one is asking GPE teachers to be perfect at including students with disabilities in GPE. Rather, all that is asked is for GPE teachers to give a good-faith effort. Try to include the student as best you can. Reflect on each lesson asking what went well, what did not go well, and what should be changed next time. Pat yourself on the back when things go well, and seek help when things do not go so well.

Social Isolation of Students with Disabilities

Although various efforts have greatly expanded the physical presence of individuals with disabilities in GPE settings, there is still a significant distance to go toward full inclusion. Research clearly shows that students with disabilities are often isolated and not socially included even though they may be physically present in GPE (e.g., Ellis, Wright, & Cronis, 1996; Goodwin, 2001; Goodwin & Watkinson, 2000; Hutzler, Fliess, Chacham, & van den Auweele, 2002; Lisboa, 1997; Place & Hodge, 2001). For example, Place and Hodge (2001) showed that three middle school students with physical disabilities had very little social contact with their peers without disabilities and little or no instruction or direction from the GPE teacher. The students were often engaged in off-task behaviors, and the vast majority of their interactions were with their peers with disabilities. Ellis et al. (1996) found similar results, with one caveat: Social contact of students with moderate to severe intellectual disabilities was influenced by how many students with disabilities were included

in a particular GPE class and how the class was organized. When an entire self-contained special education class of 11 students was incorporated into a GPE (violation of the natural proportions), the students tended to maintain their group identity (staying together as a group during GPE activities). This certainly contributed to the limited opportunities to interact with their peers without disabilities. The authors suggested that small-group settings in which only a few students with disabilities are included are the most conducive to social interactions between students with and without disabilities.

Lisboa (1997) also found that three students with autism they observed often experienced isolation when placed in GPE. These students were much more engaged in interactions with their teacher assistants than with the GPE teacher or peers. Support provided by teacher assistants is particularly important when including students with autism. Unfortunately, such support might actually inhibit opportunities for interactions with peers without disabilities. While direct instruction and one-to-one interactions between a teacher assistant and a student with autism are vital, interactions with peers without disabilities are also needed to teach the child all the social skills he or she needs to function successfully in the community.

Results of these three studies were obtained through observation of student behaviors in GPE. It should be noted that the data collection procedures in the studies did not allow the authors to reveal feelings and experiences of the students with disabilities. Fortunately, Blinde and McCallister (1998), Goodwin and Watkinson (2000), and Hutzler et al. (2002) conducted interviews with students with physical disabilities to find out perceptions of their experiences in GPE. The studies showed mixed results. For example, Goodwin and Watkinson (2000) reported that nine fifth- and sixth-grade students with physical disabilities had good days and bad days when included in GPE. Good days were marked by a sense of belonging and accommodations that allowed these students the opportunities to successfully participate in activities in GPE. Bad experiences were marked by social isolation, questioned competence, and limited opportunities to participate in GPE. Similar results were also found in Israel by Hutzler et al. (2002). Although four students with physical disabilities reported positive experiences, such as peers encouraging and even helping them to participate during games, six students reported being teased and ridiculed by their peers, such as peers imitating their walk or expressing pity. This resulted in negative feelings towards GPE as noted by comments such as "I hate it," "I am afraid," "I feel different," "I am disappointed," and "I cry." All participants, whether they had positive or negative experiences in

GPE, felt that their GPE teachers made no effort to accommodate their needs.

At least some of the participants in the studies by Goodwin and Watkinson (2000) and Hutzler et al. (2002) had positive experiences in GPE. Unfortunately, 19 of 20 students with physical disabilities studied by Blinde and McCallister (1998) reported stories of GPE that were, frankly, an embarrassment. Results from this qualitative study were consistent in that students reported receiving no accommodations, being excluded from GPE activities, and being ridiculed by the GPE teachers. For example, one student commented: "I participated in PE once, but I was just a line judge. I just sat there and cheered and did all that. I just sit and watch them and clap and stuff." Another student said, "My teacher didn't have nothing for me to do. I'd sit up on the stage from when I first got there until the end of class every day." And still another student said, "The instructor told me to leave because I was a liability. So I sat in the library for an hour every day, like having a study hall, and I got an A in PE!" Where are the individualized accommodations for these students with disabilities? What could these GPE teachers possibly have been thinking? Not surprising, the students in this study felt embarrassed, different, sad, and angry. When asked if he liked participating in GPE, one 13-year-old student said, "Well, not that much, because, about every time I get embarrassed. Because I cannot walk well, I cannot run well, [and] I cannot do volleyball that well. I cannot do any kind of sport well and [in] this here P.E. class I always get embarrassed" (p. 67).

Social development of children with disabilities depends to a great extent on the opportunities for social interactions with peers without disabilities both in school and in the community. Having friends to talk to and play with are critical. Unfortunately, study results indicate that these opportunities are often limited for students with disabilities, especially students with more severe disabilities who are accompanied by teacher assistants. If students with disabilities are physically included in GPE but never really make contact with others within the setting, or even worse are teased or ridiculed for their limitations, then inclusion is not working. Instead, student interaction should be encouraged in a way that allows a student with a disability to be included in decision-making tasks such as rule and equipment modifications. Teachers should model positive student behavior and plan interactions for both students with and without disabilities (e.g., placing students on teams in an equitable manner). In addition, students without disabilities should receive training on how to interact with their peers with disabilities (see Chapter 9 for information on how to promote social interaction between children with and without disabilities).

Summary of Research in Inclusion in GPE

Due to a low number of participants and/or descriptive, pre- or quasi-experimental designs, most of the studies described in this research review should be viewed as preliminary studies that need replication in order to generalize the findings. Still, the literature on inclusion in GPE is clearly expanding, with a growing shift from segregated special education programs to a merger between general and special education. Experiences with inclusion are both positive and negative, with research supporting the positive outweighing the negative. Many of the studies reviewed show that students with disabilities can be successfully included in GPE, there is no negative effect on peers without disabilities, and students without disabilities tend to have positive attitudes toward peers with disabilities. At the same time, other studies reveal a lack of preservice or in-service training for GPE teachers, low awareness and understanding among those without disabilities, and limited social contact available to students with disabilities. More research needs to be conducted to help us better understand why inclusion works sometimes and does not work other times. However, the scant research that has been collected does provide some guidance right now to make inclusion in GPE a positive experience for everyone involved.

SUMMARY

In summary, there is a growing shift from segregated special education programs to a merger between general and special education. As always, the bottom line in any educational program for students with disabilities is to provide quality programming designed to meet each student's individual needs. With proper preparation and support, quality programming can take place in inclusive settings. Benefits to participants both with and without disabilities provide an additional incentive to integrate students into general programs whenever possible.

A Team Approach to Inclusion in Physical Education

Shay's mother, Mrs. Beard, introduced herself to Mrs. Gilchrest, the special education teacher at Columbia Elementary School. Mrs. Beard was a pleasant woman who clearly loved her daughter and cared about her welfare. Not surprising, she also seemed to know a lot about Shay's condition. Shay was starting kindergarten at Columbia, but she was not like any kindergartner the staff and students at Columbia had ever seen. Shay was born 6 weeks prematurely and weighed only 1 pound, 15 ounces at birth. She was in the neonatal intensive care unit of Children's Hospital for 4 months before she was able to go home. While Shay's parents hoped that Shay would grow up to be a typical child, it was clear by her first birthday that Shay would have several permanent physical, cognitive, and health conditions, including severe but underdetermined cognitive impairment (intellectual disabilities), severe spastic (very stiff) quadriplegic (all four limbs involved) cerebral palsy, cortical blindness (eyes work, but optical nerve and optical receptors in the brain do not work), severe gastric problems along with oral problems that require feeding through a feeding tube, breathing difficulties requiring her to use oxygen, and fragile diabetes that requires taking a blood stick two to three times per day and taking glycogen paste orally or an injection of insulin as needed. Clearly, Shay's school attendance requires a tremendous amount of support.

Mrs. Gilchrest called a meeting with all school personnel who would work with Shay in the upcoming year. Mrs. France, the physical education teacher at Columbia, attended this meeting and turned white when she heard about Shay. How could Shay participate safely in general physical education? How could Mrs. France work with Shay while supervising and working with all of the other students in her class? What accommodations would be necessary to accommodate all of Shay's physical, cognitive, and health issues? Clearly, Mrs. France would need information and support from Shay's

parents as well as a variety of special education professionals who have more experience and knowledge about children like Shay. But to which specialists should Mrs. France turn for help? How would this help be provided? Mrs. France knew she needed help, but she did not even know where to start.

A variety of professionals are routinely involved in the development and implementation of a student's IEP, especially for children with more severe disabilities (Orelove, Sobsey, & Silberman, 2004). Although some school districts may not employ all of the professionals described in the case study, all school districts should have access to these professionals at least on a consultative basis. Together, all of those who work with a student with disabilities (including the general physical educator) are members of the student's *collaborative team* (Rainforth & York-Barr, 1997). These professionals can be invaluable resources to general and adapted physical educators who are attempting to include students with disabilities into general physical education. The purpose of this chapter is to define a collaborative team and explain the key professionals who are members of this team. Specific references to how team members can facilitate inclusion into physical education are provided. In addition, the importance of communication in collaborative teaming is discussed.

COLLABORATIVE TEAM

All students receiving special education services are required to have an IEP, which specifies in writing all aspects of their educational program. The concept of an IEP was specifically developed to guarantee that students with disabilities would receive all of the necessary services and the best educational program possible (Bateman & Herr, 2003). Many professionals are involved in the development and implementation of a student's IEP. In fact, IDEA 2004 mandates that a student's IEP be developed by a team that includes the student (when appropriate), student's parents, student's teachers, student's therapists, and a representative from the local education agency. Although IEP teams are designed to encourage team work and interaction among team members, some team members choose to work in isolation from other professionals providing therapy or services that are unrelated to the general education environment (Craig, Haggart, & Hull, 1999). In noncollaborative models, children may be pulled out of class for therapy or for adapted physical education a few times per week. Unfortunately, a pull-out model does not allow the specialist to learn about the general education environment and makes it difficult for specialists to share their knowledge about how to support the child (Craig et al., 1999). To illustrate, an adapted physical education specialist might be helping a child who uses a wheelchair to roll up and down a curb. However, if she does not share this information with the general physical education teacher, parents, or other professionals who work with this child to learn that this child never really needs to go up or down curbs to access the school building, then this isolationist approach results in inappropriate programming and limits the carryover and generalization of important skills.

Fortunately, most professionals are interested in working cooperatively and collaboratively with other professionals during the development and implementation of a student's IEP. Sharing expertise and resources among many professionals provides greater problem-solving abilities and enables all individuals involved in the student's educational program to utilize best teaching practices (Craig et al., 1999; Orelove et al., 2004; Rainforth & York-Barr, 1997). Collaborative teams meet on a regular basis to continually interact, plan, and modify a student's educational program. To illustrate, a collaborative team that meets twice per month is stumped on how to help a student who has severe autistic behaviors communicate with parents, friends, and teachers. In a monthly meeting, the speech therapist shares with team members how she uses a picture board to help this student communicate. At future meetings, the team discusses whether the new picture board program should be continued, changed, or dropped.

It should be noted that the formation of collaborative teams usually is not required by administrators. Thus, a team approach will only work if team members have a strong commitment to work together and to share information and ideas. Auxter, Pyfer, and Huettig (2005) noted that the collaborative model is a foreign concept to most general physical educators who are used to working very independently. Such an autonomous approach may work for children without disabilities, but it will not work for children with disabilities. Fortunately, most general physical educators quickly realize they need the expertise of others to safely and successfully develop and implement individualized physical education programs for their students with disabilities.

Collaborative Team Defined

Rainforth, York, and MacDonald (1992) coined the term *collaborative teamwork* to refer to the interaction and sharing of information and responsibilities among team members. As Snell and Janney clearly stated, "Collaborative teaming is two or more people working together toward a common goal (Rainforth & York-Barr, 1997). Working together can mean setting goals, identifying problems, assessing students' needs and skills, exchanging information, brainstorming, problem-solving, making plans, and implementing and evaluating plans" (2005, p. 6). Rainforth and her colleagues noted that the term was developed as a hybrid of the transdisciplinary model and the integrated therapy model. In the transdisciplinary model, parents and professionals share information and techniques. Professional boundaries are removed so that each team member is committed to promote the overall student's functional independence and participation in age-appropriate activities and routines (Craig et al., 1999). For example, physical therapists share information on positioning, while speech therapists show how to work on language development. Unfortunately, the transdisciplinary model often results in teachers' or paraprofessionals' conducting therapy in isolated, nonfunctional ways. For example, a paraprofessional may have learned how to perform range of motion activities on a student with cerebral palsy, but she may conduct the program away from the child's peers.

In the integrated therapy model, therapy is conducted within functional contexts (Craig et al., 1999). Taken together, the collaborative model focuses on team members' sharing information and working together to provide students with disabilities necessary educational and therapeutic services within functional activities (Craig et al., 1999). Thus, the paraprofessional who has learned how to perform range-of-motion activities might perform these activities during warm-ups in general physical education, and the student remains with the group while the program is performed. Thus, specialists

Table 3.1. Characteristics of collaborative teamwork

1. Equal participation in the collaborative teamwork process by family members and the educational service providers on the educational team
2. Equal participation by all disciplines determined to be necessary for students to achieve their individualized educational goals
3. Consensus decision making about priority educational goals and objectives related to all areas of student functioning at school, at home, and in the community
4. Consensus decision making about the type and amount of support required from related services personnel
5. Attention to motor, communication, and other embedded skills and needs throughout the educational program and in direct relevance to accomplishing priority educational goals
6. Infusion of knowledge and skills from different disciplines into the design of educational methods and interventions
7. Role release to enable team members who are involved most directly and frequently with students to develop the confidence and competence necessary to facilitate active learning and effective participation in the educational program
8. Collaborative problem solving and shared responsibility for students learning across all aspects of the educational program

From Rainforth, B., & York-Barr, J. (1997). *Collaborative teams for students with severe disabilities: Integrating therapy and educational services* (2nd ed., p. 23). Baltimore: Paul H. Brookes Publishing Co.; reprinted by permission.

(including the adapted physical educator) spend more time in general education (including general physical education) settings rather than pulling children out in isolated settings. Characteristics of collaborative teamwork as outlined by Rainforth and York-Barr (1997) can be found in Table 3.1. Note how equal participation, shared responsibility, interdependence, and the utilization of functional settings are critical aspects of collaborative teamwork.

The collaborative model allows team members to integrate their programs into a student's daily life routines (Craig et al., 1999). In addition, team members are encouraged to work together to help students in various settings. For example, a speech teacher along with a student's parents may accompany a student to a local YMCA to work on that student's communication skills. Parents and family members are particularly important as they can practice physical education skills at home or take their child to local recreation facilities to follow up on community-based recreation training (Horton, Wilson, & Gagnon, 2003; Kozub, 2001).

PHYSICAL EDUCATION INCLUSION TEAM

A subset of the collaborative team is needed to form a physical education inclusion team (PEIT). Generally speaking, the PEIT is comprised of all collaborative team members who can contribute to the suc-

cessful development and implementation of the physical education portion of the student's IEP. It is important to note that the PEIT does not have to meet at a special time. Rather, meetings can take place during a regular collaborative team meeting or during IEP meetings. In many cases, the special education teacher who is in charge of the general collaborative team meeting will allow the general physical educator to voice his or her concerns first to allow the GPE to quickly get back to class. In addition to the formal PEIT meeting, ongoing discussion between PEIT members should continue on a regular basis via e-mail, telephone calls, and shared notes. For example, during a collaborative team meeting, the general physical educator notes that Caleb's class will be working on a gymnastics unit and that the teacher is not sure if it is appropriate to include Caleb in gymnastics activities. The team reviews Caleb's IEP and notes that gymnastic activities are not a prioritized goal for Caleb. Through discussion among team members, it is decided that Caleb can participate with his peers during warm-ups. After warm-ups, on Tuesdays and Thursdays Caleb will work on setting up a tent provided by his parents (one of Caleb's goals is hiking/camping) in a corner of the gym with selected peers; on Mondays, Wednesdays, and Fridays, he goes hiking with the orientation and mobility specialist around the school perimeter with selected peers.

Meeting with the Physical Education Integration Team

The PEIT portion of the collaborative team meeting should be organized and run by a team leader (usually the adapted and/or general physical educator). This team solicits information from key members, documents decisions that were made during the meeting, and keeps all team members informed of pertinent information. Although it may be difficult to get all team members together for ongoing team meetings, it is imperative that all key team members, particularly the general physical educator, attend at least one preplanning meeting before the student with disabilities is included in the general physical education class.

It is important during PEIT meetings that team members introduce themselves and offer their assistance to the general physical educator. Most general physical educators are not part of the special education loop and might not be familiar with the roles of various specialists. One way of introducing team members is to utilize the concept of *role release* (Woodruff & McGonigel, 1988). Role release is a systematic way for team members to share ideas about their discipline and begin to work collaboratively to develop and implement the best possible program for a student with disabilities. Team members basically train one another to use their expertise from their various disciplines (Craig et al., 1999; Snell & Janney, 2005). Role release in introductory meetings should include the following: *role extension*, in which all team members begin to acquire knowledge about each other's disciplines (e.g., team members describe their role in the educational program of the student); *role enrichment*, in which team members begin to share information about basic practices (team members share their best teaching practices related to a particular student); and *role expansion*, in which team members exchange best teaching practices across disciplines (team members explain how other team members can utilize these best teaching practices in their setting). By the end of the first meeting, the general physical educator should feel that he or she has real resources to go to in order to get answers to answer specific questions about the student's physical education program. In addition, the general physical educator should have a greater understanding of the student's overall educational program (not just physical education) and how he or she can assist other team members in meeting other educational goals. Role release in future meetings should include *role exchange*, in which team members begin to implement teaching techniques from other disciplines, and *role support*, in which team members back each other up as team members assume the roles of other disciplines.

A great deal of information should be presented at this initial meeting so that team members can make informed decisions regarding the development of the student's individualized physical education program and strategies for inclusion. Various team members will be able to provide different aspects of the information. For example, vision teachers can provide information about a student's visual abilities, physical therapists can provide information about a student's motor abilities and physical fitness, the general physical educator can provide information about the general physical education curriculum and class format, and the student and his or her parents can provide information about a student's likes and dislikes. Key information and team members most likely to provide this information are presented in Figure 3.1.

While future team meetings are important and should be planned, some members may not be able to attend meetings on a regular basis. In such cases, the team leader should share information from team members with the team. For example, if the general physical educator cannot attend a meeting, he or she can provide information to the team leader regarding how well the student is doing, what modifications and teaching approaches have been effective or ineffective, and what the next physical education unit will include. Similarly, the student's physical therapist can provide information regarding any physical changes in the student that may affect his physical education program. Team members also should feel comfortable contacting each other with specific questions about the student's physical education program. Although formal team meetings provide the best means for discussing the student's program, team members must feel comfortable communicating with each other whenever the need arises.

Sarah is a 13-year-old student who is starting sixth grade at a local middle school. Sarah enjoys holding and throwing various-sized balls, pushing her wheelchair in various directions and being pushed really fast by her peers, bowling, listening to music, and being around her peers without disabilities. Sarah has severe, spastic hemiplegic cerebral palsy; severe intellectual disabilities; severe vision and speech impairments; and a seizure disorder. Sarah's PEIT includes her parents, special education teacher, physical therapist, occupational therapist, speech therapist, vision therapist, nurse, adapted physical educator, and general physical educator. The adapted physical educator serves as the team leader (see Figure 3.2 for an example of a team meeting agenda and minutes form).

In previous PEIT meetings, the team developed a plan for Sarah that included the following long-term goals: push her wheelchair with direction, acquire skills needed to partially participate in bowling using a ramp, swim using a flotation device, play miniature golf using a ramp, independently participate in aerobic dance, and partially participate in modified games of basketball and softball. The adapted and general physical educator reviews the progress that Sarah has made toward these goals. Sarah has just completed a unit on softball with her peers. She learned how to hold the bat using one hand and hit a ball off a tee so that it travels 5 feet in the air. In addition, she can push her wheelchair down the first base line (with verbal cuing) a distance of 10 feet in 30 seconds, a tremendous improvement from the previous month.

Other team members ask the general and adapted physical educators specific questions regarding their area of interest. For example, the speech therapist notes that Sarah's ability to communicate with a picture board taped to her lap tray is improving, and she wants to know if Sarah is using the board in physical education. The general physical educator notes that he has seen Sarah use her pictures several times to communicate with him and with peers. Similarly, the vision and physical therapist discuss changes they have seen in Sarah over the past month and query the general and adapted physical educators as to similar changes they

	P/S	SE	MD	PT	OT	VT	ST	PY	PE	APE
Information regarding the student										
Information on specific disability of the student with emphasis on how this disability will affect abilities in general physical education	X	X	X	X	X	X	X		X	
Medical and health information regarding the student, particularly as related to contraindicated activities	X	X	X	X						
Behaviors of student, including what behaviors to expect, what generally causes behavior outbursts, and what behavior program is in place for the student	X	X						X		
Communication abilities of student, including how the student communicates, how well the student understands verbal directions, and how to best communicate with the student	X	X					X			
Special equipment (if any) the student uses and whether this equipment will be brought into general physical education	X			X	X	X				X
Personal hygiene skills of student, including locker room skills, ability to dress and undress, and ability to take a shower and perform personal grooming skills	X	X		X	X					
Motor skills, including general information regarding physical fitness, fundamental motor skills, and perceptual motor abilities	X	X	X	X					X	
Specific information regarding recreation activities available in the student's community or neighborhood	X								X	X
Interests of student and student's parents, particularly as the student reaches high school and begins to develop interests in particular lifetime leisure skills and possibly sports	X									
Special sports opportunities such as Special Olympics	X			X						X
Specific goals developed for student that are not directly related to physical education but that can be worked on in the physical education setting	X	X	X	X	X	X	X	X	X	X
Activities that take place in general physical education										
Length of a typical physical education class and how the period is broken down (e.g., 10 minutes for locker room, 25 minutes for activity)									X	
The daily routine that usually takes place in general physical education									X	
The typical teaching style (movement education, direct teaching, highly structured)									X	
The minimal skills needed in the locker room									X	

Figure 3.1. Which team members to seek for specific information. (*Key:* P/S, parent and/or student; SE, special education teacher; MD, physician; PT, physical therapist; OT, occupational therapist; VT, vision therapist; ST, speech therapist; PY, psychologist; PE, general physical educator; APE, adapted physical educator.)

Team Meeting Agenda

Team meeting for: _____ Date: _____ Time: _____

Location of meeting: _____

Facilitator: _____ Recorder: _____

Agenda items and description	Outcomes desired

Figure 3.2. Form to record PEIT meeting agenda and minutes (From Rainforth, B., & York-Barr, J. [1997]. *Collaborative teams for students with severe disabilities: Integrating therapy and educational services* [2nd ed., pp. 335–336]. Baltimore: Paul H. Brookes Publishing Co.; reprinted by permission.)

Team Meeting Minutes

Team meeting for: _____ Date: _____

Start time: _____ Finish time: _____

Participants: _____

Facilitator: _____ Recorder: _____

Priority sequence	Agenda items and key points	Follow-up needed: Who? What? When?

Next meeting

Date/time: _____ Location: _____

Facilitator: _____ Recorder: _____

Agenda items: _____

_____

_____

_____

might have seen. On Fridays, Sarah goes with the adapted physical educator and several peers without disabilities to the local YMCA to swim and then to the local bowling alley. The adapted physical educator reviews the progress she has made in these IEP goals. He notes that Sarah can now push the bowling ball down the ramp without any extra verbal cues. In addition, he notes that she will take her wallet out of her purse and pay $1 for bowling shoes after a verbal cue. She also points to the picture of a shoe on her picture board after a verbal cue (the speech therapist was thrilled to hear this). The occupational therapist, who assists Sarah at the bowling alley, notes that Sarah is gaining much more control of her functional hand, and she is able to take things out of her purse and wallet independently within 30 seconds of a verbal command. Sarah has not made any notable gains in swimming, but she really enjoys using a flotation device. In addition, she is continuing to work on her dressing and undressing skills. The team comments that Sarah should continue her bowling and swimming program on Fridays.

The general physical educator then reviews the next unit, track and field. He briefly explains the activities that will take place in this unit and then asks team members for suggestions for Sarah. The physical therapist notes that Sarah should continue to work on her wheelchair mobility skills. In addition, the physical therapist gives the general physical educator some new stretches for Sarah's upper body that she can do with her assistant during warm-ups. The adapted physical educator suggests that Sarah train for specific Special Olympics wheelchair events so that she can culminate her training with actual track events. The team meeting concludes with the team leader's reviewing Sarah's program and noting on the minutes any actions that should take place by the next meeting. The next meeting is set for the first countywide in-service day (approximately 6 weeks away). At that time, team members are expected to provide brief written evaluations of Sarah's progress. For example, the speech therapist will evaluate Sarah's functional use of the picture board during general physical education class. The adapted physical educator reminds team members that they should feel free to contact each other by memo or telephone if they need more information in the interim.

COLLABORATIVE TEAM MEMBERS

A variety of professionals can be involved in the collaborative team. While each team member has specific responsibilities, the collaborative model suggests that each member assist other professionals in carrying out their responsibilities. In addition, the collaborative approach prevents holes in services or needless duplication of services for a particular student. The following describes the specific responsibilities of collaborative team members as well as how they can assist GPEs and APEs in successfully including students with disabilities in general physical education. Note that the key when determining which professional is involved in a particular student's IEP is "whether a professional's services and skills are deemed necessary for a student to benefit from his or her IEP" (Orelove et al., 2004, p. 3). For example, a collaborative team for a child who does not have a visual impairment would not include a vision specialist. However, this does not mean that the GPE or APE cannot ask this professional for advice. The general physical educator might want some general information on how to make the physical education environment more visually stimulating and visually safe for children who have trouble with activities that require tracking balls such as volleyball and basketball.

Adapted Physical Education Professionals

Many school districts in the United States require physical education for children with disabilities to be administered by a qualified adapted physical education (APE) professional who meets state requirements and competencies (Kelly, 1991; NCPERID, 1995, 2006). Qualified APE professionals usually have a master's degree in adapted physical education, extensive practical experience working with children with disabilities, and considerable knowledge in disability and physical education. One way to ensure that a school district is getting a qualified APE professional is to hire a certified adapted physical educator (CAPE). CAPEs are licensed physical education specialists who have documented practical experience and training in adapted physical education and who have successfully passed the APENS exam (NCPERID, 1995, 2006).

The major role of APE professionals is to assist in the identification and remediation of physical education-related problems of students who have disabilities (NCPERID, 1995, 2006; Sherrill, 2004). Specific services provided by APE professionals include assessment, program planning, writing individualized physical education programs, participating in IEP meetings, directly implementing habilitative programs for students with disabilities, consulting with general physical educators and parents, fitness and leisure counseling including sports for individuals with disabilities, and advocating for children with disabilities in physical education and sport (McCubbin, Jansma, & Houston-Wilson, 1993; Sherrill, 2004). While most APE professionals work directly with students with disabilities, particularly those with severe disabilities, many are increasingly working as consultants (Block & Conatser, 1999; NCPERID, 1995, 2006; Sherrill, 2004). In this role, the APE professional helps others (usually the general physical educator and parents) work more successfully with children with disabilities (Block & Conatser, 1999).

Unfortunately, fewer than 20 states have any special requirements for APE professionals other than a general physical education teaching license. Thus, many school districts employ APE professionals who do not have any specialized training, experience, or knowledge regarding children with disabilities (Winnick, 2005). Even worse, many smaller school districts do not have anyone on staff designated as an APE professional.

The APE professional can assist the general physical educator in including students with disabilities into general physical education in a variety of ways. First, the APE professional can take all of the information provided by the other team members, including specific information about the student's physical and motor skills, and present it to the general physical education specialist in a way that is meaningful and practical. Second, the APE professional can provide specific information to the general physical educator about modifying physical education activities to safely and successfully include the student with disabilities. This can be accomplished through counseling sessions, team teaching, or providing written modifications to lesson plans (Block & Conatser, 1999; Sherrill, 2004). Because the APE professional knows more about how specific types of disabilities affect physical education, he or she is the most important member of the team.

General Physical Education Professional

GPE professionals are specifically trained and licensed to teach physical education to children without disabilities. Although in the past these professionals were asked to only work with students without disabilities, changing legislation and roles require these professionals to work with all children who enter their gymnasium, including children with disabilities (Winnick, 1995). Many will enjoy their new role and become quickly acclimated to working with children who have disabilities; others will be more resistant to change. In either case, GPE professionals should be included and welcomed to the collaborative team. GPE professionals have a great deal of knowledge about all components of physical education (physical fitness, fundamental motor skills, individual and team sports and games). In addition, they have direct information on the behaviors and

attitude of the child with disability in general physical education. Perhaps of greatest importance, the general physical educator knows what units are taught at what point in the year, what teaching approach is used, what equipment is available, how many students are in each class, and the pace and dynamics of the class (CEC, 1999).

It is important to remember that most GPE professionals have had very little training or experience in working with students who have disabilities and thus may probably be a little apprehensive about including a student with disabilities into their general program (Chandler & Greene, 1995; Janney, Snell, Beers, & Raynes, 1995). Most GPE specialists have had only one survey course in adapted physical education during their formal training and very little practical experience working with children who have disabilities. It is the responsibility of all team members to make GPE specialists feel as comfortable as possible with inclusion. It is the responsibility of the GPE teacher to have an open mind about inclusion, provide opportunities for interaction between students with and without disabilities, and serve as a role model to students without disabilities by respecting the students' individual differences (Block, 1999).

According to IDEA 2004, a general educator must be included on the IEP team if the student is or may be taking part in any general education (including GPE). This does not necessarily mean that the GPE specialist must attend every IEP meeting for every child in his or her building who has a disability. However, this does mean the special education teacher should invite the GPE specialist to IEP meetings and seek his or her input into physical education programming for children with disabilities.

Special Education Teacher

The special education teacher is the primary advocate and program planner for the student with disabilities (CEC, 1999; Stainback & Stainback, 1985). His or her role is to develop and assist in the implementation the student's IEP including initiation and organization of integrated activities. In addition, the special education teacher coordinates all support and related services a student needs (Stainback & Stainback, 1985). The special education teacher knows more about the student with disabilities than any other team member with the exception of the student's parents, including the student's developmental history, health and medical background, behaviors and behavior plans, communication and cognitive skills, self-help skills, learning style, successful teaching techniques, and likes and dislikes (CEC, 1999). In addition, as coordinator of all of the student's services, the special educator can quickly communicate information to other team members. The special education teacher can also assist in training of peer tutors and paraprofessionals.

Building Principal

The building principal is responsible for everything that takes place in his or her school including physical education programs and programs for students with disabilities. Thus, while not directly involved in program planning or implementation, the building principal has a vested interest in the success of the inclusive physical education program. Principals who support inclusive physical education can have a direct impact on the attitudes of general physical education staff. In addition, principals can help team members gain important resources such as extra support, special equipment, and gym time. Finally, the principal can act as a go-between to other administrators such as directors of physical education or special education at a school-system level.

School Nurse

More students with medical problems are entering public schools (Kline, Silver, & Russell, 2001), making the school nurse an invaluable resource to the team regarding health and medical information, daily care, and emergency planning. School nurses are mainly responsible for diagnosing and treating minor injuries and illnesses, handling medical emergencies and contacting other emergency personnel, and monitoring and administering prescription medications. In some schools, nurses are also responsible for specific health care procedures such as suctioning a student's tracheostomy (hole in throat used for breathing), conducting postural drainage for students with cystic fibrosis, administering clean intermittent catheterization for students who do not have bladder control, and tube-feeding students who cannot receive adequate nutrition through oral feeding. Because the school nurse has direct access to the student's parents and physicians, he or she can act as a link between a student's parents and physicians and the school. For example, if a question arises as to the effects of vigorous exercise on a seizure disorder, the school nurse can contact the student's parents and physicians to get an immediate answer. The school nurse should act as a consultant to the team, and team members should feel free to contact the nurse if they have any questions regarding a particular student's health or medical state (Winnick, 1995). For example, the nurse should be consulted when a student with a seizure disorder is involved in activities such as swimming or gymnastics or when a student with allergy-induced asthma is planning to go outside for physical education.

Physical Therapist

According to PL 94-142, a precursor to IDEA 2004, physical therapy (PT) vaguely means "services provided by a qualified physical therapist" (Federal Register, August 23, 1977, p. 42479). According to the American Physical Therapy Association, "The physical therapist provides services aimed at preventing the onset and/or slowing the progression of conditions resulting from injury, disease, or other causes" (2005, p. 1). In school settings, PTs specialize in gross motor development (movements that involve large muscles of the body), utilizing various techniques to relieve pain and discomfort, prevent deformity and further disability, restore or maintain functioning, and improve strength and motor skill performance (Hanft & Place, 1996; Sherrill, 2004). PTs also work on activities of daily living (e.g., getting around the school building, dressing, sitting properly) and addressing architectural barriers. Techniques include therapeutic exercise, developmental therapy, and assistive devices such as gait trainers, walkers, braces, canes, crutches, and wheelchairs. The type of therapy will depend on the goals that have been set by the IEP team (Hanft & Place, 1996; Sherrill, 2004). In most states, PTs must have a written referral from the child's physician (usually an orthopedic surgeon) before they can provide therapy to children with disabilities. However, this is changing, and in many school districts now a PT can provide services without a doctor's prescription (Knoll, personal communication, February 5, 2005). The physician is supposed to provide a diagnosis, goals to be accomplished, and instructions regarding precautions and contraindications, but this often does not happen.

The PT knows a lot about the student's physical condition and should be included in decisions regarding activities or positions, selection of motor skills for training, positioning and limb use for optimum functioning, and modifications to equipment and rules of the game. For example, for a third-grade student who is learning to walk with a walker in a general physical education class, the PT can provide information regarding what warm-up activities are appropriate or inappropriate; how to modify appropriate warm-up activities and what alternative warm-ups could be used at other times; how far and how fast the student should be expected to walk; the student's aerobic capacity, strength, and flexibility; and suggestions for modifications to activities in general physical education.

Occupational Therapist

According to PL 94-142, occupational therapists (OTs) utilize various techniques to improve, develop, and/or restore functions impaired or lost through illness, injury, or deprivation; improve ability to perform tasks for independent functioning when functions are impaired or lost; and prevent, through early intervention, initial or further impairment or loss of function (Federal Register, August 23, 1977, p. 42479). According to the American Occupational Therapy Association (AOTA, 2005, p. 1), "Occupational therapy is skilled treatment that helps individuals achieve independence in all facets of their lives. It gives people the 'skills for the job of living' necessary for independent and satisfying lives." In schools, OTs focus on helping students with disabilities perform activities of daily living (ADLs) as independently as possible. Another major focus of school-based occupational therapy is the presentation of sensorimotor integration activities designed to assist children with disabilities to fully utilize and integrate vestibular information (information from the inner ear that tells a person where the head is in relation to gravity), tactile information (sense of touch and feedback from touch sensors on the skin) and visual information (Hanft & Place, 1996). The OT can be an important resource on the team regarding a student's abilities (and possible adaptations) in self-help and personal hygiene skills needed in the locker room prior to and after a physical education class; fine motor skills, fundamental manipulative skills, and sport-specific manipulative skills; and skills related to sensory integration such as static and dynamic balance, tactile awareness, and proprioception.

Recreation Therapists

According to PL 94-142, the primary responsibilities of recreation therapists (RT) include assessment of leisure function, therapeutic recreation services, recreation programs in schools and community agencies, and leisure education (Federal Register, August 23, 1977, p. 42479). According to the American Therapeutic Recreation Association (ATRA; 2005, p. 1),

> A recreational therapist utilizes a wide range of activity and technique to improve the physical, cognitive, emotional, social, and leisure needs of their clients. Recreational therapists assist clients to develop skills, knowledge, and behaviors for daily living and community involvement. The therapist works with the client and their family to incorporate specific interests and community resources into therapy to achieve optimal outcomes that transfer to their real life situations.

Basically, recreation services are used to improve functional abilities, enhance well-being and facilitate independence, teach or enhance recreation skills and attitudes that can be used throughout life, and promote health and growth through leisure and recreation experiences (Etzel-Wise & Mears, 2004; Wenzel, 2000). Recreation therapy includes an array of programs including music, art, dance, drama, horticulture, camping, and sports and fitness. Recreation therapy utilizes a child's existing skills and interests and facilitates new skills for daily living and leisure functioning (ATRA, 2005). Recreation therapy is provided by trained and licensed RT professionals who, like physical therapists, must have physician's referral before they can provide therapy to children with disabilities. For this reason, RT is more common in children's hospitals and rehabilitation centers than in public schools.

RTs can provide the team with information regarding recreation/leisure assessment, availability of community recreation facilities, and suggestions for adaptations in performing recreation/leisure programs. This information can be particularly important to physical educators who are assisting the student with disabilities make the transition from a school-based physical education program to a post-school recreation program. RT professionals also often have a good understanding of the how well the child is emotionally dealing with his or her disability.

Speech Therapist

The primary role of the speech therapist is defined in IDEA as follows:

> Identification of children with speech or language disorders, diagnosis and appraisal of specific speech or language disorders, referral for medical or other professional attention necessary for the habilitation of speech or language disorders, provision of speech and language services for the habilitation or prevention of communicative disorders, counseling and guidance for parents, children, and teachers regarding speech or language disorders. (Federal Register, August 23, 1977, p. 42480)

Speech therapists can assist team members in understanding a student's receptive and expressive language abilities and how best to communicate with certain students. For example, some students might understand verbal cues and simple demonstrations, while other students might need sign language or physical assistance. Students with disabilities communicate via speech, sign language, communication boards, and electronic devices such as Canon Communicators or speech synthesizers. Knowing how to best present information to students as well as understanding how a student might express his or her desires is extremely important for successful inclusion in physical education.

Audiologist

Audiologists are trained professionals who work with students with hearing impairments. The major role of the audiologist is to determine a student's hearing loss and abilities and recommend special augmentative hearing devices such as hearing aids. In addition, audiologists often consult with speech therapists to determine a particular student's potential for speech and language development (American Speech-Language-Hearing Association, 2005). An audiologist can assist the general physical educator by explaining a student's hearing loss and specifying his or her residual hearing abilities. In collaboration with the speech therapist, the audiologist can recommend ways to communicate with a student who has a hearing impairment. For example, an audiologist might suggest that a student who has a severe hearing loss be provided with verbal directions repeated by a peer or have demonstrations to supplement verbal commands. In addition, the audiologist can explain safety precautions for this student such as avoiding contact to the ear while he is wearing his hearing aids or taking the aids out when swimming.

Vision Specialists

Vision specialists (also called vision teachers) are certified professionals trained in meeting the educational needs of children with visual impairments (Brasher & Holbrook, 1996). Vision teachers' major goal is to help students with visual impairments become as functional and independent as possible. Specifically, for students with low vision, goals include learning orientation and mobility skills necessary to move about in various environments and learning adapted techniques for class work such as reading large print, using felt tip markers, using a magnifying glass, and using computers. For students who have very limited vision or who are blind, goals include orientation and mobility skills such as using a cane and a sighted guide and learning adapted techniques for classwork such as using braille and computers.

Vision teachers also encourage movement and introduce toys that are visually or tactually interesting, stimulate the use of all senses, teach prereading skills such as tracking and finger positioning, teach braille reading, and help with daily living skills such as eating and dressing (Brasher & Holbrook, 1996).

Vision teachers work very closely with other professionals and serve as some children's primary teacher. They can be invaluable to adapted and general physical educators. For example, a vision teacher can show how to make a student with a visual impairment feel more comfortable in the gym environment, how to appropriately interact with the student, and how to assist the student. Vision teachers can also provide ideas for adapted equipment, safety precautions, and rule modifications such as guide ropes for running, beeper balls for softball, and tandem bike riding. Many vision teachers have easy access to adapted equipment such as beeper balls and balls with bells, and many are knowledgeable about special sports programs designed for persons with visual impairments such as the United States Association for Blind Athletes (USABA).

Orientation and Mobility Specialist

Orientation and mobility (O&M) specialists (also called O&M teachers or travel instructors) are certified teachers who have specialized training in teaching children and adults with visual impairments how to travel safely and efficiently in a variety of environments (Brasher & Holbrook, 1996). Initially, O&M specialists work with children on general space awareness, body image, and directionality (over, under, left, and right). As the child progresses, O&M training moves to more specific travel skills, including traveling within a room and between rooms. Depending on the child's visual and cognitive abilities and age, the O&M specialist might have children use a sighted guide, a cane, or a dog (ACVREP, 2005). O&M specialists can be an invaluable aid by helping the child learn how to independently move from the classroom to the gym and orienting the child to the locker room, pool area, gymnasium, and any other physical education environments. Finally, the O&M specialist can help identify dangerous places in the gym, show how to help a child with a vision impairment move more safely in the gym, and give ideas for adapting equipment and rules.

Paraprofessionals

Paraprofessionals (also known as paraeducators, educational aides, instructional assistants, teaching assistants, and individualized learning assistants) are hired to assist teachers (including general physical educators) in implementing a student's IEP. Paraprofessionals work under the supervision of a teacher or other professional (including the general physical educator) who is responsible for the overall management of the class, creation and implementation of the IEP, and assessment of the student's progress (Doyle, 2002). In inclusive programs the paraprofessional is often the person who has the most one-to-one contact with the student with disabilities.

Paraprofessionals vary greatly in their background and training, from certified special education teachers to individuals with virtually no prior experience with students who have disabilities. In addition, paraprofessionals are utilized differently by different teachers. Some paraprofessionals are only responsible for noninstructional responsibilities such as clerical work (e.g., making copies, lunch count, attendance); monitoring students in the hallway, at lunch, or on the playground; setting up the classroom for the teacher; or providing specific personal care such as dressing, feeding, and repositioning (Doyle, 2002). Others have more instructional responsibilities such as observing, recording, and charting a student's behavior and academic progress; assisting in full classroom instruction; assisting with individualized instruction; tutoring small groups of students; implementing and reinforcing teacher-developed lessons; contributing ideas and suggestions regarding a child or group of children; and participating in team meetings (Doyle, 2002).

Regardless of the exact role of paraprofessionals, their close contact to the student with disabilities enables them to provide unique insight to the needs and interests of the student. Thus, paraprofessionals can provide valuable information to the team regarding the student's behaviors at certain times during the day, communication skills, likes and dislikes, preferred positions, and effective adaptations and activities. In many programs, the paraprofessional accompanies the student with disabilities to physical education class (Horton, 2001). It is important to note that paraprofessionals *are not* responsible for the initial design and development of instructional procedures for students with disabilities in physical education, assessment, or decision making (Doyle, 2002). While paraprofessionals can be included in the process, the general physical educator should be responsible for developing lesson plans and training the paraprofessional to implement these plans. In addition, the general physical education teacher must be prepared to provide the paraprofessional with some directions regarding the plan for the day, what peers should be encouraged to work on with the child with a disability, what modifications and adapted equipment to anticipate for certain activities, what activities might be inappropriate, and how to help the child work on specific skills and be part of the group (Horton, 2001).

Parents

Parents and caregivers are often overlooked resources in the education of their children with disabilities even though by law they should be an integral part in the development of IEPs (Kozub, 2001). In fact, the IDEA Amendments of 1997 strengthened the role of the parent by noting that parents' concerns, as well as the information they provide about their child, must be considered when developing and reviewing the IEP. In addition, IDEA 2004 requires one or both parents of a student with a disability to be present at each IEP meeting or at least be given the chance to participate (CEC, 1999). But more than a legal mandate, parental participation on the collaborative team is critical for developing an appropriate IEP. Parents know more practical information about their child than any professional. In addition, parents often have developed successful management and training techniques that can be useful in the classroom and in physical education.

Parents should also be encouraged to share their goals and expectations for their child as well as their personal recreation interests so that the physical educator can gear the adapted physical education program to meet the unique needs of the family (Kozub, 2001). It is much easier to get support from home when parents are included in the decision process. For example, if a family enjoys playing tennis and going hiking during their weekend leisure time, then it would make sense to target these skills for a middle school student with a disability. These skills will likely be practiced at home and, when mastered, can help the individual participate more successfully at home and school. Figure 3.3 provides a simple form that can be sent home to parents to get their input regarding the family's recreational hobbies and what physical education goals they would like to target for the child. This information can then be shared with the collaborative team during the IEP meeting.

Student with Disabilities

The student with a disability should be included on the team whenever possible (Price, Wolensky, & Mulligan, 2002). Who else knows more about his or her own abilities, interests, and needs than the student? Also, a student with disabilities who is included in the process of developing his or her educational program is more likely to be committed and motivated to work on specific program goals (MacDonald & Block, 2005). After all, the team is really in place to discuss the student's present and future (CEC, 1999). Also, participation is the first step in

Parent Physical Education Interest Form

Student's name: _____

Person filling out this form: _____

Date: _____ Student's age: _____

1. What do you do as a family for recreation (e.g., play tennis, go for walks, go swimming)?

    _____
    _____
    _____
    _____

2. What activities do you see other children in your neighborhood doing that you think your child would enjoy (e.g., bike riding, soccer, tee ball, rollerblading)?

    _____
    _____
    _____
    _____

3. What community-based recreation sport program does your child participate in or would you like to see your child participate in (e.g., tee ball, soccer, any Special Olympics or other special sport program)?

    _____
    _____
    _____
    _____

4. Do you have any fitness concerns for your child that you would like to be addressed in physical education (e.g., upper body strength, flexibility, endurance, body weight)?

    _____
    _____
    _____
    _____

5. What other specific things would you like your child to work on during physical education (i.e., what would be your dream physical education program)?

    _____
    _____
    _____
    _____
    _____

Figure 3.3. Parent physical education interest form.

helping children learn to be their own best advocate (Pennell, 2001).

Levels and kinds of participation will vary from student to student depending on age and ability to communicate and participate in the meeting. For example, an elementary-age student with spina bifida might attend a PEIT meeting to discuss alternative ways she might participate in warm-up activities when the class is doing locomotor patterns. Similarly, a high school–age student who is blind can choose a cardiovascular training program (e.g., aerobic dance, stair climber, stationary bike, walking the track) that meets his or her interests. Students who are given choices tend to more motivated learners. In addition, having the child present at team meetings helps the team focus on the child's needs rather than their own schedules and problems.

If a student with a disability is going to attend a collaborative team meeting, then someone should talk to the student ahead of time about who will be attending the meeting, what will be discussed, questions he or she may be asked by team members, and what information he or she can share with the team (CEC, 1999). Also, team members should be careful to use terminology that the student understands. For nonverbal students, interests and abilities can be shared with the group via videotapes or portfolios.

COMMUNICATION: THE KEY TO COLLABORATIVE TEAMING

Collaborative teaming is really nothing more than a simple exchange of ideas. Dougherty (1995) noted that collaboration is a human relationship and as such needs to be handled with a personal touch. He suggested that how team members communicate with each other often is more important than what they are communicating. Critical for successful collaborative teaming is being able to express ideas, articulate requests clearly and in a nonthreatening way, elicit information from others, and listen to how others feel (Hanft & Place, 1996; Kurpius & Rozecki, 1993; Sherrill, 2004; Snell & Janney, 2005). Unfortunately, communication is such a difficult process that misunderstanding and miscommunication frequently occur (Heron & Harris, 1993). The following outlines key aspects of effective communication in collaborative teaming.

Establishing and Maintaining Effective Communication

Because so much of collaboration revolves around communication, it is critical for team members to understand how to establish and maintain effective communication. Heron and Harris (1993) suggested that to establish open channels to communication team members must first gain acceptance from each other and work to minimize resistance and manage conflict.

Gaining Acceptance

Gaining acceptance and establishing rapport among team members is extremely important (Hanft & Place, 1996; Pedron & Evans, 1990). Collaborative teaming is much easier if positive relationships are established from the beginning (see Table 3.2). Hanft and Place (1996) noted that all collaboration should start with the explicit goal of establishing positive relationships between team members through effective interpersonal and communication skills. Important aspects of gaining acceptance include genuineness (conveying sincerity), positive regard (treating others with respect), empathy (understanding the other's perspective), and congruence (establishing a common ground to converse and share thoughts and feelings honestly) (Heron & Harris, 1993; Kurpius & Rozecki, 1993).

Minimizing Resistance

Related to gaining acceptance is anticipating and dealing with resistance. Establishing trust and a genuineness to the interests of other team members and the student is perhaps the best way to overcome resistance (Gutkin & Curtis, 1982; Kurpius & Rozecki, 1993; Margolis & McCabe, 1988; Snell & Janney, 2005). Margolis and McCabe (1988) provided the following suggestions for creating trust: Provide complete and unhurried attention, keep your word, listen to understand rather than to challenge, respond to request for assistance in a timely manner, use easily understood language (i.e., avoid jargon), share expertise without dominating the discussion, use active listening techniques (discussed later in this chapter), and if resistance persists use a problem-solving technique to determine how to address it.

Table 3.2. Strategies to create positive relationships

1. Honor each member's style of interaction.
2. Acknowledge caseloads or class size and the demands that accompany this workload.
3. Honor each member's teaching and management style.
4. Invite others to visit your program.
5. Bring snacks to share.
6. Write frequent thank-you notes.
7. Invite families of other professionals to participate in special events, such as open houses or other activities.

From S.L. Kasser and R.K. Lytle, 2005, *Inclusive Physical Activity: A Lifetime of Opportunities*, page 68. © 2005 by Susan L. Kasser and Rebecca K. Lytle. Adapted with permission from Human Kinetics (Champaign, IL).

Managing Conflict

Regardless of best efforts in interpersonal and communication skills, conflicts will arise. The majority of typical communications that occur during collaborative teaming are negotiations and conflict resolution (Hanft & Place, 1996). Conflict can arise for many reasons and can affect the teaming process both favorably and unfavorably (Gutkin & Curtis, 1982). Heron and Harris (1993) suggested five strategies to deal with conflict: Withdraw if neither the goal nor the relationship is important (e.g., general physical education teacher is not going to change, and the student with disabilities is reasonably accommodated); force the issue and use all of your energy to accomplish the task if it is important but the relationship is not (e.g., student is in danger or the program is completely unacceptable and your relationship with a team member is short term); smooth things over if you want to be liked and accepted and if the relationship is more important than the task (e.g., a student with disabilities is being reasonably accommodated, you want to maintain a good relationship with the adapted physical educator, and you know she will be getting more of your students in the future); compromise if the task and the relationship are important but time is limited (e.g., develop reasonable accommodations for a student with spina bifida to participate in a basketball unit that starts next week, knowing that with more time you might suggest other accommodations); and confront the situation if the task and the relationship are equally important (e.g., take time to really problem-solve how a child's unique goals and objectives can be embedded with the general physical education curriculum).

Note that confrontation is viewed as a problem-solving technique to resolve conflicts between team members (Gutkin & Curtis, 1982; Heron & Harris, 1993). As long as confrontation avoids emotional reactions such as hostility or anger, then it is a positive way for both parties to agree upon a course of action. If a team member becomes angry, Margolis and Fiorelli (1987) suggested the following: Maintain composure, listen carefully and empathetically, encourage the team member to identify and share the reasons for his or her anger and fully release the anger, resist attempts to invalidate the information that has been shared, note areas of agreement, move slowly from problem perception to problem definition, and help the team member maintain self-respect. The goal is to defuse the situation, maintain a relationship with the team member, and return to solving the problem at hand. Team members need to realize that each team member has different experiences than they do, and understanding and valuing these differences is critical for successful communication (Johnston & Wayda, 1994; Kraus & Curtis, 1986).

Listening Skills

Table 3.3 provides a list developed by West, Idol, and Cannon (1989) of the critical interpersonal and communication skills needed for effective collaboration. Of these, listening behaviors including nonverbal listening skills have been reported to be the most critical skills (Gutkin & Curtis, 1982; Kurpius & Rozecki, 1993; Snell & Janney, 2005). Communication involves more than just presenting information and asking questions (Johnston & Wayda, 1994). In fact, one of the most important communication skills in collaborative teaming is being a good listener (Covey, 1989; Snell & Janney, 2005). If a team member cannot first fully understand other team members and their unique situations, then it will be impossible to be able to discuss an appropriate solution. If a team member does not feel understood, then information might be informative and interesting but will not help them with their unique situation. Thus, no influence or change will take place.

Although most team members understand the need to be a good listener, many team members forget to listen. Covey (1989) suggested that listening with the intent to fully understand often is threatening or unnatural, because trying to fully understand someone else's perspective may cause you to change your perspective or value system. In addition, team members may not be good listeners because of the natural tendency to first be understood. Many people's first reaction to another person talk-

Table 3.3. Interpersonal and communication skills needed for consultation

Interpersonal	Communication
Caring	Listening
Respectful	Acknowledging
Empathetic	Paraphrasing
Congruent	Reflecting
Open	Clarifying
Positive self-concept	Elaborating
Enthusiastic attitude	Summarizing
Willingness to learn from others	Grasp overt meaning
Calm	Grasp covert meaning
Stress free	Interpret nonverbal
Risk-taker	communication
Flexible	Interview effectively
Resilient	Provide feedback
Manage conflict and confrontation	Brainstorming
	Nonjudgmental responding
Manage time	Develop action plan

From West, J.F., Idol, L., & Cannon, G.S. (1989). Collaboration in the schools: *An inservice and preservice curriculum for teachers, support staff, and administrators.* Austin, TX: PRO-ED; reprinted by permission.

ing is to listen with the intent to speak. For example, many team members might listen not so much to truly understand another's concerns but rather to wait for the first opportunity to give an opinion or solution. If team members are waiting to speak, then they are not fully listening. Kurpius and Rozecki (1993) suggested some other common barriers to listening, including a tendency to judge or evaluate a team member's statements, inattention or apathy, asking too many questions prematurely, feeling the need to define and solve the problem quickly, and pursuing one's own agenda regardless of the team member's needs. Unfortunately, a team member instinctively recognizes half-hearted attempts at listening, and this creates feelings of mistrust.

Collaborative teaming is more than simply one team member giving advice to another team member. Advising does not consider the other team member's preference. This is often the case when one team member tries to fix another team member's problem by telling him or her what to do (Hanft & Place, 1996). In contrast, true collaborative teaming incorporates all team members' perspectives. Solutions are reached as a team, empowering and elevating each team member in the decision-making process. As each team member takes ownership of the decision-making process, their self-esteem is enhanced as the solution becomes resolved, they become aware of their own resources and establish an increased sense of confidence.

To be a better listener, Kurpius and Rozecki (1993); Seaman, DePauw, Morton, and Omoto (2003); and Sherrill (2004) suggested the following two responses: clarification (questioning) and reflection. *Clarification* refers to asking questions in such a way as to help the team member focus more clearly on the situation. It also is a way to get the team member to talk about and elaborate on specific problems. Questions are used to gain more information about a particular issue and to clarify or confirm the information that is presented (Kasser & Lytle, 2005). Questioning has to be done delicately as to not threaten the team member, causing him or her to become defensive. Kasser and Lytle (2005) and Snell and Janney (2005) noted that open-ended questions rather than yes/no questions encourage team members to clarify their points of view. For example, a question such as "Can you give us some examples of what you meant when you said that including this student in GPE is not working right now?" encourages the GPE teacher to clarify his or her statements.

Reflection refers to team members listening to each other and then trying to rephrase the information. Reflective listening "assures the speaker that his or her message is heard and is viewed as important" (Sherrill, 2004, p. 75). For example, a GPE talks about problems he or she is having with two stu-

dents with behavior problems who are "driving me crazy." After listening for several minutes and helping the GPE clarify key points, team members help the GPE reflect by saying: "Sounds like you are really frustrated that these two boys were placed in your class without your prior knowledge and without any support from the special education staff." Note how reflection is not only rephrasing what a team member said but also includes that team member's feelings and emotions. Reflecting on a team member's feelings helps this team member feel valued, encourages this team member to continue discussing the issue, and ultimately focuses energies toward identifying and resolving the targeted problem (Gutkin & Curtis, 1982; Sherrill, 2004).

Listening requires more than picking up key words. When a team member talks, other team members need to pay close attention to body language, emotions, and tone (Gutkin & Curtis, 1982). For example, a GPE says, "I'm really all right with my situation." This phrase can be said and expressed in numerous ways with completely different meanings. Therefore, team members need to listen with their ears, eyes, and heart and then respond clearly, specifically, and contextually from within that team member's frame of reference. If complete attention is given to that team member, then other team members will be able to better understand the full message. Team members also need to convey through their body language their true interest in listening and understanding the other team members. Nonverbal communication can be just as important as verbal communication (Johnston & Wayda, 1994). Miscommunication often results from nonverbal factors such as facial expressions, vocal intonations, body postures and movement, and use of space. While usually unintentional, a team member's nonverbal behaviors can convey lack of interest or concern, lack of genuineness, and/or a general sense of uncomfortableness with other team members (Heron & Harris, 1993).

The importance of communication in collaborative teaming cannot be understated. Effective communication allows for a free flow of information between the team members. Ineffective communication leads to misunderstandings and conflicts. Team members' ability to be open, listen with the intent to understand, and reduce conflict will inspire openness and trust and increase the overall effectiveness of collaborative teaming.

SUMMARY

Many individuals are involved in the education of students with disabilities. While each may have unique goals and objectives for the student, they all want to see the student reach his or her full potential. The best way to provide services to students with disabilities is for all of these individuals to work collaboratively by sharing information and working together. Such a team approach allows a variety of professionals to provide input and assist in making important decisions regarding the student's program. In addition, each professional has information that can help other professionals do their job better.

GPEs often feel isolated and uninformed about students' abilities and disabilities. In many cases, students with disabilities are still being "dumped" into general physical education programs on the first day of school. A team approach provides the general physical educator with a wealth of resources that can help him or her develop and implement an individualized program as well as answer specific questions as they arise. Specialists can provide the general physical educator with important information that will help him or her provide the best physical education program to students with disabilities. The key to successful collaborative teaming is communication. All team members must learn how to be good listeners and work together to solve problems rather than simply giving advice to the general physical educator.

CHAPTER 4

Planning for Inclusion in Physical Education

Ekene is a 10-year-old student from Sudan who has just arrived with his parents in the United States after surviving a terrible civil war. They are refugees who have settled in Orangedale, along with several other families from Sudan. Adjusting to a new country, a new culture, a new language, and a new school is difficult for any refugee student, but adjusting has been more difficult for Ekene, who has autism. He is nonverbal, and he does not seem to understand very much (both in his native language or in English). He also is very socially withdrawn, and he seems to spend his entire day rocking a mile a minute when sitting in a chair or on the floor and even when standing and walking.

Ekene has been assigned to Orangedale Elementary School, and he has been placed in a special education classroom for children with severe developmental delays. Students in this classroom attend general physical education, adapted physical education, or a combination of both. The general and adapted physical educators, along with each student's IEP team, determine physical education placement as well as IEP goals and objectives and any necessary accommodations to instruction or equipment. But Ekene's program seems to be a little more puzzling. Not only does Ekene have autism, but he also does not speak or understand English. He does not understand anything about expectations for physical education in public schools because he never attended school back in Sudan (children with disabilities like Ekene do not attend school in Sudan). Because he has not attended any formal schooling and has not received any formal physical education, the IEP team is not sure *what* to teach Ekene. Because of his language impairments coupled with his autism, they are not sure *how* to teach Ekene. And because of all of these factors together, they are not sure *where* to teach Ekene.

Students with disabilities can receive an individualized, appropriate physical education program in the general physical education environment. However, the physical education integration team (PEIT) must address several issues before placing a student with disabilities in general physical education. For example, which students with disabilities actually need adapted physical education services? What goals will be prioritized for each student? Which goals can be incorporated into the general program? What modifications will be necessary? What in-service training should be provided to the general physical educator, paraprofessionals, and peers? Successful placement of students with disabilities in general physical education involves much more that just placing the student in the general setting. The purpose of this chapter is to outline a systematic approach for including students with disabilities in general physical education. The focus of this approach is making critical decisions utilizing an *ecological approach* to programming and preparing personnel *prior to* inclusion. Program planning should first determine what to teach the student (goals and objectives) before decisions can be made about where to work on these objectives (placement), how to work on these objectives (modifications), or who to get to work on these objectives (support). In fact, IDEA has required that IEP goals and objectives be developed prior to decisions regarding placement, teaching, and staffing (Bateman & Herr, 2003; CEC, 1999; Sherrill, 2004).

DETERMINING WHO QUALIFIES FOR ADAPTED PHYSICAL EDUCATION SERVICES

As noted in Chapter 2, all students with disabilities are required to receive physical education services, although not all will automatically qualify for adapted physical education services (Block & Burke, 1999). Therefore, the first programmatic issue to be addressed is determining who qualifies for adapted physical education services. As mandated in IDEA and its amendments, the student's IEP team should decide who qualifies for adapted physical education. Furthermore, decisions should not be based on a label, what services other students in the district receive, or what is available. For example, not all students who have been identified as having orthopedic impairments who use wheelchairs would necessarily qualify for adapted physical education services. Some students who use wheelchairs are very capable and athletic, and they can be successful in general physical education with only slight modification. But it would be wrong to not provide adapted physical education to a student with a learning disability who has significant motor and behavior problems simply because no other student with a learning disability receives adapted physical education services. Again, the key is making decisions on a case-by-case basis using formal and informal observations such as the following that examine the student's level of performance in a variety of areas:

- *Motor skills and abilities:* Norm- and criterion-referenced motor development, gross motor, and motor ability tests such as a school district-approved physical education curriculum or assessment tool, The Test of Gross Motor Development, Peabody Developmental Motor Scales, and/or the Bruininks-Oseretsky Test of Motor Proficiency

- *Physical fitness:* Norm- and criterion-referenced physical fitness tests such as school district-approved physical education curriculum or assessment tool, President's Council on Physical Fitness Test, Physical Best, and/or Fitness Gram

- *Perceptual/sensory motor:* Criterion-referenced perceptual motor tests

- *General physical education:* Informal and formal observations to determine student's ability to participate successfully in general physical education

- *Behavior:* Informal and formal observations to determine student's behaviors in general physical education, how well the student understands what is going on, and how the student's behaviors affect others in the class

Based on information gathered from these assessments and observations, the IEP team then decides whether the student with a disability qualifies for adapted physical education services. Two criteria can be used to make this determination. First, test results can be used to determine if the student is "significantly behind his or her peers" in gross motor and/or fitness development. Each school district should create its own criteria and definition of significantly behind his or her peers. Unfortunately, most school districts do not have any set criteria for who does and does not qualify for adapted physical education services. Generally speaking, a student with a disability would be considered significantly behind his or her peers if he or she is at least 1 year below the norm (2 or more years for high school students) in motor and/or fitness testing. If an eighth-grade student with intellectual disabilities performs in fitness testing similar to what is expected of fifth graders in the school district and performs motor skills (e.g., kicking, throwing, catching) similar to fourth graders, he or she is clearly 3–4 years behind in skills compared to peers and would qualify for adapted physical education services (see Chapter 5 for more detail on assessment).

However, it should be noted that simply scoring lower than peers on a gross motor and/or fitness test does not necessarily mean that a student needs adapted physical education services. Take, for instance, a tenth grader who cannot walk, run, or do any locomotor skills. This student also cannot perform many of the typical ball skills (throwing, kicking, striking) the same way that his peers perform these skills. Finally, this student cannot complete a mile run like his peers. It would seem obvious this student would require and thus qualify for adapted physical education services. However, a closer inspection shows that this student has spina bifida, a congenital birth defect that has left him paralyzed from the waist down. Although he cannot perform any traditional locomotor patterns, he is a very skilled and powerful wheelchair user who competes in both wheelchair basketball and wheelchair track and field. Although he cannot throw, kick, or strike using patterns used by his peers, he is quite skilled at throwing and striking from his wheelchair. And though he cannot complete the mile by running, his fastest wheelchair mile time is 7 minutes. Add the fact that this student loves physical activity, is very motivated to improve his motor skills and physical fitness, and has virtually no behavior problems. Now, does this student qualify for adapted physical education services?

Thus, the second criterion for qualifying for adapted physical education services is whether the student has significant problems in general physical education, including not making expected improvement on motor, fitness, and/or behavioral goals while in general physical education and/or having a significantly difficult time following directions, participating appropriately, and generally getting along with classmates and the teacher in general physical education. For example, a sixth-grade student with Asperger syndrome, a high-functioning form of autism, has significant but relatively mild delays in gross motor and fitness development (2–3 years behind his peers). However, this student has actually fallen further behind his peers in the past few years due to behavioral and social problems. He often refuses to participate in general physical education activities, has huge temper tantrums when his team loses, hates it when the gym gets loud (which is almost everyday), and has a very hard time understanding the nuances of being a peer or a teammate in games. He often spends the better part of general physical education sitting by himself against the wall. The combination of a significant motor/fitness delay and significant behavior problems qualifies this student for adapted physical education services. Significant delays in motor/fitness development *coupled with* significant problems in general physical education are required for a student to qualify for adapted physical education services. Some students (e.g., a student who displays severe behavior problems, a student who cannot follow even simple directions) may need a behavior plan or other support to be successful in general physical education. However, these students would not qualify for adapted physical education services.

If the team determines that a student qualifies for adapted physical education services, the team then continues with program planning. Alternately, the team can decide that the student with disabilities requires some accommodations to be successful in general physical education, such as help from a teacher assistant or changes in instruction, equipment, and/or activities education. Again, based on assessment information, the team decides if and what accommodations are needed for a particular student and notes them on the student's IEP (Bateman & Herr, 2003; Sherrill, 2004). For example, a student with a behavior problem might need a teacher assistant to accompany him or her to class, a student who is deaf may need an interpreter, a student who is blind may need to have written material translated into braille, and a student with intellectual disabilities may need the teacher to repeat instructions or have a peer help the student understand where to go and what to do. Accommodations are made on a case-by-case basis to ensure that each student's individual needs are met.

An Ecological Approach to Planning

Once it has been determined that a student qualifies for adapted physical education services, then the team must decide what skills to teach the student, how to embed these skills in general physical education, whether the student's IEP matches the general physical education curriculum, what modifications are needed to teach these skills in general physical education, which staff will teach these skills, and what training the staff need to teach these skills. There are many models to program planning,

but the two most common in adapted physical education are the ecological (also known as top-down or functional) approach and the developmental or bottom-up approach (Auxter et al., 2005; Block & Block, 1999; Kelly & Melograno, 2004; Sherrill, 2004).

Ecological Approach

The ecological approach reflects the interaction of the individual student and the environment in which he or she will function (Rainforth & York-Barr, 1997). In the case of physical education, an ecologically referenced program focuses on the student's abilities and interests in relation to the skills the student will need to be successful (i.e., in physical education class, on the playground, in the student's neighborhood, in community-based recreation). Team members develop an individualized plan that includes all of the skills, activities, and environments that are most important to that student (Rainforth & York-Barr, 1997).

The ecological approach is considered a top-down model in which planning begins by envisioning where the student will be upon graduation from the program and what skills the student will need to be successful in this future setting (Auxter et al., 2005; Kelly & Melograno, 2004; Rainforth & York-Barr, 1997). For example, top-down goals for a middle or high school student would reflect individually selected postschool fitness and recreation activities such as accessing a local health club, going to a local driving range, shooting baskets in the driveway of the group home, or playing on a community softball or bowling team. For a preschool or elementary student, the top of the plan could reflect goals in two areas: 1) to help prepare the student for his or her next school placement or 2) to help the student participate in age-appropriate neighborhood activities and community recreation programs such as learning how to ride a tricycle/bicycle, rollerblade, play on playground equipment, or play on a community sport team.

Assessment takes place after top-down goals are established and is referenced directly to these top-down goals (Kelly & Melograno, 2004). To illustrate, a fourth-grade student with Down syndrome would have goals that reflect individually selected skills needed to be successful in general fourth-grade physical education (middle school physical education); and intramural, neighborhood, and community-based sport/recreation programs. If the IEP team anticipates that this student is going to play on a community soccer team, then skills needed to play soccer are assessed, such as dribbling, shooting, trapping, passing, running, rules, strategies, and behaviors. Information from such an assessment would lead to programming that is directly related to skills the student will need to be successful in soccer.

Developmental Approach

With a developmental model or bottom-up approach, activities are based on the scope and sequence of typical development of young students. It is believed that lower-level developmental skills are prerequisite for the development of higher-level skills (Auxter et al., 2005; Block, 1992; Block & Block, 1999; Brown et al., 1979; Kelly & Melograno, 2004; Sherrill, 2004). However, these lower-level, prerequisite developmental skills are often targeted without regard to their relevance to skills needed by the student to be successful in current and future physical education/recreation environments. For example, balancing on one foot is a prerequisite for hopping, and hopping is a prerequisite to skipping. Thus, skipping would not be taught until balancing on one foot and hopping are mastered. With the ecological model, one would question whether balancing on one foot, hopping, and skipping are really relevant to an IEP for a particular student. If these skills are not needed to help a student acquire the skills needed to play tee ball, for example, then they are not targeted for instruction.

Another difference between the ecological and developmental models is that assessment takes place prior to the development of goals and objectives in the developmental model. Basically, goals and objectives are created for the student (e.g., skills needed to play tee ball), and then the student is assessed directly on these goals and objectives (e.g., throw, catch, hit, run) (Kelly & Melograno, 2004). Assessment before program planning is necessary to determine whether a student qualifies for adapted physical education services. In many cases, this assessment information is then used for program planning. Sometimes such order (assessment precedes program planning) makes sense. For example, a student does poorly on the object control (ball skills) section of the Test of Gross Motor Development–II. Program planning for this student logically would focus on helping this student improve ball skills.

Unfortunately, many assessment tools used to determine whether a student qualifies for adapted physical education services do not translate well to program planning (Kelly & Melograno, 2004). For example, a student is assessed using a developmental test such as the Peabody Developmental Scales–II, a fitness test such as President's Council on Physical Fitness Test, or a motor ability test such as the Bruininks-Oseretsky Test of Motor Proficiency. Results from these tests are then used to determine a student's approximate developmental age level or percentile rank compared with other students his or her age. Teachers and therapists then typically develop program goals based on the student's assessment results from these tests that move the student up the developmental scale or improve his or her percentile ranking. For example, a student who jumped only 24 inches on the Peabody Developmental Motor Scales–II would be encouraged to jump 30 inches; a student who cannot yet balance on one foot on the Bruininks-Oseretsky Test would practice one-foot balance activities; and a student who scored below the 20th percentile on sit-up performance on a fitness test would practice sit-ups. Note that these activities, while related to each student's present level of performance, are not necessarily referenced to skills the student will need to be successful in current or future life circumstances. Does it matter that a student is at the 20th percentile in sit-ups or can only jump forward 24 inches? Will these impairments in performance affect a student's success in general physical education, on the playground, in the neighborhood, or in community recreation?

Another problem with the developmental approach is how long it takes students with more significant disabilities to achieve developmental goals, if they ever do attain them (Block, 1992; Block & Block, 1999; Brown et al., 1979; Kelly & Melograno, 2004). Many students with physical disabilities such as cerebral palsy will never be able to balance on one foot, jump on two feet, or walk a balance beam. To master some of the developmental goals would take years of training and practice. If physical education programs concentrate on nonfunctional developmental skills, then students will not practice and learn ecologically relevant, functional skills that will help them to be successful in general physical education and in community recreation (Block, 1992; Brown et al., 1979). If a student can achieve developmental skills, and if these developmental skills can be related to success in general physical education and community recreation, then it makes sense to target these skills for instruction. This is often the case with students with more mild delays (1–2 years behind their peers). However, if these skills cannot be achieved in a reasonable time frame (students with more significant delays) and/or cannot be shown to have an ecological relevance to the student, then these skills should not be taught.

AN ECOLOGICAL APPROACH TO INCLUDING STUDENTS WITH DISABILITIES IN GENERAL PHYSICAL EDUCATION

The model that follows utilizes the ecological approach to program planning (see Table 4.1). The focus is on identifying what ecologically relevant, functional goals and objectives a student should work on, identifying how these goals and objectives

Table 4.1. Ecological model for including students with disabilities into general physical education

DETERMINE WHAT TO TEACH.
- Develop a long-term plan and prioritize long-term goals.
- Determine student's present level of performance.
- Develop short-term instructional objectives.

ANALYZE THE GENERAL PHYSICAL EDUCATION CURRICULUM.
- What activities match the student's IEP?
- What activities do not match the student's IEP but seem important?
- What activities are inappropriate for a particular student?
- What is the teaching style of the general physical educator?

DETERMINE MODIFICATIONS NEEDED IN GENERAL PHYSICAL EDUCATION.
- How often will student receive instruction?
- Where will student receive instruction?
- How will student be prepared for instruction?
- What instruction modifications are needed to elicit the desired performance?
- What curricular adaptations will be used to enhance performance?
- How will performance be assessed?

DETERMINE THE SUPPORT A STUDENT WITH A DISABILITY WILL NEED IN GENERAL PHYSICAL EDUCATION.
- Who will provide the support?
- What type of support will be provided?
- How often support will be provided?

PREPARE THE GENERAL PHYSICAL EDUCATOR.
- Discuss the amount of support that will be provided.
- Discuss the availability of consultation with APE and special education teacher.
- Explain that general educator is responsible for the entire class, not just the special student.
- Explain that workload should not increase.

PREPARE GENERAL EDUCATION STUDENTS.
- Talk about students with disabilities in general.
- Role play various types of disabilities.
- Invite guest speakers with disabilities to your class.
- If special class, allow students to visit special class and meet student.
- Talk specifically about the student who will be coming to GPE (focus on abilities).
- Discuss ways typical students can help student with disabilities and GPE teacher.

PREPARE SUPPORT PERSONNEL.
- Discuss specific student.
- Discuss the student's physical education IEP.
- Discuss their responsibilities in GPE.
- Discuss who can answer questions.

can be embedded within general physical education activities, identifying what support the student and staff need to implement the program, and preparing staff and peers. This approach facilitates the inclusion of students with disabilities in general physical education by carefully analyzing the general physical education environment, determining what sup-

ports a student needs to be successful in general physical education, and preparing these support people.

Determine What to Teach

The first step in the planning process is to determine what to teach. That is, what are the most critical skills a student needs to be successful in his or her present and future physical education/recreation environments? The critical skills are first defined globally by choosing a particular sport skill, recreation skill, and fitness skill. The long-term plan guides the entire educational program and helps keep the team focused on specific skills (Kelly & Melograno, 2004). The long-term plan should be based on the general physical education program, opportunities available in the student's community, and the student's unique skills and interests. For example, it does not make sense to have a long-term plan that includes swimming if there are no swimming pools in the student's school or community. Similarly, it would be inappropriate to target volleyball for a particular student if the student has a severe disability and can only play volleyball with assistance and with modifications to the game and if the only volleyball league in the community is a high-level, competitive league in which players and coaches play regulation games. Softball might be a more appropriate long-term goal if the community softball league has different divisions, including a recreation-level division in which other players would accept the modifications needed for this student.

Several factors help determine what skills to target for a student's long-term plan, including the student's general strengths and weaknesses, age, and interests; his or her parent's interests; what recreation facilities and programs are available in school and in the community; the time available to teach the skills and what support is available (see Table 4.2).

For example, the PEIT is deciding on goals for a ninth-grade student with a spinal cord injury who uses a wheelchair but has good upper body control. This student is just coming back to school after a year of rehabilitation. At the meeting, the team (which includes the student with disabilities) discusses the 1) student's overall strengths (good upper body strength, independent in wheelchair) and overall weaknesses (depressed, not very motivated, cannot use legs), 2) the student's age (ready for sports, recreation, and fitness activities), 3) the student's interests (this student played tennis before his injury; he also seems interested in weightlifting to improve his upper body strength; he does not seem interested in team sports at this point), 4) parent interests (parents belong to a club where they play tennis, they also

Table 4.2. Factors to consider when prioritizing goals and objectives and their applications to physical education

Factor	Application to physical education
What are student's strengths and weaknesses as well as current and future needs?	Consider how these fit with general physical education activities and community play/recreation activities.
How much time do you have to teach skills? What is the chance student will acquire skills?	Younger students can be exposed to more variety of skills, while older students should focus on skills needed to participate in specific lifetime leisure activities.
What are the students' interests?	What recreational/sport activities does the student prefer?
What are the parents' interests?	What recreational/sport activities do the student's parents prefer?
What are peers' interests?	What activities do peers play on the playground, in the neighborhood, and in community recreation?
What recreation facilities are available in the community?	Prioritize activities that will be available to student in community.
What equipment/transportation is available?	Consider any special equipment needs (e.g., bowling ramp, flotation devices).
What support is available?	Think about who can assist the student in physical education and recreation. Are specially trained professionals needed to work with student (e.g., vision therapist)?

used to go for a run together after work before their son's injury), 5) what is available in the community (the community has pretty much every recreation and sport activity that can be offered in both recreational and competitive forms), 6) the time to teach the skill (only the ninth- and tenth-grade physical education unless the student continues to take physical education as an elective in eleventh and twelfth grades), and 7) available supports (plenty available). After some discussion, the team decides that wheelchair tennis, weight training, and wheelchair road racing would be the most motivating and relevant activities for this student.

It may be more difficult to determine what sport, fitness, and recreation skills a student with more severe disabilities might be interested in or able to learn. In such cases, team members might informally assess the student on a variety of age-appropriate sport and recreation activities, examining the student's interests and potential for the activity. Figure 4.1 shows an example of this type of sport/recreation sampling for a 15-year-old student with severe intellectual disabilities. Note how traditional assessment information about the acquisition of motor skills, fundamental motor pattern performance, and physical fitness are embedded in the ecologically referenced assessment. Ideally, this evaluation should utilize the expertise of key members of the collaborative team. For example, the vision therapist can assist the general or adapted physical educator in assessing ball skills that require eye–hand coordination skills (e.g., striking, catching, dribbling, volleying), while the physical therapist can assist physical educators in assessing locomotor patterns and physical fitness related to specific sports. Based in this information, a long-term plan can be developed (see Figure 4.2).

Develop Long-Term Objectives

Once a long-term plan is in place, the next step is to write long-term goals. Long-term goals are part of the IEP process and describe what specific skills a teacher expects a student to acquire in the course of a year. For example, a long-term plan for Sue might be to play tennis upon graduation. A long-term goal for Sue might be demonstrating the ability to hit a tennis ball using a backhand and forehand stroke in a beginner's game of doubles. Long-term goals should be based on assessment results and a student's ability. For example, Sue's ability to grip a racket, to hit a forehand and backhand, to move around the court, and understand the basic rules of tennis should be assessed. Then, these skills are placed in a logical sequence of what is most important to least important to teach. For example, the grip would be most important, then the forehand, then the backhand, then moving to get balls, and finally the rules of the game. So, in the first year of Sue's program, a long-term goal for tennis might be holding the racket correctly and hitting a forehand and backhand using the optimal pattern.

Develop Short-Term Objectives

Once long-term goals are in place, the next step is to write short-term instructional objectives that lead to acquisition of the long-term goals. Short-term instructional objectives also are part of the IEP process and usually are written in anticipation of the student's achieving a particular objective in 2–3 months. In addition, these objectives are written in behavioral (measurable) terms so that any observer can immediately tell whether the student has acquired a particular objective (see Figure 4.3).

Present level of performance statement with reference to activities in general physical education

Tennis	Sue walks slowly in an attempt to get to balls, but she only can reach balls hit within 5 feet of her. She gets into a side position for a forehand and swings forcefully (no step or body rotation), but she misses more than she hits (two of five swings are successful). She also does not grip the racket correctly. She gets into a backhand position after verbal cues and demonstrates a backhand (no step or body rotation), but she only hits about one in five. Also, her grip is incorrect. She has the strength to hit the ball over the net from 15 feet away, and she really seems to enjoy playing and trying to hit the ball.
Golf	Sue can hold a golf club and swing with a stiff pattern (no leg or arm bend, very little body rotation) with verbal cues. She can hit the ball off a tee with a 5 iron in three of five trials, and the ball travels approximately 25 yards.
Soccer	Sue walks slowly and occasionally jogs to get the ball. She can kick with her toe so that the ball travels 10–15 feet. She can trap slowly moving balls that are kicked directly to her. She does not understand team concepts, and she often sits down in the middle of the field when she gets tired or bored.
Volleyball	Sue can set and bump a ball that is tossed directly to her with verbal cues. She can serve a ball over the net from 10 feet away. She cannot hit the ball in the course of a game, and she seems afraid of getting hit by the ball.
Basketball	Sue can dribble a ball several times while standing in place but not while moving forward. She can make a regulation basket from 5 feet away in one of five trials. She demonstrates a chest-and-bounce pass with verbal cues from 10 feet away, and she catches bounce passes (not chest passes) when ball is gently passed from 10 feet away. She does not understand team concepts and prefers to wander around the court.
Softball	Sue can hit a softball off a tee for 15–20 feet. She jogs to bases with verbal cues (often needs someone to point her in the right direction). Sue can throw overhand (no stepping or body rotation) approximately 10 feet. Sue tries to bend over and pick up grounders and catch balls tossed directly to her from 10 feet away. She tends to sit down in the outfield, but she stays more focused with verbal cues when playing catcher.
Aerobics	Sue tries to follow the routine, but she tends to be off beat compared with her peers. She does exert more effort in aerobics than any other activity, but she tires easily (after 3–4 minutes). She has adequate flexibility and strength.
Weight training	Sue performs six exercises on weight machines with verbal cues and occasional assistance for positioning. She needs assistance to set the correct weight. Her strength is similar to that of her peers.

Figure 4.1. Sample performance level for a 15-year-old with severe intellectual disabilities

At this point in the process, it is not important where the student will work on the goals and objectives or how much support or special equipment the student will need. Rather, the focus is on the overall plan and specific goals and objectives.

Analyze the General Physical Education Curriculum

Once each student has been evaluated and a long-term plan including long-term goals and short-term instructional objectives has been established, the next step is to determine if the student's IEP matches the general curriculum. This step requires a careful analysis of the general physical education curriculum including an analysis of the yearly plans for various grade levels, unit plans and daily lesson plans for specific activities, and the general teaching style of the general physical educator. This information is then used to determine when a particular student can work on his or her individual goals and when alternative activities are needed (i.e., what activities in general physical education directly match the student's IEP objectives, which activities somewhat match the student's IEP, and which activities do not match the student's IEP and require alternative activities) (see Figure 4.3). Note that no effort is made at this point to detail specific ways to accommodate a student in the general program or how to work on specific IEP goals and objectives. Such information will be determined later in the process. At this point the focus is on determining how well the student's IEP fits into the general physical education curriculum.

LONG-TERM PLAN: Sue will demonstrate the ability to participate independently (with occasional cues from peers as needed) in recreational softball and tennis and participate in fitness activities at a local health club.

Long-term goal 1:   Sue will improve her cardiorespiratory endurance.

Short-term instructional objectives:

1. Sue will pedal a stationary Lifecycle at the University Health Club at Level 2, maintaining an RPM level of 70 continuously for 20 minutes, with verbal reinforcement every 5 minutes for three of four trials.

2. Sue will participate in an aerobics class during general physical education, performing and imitating movements as best as she can so that her heart rate (as measured by a peer) is 120–150 beats per minute for 25 minutes for 3 of 4 days.

Long-term goal 2:   Sue will develop the skills needed to participate in modified and regulation individual and team sports.

Short-term instructional objectives (specific to softball):

1. Using a regulation softball bat and choking up 2 inches (using tape cue markers), Sue will hit a regulation softball off a tee so that the ball rolls at least 60 feet for three of four trials.

2. After hitting a ball off the tee, Sue will run to first base independently so that she arrives at first base in 7 seconds or less for three of four trials.

3. Sue will play catcher during a softball game, demonstrating the following behaviors independently for three of four trials:

    a. Put on face mask.

    b. Find correct position behind plate.

    c. Squat into correct position and maintain position for duration of each pitch.

    d. Move glove in direction of ball when ball is pitched.

Long-term goal 3:   Sue will demonstrate the ability to hit forehand and backhand so that the ball travels over the net 50% of the time when playing doubles tennis with peers at a beginner's level.

Short-term instructional objectives:

1. Sue will hit backhand, demonstrating the components listed next when ball is hit within 10 feet of her so that the ball travels over the net and into the opposing players' court for 5 of 10 trials 2 days in a row:

    Components of the backhand:
    - Display proper grip.
    - Stand facing opposing player.
    - Move to ball.
    - Set up in sideways position.
    - Bring arm back horizontally across body so that head of racket is behind body.
    - Shift weight and step forward with front foot.
    - Horizontally bring arm forward and contact ball slightly ahead of body.
    - Follow through, with arm and racket moving toward opposing player.

2. Sue will hit a forehand demonstrating the components listed next when ball is hit within 10 feet of her so that the ball travels over the net and into the opposing players' court for 5 of 10 trials 2 days in a row:

    Components of the forehand:
    - Display proper grip.
    - Stand facing opposing player.
    - Move to ball.
    - Set up in sideways position.
    - Bring arm back horizontally away from body so that head of racket is behind body.
    - Shift weight and step forward with front foot.
    - Horizontally bring arm forward and contact ball slightly ahead of body.
    - Follow through, with arm and racket moving toward opposing player.

Long-term goal 4:   Sue will develop the skills needed to participate in community-based leisure activities in integrated environments. (Sue participates in community-based recreation instead of general physical education two times per week.)

Short-term instructional objectives:

1. Sue will enter the University Health Club, show her identification card, locate locker room, put gym bag in locker, lock locker, then locate weight room using natural cues only (including asking Health Club staff for assistance) with 100% accuracy for 4 of 5 days.

2. Sue will follow picture cards and complete a six-machine Nautilus weight training circuit, performing the exercise for each machine correctly and completing one set of 10–12 repetitions per machine independently (or asking Health Club staff for assistance) with 100% accuracy for 4 of 5 days.

3. Sue will demonstrate appropriate behavior in the locker room and weight room as noted by changing clothes quickly without acting silly, saying only hi to strangers or responding appropriately when a stranger initiates a conversation in the locker room, and not acting silly or talking while others are working out unless others initiate conversation in the weight room 100% of the time for 4 of 5 days.

Figure 4.2.   Sample long-term plan, long-term goals, and short-term instructional objectives for a 15-year-old with severe intellectual disabilities

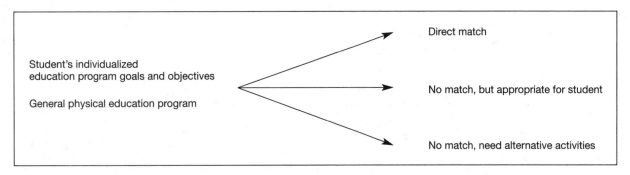

Figure 4.3. Possible outcomes of analysis of general physical education curriculum.

Analyze the Yearly Plan

Figure 4.4 contains a yearly plan for a typical second-grade physical education program with initial considerations for including John, a student who is blind; Figure 4.5 contains a yearly plan for a typical tenth-grade physical education program with initial considerations for including Sue, a student with severe intellectual disabilities. Note that the activities in general physical education at the lower elementary level (kindergarten through third grade) are generally going to match the goals and objectives for most students with disabilities because most elementary-age students need some foundational skills before they can apply these skills to popular sports and recreational activities. John, for example, needs to work on understanding movement concepts and developing skillful locomotor and manipulative patterns—goals that match very nicely with the general program (even though he may need special accommodations to participate and receive instruction). Even when

his IEP does not directly match what the other students are doing (e.g., gymnastics and rhythms), these activities are deemed important and beneficial enough to John that he participates in these activities with his peers.

Sue, however, can only work on her IEP goals while her peers participate in the tennis unit in September, aerobics unit in December, weight training unit in February, and softball unit in May. The other units do not match Sue's IEP goals, so Sue may need to participate in alternative activities (i.e., her IEP goals and objectives) during these times. For example, when the class is playing soccer in October, Sue could go to the tennis court to work on her tennis goals with peers rotating in to assist and play with her. Similarly, Sue could work in the weight room with various peers in March when the class is working on field hockey and lacrosse. Sue certainly could benefit from the endurance and stretching activities in track and field (perhaps walking around the track with peers at a vigorous pace and partici-

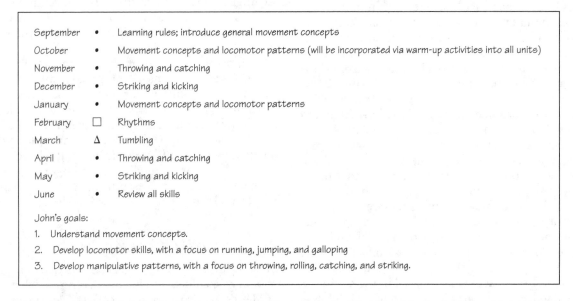

September	•	Learning rules; introduce general movement concepts
October	•	Movement concepts and locomotor patterns (will be incorporated via warm-up activities into all units)
November	•	Throwing and catching
December	•	Striking and kicking
January	•	Movement concepts and locomotor patterns
February	□	Rhythms
March	Δ	Tumbling
April	•	Throwing and catching
May	•	Striking and kicking
June	•	Review all skills

John's goals:

1. Understand movement concepts.
2. Develop locomotor skills, with a focus on running, jumping, and galloping
3. Develop manipulative patterns, with a focus on throwing, rolling, catching, and striking.

Figure 4.4. Yearly physical education plan for second-grade physical education. (*Key:* • = activity directly matches John's individualized education program [IEP] goals; □ = activity does not directly match but is appropriate for John to participate in; Δ activity does not match John's IEP goals and is inappropriate for John.)

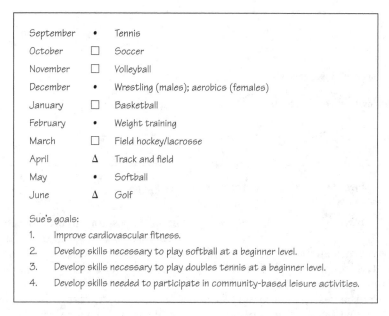

September	•	Tennis
October	☐	Soccer
November	☐	Volleyball
December	•	Wrestling (males); aerobics (females)
January	☐	Basketball
February	•	Weight training
March	☐	Field hockey/lacrosse
April	Δ	Track and field
May	•	Softball
June	Δ	Golf

Sue's goals:

1. Improve cardiovascular fitness.
2. Develop skills necessary to play softball at a beginner level.
3. Develop skills necessary to play doubles tennis at a beginner level.
4. Develop skills needed to participate in community-based leisure activities.

Figure 4.5. Yearly plan for tenth-grade physical education. (*Key:* • = activity directly matches Sue's individualized education program [IEP] goals; ☐ = activity does not directly match but is appropriate for Sue to participate in; Δ activity does not match Sue's IEP goals and is inappropriate for Sue.)

pating in warm-ups), so she could be included in this unit. Similarly, Sue could participate with golf with her peers to see if she enjoys this activity (golf may replace tennis as a lifetime sport if Sue really enjoys it).

The important point is that inclusion does not necessarily mean that students with disabilities have to do the same activities the same way as their peers without disabilities. Most students without disabilities can be exposed to a variety of activities in general physical education (i.e., try a lot of activities but not necessarily master anything) and still leave the program with the ability to successfully participate in two or more lifetime leisure activities. Students with moderate and severe disabilities, however, will only acquire critical lifetime leisure skills if training focuses intensely on these skills (Block, 1992; Brown et al., 1979; Kelly & Melograno, 2004). Thus, decisions need to be made as to what activities will be most beneficial for the student.

This does not mean that a student will require programming away from general physical education. Sue certainly can participate in warm-up activities with her peers during general physical education. In addition, while Sue's peers are working on their activities such as basketball in the gym, Sue could be practicing hitting a tennis ball back and forth with a peer or hitting a softball off a tee with a peer in the corner of the gym or in the hall. Peers without disabilities can be rotated in the station to assist and actually participate with Sue so that Sue still receives the social benefits of inclusion while working on her specific IEP goals.

Analyze Specific Units

The next step is to analyze each physical education unit that matches the student's program. Unit plans usually can be obtained from general physical education specialists a week or so prior to the introduction of that unit (more seasoned teachers may have their unit plans from previous years on file). Figure 4.6 contains an example of a tenth-grade softball unit plan. An analysis of the softball unit suggests that Sue can work on many of the softball skills highlighted in her IEP during this unit (with modifications as needed). In addition, Sue could easily be accommodated in the modified game that includes peers without disabilities.

Some physical education programs at the high school level only focus on the actual game. It would be much more difficult to integrate Sue in such a program because her softball skills are very weak. By analyzing the unit ahead of time (even 1 week before the unit begins), you can begin to make decisions about how Sue will work on her goals during the unit, including what modifications might be needed to make Sue more successful. Again, more detailed accommodations and modifications will be developed later in the process.

Analyze the Daily Lesson Plan

Finally, an analysis of a general daily lesson plan should be conducted to further determine when the student's IEP goals and objectives can be implemented and when the student may have difficulty with specific activities. Again, most general physi-

WEEK 1

Introduce game.

- Equipment
- Field dimensions
- Basic rules
- Basic concepts and positions

Introduce warm-up activities.

- Stretching major muscles of upper and lower body
- Strengthening abdominal, arm, and leg muscles
- Cardiovascular endurance activities (e.g., jogging around the base path)

Introduce to basic softball skills (with emphasis on learning correct movements).

- Striking
- Throwing
- Fielding
- Base running

Have lead-up games to work on skills.

- Base running relays, hot-box, 500
- Pepper, 500
- Home run derby, spot hitting

WEEK 2

Continue warm-up activities (have students lead warm-ups).

Present team concepts and strategies.

- Base running strategies, hitting ball to various places in field, hitting to cut-off person
- Viewing videotape of softball game that shows these techniques

Continue refinement of skills.

- Throwing from greater distances, throwing with varying force
- Fielding balls hit to the side, fielding high flies in the outfield
- Hitting faster pitched balls, hitting balls in different parts of strike zone

WEEK 3

Continue warm-up activities (have students lead warm-ups).

Review all softball skills.

Introduce games.

- 10 players versus 10 players, with outfield players practicing throwing balls back and forth during down time and batting team practicing hitting balls off a tee behind backstop while waiting for turns at bat
- Modified game of softball for students who have less skill (including students without disabilities who have limited softball skills)

WEEK 4

- Continue warm-up activities (have students lead warm-ups).
- Continue to review softball skills.
- Continue games with less instruction (both regulation and modified).

Some anticipated accommodations for Sue

1. Have peer assist Sue during warm-ups (demonstration and occasional physical prompt).
2. Have peer assist Sue as she moves from station to station and at station as needed.
3. Have adapted physical educator write activities for Sue to do at each station.
4. Use smaller ball (tennis ball) for throwing and catching with mitt.
5. Use lighter bat (Wiffle ball bat) and have ball on tee for striking.
6. Have Sue play in outfield with peer during games or have Sue play catcher, with batter assisting her.
7. Allow Sue run to a shorter-distance base when running to first, and allow peer to run with her around other bases until she understands where to go.
8. Have Sue play in recreational games.

Figure 4.6. Sample 4-week softball unit plan.

cal educators can quickly outline their typical daily lesson plan. Most physical education lesson plans begin with a warm-up activity, followed by a skill activity, followed by a game activity. In addition, physical education at the middle and high school levels will include locker room activities (e.g., dressing, showering, grooming) immediately prior to and after each physical education class. Figure 4.7 outlines a typical daily lesson plan for a tenth-grade class with considerations for Sue.

An alternative way to determine what activities take place in a typical general physical education class is called an ecological inventory (Brown et al., 1979). An ecological inventory provides a detailed analysis of all the activities students typically do during a particular activity (in this case, general physical education). The analysis begins with identifying subenvironments and activities that take place within each subenvironment. This is followed by a discrepancy analysis, which determines how the student with disabilities currently performs each activity and provides suggestions for modifications so that the student could be more successful. Figure 4.8 provides an example of an ecological inventory with discrepancy analysis. While the ecological inventory is more difficult to develop compared with a simple daily lesson plan, the information provided gives much more detailed information regarding daily routines and potential modifications to GPE. Special education teachers often have experience developing ecological inventories and, with the assistance of the general physical educator, can quickly develop such an inventory for the PEIT.

One final analysis of the general curriculum is of a teacher's particular *teaching style* (see Chapter 6 and Mosston & Ashworth, 2002, for a more thorough review of teaching styles). There are many different teaching styles, but most revolve around two

basic types: *direct approaches* (teacher directed, with a goal of reproducing a movement pattern) or *indirect approaches* (student directed, with the goal of producing something new) (Mosston & Ashworth, 2002). In direct approaches each student performs the same basic movement under the direct guidance of the physical educator. This physical educator is responsible for most decisions. The teacher tells or shows students exactly what is expected of them, how particular skills are to be performed, when to perform these skills, and where to perform these skills. Obviously, such an approach provides tremendous control over a class yet still allows for some individualization. However, creativity and the process of learning how to learn or discovering the best way to perform a particular skill are not provided in this approach. For example, a teacher might be working on the overhand throw with a second-grade class. She might have all students stand a certain distance from the wall and, on her verbal cue, shift weight to back foot, reach back with throwing arm, shift weight forward, rotate body, and throw ball to wall. Some teachers who use this approach are quite inflexible, expecting all students to perform a particular movement the same way, at the same time, and with the same requirements for success. Such a rigid interpretation of the direct approach would not be very accommodating for a student who has a disability. However, teachers can use the direct approach and still accommodate varying abilities. For example, when teaching second graders to throw, another teacher might allow some students to stand closer to or farther away from the wall, may give some students larger balls and other students smaller balls, or may allow a student with cerebral palsy to throw using a different pattern.

In indirect approaches students are encouraged to discover the best way to perform certain skills by

---

1. **Locker room:** Change into physical education uniform (approximately 5 minutes).

2. **Squads/attendance:** Students sit in squads while attendance is taken (2 minutes).

3. **Warm-ups:** Students are led by teacher in several stretching, strength, and aerobic activities (7–10 minutes).

4. **Skill focus:** Work on specific skills related to team or individual sport (as little as 5 minutes to as many as 30 minutes, depending on where class is in unit; beginning of unit focuses more on skills, end of unit focuses more on games).

5. **Game:** Play lead-up and regulation games related to team or individual sports (5–30 minutes).

6. **Locker room:** Shower, groom self, put on street clothes (approximately 10 minutes).

Sue will need assistance in the locker room both before and after class (teacher assistant can assist initially, but peers whose lockers are near Sue's will eventually learn how to assist Sue). Sue should be able to participate in warm-ups with minimal cues from peers. Sue will need modified ways to practice skills and to participate in group activities (have adapted physical education specialist or team members provide suggestions).

Figure 4.7. General daily lesson plan for tenth-grade physical education with comments regarding Sue. (*Source:* Morris & Stiehl, 1999.)

Ecological Inventory with Discrepancy Analysis

Student's name ___Jonathan Smith___   Student's birth date ___8-10-90___   Teacher ___M. Block (APE specialist)___

Environment ___General PE class, soccer unit___   Dates of unit ___9/21–10/21___   Suggested assistant ___Steve Smith (peer tutor)___

Subenvironment and activity	What are the steps that a person without disabilities uses?	What assistance does the student with disabilities currently need?	What adaptations or levels of assistance might help this student?
Locker room			
Activity 1	Locates locker room	V	Teach Jonathan to use natural cues on wall; add arrows on walls.
Activity 2	Enters locker room	I	None needed
Activity 3	Locates empty locker	V	Teach Jonathan to identify lockers without locks; color code one locker.
Activity 4	Takes off clothes	PP	Jonathan can wear pull-on clothes and practice dressing at home; use Velcro instead of buttons.
Activity 5	Places clothes in locker	I	None needed
Activity 6	Puts on exercise clothes	P	Jonathan can use pull-on clothes; equip shoes with special ties; use Velcro instead of buttons.
Activity 7	Locks locker	P	Use repeated practice; perhaps use longer lock, key lock might be easier than combination lock.
Gym: attendance			
Activity 1	Locates gym	V	Jonathan can use natural cues on walls; use additional wall cues.
Activity 2	Finds squad and sits down	V	Teach Jonathan to identify members of squad; have squad members cue Jonathan if he appears lost.
Activity 3	Sits quietly with squad	I	None needed
Gym: warm-up			
Activity 1	Stands up with squad	V	Have peers provide cues.
Activity 2	Performs 10 jumping jacks	VP	Have peers provide cues; have Jonathan do arm-only jumping jacks.
Activity 3	Performs leg stretches	VP	Have peers provide cues; have Steve provide physical assistance as needed.
Activity 4	Performs 10 sit-ups	VP	Pair Jonathan with Steve; perform 5 rather than 10 sit-ups.
Activity 5	Performs 10 push-ups	VP	Have peers provide cues; have Jonathan perform modified knee push-ups.
Activity 6	Runs continuously for 3 minutes	V	Have peers provide cues; have Jonathan alternate running and walking for 10 minutes.
Gym: soccer stations			
Activity 1	Locates squad and station	V	Have peers provide cues.
Activity 2	Practices shooting	VP	Have Jonathan shoot from closer distance; shoot at wider goal; use lighter ball.
Activity 3	Waits turn	I	None needed
Activity 4	Moves to next station	V	Have peers provide cues.
Activity 5	Works on passing/trapping	VP	Have Jonathan stand closer to peer; use deflated ball; use tape markings on foot to cue correct contact point, pass to stationary partner.
Activity 6	Waits turn	I	None needed
Activity 7	Moves to next station	V	Have peers provide cues.
Activity 8	Works on dribbling	VP	Jonathan can dribble with deflated ball or Nerf ball; work on dribbling straight ahead without obstacles; work on walking then jogging while dribbling.
Activity 9	Waits turn	I	None needed
Activity 10	Goes back to original squad	V	Have peers provide cues.

(continued)

Figure 4.8. Sample ecological inventory with discrepancy analysis for tenth-grade physical education. (*Key:* I, independent; V, verbal cues or reminder; PP, partial physical assistance; P+, physical assistance [student tries to help]; P, physical assistance [student is passive]; P–, physical assistance [student fights assistance].)

Figure 4.8.   *(continued)*

Subenvironment and activity	What are the steps that a person without disabilities uses?	What assistance does the student with disabilities currently need?	What adaptations or levels of assistance might help this student?
Gym: soccer game			
Activity 1	Listens to instructions	V	Have Steve reexplain rule from teacher in simpler terms.
Activity 2	Puts on assigned penny	PP	Have peers provide assistance.
Activity 3	Goes to assigned position	V	Have peers provide cues.
Activity 4	Plays game	VP	Jonathan will play a wing fullback, and a nonskilled peer will go against him.
Activity 5	Watches flow of game	V	Have peers provide cues.
Activity 6	Interacts with teammates	V	Have peers provide cues.
Activity 7	Shakes hands with other team	V	Have peers provide cues.
Activity 8	Takes off penny	PP	Have peers assist Jonathan.
Activity 9	Puts penny away	V	Have peers provide cues.
Activity 10	Walks to locker room	V	Have peers provide cues.
Locker room			
Activity 1	Locates locker room	V	Jonathan can use natural cues on wall; use additional wall cues.
Activity 2	Enters locker room	I	None needed
Activity 3	Locates locker	V	Tape colored sign on locker; have peer provide cues as needed.
Activity 4	Takes off gym clothes	PP	Have peers assist as needed.
Activity 5	Places exercise clothes in gym bag	I	None needed
Activity 6	Gets towel, soap, shampoo	V	Have Steve provide cues as needed.
Activity 7	Locates shower	V	Place extra sign on wall; have peer provide cues.
Activity 8	Turns on water and modulates water temperature	PP	Jonathan can practice starting with cold and gradually add hot; have Steve assist.
Activity 9	Shampoos hair; washes self	PP	Jonathan can start from top and work down; Jonathan can practice at home; have peer provide assistance
Activity 10	Turns off shower	PP	Jonathan can step away from water, then turn off hot then cold; have peer assist as needed.
Activity 11	Dries self off	V	Jonathan can start from top and work down; practice; peer can give verbal cues as needed.
Activity 12	Locates and uses deodorant	V	Have peer provide cues as needed.
Activity 13	Puts on street clothes	P	Jonathan can use pull-on clothes; use special ties for shoes; have peer assist as needed.
Activity 14	Goes to mirror and combs hair	V	Jonathan can start from top and work down, checking appearance: hair combed, shirt tucked in, shoes on correct feet. Peer can give cues as needed.
Activity 15	Places all personal belongings in gym bag	V	Teach Jonathan to check area and locker; use picture cue card; peer gives cues.
Activity 16	Leaves locker room and goes to class	V	Use natural cues on wall; use additional wall cues; have peer assist.

actively exploring and experimenting with equipment, rules, distances, and patterns. Such an approach allows for more creative learning and encourages students to problem solve. The student is responsible for most decisions (Mosston & Ashworth, 2002). However, it may be more difficult to control a class using an indirect approach, learning specific skills often takes longer compared to a direct approach, and some students may not achieve the goal in the way you prefer (e.g., some may never throw overhand even though you had hoped that

they would discover that is the best way to throw a small ball for distance). Indirect instruction tends to be very accommodating to students with disabilities, particularly students with physical disabilities who are encouraged to discover their best way to perform particular movements. However, such an approach can be confusing to students with intellectual disabilities, autism, and attention-deficit/hyperactivity disorders, and the freedom allowed in such programs can promote behavior problems in students with emotional disturbances.

At this point in the process, simply focus on getting a feel of the general physical educator's teaching approach and how this approach matches the unique abilities of the student with disabilities. Ideally, a student will be placed in a class in which the teacher uses an approach that matches the student's learning style. Realistically, this may not happen. Still, general physical educators can be encouraged to teach the group of students one way and a particular student with disabilities another way. For example, a teacher might use a command approach when teaching throwing to most of the class while encouraging a student who has cerebral palsy to explore different ways to throw to see which method is most effective given the student's unique movement abilities (see Chapter 6 for more detail on various teaching approaches).

Determine Modifications Needed in General Physical Education

At this point you should know each student's present level of performance; long-term plan, including long-term goals and short-term instructional objectives; and generally where the student will be able to work on these goals and objectives within the general physical education program. The next step is to determine what specific modifications are needed. Rainforth et al. (1992) outlined several questions to guide the decision process when determining specific instructional modifications for students with disabilities (listed in Table 4.3 and discussed next).

1. *How often will instruction occur?* Students with disabilities may need more instruction than their peers without disabilities to learn even simple skills. Therefore, one of the first decisions to be made is how often the student with disabilities will receive instruction. For example, if elementary-age students receive physical education twice per week, you may want to request that a student with severe disabilities receive general physical education with peers without disabilities twice per week plus an additional two sessions with a small group of students (composed of both students with and without disabilities) who need extra help on specific skills each week.

   Another possibility is working with the student one-to-one on Mondays on activities that will take place during the week, giving the student extra practice on skills and explaining and practicing some of the upcoming activities (see Kelly & Melograno, 2004, for a detailed description of how to determine how often a student should receive physical education).

The question of how often also can include how often an adapted physical education specialist team-teaches with the general physical educator or how often particular support personnel assist the student with disabilities. For example, a speech teacher may come to general physical education once per week to assist a student with autism in physical education activities as well as in using verbal language. Having this professional assist the student (with guidance from the general and/or adapted physical educator) may optimize the student's time in general physical education, thus giving him or her even more instruction and practice in critical skills. Similarly, the adapted physical education specialist may come to general physical education once each week to work with the student along with other students without disabilities who need extra help. Such a team approach allows the general physical educator time to work with a smaller, more skilled group of students without disabilities while the adapted physical educator works with a smaller group of less skilled students (including the student with disabilities).

2. *Where will student receive instruction?* The second related question is where instruction will occur. Because our focus is on inclusion, in most cases instruction will occur in general physical education. Activities that are directly related to the student's IEP can be modified so that the student can work on these goals in a safe and successful setting. Even when general physical education activities do not match the student's IEP, alternative activities can be presented within the general setting. For example, an elementary-age student working on independent walking can practice this skill (with assistance as needed) while his or her peers without disabilities work on kicking skills. In either case, you should note where specific IEP objectives (including objectives from other team members) could be embedded in the typical daily physical education routine (see Figures 4.9 and 4.10).

Table 4.3. Considerations when determining a student's individual instructional program

- How often will student receive instruction?
- Where will student receive instruction?
- How will student be prepared for instruction?
- What instructional modifications are needed to elicit desired performance?
- What curricular adaptations are needed to enhance desired performance?

From Rainforth, B., York, J., & MacDonald, C. (1992). *Collaborative teams for students with severe disabilities* (p. 186). Baltimore: Paul H. Brookes Publishing Co.; adapted by permission.

Activity	IEP objectives (written generally)			
	Improve endurance.	Develop softball skills.	Develop tennis skills.	Use local health club.
Walks to locker room	X			
Changes clothes; puts clothes in locker				X
Goes to squad				X
Sits in squad				X
Does warm-ups	X			
Participates in skill activities (choosing stations)		X	X	
Participates in game	X	X		
Walks to locker	X			X
Showers; changes clothes				X
Walks to class	X			

Figure 4.9. Sue's individualized education program (IEP) objectives for general physical education and where they will be embedded within general physical education.

In other cases, general physical education may not be the most appropriate setting for particular students, and alternative settings should be identified that include interaction with peers without disabilities. (Table 4.4 provides a list of factors to help determine where a student with disabilities should receive physical education instruction.) For example, students with autism-like behaviors who cannot deal with the stimulating environment of a large gymnasium of 20 or more peers may need to begin their program in a quieter, less threatening setting. Such a setting may be in the cafeteria or in a workroom with one or two peers without disabilities. Gradually, a student can be weaned into the more stimulating general physical education setting. Finally, older students should receive part of their physical education instruction (i.e., instruction in community-based recreation) at local recreation facilities such as health clubs, bowling alleys, and recreation centers. Again, peers without disabilities can be included in these outings to promote appropriate social skills. Decisions regarding how often and where to teach particular skills, like all decisions, should be student-based (i.e., what is best for the student). Factors such as age and severity of disability, availability of support personnel, and availability of transportation and recreation facilities in the community will influence the team's decision as to how often and where the student will receive community-based physical education.

One cautionary note: Other team members may wish to target physical education to work on their goals. For example, a physical therapist might ask physical education staff to do particular stretching activities during physical education for a student with cerebral palsy, a speech teacher may ask physical education staff to encourage a particular student to practice answering "wh-" questions (who, what, where, why), or an occupational therapist might ask you to assign a peer to a student to help a student with spina bifida in the locker room so that the student can work on independent dressing and undressing skills. While these requests are often appropriate and easily implemented by physical education staff, these particular goals should not take precedent over specific physical education goals. For instance, some special education teachers integrate their students with disabilities into general physical education to improve social and communication skills without regard to whether the students improve in physical education/recreation. Such teachers may push to have a student participate with his or her peers without disabilities in all general physical education activities including activities that are not safe or appropriate (e.g., an 18-year-old student who is blind participating in field hockey, when your goal is to have this student acquire skills needed to participate independently in beep baseball, weight training, aerobics, swimming, and hitting golf balls at a driving range). In such

Activity	IEP objectives from other team members (written generally)				
	Walk/move faster.	Use appropriate behavior.	Develop dressing/ undressing skills.	Make choices.	Follow one-cue directions.
Walks to locker room	X	X			
Changes clothes; puts clothes in locker			X		
Goes to squad	X	X			
Sits in squad		X			X
Does warm-ups	X	X			X
Participates in skill activities (choosing stations)		X		X	
Participates in game	X	X		X	
Walks to locker	X	X			
Showers; changes clothes		X	X		
Walks to class	X	X			

Figure 4.10.   Sample objectives from Sue's individualized education program (IEP) from other team members and where the objectives will be embedded within general physical education.

cases it is important to help teachers understand that participating in general physical education activities just so that the student can socialize with his peers is not good use of his physical education period (Block & Garcia, 1995). Furthermore, by participating in field hockey, this student is missing out on necessary practice time in his targeted activities. Again, most requests are reasonable and can be easily accommodated, but make sure all team members understand that the purpose of physical education is to teach students specific motor, fitness, sport, and recreation skills and should not be considered a dumping ground for everyone else's goals and objectives.

3. *How will the student be prepared for instruction?* Preparation for instruction can involve several factors. For students with physical disabilities such as cerebral palsy, preparation might include relaxation techniques, techniques to normalize muscle tone, range-of-motion activities, and positioning to facilitate active independent movement (Rainforth & York-Barr, 1997). Physical educators can incorporate specific range-of-motion and relaxation activities in their warmups (either have the entire class do them or have the student do these activities while his or her peers do other forms of warm-ups). Such exercises can help the student demonstrate more functional arm or leg use during physical educa-

tion. In other situations, preparation may take place back in the classroom. For example, a student with a severe physical disability usually sits in a wheelchair during academic classes. Although sitting in the chair might be the best position for this student in terms of academic work such as using eye-gaze when working on the computer, sitting in a chair may not be the best position for functional arm and hand use. This student might be better positioned in a prone stander or side-lyer so that he or she has more range of motion for pushing balls down a ramp (see Table 4.5 for an example of a positioning decision). The student's physical therapist would be the best resource to determine how to help the student warm-up and what the best position is for the student during certain activities. Therapists also can develop easy-to-follow picture cards that show how to warm-up and position students. In some cases, the teacher or teacher assistant can warm-up the student and place him or her in particular pieces of equipment prior to physical education class.

Another consideration for preparing students for instruction is working with students who have behavior problems or intellectual disabilities. Some of these students may have difficulty making the transition from quiet, classroom activities to the stimulation of the gymnasium. These students may need to be reminded several

Table 4.4. Where to teach targeted skills

GPE no support	GPE support by peer/TA	APE in GPE environment	1/2 GPE; 1/2 pull-out APE	Full-time pull-out APE
Individualized education program (IEP) goals match GPE 85% of time.	IEP goals match GPE 50%–80% of time.	IEP goals match GPE 25%–50% of time.	50% of IEP goals cannot be worked on in in GPE	Student does not benefit at all from GPE.
Student can safely work on IEP goals with few to no modifications.	Student can safely work on IEP goals with support.	Student can safely work on IEP objectives with more specialized support.	Student can safely work on IEP goals part of the time, but GPE is unsafe part of time.	GPE environment is not safe for student.
Student does not affect program for peers.	Student does not affect program for peers with support.	Student does not affect program for peers with support.	Student does not affect program for peers half of the time, but does affect program for peers half of the time	Student is disruptive even with support or is a danger to peers.
Student benefits and learns from peers and enjoys being with peers.	Student benefits and learns from peers and enjoys being with peers if supported.	Student benefits and learns from peers and enjoys being with peers if given specialized support.	Student benefits and learns from peers and enjoys being with peers sometimes.	Student never benefits from or learns from peers and does not seem to enjoy being with peers.
Environment does not cause undue anxiety in student.	Environment does not cause undue anxiety in student if student is supported.	Environment does not cause undue anxiety in student if student is given specialized support.	Environment sometimes is okay for student, but other times it can cause extreme anxiety even with support.	Environment always causes extreme anxiety for student, even with support, such that student cannot learn in setting.

GPE, general physical education; APE, adapted physical education.

Adapted by permission from class project submitted by Mel Mitchell at The University of Virginia.

times that physical education is their next class. In addition, some students such as those with autism may need strategies to help them cope with transition such as using a picture schedule, being the first or last person in the gym, sitting in a smaller squad, sitting at the end of a squad, sitting and watching the first few warm-up activities, and so forth. Students who have behavior problems might need extra reminders of the rules of the gymnasium and any specific conse-

Table 4.5. Considerations in selecting positions for students with severe physical disabilities

Considerations	Warm-ups	Basketball skills
What positions do peers use when they engage in the activity?	Lying down, standing, moving	Standing, moving
Which of these positions allow easy view of an access to activity materials and equipment?	Sitting better than standing	Standing better than sitting
Do the positions allow for proximity to peers?	Yes, sitting on mat with peers	Yes, stander is easy to move near peers.
Do the positions promote efficient movement as needed to perform the task?	Sitting on mat allows participation in many warm-up activities.	Standing allows free movement of hands for holding/pushing.
What positions provide alternatives to overused postures and equipment?	Usually sits in chair; stretching on mat is good alternative	Usually sits in chair; stander is good alternative
If positioning equipment is required, is it unobtrusive, cosmetically acceptable, and not physically isolating?	None needed	Prone stander, while fairly obtrusive, is nicely decorated; peers are used to it.
Is the positioning equipment safe and easy to handle?	None needed	Should be placed in stander by therapist or teacher; easy to move
Is the equipment individually selected; modified to individual learner needs?	None needed	Fit to student by physical therapist
Is the equipment available and easily transported to natural environments?	None needed	Available from special education class
FINAL POSITION	*ON MAT*	*PRONE STANDER*

From Rainforth, B., York, J., & MacDonald, C. (1992). *Collaborative teams for students with severe disabilities* (pp. 182–195). Baltimore: Paul H. Brookes Publishing Co.; adapted by permission.

Table 4.6. Instructional modifications to accommodate students with disabilities

- Teaching style (direct, indirect)
- Class format and size of group (small/large group, stations/whole-class instruction)
- Level of methodology (verbal cues, demonstrations, physical assistance)
- How student communicates with you (verbal, sign language, pointing to pictures)
- Starting/stopping signals (whistle, hand signals)
- Time of day when student is included (some do better in morning versus afternoon)
- Duration of participation (of instruction, expected participation, length of activities)
- Order of learning (in what order will you present material and instruction)
- Instructional setting (indoors/outdoors; part of gym/whole gym)
- Elimination of distractions (extra lighting, temperature)
- Structure of class (set organization of instruction each day)
- Level of difficulty (control complexity of instruction, presentation of information, organization)
- Levels of motivation (make setting and activities more motivating)

Table 4.7. Curricular adaptations to accommodate individuals with specific limitations

Students with limited strength, power, or endurance
- Lower targets.
- Reduce distance/playing field.
- Reduce weight/size of striking implements, balls, or projectiles.
- Allow students to sit or lie down while playing.
- Use deflated balls or suspended balls.
- Decrease activity time/increase rest time.
- Reduce speed of game/increase distance for peers without disabilities.

Students with limited balance
- Lower center of gravity.
- Keep as much of body in contact with the surface as possible.
- Widen base of support.
- Increase width of beams to be walked.
- Extend arms for balance.
- Use carpeted rather than slick surfaces.
- Teach students how to fall.
- Provide a bar to assist with stability.
- Teach students to use eyes optimally.
- Determine whether balance problems are related to health problems.

Students with limited coordination and accuracy
- For catching and striking activities, use larger, lighter, softer balls.
- Decrease distance ball is thrown and reduce speed.
- For throwing activities, use smaller balls.
- In striking and kicking, use stationary ball before trying a moving ball.
- Increase the surface of the striking implement.
- Use backstop.
- Increase size of target.
- In bowling-type games, use lighter, less stable pins.
- Optimize safety.

Source: Sherrill (2004).

quences or reinforcers that may be presented during physical education. Such simple reminders prior to entering the gymnasium often help the student refocus on appropriate behaviors. A concerted effort by the classroom teacher and physical educator to make transitions smoother for students with disabilities can prevent many behavior problems.

4. *What instructional modifications are needed?* Many factors related to instruction can be modified to accommodate students with disabilities in general physical education. Such factors as teaching style, length of instruction, types of cues given, and type of structure are just a few instructional factors under the control of the teacher (see Tables 4.3 and 4.6). Making simple adjustments in how you present various aspects of your lesson can help students with disabilities be more motivated, more successful, follow directions, and improve the quality of their practice and rate of skill development. For example, will the student respond to verbal cues or will some other form of instruction be necessary? Will the student respond to the same start/stop signal that the other students respond to, or will the student need some other signal? Can the student sit and wait his or her turn as long as other students, or will some adjustment in waiting have to be made? The team should work together to determine how instruction will be modified to meet the unique needs of students with disabilities. Chapter 5 provides more detailed information on various instructional fac-

tors and how they can be used to facilitate inclusion in physical education.

5. *What curricular adaptations will be used to enhance performance?* Perhaps the greatest challenge to the physical education team is finding ways to accommodate students with disabilities who cannot perform the skill in the same way or at the same level as their peers. The goal at this level is to create adaptations that allow the stu-

Table 4.8. Curricular adaptations when modifying group games and sports

- Can you vary the purpose/goal of the game?
- Can you vary number of players?
- Can you vary movement requirements?
- Can you vary the field of play?
- Can you vary objects used?
- Can you vary the level of organization?
- Can you vary the limits/expectations?

Source: Morris and Stiehl (1999).

Table 4.9. Determining appropriateness of physical education adaptations

Consideration	Application to physical education
Will the adaptation increase active participation in the activity?	A lower basket or shorter distance to first base allows student to play team sports with peers.
Will it allow the student to participate in an activity that is preferred or valued by the student, friends, or family members?	Modifications allow student to participate in team sports, popular group games, playground activities, and community sports.
Will it continue to be useful and appropriate as the student grows older and starts using other environments?	Bowling ramp can be used in regular bowling facilities, flotation devices can be used in community pools, adapted golf club can be used at local driving range.
Will it take less time to teach the student to use the adaptation than to teach the skill directly?	Use flotation device rather than teaching swimming, having student hit ball off tee rather than hit pitched ball.
Will the team have access to the technical expertise to design, construct, adjust, and repair the adaptation?	Special switches to hit or toss balls (will physical educator be taught how to use equipment and do simple maintenance?).
Will use of the adaptation maintain or enhance related motor and communication skills?	Adapted switch promotes independent arm and hand movements, participating with peers promotes socialization and communication.

Source: Udvari-Solner, Causton-Theoharis, and York-Barr (2004).

dent to participate and acquire skills in a safe, successful, and challenging environment. There are many ways to adapt specific situations, skills, or activities to enhance a person's performance. For some, adaptations might be as simple as giving a student with limited strength a lighter bat. For other students, such as those with visual impairments, a simple adaptation might involve assigning a peer to assist in retrieving balls. Still other students with more severe disabilities may need special equipment such as ramps, special switches, or major changes to the rules of games to successfully participate in general physical education.

Chapters 6 and 7 provide an extensive review of specific strategies for modifying the curriculum to accommodate students with disabilities in general physical education (see Tables 4.7 and 4.8 for a list of some of these strategies). Suggestions include accommodating students who have problems with fitness, accommodating students who have problems with balance, accommodating students with problems with coordination, and making specific modifications to traditional games and team sports. The PEIT members should work together to examine the students abilities referenced to the requirements of specific skills and rules of games to determine

Table 4.10. Chronological-age–appropriate activities and sample modifications for elementary-age students with severe disabilities

Age-appropriate activities	Modifications
Manipulative patterns	
Throwing	Pushing a ball down a ramp, grasp and release
Catching	Tracking suspended balls, reaching for balloons
Kicking	Touch balloon on floor, push ball down ramp with foot
Striking	Hitting ball off tee; hitting suspended ball
Locomotor patterns	
Running	Being pushed in wheelchair while keeping head up
Jumping/hopping	Lifting head up/down while being pushed in wheelchair
Galloping/skipping	Moving arms up and down while being pushed in wheelchair; also, student can use adapted mobility aids such as scooter boards and walkers
Perceptual-motor skills	
Balance skills	Propping up on elbows, prone balance over wedge, body awareness, accept tactile input, imitate simple movements
Spatial awareness	Moving arms in when going between, ducking head under
Visual-motor coordination	Track suspended objects, touch switches
Physical fitness skills	
Endurance	Tolerate continuous activity, move body parts repeatedly
Strength	Use stretch bands, use isometric exercises
Flexibility	Perform range of motion activities as suggested by PT

From M.E. Block, "What is Appropriate Physical Education for Students with Profound Disabilities," in *Adapted Physical Activity Quarterly,* 9(3) © 1992 by Human Kinetics. Reprinted with permission from Human Kinetics (Champaign, IL).

Table 4.11. Chronological-age–appropriate activities and sample modifications for middle school/high school/young adulthood

Age-appropriate activities	Modifications
Team sports	
Soccer skills	Passing/kicking/shooting—push ball down ramp using foot
Soccer game	Set up special zones, use ramps for kicking
Volleyball skills	Track suspended balls, reach and touch balls
Volleyball game	Buddy catches ball, student has 3 seconds to touch ball
Basketball skills	Using switch that shoots ball into small basket, keeping head up and arms out on defense; pushing ball off tray for passing
Basketball game	Buddy pushes student into offensive or defensive zone, ball passed to buddy, student has 5 seconds to activate switch that shoots his ball into small basket
Individual sports	
Bowling	Use a ramp (play at community facility when possible)
Bocce (lawn bowling)	Same as above
Miniature golf	Push ball down ramp using mini-putter
Golf (driving range)	Activate switch that causes ball to be hit
Physical fitness skills	
Endurance	Moves body parts during aerobic dance program
Strength	Use stretch bands, isometrics, free weights
Flexibility	Perform range of motion activities as suggested by PT during aerobics or during warm-up activities prior to team sports

Note: In all activities, utilize the principle of partial participation to ensure that the student is successful.

From M.E. Block, "What is Appropriate Physical Education for Students with Profound Disabilities," in *Adapted Physical Activity Quarterly, 9*(3) © 1992 by Human Kinetics. Reprinted with permission from Human Kinetics (Champaign, IL).

which adaptations to implement. Chapter 7 also provides detailed information on how to modify select individual and team sport activities for students with specific types of disabilities.

Deciding which modifications to employ should take into account a student's age, what equipment is used by peers without disabilities, and what equipment is available in the community, for example (see Table 4.9). For example, a seventh-grade student with severe intellectual disabilities participating in an introductory tennis unit has limited strength and coordination; therefore, this student is given a shorter, lighter racket (racquetball racket) and is allowed to hit a ball off a tee. These adaptations allow the student to practice the skill and improve performance. These adaptations will not affect the student's ability to participate in tennis in the community later in life.

Even students with very severe disabilities can be accommodated via adaptations to equipment and rules (see Tables 4.10 and 4.11). As with considerations regarding prompts and cues, each student should be provided the necessary adaptations that will promote meaningful participation and success. Still, special equipment and changes to rules should be systematically faded away whenever possible so that students can participate in activities using the same rules and equipment as their peers. In addition, caution should be taken when making adaptations that

stigmatize the student or dramatically change the game for students without disabilities. For example, allowing a high school student to use a Mickey Mouse balloon as a substitute for a volleyball only accentuates the difference rather than similarities between this student and his or her peers. A better adaptation might be having a peer catch a regulation volleyball for this student and then hold it while he or she hits it. Similarly, forcing all students to walk rather than run in a soccer game to accommodate a student who uses a walker would ruin the game for the students without disabilities. A better solution could be setting up a small zone for this student in which he or she is the only player allowed to kick the ball (see Chapter 6 and 7 for more detail on modifications).

Determine the Support the Student with a Disability Will Need in General Physical Education

While many general physical educators are quite competent and interested in including students with disabilities into their general program, from time to time some students will present such unique challenges that support will be necessary. York, Giangreco, Vandercook, and Macdonald (1992) noted that the need for support should not be a re-

Table 4.12. Student challenges and respective support personnel

Student challenge	Potential support
Cognitive/learning	
Curricular/instructional adaptations	General educator, general physical educator (PE), adapted physical educator (APE), special educator, speech therapist, occupational therapist (OT), vision or hearing specialist, classmates
Organizing assignments, schedules	General educator, GPE, APE, special educator, speech therapist, OT
Communication/Interactions	
Nonverbal communication	Speech therapist, special educator, family member, classmates
Socialization with classmates	Speech therapist, special educator, psychologist, classmates
Behaving in adaptive ways	General educator, GPE, special educator, psychologist, speech therapist, classmates
Physical/motor	
Functional use of hands	OT, physical therapist (PT), special educator
Mobility and transitions	APE, OT, PT, orientation and mobility, special educator
Posture (body alignment)	PT, OT
Fitness and physical activity	General PE, APE, PT, nurse
Sensory	
Vision	Vision specialist, OT, orientation and mobility
Hearing	Audio, hearing specialist, speech therapist
Health	
Eating difficulties	OT, speech therapist, PT, nurse, special educator
Medications	Nurse
Other health needs	Nurse, physician, selected health care professionals
Current and future living	
Career and vocational pursuits	Vocational educator, counselor, special educator
Leisure pursuits	Special educator, OT, GPE, APE, recreation personnel
Support from home and community	Social worker, counselor, special educator, general educator

From York, J., Giangreco, M.F., Vandercook, T., & Macdonald, C. (1992). Integrating support personnel in the inclusive classroom. In S. Stainback & W. Stainback (Eds.), *Curriculum considerations in inclusive classrooms: Facilitating learning for all students* (p. 108). Baltimore: Paul H. Brookes Publishing Co.; adapted by permission.

flection of the general physical educator's shortcomings. Rather, support should be viewed as a reminder to all team members that no one, regardless of their training, experience, or attitude, has the ability to meet the needs of all students who participate in inclusive physical education programs. Therefore, a key step in developing a physical education program for a student with disabilities is to determine who (if anyone) will provide assistance as well as the level of intensity of support (AAMR, 1992; Rainforth & York-Barr, 1997; York et al., 1992).

Some students such as those with spina bifida or mild intellectual disabilities may not need any special assistance, while students with severe learning disabilities or intellectual disabilities may need peers to give them extra cues to follow directions occasionally. Students with more severe disabilities or those with medically fragile conditions may need a trained professional to provide assistance on a regular basis. Decisions regarding what type and how much support a student receives should be based on a case-by-case basis. For example, one student with Down syndrome might need a teacher assistant while another student with Down syndrome may not need any support to be successful in general physical education. Each of these students with the same diagnosis should be viewed as an individual with unique abilities and needs. How much and what type of personal support a student will need will depend on each individual student's age, medical and health concerns, the type of activities being presented, and physical, cognitive, and social skills.

Determine Who Will Provide Support

Rainforth and York-Barr (1997) suggested that teams should first determine the primary challenges faced by an individual student in accomplishing his or her educational goals. These challenges can include such general areas as cognitive/learning, communication/interaction, physical/motor, sensory, health, and current/future living (York et al., 1992). Next, teams should identify members with specific competencies who can address these challenges and provide necessary support (see Table 4.12). For example, classmates could assist a student with moderate intellectual disabilities and no behavior or medical problems during physical education. The physical educator might tell the class, "If you are near John and he looks confused or looks like he needs help, please assist him." Similarly, a student with muscular dystrophy may only need a classmate to retrieve balls in a throwing activity. However, the general physical educator might also want consultation with an adapted physical education specialist and physical therapist to learn more about this student's posture, fitness abilities, physical activity capabilities, and possible curricular modifications. A student who is blind could have a peer help him move from one station to another and participate in various activities. In addition, this student's orientation and mobility specialist might come in to general physical education on Mondays and the APE specialist might come on Wednesdays to work with the student and support the general physical educator.

Even students with more severe disabilities can be assisted by classmates in general physical education with the additional support of other professionals. For example, a student with severe spastic cerebral palsy is in a ball skill unit in first grade. The class is broken down into stations, and this student relies on assistance from his classmates to help him at each station. At a throwing station, peers who are either resting or waiting their turn assist this student. The adapted physical educator has taught these peers how to place the ball in this student's hand and how to position his chair so that he can throw. These peers also push the student from station to station during transitions. This student's physical therapist comes to general physical education once per week and the APE specialist comes twice per week to support this student, work on individualized prescribed goals, provide information to the general physical educator, and provide information and training to classmates.

Students with severe medical or health conditions or a severe behavior problem that pose a risk to the student and/or his or her classmates will require more specialized support. For example, a trained teacher assistant, special education teacher, and/or APE specialist should support a high school student with severe intellectual disabilities and aggressive behaviors. These professionals also should be trained in how to help the student acquire IEP objectives while in general physical education. Similarly, a nurse might support a student with a severe medical condition in general physical education so that medical emergencies can be handled quickly and appropriately. Again, these support staff, while trained in dealing with the student's medical condition, should be given specific direction on how to help the student work on his or her physical education goals.

Determine Type of Support to Be Provided

Once a decision has been made as to who will provide the support, the next step is to decide what type of support is to be provided. There is a delicate balance between providing necessary support that facilitates inclusion and too much support that actually has a negative effect on inclusion (Block, 1999; Bricker, 1995; Ferguson, 1995; York et al., 1992). For example, a student with a disability has a teacher assistant who accompanies her to general physical education. When the general physical educator asks students to partner up to do sit-ups, the teacher assistant is the partner for the student with disabilities. Although the teacher assistant means well, she actually has a negative effect on helping this student interact with peers and be a true member of the group (Block, 1999).

York et al. (1992) identified four types of support that can be applied to including students with disabilities in general physical education:

1. *Resource support* consists of providing the general physical educator, classmates, and the student with tangible material (e.g., adapted equipment such as beep balls), financial resources (e.g., funds to provide an off-campus aquatics program), information resources (e.g., literature about community sport programs and summer camps), or human resources (teacher assistants, other professionals). York and her colleagues noted that resources alone would not ensure a successful inclusive program. Team member must still implement the prescribed inclusive program properly.

2. *Moral support* refers to person-to-person interactions in which the support person empathetically and without judgment listens to the gen-

eral physical educator share his or her concerns about the program and then mutually identifies and solves specific problems. Although the support person may not always agree with the general physical educator, the important part of providing moral support is to acknowledge the general physical educator's concerns.

3. *Technical support* refers to helping the general physical educator find specific strategies, methods, approaches, ideas, and adaptations to make inclusive physical education successful. Technical support involves hands-on delivery of support, such as in-service training, staff development activities, on-site collaboration, peer coaching, team teaching, and demonstrations. Thus, technical support should be highly individualized and more directly relevant to the general physical educator than resource support. Technical support may be more critical at certain times during the year such as in the beginning of school when both the general physical educator and peers without disabilities are adjusting to having a new student with a disability.

4. *Evaluation support* refers to assisting the general physical educator in collecting information needed to monitor and adjust support services. For example, an APE specialist can provide a general physical educator with a simple observation instrument that allows her to more objectively determine if the student with a disability is being successfully included. Evaluation support also refers to assisting the team in determining the impact of support on classmates, family members, and other team members.

One other type of support that is very applicable to general physical education is befriending (AAMR, 1992). Befriending refers to things that the general physical educator and general education classmates can do to help the student become more successful in general physical education and feel more a part of the group (Block & Brady, 1999). For example, a general physical educator can befriend a student with a disability by simply talking to and instructing the student with disabilities, making an effort to modify activities to facilitate inclusion of this student, and generally acknowledging the student as an important member of the class. Similarly, classmates can befriend a peer with a disability by associating and socializing with the student with disabilities, including him or her in their groups, helping the student as needed, and doing whatever they can to help the student feel welcome (Block & Brady, 1999). Of all the various types of supports that can be provided, befriending may be the simplest and least expensive support yet the most important for successful inclusion.

Determine How Often Support Is to Be Provided

Another important yet difficult decision the team must make is how often support will be provided for individual students. The AAMR defined four levels of intensity of support that vary from intermittent support (as needed) to pervasive support (virtually the entire school day) (see Table 4.13). However, the AAMR noted that decisions regarding support must be made on a case-by-case basis and should be based not only on the student's needs but also on the student's immediate environment (AAMR, 1992). In terms of physical education, the student's immediate environment that may affect the amount of support provided include the general physical educators attitude towards and capacity to successfully include the student, grade level of general physical education class, the nature of the general physical education curriculum (e.g., sports and games versus skill focus), the number of students without disabilities in general physical education (some programs have as many as 150 students at one time in general physical education), and the general physical education environment (inside and outside spaces and facilities). For example, a motivated, experienced general physical educator might require only consultative support by an APE specialist one or twice

Table 4.13.　Definition and examples of intensities of support

Intermittent

Supports on an "as needed basis." Characterized by episodic nature, person not always needing the support(s), or short-term supports needed during life-span transitions (e.g., job loss or an acute medical crisis). Intermittent supports may be high or low intensity when provided.

Limited

An intensity of supports characterized by consistency over time, time-limited but not of an intermittent nature, may require fewer staff members and less cost than more intense levels of support (e.g., time-limited employment training or transitional supports during the school to adult provided period).

Extensive

Supports characterized by regular involvement (e.g., daily) in at least some environments (such as work or home) and not time limited (e.g., long-term support and long-term home living support).

Pervasive

Supports characterized by their constancy, high intensity; provided across environments, potential life-sustaining nature. Pervasive supports typically involve more staff members and intrusiveness than do extensive or time-limited supports

a month to successfully include a second grade student with severe intellectual disabilities into a second-grade general physical education class of 25 students that is working on throwing and catching skills. However, a general physical educator may require daily, direct support to successfully include a similarly functioning student in seventh grade general physical education class of 75 in which the focus of the class is playing regulation team sports.

The important point when making decisions regarding support is that all decision should be made on an individual basis through a thoughtful, team process rather than simply assigning a peer, volunteer, or assistant to work with a student. In addition, it is extremely important that support personnel go through a formal training program prior to working with specific students and receive on-going training so that these individuals provide appropriate, safe support to students with disabilities. In addition, the general educator and/or APE specialist should take responsibility to inform support personnel about changes to the daily or weekly routines, when new units will start, what modifications are appropriate for particular activities, and so forth. Block and Krebs (1992) described a continuum of support to general physical education in which they described how to make decisions regarding personnel who can support students with disabilities in general physical education (see Table 4.14).

Table 4.14. A continuum of support to general physical education (Block & Krebs, 1992)

LEVEL 1: NO SUPPORT NEEDED
  1.1 Student makes necessary modifications on his/her own.
  1.2 GPE teacher makes necessary modifications for student.

LEVEL 2: APE CONSULTATION
  2.1 No extra assistance is needed.
  2.2 Peer tutor watches out for student.
  2.3 Peer tutor assists student.
  2.4 Paraprofessional assists student.

LEVEL 3: APE DIRECT SERVICE IN GPE 1x/WEEK
  3.1 Peer tutor watches out for student.
  3.2 Peer tutor assists student.
  3.3 Paraprofessional assists student.

LEVEL 4: PART-TIME APE AND PART-TIME GPE
  4.1 Flexible schedule with reverse mainstreaming.
  4.2 Fixed schedule with reverse mainstreaming.

LEVEL 5: REVERSE MAINSTREAM IN SPECIAL SCHOOL
  5.1 Students from special school go to general physical education regular school 1–2× per week.
  5.2 Students without disabilities come to special school 2–3× per week for reverse mainstreaming.
  5.3 Students with and without disabilities meet at community-based recreation facility and work out together.

From M.E. Block and P.L. Krebs, "An Alternative to Least Restrictive Environments: A Continuum of Support to Regular Physical Education," in *Adapted Physical Activity Quarterly, 9*(2): page 104. © 1992 by Human Kinetics. Reprinted with permission from Human Kinetics (Champaign, IL).

Preparing Team Members for Inclusion

This model allows you to determine what goals a particular student has and how these goals can be met in general physical education. In addition, support personnel have been identified to help implement the program. You are just about ready to include the student in general physical education, but first you must make sure that the general physical education teacher and students without disabilities feel comfortable having a student with disabilities in their general physical education class (Morreau & Eichstaedt, 1983). You should also make sure the support staff (teacher assistants, volunteers, peer tutors) know the student they are working with as well as their responsibilities to the team. One of the primary reasons why inclusion fails is that those directly involved with the program are not adequately prepared (Block, 1999; Grosse, 1991; Lavay & DePaepe, 1987). The next three steps discuss ways to prepare key personnel for inclusion.

Prepare the General Physical Educator

The first and most important person to prepare is the general physical educator. The PEIT often assumes that general physical educators are receptive to inclusion and have the skills necessary to successfully accommodate the unique needs of the student with disabilities. Although some general physical educators feel comfortable having a student with disabilities in their program, many others feel very threatened (Minner & Knutson, 1982; Santomier, 1985). Those who feel uncomfortable having students with disabilities in their program argue that they do not have the training, that the student with disabilities will take too much of their time, that it will be dangerous, and that typical students will not accept the special student, among many other reasons. Although these may sound like excuses, most general physical educators rarely have the in-depth training needed to successfully include students with disabilities. For example, a typical undergraduate physical education teacher preparation program includes only one course on adapted physical education, which usually focuses on identifying various types of disabilities rather than practical suggestions for developing and implementing individualized programs.

One of the most important steps in preparing general physical educators is to define his or her specific role. Vandercook and York (1990) described the roles of general education teachers in facilitating the inclusion of students with disabilities into their general education classes. This role can be applied to general physical educators as follows: The general physical education teacher should view the student with disabilities as a member of the class rather than as a visitor; the general physical educator should contribute information about the general physical education curriculum, instructional strategies, teaching style, management techniques, routines, and rules; the general physical educator should work collaboratively with support personnel, family members, and peers in developing physical education programs and in including the student with disabilities into typical physical education activities; the general physical educator should provide a model of appropriate interaction and communication with student with disabilities (set expectations for acceptance and inclusion that would transfer to peers without disabilities); and the general physical educator should be willing to give it a try. This last role should not be taken lightly. Many physical educators absolutely refuse to allow the student to participate in general physical education, or if they allow the student into the gym, they make no effort to appropriately include the student in physical activities.

For inclusion to be truly successful, the general physical education teacher must learn to feel comfortable with the notion of having students with disabilities in his or her class. This can be accomplished in several ways. First and foremost, those physical educators who feel most threatened should be assured that they will receive both direct and consultative support from an adapted physical education specialist and special education teacher to assist in the development of the individual program for the student with disabilities, obtain and set up adapted equipment, and develop appropriate modifications to the general program. The special educator can also provide specific information about students' specific skills and weaknesses, any medical/health concerns, communication skills, behaviors, and likes and dislikes. In addition, general physical educators should be assured that students with disabilities, especially students with severe disabilities, will receive support through peer tutors, paraprofessionals, the special education teacher, or the adapted physical educator. The general physical educator should never be left alone with the student until he or she feels comfortable with the situation. Finally, assurance should be made that including a student with disabilities should not cause the general physical educator any more work. In fact, with others' help the physical educator's job might actually be easier. For example, if a teacher assistant comes into the gym with a particular student, the general physical educator could send several students who need extra practice (along with instructions for the teacher assistant) to work with the teacher assistant and special student. This way the general physical educator could work with a smaller group of students on specific skills and strategies.

Another method of helping the general physical educator is to provide desensitizing workshops. These workshops can change preconceived notions about persons with disabilities, foster more positive attitudes, and provide suggestions for modifications. Clark, French, and Henderson (1985) outlined several activities which could be used to desensitize the general physical education teacher, including hosting guest lecturers who have disabilities, visiting special education classes, and getting to know the students better, showing videotapes on athletes with disabilities, role-playing activities in which the general physical educator has to move about in a wheelchair or is blindfolded while doing typical physical education activities, brainstorming with team members about modifications for specific physical education units, visiting other schools that are successfully integrating students with disabilities into general physical education, having an adapted physical educator team teach with the general physical educator early in the semester to show some concrete ways of accommodating the student with disabilities. When provided prior to inclusion, these and similar activities can facilitate acceptance and confidence in general physical educators.

Finally, it is extremely important that the general physical educator understand that his or her responsibilities are still with the entire class, not just one or two students. The general physical educator should not spend any more time with the student who has disabilities compared to his or her students without disabilities. However, the general physical educator should feel comfortable talking with, correcting, and reinforcing the special student just as he or she would typical students. In addition, activities should continue to be challenging to all students, and the general program should not be compromised (see Chapters 6 and 7). For example, skill hierarchies could be extended to accommodate students with disabilities yet could provide challenging activities at the end of the hierarchy for more skilled students (see Figure 4.11). Similarly, modifications to group activities and team sports should be made so that students with disabilities can be included. However, these modifications should not detract from the program for the students without disabilities. It is important that general physical educators understand how certain modifications to games affect the entire class, and they should strive to implement only those modifications that allow a student with disabilities to participate without drastically affecting the rest of the class.

Prepare General Education Students

Peer acceptance can be the critical difference between successful and unsuccessful inclusion. Research suggests that many students without disabilities

Extension of Traditional Skill Station for Dribbling a Basketball

_____ will

1. __ __ __ __ __ Hold ball on lap tray while student is pushed in wheelchair around gym
2. __ __ __ __ __ Push ball off lap tray
3. __ __ __ __ __ Drop ball to floor
4. __ __ __ __ __ Drop ball to floor then reaches down to touch ball before it bounces 3x
5. __ __ __ __ __ Drop ball to floor then reaches down to touch ball before it bounces 2x
6. __ __ __ __ __ Drop ball to floor then reaches down to touch ball before it bounces 1x
7. __ __ __ __ __ Push ball to floor with two hands so that ball bounds up to approximately waist height
8. __ __ __ __ __ Push ball to floor with two hands two times in succession
9. __ __ __ __ __ Push ball to floor with two hands three times in succession
10. __ __ __ __ __ Push ball to floor with one hand two times in succession
11. __ __ __ __ __ Push ball to floor with one hand three times in succession
12. __ __ __ __ __ Push ball to floor with one hand five times in succession
13. __ __ __ __ __ Push ball up and down repeatedly with one hand
14. __ __ __ __ __ Dribble ball while standing still for 10 seconds
15. __ __ __ __ __ Dribble ball while standing still for 20 seconds
16. __ __ __ __ __ Dribble ball while walking forward slowly
17. __ __ __ __ __ Dribble ball while walking forward at normal walking speed
18. __ __ __ __ __ Dribble ball while walking forward quickly
19. __ __ __ __ __ Dribble ball with dominant hand while jogging forward
20. __ __ __ __ __ Dribble ball with dominant hand while running forward
21. __ __ __ __ __ Dribble ball with non-dominant hand while walking forward
22. __ __ __ __ __ Dribble ball with non-dominant hand while jogging forward
23. __ __ __ __ __ Dribble ball with non-dominant hand while running forward
24. __ __ __ __ __ Dribble ball with either hand while weaving through cones
25. __ __ __ __ __ Dribble ball using a cross over dribble while weaving through cones
26. __ __ __ __ __ Dribble ball with either hand while moving in a variety of directions
27. __ __ __ __ __ Dribble and protect ball while guarded by opponent going at full speed

Cue key

(Prompts can be given by physical educator, teacher assistant, or peer tutor.)

I	Independent	T	Touch prompt
IN	Indirect cue	PP	Partial physical assistance
V	Verbal cue	P	Physical assistance (student actively participating)
G	Gestural cue	P+	Physical assistance (student passively participating)
M	Model	P–	Physical assistance (student fighting assistance)

Performance key

+ Student performs skill for four of five trials.

+/– Student performs skill, but for fewer than four of five trials.

– Student does not perform skill.

A Teacher's Guide to Including Students with Disabilities in General Physical Education, Third Edition, by Martin E. Block.
Copyright © 2007 by Paul H. Brookes Publishing Co., Inc. All rights reserved.

Figure 4.11. Extension of traditional skill station for dribbling a basketball. (From Block, M.E., Provis, S., & Nelson, E. [1994]. Accommodating students with special needs in regular physical education: Extending traditional skill stations. _Palaestra, 10_[1], 32–35 [Table 1, p. 34]. PALAESTRA is a publication of Challenge Publications, Ltd., Macomb, IL; adapted by permission of Challenge Publications, Ltd./PALAESTRA.)

Table 4.15. Disability awareness activities for classmates without disabilities

1. Bring in guest speakers who have disabilities but who have made a name for themselves despite their disability (e.g., Paralympics or Special Olympics athletes from the community).
2. Set up role playing situations so that students without disabilities can experience what it is like to have a disability.
3. Discuss the purpose of sport rules and how these rules can be modified to successfully include all students. Focus on the notion of "handicapping" (e.g., bowling, golf, horse racing).
4. Have students fill out a questionnaire that has statements about students with disabilities. Then discuss with the group how each person in the class responded and why they responded that way.
5. Lead a discussion about famous people who have disabilities and how they achieved greatness in their chosen fields despite having a disability.
6. Lead a Circle of Friends discussion.
7. Have students look through books, the local newspaper, or the Internet to find information about people with disabilities.
8. Discuss with classmates the specific disabilities (and abilities) of the student who will be integrated into general physical education.

Note: See Chapter 9 for details on how to implement these and other disability awareness activities.

have positive attitudes toward including classmates with disabilities in physical education and sports activities (Block, 1995b; Block & Malloy, 1998). For example, Block and Malloy found that girls ages 11–13 overwhelmingly accepted a student with a disability into their competitive, fast-pitch softball league. Furthermore, they were willing to allow modifications to make sure this peer was successful. Unfortunately, the initial response of many peers without disabilities may be negative just because they have no experience with peers who have disabilities. Some will be scared of students with disabilities, particularly students with physical disabilities. Others will immediately reject students with disabilities because they feel that these students will ruin their physical education program. Still others may be sympathetic toward students with disabilities and try to mother these students. Although none of these responses will facilitate successful inclusion, they are understandable given that most students without disabilities know very little about students with disabilities. Thus, an important part of the process of including students with disabilities is to prepare classmates.

Several authors have suggested ways in which teachers can help peers without disabilities develop a more positive attitude toward students with disabilities (e.g., Auxter et al., 2005; Block & Brady, 1999; Clark, French, & Henderson, 1985; Getskow & Konczal, 1996; Lieberman & Houston-Wilson, 2002;

Stainback & Stainback, 1985; see Table 4.15; see also Chapter 9. The general physical education teacher, the adapted physical education teacher, the special education teacher, the student, his or her parents, or other knowledgeable team member can conduct each disability awareness activity. For example, the vision specialist, with the help of a student who is blind, might know a great deal about visual impairments; together they could organize activities to help peers learn what it is like to have a visual impairment. The key is helping classmates become more knowledgeable about disabilities, avoid myths and stereotypes, learn how to view people with disabilities in a positive manner, and learn specific ways to welcome and help the student with disabilities who will be in their physical education class. Classmates generally will be receptive to having a student with a disability in their physical education class if they are given information and training.

Preparation should not stop once the student enters the program. Too often students with disabilities are ignored in physical education because their classmates do not know how to interact or assist the student with a disability (Block & Brady, 1999; Place & Hodge, 2001). The teacher should provide ongoing encouragement to peers (both through modeling and direct suggestion) to talk to the student with disabilities, to provide feedback and positive reinforcement, to gently correct or redirect the student when he misbehaves, and to ask the student if he or she needs assistance. Rather than having one peer assigned to one student, the entire class should take responsibility for the special student. For example, if a student who has intellectual disabilities does not know which station to go to, one of his peers can assist him. Similarly, if a student who is blind has lost the ball he was dribbling, one of his peers can retrieve it for him. Students should be continuously prompted and reinforced for interacting with the student with disabilities. As the year progresses and classmates begin to feel more comfortable with the student who has a disability, then interactions will become more spontaneous.

Prepare Support Persons

One final, often neglected step is preparing support persons who will be assisting the student with disabilities in general physical education. These support persons, whether trained teacher assistants, peer tutors, or community volunteers, are committed to helping the student with disabilities, yet they often have no formal training or experience working with these students or in physical education (Doyle, 2002). Although such support persons are given some direction by the special education teacher in how to work with the student in general education

Table 4.16.   Common paraprofessional responsibilities with application to physical education

Noninstructional responsibilities	Application to physical education
Perform clerical and organizational tasks.	Help with attendance, help with fitness and other testing for the student with disabilities as well as other students in the class (e.g., attendance, records, lunch count).
Monitor students in the hallway, on the playground, and at the bus stop.	Monitor student going to and from physical education, in the locker room, and in the gym.
Assist with supervision during meals/snacks.	Not applicable
Operate audiovisual equipment.	Operate CD player when music is playing, can assist in setting up VCR and monitor when sport films are being shown, can assist in videotaping students performing motor skills.
Provide specific personal care for students.	Assist student in locker room and in rest room.

Instructional responsibilities	Application to physical education
Observe, record, and chart student's behavioral responses to teacher demonstration.	Observe, record, and chart student's motor, fitness, and behaviors during physical education.
Assist with classroom management.	Implement behavior management plan created by classroom or general physical education teacher; provide reinforcement and assist in data collection behaviors in general physical education.
Implement teacher-designed instruction with individual students, small groups, and large groups.	Assist PE teacher in instructing the entire group or small groups (e.g., helping supervise during warm-ups). Provide individualized instruction such as additional cues, different equipment, or modified curricula in physical education. Implement general PE curriculum when appropriate, and implement teacher-directed alternative PE program when cued by PE teacher.
Tutor individual and/or small groups.	Work with student with disabilities one-to-one with or away from the group when appropriate. Assist not only the student with a disability but other students who may need assistance in PE.
Contribute ideas and suggestions related to general instruction.	Contribute ideas related to physical education for the student with a disability as well as for other students who might be having trouble with the regular PE curriculum and instruction.
Participate in team meetings.	Discuss what is happening in PE, both positive and negative, and share suggestions with team members, including general PE teacher.

From Doyle, M.B. (2002). *The paraprofessional's guide to the inclusive classroom* (2nd ed., p. 91). Baltimore: Paul H. Brookes Publishing Co.; adapted by permission.

classrooms, they are rarely given direction when in physical education. This is probably due to miscommunication between the general physical educator and the special educator. That is, the general physical educator assumes the special educator has briefed the support person and provided her with a list of physical education activities, while the special educator assumes that the general physical educator is guiding the support person on how to provide specific physical education activities to the student with disabilities. What results are confused and often frustrated support persons who have no idea what they should be doing with the student with disabilities in general physical education and often make up their own physical education program.

Obviously, such a situation prevents the student from developing necessary motor, fitness, and leisure skills and can even be dangerous, depending on what activities the support person chooses to attempt. For example, a student with Down syndrome might have positive atlantoaxial instability, and this student should not be allowed to participate in forward rolls during a gymnastic unit. Yet, no one has informed this student's teacher assistant of this problem, and he has been given no direction on what to do and what not to do by the general physical educator. Seeing other students in the class doing forward rolls during a gymnastics unit, the teacher assistant assumes that his student should be doing the same activity. Such a scenario is frightening, yet this scenario and similar ones take place all too often because no one takes responsibility in preparing support persons.

Training of support persons should be an ongoing responsibility of all team members. This training should focus on both general information about the role as a support person as well as specific information about the student they will be working with and how they will facilitate the inclusion of the student into general physical education (Doyle, 2002).

Following are some suggestions about information to provide support persons: general information (perhaps a brochure or handout) regarding his or her role as a support person and listing expectations; information regarding the philosophy of the program and the general goals that have been developed for all students (i.e., opportunities to interact with typical peers, improved social behavior, improved communication skills, improved independence in a variety of functional skills); resources and key personnel who can answer questions; detailed description of the student, including IEP objectives, medical/health concerns, unique behaviors, likes and dislikes, special friends; specific information regarding safety/ emergency procedures (e.g., what to do if a student has a seizure or an asthma attack); specific information regarding what typically happens in physical education including yearly outline, unit and daily lesson plans, daily routines, rules and regulations, typical teaching procedures, measurement and record keeping procedures; general suggestions for modifying activities (e.g., use a balloon or suspended ball when speed and weight of ball are a concern; lower goals or targets, make them larger, or bring them closer to student for more success); several alternative activities when general program activities are deemed inappropriate (e.g., when a forward roll is contraindicated, student can be working on fitness goals or fundamental motor patterns, when the class is playing field hockey, the student can be working on alternative striking activities that would facilitate the acquisition of lifetime leisure skills such as croquet, golf or tennis); and several suggestions for facilitating interactions with peers without disabilities. Table 4.16 provides a list of common paraprofessional responsibilities with application to physical education.

SUMMARY

Once a school system or school adopts a philosophy of inclusion, it is tempting to immediately place students with disabilities into as many general programs as possible. One of the first places students will be placed is general physical education since physical education is viewed as a non-academic program. Unfortunately, the general physical educator often has the least training in terms of working with students with disabilities. This can lead to poor attitudes toward the student with disabilities (which quickly transfer to all of the students), haphazard programming or no programming at all, and ultimately a waste of valuable learning time for the student with disabilities. Preparing all key personnel prior to inclusion can prevent such a downward spiral. Preparation should include team members developing individual goals for the student, comparing individual goals to what takes place in general physical education, anticipating the need for certain modifications and adjustments prior to implementation and developing appropriate accommodations, and finally preparing general physical educators, typical peers, and support persons. Although carefully preparing for inclusion might take several weeks or even months, the end result is smooth and positive transition into general physical education that is supported by general physical education staff and peers without disabilities.

Assessment to Facilitate Successful Inclusion

Marissa is a 14-year-old who will be attending Southern Montgomery County High School in the fall. Like most of her middle school peers, she is excited but nervous about starting high school. Marissa is a little more nervous than her peers because transitions to new schools can be challenging for her. Marissa was born with spina bifida, is paralyzed from the waist down, and uses a wheelchair for mobility. She does not have any cognitive impairments. In fact, she is going to be in the highest-level math and science classes when she enters high school. Middle school was fun and fulfilling for Marissa, as she encountered very few problems. Unfortunately, her middle school physical education experience was not as good as it could have been. She often watched from the sidelines because her general physical education teachers did not seem to understand how to accommodate her wheelchair into their physical education curriculum. This was obviously frustrating for Marissa, especially considering that she is actually quite athletic; she plays basketball twice per week for a junior wheelchair basketball team, and she is learning how to play wheelchair tennis. So, Marissa's apprehension, especially regarding high school physical education, was not surprising.

When Marissa went to her IEP meeting in early August with her parents, she was surprised to find Mr. Coleman (the general physical education teacher at Southern Montgomery County High School) at the meeting. (Her middle school physical education teachers never attended any of her IEP meetings.) When the issue of physical education came up, Mr. Coleman shared his previous experiences with students who used wheelchairs. He noted that accommodations for Marissa should not be too difficult, and he was confident that she would have a successful experience in physical education. Mr. Coleman went on to discuss the assessment plan he would like to use with Marissa. First, he wanted to give her and her parents a simple sports and recreation interest survey he created to find out what sports Marissa would like to learn in high school. Once

she selected two or three sports, he would then test her on the various skills related to these sports. This way he would know exactly what Marissa needed to work on. Then he would like to use some simple assessment tools he created for other students he had who used wheelchairs to determine what adapted equipment Marissa might need for her selected sports. He then mentioned that he would like Marissa to attend general physical education as much as possible, but he noted that there were units that were probably not appropriate for Marissa, including soccer and football in the fall. He noted that he would evaluate each unit and then discuss it with Marissa to determine if Marissa should participate or if it made more sense for her to practice her chosen sports with a select handful of her classmates. (Mr. Coleman said he did not want Marissa doing something by herself, and he was sure that several of her classmates would enjoy playing with her away from the general physical education class.)

Marissa was thrilled with Mr. Coleman and his very positive approach to her physical education program. She was impressed with his obvious experience and confidence in working with students like her; she never heard of someone who so carefully used assessments to make sure students were involved in appropriate activities, working on the correct level of skills required in each activity, using the correct adapted equipment for each activity, and placed appropriately for physical education. Marissa was sure her high school physical education experience was going to be much more enjoyable than her middle school experience.

The previous chapter outlined an ecological approach to decision making for developing and implementing a physical education program for students with disabilities in general physical education classes. However, all programming decisions should be based on information obtained from ecologically relevant assessment data. That is, assessment should be closely tied to what skills and behaviors the child needs to be successful in his or her current and future environments (Block & Block, 1999; Kelly & Melograno, 2004). In addition, assessment should be sensitive to the interests of key people in the child's life such as his or her parents and peers. Without such assessment data, programming decisions would be based on irrelevant information or assumptions, which, in turn, could result in a poor or inappropriate physical education program.

Assessment is a critical yet often misused part of the overall program. According to the Individuals with Disabilities Education Improvement Act (IDEA) of 2004 (PL 108-446), part of the IEP process must include assessing all students with disabilities to determine their present level of performance. Assessment data can then be used by the collaborative team to make informed decisions regarding specific diagnoses, types and intensity of services, instructional plans, amount and type of supports, and least restrictive placements (Horvat, Block, & Kelly, in press). In addition, assessment should be an ongoing process that begins with the development of the student's IEP and continues during the implementation of the program. Unfortunately, often assessment tools are used improperly, assessment data are misinterpreted, or decisions are made based on a specific disability label or school philosophy (Horvat, Block, & Kelly, in press).

The purpose of this chapter is to outline assessment procedures that can facilitate the integration of students with disabilities into general physical education. The chapter begins with a brief review of the legal basis for assessment as outlined in IDEA 2004. This is followed by a review of traditional assessment procedures, then a detailed review of an ecological approach to assessment. Finally, an example of how an ecological assessment is conducted is presented. It should be noted that the term *assessment* is used synonymously with the term *evaluation*, which is used in IDEA 2004. That is, *assessment* is defined rather broadly as the process of collecting and interpreting data in order to plan and implement a physical education program for students with disabilities. The term *test* is used to describe specific tools to collect assessment information.

LEGAL BASIS FOR ASSESSMENT IN PHYSICAL EDUCATION

Assessment has always been a critical part of federal special education legislation. From the beginning back in 1975, IDEA included very specific information and procedures on assessment in an effort to ensure that children with disabilities were appropri-ately diagnosed, provided appropriate services, and placed in the least restrictive environment (Horvat, Block, & Kelly, in press). These evaluation procedures have remained basically the same through the many revisions of IDEA, including IDEA 2004. The regulations governing the implementation of IDEA 2004 are available at http://access.gpo.gov/nara/cfr/waisdx_06/34cfr300_06.html. They include procedures for the evaluation and determination of eligibility (§§ 300.530–300.536). The regulations describe highly individualized procedures for assessment and decision making, use of collaborative teams rather than one individual doing all of the assessment and decision making, and the important role of parents.

All of the procedures outlined in the regulations should be adhered to when conducting a physical education assessment. For example, placement decisions (including the decision whether to place student in a general physical education class or a separate physical education setting) cannot be made until a student is given a full and individual evaluation of motor needs. This evaluation should be conducted by "trained personnel" (ideally an adapted physical educator), and the evaluation should draw upon information from all team members, including the preferences of the student and his or her parents. In addition, testing materials must be appropriate for the student's age and abilities. For example, it would be inappropriate to give an 18-year-old the Peabody Developmental Motor Scales, which are designed for children birth to 6 years old. Similarly, it would be inappropriate to give a student who uses a wheelchair a standard physical fitness test designed for students without disabilities. Finally, decisions regarding placement and scope of program should be based on an ecologically relevant assessment that is directly related to the student's needs, abilities, and current and future environments (Block & Block, 1999; Kelly & Melograno, 2004). Unfortunately, not all adapted physical education assessments are conducted this way. The following contrasts traditional approaches to assessment in adapted physical education versus an ecological approach to assessment.

TRADITIONAL APPROACH TO ASSESSMENT IN ADAPTED PHYSICAL EDUCATION

The ways in which adapted physical education decisions are made vary from school system to school system. Still, there are fairly traditional ways in which adapted physical educators (or other team members responsible for physical education for students with disabilities) administer and use assessments. Traditional procedures can be broken down into four major categories: classification, development of the IEP, placement, and instruction.

Classification

Traditionally, the first step in the assessment process is to determine if a student needs specialized physical education services. In some school districts, students qualify for adapted physical education services simply because they have a particular diagnosis. As noted in Chapter 4, students with learning disabilities often do not get adapted physical education services because it is assumed that they do not have any special motor or fitness needs. However, students who use wheelchairs usually qualify for adapted physical education because it is assumed that the goals for these students are completely different from their peers without disabilities. Such practices are in direct violation of the law, which specifically mandates that all students with disabilities be evaluated to determine if they require special physical education services (Bateman & Herr, 2003; IDEA 1997; Osborne, 1996; Wright & Wright, 2004). More important, no one has taken the time to assess each student's strengths and weaknesses before determining who qualifies for adapted physical education. Many students with learning disabilities, in fact, have motor and learning impairments, which justify specialized physical education, while many students who use wheelchairs can do quite well in general physical education without any special support.

Others who try to determine if a student qualifies for adapted physical education use norm-referenced or standardized tests. A standardized test is one in which a student's score is compared with the scores of others on the same test—that is, compared with a set of norms (Horvat, Block, & Kelly, in press; Kelly & Melograno, 2004). Norms are established by testing a representative sample from a particular population. For example, for a test to be valid for children 2–6 years of age, a large sample of children ages 2–6 should be tested to develop norms. These norms can then be analyzed and organized to describe scores that correspond to a certain percentage of the population. To illustrate, a particular score on a test might represent a point where 75% of the norm sample scored below that particular score (75th percentile). School systems can then establish minimal cut-off scores that correspond to who does or does not qualify for adapted physical education. Such an approach is by far the most widely used approach in adapted physical education (Ulrich, 1985). Many states even have set criteria based on standardized test results for determining who qualifies for adapted physical education services. Sherrill

(2004) noted that students in Alabama and Georgia who score below the 30th percentile on standardized tests of motor performance qualify for adapted physical education services. Sherrill suggested that students who consistently score below the 50th percentile should qualify for special physical education service.

For example, the Bruininks-Oseretsky Test of Motor Proficiency (BOT), the standardized test most often used by adapted physical education specialists (Ulrich, 1985), is often used to determine which students qualify for adapted physical education (see Figure 5.1). The BOT is a valid, norm-referenced test designed to measure specific motor abilities of children $4\frac{1}{2}$–$14\frac{1}{2}$ years of age. Areas evaluated include running speed and agility, balance, bilateral coordination, response speed, strength, upper limb coordination, visual-motor coordination, and upper limb speed and dexterity. A school system might decide that a student with a total score below the 30th percentile qualifies for adapted physical education.

Although the BOT is valid and reliable, one has to question whether the information obtained from this type of test is ecologically relevant to the needs of individual children. What information does data collected from the BOT give the team that would help the team determine if a student needs adapted physical education services? Will a student who performs at the 20th percentile have difficulty in general physical education activities? Will a student who does poorly on subtest items such as response speed or bilateral coordination do poorly with activities in general physical education without extensive support? Does the BOT reliably predict how well a second-grade student will do in a unit that focuses on locomotor patterns or how well a middle school student will do in a softball unit?

Similarly, why does performance at or below the 20th percentile on the Physical Best Fitness Test qualify a student for adapted physical education services? Physical Best measures health-related physical fitness for students ages 5–18 years. Areas evaluated include cardiovascular endurance (1-mile run), percent body fat (skinfold), muscular strength (sit-ups and pull-ups), and flexibility (sit and reach). Does a student's poor performance on any or all of these items predict how well a student will do in general physical education? Will limited abdominal strength as measured by sit-ups help determine if a high school student will be unsuccessful or need modifications to popular lifetime leisure activities such as softball, tennis, or golf? It should be clear that the BOT, Physical Best, and similar tests are not related to what really takes place in general physical education. Yet, these types of tests are used to make decisions regarding who qualifies for adapted physical education services.

SUBTEST 5/Item 7
Touching Nose with Index Finger—Eyes Closed

With eyes closed the subject touches any part of his or her nose first with one index finger and then with the opposite index finger, as shown in Figure 26. The subject is given 90 seconds to touch the nose four consecutive times. The score is recorded as a pass or a fail.

Trials: 1

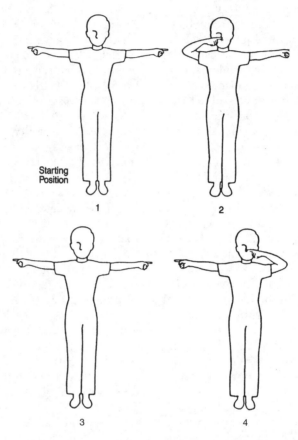

Starting
Position

1   2

3   4

Figure 26   Touching nose with index fingers—eyes closed (Subtest Item 7)

Administering and Recording
Have the subject stand facing you. Say: **Hold your arms straight out to the side. Close your hands and point with your first** (index) **fingers** (demonstrate). **Touch your nose with the tip of one of your fingers and then put your arm straight out again** (demonstrate). **Then touch your nose with the other fingertip and put that arm straight out again** (demonstrate). **Now do it with your eyes closed and your head still. Keep touching your nose until I tell you to stop. Ready, begin.**

Begin timing. If necessary, provide additional instruction. For example, remind the subject to touch the nose with the tips of the index fingers and to return one arm to an extended position before moving the other arm. Start counting as soon as the subject is moving the arms and touching the nose correctly in a continuous movement. During the trial correct the subject and start counting over if she or he:
a.   fails to maintain continuous movements
b.   fails to touch the nose with the index finger
c.   fails to alternate arms
d.   fails to extend arms fully after touching nose
e.   moves head to meet the finger
f.   opens eyes

Allow no more than 90 seconds, including time needed for additional instruction, for the subject to touch the nose correctly four consecutive times (twice with each finger). After 90 seconds, tell the subject to stop.

Figure 5.1.   Select items from the Bruininks-Oseretsky Test of Motor Proficiency. (From Bruininks, R.H. [1978]. *Bruininks-Oseretsky Test of Motor Proficiency: Examiner's manual* [pp. 82–85]. Copyright © 1978. Published and distributed exclusively by NCS Pearson, Inc., P.O. Box 1416, Minneapolis, MN 55440. Reproduced with permission by NCS Pearson, Inc.)

SUBTEST 5/Item 8
Touching Thumb to Fingertips—Eyes Closed

With eyes closed, the subject touches the thumb of the preferred hand to each of the fingertips on the preferred hand, moving from the little finger to the index finger to the little finger, as shown in Figure 27. The subject is given 90 seconds to complete the task once. The score is recorded as a pass or fail.

Trials: 1

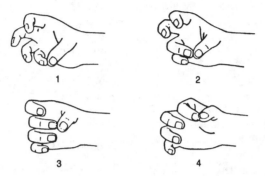

1   2

3   4

Figure 27 Touching thumb to fingertips—eyes closed (Subtest 5 Item 8)

Administering and Recording
Have the subject sit beside you at a table. Have the subject extend the preferred arm. Then say: You are about to touch your thumb to each of the fingertips on this hand. Start with your little finger and touch each fingertip in order. Then start with your first finger and touch each fingertip again as you move your thumb back to your little finger (demonstrate). Do this with your eyes closed until I tell you to stop. Ready, begin.

Begin timing. If necessary, provide additional instruction. During the trial correct the subject and have the subject start over if he or she:
a.   fails to maintain continuous movements
b.   touches any finger except the index finger more than once in succession
c.   touches two fingers at the same time
d.   fails to touch fingers above the first finger joint
e.   opens eyes

Development of the Individualized Education Program

Once it has been determined that a student requires special services, the next step is to determine what specific skills to target. The development of the student's individualized education program (IEP) is an important process, because the IEP will guide the student's specific activities for the next year (Bateman & Herr, 2003; Wright & Wright, 2004). Usually, information taken from the classification assessment is used to develop the student's IEP. This makes the assessment tools used for classification critical. Unfortunately, in the traditional approach, the use of standardized tests forces practitioners to follow a developmental or "bottom-up" approach. In the bottom-up approach, impairments at the lower end of the developmental continuum become the focus of a student's physical education program without regard to how these skills affect the acquisition of real-life skills (Block, 1992; Brown et al., 1979; Kelly & Melograno, 2004). In practice, IEP goals and objectives become items a student fails on developmental tests or tests of motor abilities. For example, a student who does poorly on upper limb speed and dexterity (e.g., sorting cards quickly) might have as a goal on his IEP to improve upper limb response speed with specific activities as repeatedly touching nose with index fingers, touching thumb to fingertips, or pivoting thumb and index finger. Similarly, a student who cannot stand on tiptoes for 5 seconds with eyes open or stand on one foot with hands on hip for 5 seconds (items on the Peabody Developmental Motor Scale) would have an IEP goal to improve static balance and a short-term instructional objective of standing on tip-toes and balancing on one foot. While upper limb response speed and static balance may be problematic for this student, is working on these nonfunctional skills in isolation appropriate? How do these goals relate to skills the student will need to be successful in current and future physical education and recreation environments? Again, while the long-term goals may be appropriate, the short-term instructional objectives are nonfunctional and bear no relation to the skills a student needs to be successful in general physical education.

Placement

Once it has been determined that a student qualifies for adapted physical education services and has an IEP, the next step in the assessment process is to make a decision regarding where the student will receive services. IDEA 2004 mandates that placement decisions be based on the concept of the least restrictive environment (LRE). Students with disabilities must be educated with their peers without disabilities, and separate programming should only occur when education in the general setting cannot be satisfactorily achieved with the use of supplementary aids and services (Bateman & Herr, 2003; Block, 1996). Placement in general education with supplementary aids and supports has been re-emphasized in IDEA 2004. Therefore, assessment data should be used to first determine how much support a student with a disability needs to be successful in general physical education. Only after it has been clearly and objectively found that the child with a disability cannot be successfully placed in general physical education can a student with a disability be placed in an alternative physical education setting (Block, 1996; Block & Krebs, 1992; Sherrill, 2004).

In theory, information obtained from assessment data should be used to determine how much support a child needs to be successful in general physical education and, if the child cannot be successful in general physical education with support, what alternative placement would be appropriate for the student. In reality, placement decisions tend to be an either/or decision process: general physical education with no support or separate physical education (Jansma & Decker, 1990). In addition, decisions tend to focus on placement options rather than on the provision of support to help the child be successful in general physical education (Block & Krebs, 1992). Again, there tends to be a domino effect: The use of a standardized assessment tool determines classification, which influences IEP goals, which influences placement. The use of standardized tests to develop IEP goals usually results in goals and objectives that bear no resemblance to activities that take place in general physical education. Furthermore, these types of assessment data do not help the team determine whether the child will be successful in general physical education or what types of supports are needed for the child to be successful in general physical education. For example, it is difficult for general physical educators to see how working on upper limb speed and dexterity (IEP goals based on results of standardized assessments) are related to lessons on locomotor patterns and body awareness. Thus, the teacher concludes that the student should be placed in a separate adapted physical education class. The use of assessment data that is not related to the child's current and future environments often leads to inappropriate placement decisions.

Instruction

The last and perhaps most relevant aspect of assessment is how to help a student acquire the targeted goals on his IEP. Unfortunately, decisions at this level are usually based on standardized test results, which focus on motor abilities, developmental level, and physical fitness. Again, these tests usually bear no relation on how to adapt instruction to help a student acquire critical physical education skills and be successful in general physical education. For example, poor performance on sit-ups on the Physical Best test does not indicate why the student is having trouble doing sit-ups or how to help this student improve his physical fitness. A poorly motivated student may need a different type of instruction from a student who actually has poor abdominal strength. Similarly, how do you cue a student who has trouble with upper limb activities? Do you give him extra practice on upper limb skills, or do you need to modify instruction? Perhaps the skill needs to be broken down into smaller steps; perhaps the student needs physical assistance; perhaps the student needs adapted equipment. Unfortunately, information from standardized assessment tools does not provide information regarding instruction. Thus, teachers are forced to make instructional decisions based on what they think is best for a particular student.

AN ECOLOGICAL APPROACH TO ASSESSMENT

Many professionals recommend a functional or ecologically relevant approach to assessment in which programming decisions are based on a "top-down" model (Block & Block, 1999; Horvat, Block, & Kelly, in press; Kelly & Melograno, 2004). As described in the previous chapter, the ecological approach to programming provides a much more real-world approach that emphasizes outcomes. Thus, the first step in a top-down assessment model is to identify current and future recreation environments that are appropriate for each student. This is followed by assessment to determine what specific skills are needed for a student to be successful in the identified recreation environments, which of these skills a student currently possesses, and which skills a student still needs to acquire. Kelly and Melograno (2004) viewed this process in terms of a pyramid in which the top of the pyramid represents the ultimate goal of the program, with lower levels representing skills needed to get to the top (see Figure 5.2).

Using the top-down approach, teachers focus on critical skills a student needs to be successful in current and future recreational environments and eliminate less functional items. For example, activities such as crawling reciprocally, standing on tip-toes, walking along a circle, and skipping are items on developmental tests that rarely are related to any functional end-goals. Yet, these and other nonfunctional items often appear in a student's physical education IEP goals because the student was unable to perform these items on a particular developmental test. These items would not have to be taught in a top-down approach because these skills are not related to functional outcomes.

The ecological assessment model can be broken down into six interrelated phases, which help answer the following six real-life questions (see Table 5.1):

1. Who do we teach (i.e., who qualifies for APE services)?

2. What do we teach (i.e., long-term plan and goals and objectives)?

3. How do we teach it (instructional planning)?

4. Where do we teach it (placement decisions)?

5. Who will teach it (support needs)?

6. How effective is our program (evaluation)?

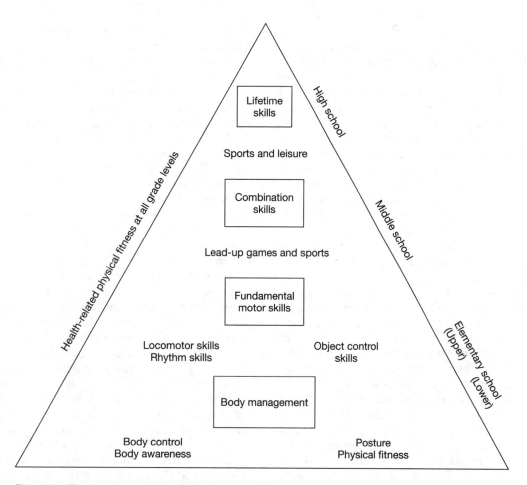

Figure 5.2. Top-down pyramid. (From Kelly, L.E., et al. [1991]. Achievement-based curriculum: Teaching manual. Charlottesville: The University of Virginia; adapted by permission.)

Table 5.1. Six phases of an ecological approach to assessment in adapted physical education

Phase 1	Determine WHO qualifies for APE services
Phase 2	Determine WHAT to teach
	a. Define top-down plan and targeted skills
	b. Determine student's present level of performance on targeted skills
	c. Develop student's IEP based on present level of performance
Phase 3	Determine HOW to teach targeted skills
Phase 4	Determine WHERE to teach targeted skills
Phase 5	Determine WHO will teach targeted skills
Phase 6	Determine HOW WELL we taught targeted skills (ongoing evaluation)

Who Do We Teach?

Determining who qualifies for adapted physical education services seems like an easy task. Simply assess the child on some norm-referenced test and then compare the child's results to the norm tables provided on the test. If the child scores below age level or percentile rank defined by the school district, then he or she qualifies for adapted physical education. However, any general or adapted physical educator will tell you that determining who qualifies for adapted physical education is an extremely difficult task. First, most school districts do not have a districtwide recommended assessment tool. Second, most school districts do not have any set criteria to determine who qualifies. Thus, it is usually left up to the general and/or adapted physical educator to come up with a system to determine who qualifies for adapted physical education services. Even if a district does have a specific norm-referenced test and clear cut-off scores, such an approach does not provide information on how successful the child is in general physical education. Furthermore, information from this type of assessment does not translate well to the development of appropriate IEP goals and objectives.

Therefore, the ecological approach to assessment is recommended. Ecologically relevant areas for elementary physical education assessment might include motor skills in the general elementary curriculum, fitness as it relates to a child's abilities to be successful in general elementary physical education, behaviors and social skills as they relate to a child's ability to be successful in elementary general physical education, cognitive skills as they relate to a child's ability to be successful in general elementary physical education, and ability to participate in community recreation with peers. Ecologically relevant areas for middle/high school physical education assessment might include individual and team

sport skills, fitness as it relates to participation in middle/high school physical education as well as overall health-related fitness, behaviors and social skills as they relate to a child's ability to be successful in general middle/high school physical education, cognitive skills as they relate to a child's ability to be successful in general middle/high school physical education, and ability to participate in community recreation and recess with peers.

To qualify for adapted physical education services using the ecological model, a student would need to have significant impairments in ecologically relevant motor/sport skills and/or physical fitness and significant impairments in ecologically relevant behaviors, cognitive skills, and/or social skills. For example, using the assessment form in Figure 5.3, a child could qualify if he or she has 50% or more "significantly inadequate" scores on ecologically relevant motor/sport skills and social/behavioral skills. A child who is doing well in general physical education, however, would have mostly "adequate" and perhaps some "needs improvement" scores and would not qualify for adapted physical education services. Figure 5.4 shows an assessment report based on data collected from the assessment tool in Figure 5.3 for a child who does not qualify for adapted physical education services.

Some might argue that such an approach when determining whether a child has significant delays is too subjective. Others might argue that their school district requires a real number (e.g., 2 years delayed). A more objective yet still ecologically relevant method is to compare a child's motor skill development to his or her peers without disabilities on the general physical education curriculum. For example, a third-grade child with intellectual disabilities has mastered most locomotor patterns (e.g., still cannot hop and skip) but has mastered only a few ball skills (e.g., has not mastered the basketball dribble, soccer dribble, soccer kick; has mastered the underhand roll and underhand toss). Based on data collected by elementary physical education teachers from the school district, this child is about 2 years delayed in motor development (she has mastered skills expected of a first grader). This objective motor data can then be coupled with subjective behavior/social skill behavior to determine whether this child qualifies for adapted physical education. This third grader is well behaved, but she has a very hard time following directions and staying on task. Even with the support of peers, she often is confused in general physical education and asks the general physical educator for help. Thus, this child would qualify as having a significant motor delay and cognitive impairments. It should be noted that this approach to assessment assumes that the school district has a

University of Virginia Adapted Physical Education
Initial Observation and Referral Form

Child's name: _____   Evaluator: _____

School: _____   Date: _____

Use this form when first observing a child with a disability who has been referred for adapted physical education. Rate each item based on how the child compares with other children in his or her physical education class.

FITNESS OR MOTOR SKILLS	Adequate	Needs improvement	Significantly inadequate	Not observed
Physical fitness				
Performs activities that require upper body strength (e.g., push-ups, throwing, chest pass)				
Performs activities that require lower body strength (e.g., running, hopping, kicking)				
Performs activities that require flexibility (e.g., stretching, bending, tumbling)				
Performs activities that require endurance (e.g., mile run, games that involve endurance)				
Body composition (e.g., child's weight and general appearance)				
Gross motor skills				
Performs nonlocomotor skills (e.g., twisting, turning, balancing, bending)				
Moves safely around environment (e.g., dodging, using space awareness)				
Uses physical education equipment (e.g., balls, bats, scooters)				
Performs locomotor skills (e.g., running, jumping, galloping, hopping, skipping)				
Performs manipulative skills (e.g., throwing, catching, kicking, striking)				
Performs dance skills (e.g., rhythm, patterns)				
Plays low organized games (e.g., dodge ball, relays, tag, teacher-made games)				
Displays sports skills (e.g., throwing in softball, kicking in soccer, serving in volleyball, hitting a tennis ball)				
Plays organized sports (e.g., basketball, soccer)				

Comments: _____

_____

_____

_____

A Teacher's Guide to Including Students with Disabilities in General Physical Education, Third Edition,
by Martin E. Block. Copyright © 2007 by Paul H. Brookes Publishing Co., Inc. All rights reserved.

_____

(continued)

Figure 5.3.   The University of Virginia adapted physical education initial observation and referral form.

Figure 5.3. *(continued)*

BEHAVIORS, COGNITIVE ABILITIES, AND SOCIAL SKILLS	Adequate	Needs improvement	Significantly inadequate	Not observed
Transition to and from physical education				
Enters without interruption				
Sits in assigned area				
Stops playing with equipment when asked				
Lines up to leave when asked				
Responding to teacher				
Remains quiet when teacher is talking				
Follows directions in a timely manner during warm-up				
Follows directions in a timely manner when working on skills				
Follows directions in a timely manner when playing games				
Accepts feedback from teacher				
Uses positive or appropriate language				
Relating to peers and using equipment				
Works cooperatively with a partner when asked (e.g., shares, take turns)				
Works cooperatively as a member of a group when asked				
Uses positive or appropriate comments to peers				
Seeks social interactions with peers				
Displays sportsmanship by avoiding conflict with others				
Uses equipment appropriately				
Displays effort and self-acceptance				
Quickly begins activity once instructed				
Continues to participate independently throughout activity				
Adapts to new tasks and changes				
Strives to succeed and is motivated to learn				
Accepts his or her own skill whether successful or improving				
Cognitive abilities				
Understands nonverbal directions				
Understands verbal directions				
Processes multistep cues				
Attends to instructions				

Comments: _____

_____

_____

Results from Ecologically Based Qualifying Assessment in Adapted Physical Education

Name: Tamara Jones   Date: September 14, 2006

Date of birth: July 15, 1998   Evaluator: Chandra Martin, CAPE

Grade/Class: Second grade/Ms. Jacobs

Introduction
Tamara is an 8-year-old girl in Ms. Jacobs's second-grade class. Tamara has paraplegic spastic cerebral palsy (i.e., affects her legs but not her arms). She independently uses a manual wheelchair for mobility. She has typical intelligence but has some speech and auditory processing delays. She receives physical therapy once per week for 30 minutes per session and speech therapy twice per week for 30 minutes per session. Her special education teacher has recommended an adapted physical education evaluation because of suspected delays in gross motor development.

Abilities in reference to general physical education curriculum
The general physical education (GPE) curriculum for kindergarten through second grade focuses on mastery of body and space awareness, mastery of movement concepts, mastery of basic rhythms, mastery of locomotor patterns, introduction to manipulative patterns, and introduction to physical fitness concepts. Tamara has mastered body and space awareness concepts, movement concepts, and basic rhythms. She is unable to perform any locomotor patterns due to her disability, but she can independently move her manual wheelchair quite well around the gym and the playground (including going forward and backward, going fast and slow, and avoiding peers and obstacles). She cannot kick or punt due to her disability, but she has learned to catch and throw in her wheelchair using a modified pattern. She has good upper body strength and flexibility, and she has very good endurance.

Behavioral, cognitive, and social abilities in reference to general physical education curriculum
Tamara is an extremely well-behaved and enthusiastic student in GPE. She really wants to please and follow directions, although the GPE teacher or a peer sometimes has to repeat complex directions for her. She is a very social child who interacts well with peers, and her peers seem to enjoy interacting with her.

Motor abilities with reference to recess and community-based recreation
Tamara's parents report that she is a very active participant in activities with peers at home. She plays in a tee ball league with no modifications other than using her wheelchair. She also plays with neighborhood children without too much difficulty, again using her wheelchair rather than walking or running. Tamara's classroom teacher notes that she is able to participate in most recess activities including dodging and fleeing games, four-square, and the swings. She cannot climb up on the playground structure independently, but that does not seem to bother her.

Recommendations
Based on this ecologically based assessment, it seems that Tamara functions quite well in general physical education, in her neighborhood, and during recess. Therefore, I do not recommend APE services at this time. However, as Tamara moves to upper elementary and middle school, she may need to be reassessed.

Figure 5.4. Report of results from ecologically based qualifying assessment in adapted physical education.

physical education curriculum, general physical educators in the district follow this curriculum, and the district has collected data on when children master various skills in the curriculum. Unfortunately, this is not the case in many school districts.

The key to this phase of assessment is to determine whether the child actually has significant impairments that affect his or her ability to participate successfully in general physical education. Because the ability to participate in general physical education is key, it makes sense that assessment information at this point of the process focus on those skills and behaviors necessary for general physical education. This provides the ecologically relevant part of the assessment.

What Do We Teach?

It is impossible to teach all skills to all students. Many students without disabilities will learn a variety of lifetime leisure skills. However, students with mild disabilities often will take longer to learn fewer skills, and students with severe disabilities often take much longer to learn just a few skills. Therefore, it is important to target key skills for particular students (Block, 1992; Brown et al., 1979; Kelly & Melograno, 2004).

Developing the Vision

First, define what skills are critical in the student's present and future environments (Kelly & Melograno, 2004; Rainforth & York-Barr, 1997). One way to begin this process is to use Making Action Plans (MAPs), formerly known as the McGill Action Planning System (MAPS), in which team members together discuss a series of questions about the child with a disability (Rainforth & York-Barr, 1997; Vandercook, York, & Forest, 1989) (see Figure 5.5). Although such a model does not delineate specific skills to be targeted for instruction, information from this type of assessment can be helpful to guiding the planning process. For example, parents and team members note that an 11-year-old boy with a learning disability and emotional problems is struggling with self-esteem in physical education class. This child does not like physical education and believes he is not good enough to play any sports in the community. The dream for this child is to develop some skills in a particular sport as well as improve general fitness so that he can feel better about himself in physical education and use his leisure time more appropriately. The nightmare for this child is that he continues to hate physical education, drops physical education as soon as he can in high school, and becomes an inactive, overweight adult.

Targeting Specific Goals

With a vision for the child now in place, the team can now focus on specific goals and objectives to help the child reach the dream and avoid the nightmare. As noted in Chapter 4, the team can begin to define specific sports, recreation activities, or skills. One rather simple way of determining which activities are important for a particular student is to ask key people in the student's life (e.g., student, parents, peers) what they perceive to be critical skills (Voeltz, Wuerch, & Bockhaut, 1992). Examining what the student's peers do in physical education, during recess, and in their neighborhood also is a simple way to target activities.

This information can then be used to determine what activities are popular. Activities that are appropriate and important for students without disabilities are usually appropriate for students with disabilities (with modifications as needed to accommodate individual abilities). This information can then be used to develop a list of critical activities and skills for particular students. Figure 5.6 provides a simple checklist for noting the student's, parents', and peers' preferences for making curriculum decisions. Note that a student's particular abilities (or disabilities) are not the focus at this point in the assessment process. Only after specific activities and skills are defined do we begin to ask how well can the student perform these skills and what modifications are needed for the student to be successful.

Other factors to consider when prioritizing goals for students with disabilities include availability of transportation, availability of assistance, and chance the student will acquire the skills needed to participate in the activity with minimal support and modifications. Helmstetter (1989) described a checklist that was designed to weigh these criteria when prioritizing goals for students with disabilities (see Figure 5.7). Activities in which the majority of criteria are met should be high-priority activities. For example, the team lists 10 activities as possible targets for a 13-year-old student who uses a wheelchair. All 10 activities are popular activities that are available at some level in the student's school and in the community. The team then examines these 10 activities to determine which of these activities are most appropriate for this particular student. Weight training, aerobics, and swimming at a local health club as well as wheelchair tennis score the highest on the checklist. Thus, these activities become prioritized activities for this particular student.

Determining Student's Present Level of Performance

Rather than assessing all of the possible motor patterns, motor and perceptual-motor abilities, and fitness attributes of a particular student, as the student only needs to be assessed on the critical skills and abilities directly related to the targeted activities (e.g., throwing, catching, striking, and running skills if softball is targeted). These motor skills will be measured in terms of how well the student performs the skill (qualitative assessment) as well as how much of the skill the student can do (quantitative assessment such as how far, how many, how fast) (see Figure 5.8). Note that there is no need to measure kicking or skipping skills or other skills that are not related to the overall goal of the program. As noted in Chapter 4, skills or characteristics associated with skilled performance such as physical fitness, general motor abilities, and perceptual skills also should be measured, but only as they relate to the skills under each targeted activity.

For example, cardiovascular endurance is usually measured by having a student run or walk a certain distance for time. Although this may be useful to determine a student's overall cardiovascular integrity, it does not indicate if the student has adequate cardiovascular endurance to participate in real-life activities such as softball, soccer, basketball, swimming, or other targeted activities. A better measure of cardiovascular endurance for younger children would be an appraisal of their ability to sustain various animal walks and locomotor patterns during the course of a physical education class. If a student needs to stop and rest after just a few locomotor patterns (maybe 2 minutes of exercise), whereas his peers do not need to rest until they complete several locomotor patterns (up to 10 minutes), then the student is functionally deficient in cardiovascular endurance.

Making Action Plans for Physical Education Planning

Student's name: _____

Person filling out this form: _____

Date: _____ Student's age: _____

1. What is _____'s history regarding motor development, recreation, and fitness?

2. What is your dream for _____ with reference to physical education and recreation?

3. What is your nightmare?

4. Who is _____ with reference to physical education and recreation?

5. What are _____'s strengths, gifts, and abilities with reference to physical education and recreation?

6. What does _____ need to make the dream come true and avoid the nightmare?

7. What would _____'s ideal day in physical education look like, and what must be done to make it happen?

8. What is our plan of action for physical education?

Figure 5.5. Making Action Plans (formerly known as McGill Action Planning System), adapted for physical education planning. (From Vandercook, T., York, J., & Forest, M. [1989]. The McGill action planning system [MAPS]: A strategy for building the vision. *Journal of The Association for Persons with Severe Handicaps, 14,* 205–215; adapted by permission.)

Making Curriculum Decisions

Student's name: _____

Person filling out this form: _____

Date: _____ Student's age: _____

List all of the activities that are preferred or typically engaged in under the following headings. Then, read the list and place activities that are in more than one column under *Targeted activities.*

Student's preferences	Parents' preferences	Activities in general physical education	Neighborhood activities played by peers	Community leisure activities
_____	_____	_____	_____	_____
_____	_____	_____	_____	_____
_____	_____	_____	_____	_____
_____	_____	_____	_____	_____
_____	_____	_____	_____	_____
_____	_____		_____	_____

Targeted activities: 1. _____   2. _____   3. _____   4. _____

A Teacher's Guide to Including Students with Disabilities in General Physical Education, Third Edition,
by Martin E. Block. Copyright © 2007 by Paul H. Brookes Publishing Co., Inc. All rights reserved.

Figure 5.6. Making curriculum decisions.

For older students, a better measure of cardiovascular endurance is determining how long the student can be active in the targeted individual and team sports. Such a measure, while not standardized or norm-referenced, can be objectively collected during the course of the semester. If, for example, a student needs to sit out and rest after 2 minutes of a game of soccer, improvement can be gauged by measuring how long the student can stay actively engaged in the game by the end of the unit. Other fitness measures such as strength and flexibility as well as measures of motor abilities, perceptual motor abilities, and functional motor patterns also should be measured with specific reference to how these factors relate to the skill targeted for the student (see Figure 5.8).

Developing the Student's IEP

Now that we have targeted specific activities and know the student's present level of performance on these activities, we can formulate the student's IEP including long-term goals and short-term instructional objectives. This should be a fairly simple process. For example, tennis is one key activity for a particular student, and we have evaluated the student on his forehand, backhand, serve, and volleying skills. In addition, we have measured such fitness skills as strength (being able to hit the ball over the net from various distances), flexibility (ability to demonstrate adequate range of motion in strokes and adequate range of motion for running and positioning legs), perceptual skills such as eye–hand coordination (ability to hit stationary or moving ball at various heights, speeds, and trajectories), and balance (ability to move, stand, and hit ball without losing balance or falling) (results of this student's assessment are in Figure 5.9). Based on the results of this assessment, long-term goals and short-term instructional objectives have been established for this student (see Figure 5.10).

Note how these goals and objectives are directly related to the student's overall program goal (i.e., to play a functional game of tennis). In addition, note how the goals and objectives are directly related to the student's present level of performance on tennis skills. It should be clear that the type of assessment that is used is critical in determining what types of IEP goals and objectives are established. Remember how in the traditional approach standardized tests

Checklist for Prioritizing Goals

Student's name: _____

Person filling out this form: _____

Date: _____ Student's age: _____

Activity 1: _____ Activity 5: _____ Activity 9: _____

Activity 2: _____ Activity 6: _____ Activity 10: _____

Activity 3: _____ Activity 7: _____ Activity 11: _____

Activity 4: _____ Activity 8: _____ Activity 12: _____

Criteria	1	2	3	4	5	6	7	8	9	10	11	12
1. Activity can be done in current environments.	—	—	—	—	—	—	—	—	—	—	—	—
2. Activity can be done in future environments.	—	—	—	—	—	—	—	—	—	—	—	—
3. Activity can be done in four or more different environments.	—	—	—	—	—	—	—	—	—	—	—	—
4. Activity affords daily opportunities for interaction.	—	—	—	—	—	—	—	—	—	—	—	—
5. Activity increases student independence.	—	—	—	—	—	—	—	—	—	—	—	—
6. Activity helps maintain student in, or promotes movement to, a least restrictive environment.	—	—	—	—	—	—	—	—	—	—	—	—
7. Activity is chronologically age appropriate.	—	—	—	—	—	—	—	—	—	—	—	—
8. Student will acquire in 1 year the necessary skills to participate in the activity.	—	—	—	—	—	—	—	—	—	—	—	—
9. Parents rate the activity as a high priority.	—	—	—	—	—	—	—	—	—	—	—	—
10. Activity promotes a positive view of the individual.	—	—	—	—	—	—	—	—	—	—	—	—
11. Activity meets a medical need.	—	—	—	—	—	—	—	—	—	—	—	—
12. Activity improves student's health or fitness.	—	—	—	—	—	—	—	—	—	—	—	—
13. If able to, student would select the activity.	—	—	—	—	—	—	—	—	—	—	—	—
14. Student shows positive response to the activity.	—	—	—	—	—	—	—	—	—	—	—	—
15. Advocacy, training, and other support can be arranged so that student can participate in the activity in the absence of educational services.	—	—	—	—	—	—	—	—	—	—	—	—
16. Related services staff support the activity selection.	—	—	—	—	—	—	—	—	—	—	—	—
17. Transportation is no barrier.	—	—	—	—	—	—	—	—	—	—	—	—
18. Cost is no barrier.	—	—	—	—	—	—	—	—	—	—	—	—
19. Staffing is no barrier.	—	—	—	—	—	—	—	—	—	—	—	—
20. Environments are physically accessible.	—	—	—	—	—	—	—	—	—	—	—	—
TOTAL	—	—	—	—	—	—	—	—	—	—	—	—

Figure 5.7. Checklist for prioritizing goals: 20 examples of criteria used for setting priorities for 12 activities. (Rating: 3, *strongly agree with statement;* 2, *agree somewhat with statement;* 1, *disagree somewhat with statement;* 0, *disagree strongly with statement.*) (From Helmstetter, E. [1989]. Curriculum for school-age students. In F. Brown & D.H. Lehr [Eds.], *Persons with profound disabilities: Issues and practices* [p. 254]. Baltimore: Paul H. Brookes Publishing Co.; originally adapted from Dardig, J.C., & Howard, W.L. [1981]. A systematic procedure for prioritizing IEP goals. *The Directive Teacher, 3,* 6–7. Adapted by permission.)

Quantitative Analysis of Catching Skill for Preschool Children

Class: _____ Date: _____

Age and grade: _____ Teacher: _____

School: _____ Objective: _____*Catching a ball*_____

Name	Catch balloon tossed from 2 feet	Catch balloon tossed from 4 feet	Catch 8" Nerf ball tossed from 2 feet	Catch 8" Nerf ball tossed from 4 feet	Catch 8" Nerf ball tossed from 6 feet	Catch tennis ball tossed from 3 feet	Catch tennis ball tossed from 6 feet	Catch tennis ball tossed to side from 6 feet
	1	2	3	4	5	6	7	8
1								
2								
3								
4								
5								

Figure 5.8a. Quantitative analysis of catching skill for preschool children.

resulted in nonfunctional goals and objectives such as standing on one foot for increasing periods of time or doing more sit-ups. In contrast, balance and fitness skills are incorporated into functional goals and objectives (in this case, functional tennis goals) in the ecological approach.

How Do We Teach?

The next decision is how to help the student achieve the goals outlined in his or her program. Again, Chapter 4 outlined several factors that should be considered when making instructional decisions. At this level, you are trying to find out whether the student does not know the correct components of the skill and just needs instruction and feedback or knows the correct components of the skill but cannot perform the skill because of specific motor or

sensory impairments. If the student does not know the components, instruction could be as simple as showing the student how to perform the skill using verbal cues, physical assistance, demonstration, and environmental cues. For example, a 7-year-old student with mild intellectual disabilities has had little instruction on how to perform a skillful, two-handed catch. In this case, instruction might only require giving her information about the correct pattern, specific instruction with corrective feedback, and time to practice the skill. Another 7-year-old student with a learning disability is not able to perform a two-handed catch because of problems with visual-motor perception and body awareness. This student might need supplemental practice and instruction to improve visual-motor perception and body awareness in addition to specific instruction in the components of the catch. Figure 5.11 provides a simple checklist to aid in deciding which students

Qualitative Analysis of Catching Skill for Preschool Children

Class: _____ Date: _____

Age and grade: _____ Teacher: _____

School: _____ Objective: _*Catching a ball*_____

Write students' names in the first column below. For each numbered skill within each skill level, rate whether the item was achieved by each student (X = achieved; 0 = not achieved; / = partially achieved). In the Comments column, rate each student's primary response(s).

	Skill level I			Skill level II			Skill level III	Primary responses:
	Three consecutive times							N Not attending
								NR No response
								UR Unrelated response
								O Other (specify in comments)
Name	Focuses eyes on ball	Stops ball with hands or hands and arms	Focuses eyes on ball	Extends arms in preparation to catch ball, with elbows at sides	Contacts and controls ball with hands or hands and arms after one bounce	Bends elbows to absorb force of ball	Two or more students play game or activities at home or school, demonstrating skill components over 6-week period	Comments
	1	2	3	4	5	6	7	
1								
2								
3								
4								
5								

Recommendations: Specify changes or conditions in planning for instruction, performance, or diagnostic testing procedures or standards. Please describe what worked best.

_____

_____

_____

_____

_____

_____

Figure 5.8b. Qualitative analysis of catching skill for preschool children. (Qualitative analysis from Wessel, J.A., & Zittel, L.L. [1995]. *Smart Start: Preschool movement curriculum designed for children of all abilities* [p. 271]. Austin, TX: PRO-ED; adapted by permission.)

Forehand and backhand: Demonstrates full range of motion in stroke. Has adequate strength to hold regulation racket. Has strength to hit ball over net into server box from 20 feet away (near baseline). Can hit ball off tee consistently, but can only hit moving ball when ball is tossed from 5 feet away in one of five trials. Qualitatively, student shows side orientation, brings arm back horizontally, and swings forward horizontally. Has problem with keeping eye on ball and timing.

Serving: Demonstrates full range of motion in stroke. Has adequate strength to hold regulation racket. Has strength to hit ball over net into server box from 10 feet away (not from baseline). Hits self-tossed ball in 1 of 10 trials. Qualitatively, student stands facing net, tosses ball by bending legs and tossing underhand with arm, brings racket up overhead, and strikes into ball with good follow-through toward ground. Problems appear to be accuracy in toss, keeping eye on ball, and timing.

Figure 5.9. Functional assessment of tennis skills for high school student with Down syndrome.

need general instruction and which students need supplemental instruction.

Instructional Modifications

Figure 5.12 presents a checklist to guide the decision process regarding implementing instructional modifications. Such factors include information on teaching style, class formats, and how to present material to the student (see Chapter 6 for more specific information about each of these instructional modifications). This checklist should be viewed as a tool to help the team and the general physical educator brainstorm about instructional modifications. It is important to understand that different children will need different types or levels of instruction to be successful in general physical education. Some children may respond to verbal cues; others will need physical assistance. Most children stop when they hear a whistle, but a child who is deaf may need a hand signal. Typically developing children might be motivated just because they enjoy the activity, while a child with autism or intellectual disabilities might need alternative forms of motivation or reinforcement. Physical educators need to understand that not all children can be taught the same way. For inclusive physical education to be successful, physi-

cal educators have to be able to utilize a variety of instructional techniques.

Communication

As noted in Chapter 4, one of the most important questions regarding instruction is how to communicate with the student. One simple way to determine how to communicate with the student is to set up a meeting with the student's speech therapist. She can describe the best ways to communicate with the student. A more ecologically valid approach (i.e., directly related to physical education) is to actually evaluate how the student responds to different types of cues in different physical education situations (see Figure 5.13 for a simple checklist). For example, with a student who has a visual impairment, a combination of verbal cues and physical assistance may seem to work best. For another student who has autism, environmental cues such as pictures or symbols on the wall or on the floor might work best. Again, the speech therapist, special education teacher, parents, and/or adapted physical education specialist can assist with this process in general physical education. Once you have a general idea of how to communicate with particular students, repeat the same process (informally as you in-

Long-term plan: Sarah will develop the skills needed to play a beginner-level game of tennis with peers.

Long-term goal: Sarah will demonstrate the ability to perform a functional forehand and backhand so that she can hit a ball with instructor.

Short-term instructional objectives:
1. Sarah will demonstrate the ability to hit a tennis ball that is tossed to her from 5 feet away using the components of a skillful forehand so that she contacts tennis ball for four of five trials and so that the ball travels over net for three of five trials.
2. Sarah will demonstrate the ability to hit a tennis ball that is tossed to her from 5 feet away using the components of a skillful, two-handed backhand so that she contacts tennis ball for four of five trials and so that ball travels over net for three of five trials.

Figure 5.10. Individualized education program goals and objectives based on functional assessment of tennis skills.

Checklist to Determine Method of Instruction to Use

Student's name: _____

Person filling out this form: _____

Date: _____ Student's age: _____

	Yes	No	Comments
Does student appear to have typical sensory awareness?			
Does student appear to have typical body awareness?			
Does student appear to respond to specific instructional cues related to targeted skill?			

If answers to any of these questions is no, then student should be checked for perceptual issues such as visual-motor problems or problems with body awareness (consult with other team members; e.g., occupational therapist). If the student does have perceptual problems, he or she may need supplemental instruction or modifications.

Figure 5.11. Checklist to determine method of instruction to use.

ternalize the various types of communication techniques) in various teaching-learning situations to make sure the student understands the cues you are giving.

Alternative Ways to Perform Skills

For some students, breaking down a skill into smaller components may not be enough (Figure 5.14). For example, students with physical disabilities due to spinal cord injuries or cerebral palsy may not be able to perform skills the way that other students do. These students would be frustrated and perhaps noncompliant if asked to learn how to perform a fundamental skill using a particular pattern. These students should be given alternative ways to perform the skill that meets their unique abilities. Figure 5.14 provides a checklist that can help guide this decision.

Caution should be taken when deciding to introduce an alternative pattern to particular students. If the pattern does not give the student any advantage and even a disadvantage, then it may not be appropriate. For example, if a student is having difficulty kicking a soccer ball due to spasticity in his legs, he may be allowed to pick up the ball and throw

it as an alternative pattern. However, this student would not be allowed to use this alternative pattern in little league soccer games, so this type of adaptation may not be very functional if the goal was for the student to be integrated into a regular soccer league (but may be okay in general physical education). If a student with severe spastic cerebral palsy is allowed to throw backwards over her head rather than throwing forward to get maximum distance, then this student could then use this skill when playing horseshoes, playing lawn darts, or competing in the Indian club throw in cerebral palsy sports.

Curricular Adaptations

It is important to determine whether the student needs some type of curricular adaptation or adapted equipment, such as flotation devices or a shorter racket, to allow the student to perform functional, lifetime leisure skills more independently. However, most students should be given every opportunity to learn skills without modifications or special equipment because such adaptations can be costly and difficult to transport and can heighten the difference between students with and without disabilities. When considering curricular adaptations or adapted

---

Checklist to Determine Instructional Modifications

Student's name: _____

Person filling out this form: _____

Date: _____ Student's age: _____

PE class/teacher: _____

Who will implement modifications? (circle one)   General PE teacher   classmates   peer tutor   teacher assistant   specialist

Instructional component	Things to consider	Selected modifications (if any) and comments
Teaching style	Command, problem solving, discovery	_____
Class format and size of group	Small or large group; stations or whole class instruction	_____
Level of methodology	Verbal cues, demonstrations, physical assistance	_____
Starting/stopping signals	Whistle, hand signals, physical assistance	_____
Time of day	Early A.M., late A.M., early P.M., late P.M.	_____
Duration of instruction	How long student will listen to instruction	_____
Duration of expected participation	How long student will stay on task	_____
Order of learning	Order in which you will present instruction	_____
Instructional setting	Indoors/outdoors; part of gym/whole gym	_____
Elimination of distractions	Lighting, temperature, extra equipment	_____
Structure	Organization of instruction each day	_____
Level of difficulty	Complexity of instructions/organization	_____
Level of motivation	Making setting and activities more motivating	_____

Figure 5.12. Checklist to determine instructional modifications.

---

equipment, the questions in Figure 5.15 may be helpful. Once the decision has been made to utilize some curricular adaptations or adapted equipment, checklists in Figures 5.16 and 5.17 can be used (see Chapter 6 for more details on curricular adaptations).

Note that some curricular adaptations and pieces of adapted equipment can be used temporarily to motivate or assist a student in learning a particular skill. If modifications or equipment are to be used temporarily, a plan should be developed to quickly and easily wean the student from these adaptations. For example, arm flotation devices are often used to give young swimmers confidence in the water, but these young swimmers often become dependent on them and it becomes extremely difficult

to teach the students to swim more independently. A systematic plan should be set up to gradually help the student swim without the aid of such devices.

Where Do We Teach It?

Once a list of activities and skills have been delineated, the student's present level of performance determined, the IEP written, and plans laid out for how to teach each skill, the next decision is where best to teach these skills. As noted in Chapter 4, data collection at this level involves comparing the student's targeted goals to the activities that take place in general physical education or community recre-

---

Sample Checklist to Determine Communication Skills

Student's name: _____

Person filling out this form: _____

Date: _____   Student's age: _____

Instruct student in various situations. Note how student responds to each type of cue or combination of cues. You may need to repeat in various instructional situations (e.g., outside versus inside; simple skill versus more complex skill).

Cue(s)	Responds correctly	Delayed response (5–10 seconds)	Does not respond
Verbal cues			
Gestures			
Demonstration			
Environmental cue			
Physical assistance			

Situations in which assessment was conducted:

_____ Inclusive physical education setting with peers without disabilities (large group)

_____ Inclusive physical education setting with small groups (five to seven students)

_____ Inclusive physical education setting: one-to-one instruction

Figure 5.13.   Checklist to determine communication skills.

---

ation (see Figure 5.18, for example). There will likely be plenty of overlap, in which case the student should be placed in general physical education with support as needed. Even if some general physical activities appear to be different from those targeted for the student, the student's targeted activities can be worked on in general physical education.

For example, softball, bowling, swimming, and fitness are targeted goals for a particular student, but the general physical education program is beginning a basketball unit. While other students work on shooting skills, the student can work on hitting a softball placed on a tee into a modified basket. While other students are working on dribbling, the student can work on pushing his wheelchair toward base, and while other students work on passing, the student can work on throwing a ball to a peer.

Note that placement decisions are made on skills that are needed in present and future environments, and students should receive training in the environments where these skills will be used. For elementary-age children, most critical skills will take place in general education classrooms. This is true for physical education where activities conducted in general physical education often are important for students with disabilities. As students reach middle school and high school, a greater number of skills may be more appropriately taught in the community (Brown et al., 1991; Sailor, Gee, & Karasoff, 1993). For example, upper-level high school students may spend 75% or more of their school day in the community learning job and community skills (Brown et al., 1991). In terms of physical education, lifetime leisure skills may be taught in the community environment where they will be eventually used. Thus, if a student's program is vastly different from the general physical education program and if this program involves lifetime leisure activities, instructional training should take place in the community. To provide opportunities for inclusion, classmates without disabilities should be invited on these community trips to participate alongside the student with a disability.

Another aspect of where to teach the student is how well the student performs routines in general physical education. These routines can be evaluated

Checklist to Determine Whether Student Needs Alternative Way to Perform a Skill

Student's name: _____

Person filling out this form: _____

Date: _____   Student's age: _____

Does the student need an alternative way to perform the following skill: _____?

	Yes	No	Comments
Does student have a physical disability that appears to preclude typical performance?			
Is student having extreme difficulty performing the skill?			
Is the student making little to no progress over several months or years despite instruction?			
Does student seem more comfortable and motivated using a different pattern?			
Will the alternative pattern be functional in the targeted environments?			
Will the alternative pattern increase student's ability to perform skill?			
If the answer to any of the above questions is yes, student may need adapted pattern.			

Figure 5.14. Checklist to determine whether student needs alternative way to perform a skill.

to determine what skills the student can do independently, what skills the student might need assistance with, and what activities might need to be modified. As noted in Chapter 4, one way of analyzing the regular routine and how well a particular student performs these routines is an environmental inventory with a discrepancy analysis. Such information can assist the general and adapted physical education specialists in determining what tasks the student can do independently or with support, what tasks need training, and what tasks need to be modified to meet the student's unique needs.

Who Will Teach It?

The final item before actually implementing the program is to determine how much support a particular student will need and who will provide this support. Some students can do quite well in general physical education with no extra support, while other students will need support in the form of peers,

volunteers, teacher assistants, or specialists. Again, ecologically referenced assessment data should guide this decision process. As noted by Rainforth and York-Barr (1997), collaboration is needed to determine the amount and type of support needed by particular students.

Important factors that should be considered when determining level of support are the student's characteristics, the physical educators' and peers' characteristics, and the general physical education setting. These factors taken together will help the team determine the best type of support to provide. For example, York, Giangreco, Vandercook, and Macdonald (1992) noted that student characteristics such as particular abilities, previous experiences, and/or their intellectual, communication, social, physical, sensory, or health functioning are important factors to consider when determining levels of support. In addition, the student's behaviors in terms of his or her ability to follow directions, stay on task, and maintain control in a crowded, noisy environment is important.

Checklist to Determine Whether Student Needs Adapted Equipment

Student's name: _____

Person filling out this form: _____

Date: _____ Student's age: _____

Does the student need adapted equipment?

	Yes	No	Comments
Will adapted equipment increase active participation in activity?			
Will adapted equipment allow the student to participate in an activity that is preferred or valued by the student, friends, and family members?			
Will it take less time to teach the student to use the adapted equipment than to teach the skill directly?			
Will the team have access to the technical expertise to design, construct, adjust, and repair the adapted equipment?			
Will the use of the adapted equipment maintain or enhance related motor/communication skills?			

If the answer to most of these questions is yes, then the student may need adapted equipment.

A Teacher's Guide to Including Students with Disabilities in General Physical Education, Third Edition,
by Martin E. Block. Copyright © 2007 by Paul H. Brookes Publishing Co., Inc. All rights reserved.

Figure 5.15. Checklist to determine whether student needs adapted equipment.

Also important are the characteristics of the physical educator and peers without disabilities. Physical educators and peers who have knowledge about the student being included, knowledge about successful ways to include students with disabilities, and previous experience with inclusion may need less support; a physical educator who has limited knowledge of inclusion and is experiencing inclusion for the first time may need more support. Finally, expectations of the setting, in this case general physical education, will affect how much support a particular student will need. Figure 5.19 presents a checklist to help facilitate decisions regarding supports. This form reads like a flow chart in which the general physical educator, in collaboration with other team members, determines how much support he or she would need to safely and successfully provide an appropriate, quality physical education program to the student with disabilities as well as to students without disabilities.

In making this important decision, the team should weigh such factors as personal needs of the student (e.g., ability to dress, sit and wait turn, interact with peers), physical needs of the student (e.g., performing all of the physical education activities), sensory needs of the student (e.g., receiving information, following directions, locating certain places in the gymnasium), comfort level of regular physical educator, teaching style of general physical educator, level of structure in class, and general behaviors of general physical education students.

In many cases, peer tutors and volunteers can provide support to students with more mild disabilities; specialists may be needed to provide more support for students with more severe disabilities (Block & Krebs, 1992). Support provided by specialists often can be faded away so that the student is responding to more natural cues in the environment with occasional support from peers (Block, 1999). For example, a student with severe, spastic diplegic cerebral palsy (needs assistance to move his wheelchair) might need a physical therapist or adapted physical educator to provide assistance in general physical education. However, as the peers become

Checklist to Determine Curricular Adaptations

Student's name: _____

Person filling out this form: _____

Date: _____ Student's age: _____

ASSESSING THE STUDENT'S STRENGTH

Adaptations to consider

Shorten distance to move or project object.

Use lighter equipment (e.g., balls, bats).

Use shorter striking implements.

Allow student to sit or lie down while playing.

Use deflated or suspended balls.

Change requirements (e.g., jump a few times, then run, rather than jump across gym).

Selected modifications (if any) and comments

_____

_____

_____

_____

_____

_____

ASSESSING THE STUDENT'S SPEED

Adaptations to consider

Shorten distance (or make it longer for others).

Change locomotor pattern.

Make safe areas in tag games.

Selected modifications (if any) and comments

_____

_____

_____

ASSESSING THE STUDENT'S ENDURANCE

Adaptations to consider

Shorten distance.

Shorten playing field.

Allow safe areas in tag games.

Decrease activity time for student.

Allow more rest periods for student.

Allow student to sit while playing.

Selected modifications (if any) and comments

_____

_____

_____

_____

_____

_____

ASSESSING THE STUDENT'S BALANCE

Adaptations to consider

Provide chair/bar for support.

Teach balance techniques.

Increase width of beams to be walked.

Use carpeted rather than slick surfaces.

Teach students how to fall.

Allow student to sit during activity.

Place student near wall for support.

Allow student to hold peer's hand.

Selected modifications (if any) and comments

_____

_____

_____

_____

_____

_____

_____

_____

ASSESSING STUDENT'S COORDINATION AND ACCURACY

Adaptations to consider

Use stationary balls for kicking/striking.

Decrease distance for throwing, kicking, and shooting

Make targets and goals larger.

Use larger balls for kicking and striking.

Increase surface of the striking implements.

Use backstop.

Use softer, slower balls for striking and catching.

In bowling-type games, use lighter, less stable pins.

Optimize safety.

Selected modifications (if any) and comments

_____

_____

_____

_____

_____

_____

_____

_____

_____

Remember, you can implement some or all of these modifications. Also, these modifications can be implemented for one child, for several children, or for the entire class to make the activity more challenging and success oriented.

Figure 5.16. Checklist to determine curricular adaptations.

Checklist to Determine Curricular Modifications for Group Games and Sports

Student's name: _____

Person filling out this form: _____

Date: _____   Student's age: _____

Modifications to consider	Selected modifications (if any) and comments
Can you vary the purpose/goal of the game (e.g., some students play to learn complex strategies, others play to work on simple motor skills)?	_____
Can you vary number of players (e.g., two-on-two basketball)?	_____
Can you vary movement requirements (e.g., some students walk, others run; some hit a ball off a tee, others hit pitched ball; skilled students use more complex movements, less skilled use simpler movements)?	_____
Can you vary the field of play (e.g., designate special zones for students with less mobility; make the field narrower or wider as needed; shorten the distance for students with movement problems)?	_____
Can you vary objects used (e.g., some students use lighter bats/larger balls; some use a lower net/basket)?	_____
Can you vary the level of organization (e.g., vary typical organizational patterns; vary where certain students stand; vary the level of structure for certain students)?	_____
Can you vary the limits/expectations (e.g., vary the number of turns each student receives; vary the rules regarding how far a student can run or hit; vary how much you will enforce certain rules for certain players)?	_____

A Teacher's Guide to Including Students with Disabilities in General Physical Education, Third Edition,
by Martin E. Block. Copyright © 2007 by Paul H. Brookes Publishing Co., Inc. All rights reserved.

Figure 5.17.   Checklist to determine curricular modifications for group games and sports. (*Source:* Morris & Stiehl, 1998.)

more comfortable with the student, the specialist can begin to train peers how to assist the student in throwing balls, pushing his wheelchair, and performing other physical education activities. Again, there is no clear-cut way to determine how much support a particular student will need. The team should work together to make an informed decision based on as much information as they can collect regarding the student, the teacher and peers, and the environment.

How Effective Is Our Program?

Ongoing evaluation is critical to determine if the student is making progress toward his or her targeted goals. If he is not making adequate progress, then ongoing evaluation can quickly discover the problem. If ongoing evaluations are not conducted at all or conducted at the end of a unit or semester, then a student might be working on skills in incorrect ways receiving inadequate instruction and feedback (Kelly & Melograno, 2004). For example, it was decided that a high school student with Down syn-

drome would use a racquetball racket rather than a tennis racket. However, evaluation of the student at the end of the first day reveals that he does very well with the racquetball racket but cannot reach most balls hit toward him. A lighter regulation tennis racket was tried the next day, and the student was able to hold the racket while playing tennis and reach many more balls. If evaluation had only been conducted at the end of the unit, this student would have had to use an inappropriate piece of equipment the entire time and would probably have had to relearn how to strike a tennis ball using a regulation tennis racket.

Evaluating what was taught can be as simple as talking with the student, his parents, and his peers to find out how they perceive the program. If they all perceive that the program is going well and the student is involved in appropriate activities, then the program has social validity. In addition to determining if the general program is appropriate, another important part of the evaluation process is to reevaluate the child's present level of performance in targeted skills. Student progress and the effectiveness of modifications can be measured by the student's progress toward his targeted goals as well as

Comparison of Student's Individualized Education Program Goals with General Physical Education Activities

Student's name: _____

Person filling out this form: _____

Date: _____ Student's age: _____

List the activities/goals targeted for the student in the left-hand column, activities that take place in general physical educa-tion (GPE) or community recreation in the second column, and how well these activities match in the third column (using the key shown below). Then provide suggestions how the student can participate in general physical education/community recreation.

Student's goals	Activities in GPE/recreation	Match	Suggestion for placement
_____	_____	_____	_____
_____	_____	_____	_____
_____	_____	_____	_____
_____	_____	_____	_____
_____	_____	_____	_____
_____	_____	_____	_____
_____	_____	_____	_____
_____	_____	_____	_____
_____	_____	_____	_____

Key:

+   Activities directly match.
+/–   Activities can reasonably be modified.
–   Activities have no relation to student's goals; alternative activities are needed in GPE.
O   Activities have no relation to student's goals; alternative activities are needed outside of GPE.

A Teacher's Guide to Including Students with Disabilities in General Physical Education, Third Edition,
by Martin E. Block. Copyright © 2007 by Paul H. Brookes Publishing Co., Inc. All rights reserved.

Figure 5.18. Comparison of student's individualized education program goals with general physical education activities.

how his special education teacher, teacher assistant, general physical education teacher, and peers per-ceive he is doing in general physical education. As the student progresses and acquires new skills, changes should be made to his present level of per-formance and expectations for future progress mod-ified.

Evaluating how the teaching occurred can uti-lize the same evaluation forms as in the pre-assess-ment. Nothing needs to be noted if the child con-tinues to need the same modifications to instruction as in the initial assessment. However, if the child has progressed to the point where fewer modifica-tions are needed or if it is determined that the child needs more or different modifications, then this should be noted on the assessment forms.

Finally, evaluate where the skill was taught and how much support was needed to teach the skill by talking with the student, his peers, and the regular physical educator. If the student is having difficulty in any area on the ecological inventory or is not making anticipated progress on tasks that have been targeted for training, more support might be needed. For example, the ecological inventory and discrep-ancy analysis suggested that a student needed a peer to help him change into his clothes for physical ed-ucation. However, the student is taking much longer than expected in the locker room, and he and the peer are missing warm-up activities. It was de-cided to change the support person from a peer to a teacher assistant. In addition, the student comes down to physical education 5 minutes earlier than his peers to make sure he has enough time to change into his uniform. Again, the use of the ecological in-ventory described in Figure 4.8 can be used to con-duct ongoing evaluations.

Checklist for Determining Supports in General Physical Education

Student's name: _____

Person filling out this form: _____

Date: _____   Student's age: _____

	Locker	Warm-Up	Skills	Games
Can you handle having _____ in these situations without extra support?				
If *no*, could you handle situation with consultation from specialists?				
If *yes*, which specialists would you like to provide consultative support?				
Can you handle these situations on your own with consultative support?				
If *no*, could peers in class provide enough extra support (without drastically affecting their program)?				
If *no*, could an older peer tutor or volunteer provide enough support?				
If *no*, could a trained teacher assistant provide enough support?				
If *no*, could regular visits from a specialist provide enough support? (If *yes*, which specialists would you like to provide support)?				
Comments:				

Figure 5.19. Checklist for determining supports in general physical education.

EXAMPLE OF ECOLOGICAL ASSESSMENT TO FACILITATE INCLUSION IN PHYSICAL EDUCATION

The following is an example of how the ecological approach to assessment might look for John, a 10-year-old boy who has recently moved into a particular school district. John has been diagnosed as having mild intellectual disabilities; diplegic, spastic cerebral palsy with very limited movement in his legs and some control over his arms; and a seizure disorder that is controlled with medication. John uses a manual wheelchair for mobility, and he can push it forward and maneuver it around obstacles slowly but independently. John communicates verbally with one- to two-word statements, and he seems to understand most simple directions. John can go to the bathroom and take care of his personal needs with minimal assistance (needs help pulling up pants,

buttoning shirt, and transferring out of chair). John enjoys being with his peers and doing the same things they do. He is a big baseball fan, and his favorite team is the Chicago Cubs. John received special education services in his previous school, but he did not have a specific IEP for physical education. The collaborative team has scheduled a meeting. The adapted physical education specialist, in conjunction with the general physical education specialist and special education teacher, has been asked to assess John in order to make recommendations to the team regarding physical education services.

Does John Qualify for APE Services?

John's IEP team asked the general and adapted physical educator to comment on John's abilities in general physical education and their recommendations for services (see Figure 5.20). Note how the results are

---

Name: _John Armstrong_   **Date:** _September 14, 2006_

Date of birth: _7-15-96_   **Evaluator:** _Susan Carter, CAPE_

Grade/class: _Fifth grade/Ms. Karish_

Introduction

John Armstrong is a 10-year-old boy in Ms. Karish's fifth-grade class. John has mild mental retardation; diplegic, spastic cerebral palsy such that he has very limited movement in his legs and some control over his arms; and a seizure disorder that is controlled with medication. John uses a manual wheelchair for mobility, and although he pushes it forward and maneuvers around obstacles slowly, he does so independently. John communicates verbally with one- to two-word statements, and he seems to understand most simple directions. John currently receives physical therapy twice per week for 30 minutes each session and speech-language therapy once per week for 30 minutes per session. His special education teacher recommended John for an adapted physical education evaluation due to suspected delays in gross motor development.

Abilities in reference to general physical education (GPE) curriculum

The GPE curriculum for third through fifth grades focuses on mastery of locomotor patterns, manipulative patterns, passing the physical fitness test, and introduction to individual team sports and dance. John is unable to perform any locomotor patterns due to his disability, but he can independently move his manual wheelchair slowly around the gym and the playground. He cannot kick or punt due to his disability, but he has learned to catch and throw in his wheelchair using a modified pattern. He also can hit a ball off a tee using his hand. Although John has good upper body strength, he has very limited flexibility in his arms and, particularly, in his legs. He appears to have adequate endurance.

Behavioral, cognitive, and social abilities in reference to the GPE curriculum

John is an extremely well behaved and enthusiastic student in GPE. He really wants to please and follow directions, although the GPE teacher or a peer often has to repeat complex directions for him. He interacts very well with his peers, and his peers seem to enjoy interacting with him. He tries to do what he is supposed to do.

Motor abilities with reference to recess and community-based recreation

John's parents report that John plays on the Challenger baseball team, in which children with disabilities are provided with certain modifications. John's parents note that John does not play with other children in the neighborhood due to his limited mobility. John's classroom teacher notes that he is able to participate in very few recess activities independently. He seems to enjoy watching his peers play, and sometimes they let him play basketball or dodging games with them.

Recommendations

Based on this ecologically based assessment, it seems that John functions quite well in GPE, although he is significantly delayed compared with his peers. As he gets older and moves to middle school physical education, we think that he will fall further behind. In addition, we believe that John needs to focus on a few long-term goals and learn them well rather than doing all of the activities offered in GPE. Therefore, we recommend adapted physical education (APE) services for John to be carried out within GPE that focus on unique goals/objectives for John (APE specialist goes into GPE with John two times per week.) John will have a teacher assistant accompany him to GPE the other day.

Figure 5.20. Professionals' report with comments and recommendations for John.

---

directly applicable to John's abilities in general physical education. One of the results suggests that general physical education activities are quickly becoming inappropriate for John. However, given John's excellent behavior and the fact that that he will receive support from the APE specialist and teacher assistant, the APE and GPE specialists felt the most appropriate placement for John is still in general physical education.

Phase 2: What to Teach John

Determining the Vision

John's parents discussed their dreams and nightmares with reference to physical education and recreation for John using MAPs (see Figure 5.21). This helped the team focus from the top down on what John needs to be successful now and in the future. Results suggested that John's parents want him to participate with peers in general physical education whenever possible and develop some independent lifetime leisure skills. Their nightmare for John was that he would have no skills and no one to recreate with when he was older.

In this phase information is collected in order to find out what John likes to do, what his parents like to do, what his peers like to do, and what young adults in the community like to do (see Figure 5.22). First, the adapted physical education specialist asks John what he would like to learn in physical education. Because he is a big baseball fan, John wants to learn how to play baseball. He also mentions tennis; John's father notes that the family often plays tennis, but John watches from the sidelines. Both John and

---

Making Action Plans for Physical Education Planning

1. What is _____John_____'s history regarding motor development, recreation, and fitness?

   John has been delayed in motor development and fitness all his life due to cerebral palsy. He will never be able to move like children without disabilities, so we are more interested in him learning how to move within his abilities. John has always enjoyed watching sports on television and trying to play with the family, especially tennis and baseball.

2. What is your dream for _____John_____ with reference to physical education and recreation?

   To be able to develop skills needed to be somewhat independent in an active recreation activity
   To be able to interact and participate with peers in general physical education
   To have friends with similar recreation interests

3. What is your nightmare?

   For John to be isolated from his peers or to have none of the skills necessary for him to do something with his leisure time; to be alone as an adult with no friends

4. Who is _____John_____ with reference to physical education and recreation?

   John is a boy who wants to be active but is limited by his disability. John really enjoys sports and being with his peers and family in physical education and recreation, even if he is cheering others on.

5. What are _____John_____'s strengths, gifts, and abilities with reference to physical education and recreation?

   John's enthusiasm for life, his up-beat attitude about everything, his love of friends and being part of the group, his unique way of making others feel good about themselves, his unselfishness

6. What does _____John_____ need to make the dream come true and avoid the nightmare?

   John needs support during general physical education to participate successfully and some extra practice in targeted lifetime leisure skills. The general physical education teacher needs support to make modifications for John, and peers need training to understand how to help and accept John.

7. What would _____John_____'s ideal day in physical education look like, and what must be done to make it happen?

   Participation in general physical education with peers who support, respect, and appreciate him; participation in some general physical education activities with modification so he can be successful; time to work on his targeted skills

8. What is our plan of action for physical education?

   Placement in general physical education to work on these goals and to provide opportunities to interact and participate with peers; extra time to work on his unique goals

Figure 5.21. Making Actions Plans questions completed for John. (From Vandercook, T., York, J., & Forest, M. [1989]. The McGill action planning system [MAPS]: A strategy for building the vision. *Journal of The Association for Persons with Severe Handicaps, 14,* 205–215; adapted by permission.)

his parents would like to see John play tennis with the family on these weekly outings. Finally, John's mother says that she would like to see John move his wheelchair faster, for longer periods of time, and with more precision around obstacles such as when he goes to the mall or to a grocery store.

Next, the adapted physical education specialist conducts a simple survey in John's school to determine what activities students without disabilities John's age like to do during recess and in their neighborhood after school. This information provides social validity as to the potential activities that might

Making Curriculum Decisions

List all of the activities that are preferred or typically engaged in under the following headings. Then, read the list and place activities that are in more than one column under *Targeted activities*.

Student's preferences	Parents' preferences	Activities in general physical education	Neighborhood activities played by peers	Community leisure activities
Baseball/softball	Tennis	Lead-up games	Bike riding	Softball
Tennis	Wheelchair	and skills for a	Soccer	Swimming
	Mobility	variety of team	Basketball	Weight training
		sports	Softball	Aerobics
			Fishing	Wheelchair
				mobility

Targeted activities: 1. _Softball_   2. _Wheelchair mobility_   3. _Tennis_   4. _General fitness_

Figure 5.22. Curriculum decisions for John.

be targeted for John. The results of the survey revealed that the most popular recreational activities (other than computer games and watching TV) are riding bikes, playing soccer in the fall, basketball in the winter, and softball in the summer, and fishing and playing in the creek. Some of these activities can be targeted for John's physical education IEP; others can be recommended to other team members, including John's parents, in terms of activities they might want to focus on with John.

Next, the adapted physical education specialist conducts a second survey in the community in which John lives to determine what recreation activities are popular for young adults. While John will not be graduating from school for some time, the severity of his physical and mental disabilities indicates that he will learn skills very slowly. Therefore, some critical skills that John will need upon graduation should be targeted immediately in John's IEP. The survey revealed that the most popular active recreational activities in John's community include bowling, golf, tennis, aerobic dance, weight lifting, softball, soccer, hiking, biking, and swimming. The team can then make a determination regarding which of these community-based recreation activities are realistic for John. For example, even though adult co-ed soccer is a popular sport in John's community, the program is very competitive. There is only one division, and only skilled players participate in the league. This activity would not be appropriate for John given its current parameters.

Adult co-ed softball is another popular sport in John's community, and this program is large enough to have several divisions. Division C is specifically designed for those just learning how to play softball or for those who just want to have fun. It would seem plausible that such a division would accept John into the league, especially if John can learn some of the key softball skills such as batting, pushing his chair toward first base, tossing a ball to a peer, and understanding the general rules and etiquette of the game (see Table 5.2). Swimming, weight training, and aerobics also are activities that might be targeted for John since these activities can easily be adapted to accommodate John's unique needs.

Based on this preliminary assessment, it appears that softball, tennis, wheelchair mobility, and fitness (strength and endurance in pushing his wheelchair) should be the main focus of John's program (see Figure 5.22).

Determining John's Level of Performance

The team sets out to determine John's present level of performance in motor skills, physical fitness, motor abilities, perceptual motor abilities, and cognitive abilities in reference to skills needed in tennis, softball, and mobility. For example, softball skills John needs include throwing, catching, striking, and wheelchair mobility. These skills will be measured both qualitatively and quantitatively. Qualitative measurement involves analyzing how John per-

Name: _John Armstrong_　　　　Date of assessment: _September 20, 2006_

Evaluator: _Martin Block_　　　Skill: _functional batting in baseball/softball_

Quantitative Assessment

How consistently can John hit the ball?

Hits ball off tee in three of four trials; hits pitched ball from 10' away in 1 of 10 trials

How far can John hit the ball?

Hits 10' off tee or when pitched

Qualitative Assessment

Components of batting (modified for John)

X, demonstrates component; 0, does not demonstrate component

Trials

_X_ _X_ _X_　Turns chair into orientation to tee

_X_ _X_ _X_　Keeps eye on ball

_0_ _0_ _0_　Holds bat with right hand on bottom and left hand on top of bat (he is right-handed)

_0_ _0_ _0_　Bends elbows so that arms are almost straight when bat contacts ball

_0_ _0_ _0_　Rolls wrists and follows through so that bat goes toward back

Figure 5.23. Quantitative and qualitative analysis of John's softball skills.

forms these skills and the underlying fitness and perceptual abilities needed to perform these skills (see Figure 5.23).

John's wheelchair mobility skills on the softball field were limited. He could push his wheelchair forward slowly toward first base but not fast enough to be safe in most situations. John was able to hit the ball off a tee in three of four tries so that the ball traveled approximately 10 feet. Cognitively, John understood the general concept and rules of softball. He was able to stay on task during the entire assessment process (15 minutes), and he seemed motivated and receptive to instruction. Notice how the information obtained from this type of assessment is directly applicable to what John needs work on in relation to his targeted skills and how the teacher might go about teaching the skills (e.g., shortening the distance to first base for John. allowing him to hit a ball off a tee, having assistance when playing the field to compensate for John's limited skills.

Developing John's IEP

The bulk of the information regarding the physical education portion of John's IEP is based on the assessment of his present level of performance on the targeted skills. Figure 5.24 shows the softball portion of John's IEP. Note how the team arrived at these objectives based on the long-term goal they had for John on the targeted goals they established for John, and finally on his present level of performance on these targeted goals.

How to Teach John Skills

Information that is needed to help John work on his goals and objectives includes general information about possible instructional modifications as well as specific information regarding John's communication skills, if John has any perceptual or motor impairments, if John can perform the movement in the traditional way, and if John needs adapted equipment. For example, John responds quite well to verbal cues and physical assistance but does not do well with demonstration. Similarly, John seems to have the range of motion, strength, and perceptual skills needed to respond to general instructional cues; he should be able to perform the skill the same way his peers do; and there are modifications that seem appropriate such as using a lighter bat for softball, pushing his chair to a closer base, and having a peer

---

Long-term plan: John will demonstrate the skills needed to play in a modified game of softball with peers in school and in the community.

Long-term goal: John will demonstrate functional competency in striking a pitched ball, pushing wheelchair to first base, and throwing ball to peer in practice situations.

Short-term instructional objectives:
1. John will demonstrate the ability to push his wheelchair from home to first base that is 30 feet away (half the distance of regulation softball) in 30 seconds or less in three of four trials.
2. John will hit a pitched Nerf ball holding two hands on the bat and using a horizontal striking pattern that includes follow-through across body when the ball is tossed slowly from 10 feet away for three of four trials.
3. John will throw a ball overhand so that the ball travels a distance of 10 feet and within 1 foot to either side of a peer for three of four trials.

Figure 5.24. Softball portion of John's individualized education program (IEP).

assist him in the field. This information can be supplemented by more specific information from teach members such as physical and speech therapists. In addition, John should be encouraged to try moving in different ways to see what works best for him.

Determine Where to Teach John These Skills

Determining where to teach John is accomplished by examining the curriculum for the fifth, sixth, and seventh grade at John's school. The philosophy of the physical education program at John's school is to expose students to and provide some foundational skills in a variety of individual and team sports including lifetime leisure skills. A basic foundation in a variety of activities will help these students make informed choices as to what activities they want to focus on when they go to high school (high school physical education follows and elective format). Table 5.2 lists specific activities and when they are targeted during the year.

A general inspection of the middle school physical education curriculum suggests that John's peers will be working on softball in the spring of the fifth grade and tennis in the fall of the sixth grade. John should be integrated into these units (with modifications as needed) so that he can work on his targeted goals. Badminton in the seventh grade is similar to tennis, and in fact the lighter racket and birdie might prove to be a useful adaptation for John. Thus, John should probably stay in general physical education for this activity. Similarly, aerobics, weight training, and roller skating/blading can help John improve his strength, flexibility, and endurance. Weight training (improving strength and flexibility) can concentrate on the muscle groups that John uses

to propel his wheelchair, and aerobics can improve John's endurance. For roller skating/blading, John can practice pushing his wheelchair following the same course his peers follow on their skates/blades. When the class goes to a local roller rink at the end of the unit, John can go along and push his wheelchair. Golf, bowling, and archery are lifetime leisure activities that are available in John's community. John might find these lifetime leisure sports enjoyable, and some or all of these activities might be so interesting to John that they might become targeted goals for him when he enters high school. Therefore, he will stay in general physical education part of the time for these activities (two days per week). He will receive specialized adapted physical education the other three days to work on his targeted goals.

While soccer, volleyball, and basketball can be accommodated so that John can have a safe and successful experience, they do not appear to be high-priority goals for John. It is going to take John a long time to learn to master the basic skills of tennis and softball, and exposing John to these other activities would take away important instructional time (Kelly & Melograno, 2004). However, these team sports are popular with John's peers during various seasons of the year, and it would be nice if John had a least a

Table 5.2. General physical education activities and quarter in which they are targeted in different grades

	Fifth grade	Sixth grade	Seventh grade
1st quarter	Soccer	Tennis	Roller skating/blading
2nd quarter	Volleyball	Aerobics	Badminton
3rd quarter	Basketball	Weight training	Bowling
4th quarter	Softball	Golf	Archery

general understanding of the skills, rules, and flow of the game. In addition, some of John's fitness and mobility goals can easily be incorporated into these sports. The team decides that John will work on tennis during the soccer unit because it is difficult to get John to the soccer field and move his wheelchair on the grass. However, the team recommended that John participate in volleyball and basketball 2 days per week and work on his targeted skills the other three days. It is understood that John will not acquire the skills for these sports but simply gain exposure to them. John's teacher assistant and five to seven of John's peers will go with him on the days when he is pulled out of general physical education. These students are not peer tutors but friends of John who will participate alongside John in his targeted activities. Different students are picked randomly each day (thus, each student would only miss one day of physical education if he or she is picked).

Next, daily routines in general physical education are measured, including the communication, self-help, social/emotional, and motor skills needed on a daily basis. This information will help determine what specific skills John will need to be safe and successful in general physical education as well as suggestions for support and accommodations. Information from the ecological inventory and discrepancy analysis revealed that John can follow most routines independently. A peer could help John on the skills that he has difficulty with. John does have self-help problems, and he will need assistance changing into his physical education clothes. A peer can help John change his clothes in the locker room. The occupational therapist has suggested that John wear pants with an elastic waist and pullover shirts so that he can dress faster and more independently. It does not appear that John will need more time than his peers to change into his gym clothes. The discrepancy analysis also showed that John did not have any communication problems, although a peer might have to repeat more complex directions to him. John is a motivated, well-behaved learner who has no major behavior problems.

Who Will Teach John?

John will need some support in general physical education if he is going to be successful. However, he does not have behavior problems, and the general physical educator and peers without disabilities feel very comfortable with John. Therefore, the team decides that the physical therapist and adapted physical educator could provide information to the general physical educator and peers on how to work with John, how to position him, how to help him get dressed and undressed, and how to practice skills. These specialists can monitor how well the peers assist John and, eventually, become consultants, perhaps coming in to see John and discuss his program with the general physical educator at the beginning, middle, and end of each unit.

How Effective Was John's Program?

Ongoing evaluation is critical to determine if John is making progress toward his targeted goals, and if he isn't, why not. For example, John's APE teacher initially decided that a large whiffle ball bat was better for John than a regulation bat, but this bat proved to be too heavy and long for John. Because John's goals include tennis as well as softball, a lighter tennis racket was then used for striking in softball; this helped John to be much more successful. Similarly, John has begun to demonstrate slight rotation in his trunk when he throws the ball, and his program has been adjusted so that greater rotation during throwing is targeted.

John is making slower than expected progress on pushing his wheelchair to first base. Discussions with John, his peers, and his teachers as well as observations revealed that John has difficulty keeping his chair on the base path that causes him to run onto the infield grass. A peer is assigned to John to help him keep his chair straight, and extra work in physical education, in the classroom, and at home is implemented to help John push his chair with greater accuracy. Finally, it was determined that John was having difficulty getting out of his chair (even with assistance from a peer) to do push-ups and sit-ups during warm-ups. In fact, John takes so long to get out of his chair that he never gets a chance to do these exercises. A new modification was suggested in which John stays in his chair and works on pushing himself up out of his chair (actually, a more functional strength activity for John) and on sit-ups by isometrically contracting his abdominal muscles on one count and stretching his lower back by bending forward on the next count.

SUMMARY

Assessment is a critical aspect of the overall physical education program. Yet, physical educators often assess their students in such a way that the information they gain does not help them decide what to teach, how to teach it, where to teach it, or what supports are needed to teach it.

The ecological model of assessment provides specific information that is relevant to teaching students with disabilities in general physical education. The model includes six distinct but sequentially related phases of assessment.

Note that the checklists described in this chapter are not the only means available for determining programming decisions. They are simply samples of tools designed to assist the team in making informed decisions. Assessment also can take the form of informal observations and discussions with team members. Still, formal assessments should be used whenever a programmatic decision is made to ensure that the student is receiving the most appropriate program possible.

CHAPTER 6

Instructional Modifications

There was no doubt that DJ could be a challenge. Everyone at Henry Elementary School knew about DJ. In fact, several neighbors and even a local convenience store near Henry Elementary knew about DJ. DJ has autism, and ever since he started at Henry, he has been a ball of energy. Despite having a teacher assistant assigned to him, several times DJ has managed to escape school grounds and run through the neighborhood and into the convenience store. Now, as a rising third grader, DJ is only slightly more controllable than he was when he was a kindergartner.

Mrs. Garrison, the physical education teacher at Henry, was on maternity leave for the entire year, so Ms. Bowers has taken over. Ms. Bowers recently graduated from college, and she is eager to start her first job as an elementary physical education teacher. During the week of in-services, she met with DJ's special education teacher and teacher assistant, but Ms. Bowers did not seem to be too rattled by what she heard. Ms. Bowers worked with some children with Asperger's syndrome when she did her student teaching, and she was able to handle those children without any problem. But, Ms. Bowers was soon to find out that those children were nothing like DJ!

Ms. Bowers met DJ along with the third-grade class at 9:15 on a sunny, warm Monday morning. It did not take long for DJ to show his true colors. While Ms. Bowers was talking to the class about her rules for the gymnasium, DJ was rocking and making odd sounds. Then, while the students were sitting and listening to Ms. Bowers talk about all of the things they were going to do that year, DJ stood up and ran around the room, touching all of the pictures that Ms. Bowers so carefully put up the previous week. When Ms. Bowers asked DJ to return to the group, DJ decided he had enough and ran out the rear exit door onto the playground. Both DJ's teacher assistant and Ms. Bowers quickly ran after DJ and caught him on a swing.

DJ certainly was not like the children Ms. Bowers worked with during her student teaching. How was she going to communicate with DJ? How was she going to help him understand what he was supposed to do when he was in physical education? How was she going to get him to stop and start (she used the word "freeze" during her student teaching, but she was pretty sure that was not going to work with DJ)? Was DJ going to be able to handle large group activities, or would DJ do better with a partner and small group activities? Could DJ handle the guided discovery model of teaching that Ms. Bowers became so fond of during her student teaching, or would he need more direct instruction? Ms. Bowers recalled something she heard in her undergraduate adapted physical education class about picture schedules, but would that work with DJ?

Students with disabilities often can be safely and successfully included in general physical education without drastically changing the program or causing undue hardship for the general physical education teacher. However, the general physical educator (with support from the collaborative team) must be prepared to make modifications to how the class is organized, how information is presented, and how support personnel are utilized. The first step in accommodating students with disabilities in general physical education is to determine how you organize your class and present information. Once you understand how you teach, then you can make modifications to accommodate students with disabilities. Instructional modifications can make a tremendous difference between success and failure for students with special needs, and most modifications are relatively easy to implement. For example, students with visual impairments would not understand what to do in physical education if you used only demonstrations. The simple addition of verbal cues would allow these students to be successful.

The purpose of this chapter is to introduce a variety of instructional modifications to accommodate students with disabilities in general physical education. These instructional modifications (adapted in part from Eichstaedt & Lavay, 1992; Seaman, DePauw, Morton, & Omoto, 2003; and Sherrill, 2004) illustrate how subtle changes in how you organize your class and present information can better accommodate students with disabilities (see Table 6.1). The goal of these modifications is to allow all students, including students with disabilities, to participate in a general physical education setting that is safe and challenging and affords opportunities for success. Which techniques you choose to implement will depend on the particular needs of the student with disabilities, the age group you are working with, the skills you are focusing on, the make up of your class, availability of equipment and facilities, availability of support personnel, and your own preference. Although specific examples are provided, it is important that you focus on the general process of how to modify. If you understand the general process of creating and implementing appropriate instructional modifications, then you can apply this process to a variety of situations.

In many cases you will be able to individualize your presentation to meet the unique needs of students with disabilities without changing your presentation for the rest of the class. For example, you can demonstrate a particular skill to the group and have them begin the activity. You can then provide extra verbal cues and physical assistance to a student who has an intellectual disability so that he or she understands the task. Similarly, you can use a movement exploration approach when teaching body control skills and movement concepts to your first-grade class. At the same time, you can provide direct cues and physical assistance to a student who has autism who is having difficulty exploring his or her environment independently. In this way, you are making subtle additions to your instruction to accommodate the needs of students with disabilities.

Table 6.1. Instructional modifications that can facilitate inclusion

Class organization
- Teaching style
- Class format

Information presentation
- Verbal cues
- Demonstrations
- Level of methodology
- How students communicate with you
- Starting and stopping signals
- Time of day
- Duration
- Order of learning
- Size and nature of group
- Instructional setting
- Eliminating distractors
- Providing structure
- Level of difficulty
- Level of motivation

You should utilize peers and support personnel whenever possible when developing and implementing any modification. Chapter 3 reviews members of the collaborative team who can offer support, and Chapter 4 explains how these team members can be used to help determine which types of modifications are most appropriate for particular students. Peers and support persons also can be used to assist the general physical educator in implementing specific modifications. Support persons can include classmates, older peer tutors, volunteers, teacher assistants, or specialists. All of the instructional modifications outlined in the following section (as well as the curricular modifications outlined in Chapters 7 and 8) can be more effectively implemented if support personnel are in the gymnasium to assist the general physical educator. Even having a parent volunteer or the school custodian for a few minutes to provide individual assistance to a student with disabilities can make a tremendous difference. For example, a student who is learning how to walk with a walker might only need extra assistance to prevent him or her from falling. During warm-up activities when the class is moving about using different locomotor patterns, a parent volunteer can come assist this student, leaving the general physical educator free to focus on the larger group.

DETERMINING WHETHER A MODIFICATION IS APPROPRIATE

Not all instructional modifications are necessarily good. For example, perhaps you consider slowing down your speech when talking to the entire class to accommodate a child who is has trouble with understanding verbal directions. Although such an accommodation will help this one student, it would also highlight his differences. Furthermore, such an accommodation would waste the time of peers without disabilities, who before long would come to resent having this student with a disability in their class. Before implementing an instructional modification, it is important to determine whether a particular modification might have a negative effect on the student with disabilities, peers without disabilities, or the general physical educator. If the modification has a negative effect on any or all of these individuals, then it probably is not the most appropriate modification. Lieberman and Houston-Wilson (2002) created a checklist to help determine the appropriateness of modifications (see Table 6.2). In addition, the following four criteria should be used whenever considering a particular modification:

    1. *Does the change allow the student with disabilities to participate successfully yet still be chal-*

Table 6.2.　Adaptation checklist

- Is the adaptation safe?
- Does the modification maintain the concept of the game?
- Was the child included in the adaptation, and does he or she embrace the concept?
- Is the game still age-appropriate?
- Is the child still included successfully?
- Is the adaptation holding the child back and not affording a challenge?
- Does the adaptation still allow the child with a disability to work on either class goals or IEP goals?
- Does the adaptation alienate the child from the rest of the class?
- Other?

From Lieberman, L.J., & Houston-Wilson, C. (2002). *Strategies for inclusion: A handbook for physical educators* (p. 63). Champaign, IL: Human Kinetics; reprinted by permission.

lenged? Finding the balance between success and challenge can be very difficult, but it is critical for children with disabilities. Not providing necessary accommodations can cause the child with disabilities to be confused or to fail, but providing too much support makes the activity too easy for the child. For example, a child who is blind might simply need to have a peer help her find a throwing station, find the bucket of balls, and then face the correct direction. This student can then do the activity independently. There is no need for the teacher, teacher assistant, or peer to then provide physical assistance to this student.

2. *Does the modification make the setting unsafe for the student with a disability or for peers?* Safety should always be a top priority when determining accommodations. Often simple instructional accommodations can make the setting safer for all students. For example, an impulsive student often gets distracted by extraneous equipment such as mats stored to the side of the gym. He has been known to leave the group, climb on the mats, and then jump down before the teacher even knows he is gone. To accommodate this child (and others who have been distracted by the stack of mats), the teacher has stored the mats behind a curtain on a corner of the stage that is connected to the gym. Now this student is not distracted by the mats.

3. *Does the change affect peers without disabilities?* As noted, some accommodations can affect the entire class and should be used cautiously.

4. *Does the change cause an undue burden on the general physical education teacher?* One of the greatest concerns of general physical educators is that accommodations are going to be too difficult to implement. Yet, many modifications can be very simple to implement. For example, a student with an intellectual disability might not be able to under-

stand the teacher's verbal cue to stop. One simple solution might be to have peers near the child give him an extra cue or a hand signal. This simple accommodation allows the student to be successful without causing an undue hardship on the physical education teacher.

CLASS ORGANIZATION ACCOMMODATIONS

Teaching Style

Teaching style refers to the learning environment, the general routine, and how the lesson is presented to the class. Mosston and Ashworth (2002) described several different teaching styles commonly used by physical educators (see Table 6.3). They suggested these various teaching styles could be arranged across a spectrum that reflected decisions made by the teacher and by the student. On one side of the spectrum, teachers make all or most of the decisions for students regarding what to do, when to do it, how to do it, how long to do it, who (if anyone) to do it with, and with what equipment to do it with. These styles are referred to as *reproductive styles* because students are supposed to reproduce or replicate a particular movement pattern. For example, students learning how to shoot a basketball are given a basketball and asked to follow the step-by-step directions given by the teachers. The goal is for students to copy the teacher's pattern as accurately as possible (see Figure 6.1). The major advantage to these types of styles is that students know exactly what they are supposed to do and teachers are more apt to have control over the class. The major disadvantage

Table 6.3. Mosston and Ashworth's teaching styles

REPRODUCTIVE STYLES

Command	To learn to do the task accurately and within a short period of time, following all decisions made by the teacher. Invokes an immediate response to a stimulus. Performance is accurate and immediate. A previous model is replicated.
Practice/task	This style offers the learner time to work individually and privately and provides the teacher with time to offer the learner individual and private feedback. The essence: Time is provided for the learner to do a task individually and privately, and time is available for the teacher to give feedback to all learners, individually and privately.
Reciprocal	In this style learners work with a partner and offer feedback to the partner, based on criteria prepared by the teacher. The essence: Learners work in a partner relationship; receive immediate feedback; follow criteria for performance designed by the teacher; and develop feedback and socialization skills.
Self-check	The purposes of this style are to learn to do a task and to check one's own work. The essence: Learners do the task individually and privately and provide feedback for themselves by using criteria developed by the teacher.
Inclusion/invitation	The purposes of this style are to learn to select a level of a task one can perform and to offer a challenge to check one's own work. The essence: The same task is designed for different degrees of difficulty. Learners decide their entry point into the task and when to move to another level.

PRODUCTIVE STYLES

Guided discovery	The purpose of this style is to discover a concept by answering a sequence of questions presented by the teacher. The essence: The teacher, by asking a specific sequence of questions, systematically leads the learner to discover a predetermined target previously unknown to the learner.
Convergent discovery	Here learners discover the solution to a problem and learn to clarify an issue and arrive at a conclusion by employing logical procedures, reasoning, and critical thinking. The essence: Teachers present the question. The intrinsic structure of the task (question) requires a single correct answer. Learners engage in reasoning (and other cognitive operations) and seek to discover the single correct answer/solution.
Divergent discovery	The purpose of this style is to engage in producing (discovering) multiple responses to a single question. The essence: Learners are engaged in producing divergent responses to a single question. The intrinsic structure of the task (question) provides possible multiple responses. The multiple responses are assessed by the possible-feasible-desirable procedures, or by the verification "rules" of the given discipline.
Learner's individual designed program	The purpose of this style is to design, develop, and perform a series of tasks organized into a personal program with consultation with the teacher. The essence: The learner designs, develops, and performs a series of tasks organized into a personal program. The learner selects the topic, identifies the questions, collects data, discovers answers, and organizes the information. The teacher selects the general subject matter area.

Source: Mosston and Ashworth (2002).

of these styles is that students are more passive rather than active learners (they are told what they are supposed to learn rather than discovering what is important to learn) and students are less likely to be creative and discover unique and different ways to solve movement problems.

On the other end of the spectrum, students make most or all the decisions. Teaching styles on this side of the spectrum are referred to as *productive styles* because students are supposed to as produce or discover the most appropriate movement pattern to solve a particular movement pattern (see Figure 6.2). In some cases, there is no absolute right or wrong movement pattern, and students learn through discovery which pattern fits best with which particular situation. For example, a teacher might want her students to discover which throwing pattern is the best for bowling, for playing catch with a water balloon, and for throwing a basketball and softball. Obviously, each situation requires a unique movement pattern. Students who learn by actively experimenting and dis-

covering for themselves the most appropriate patterns tend to be more invested in their learning and retain what they have learned longer.

Some objectives in physical education can be achieved more effectively with certain styles. For example, accurate replication of a precise movement pattern such as learning how to grip and swing a golf club might best be taught through various reproductive styles. In contrast, creating different types of pyramids in a gymnastics unit or developing a repertoire of locomotor patterns and movement concepts might best be taught through various productive styles. In addition, some students will respond better to certain teaching styles. For example, children who need more structure and direction such as students with attention deficit-disorders, autism, or an intellectual disability do better in reproductive learning styles such as command or reciprocal styles. Students with unique movement abilities but typical intelligence such as children with cerebral palsy or muscular dystrophy may learn to compensate by

We are going to learn how to shoot a basketball today. Everyone has a basketball.

1. Okay, I want you to hold the basketball in your dominant hand (the one you use to write with).

2. Okay, now pretend that you are a waitress holding a tray of food and hold the ball with your palm facing upward. You want the ball to be even with and slightly to the side of your face. In this position, I also want you to make sure your elbow (the arm holding ball) is pointing toward your target.

3. Okay, now place your other hand gently to the side of the ball. This hand is used to keep the ball aiming straight and not falling out of your other hand.

4. Let's quickly check hand positions; your dominant hand is behind the ball with your elbow facing your target, and your nondominant hand is to the side of the ball.

5. Okay, stand so that you are facing your target (stomach facing target) with your feet about shoulder-width apart.

6. Now we are going to bend our knees slightly, maybe 3 or 4 inches.

7. This is going to be tricky: Straighten your knees and your arms at the same time to shoot your basketball. If you time this correctly, you will be able to shoot the ball from pretty far away.

8. One more important thing: When you finish shooting, your shooting arm should be straight, with your hand pointing toward the target. Try and let the ball roll off your fingertips by snapping your wrist like you are reaching into a cookie jar. Hold this position for a few seconds like a statue so you can really feel the correct follow-through.

9. Okay, get your ball and find a place near a wall on the gym to practice shooting. I want you to focus on the correct form of the skill like we just practiced. You are going to shoot the ball 10 times. This is not a race; I want you to practice the correct form.

10. Each time you prepare to shoot say the following cue words to yourself:
    a. Waitress
    b. Elbow
    c. Bend
    d. Jump
    e. Cookie

Figure 6.1. Scripts for the reproduction style of teaching: elementary school basketball shooting

discovering for themselves the best way to move. It is important to recognize the importance of the objectives of the activity and how each student learns. Then and only then can the teacher choose the most appropriate teaching style.

With inclusive physical education classes, it may be necessary to provide different teaching styles for different students in the same class. Teachers can still employ the general principles of one particular teaching style to help a particular student while using another style for the majority of the class. For example, in the context of a command style used to teach the overhand throwing pattern, a teacher could allow a student who has cerebral palsy to explore different throwing patterns (guided discovery) that meet his or her unique needs. Similarly, a teacher presenting body awareness concepts in a divergent (productive) style could give very specific information on what to do, how to do it, when to do it, and where to do it using a command (reproductive) style for a student with an intellectual disability. Again, the key is deciding on objectives for the class as well as individual students, how the class learns best as well as how individual students learn best, and which teaching style will be most effective.

Class Formats

Class formats refers to how members of the class are organized. Seaman et al. (2003) outlined seven class formats commonly used in physical education settings:

1. One-to-one instruction: one teacher or assistant for every student

2. Small groups: 3–10 students working together with a teacher or teacher assistant

3. Large group: entire class participating together as one group

4. Mixed group: using various class formats within one class period

5. Peer teaching or tutoring: using classmates or students without disabilities from other classes for teaching and assisting students with disabilities

6. Teaching stations: several areas in which smaller subsets of the class rotate through to practice skills

7. Self-paced independent work: each student works on individual goals at their own pace following directions on task cards or with guidance from teacher and teacher assistants

In addition, *cooperative learning* and *reverse mainstreaming* are class formats that can facilitate inclusion in physical education. The following briefly reviews selected class formats and how they can be used in inclusive physical education settings. Again, no class format is necessarily wrong or right. It is just important that the goals of your lesson match the learning needs of your class. You want to find the best class format to help your students (including the student with a disability) achieve your goals for the lesson.

Peer Tutoring

Peer tutoring involves students helping students. Because it can be difficult for a general physical education teacher to work individually with children with disabilities, peers without disabilities can be trained and then assigned to provide extra instruction and support. In addition, peer tutoring creates a setting in which the student with a disability receives one-to-one instruction and increased practice and reinforcement (Lieberman & Houston-Wilson, 2002). There are three basic peer tutoring models: classmates in the same class working together to provide each other feedback (e.g., Mosston & Ashworth's [2002] reciprocal style), classmates in the same class assigned to help a particular classmate with a disability, and older students from other classes coming to a general physical education class to help a particular student with disabilities (cross-age peer tutoring) (Block, Oberweiser, & Bain, 1995; Houston-Wilson, Lieberman, Horton, & Kasser, 1997; Lieberman & Houston-Wilson, 2002). Cross-age peer tutoring is a popular model. Some schools allow peer tutoring to count toward required community service. Other schools have peer tutoring classes in which students register for credit, go through training, and meet on a regular basis to discuss tutoring. In addition, these older peers may take their tutee out to high school events or out to eat pizza. One advantage is that older peers often are more reliable and focused than same-age classmates, and older peers often can handle more responsibility. In addition, some students with disabilities might behave better with an older peer rather than a classmate. However, it may be difficult to free up older students from their academic classes to come and help in physical education (see Houston-Wilson et al., 1997, for more information on cross-age peer tutors).

Having classmates in the same class provide extra instruction and support is the most cost-effective and easiest to set up. They are already in class and available, and classmates know each other and are familiar with the routine of that class. However, using classmates as peer tutors can cause problems. First and foremost, one has to be careful not to assign one classmate to work with a child with a disability for an entire class period. This would sacrifice the peer tutor's physical education experience. Rather, several children can be assigned to work with a child with a disability and then take turns assisting. Second, using classmates as peer tutors can change the dynamics of the relationship between children with and without disabilities. Peers who tutor can begin to view the child with a disability as

---

We are going to try lots of different ways to move. There is no right or wrong way; I want to see you be really creative when you move. Okay, here we go:

1. Show me how you can travel using any locomotor pattern you want; be sure to use different pathways (straight, curvy, or zigzag).

2. Now pick a different way to travel, and try different levels—high, medium, or low.

3. Now pick a different way to travel, and this time try different speeds—fast, medium, or slow.

4. Now pick a different way to travel, and this time you can be really loose and floppy or you can be really stiff and straight.

5. Now pick a different way to travel, and this time move really loudly or really softly with your feet.

6. Okay, now pick your favorite way to travel, and this time pick a pathway and a speed.

7. Okay, now pick your second favorite way to travel, using a different level and different force.

Middle/High School Soccer Unit

There are several different ways to dribble around your opponent in soccer, including a stop and go, faking to the left or right, and a double fake. There are many other ways. For the next several minutes I want you to choose a partner and try different ways of dribbling around your partner. There is no right or wrong way; the goal is to find a few different ways that work best for you. Be creative.

Figure 6.2.   Script for the production style of teaching: lower elementary school locomotor patterns and movement concepts

someone who needs help rather than as a classmate (Block, 1999). This can be prevented in two ways. First, all children can be partnered in a classwide peer tutoring session (Block et al., 1995; Houston-Wilson et al., 1997). After several minutes with one partner, students can switch and work with another partner. Second, no one classmate is assigned to a specific student with a disability but, rather, the entire class is cued to help all children who may need extra assistance. For example, a teacher might say to the class, "Practice dribbling your ball while walking forward, backward, or sideways. If you see a friend who drops the ball or who is having trouble, you may ask this person if he or she needs some help." This way the child with a disability is not the only student who is targeted for assistance.

Regardless of the model used, training peer tutors is critical for success (Lieberman & Houston-Wilson, 2002). Block (1995b), Houston-Wilson et al. (1997), and Lieberman and Houston-Wilson (2002), suggested the following be included in a peer tutoring training program: disability awareness, communication techniques, teaching techniques, reinforce-ment techniques including how to provide specific feedback, skill analysis including what components of a skill to look at, and how to collect ongoing data. Training can be formal such as a partner club (Eichstaedt & Lavay, 1992; Sutherland, 1999) or informal and part of the general physical education class. Training can take several days or can be conducted in two or three general physical education class sessions (see Chapter 9; Lieberman & Houston-Wilson, 2002).

One way to simplify training and provide ongoing information for peer tutors is to use task sheets. Task sheets provide information to help peer tutors be better at their duties. Task sheets include information such as the components of the skill that the student should work on, a picture of the component, reminders of how to communicate with the child and deal with behaviors, suggestions for how to give feedback, and a place to record data (Block, 1995b; Houston-Wilson et al., 1997; see Figure 6.3). Peer tutoring has been effective in several different inclusive physical education settings (see Houston-Wilson et al., 1997; Lieberman et al., 2000; Lieberman et al., 1997; Webster, 1987).

Peer Tutoring Task Sheet

Student: _____   Peer tutor: _____

Student's goals: _____

_____

_____

Directions for the peer tutor: Circle the type of prompt, reinforcement, or method of communication used with the tutee. Then watch the tutee perform the skill while you focus on and comment on one component of the skill. Give the tutee a plus (+) if he or she performs the component correctly and a minus (–) if he or she does not perform the skill component correctly. After five trials, switch roles with the tutee so that you are the tutee and your partner is the tutor.

Types of prompts	Types of reinforcers	Communication
Natural	"Good job"	Talking
Verbal	High five	Show how
Gestures	Pat on the back	Pictures
Demonstration	Shooting baskets	
Partial physical	Token	
Physical assistance	Food	

Components of skill

Dominant hand above nondominant hand	__ __ __ __ __ __ __ __
Side orientation	__ __ __ __ __ __ __ __
Weight transfer	__ __ __ __ __ __ __ __
Follow-through	__ __ __ __ __ __ __ __

Figure 6.3. Peer tutoring task sheet.

Teaching Stations

Task teaching (also called station learning or learning centers) is a simple and popular way to organize inclusive general physical education classes (Block et al., 1995; Graham, Holt-Hale, & Parker, 2004). The teacher sets up three or more places around the gym with various activities. Children are assigned to a station and rotate to a different station when they have completed certain activities or when the teacher signals the group to move to a new station. For example, a teacher might set up hierarchical or progressive stations in which students are placed according to level of skill. As they progress in skill level or master some aspect of a skill, they move to a new station. Alternately, a teacher might simply assign groups of five to seven students to a station. After 3–5 minutes, the teacher signals students to rotate to the next station.

Stations can be independent, unrelated activities (e.g., jumping rope, throwing and catching, sit-ups/push-ups, tumbling) or can revolve around a theme (e.g., throwing at targets, throwing to a partner, throwing into a curtain, throwing over a net). In either case, there should be multiple challenges at each station to accommodate the varying abilities of children in the class. For example, the teacher might set up a kicking station in which students stand at different distances from the target, use different size balls, and have different size targets to hit. This way, each child who comes to the station is challenged at his or her own level and has the opportunity to be successful. In addition, the teacher might have a list of different ways to perform the skill to make it more challenging (e.g., at the kicking station: use your opposite leg, try to kick a moving ball, or try and chip the ball into the air). Again, this allows more skilled students to work at the same station as less skilled students.

Because stations accommodate children of different abilities, they are ideal for including children with disabilities. For example, a 12-year-old girl with severe cerebral palsy is in a swimming class at her middle school. Some students in the class swim year-round; others can swim but need work on stroke refinement; others are learning basic strokes. In order to accommodate the range of abilities in this class, the physical education teacher has set up different stations for students in the class to work on the following skills: butterfly/breaststroke, backstroke, free style, and diving. The physical education teacher directly supervises the diving station while she watches the other stations from afar. A lifeguard also watches the swimmers. The student with cerebral palsy has a teacher assistant helping her. Students were previously tested on the various strokes and know what components of each stroke on which to focus. The teacher divides the class, sending seven students to each station. At the station is a list of activities including swimming a distance in a given period of time, swimming a particular distance using a particular stroke, and swimming using a kickboard focusing on one or two aspects of the stroke (see Figure 6.4). Each student knows to

---

Breaststroke/Butterfly Station

Practice your personal challenge based on your pretest results (which are posted in the gym). When you have mastered a particular challenge, move to the next challenge. Help and encourage peers.

Challenges

_____ Lie on stomach and lift head out of water. Repeat several times.

_____ Hold onto gutter and perform correct leg movements for breaststroke 20 times.

_____ Hold onto kickboard and perform correct leg movements for breaststroke 20 times.

_____ Place kickboard under stomach, and practice correct arm movements for breaststroke 20 times.

_____ Place kickboard under stomach, and practice correct breathing pattern for breaststroke 20 times.

_____ Place kickboard under stomach, and practice correct arm and breathing pattern for breaststroke 20 times.

_____ Without kickboard, do complete breaststroke for five strokes.

_____ Do complete breaststroke for 10 strokes.

_____ Do breaststroke for length of pool.

_____ Do breaststroke for length of pool as fast as you can. Record your time: _____. Rest and repeat.

_____ Students on swim team: Do complete butterfly for length of pool as fast as you can. Record your time: _____. Rest and repeat.

Figure 6.4. Breaststroke/butterfly station.

work independently on his or her own tasks, but students also are encouraged to help each other improve their strokes. For example, while resting after doing the butterfly for 25 meters in less than 2 minutes, a student watches and gives feedback to another student who is trying to gather enough courage to put his face in the water during the breaststroke. At the same station, the child with cerebral palsy is learning how to lie on her stomach and lift her head out of the water to clear an airway. A teacher assistant helps her do this task while a peer provides encouragement as he rests after his swim.

Cooperative Learning

Another class format option is *cooperative learning* in which students work together to accomplish shared goals. Group goals can only be accomplished if individual students in the group work together (Grineski, 1996; Johnson & Johnson, 1999). In cooperative learning, students are instructed to learn the assigned information and to make sure that all members of the group master the information (at their level). For example, each child in the group must perform a set number of push-ups for the team to reach its shared goal of 180 push-ups. One girl who is very strong and who is trying to break the school record is trying to do 100 push-ups. Another child in the group usually can do 35 push-ups, two other children in the group are trying to do 20 push-ups, and a child with an intellectual disability is trying to do 5 push-ups. In order for the team to be successful, each person must meet his or her individual goal. Members of the team encourage each other to reach these goals that, in turn, help the team reach their shared goals.

Often individuals in the group are given specific jobs or tasks that contribute to goal attainment. Cooperative learning encourages students to work together, help each other, and constantly evaluate each member's progress toward individual and group goals. For example, in a gymnastics unit a team of four members must balance so that a total of two feet, two hands, two elbows, and two knees touch the ground. The team, which includes a child who is blind and has poor balance, together decides the best way to solve the challenge. After much discussion and experimentation, the team comes up with the following solution: The child who is blind stands on two feet and holds the ankles of another student who is standing on her hands (she needs the support or she will fall). Another student gets on his elbows and knees (feet up) while a fourth student sits on his back. The student sitting on his back helps balance the person standing on his hands. The only way this team could be successful was for everyone to work together.

For cooperative learning to be effective, students must perceive that they are positively linked to other students in their group and that each member can and must contribute to the success of the group. In addition, each member of the group must understand his or her role in the group (Grineski, 1996). Less skilled students, including students with disabilities, could be perceived to be the weak link in the group if all members believe that they must each perform the same task. However, if the group understands that each member has a unique task that maximizes his or her skills and contributes to the group goal, then the method will be effective. For example, a group of third graders is working on the skill of striking. The teacher divides the class into small groups of three to four students. The cooperative task for each group is to hit 50 paper and yarn balls across the gym with each member hitting each ball only once, with each student working on one key aspect of a skillful striking pattern. Because no student can hit the ball across the gym by him- or herself, only through group cooperation can the ball get across the gym. In Group A, a skilled student begins the process by hitting a pitched ball as far as possible (pitched by one of the group members). This student is working on timing and hitting the ball up into the air. A less skilled group member then walks to where the ball lands, picks up the ball, places it on a batting tee, then hits the ball forward as far as possible. This student is working on shifting weight and stepping, and the skilled student provides feedback to the less skilled student. Finally, the tee is moved to where the ball landed and is placed on the tee for a student who is blind. This student is working on hitting the ball off the tee with his hand using proper preparatory position, stepping, and using a level swing. Both the skilled and non-skilled students help position the student and provide him with feedback. The process is repeated until the group hits 50 balls. The group must work together to accomplish its goal, and each student must contribute in his or her own way. In addition, it benefits the group if each member improves his or her skill level. If a group member uses better form, then the ball will be hit farther and, in turn, help the team accomplish its goal (see Grineski, 1996, for more details on cooperative learning in physical education; see Ellmo & Graser, 1995; Grineski, 1996; & Orlick, 1982, for excellent examples of cooperative learning activities for physical education).

Reverse Mainstreaming

In some situations it makes sense to have a self-contained physical education class comprised of just students with disabilities. In these situations, interactions with peers without disabilities can be facilitated through *reverse mainstreaming*. In this format several students without disabilities are included in a class of children who have disabilities. Students without disabilities are not peer tutors but rather participate in the activity alongside students with disabilities (Dunn, 1997). Students without disabilities provide good role models for students with disabilities and allow for team sports and games that require more players. For example, once a week an adapted physical education class of seven middle school students with moderate intellectual disabilities invites seven middle school students without disabilities to participate with them in physical education. The current unit in both adapted physical education and general physical education is soccer. In reverse mainstreaming, all of the students begin with a warm-up activity. Students without disabilities tend to use better form in stretching, providing a good model for their peers with intellectual disabilities. Similarly, peers without disabilities provide a good pace during warm-up laps. Following warm-ups, students pair up (student with and without an intellectual disability paired together) to work on various soccer skills. Peers without disabilities can pass the ball directly to students with intellectual disabilities at a slow speed so that the student with an intellectual disability can practice trapping the ball (when students with an intellectual disability are paired together in the adapted class they have trouble accurately passing the ball back and forth to each other). The class culminates with a modified game of seven-on-seven soccer. (It is difficult playing soccer with a class of only seven students.) Rules are modified so both students with and without intellectual disabilities are challenged (students without disabilities have to kick the ball with their opposite foot, cannot kick the ball in the air, and cannot use their hands if they are playing goalie). Students with intellectual disabilities find the game more motivating and challenging when peers without disabilities participate, and they can be successful because of the smaller game size and rule modifications.

Using Multiple Formats

The best format for any situation will vary, based on numbers, attitudes, and types of students with and without disabilities; type and flexibility of the facility; and availability of resources. In most situations, a combination of the class formats is most effective. For example, a student with severe disabilities can be included in a high school physical education class during a basketball unit in which the teacher utilizes a combination of peer tutors, stations, self-paced learning, and large-group instruction. Students begin the class by following the teacher through various warm-up activities (*large group*). The student with severe disabilities is assisted in these warm-up activities by his physical therapist who works on specific stretching and strengthening activities. Following warm-ups, students rotate through several basketball *stations* at their own pace, working on tasks geared to their ability level. Students choose which station to go to, but they can only stay at one station for 10 minutes and no more than seven students can be at any one station at one time. All students have a task card with a hierarchy of tasks that they move through at their own pace. In order to move to the next level on a hierarchy, the student must have another student confirm that he or she can perform the skill in four of five trials (*stations/self-paced learning*). Peers who chose the same station as the child with disabilities are cued by the teacher to help this child as needed (*peer tutoring*).

The culminating activity for the day is a game of basketball. Skilled students go with a class leader and play regulation games of five-on-five basketball, learning set plays and strategies (*small group*). Less skilled students, including the student with severe disabilities, go with the general physical education teacher who organizes a modified game. In today's version of the game, the defense must play a passive zone defense (cannot steal the ball unless it is passed directly to them). In addition, every player on the offensive team must touch the ball one time before a player can shoot, and students can get points for hitting the backboard (1 point), rim (2 points), or making a basket (3 points). Students who cannot reach a 10-foot basket can shoot at an 8-foot target on the wall, and the student with severe disabilities can score by pushing the ball off of his lap tray into a box on the floor with assistance from a peer.

ACCOMMODATIONS IN HOW INFORMATION IS PRESENTED

Verbal Instructions

Verbal instructions refer to the length and complexity of commands or verbal challenges used to convey information to the class. Students with autism or intellectual disabilities who cannot understand complex commands or students with hearing impairments who cannot hear verbal commands may need to have instruction delivery modified. Seaman et al. (2003) suggested the following ways in which instructions can be modified for students who have difficulty understanding verbal language: simplify words used, use single-meaning words (e.g., run to the base versus go to the base), give only one command at a time, ask the student to repeat the command before performing it, say the command and then demonstrate the task and or physically assist the student.

Although these modifications might be helpful for a student with a language disorder, such modifications might not be needed for the majority of students in the class. These modifications can still be implemented without changing the way instruction is delivered to the rest of the students. For example, a teacher might give complex verbal directions including information about abstract strategies and team concepts to the class. When the teacher is finished instructing the class, a peer could repeat key directions to the student with an intellectual disability. The peer can demonstrate some strategies and concepts, while abstract concepts can be translated into more concrete examples or skipped altogether. Similarly, a peer can demonstrate and mimic directions to a student with a hearing impairment after the teacher presents verbal directions to the class.

Demonstrations

Demonstrations involve who gives demonstrations, how many are given, how often they are given, and the best location for a demonstration. Again, the teacher can provide a level of demonstration that is appropriate for the majority of the class while presenting extra demonstrations (or having a peer present extra demonstrations) for students with special needs. Modifications to demonstrations could be as simple as having students with poor vision stand close to the teacher. For students with intellectual disabilities, the teacher might need to highlight key aspects of the demonstration or have a peer repeat the demonstration several times. For example, the teacher could demonstrate the starting preparatory position, backswing, trunk rotation, and follow-through for the overhand throw to the class. For a student with an intellectual disability just learning to throw, the teacher (or peer) might repeat the demonstration, focusing on just one aspect (stepping with opposite foot) so that this student knows what component he should focus on.

Visual Supports

Visual supports refer to any kind of visual prompt that helps a student understand and interact with his or her world. Visual supports are particularly helpful for students with autism (Bondy & Frost, 2001; Savner & Myles, 2000). Visual supports help students understand and follow rules, know what is happening in their day, understand how to complete an assignment and when an assignment is complete,

transition from one activity to another, and make choices about what they want. Visual support also allows the student to become more independent (Bondy & Frost, 2001; Savner & Myles, 2000). There are many different kinds of visual supports. Savner and Myles (2000) suggested four major types of visual supports for students who have difficulty with auditory cues:

1. *Visual schedules:* Visual schedules set out a plan for the entire day, for part of the day, or for a particular class (e.g., for physical education). The amount of time as well as the number of activities placed on a schedule varies from student to student. For example, one child might have a daily picture schedule that includes pictures of people and places he will go during the day. Pictures include his classroom teacher and her classroom, the music teacher and her room, the physical education teacher and the gymnasium, the cafeteria worker and the cafeteria, the playground, the occupational therapist and the therapy room, and the bus driver and the bus. By having visual cues to remind the child of all of the activities during the day, he will be less likely to get confused and upset during transitions. New activities such as field trips or assemblies can easily be added to the child's picture schedule each morning.

   Picture schedules also can be used for a particular class period such as physical education (see Figure 6.5). For example, a student with autism is given a new physical education schedule each day. Before class, the general physical educator places select pictures on a special clipboard. The pictures show the child doing various activities in the order in which these activities will be presented during physical education that day. Every time an activity is completed, the student is prompted to point to the next picture on the schedule. This type of schedule helps this child understand the physical education activities of the day.

2. *Information sharers:* Many children with disabilities cannot answer the question, "What did you do in school today?" Information sharers help these children communicate with parents and siblings. Information sharers also prompt verbal students to answer and elaborate on questions about the day. For example, when a student returns from physical education class, the classroom teacher asks, "What did you do in physical education today?" The student has a picture of a ball, which prompts him or her to say, "Played volleyball." Information sharers also can be used for safety purposes.

Figure 6.5. Sample picture schedule for physical education. Once activities have been completed, they would be moved to the "FINISH" column.

3. *Checklists/organizers:* Checklists and organizers break skills into manageable steps so that the student can complete them. Many students can complete the beginning or end of a task or perhaps one or two steps in the middle of a task. Checklists and organizers promote independence by prompting the student to remember and then execute the various steps needed to complete a task. For example, a checklist in physical education might have pictures of the 10 stretching and strengthening activities that all students are expected to do upon arrival into the gym. Checklists also can be used to help middle and high school students become more independent in the locker room by visually reminding them exactly what to do.

4. *Visual behavioral supports:* Visual behavioral supports remind the student of behavior expectations. Visual behavioral support systems usually include the expected behaviors, such as how to act in physical education, along with reinforcement. For example, Jessica has trouble sitting and keeping her voice down when the teacher takes role at the beginning of her middle

school physical education class. After Jessica dresses out and sits in her squad, she looks at her visual behavioral support (a file card she brings with her to physical education). The card has a small picture of Jessica sitting nicely in her squad. It also has a picture of a person with their mouth closed. A smiley face reminds Jessica that if she sits quietly in her squad during role, she will earn a star. Jessica has learned that if she receives five stars during physical education, she can help the general physical educator put the equipment away (a favorite activity of Jessica's). Again, this visual behavior prompt allows Jessica to be more independent in general physical education and more responsible for her own behavior.

Level of Methodology

Sometimes it is important to decide whether you need a completely different way to communicate and instruct particular students. *Levels of methodology* refer to the various methods a teacher can use to present information and communicate with a student. Some students will respond quite well to verbal cues given to the class, while other students may need extra verbal cues, demonstrations, visual cues, or even physical assistance to understand directions and perform skills correctly.

One consideration when instructing students is level of cues presented or prompt hierarchy (Snell & Brown, 2000). Prompts are cues given to students. Instructional prompts range from nonintrusive prompts such as a student following natural cues in the environment (student sees peers stand up and run around the gym, and the student quickly stands up and runs with peers) to intrusive prompts such as physical assistance (physically helping student hold a bat and then strike a ball off a tee) (see Figure 6.6). Each type of prompt can be further broken down into levels. For example, physical assistance can vary, from physical assistance in which the student passively allows the teacher to help him to physical assistance in which the student actively tries to perform movement. Ideally, students will follow natural prompts in the environment, but many

Responds to natural cues in environment
Responds to verbal cues
Responds to pointing and gestures
Uses picture cards
Requires demonstration
Requires physical prompting

Figure 6.6. Least to most intrusive level of prompts

students with disabilities will need extra prompts to understand directions and instruction. Students with severe intellectual disabilities or autism often benefit from a multisensory approach in which several types of prompts are provided (e.g., verbal cue, then demonstration, then physical assistance).

Speech therapists or special education teachers can help physical educators decide which level of prompt is needed for a student to understand directions and instruction. However, most physical educators will quickly discover on their own how best to prompt students.

If it is clear that a student will not be able to respond to a verbal cue or demonstration, then the physical educator or tutor should start with physical prompts or assistance so that the student will not fail the task or be confused (Snell & Brown, 2000). For example, if you know one of your students with cerebral palsy needs physical assistance to toss a ball, it makes no sense to first give him a verbal cue, then point, then gesture, then demonstrate, then touch, and finally physically assist the student. Time was wasted, and the student experienced failure for five of six cues. Because the ultimate goal is to have students follow natural cues whenever possible, however, an attempt should be made to systematically fade extra prompts during the course of the program. For example, students with intellectual disabilities can learn to focus on natural cues in the locker room at the YMCA for locating an empty locker and walking to the weight room independently.

How Students Communicate

Another consideration when instructing students with disabilities is to determine *how they will communicate* with you. Many students with disabilities will be able to respond using clear, concise speech. Some students will speak in one- or two-word sentences, other students may communicate with gestures or signs, others may communicate by pointing to pictures, and still others may use sophisticated computer-assisted speech synthesizers or keyboards. Regardless of how a student communicates, it is important that you understand each student's mode of communication. Not being able to communicate can be frustrating for the student and can sometimes lead to behavioral outbursts.

Starting and Stopping Signals

It is also important to find the best way to give *starting and stopping commands* to students who do not respond to traditional signals. Students with hearing impairments may need hand signals, and students with autism or severe intellectual disabilities may need physical assistance to stop. Accommodating a student who needs different starting and stopping signals does not mean the general physical educator has to change what she has used successfully for years. The general physical educator can use one cue for the entire class and also provide hand signals or physical assistance to students who need extra cues. For example, the teacher could use a whistle to indicate when to stop and start for fouls and throw-ins in a soccer game during a high school physical education class. When students hear the whistle, they know to locate the student with a hearing impairment and raise their hand (indicating to stop or start).

Time

Time of day or season that a child is going to be included is another important consideration. Some students who receive medication (e.g., children with attention-deficit disorder) might be placed in a general physical education class that meets in the afternoon, after they have taken their medicine. Students who tire might be better served in a morning general physical education class. Changing the time a student goes to physical education can be tricky, so whenever possible such modifications should be decided before school starts.

Duration

Duration refers to how much time a student will be engaged in an activity. Duration can include number of weeks for a particular unit, number of physical education periods per week, how long the student will participate each period, or how long the student will be engaged in each activity during the period. For example, a student with an intellectual disability might need 6 weeks to reach his goals, while her peers without disabilities need only 3 weeks. A student with an attention-deficit disorder can tolerate a station or activity for 1 minute, while his peers are expected to stay at a station for up to 5 minutes. A student with an intellectual disability might need to stay at that station for 10 minutes. The key is to be flexible in allowing some students with disabilities to come to physical education more often than most other students in the school or allowing some students to participate in only some of the activities during general physical education.

Duration also refers to how long a student will stay in a game situation. A student with asthma or a heart condition might play the game for 2 minutes, then rest on the sideline for 2 minutes. Although many programs are locked into daily schedules, adjustments can usually be made to accommodate students with special needs. For example, a student with an intellectual disability has a goal of learning the skills needed to play softball. The softball unit in general physical education lasts 3 weeks, during which time this student has not acquired the targeted softball skills. While the class moves to volleyball, this student can continue to work on softball skills with a peer who already has good volleyball skills (does not need extra practice in volleyball), with another student who also needs extra work on softball, with a cross-age peer tutor, with a teacher assistant, or with a volunteer. The student can still do warm-ups with the general class.

Order of Learning

Order of learning refers to the sequence in which various aspects of a particular skill are presented. Most teachers teach skills such as the sidearm strike in tennis by teaching the whole task in order from first to last components (preparatory position, step, swing, and follow-through). A student with a learning disability, however, might need to focus on one aspect of the movement at a time: first learning to step and swing, then learning the preparatory position, and finally learning the follow-through. Other students might benefit from even smaller skill steps. The teacher can present the whole task to the majority of the class, then change the order of learning or break down the skill more slowly (or have a peer do this) for a student with a learning disability.

Size and Nature of Group

Size and nature of the group refer to how many students will be at a station or in a game as well as the make-up of the group. Students who have trouble working in large groups can be placed in smaller groups during station work. Students with an intellectual disability who are slower and less skilled than their peers can be placed on a team that has more players than their opponent's team. Similarly, the teacher can select teams so that each team has an equal number of skilled, average, and unskilled players. Players of similar ability can then be paired up against each other in the game (e.g., guarding each other in a game of soccer or basketball). The teacher should select teams so that students with lower abilities (or disabilities) are not always picked last. Also, skilled students should be encouraged to use appropriate sportsmanship during the selection process (see Chapter 8 for more detail on modifying games).

Instructional Setting

Instructional setting refers to where the class is conducted, including indoors or outdoors, temperature, lighting, floor surface, boundaries, and markings on walls. Most teachers cannot make major changes to their instructional setting to accommodate students with special needs, but there are some simple modifications that can make a setting more accommodating. For example, cones or bright colored tape can be used to accentuate boundaries. Carpet squares or small tumbling mats can cushion falls. Carpet squares, poly spots, or hula hoops can be used to mark a student's personal space. Partitions can be used to block off parts of the gym for students who are easily distracted.

Eliminate Distractions

It is important to reduce or eliminate *extraneous noises, persons, or objects* so that the student can focus on instruction. Many students are easily distracted and have difficulty focusing on important instructional cues. For example, balloons and cones set up in the environment for a later activity might be extremely distracting for a student with an intellectual disability or attention-deficit disorder. To help students focus, position them so that they are facing away from distractions. Also, avoid setting up equipment until it is actually to be used. Store equipment in a barrel, box, or bag or cover it with a tarp until they are needed. In many elementary schools, gymnasia double as the cafeteria, and teachers and students walk through the gym/cafeteria in the morning to give the lunch count to cafeteria workers. Students with attention-deficit disorders can be placed in a physical education class later in the day when no one walks through. Similarly, some gyms have stages where music or drama classes are conducted. Schedules should be established so that no other classes are in session. Finally, teachers can help students focus on the task at hand by providing extra cues and reinforcement and by making instruction more enticing. For example, using music during warm-ups can drown out the sound of noisy distractions in the environment. When the music is turned off and the environment is relatively quiet, the teacher can then give directions. Whistling and loud clapping are other ways to return a student's focus to the teacher.

Provide Structure or Routine

All children learn best and are most cooperative when they know the class routine and what is expected of them. Although most students can handle

1. Do 10 toe-touches.

2. Lie on back, bend knees, fold arms in front of chest, and do 10 sit-ups.

3. Roll over on stomach, put hands to either side of face, bend knees, cross left foot over right foot, and do 10 modified push-ups.

4. Roll over and sit on bottom, bring bottoms of feet together so that they touch, hold onto ankles, try to push knees toward ground, and hold for 10 seconds.

5. Stay in sitting position, stretch both legs in front, keeping legs together and legs straight. Start with hands on knees and slowly crawl hands down toward ankles. Stop when you feel a good stretch, and hold for 10 seconds.

6. Stand up, place hands on hips, keep body straight, and turn from side to side 10 times.

7. Stand up, gently roll head in a circle so that you are looking down at your toes, then to the side, then up to the ceiling, then to the other side, and then back down to the ground again. Do this 5 times.

Figure 6.7.   Sample checklist for a child with high-functioning autism during warm-up

occasional changes to *class structure or routines,* change can lead to confusion, withdrawal, misbehavior, and even self-abuse in some children with disabilities. It is important that class structure remain as constant as possible for students who do not do well with change. Even if you do not have a routine for most students, it is important to establish set routines for the students with disabilities. Even if most students do different warm-ups every day, establishing a set warm-up routine for a student with autism will make it less likely that he is confused or upset (see Figure 6.7).

Level of Difficulty or Complexity

Complexity refers to the difficulty level of skills, formations, game rules and game strategies. Again, a teacher can vary the level of difficulty for particular students without changing the difficulty level for the rest of the students. For example, a team might play a complex zone defense in basketball, but all a student with intellectual disabilities needs to know is to stand on a poly spot and keep his hands up. Similarly, most students can work on stepping, rotating their body, and lagging their arm in the overhand throw, while a student just learning how to throw can work on simply getting his arm into an overhand position while throwing. Specific examples of how to modify skills and group activities are presented in Chapter 8.

Levels of Motivation

Level of motivation refers to how much and types of reinforcement particular students need to be moti-

vated to participate in physical education activities. Many students without disabilities are intrinsically motivated to participate in physical education. Students who know that they have difficulty in physical education might need more encouragement, such as verbal praise, extra privileges, free play, tokens, or even tangible reinforcers such as food. For example, a student with a severe emotional disturbance can be reinforced for staying engaged in a physical fitness activity for 10 minutes by allowing the student to do an activity he really likes for a few minutes after the fitness activity.

SUMMARY

Students with disabilities often have difficulty understanding what to do in general physical education classes. Yet, simple modifications to how the class is organized and how information is presented can make a tremendous difference in the success of these students. Many of the instructional modifications outlined in this chapter can help children without disabilities, too, who will respond to accommodations in class formats. Similarly, providing a variety of cues and stopping and starting signals and eliminating distractions will help all students understand what is expected of them in general physical education.

As outlined in this chapter, most instructional accommodations can be implemented without affecting the program for children without disabilities. However, remember that any changes that are made to accommodate a student with a disability should be viewed cautiously and should meet the four criteria.

Curricular Modifications

harmaine is a 7-year-old girl who loves physical education, but she and her elementary physical education teacher Mr. Harper know that physical education can be a real challenge for Charmaine. Charmaine has spastic, diplegic cerebral palsy (stiff in all four limbs but more in her legs than her arms). She comes to general physical education in a walker that she uses fairly competently. She does not have any cognitive impairments, so she understands exactly what she is supposed to do, but her body is not able to respond. Specifically, Charmaine has trouble in games and activities that require speed (tagging games), accuracy and coordination (catching and throwing activities and jumping rope), and strength (throwing a ball across the gym, kicking a ball hard, shooting a ball up into a basket). In other words, Charmaine has challenges with pretty much every general physical education activity. Mr. Harper really wants to help Charmaine, but he is stumped. Kindergarten and first-grade physical education activities were fairly easy to modify, but the kids in second grade are bigger, faster, and more skilled. Mr. Harper worries that Charmaine will not be successful without major modifications to the activities and games in general physical education; he also worries that these major modifications are going to "water down" the program for his students without disabilities. What can Mr. Harper do?

Nick is a ninth grader at Middlebrooke High School. He enjoys listening to his favorite college teams–the University of Maryland football and basketball teams–on the radio. He also attends as many games as he can with his dad providing play-by-play and Nick reacting intently to the sounds of the crowd. Nick relies on his listening skills because Nick is blind. Nick lost his sight gradually due to an optic nerve disease and now is almost totally blind. Nick loves sports, but he needs a lot of modifications to be successful when participating in sports in physical education. High school will be a real challenge for Nick and his physical education teachers. Clearly, activities that use balls (soccer, volleyball, basketball, football) are going to be the greatest challenge for Nick. Are there ways that Nick's physical education teachers can modify these activities so that Nick can participate in skill work and lead-up games? What types of modifications would work for someone like Nick?

Curricular modifications refer to any adaptation made to the general education curriculum in order to prevent a mismatch between a student's skill level and the lesson content and promote student success in learning targeted IEP objectives and appropriate skills (Block & Vogler, 1994; Giangreco & Putnam, 1991). Curricular modifications might include changes to equipment and changes to the rules of games.

As with instructional modifications, some modifications will only affect the student with a disability (e.g., lowering a basket, making a target larger); other modifications may affect the entire class (e.g., having all students do a simpler locomotor pattern during warm-ups). Changes that affect the group should be implemented cautiously to avoid negatively affecting the program for students without disabilities. However, as with instructional modifications, some changes that affect the entire class can be positive. For example, giving all students choices in the equipment they use and offering multiple activities not only can help less skilled students be more successful but also still challenge more skilled students.

The purpose of this chapter is to introduce a variety of curricular modifications that can be used to accommodate students with disabilities in general physical education. These modifications have been organized as follows: a general model for making curricular modifications for all students, specific curricular modifications for students with functional impairments, and modifications for children with specific types of disabilities. The goal of all of these modifications is to allow all students to participate in a general physical education program that is safe and challenging and affords opportunities for success. As noted in the previous chapter, which techniques you choose depends on the particular needs of the student with disabilities, the age group of your students, the skills you are focusing on, the make-up of your class, availability of equipment and facilities, availability of support personnel, and your own preference. Although specific examples are provided, it is important that you focus on the general process of how to modify your physical education programs. If you can understand the general process of creating and implementing appropriate modifications, then you can apply this process to a variety of situations.

DETERMINING WHETHER A CURRICULAR MODIFICATION IS APPROPRIATE

Not all modifications are necessarily appropriate for a particular child with a disability in a particular situation. One simple way to determine which modification to use is to ask what effect that modification will have on the student with disabilities, peers, and the general physical educator. If the modification has a negative effect on any or all of these individuals, then it probably is not the most appropriate modification. The following four criteria as well as the checklist in Table 6.2 in Chapter 6 should be used whenever considering a curricular modification. If the modification does not meet these standards, then alternative modifications should be considered.

1. *Does the change allow the student with disabilities to participate successfully yet still be challenged?* For example, a student with intellectual disabilities might not be able to kick a regulation soccer ball back and forth with a partner. A simple modification might allow the student and his partner to kick a large playground ball or volleyball trainer back and forth with his partner. Such a modification allows the student to be successful yet challenges him at his level.

2. *Does the modification make the setting unsafe for the student with a disability or for peers?* For example, you want to include a student who uses a wheelchair at a soccer dribbling station, but you are worried other children will bump into this child. One solution is to mark off an area with cones for the child who uses a wheelchair. You also should remind peers at the beginning of the class and several times during the class to be careful around the student.

3. *Does the change affect peers without disabilities?* Making all targets larger and making all students stand closer to the targets is unnecessary and unfair for all students. Similarly, making all children walk during warm-ups to accommodate a child who uses a walker does not make sense. Rather, make accommodations that only affect the student with disabilities. For example, allow students to choose the target and a distance that challenges them.

4. *Does the change cause an undue burden on the general physical education teacher?* For example, a general physical educator wants to include a student who has cerebral palsy and is learning how to walk with a walker in warm-up activities that include performing locomotor patterns to music. Because this student needs help to walk with his walker, the general physical educator feels that it is her duty to assist this student during warm-ups. This affects her ability to attend to and instruct the other students. A better modification might be assisting this student for part of warm-ups and then letting him creep on hands and knees (still his most functional way of moving). Or, if walking with the walker is a critical goal for this student, older peer tutors, a teacher assistant, a volunteer, or the physical therapist can come into physical education (at least during warm-ups) to assist this student.

GENERAL CATEGORIES OF CURRICULAR MODIFICATIONS

Although specific modifications vary from student to student, generally speaking three distinct categories of curricular modifications may be necessary: *multilevel curricular selection, curricular overlapping, and alternative programming* (Block & Vogler, 1994; Giangreco & Putnam, 1991).

Multilevel Curricular Selection

Multilevel curricular selection is designed for children with mild disabilities who can follow the general education curriculum with only slight accommodations. In other words, the general education curriculum is appropriate but the level at which the curriculum is presented may be above the child's ability level. For example, a child with Asperger's syndrome is in a general physical education throwing and catching unit in fourth grade. Throwing and catching are appropriate activities for this child, but he cannot throw and catch as well as his peers. To accommodate his needs, the teacher allows him to stand closer to targets when throwing, throw at a larger target, stand closer to peers when catching, and use a lighter, larger ball when catching. In fact, this teacher offers all children the opportunity to choose how close they stand to the target, which size target to throw to, and which balls to catch. Each child works on the same curricular content but at a level that accommodates his or her individual abilities.

Curricular Overlapping

The general education curriculum may be inappropriate for children with more severe disabilities. In such cases, the student should work on his or her unique physical education IEP objectives. But rather than working on these objectives away from his or her peers, these objectives can be embedded or overlapped within the general physical education curriculum. Such a model is known as *curricular overlapping*. For example, a second-grade child with severe cerebral palsy is learning how to walk with a walker. The general and adapted physical education teachers note that learning to use a walker is not included on the general physical education curriculum. However, within a chasing and fleeing unit this student can work on walking while other students work on chasing and fleeing. The student gets to participate with peers in the activities, but her focus is on her unique objectives. Figure 7.1 provides other examples of how a child's unique IEP objectives are overlapped within the general physical education curriculum.

Alternative Activities

Some children's unique IEP objectives cannot be safely and/or meaningfully overlapped within the general physical education curriculum. In such cases, the child with disabilities needs to work on his or her unique IEP objectives separately. For example, a high school student with severe intellectual disabilities and severe cerebral palsy might get hurt in a regulation or modified game of volleyball, plus these activities do not match his or her IEP objectives for physical education. In order to make this student's alternative activities inclusive, peers without disabilities can rotate away from the game to participate in the alternative activity. This allows the child with disabilities to work on his unique objectives while affording opportunities to interact with peers without disabilities.

Student: Emilio   **Grade:** Fourth grade

Age: 10 years   **Unit:** Introduction to soccer skills

Activities in GPE soccer unit	Emilio's IEP objectives for physical education				
	Walk with walker	Throw overhand	Catch	Sidearm strike	Upper-body strength
Move from class to gym	X				
Warm-ups	X				X
Chipping station				X[1]	
Passing/trapping station		X[2]	X[2]		
Shooting station		X[3]			
Dribbling station	X[4]				
Lead-up game	X				
Move from gym to class	X				

Key:

X[1] Emilio uses a bat to hit soccer balls placed on a cone to practice his striking goals.

X[2] Emilio bends over to pick up balls that are passed to him by a partner; he then throws the ball back to his partner, who has to trap it.

X[3] Emilio throws smaller playground balls into the goal rather than trying to kick the ball into the goal.

X[4] Emilio kicks and then walks after the soccer ball, with a focus on walking with his walker in a cluttered area.

Figure 7.1. IEP objectives overlapped within general physical education (GPE) activities.

GENERAL MODELS FOR MAKING CURRICULAR MODIFICATIONS

Rather than specific guidelines for specific students, the model outlined here provides a process that general physical educators and other team members can use to accommodate students with disabilities in general physical education. Again, once you understand the process of manipulating the equipment and the task, you can accommodate any student who enters your program. The following provides general guidelines for making curricular accommodations for students with a wide range of disabilities.

Developmental Task Analysis

A variety of task and environmental factors can influence motor performance. The teacher can modify many of these factors to make the activity easier or more challenging for particular students. Herkowitz's (1978) *developmental task analysis* is designed to systematically identify task and environmental factors that influence movement patterns. The model includes two components: 1) general task analysis (GTA), and 2) specific task analysis (STA). GTA involves outlining all task and environmental factors that influence movements of children in general categories (e.g., striking, catching, jumping). These factors are then listed hierarchically in terms of levels of difficulty from simple to complex. Figure 7.2 provides an example of a GTA for striking. Note how this grid provides the general physical educator with information on how various task factors influence specific movements. The general physical educator could then use this information to modify these factors to make a movement simpler or more complex.

Once the teacher has a general understanding of how task and environmental factors affect movement, an STA can be developed that examines in greater detail how select factors influence a specific movement. STAs are developed by creating activities that utilize two to four factors from the GTA. Like the GTA, these factors are then broken down into levels of difficulty and listed hierarchically from simple to complex. In the STA, however, levels of difficulty refer to specific factors. Figure 7.3 provides an example of an STA for striking. Note how more specific, observable information is provided in this STA. The teacher can quickly evaluate how specific levels of difficulty in various factors influence movement performance in various children. The goal is to get the student to perform the task under the most complex circumstances, in this case using a 36-inch plastic bat to strike a tennis ball. STAs also can be used to help less skilled students and students with disabilities become more suc-

cessful in a particular task. For example, a student who has limited strength could use an 18-inch wooden dowel rather than a 36-inch plastic bat to strike, or a student who has difficulty contacting a tennis ball can hit a 9-inch beach ball rather than a tennis ball. Limitations such as strength and visual-motor coordination can mask a student's ability to perform a task using a more skillful pattern. By simply altering task and environmental demands, these students might be able to demonstrate more skillful patterns. Teachers also can use STAs to evaluate a student's present level of performance (circumstances under which a student can perform a given task) as well as progress the student is making (see Herkowitz, 1978, for examples of STA evaluation grids).

Ecological Task Analysis

Davis and Burton (1991) developed a type of task analysis that extends Herkowitz's (1978) developmental task analysis. They noted that while a great beginning in skill analysis, Herkowitz's model has two major flaws: The model 1) did not consider the goal of the given task, and 2) did not consider the attributes of the mover.

The goal of the task can have a tremendous influence on the movement pattern a mover displays. For example, a mover might throw using what appears to be a very inefficient movement pattern (not stepping or stepping with the same-side foot, not extending his arm in back swing, having very little follow-through). If the goal of the task was to throw a dart at a dartboard from 10 feet away, this movement pattern might be very appropriate. In such situations, the student might appear to be displaying movement patterns that are different than what the teacher wants. For example, a student might demonstrate a chopping movement with very little bat motion in his striking pattern because he wants to hit the pitched ball (goal is perceived as hitting ball), while the teacher was hoping that the student would take a full, horizontal swing at the ball including rotating the body (goal is perceived as using a certain striking pattern). The intended goal of the task is critical to eventual performance of the movement, yet the goal of the task is not discussed in Herkowitz's (1978) model.

The second weakness noted by Davis and Burton (1991) is the absence of the person in the task analysis equation. Herkowitz's (1978) developmental task analyses focus on the characteristics of the task rather than the characteristics of the mover. Yet, movers with different capabilities and physical characteristics respond quite differently to changes in task factors. For example, Herkowitz listed ball

Factors	Size of object to be struck	Weight of object to be struck	Speed of object to be struck	Predictability of trajectory of object to be struck	Length of striking implement	Side of body to which object is traveling	Anticipatory locomotor spatial adjustments
Simple	Large	Light	None Slow	No movement	None	Favored side	No adjustment
↓	Medium	Moderate	Moderate	Down incline	Short	Nonfavored side	Minimal adjustment
Complex	Small	Heavy	Fast	In air	Long	Midline	Maximal adjustment

Figure 7.2. General task analysis (GTA) for striking. (From Herkowitz, J. [1978]. Developmental task analysis: The design of movement experiences and evaluation of motor development status. In M. Ridenour [Ed.], *Motor development: Issues and applications* [p. 141]. Princeton, NJ: Princeton Book Co.; adapted by permission.)

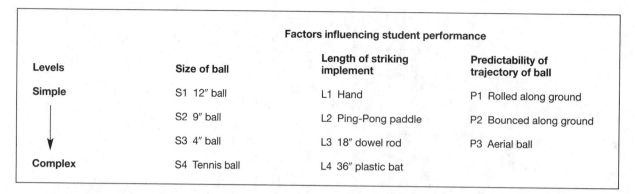

Figure 7.3. Specific task analysis (STA) for striking. (From Herkowitz, J. [1978]. Developmental task analysis: The design of movement experiences and evaluation of motor development status. In M. Ridenour [Ed.], *Motor development: Issues and applications* [p. 143]. Princeton, NJ: Princeton Book Co.; adapted by permission.)

size and balance requirements of the task as factors that can affect throwing performance. However, the size of a mover's hand and his or her own innate balance abilities will affect how much ball size and balance requirements affect performance. For some children with large hands, subtle changes in ball size might not affect throwing performance. For children with smaller hands, a slightly larger ball will change the throwing pattern from one handed to two handed (Block & Provis, 1992). Similarly, balance requirements in the task might not negatively affect a student who has good balance; yet such requirements could have a dramatic effect on a student with ataxic cerebral palsy who has difficulty with even simple balance tasks. Performer characteristics, like the goal of the task, are critical determinants to performance.

In an effort to correct flaws found in Herkowitz's (1978) models, Davis and Burton (1991) proposed the *ecological task analysis model* (ETA). Three of the major tenets of ETA are as follows:

1. Actions are the result of the complex relationship between the task goal, the performer, and the environment. ETA includes a description of the task goal and the performer as critical factors in movement outcome.

2. Tasks should be categorized by function and intention rather than movement pattern or mechanism of performance. The same function can be achieved through very different movement patterns. While a particular pattern might be most efficient for a group of movers who have similar abilities and physical characteristics, other movers with different abilities and characteristics might find a different movement pattern more efficient. This is particularly true for students with disabilities, who often have very unique abilities and characteristics. Rather than describing a movement pattern such as skipping or throwing, ETA utilizes a functional task category that describes the general intent of the movement. Skipping thus becomes one form of the function: *locomotion,* to move from one place to another; and throwing becomes one form of the function: *propulsion,* to propel a stationary or moving object or person. Within each functional task category is criteria for performance. For example, under locomotion (to move from one place to another), criteria include to move with efficiency, precision, accuracy, speed, and/or distance. Each mover might use a different pattern to accomplish a given function and criteria.

3. Invariant features of a task and variations within a task may be defined in terms of essential and nonessential variables, respectively. Essential variables describe the invariant characteristics of the movement, the underlying patterns that organize and define a movement. Relative timing between the two lower limbs in walking or galloping is an example of an essential variable. For practical purposes, broader descriptors of patterns of coordination such as arm action in throwing also can be viewed as essential variables. Nonessential variables refer to dimensions or control parameters that, when scaled up or down, may cause the mover to change to a new, qualitatively different pattern of coordination (new essential variable). These control variables can include physical dimensions of the mover such as limb length or weight, body proportions, or postural control; or they can refer to task factors such as ball size, weight of striking implement, or size of target. For example, throwing a ball at a wall from 5 feet away would result in the student's displaying a pattern of coordination (essential variable) that is characterized by no stepping, no preparatory back swing, and no trunk rotation. As the student moves away

from the wall (scale up nonessential variable of distance to throw), his throwing pattern will stay intact up to a critical distance. At that critical distance (given that the student has the underlying ability to display a different throwing pattern), the student's pattern will abruptly change to a qualitatively different throwing pattern, stepping with opposition, trunk rotation, and preparatory back swing.

According to Davis and Burton (1991), using the ETA a teacher can more accurately determine under which set of conditions the student is able to achieve the task, the set of conditions that elicit the most efficient and effective pattern (optimal performance), and the dimension values at which the student chooses to use a different skill to perform a task (e.g., changes from galloping to running). ETA appears to be a viable approach to understanding how a student prefers to move and how changes in task variables affect movement. (For more practical application of the ETA model, refer to Gagen & Getchell, 2004.)

ACCOMMODATIONS FOR STUDENTS WITH SPECIFIC FUNCTIONAL IMPAIRMENTS OR SPECIFIC DISABILITIES

Some physical educators feel more comfortable with specific suggestions on how to accommodate students with distinct impairments or disabilities. This section presents modifications designed to accommodate students with specific impairments or disabilities. Although it is difficult to generalize modifications across categories, the specific modifications reviewed in this chapter should give general physical educators and other team members ideas on how to modify activities. Still, it important to focus on the functional strengths and weaknesses of your particular students rather than their diagnostic labels. For example, functionally students with cerebral palsy can be quite different. Some may have trouble with coordination, others might have trouble with strength. As you read this section on specific disabilities, try to think of the specific functional impairments that your students have. As always, utilize team members to provide more specific information regarding particular students.

Finally, include the student with a disability whenever possible when deciding how to adapt an activity in general physical education. Lieberman and Houston-Wilson (2002) noted that many students with disabilities are happy to have activities modified to help them become more successful in general physical education. These students also know which modifications have worked and which

have not worked in previous general physical education and recreation settings (MacDonald & Block, 2005). However, Lieberman and Houston-Wilson (2002) pointed out that some students with disabilities prefer to fit in rather than being successful, and these students may not want any modifications. It is important to honor a student's wishes regarding modifications to general physical education activities.

Accommodations for Students with Specific Functional Impairments

Functional impairments, such as challenges with strength or endurance can often be remediated so that the student can perform the skill at a higher level. *Structural impairments*, however, such as extreme short stature (dwarfism), visual impairments, or a physical disability cannot be remediated. In these situations, modifications to activities can allow the student to perform the skill more successfully. The following sections (adapted from Arbogast & Lavay, 1986; Herkowitz, 1978; and Sherrill, 2004) outline general factors that can be manipulated to accommodate students with specific impairments (see Table 7.2).

Specific Adaptations for Students with Impairments in Strength, Power, and Endurance

Students who do not have the strength to get an object to a target can have the target lowered. For example, a student who cannot reach a 10-foot basket in basketball can shoot at a 6- or 8-foot basket. Similarly, a student who cannot hit a ball over a regulation volleyball or badminton net can have the net lowered. By lowering the target, students will have a greater opportunity for success that in turn will encourage them to continue to practice the skill. Targets set at reasonable heights also facilitate desired movement patterns. For example, students who cannot reach a 10-foot basket with a basketball using a "typical" shooting pattern often resort to different, less effective shooting patterns (e.g., sidearm hurl, underhand, tossed backward over their head).

Many physical education activities require students to throw, pass, serve, or shoot a ball or run a certain distance. These distances, while necessary when playing intramural or interscholastic games, can be altered when teaching skills or playing lead-up or recreational games in physical education. Distances can be reduced so students with disabilities can be successful. For example, a student could push his wheelchair to a first base that is half the distance of the general first base to accommodate his limited speed. Such accommodations do not give either

Table 7.2. Adaptations for students with functional impairments

Students with impairments in strength, power, and endurance
- Lower targets.
- Reduce distance/playing field.
- Reduce weight and/or size of striking implements, balls, or projectile.
- Allow student to sit or lie down while playing.
- Use deflated balls or suspended balls.
- Decrease activity time/increase rest time.
- Reduce speed of game/increase distance for peers without disabilities.

Students with limited balance
- Lower center of gravity.
- Keep as much of body in contact with the surface as possible.
- Widen base of support.
- Increase width of beams to be walked.
- Extend arms for balance.
- Use carpeted rather than slick surfaces.
- Teach students how to fall.
- Provide a bar to assist with stability.
- Teach student to use eyes optimally.
- Determine whether balance problems are related to health problems.

Students with problems of coordination and accuracy
- For catching and striking activities, use larger, lighter, softer balls.
- Decrease distance ball is thrown and reduce speed.
- For throwing activities, use smaller balls.
- In striking and kicking, use stationary ball before trying a moving ball.
- Increase the surface of the striking implement.
- Use backstop.
- Increase size of target.
- In bowling-type games, use lighter, less stable pins.
- Optimize safety.

Sources: Arbogast and Lavay (1986); Herkowitz (1978); Sherrill (2004).

team any advantage yet allow the student with disabilities an opportunity to be successful. For games that require running up and down an entire floor or field (e.g., basketball or soccer), games can be played using the width of the field rather than the length, or half court games can be played. Another modification that would not affect the entire class is allowing a particular student to play in just half the field (just play defense or offense, or place the student in a position that requires less movement (playing defensive back in soccer rather than midfielder; playing lineman in football rather than wide receiver).

Students with limited arm or grip strength or who have smaller than normal hand size may have difficulty holding large/heavy striking implements or balls. For example, a regulation tennis racquet might be too long and heavy for a student with muscular dystrophy. Allowing this student to use a racquetball or badminton racket or a tennis racket with the handle cut off would allow this student more success. Some students might need to simply be encouraged to choke up on the racket. Similarly a student with small hands might have difficulty gripping a softball with one hand and resort to throwing the softball with two hands. Balloons, beach balls, or nerf balls can be a good substitute for balls that are too heavy or too intimidating for a student.

Allow Student to Sit or Lie Down While Playing
Activities played while lying or sitting demand less fitness than games played while standing or moving. Students with limited strength and endurance can be allowed to sit down when the ball is at the other end of the playing field or while playing in the outfield. These students also can be allowed to sit while practicing some skills. For example, a student with a heart condition who tires easily can warm-up with the class by performing every other locomotor pattern the class performs. The student can be allowed to sit down when he is not performing a locomotor pattern.

Use Deflated Balls or Suspended Balls
By their nature, balls tend to roll when put in motion. Although most young children enjoy chasing balls, students who fatigue easily may use up all their energy and miss out on important practice trials. Balls that are deflated or paper balls (crumpled up piece of paper wrapped with a few pieces of masking tape) do not roll away. Also, balls suspended from a basket or ceiling or balls tied to a student's wheelchair are easy to retrieve.

Decrease Activity Time/Increase Rest Time
Games and practice sessions can be shortened for students who fatigue easily. Students can be allowed to play for 5 minutes, then rest for 5 minutes, or all students play for 3 minutes, then rotate to an activity that requires less endurance. For example, a game of sideline basketball could be played in which three players from each team play for 3 minutes while the other players on each team stand on opposite sidelines prepared to assist their teammates. Another possibility is to allow free substitutions in a game. For example, a student with asthma can come out of a soccer game every 2 or 3 minutes.

Reduce Speed of Game/Increase Distance for Peers without Disabilities
Many games move quickly, leaving slower players and players with limited endurance behind. Modifications can be made so that races and games are fairer for students with limits in speed and endurance. For example, slower students in a relay race need only go up and

back one time, while more skilled students go up and back two times. Similarly, a special zone in soccer can be marked off for a student who has limited speed. When the ball goes into the zone, this student is the only one who can kick the ball.

Specific Adaptations for Students with Limited Balance

Lower Center of Gravity   Allow student to perform activities while sitting down or on hands and knees. Also, encourage student to bend knees while moving, stopping, and standing. For example, a student should be encouraged to land with his feet apart when jumping down from a box. When performing locomotor patterns, students should be encouraged to perform animal walks that lower the center of gravity (crawling, creeping, bear walking) or to move with knees bent when performing locomotor patterns such as running and jumping.

Keep as Much of Body in Contact with the Surface as Possible   Allow students to walk or run flat-footed rather than on tiptoes, or allow student to perform balance activities on three or four body parts rather than on one or two body parts. For example, allow a student to jump on two feet while his classmates hop on one foot.

Widen Base of Support   Encourage students to stand with feet farther apart to provide more stability, for example while preparing to catch a ball. Similarly, allow students to walk or run with feet apart until they develop more postural control.

Increase Width of Beams   Students should be allowed to walk on the floor or on wider beams until they develop more postural control. For example, a balance station could have 2″ × 4″, 2″ × 6″, 2″ × 8″, and 2″ × 10″ beams. In addition, a hierarchy of challenges can be set up, beginning with walking with one foot on and one foot off the beam, using a shuffle step across the beam, and walking across the beam holding on to the wall or a peer's hand.

Extend Arms for Balance   Encourage students to hold their arms out to the side when performing balance activities. For example, have a student hold arms out to the side while walking on a beam or when learning how to walk, run, jump, or hop.

Use Carpeted Rather than Slick Surfaces   When possible, provide surfaces that increase friction. For example, learning how to roller skate on a tumbling mat or carpeted surface is easier than learning how to skate on a gym floor. Similarly, it is easier to per-

form various locomotor patterns on a carpeted surface as opposed to a slick surface. Finally, encourage students to wear rubber-soled footwear rather than shoes with slick bottoms.

Teach Students How to Fall   Students who have problems with postural control will fall often. Teach these students how to fall safely by practicing how to fall on mats. For example, a simple game like "Ring around the rosy" requires all students to fall, affording them practice in falling forward, backward, and sideward.

Provide a Bar to Assist with Stability   During activities that require balance, such as walking across a balance beam or kicking, allow student to hold on to a wall, bar, chair, or table for extra stability. Allowing students to use balance aids may enable them to exhibit more advanced motor patterns. The balance aid can be gradually faded away as the skill becomes more engrained.

Teach Student to Use Eyes Optimally   Vision plays a critical role in postural control. Teach students how to use their vision to facilitate balance. For example, student can be taught to focus their vision on a stationary object on a wall while walking a beam or while performing standing balance activities.

Determine Whether Balance Problems Are Related to Health Problems   Balance problems may be related to health problems such as inner ear infections. Talk to the student's special education teacher, parent, or physician to determine whether there are any health problems that might negatively affect balance. In addition, find out if the student is taking any medication that might affect balance. Balance difficulties due to health problems or medication might be acute in nature, in which case you might want to have the student avoid activities that require balance. If the problem is more chronic, then you should implement some of the modifications described above.

Specific Adaptations for Students with Problems of Coordination and Accuracy

Use Large, Light, Soft Balls   Large balls are easier to catch and strike than smaller balls. However, large balls may promote an immature catching pattern (scooping into body rather than using hands). If a student is unsuccessful or frightened of small, hard balls (e.g., softball) then the use of a large Nerf ball, balloon, or punch ball is appropriate. Gradually introduce a small ball to elicit a more skillful pattern. In addition, balls tossed directly to a student are easier to catch than balls tossed to a student's side, while balls tossed to a student's side are easier to strike than balls tossed directly at student.

Decrease Distance Ball Is Thrown and Reduce Speed   Reduce the distance that balls are thrown for students who have difficulty tracking balls. For example, one student might be allowed to hit a ball pitched from 10 feet away in a game of softball while other students are expected to hit a ball pitched from 20 feet. Similarly, a ball can be tossed slowly for some students, faster for others, and still faster for more skilled students. Ideally, you will vary distance and speed so that each student is challenged at his or her level yet has an opportunity to succeed.

Throw Small Balls   Allow students who have trouble gripping to use smaller balls or yarn balls, Koosh balls, paper balls, or bean bags. Have a variety of balls available.

Strike or Kick Stationary Balls   Allow students to first kick a stationary ball or strike a ball on a tee. Suspended balls that move at slower speeds and at a known trajectory are also easier than moving balls. Again, allow the student to be successful and demonstrate a skillful pattern with adaptations, then gradually fade away the adaptations as the student gains confidence and skill.

Increase the Surface of the Striking Implement Allow students to use lighter bats with a larger striking surface or a racket with a larger striking surface. Again, have a variety of striking implements for students to choose from.

Use Backstops   Students who miss the ball often may spend most of their time retrieving the ball rather than practicing the skill. This does not promote good use of practice time, and it can become very frustrating for the student. When working on striking, kicking, or catching activities, have a backdrop, backstop, net, or rebounder available. You can also attach a string to a ball and then to a student's wheelchair for ease of recovery.

Increase Size of Target   Allow students to throw or kick to larger targets, or allow students to shoot at larger basket. In addition, give points for coming close to target such as hitting the rim or backboard in basketball. Less skilled students can be allowed to stand closer to the target in order to promote initial success, and then gradually allow them to move back as they become more accurate.

Use Light, Unstable Pins When Bowling   In games or activities in which the goal is to knock something down, use light objects (e.g., milk cartons, aluminum cans) so that any contact with the object will result in success. In addition, use more pins and spread them out farther than normal so that tosses or kicks that would normally miss the target still result in success.

Optimize Safety   Students who have trouble with coordination are more prone to injury, especially in activities that involve moving balls. These students should be allowed to wear glasses protectors, shin guards, helmets, and face masks. When necessary, provide a peer tutor who can protect the student from errant balls.

ADAPTATIONS FOR STUDENTS WITH SPECIFIC TYPES OF DISABILITIES

This section provides information regarding adaptations for students who have physical disabilities, intellectual disabilities, hearing impairments, visual impairments, orthopedic disabilities, and health disorders. As noted, a diagnostic label does not provide much information about a student's functional abilities. As you think of your particular students, cross-reference the modifications presented in this section with modifications outlined in the previous section on functional impairments.

Students with Physical Disabilities

Determine Exact Nature of Disability

Make sure you get medical information from the student's parents, physician, and physical therapist, including contraindicated activities, activities that need modifications, and precautions for safety. Adhere to these restrictions. For example, a student's physical therapist can provide information regarding the student's range of motion in various joints and the best position for functional movement.

Prepare Classmates

Provide students with general information about physical disabilities as well as specific information about the particular student to be included. Talk about wheelchairs, and allow students to sit in and move a wheelchair. Talk about ways that students without disabilities can informally help a student who uses a wheelchair. For example, students without disabilities can retrieve errant balls or help push a student to a station. Encourage students to welcome the student with disabilities into their class (see Chapter 9 for more information on facilitating social acceptance).

Think Safety

Teach students without disabilities to be vigilant of peers who use wheelchairs or crutches. Peers can be assigned to stand near the student who uses a wheelchair to protect him from any danger.

Include Students in Decision Making

The student with physical disabilities but no cognitive disabilities probably knows better than anyone his movement capabilities and how best to accommodate his abilities and limitations (MacDonald & Block, 2005). For example, if you are working on locomotor patterns, a student who uses a wheelchair can decide how he is going to move his chair to simulate hopping (using one arm) skipping (moving arms rhythmically) or how best to throw a ball (maybe backwards over their head rather than the traditional forward way).

Make Accommodations for Limited Strength, Endurance, and Flexibility

Simple modifications can help a student overcome problems with physical fitness and can improve a student's success and ability to participate with peers in a variety of group games and sports. Encourage students to find their own modifications to accommodate their limitations.

Make Accommodations for Limited Coordination and Reaction Speed

Use Herkowitz's (1978) developmental task analysis to determine how to modify such task factors as size of the ball, speed of the ball, and trajectory of the ball.

Use Rebounders or Tie Balls

For example, a student can practice throwing a ball that is tied to his chair with a 20-foot string. After the throw, the student simply pulls the string to retrieve the ball.

Reduce Playing Area

While students without disabilities can be allowed to use the whole field or court, a student who is learning how to push his wheelchair can be allowed to move in a smaller space.

Use Game Analysis Techniques

Use game analysis techniques to determine best ways to accommodate students who use wheelchairs in traditional games and sports (Morris & Stiehl, 1999; see also Chapter 8). Allow students without disabilities to participate in decisions regarding game modifications so that they feel the modifications are not dictated to them. Use cooperative and initiative games and encourage group to figure out ways to safely include student who uses a wheelchair.

Utilize Sports Rules

Wheelchair Sports, USA, National Disability Sports Alliance (NDSA), and Disabled Sports all have specific rule modifications for various sports that can be utilized by persons with physical disabilities (see resource section in the back of this text for contacts for these and other special sports associations).

Students with Intellectual Disabilities

Confer with Collaborative Team

Determine a student's mental abilities and limitations. Also, obtain information from the student's parents, special education teacher and speech therapist regarding ability to comprehend verbal cues. The special education teacher and speech therapist also can give you vital information regarding how best to communicate with the student, and the physical and occupational therapists can tell you if the student has any motor problems. Finally, ask the special education teacher whether the student has any behavior problems and, if so, what behavior management techniques to use.

Prepare Classmates without Disabilities

Provide information in general about intellectual disabilities and specifically about the student who will be included in their class. Encourage peers without disabilities to help the student with intellectual disabilities understand directions and how to practice skills correctly. Also, encourage students to invite the student to join their station or group. Praise students without disabilities for befriending the student with intellectual disabilities, and sternly reprimand students who tease, ridicule, or take advantage of the student with intellectual disabilities. Peers without disabilities should realize that the student with intellectual disabilities wants to do well in physical education and wants to be friends with other students even though he may be shy or uncomfortable at first. Peers without disabilities can help the student feel more comfortable (see Chapter 9 for more details on facilitating social inclusion).

Do Not Underestimate Students

Given enough instruction, practice, and time, many students with intellectual disabilities can learn skillful movement patterns. For example, most individuals with intellectual disabilities, particularly students with mild or moderate intellectual disabilities, can be expected to demonstrate skillful throwing, striking, and catching patterns. Only after exhaustive efforts should you accept less skillful movement patterns (e.g., hitting a ball off a tee, throwing without rotating trunk). Most students with intellectual disabilities also can learn to follow the basic rules of individual and group games and sports. Many Special Olympics athletes play team sports such as basketball, volleyball, softball, and soccer. These players not only adhere to the rules of the game without any special modifications but also use more complex strategies and team concepts such as zone defenses in basketball and set plays for corner kicks in soccer. Again, more instruction, practice, and time may be needed for these students to learn rules and concepts, but every effort should be made to give them an opportunity to learn how to play the game correctly. Then these students will have an opportunity to participate in integrated, community sport programs.

Select Activities Based on Chronological Age

Selecting activities based on chronological age is particularly important for middle and high school students. Although students with intellectual disabilities may be delayed by 2 years or more in mental and skill development compared to their peers without disabilities, it is important to teach skills that will allow these students to interact with their peers and develop recreation and fitness skills for life. For example, a high school student with severe intellectual disabilities has the mental abilities and motor skills of a 5-year-old. While it may seem reasonable to work with this student on activities appropriate for a 5-year-old, such activities will not help this student participate in activities his high school peers play or help him acquire skills necessary to independently participate in recreation skills as an adult.

Think Safety

Children with intellectual disabilities often cannot anticipate potential dangers such as walking in front of a soccer goal when other children are shooting. Remind children with intellectual disabilities of the safety rules, and tell classmates without disabilities to be a little more cautious when moving around a peer with intellectual disabilities.

Provide Direct Instruction

Children with intellectual disabilities may not understand how to play with toys and equipment or how to interact with peers or teammates. Provide direct instruction (i.e., actually show students how to throw bean bags, walk on beams, toss and catch balloons). Have other students act as role models for appropriate play, and encourage other students to invite students with intellectual disabilities to play with them. If you are doing an activity that encourages exploration with equipment, have a peer help the student with intellectual disabilities think of different ways to explore the equipment.

Keep Verbal Directions to a Minimum

Also use extra demonstration and physical assistance when providing instruction. Students with intellectual disabilities do not understand verbal directions as well as their peers without disabilities, and they may miss key points in demonstrations. Help students focus on critical aspects of a movement by giving extra, specific verbal cues, demonstrating key movement aspects, and even physically assisting student to perform movement correctly. A peer can be trained to provide this extra instruction while the general physical educator is supervising the class. Even if you are using a movement exploration approach, you may need to provide some physical assistance to students with intellectual disabilities.

Break Skills into Smaller Components

For example, if you are working on the task of hopping with a class of kindergartners, most students can learn the skill by breaking it down into three or four critical steps: preparatory position, place arms out to side, bend knee, simultaneously extend knee and hip to lift body up. For students with intellectual disabilities, you may need to extend this task analysis into 10 steps.

Measure Progress

Students with intellectual disabilities do learn, but their progress is much slower than their peers without disabilities. Use various ways of detecting and reinforcing progress. For example, progress can include less intrusive levels of assistance (going from physical assistance to demonstration), throwing a ball farther or with more accuracy measured in inches rather than feet, or noting use of one or two more components in the overall locomotor or manipulative pattern.

Be Aware of Limited Motivation

Plan on providing external reinforcers (tokens, free play) to encourage students with intellectual disabilities to perform activities that are difficult such as running laps, sit-ups and push-ups, or practicing the correct pattern for throwing. Also, allow and then reinforce completion of part of a fitness task such as running the straight-aways and walking the curves when running the mile or doing 5 sit-ups when the class has been asked to do 10 sit-ups. Then encourage the student to try to improve his fitness by gradually increasing fitness demands, but be sure to reinforce even small amounts of progress.

Let Students Know that They Will Not Be Ridiculed

Even if the student performs a movement or activity incorrectly or more slowly than their peers, reinforce the student for trying new activities even if he or she does the activity incorrectly. Also, encourage peers without disabilities to be patient with students with intellectual disabilities and to reinforce him or her for trying difficult activities.

Help Students Maintain and Generalize Skill

For maintenance, you will need to give the student many extra trials after he or she acquires a skill. Similarly, students with more severe intellectual disabilities may not generalize skills from one environment to another. That is, if a student is taught how to bowl in the gym, he may not be able to perform this skill at a bowling alley. Therefore, you may need to teach critical lifetime skills in the actual environment where they will take place. This is especially true for high school students who soon will graduate from school and use their community recreation settings.

Provide Compensations

Students with intellectual disabilities may not be able to process complex verbal instruction as quickly as their peers. Give them extra time to process information, and be prepared to repeat directions. Ask the student to repeat key parts of the verbal instructions to check for understanding. Similarly, some students with intellectual disabilities may have problems taking in visual or auditory information or they may have problems with spatial awareness. Actually set up activities in which the student can work on improving perception. For ex-

ample, an activity at one station can include practicing going over, under, and between obstacles without touching them. A peer at the station can change the heights of obstacles to encourage the student with intellectual disabilities to practice making correct decisions.

Students with Hearing Impairments

Confer with Collaborative Team

Seek out especially the student's parents, audiologist, and speech teacher. Ascertain how to best communicate with the student. Learning sign language may be difficult for most general physical educators, but learning a few key signs will help you convey instructional and management cues to the student more effectively. For example, simple signs such as STOP, GO, SIT, STAND UP, RUN, WALK, LINE UP, and COPY ME are relatively easy to learn. Often, your student can teach you these signs. Most students with hearing impairments learn to become good imitators, so often a good demonstration is all that is needed.

Prepare Classmates

Give classmates general information about hearing impairments and specific information about the student who will be included. Explain the best way to communicate with the student, and encourage students to learn a little sign language so they can communicate with the student. Also, encourage classmates without disabilities to interact and befriend the student who has a hearing impairment and to invite him or her to join their stations or groups. Encourage peers to offer to be a buddy to the student in terms of repeating directions, providing extra demonstrations, and generally watching out for the student if he or she looks confused.

Position the Student Close to You

If student has residual hearing, you may want him to actually stand next to you. If the student is reading your lips, he should have a good view from the front of the class. Do not speak any slower or more exaggerated than normal, and, remember, even good lip readers understand only about 30% of what the speaker is saying. Be prepared to repeat verbal directions, or have a peer repeat, to the student individually after you have given directions to the entire class.

Provide Extra Demonstrations

After you present information to the class, pull the student with a hearing impairment off to the side and give him a brief demonstration focusing on the exact component of the skill you want the student to focus on. Demonstrations also can be presented by a peer. Point to the student and have him repeat the demonstration to make sure he understands what he should be working on (check for understanding).

Use Extra Visual Cues

Written directions or pictures can describe exactly what you want the student to do. For example, you can have a picture of the correct throwing pattern taped to the wall of a station. Point to the particular aspect of the movement on which you want the student to focus. Also, give the student written information regarding rules and strategies.

Make Sure the Learning Environment Has Adequate Lighting

When outside, do not have the student face the sun; this will make it difficult for him to read your lips and see your demonstrations. In the gymnasium, make sure that there is bright lighting and that stations are set up under good lighting. Position yourself so that the student is not looking directly into the light coming through a window or light fixture.

Encourage Use of Residual Hearing

Discuss the student's hearing ability with the collaborative team, and determine how much residual hearing the student has. Also determine if one ear hears better than the other, and if speaking into that ear would be helpful.

Avoid Excessive Noise

Physical education classes tend to be noisy, but you can ask for quiet during critical instruction time. Again, if the environment is too noisy when you are relaying information to the class, repeat the directions (using demonstrations and gestures as needed) off to the side.

Be Cautious of Students' Hearing Aids

Students should be encouraged to wear their hearing aids during physical education to assist them in picking up verbal cues and sounds, but they should be aware of these aids in contact activities. Removal of aids in combative and contact activities such as wrestling, karate, football, and basketball is probably appropriate, but check with the student's audiologist or physician.

Utilize Peer Tutors

Peer tutors can repeat directions, give extra demonstrations, and to help student understand what to do and where to go. For example, if the teacher gives complex directions regarding which station to go to and how to perform an activity, a peer can repeat the information to the student with a hearing impairment via gestures and demonstrations. Some students without disabilities enjoy learning sign language and may be able to learn enough to communicate more detailed cues to the student.

Students with Visual Impairments

Confer with the Collaborative Team

Obtain information from the student's parents, ophthalmologist, and vision specialist. For example, students with a detached retina can lose what little vision they have if they receive a direct blow to their head. Caution should be taken when exposing these students to activities using balls, and most contact activities (e.g., wrestling, karate, football) are contraindicated for these students.

Think Safety

If the student wears glasses, consider having him wear glass protectors during activities in which balls will be used. Assign a peer to the student when you are not sure that the student with a visual impairment can protect him- or herself in an activity (e.g., playing outfield in softball or wing fullback in soccer, performing locomotor pattern in a scattered formation). For example, a student with a visual impairment can play deep center field in softball with a peer playing short center field to protect the student from line drives and hard hit balls. When possible, replace hard balls with Nerf balls. Also try the firmer sponge balls, which have the bounce and feel of softballs, basketballs, and soccer balls.

Offer a Variety of Activities

While gymnastics, swimming, and bowling are relatively easy activities for students who are blind to learn, many students who are blind will want to participate in the same activities as their peers. With modifications and extra assistance, these students can participate in team sports. Although students who are blind might not be able to play these sports independently, they can learn the rules of these sports and gain a better understanding of the various positions and strategies used in the game. This will enhance their enjoyment when listening to high school, college, or professional games, and many students may learn to enjoy working on the skills used in the game, such as shooting basketballs or hitting a tennis ball with verbal cues.

Assist Students in Moving Safely and Independently

Have a peer show the student where the bathrooms, showers, and lockers are as well as gym boundaries and where equipment is located. Pay particular attention to stored equipment. When changing the environment so that new equipment is placed around the gym, take time to show the student where the equipment is, what it is used for, and how it feels. Encourage the student to tactually explore balls, bats, and other pieces of equipment in order to better understand their use.

"Anchor" Student to Play Area

Anchoring means telling the student who to sit next to when he or she comes into the gym. This can be as easy as having the student sit next to the same students every time he or she comes to the gym (e.g., in the same squad). If students sit randomly, have students without disabilities next to the student who is blind introduce themselves.

Prepare Classmates

Classmates without disabilities should know a little about visual impairments in general and about the specific visual skills of the student being included. They should be encouraged to informally assist the student. Also, encourage peers without disabilities to befriend a student who has visual impairments, share team strategies, and help the student understand where other students are positioned around the playing area.

Use Brightly Colored and Contrasting Objects

For example, use yellow balls when playing on grass or use blue balls when playing on an orange gym floor. Use bright colored cones or tape to mark boundaries. Ask the student which colored ball is easiest for him or her to see.

Use Tactile or Auditory Boundaries

For example, use cones or change the surface (from grass to gravel) to indicate a boundary. Hang crepe paper from the ceiling, or mark floor with tape that the student can feel with his toes or hands. Use beeper cones or music (a tape player works well) to indicate the location of a target. For example, placing a radio under the basket helps a student locate in which direction he should shoot a basketball. Again, when in doubt ask the student which modality and modifications he or she prefers.

Give Specific Verbal Directions and Physical Assistance

For example, you will have to tell a student (or have a peer tell the student) exactly how he or she missed the target ("You missed the target by throwing the ball 1 foot too high and 6 inches to the left"). You also need to give explicit feedback regarding a student's movement pattern (e.g., "Bend your elbow so that it is at a 90-degree angle when getting into the backswing position of backhand in tennis"). In most cases, students with visual impairments will learn best if you provide them with physical assistance. You can physically assist the student through the appropriate pattern so that the student gets a feel for how he should move, or have the student hold onto you while you perform the movement. This technique (called reverse manual assistance) works well as a supplement to more traditional physical assistance and explicit verbal cues. Auxter et al. (2005) noted that you can present a demonstration to the class by using the student with a visual impairment as an assistant. You demonstrate the movement and physically assist the student who is blind. This way you are giving direct tactile feedback to the student who is blind while benefiting the rest of the class.

Allow Special Equipment

For example, place bowling guides parallel to the student so that he or she can tell boundaries. Another simple modification is to attach a string to balls and to the student's hand so that balls do not get away so easily. That way, students who are blind can throw the ball, then retrieve it by pulling the string toward them. Other simple adaptations include having a guide rope or using beeper cones when running, wrapping a ball in a plastic grocery bag, or dangling crepe paper as reference points throughout the gym.

Translate All Materials into Braille

Have the vision specialist translate all handouts and cognitive concepts such as rules of games, strategies, and names of equipment into braille. Students who are blind also should be allowed to take written tests orally.

Utilize Special Game Rules

Utilize rules from the United States Association for Blind Athletes (USABA). This sports governing body specifically for students who have visual impairments has a variety of suggestions for modifying traditional sports such as swimming, track and field, and gymnastics. In addition, they offer information and rules for unique sports designed specifically for students with visual impairments such as beep baseball and goal ball. These games can be fun to introduce to blindfolded students without disabilities to show them what it is like to have a visual impairment.

Students with Emotional Disturbances and Autism

Confer with Collaborative Team

Discuss any activities that might set the student off or make the student feel uncomfortable, and discuss simple ways that such situations can be modified (e.g., providing a visual schedule). Determine which activities, teaching methods, instructional formats, or pieces of equipment (if any) should be avoided for particular students. For example, some students might fear loud sounds such as balloons popping. If you are planning on using balloons with a first-grade class, this student might work at a station away from the balloons or in the hallway with a teacher assistant during this particular activity. Similarly, some students do not do well in large-class formats where there is a lot of noise and stimulation. These students might be included gradually. Finally, some students do not like being touched. These students should be given directions verbally and by demonstration. Physical assistance can be provided in small doses, but the student should be told ahead of time that he or she will be touched for a few seconds.

Prepare Classmates

Classmates should be taught a little about emotional disturbances and autism and how this particular student behaves in certain situations. They should be encouraged to interact with the student, but they should also learn when to back off from the student. You may need to hand-pick groups so that children who set each other off are separated.

Ensure Success

This will help the student feel good about himself and about physical education. As the student feels comfortable with you and the class structure, you can begin to introduce challenges that may result in occasional failures. For example, initially you can have the student shoot at a lower basket in basketball so that he will be successful. Later, you can introduce shooting at a higher basket for part of the class, reinforcing the student for good efforts as well as successful baskets. You may even want to set up a scoring system that reinforces good efforts. For example, a student can be reinforced for touching a ball with hands when practicing catching (not just being able to catch the ball).

Teach Students to Accept Failure

Spend some early class sessions teaching appropriate sportsmanship. Set up structured situations, warn students ahead of time that one team will lose, and explain how to lose properly. Also, play more cooperative and initiative games as well as competitive games that deemphasize winning and losing. For example, play games in which points are scored by passing the ball to teammates, or play a tag game in which players tagged do five jumping jacks and then can go back into the game.

Provide a Release for Aggressive Students

If a student is prone to hitting other children or throwing things when he is angry, have a special station set up where he can throw bean bags at a target. Explain to the student that it is okay to get angry, but throwing bean bags at a target is more appropriate than hitting other students. Encourage the student to think of other appropriate ways to vent his anger and frustration.

Help Students Focus

Many students with emotional disturbances (especially those with attention-deficit disorders) and autism have difficulty focusing on the targeted activities. By making the activities more fun and reinforcing, students will be more apt to pay attention and stay on task. For example, having a student hit balls off a tee against a wall is not as stimulating as hitting old coke bottles, which make a lot more noise.

Provide External Reinforcers

Some students with emotional disturbances or autism (like many students without disabilities) are not intrinsically reinforced by physical education activities. Be prepared to provide extra reinforcers to help motivate these students to try new and challenging physical education activities. Without bribing them, use a simple Premack principle (e.g., "If you do a good job with this activity, then you can have a few minutes of free play"). Another technique is a token system in which students receive tokens for good behavior, following directions, or good effort. Students can then trade in tokens for something they want to do (e.g., playing a special game, using a special piece of equipment, playing with a special partner). Discuss possible behavioral programs with the student's special education teacher.

Clearly State Consequences

Students need to know exactly what will happen when they perform the desired activities and when they misbehave. Describe in detail both positive and negative consequences to students *prior to* implementing the program. You may want to practice the consequences one or two times in a nonthreatening way so that a student clearly understands. Once the student knows the expectations and consequences, make sure you follow-through with these consequences when the student misbehaves. Do not give warnings unless they are part of the behavior program. Students will test the program in its early stages, and if you waver in your delivery of consequences, he or she will think he can get away with misbehavior. Again, confer with the team regarding specific behavior management techniques.

Be Flexible

Some students will come to your gym with a chip on their shoulder from something that happened at home or in the classroom. If you force participation at these times, you will no doubt have to deal with a major behavior problem. Let the student know that you realize he is having a hard day and can choose whether he wants to participate with the group. Point out that this is a special situation and that usually he would be expected to participate.

Students with Health Conditions

Confer with Collaborative Team

Particularly important is information from the student's parents and physician. Adhere to these guidelines when planning and implementing your program. For example, a student with a congenital heart defect might be able to participate in all physical education activities except those that raise his heart rate over a long period of time such as long distance running, basketball, and soccer. However, the student might be allowed to play basketball and soccer if he only plays for 2-minute periods, rests for 5 minutes, then plays another 2 minutes. Any modifications should be approved by the student's physician.

Prepare Classmates

In many cases, no one except the general physical educator needs to know about a student's health disorder. If the student's condition is under control and no modifications are needed in general physical education, then there is no need to share any information with the class. However, if modifications are needed or there is a chance that the student may

have a medical emergency during class, then it makes sense to talk to the class about the student's health condition. Be careful not to give information that will affect the student's right to privacy or cause him any ridicule. Many parents of students with health conditions are happy to talk to the class about the student's condition. They should be encouraged to interact with the student, and invite him to participate with them in their stations or on their teams. Right to privacy is a tricky situation, particularly for students with acquired immunodeficiency syndrome (AIDS), so you will need to confer with the team about how much information to share.

Think Safety

Although including students with health conditions is important, it is even more important that the student participates safely. Care should be taken that participation will not jeopardize the student's health and safety. For example, a student who has a seizure disorder should not be allowed to participate in climbing activities but can participate in low ropes or low gymnastic activities with spotters and mats. Again, safe modifications should be a team decision. Students with health disorders should not be immediately dismissed from physical education nor should they be tossed in without considering their individual condition. Students with AIDS or hepatitis pose a unique health risk to the teacher and other students in the class. Utilize universal precautions in situations in which cuts or scrapes may occur. Use gloves when treating bloody injuries, and do not allow other students near the student when he is bleeding. Confer with the school nurse for specific injury procedures.

Be Aware of the Effects of Medication

Some students who have health disorders take medications with side effects. For example, some seizure medications can make a student's gums weak and prone to bleeding. These students can participate in physical activity, but they may need to be extra careful not to take a blow to their face. Similarly, some medications affect a person's balance. Such individuals should be given a balance aid (as simple as a chair) or an assistant (could be a peer) in activities for which balance is needed. Some students might need to wear a helmet during physical education.

Be Aware of How the Time of Day or Seasons Affect Particular Students

Some students do better once their medication has kicked in. Other students gradually tire throughout the day. Still other students might be affected by the season. Whenever possible, accommodations should be made to accommodate these conditions. For example, students with allergy-induced asthma might receive physical education inside during particularly bad pollen days in the fall and spring.

SUMMARY

This chapter has reviewed a variety of ways that curricular modifications can accommodate students with disabilities into general physical education. Children with mild disabilities can be included in general physical education with multilevel curricular selection in which they work on the same content as their peers but at a different level. Children with severe disabilities can be included in general physical education while working on their own IEP objectives—either overlapped within general physical education activities or presented through an alternative activity.

Each child should be viewed as an individual with unique strengths and weaknesses, and any modifications should be developed based on each child's unique needs. The goal of any modification is to allow the child to be safely, successfully, and meaningfully included in general physical education, work on his or her unique IEP objectives, and have the opportunity to interact with peers who do not have disabilities. Modifications must be made carefully and thoughtfully if they are to be effective.

CHAPTER 8

Modifying Group Games and Team Sports

Travis is an 11-year-old who is excited to be starting middle school in the fall. Travis had a very positive experience in elementary school. He particularly enjoyed his experiences in general physical education with Mrs. Carr, his general physical education teacher. Mrs. Carr always seemed to know how to present activities in a way that allowed Travis to be successful. Travis was born with a rare physical condition known as arthrogryposis. Arthrogryposis begins during fetal development and causes the child to have no muscles or extremely atrophied muscles in arms and legs and the student's elbow and knee joints (and sometimes ankle, hip, wrist and shoulder joints) to be frozen. In Travis's case, this condition has not affected his cognitive development. Travis uses a manual wheelchair to move around school and is pretty independent in the classroom, bathroom, and cafeteria (needs a little help with carrying a tray in the cafeteria and pulling up his pants in the bathroom).

As noted, Mrs. Carr did a wonderful job accommodating Travis in physical education. For locomotor patterns, Travis would use his wheelchair. For ball skills, Travis figured out his own way to throw, catch, strike, and kick. He was well liked by his peers, and they had no problem modifying games so that Travis could have as much of a chance as his peers to be successful. However, middle school general physical education may pose some problems for Travis. Most notably, the middle school program at Travis' school focuses on team sports such as basketball, soccer, and volleyball; for the most part these games are played using regulation equipment following standard rules. Travis will not be successful in team sports played using regulation equipment following standard rules. The general physical educators are willing to accommodate Travis but are concerned that accommodations will ruin the game for the peers in the class without disabilities. They also are concerned that even with accommodations, Travis will not be able to participate safely in any team sports.

Group games and team sports are popular activities in general physical education. When used properly, group games and team sports can facilitate skill development as well as promote an understanding of rules, strategies, and concepts. Some group games also can be designed to promote sportsmanship, cooperation, and teamwork. Unfortunately, group games and team sports often promote competition and adherence to rules designed for very skilled athletes (Kasser, 1995; Morris & Stiehl, 1999). For example, it is not unusual to see upper-level elementary school physical education children playing regulation basketball games in which 10-foot baskets are used and professional rules are strictly followed even though most students at this age cannot reach a 10-foot basket or follow the rules of the game. Skilled students might enjoy these games, but the majority of students quickly become frustrated and passive, unhappy participants. Many general physical educators assume that group games and team sports are beyond the skill level or cognitive ability of students with disabilities, so these students are relegated to watching from the sideline, keeping score, or keeping time. When allowed to participate in the game, they rarely have success because they cannot perform the skills as quickly or as accurately as their peers.

Fortunately, many general physical educators modify games and team sports so that all students can successfully participate. Some modifications can be relatively simple such as allowing a child to hit a ball off a tee in softball or standing closer when serving in volleyball. Other modifications might require changes for everyone such as requiring all players to touch the ball one time before shooting in basketball. Still other modifications might change a game so much that a teacher might want to offer two or three different types of games: one volleyball game that is played with regulation rules, one in which children use a volleyball trainer and are allowed to stand closer when serving, and one with a lower net that has a cooperative rather than a competitive focus.

This chapter presents a variety of modifications to group games and team sports that can be used when including children with disabilities in general physical education. As with the previous two chapters, the first part of this chapter focuses on a general process or model for making modifications to group games or team sports. Once a physical educator understands the general process for modifying group games and the components of games that can be manipulated, then he or she can apply this process to a variety of game situations. The second part of this chapter presents a variety of alternative ways to present group games including adventure activities, cooperative games, and new games. Finally, a list of modifications to popular individual and team sports is presented with suggestions for children with physical disabilities, intellectual disabilities, and visual impairments. The specific type of game modification will vary based on each individual child's needs, the abilities and competitive nature of the class, and the purpose of the game. All children with a similar disability will not benefit from similar modifications; each child and each situation should be analyzed separately.

BASIC PRINCIPLES FOR MODIFYING GAMES AND SPORTS

Group games and team sports can facilitate skill development, promote an understanding of rules and strategies, and teach concepts such as sportsmanship and teamwork. Unfortunately, general physical educators often feel compelled to strictly follow the regulation rules of group games and team sports, which may lead to limited success and even the exclusion of lesser skilled students and students with disabilities. General physical educators should be aware of several basic principles regarding the use of group games and sports in their program.

1. *Games are not sacred; kids are.* If a game is not appropriate for even a single player, it is worth examining and altering to accommodate that player. The design of a game strongly influences each student's experience. Children who always get tagged or are never given the ball are probably not benefiting from the intended purposes of the game (Morris & Stiehl, 1999).

2. *Not all games are for everyone, at least not in their traditional configurations.* For example, in its current form, professional baseball might be ideal for some players. Few would argue, however, that professional rules, equipment, and expectations are appropriate for third graders. Instead, to accommodate this group, substantial alterations are necessary. There are many different ways to play games. If the purpose of your physical education program is to include everyone regardless of ability level, experience, or motivation, then a single, standard game design with strict rules might not be appropriate (Morris & Stiehl, 1999).

3. *You can modify any game to include anyone,* accommodating a wide spectrum of abilities, interests, needs, and resources. This will require modifications to various components of games such as the number of players, equipment, and how a player moves (see the Games Design Model below). Some modifications might be for only one child (e.g., allowing a child who moves slowly a safe area in a tag game); other modifications might involve several children (e.g., children who miss their first serve in volleyball get to take a step closer and try again). The key is thinking of alternative ways to play the game to accommodate all children (Morris & Stiehl, 1999).

4. *Whenever possible, include the students with a disability when making decisions* regarding adaptations to games and activities. Some students with disabilities will know through past experiences how best to modify an activity to meet their individual needs. Other students may not want any special modifications to games, choosing instead to do the best they can following the regulation rules. In either case, the student with a disability should have a say in modifications that will affect his or her successful participation (Lieberman & Houston-Wilson, 2002; MacDonald & Block, 2005).

5. *Get input from classmates without disabilities before creating and implementing modifications.* Classmates without disabilities will be more likely to embrace modifications to games and sports if they contribute to these modifications. For example, rather than telling the class about three modifications to a softball game to accommodate a student in a wheelchair, ask the group how they can modify the game so that students who cannot hit a pitched ball can still participate successfully.

6. *Give the student as many choices as possible.* Usually there is more than one way to modify a game. Choices allow the student with a disability to to be more comfortable in the game.

Choices also allow the student with disabilities more ownership in the modifications, which will motivate the student (Lieberman & Houston-Wilson, 2002).

7. *Participating with physical assistance is an acceptable way to participate in an activity,* especially when the alternative is not participating. Students with more severe disabilities may need physical guidance and even hand-over-hand assistance to safely and successfully participate in many games. It is easy to dismiss a student with severe, multiple disabilities from participation. However, these students can still enjoy the excitement and camaraderie of playing a game or being a member of a team, even if participation requires a great deal of assistance.

8. *On occasion, play multiple games simultaneously with some games following regulation rules and others having modifications.* Skilled students without disabilities should be allowed to play regulation games to challenge and improve their skills. Too often, modified games are forced onto skilled students without disabilities, and these students may come to resent having a peer with a disability in their general physical education class. A good solution is to occasionally allow regulation games for the skilled students and modified games for less skilled students. For example, at the end of a high school volleyball unit, the general physical educator has the students play competitive games. However, this general physical education class of 50 students is very diverse, including some girls who play on the varsity volleyball team, some boys and girls who are very athletic, some boys and girls who are not very athletic, a child with autism, and a child with muscular dystrophy who uses an electric wheelchair. To accommodate this range of abilities, the general physical educator has set up three nets. The first net is set at regulation height for 18 students (three teams of six per team), who are very skilled at volleyball. These 18 students will play following the regulation rules of volleyball. It is not uncommon to see overhand serving and bump, set, and then a spike during the game, and the goal is clearly to win. The second net also is set at the regulation height for 18 students divided into three teams who understand the game of volleyball but who play at more of a recreational level. A volleyball trainer (larger, lighter volleyball) is used instead of a regulation volleyball. Underhand serving is popular in this game, and rarely does anyone spike the ball. Rules such as carrying the ball and double hits are relaxed, and students are allowed to stand closer to the net when serving. Although someone does keep score, clearly winning is less important than playing the game. The third net is set at the height of a tennis net, and 14 students (including the student with autism and the student with muscular dystrophy) are assigned to this group. Students in this court are still learning the very basics of volleyball, and most have very limited volleyball skills. A beach ball is used instead of a volleyball, and rules are very relaxed. Students keep score and the game is competitive, but the goal is to have fun.

Determining Whether an Accommodation Is Appropriate

Not all modifications are appropriate for a particular child with a disability in a particular situation, especially in group games in which some modifications can change the game so drastically that it is no longer fun or motivating for children without disabilities. One simple way to determine which game modification to use is to consider the effect of the modification on the student with disabilities, other classmates, and the general physical educator. If the game modification has a negative effect on any of these individuals, then it probably is not the most appropriate modification. The following four criteria should be used whenever considering a particular game modification. If the proposed game modification does not meet the standards set by these criteria, then an alternative modification should be considered:

1. *Does the game modification allow the student with disabilities to participate successfully yet still be challenged?* For example, in a softball game a student with an intellectual disability might not be able to hit a softball pitched from the regulation mound. However, this student can hit the ball if the pitcher stands a little closer and tosses it over the plate. Such a modification allows the student to be successful but also challenges him. Game modifications should be designed to meet each individual child's unique needs.

2. *Does the game modification make the setting unsafe for the student with a disability or for peers?* For example, to include a student who uses a wheelchair in a game of volleyball, you say that the student must play one of the back positions so that other students are less likely to bump into the student. In addition, you place cones around the student's chair so that classmates without disabilities who get too close to the student hit the cones before the wheelchair.

Finally, you remind peers at the beginning of the class and several times during the class to be careful around the student who uses a wheelchair. Peers will quickly learn to be careful, and the student can safely participate in the activity.

3. *Does the game modification negatively affect peers without disabilities?* This point is particularly important when playing group games. For example, an elementary class playing a game of tag includes a student who has autism-like behaviors and is not aware of the rules of the game. To include this student you specify that when he is the tagger, all students must sit down and let him tag them. Obviously, students without disabilities are not thrilled with the idea of sitting down and letting another student tag them, regardless of his ability. Better modifications would be making the game space smaller, eliminating safe places, and assisting the student to tag his peers. Similarly, it might be fun for a high school class to play sit-down volleyball for 1 day to accommodate a student who uses a wheelchair or beep softball to accommodate a student who is blind, but such changes implemented for an entire unit negatively affect the program for students without disabilities.

4. *Does the game modification cause an undue burden on the general physical education teacher?* For example, a ninth grader with advanced muscular dystrophy who uses an electric wheelchair is fully included in general physical education. For a unit on soccer, you could consider changing the game to accommodate this student. However, this would be difficult. Another solution is to work with this student off to the side of the field one-to-one; however, this prevents you from supervising and instructing the other students. A better solution is to have this student play a permanent throw-in position. The student moves his electric wheelchair along the sidelines of the field. When the ball goes out of bounds, a player retrieves the ball, gives it to the student in a wheelchair, and then the student in the wheelchair throws it back into play (pushing the ball off his lap). This way the student is part of the game and works on his goals of moving his electric wheelchair and moving his arms. Furthermore, this simple modification is relatively easy for the general physical educator to implement.

GAMES DESIGN MODEL

Morris and Stiehl (1999) developed a systematic approach for analyzing and changing group games, built around three premises: 1) games are not sacred,

kids are; 2) games are for everyone, but not in their traditional configurations; and 3) any game can be modified to include anyone. Their approach follows three basic steps.

Understand Any Game's Basic Structure

First, key aspects of any game can be analyzed and then modified to accommodate the needs of students of varying abilities. Table 8.1 outlines how Morris and Stiehl (1999) conceptualized six major aspects of games and variations that can change the nature of the game.

Purposes of games can vary from one simple focus (e.g., improving one motor skill) to expecting students to acquire a variety of skills, concepts, and behaviors. Not all students involved in a game necessarily have to work on the same goals. For example, a locomotor game played by all students in a kindergarten physical education class could have various goals for various students, including improving walking gait for a student with cerebral palsy, improving hopping skills for students with limited locomotor abilities, and improving skipping, levels and general space awareness in skilled students. Similarly, goals for a game of soccer played by all students in tenth-grade physical education could include improving cardiovascular fitness for a student with Down syndrome, improving range of motion for a student with cerebral palsy, developing basic skills and understanding of the rules of the game for lower ability students, and using various strategies for skilled students.

Players involved in the game can vary in two major ways: how they are grouped, and number of players involved. Players can be grouped homogeneously by gender, size, or skill level; players can be grouped heterogeneously so that each team has an equal representation of skilled and unskilled players; or players can be randomly assigned to groups. The number of players involved in a game can vary by having more than, less than, or the same number of players than a particular game calls for. Group size can be varied so that a particular team might have more or less players than other teams. How players are selected for a particular group as well as the number of players involved in a game will have a profound effect on how successfully a student with disabilities is included. For example, a teacher needs to break down her seventh-grade physical education class into four teams for a modified game of volleyball. The class includes a student named Bill who has muscular dystrophy, uses an electric wheelchair, and has limited strength and mobility in his upper body. The teacher decides to group the teams by skill level, with each team having skilled players, average players, and unskilled players. Bill is assigned to Team A. Teams B–D also have unskilled

Table 8.1. Games Design Model: Components to be manipulated

Purposes	Players	Movements	Objects	Organization	Limits
Development of motor skills	Individuals	Types	Types/uses	Types	Performance
Enhancement of self worth	Groups	Location	Quantity	Location	Environment
Improvement of fitness	Numbers	Quality	Location	Quantity	
Enjoyment	Relationships				
Satisfaction		Quantity			
Development of cognitive skills		Sequences			

From G.S. Morris and J. Stiehl, *Changing Kids' Games*, 2nd ed., page 18. ©1999 by Gordon S. Morris and Jim Stiehl. Adapted by permission from Human Kinetics (Champaign, IL).

players, so this will not be an unfair disadvantage to Team A.

Movement refers to the types of movements involved in a particular game and how these movements are used. Types of movements include different types of locomotor, non-locomotor, manipulative, and body awareness skills. Type of movements can be varied so that skilled and non-skilled students work on different skills during the game; a student with disabilities might work on even different skills. Other ways in which Morris and Stiehl (1999) suggested that movements could be modified include locations of movement (personal space, general space, following certain directions, levels, or pathways), quality of movement (variations in force, flow, and speed requirements), quantity of movement (several repetitions, a few repetitions), variations in relationships (moving with or without object or other players), and sequences (following a particular sequence or having no sequence). Modifications in movement are excellent ways to ensure that students with disabilities are appropriately and successfully engaged in general physical education activities.

For example, Susie is a third grader who has severe intellectual disabilities and autism-like behaviors. Susie's class is working on the ball skills of dribbling and passing a playground ball, skills that Susie does not do independently. The class consists of 40 students who have varying abilities, so the teacher has modified the movement requirements so that all students are challenged yet successful in the activity. More skilled students are working on dribbling the ball while running in and out of cones and passing by playing a game of keep-away with one person in the middle trying to steal the pass from two players who pass the ball back and forth using different passing patterns. Students who can dribble and pass but who still need practice on these skills are working on dribbling the ball while jogging forward and passing the ball back and forth with a peer from various distances depending on each student's strength. Students who are just learning how to dribble and pass are working on dribbling a ball while standing in one place and passing a ball so that it hits a large target on the wall. Finally, Susie is working on drib-

bling by dropping the ball and catching it before it bounces again (with assistance from different peers in her class). Susie works on passing by handing the ball to a peer upon a verbal request. During relay races at the end of class each student uses the skills they have been working on. That is, some students have to dribble between cones, some students have to dribble while jogging forward, some students have to dribble the ball 10 times, and Susie has to drop and catch the ball with assistance. The basic movements are similar, but how these movements are operationalized during practice as well as during the game vary from student to student depending on each student's abilities.

Objects refer to any equipment used during practice or during a game. Objects can vary in terms of how a student moves in relation to the object (e.g., going under, over, or through hoops; catching, kicking, or throwing a ball), how the object moves a student (e.g., scooter boards, skates, tricycles), how an object is used to send other objects away (e.g., bats, hockey sticks, rackets, feet), or how objects are used to gather other objects in (e.g., gloves, hands, lacrosse sticks, milk cartons). In addition, the number and placement of objects in the environment can vary depending on the needs of each student. For example, some students might use regulation-size bats to send objects away from their body; other students might use slightly larger bats; still other students might use a very large bat and hit a very large ball. Varying the objects will ensure that each student is working at a level that meets his or her unique needs.

Organization refers to decisions regarding the patterns, structure, and location of players. Some games might have very strict patterns to follow, such as relay races in which students are expected to line up behind each other. However, the structure can be altered in which players are allowed to move anywhere they wish in the environment. Modifications can also be made to the location of players and objects within the boundaries. For a student with limited mobility or strength, a fair accommodation would be to have another student stand near him when it is his turn to toss a ball to them or to tag them. Similarly, how far each student has to run in a relay race could vary based on individual abilities.

Limits refer to the general rules for players. Some games might have movements that are deemed acceptable or necessary. For example, it might be necessary for a skilled student to dribble through several cones in a relay race. It might be unacceptable for skilled students to spike a volleyball unless it goes into a certain zone. Limits also refer to the physical aspects of the environment and activity. Physical aspects of the environment can vary in terms of the width of the field, size and type of equipment, and number of players in the game. Activity conditions can vary in terms of how long the game is, how long a particular student plays, scoring, or rules. For example, a skilled student might get one pitch in a softball game, a less skilled student gets three pitches, and a student with disabilities hits the ball off the tee.

Modify a Game's Basic Structure

The second level of game analysis involves applying the components outlined previously to specific games. That is, devise and modify games based on the purpose of the game, how many players will be involved, and the game's movements and objects, among others.

Modifying a game's basic structure can take two distinct forms. The components can be manipulated to make up a completely new game (see Table 8.2).

For example, if students are to develop and improve kicking skills, a game could be devised in which equal teams of three players are given one large box to kick. The object of the game is to kick the box across the gym. Each player on the team must kick the box at the same time, and players cannot touch or kick anyone else's box. This novel game ensures that teammates work together and that each player gets many turns to practice the skill of forceful kicking.

A second way of manipulating game components is to modify traditional games. Game analysis can be used to modify traditional sports that tend to be dominated by a few skilled players so that everyone has an opportunity to participate, improve skills, and contribute. For example, basketball can be changed to focus on improving passing skills and teamwork. Six teams of five players are selected by the teacher so that each team has an equal representation of skilled and non-skilled players. Points can be scored by making baskets, but a team that passes the ball to each player before someone shoots gets double points for every basket. In addition, every time a different player makes a basket, the team gets 5 bonus points. This encourages teammates to pass the ball before shooting. In addition, some players must shoot at a 10-foot basket, while other players can shoot at an 8-foot basket. Manipulating game components is an easy way to ensure that the class is focused on specific goals and that maximum participation and practice is afforded to each student.

Table 8.2.   Sample modifications for a soccer game

Component	Skilled child	Typical child	Child with Down syndrome
Purposes	Use opposite foot; cross ball to far post	Improve basic skills of passing, dribbling, shooting, and playing defense	Work on fitness (moving and running)
Players	11 versus 11 or 5 versus 3 With skilled players only having three players	11 versus 11 or 7 versus 7	7 versus 7 or 5 versus 3 Put player with Down syndrome on team with more players
Movements	Practice one-to-ones to beat an opponent off the dribble; work on changing speeds	All regular movement	Allow moving slower and even walking when child gets tired
Objects	Regulation ball; smaller goals to make it more challenging	Regulation ball	Regulation ball when playing on playground; Nerf ball when playing in modified game; larger goals when playing in modified game
Organization	Regulation boundaries	Regulation boundaries or smaller field	Play "zone soccer" in which players have to stay in particular zones. Place one or two players from each team with similar abilities in zones. Put player with Down syndrome in the same zone as lesser skilled players or those who will share the ball.
Limits	Cannot dribble (has to trap and then pass ball); has to use opposite foot when shooting; cannot go past midfield when playing defense or offense	No limits	No one can steal the ball from player with DS; player with DS is allowed free pass to teammates and a free shot at goal

Manage a Game's Degree of Difficulty

The third level of analysis is the most important in terms of accommodating students with disabilities. This step involves analyzing each of the game components and then creating a continuum from easy to difficult that is used to make a game or skill easier or more difficult for particular students. Skilled students can be challenged by making the activity more difficult, and students with lower abilities or specific disabilities can become more successful by making the activity easier. Morris and Stiehl (1999) outlined the following strategy for identifying degree of difficulty.

1. *Identify factors that may limit a player's performance.* List the various aspects of the task that can be manipulated. External factors such as ball size, size of targets, and speed of objects should be the focus at this level. A student's personal abilities such as visual perception or strength should not be considered at this level of analysis because these factors cannot be influenced directly by game analysis. However, personal limitations can be accommodated by making simple changes in task complexity. For example, a larger, slower moving ball can be used for kicking or striking by a student who has a visual perception problem or a visual impairment.

2. *Diagram the task complexity spectrum.* Factors identified are sequenced along a continuum from less difficult to more difficult. For example, ball speed in kicking might be listed (see Figure 8.1). All of the factors related to targeted skills should be sequenced. These sequences will begin to help you understand how to modify activities to accommodate varying abilities.

3. *Begin to create tasks that vary in difficulty.* Finally, compile all of the factors and sequences into a *task complexity (TC) spectrum* for a particular skill. An example of one of Morris and Stiehl's (1999) TC spectrums is presented in Figure 8.2.

Game categories (e.g., limits, players) also can be modified to make a particular game easier or more difficult for a group of children. For example, having four teams and four separate goals in soccer would make the game more difficult; having two teams of just three players on each team would make the game easier. Similarly, having a smaller playing field would make soccer easier for players with limited endurance, but a smaller tennis court would make the game more difficult for a skilled player. The TC spectrum shows in one schematic how several factors can be manipulated to accommodate a student

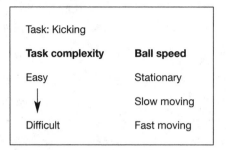

Figure 8.1. Sequence of factors for kicking.

with disabilities, make a task slightly less difficult for a student just learning a skill, or make an activity more challenging for a skilled player.

Functional Approach for Modifying Movement Experiences

Another model for analyzing and modifying games is the *Functional Approach for Modifying Movement Experiences* (FAMME) model (Kasser & Lytle, 2005). Similar to Morris and Stiehl's (1999) model, the FAMME model is designed to help the general physical educator systematically analyze a child's strengths and weaknesses as they relate to the skills needed in a particular game. This information is then examined to create individually determined modifications that facilitate the successful participation of a child with a disability. (Table 8.3 shows the FAMME model applied to a game of tag.) The model has the following four steps.

Determine Underlying Components of Skills

The first step in the model involves carefully examining the underlying requirements of a particular game or activity. These components are the basic prerequisites that any student needs to successfully participate in an activity. The first column of Table 8.3 shows the basic requirements for playing tag. Most games require some basic elements such as a certain amount of strength, flexibility, endurance, speed, and agility. For a game of tag, strength and flexibility are not as important as speed, agility, and endurance. Softball, however, requires upper body strength and eye–hand coordination but does not require much agility, speed, or endurance. Underlying components of any game will be unique depending on the specific nature of the game. In addition to physical requirements of games, students must understand the basic concept or goal of the game as well as rules that govern the game. For example, in

TC	Size of support base	Center of gravity	Speed	Time
Easy	Eight body parts	Directly over and close to base of support	Slow	8 seconds
↓	Four body parts	Slightly off center and above base of support	Fast	18 seconds
Difficult	One body part	Moderately off center and far above base of support	Faster	30 seconds

Figure 8.2. Task complexity: Balance factors. (From G.S. Morris and J. Stiehl, *Changing Kids' Games,* 2nd ed., page 139. ©1999 by Gordon S. Morris and Jim Stiehl. Reprinted with permission from Human Kinetics [Champaign, IL].)

a simple game of tag, a student needs to know the goal and the rules.

Determine Current Capabilities of the Individual

The general physical educator identifies the student's abilities and disabilities as they relate to a particular activity or game. As noted in Chapter 7, it is more important to understand a student's functional abilities and impairments rather than simply rely on a label. Knowing that a student has cerebral palsy or an intellectual disability does not really predict how well a student will do in a volleyball game or what modifications might be necessary. Kasser and Lytle (2005) suggested focusing on the following major functional areas: strength, flexibility, balance/postural control, coordination, speed/agility, endurance, concept understanding, attention, self-responsibility/self-control, and sensory perception. When possible, match these

functional characteristics to the specific requirements of an activity or game. For example, it is important to note that a student has limited endurance in a game such as tag or soccer. However, limited endurance would not be an issue in a bowling unit.

Match Modification Efforts to Capabilities

In this step, specific modifications are prescribed that help a student who has a particular functional impairment (e.g., strength) be successful in an activity or game that requires strength (e.g., serving a volleyball over the net). For example, tagging requires understanding the basic concept of tag and rules of the game. A student with autism has difficulty understanding the concept and rules of tag. Therefore, a modification is needed for this student to participate safely and successfully in tag. The suggested modification focuses on a peer or teacher as-

Table 8.3.   Application of FAMME model for game of tag

Underlying components of tag	Child's functional differences	Modifications
Concept understanding	Does not understand rules of tag	Peer to TA helps student move around setting and avoid being tagged. Make space smaller when student is tagger; have peer or TA help student find people to tag
Balance	Okay	None needed
Coordination	Okay	None needed
Agility/speed	Slower than peers	Peers and TA help student avoid tagger. Make space smaller when student is tagger; have peer or TA help student find people to tag
Sensory perception	Okay	None needed
Strength (legs)	Okay	None needed
Endurance	Tires after about 3 minutes	Allow student to sit out and rest for 1 minute every 3 minutes.
Flexibility	Okay	None needed
Attention	Maintains attention for only a few seconds	Peers or TA help student stay on task
Self-control	Can easily lose control and tantrum	Peers or TA calm student; if student begins to get upset, allow him to leave setting and get a drink of water

From S.L. Kasser, *Inclusive Physical Activity: A Lifetime of Opportunities,* pages 159–160, Table 6.7 © 2005 by Susan L. Kasser. Adapted with permission from Human Kinetics (Champaign, IL).

Note: Targeted student is a second grader with autism who comes to GPE with a teacher assistant.

sistant helping this student to move away from the tagger. When this student is the tagger, the space is reduced and a peer or teacher assistant assists this student in moving towards and tagging peers.

Evaluate Modification Effectiveness

The final step in the FAMME model is evaluating the effectiveness of the modification. Kasser and Lytle (1995) created a list of seven questions that a general physical educator can use to determine a modification's effectiveness.

1. Is the modification age appropriate?

2. Is the modification functionally appropriate?

3. Does the modification allow the participant to be as independent as possible?

4. Does the modification ensure maximum participation of the participants?

5. Does the modification avoid singling out or spotlighting high or low ability participants?

6. Does the modification allow for optimal challenge for everyone in the activity?

7. Is safe participation ensured for all participants once the modification is implemented?

UNIQUE GAMES AND GROUP ACTIVITIES THAT CAN FACILITATE INCLUSION

Adventure and Initiative Games

Project Adventure (PA) is based on the

> Philosophy that people are usually more capable (mentally, emotionally, and physically) than they perceive themselves to be. PA games and activities give people opportunities to challenge themselves and to take risks within the supportive atmosphere of a group. Adventure means any new experience that elicits excitement. (Ellmo & Graser, 1995, p. 4)

Goals of the adventure program are as follows:

1. To increase the participant's sense of personal confidence

2. To increase mutual support within a group

3. To develop an increased level of agility and physical coordination

4. To develop an increased joy in one's physical self and in being with others

5. To develop an increased familiarity and identification with the natural world

These goals are achieved through the use of noncompetitive games, group problem solving, initiatives, and rope course events to create that excitement and achieve their goals of facilitating personal learning and growth (Rohnke, 1989; Rohnke & Butler, 1995). Group initiative activities are designed "to increase a student's ability to be an active member of a group which has a problem to solve. This problem-oriented approach can be useful in developing each student's "awareness of decision-making, leadership, and the obligation of each member within a group" (Rohnke, 1977, p. 65). In terms of including students with disabilities, group initiative activities can be used to highlight the importance of including all students in the class to achieve a team goal. The rules of the game do not permit exclusion of any participants. In fact, initiative games help team members focus on each person's strengths and how they can best contribute to the solution to the problem. Students can then apply cooperative problem-solving skills learned in initiative games to include students with disabilities into more traditional team sports.

An example of a simple initiative game is *Reach for the Sky* (Rohnke, 1977). The object of the game is to place a piece of tape as high as possible on a wall. Teams of as few as 3 and as many as 15–20 players work together to build a human tower to place the tape as high as possible on the wall. Groups quickly realize that heavier students should be on the bottom supporting smaller players. A person who uses a wheelchair can be a good support on the bottom of the tower, using his wheelchair as a base and having him use his arms to help hold a person in place. Smaller students, such as those with fetal alcohol syndrome (FAS), can be near the top of the tower. Thus, person's strengths are highlighted rather than their weaknesses, and students without disabilities learn to appreciate how each person can contribute to team efforts.

Transferring this concept to traditional games, students without disabilities can focus on both a student's strengths and weaknesses when modifying the game. For example, in a game of basketball, a student who uses a wheelchair can be seen as a tough obstacle to get around as a point guard positioned in a 2-1-2 defense alignment. The student with attention-deficit disorder might be a chaser while playing defense, chasing the ball and harassing any player who has the ball. In a game of football, the student who uses a wheelchair can be an offensive lineman, protecting the quarterback by moving his wheelchair so that on-coming rushers must run around him. Make sure that you talk to the group about safety, especially being aware of a student who uses a wheelchair. In addition, you might want to make special rules for the student who uses a wheelchair, limiting the range in which they can move so that students without disabilities have safe areas. Students will learn quickly with proper instruction.

One of the nice aspects of group initiative games is that there are no set solutions or answers. Solutions will depend on the unique characteristics of each member and how these characteristics interact with those of other group members. This fact should be pointed out to the group at the end of each initiative game or at the end of a class that included several initiative games. Group discussions are a critical part of the adventure process, and participants are encouraged to share how they solved problems during the activity. Group discussion is a good place to help focus on how each member of the team contributed to the group goal. Group discussions also can be used to guide students to think of how children with different disabilities/abilities can be included in an activity and contribute to the team (see Ellmo & Graser, 1995; Rohnke, 1977, 1989; and Rohnke & Butler, 1995, for samples of adventure games and initiative games).

Cooperative Games

Cooperative sports and games are designed to help students work together to overcome challenges rather than against one another to overcome other people. The major goal of cooperative games is to create an environment that helps

> Children play together for common ends rather than against one another for mutually exclusive ends. In the process, they (children) learn in a fun way how to become more considerate of one another, more aware of how other people are feeling, and more willing to operate in one another's best interests. (Orlick, 1982, p. 4)

The major difference between traditional games and cooperative games is the focus and structure. As Orlick explained, traditional games such as *King of the Mountain* have one person as king, all others are to be pushed down the mountain. Players are compelled to work against each other, and only one player can achieve the goal of the game. Thus, the game has an inherent competitive focus and structure. In contrast, a cooperative version of the same game, *People of the Mountain,* has a completely different focus in which the objective is to get as many people as possible to the top of the mountain, requiring children to work together. The focus of the game is inherently cooperative and encourages classmates

to help and support each other. In addition, everyone is a winner in this game.

Many physical education programs present skill development through competitive activities. Although fun and motivating for skilled students who can win competitive games, students with less ability (including students with disabilities) rarely have an opportunity to win. In addition, competitive team sports force skilled players to pressure less skilled players. Mistakes are more glaring, and often more skilled players dominate the game. Less skilled players lose confidence and self-esteem and learn how to avoid fully participating in the game. For example, after miskicking a soccer ball during a soccer game and being ridiculed by his teammates and teased by his opponents, a less skilled player avoids kicking the ball by positioning himself away from the action. An alternative to competition in physical education is cooperation. Cooperative games can be implemented at various levels.

One alternative is to play only cooperative games such as *People of the Mountain* in which the focus of all activities is cooperation. This approach is most appropriate for elementary children who are learning how to work together and who have not been exposed to traditional sports. A second alternative is to play within a traditional competitive structure but focus on cooperation rather than competition. For example, a game of volleyball can focus on how many different players on a team can hit the ball before it goes over the net. Such an approach is appropriate for students just learning skills who need practice in a game atmosphere without the added pressure of competition. A third alternative is to include self-paced activities that are not assessed or scored. For example, Clean Out Your Backyard is a fun throwing game for young children in which yarn balls are thrown back and forth toward each other. For older students, a basketball game can be less competitive by simply not keeping score. Finally, a fourth alternative includes goal-oriented play in some situations and light-hearted play in other situations. For example, some days the class can work on basketball following traditional rules; on other days the focus can be on which team passes the ball the most before shooting and which team has the most players score.

Most traditional physical education activities including group games and team sports can easily become more cooperative by making just a few changes. The Cooperative Games Book (Orlick, 1978) and The Second Cooperative Games Book (Orlick, 1982) present several suggestions for making traditional competitive games cooperative. For example, *Musical Hoops* is a cooperative version of Musical Chairs. In traditional Musical Chairs, chairs are taken away and children compete against each other for a chair.

The quickest children usually get to sit in the remaining chairs, while less skilled players, including students with disabilities, are the first to be eliminated. In Musical Hoops, when the music stops and hoops are taken away, players must share the remaining hoop. Imagine an entire class of kindergartners, including a student who is blind and another with cerebral palsy who is much slower than his peers, working together to fit into one hoop!

Another example is *Alaskan Rules Baseball.* One of the problems in traditional baseball is that players in the field stand around waiting for the ball to be hit to them. Even if a ball is hit to a less skilled player or a player with a disability, chances are that a more skilled player will run over and try to field the ball. What results is skilled players getting more turns while less skilled players and players with disabilities get fewer practice turns and are bored. In Alaskan Rules Baseball, all players in the field must touch the ball before a player is out. The first player who gets to the ball picks it up, and all other players on the team line up behind that player. The ball is then passed (or tossed) from player to player. When the last player has the ball, he yells "stop," at which time the player's turn is over. The batter gets one run for every base he touches.

New Games

New Games are games that allow individuals of all ages and abilities to play in an atmosphere of fun and creativity. The following are the major philosophies of New Games (Fluegelman, 1976):

1. Individuals choose games and make changes to rules as needed so that everyone can be involved.

2. Modifications can occur at any time during the game (even in the middle of the game).

3. Everyone should enjoy the activities. If everyone is not having fun, then modifications are probably needed.

4. Fair, fun competition is important, but winning is de-emphasized.

The *New Games Book* (1976) and *More New Games* (Fluegelman, 1981) have descriptions of hundreds of games that can be played by as few as two players and as many as 100 players. Games are also categorized by how active the participants are. New Games lend themselves nicely to including students with disabilities and can be a fun rainy day activity for students without disabilities. The following are two examples of New Games that can easily accommodate students with varying abilities.

People to People

Pairs of students stand in a circle facing one player who is the leader. The leader calls a name of two body parts (e.g., back to back), and the partners must touch their backs together. When everyone is touching backs, the leader then calls two more body parts (e.g., head to knee) and the partners must touch their head to their partner's knee. The game continues until the leader says "people to people" at which time everyone (including the leader) tries to find a new partner. Whoever is left without a partner is the new leader.

Amoeba Tag

Players scatter about the playing area, and one player is designated "it." Players move about the playing area, while "it" tries to tag a player (every so often change the way players move such as galloping, skipping, jumping, hopping, traveling at different levels or following different pathways). When a player is tagged, he or she holds "its" hand, and both players become it. When another player is tagged, he or she holds hands with the two-person "it" to form a three-person "it." As new people are tagged, they join the ever-increasing "it." Eventually, all but one player is "it."

SPECIFIC MODIFICATIONS TO TRADITIONAL TEAM AND INDIVIDUAL SPORTS

Many middle and high school physical education programs focus on traditional individual and team sports. It may be easier for physical educators in these types of programs to focus on simple modifications to traditional sport activities rather than use the game models discussed previously. The chapter appendix provides information on specific ways to modify selected individual and team sports to meet the needs of students with disabilities. Information includes general suggestions for modifying skill work, general suggestions for modifying games, and modifications for students with specific disabilities. This is not a comprehensive list but rather suggestions for modifying traditional individual and team sports. As you begin to learn more about the functional skills of your students as well as how to utilize these modifications, you will quickly begin to incorporate your own modifications that meet the needs of your particular students.

SUMMARY

Some accommodations may be necessary if students with disabilities are to be successfully and meaningfully included in group games and team sports.

These modifications can be implemented without necessarily changing the general format of the game or forcing skilled students to play at a lower level (e.g., simply allowing the student to use a lighter racquet in tennis or slightly shortening the bases in softball). However, modifications can include specific changes to rules of games such as giving students free passes in basketball or setting up special zones in soccer. In either case, these accommodations can be the difference between successful inclusion and frustration for students with and without disabilities.

This chapter has outlined Morris and Stiehl's (1999) Games Design Model and Kasser and Lytle's (2005) FAMME model for modifying group games and team sports; unique games modifications including initiative games, cooperative games, and new games, and specific modifications to traditional individual and team sports (in chapter appendix). As noted in the previous two chapters, these modifications are not meant to be an exhaustive list but rather help general physical educators and other team members begin to think of simple yet innovative ways to safely and successfully include students with disabilities into group games and team sports. As noted throughout this chapter, it is important to focus on the functional abilities and impairments exhibited by each of your students.

Accommodations to Team and Individual Sports for Students with Disabilities

Although the suggestions in this appendix are presented by disability labels, determining the exact modification to use should be based on each child's unique abilities and needs as well as on the nature of the sport and the focus of your lesson. A successful modification for one child with a disability may not necessarily work for another child with a similar disability.

TEAM SPORTS

Basketball

Dribbling

General

Use larger or smaller balls.

Use playground balls, Nerf balls, or punch balls (large balloons).

Vary distance required to travel.

Vary speed required.

Have student use only dominant hand.

Students who use wheelchairs (normal upper body strength and control)

Hold ball on lap and push wheelchair.

Push wheelchair a few rotations, bounce ball one time, and then push wheelchair again.

Students who use wheelchairs (limited upper body strength and control)

Have peer push wheelchair while student holds ball in lap or in hands.

Have peer physically assist student in bouncing ball.

Have student repeatedly hit ball when it sits on lap tray while student is being pushed.

Students with visual impairments

Allow student to dribble in place.

Allow student to use two hands to dribble.

Allow student to dribble in place a few times, then walk forward toward sound of peer.

Allow student to walk forward while dropping and catching ball for dribbling.

Attach string to ball and to student's wrist so that ball is easy to retrieve.

Have student stand in corner of gym while dribbling so that ball is less likely to bounce away from him or her.

Put bell or beeper in ball so that student can retrieve it when it bounces away.

Have peers assist student by giving verbal cues for direction and by retrieving balls that get away from student.

Students with intellectual disabilities or autism

Allow student to walk while dribbling.

Allow student to stand, bounce, and catch ball.

Allow student to walk while holding ball.

Allow student to use two hands to dribble.

Allow student to walk forward while dropping and catching ball to encourage proper technique.

Passing and Catching

General

Use suspended balls.

Use larger or smaller balls.

Use textured balls.

Use playground balls, Nerf balls, or punch balls (large balloons).

Vary distance required to pass (have peers stand closer).

Toss ball slower as required.

Toss ball at known trajectory.

Students who use wheelchairs (normal upper body strength and control)

Encourage student to find best way to pass (overhead versus chest versus sidearm).

Use soft balls (Nerf balls) for safety as needed.

Students who use wheelchairs (limited upper body strength and control)

Use soft balls (Nerf balls) for safety.

Have student push ball down ramp.

Have student push ball off lap.

Have student swing arm and hit ball held by peer.

Have student kick ball if legs have more control than arms.

Have student hit ball off tee (or held by peer) with head.

Students with visual impairments

Use soft balls (Nerf balls) for safety.

Use verbal cues (tell student when ball is released for catching; tell student where to pass).

Use bounce pass (ball makes sound).

Put bells or beeper in ball.

Use physical assistance to instruct student.

Students with intellectual disabilities or autism

Use soft balls (Nerf balls) for safety.

Start with a balloon and gradually work toward faster-moving balls.

Use suspended balls.

Use physical assistance when teaching skill.

Encourage proper technique.

Shooting

General

Use larger or smaller balls.

Use playground balls, Nerf balls, or punch balls (large balloons).

Vary distance required to shoot.

Vary height of basket.

Vary size of basket (use large box for basket or hang Hula-Hoop on wall).

Students who use wheelchairs (normal upper body strength and control)

Encourage student to find best way to shoot (overhead versus chest versus sidearm).

Use soft balls (Nerf balls) for safety as needed.

Students who use wheelchairs (limited upper body strength and control)

Use soft balls (Nerf balls) for safety.

Have student push ball down ramp into box.

Have student push ball off lap into box.

Have student swing arm and hit ball held by peer into box.

Have student kick ball into box if legs have more control than arms.

Have student hit ball off tee (or held by peer) with head into box.

Students with visual impairments

Use soft balls (Nerf balls) for safety.

Use verbal cues to tell student where to shoot.

Give student specific verbal feedback to tell him or her how close his or her shot was to the basket.

Use physical assistance to instruct student.

Tie string to ball and to student's wrist so that ball is easy to retrieve.

Place radio under basket to cue student.

Put bells or beeper in ball.

Students with intellectual disabilities or autism

Use soft balls (Nerf balls) for safety.

Use physical assistance when teaching skill.

Place hand-prints on ball to show proper technique.

Encourage proper technique.

Basketball

General

Encourage students to develop modified rules that will be fair for everyone, including student with disabilities.

Allow student to shoot at lower basket.

Allow student to use different ball when it is his or her turn to dribble or shoot.

Make rule that no student can steal ball when student is dribbling.

Make rule that no student can block or interfere with student's pass.

Have student play a zone position away from the basket.

Match student with disability against a lower-ability student without disability.

Give student a peer to assist him or her during game.

Allow free substitution for student if he or she tires easily.

Give student's team an extra player (six versus five game).

Allow student to play only offense or defense if he or she has limited mobility.

Split the class and allow skilled students to play competitive, full-court games while allowing less skilled players (including student with disabilities) to play slower, less competitive games (half-court, three versus three, run set plays).

Play lead-up basketball games such as half-court basketball, horse, relays, and so forth.

Students who use wheelchairs (normal upper body strength and control)

Caution peers about wheelchair.

Have student play away from basket on defense and offense for safety.

Students who use wheelchairs (limited upper body strength and control)

Provide student with peer to assist him or her.

Allow student to use adapted equipment practiced during skills (e.g., ramps).

Bring basket (can be box or trash can) to student.

Students with visual impairments

Have peer guide student around court.

Have a guide rope across gym so student can move up and down court.

Place carpet squares on floor to mark where student should stand for defense and offense.

Have teammates give extra verbal cues to student to describe where he or she is, where teammates are, and where opponents are.

Use ball with bell.

Place radio under basket.

Have teammates wear brightly colored pennies.

Use brightly colored ball.

Put brightly colored ribbons or streamers on basket.

Students with intellectual disabilities or autism

Give student peer to assist him or her during game.

Give student extra time to pass and shoot without being defended.

Give student free shot at basket.

Soccer

Dribbling

General

Use larger or smaller balls.

Use playground balls, Nerf balls, or punch balls (large balloons).

Vary distance required to travel.

Vary speed required (allow student to walk).

Have student use only dominant foot.

Students who use wheelchairs (normal upper body strength and control)

Hold ball on lap and push wheelchair.

Students who use wheelchairs (limited upper body strength and control)

Have peer push wheelchair while student holds ball in lap or in hands.

Have peer physically assist student in moving foot to kick ball.

Have student repeatedly hit ball when it sits on lap tray while being pushed.

Students with visual impairments

Tie string to ball and to foot so that ball can be retrieved.

Pair student with peer to guide him or her in correct direction.

Put bells or beeper in ball.

Dribble toward sound of peers.

Use deflated ball.

Place student along wall or fence so that he or she can place hand against wall for balance and for reference.

Students with intellectual disabilities or autism

Allow student to walk while dribbling.

Allow student to use deflated ball.

Tie ball to student foot so that ball does not get away.

Have student practice on grass (ball moves slower).

Have peer assist student (with extra verbal and physical cues).

Encourage proper technique.

Passing and Trapping

General

Use suspended balls.

Use larger or smaller balls.

Use playground balls, Nerf balls, or punch balls (large balloons).

Vary distance required to pass (have peers stand closer).

Pass balls slower as required.

Pass ball directly to student.

Students who use wheelchairs (normal upper body strength and control)

Allow student to throw or roll ball for passing.

Encourage student to find best way to pass (overhead versus chest versus sidearm).

Use soft balls (Nerf balls) for safety as needed.

Students who use wheelchairs (limited upper body strength and control)

Use soft balls (Nerf balls) for safety.

Have student kick (push with foot) ball down ramp.

Have student kick ball held by peer.

Have student push ball off lap.

Have student hit ball off tee (or held by peer) with head.

Students with visual impairments

Use soft balls (Nerf balls) for safety.

Use verbal cues to help student stand in correct direction.

Use verbal cues (tell student when ball is released for trapping; tell student where to pass).

Put bells or beeper in ball.

Use physical assistance to instruct student.

Students with intellectual disabilities or autism

Use soft balls (Nerf balls) for safety.

Start with a balloon and gradually work toward faster-moving balls.

Use suspended balls.

Use physical assistance when teaching skill.

Encourage proper technique.

Shooting

General

Use larger or smaller balls.

Use playground balls, Nerf balls, or punch balls (large balloons).

Use balls with varying texture.

Vary distance required to shoot (allow student to stand closer).

Vary size of goal (larger for less skilled students).

Students who use wheelchairs (normal upper body strength and control)

Allow student to substitute throwing for shooting.

Encourage student to find best way to shoot (overhead versus chest versus sidearm).

Use soft balls (Nerf balls) for safety as needed.

Students who use wheelchairs (limited upper body strength and control)

Use soft balls (Nerf balls) for safety.

Have student kick ball or push ball down ramp toward goal.

Have student push ball off lap toward goal.

Have student kick or swing arm and hit ball held by peer toward goal.

Have student hit ball off tee (or held by peer) with head toward goal.

Allow student to kick or strike ball into box next to chair as goal.

Students with visual impairments

Use soft balls (Nerf balls) for safety.

Use verbal cues (goalie) to tell student where to shoot.

Give student specific verbal feedback to tell him or her how close his or her shot was to goal.

Use physical assistance to instruct student.

Place radio in middle of goal to cue student.

Put bells or beeper in ball.

Use target that makes noise when hit.

Students with intellectual disabilities or autism

Use soft balls (Nerf balls) for safety.

Use overinflated playground balls (travel farther with less strength).

Use physical assistance when teaching skill.

Encourage proper technique.

Soccer Game

General

Encourage students to develop modified rules that will be fair for everyone, including student with disabilities.

Set up special zone for student where only he or she can play ball.

Allow student to shoot at wider goal.

Allow student to use different ball when it is his or her turn to dribble or shoot.

Make rule that no student can steal ball when student is dribbling.

Make rule that no student can block or interfere with student's pass.

Have student play a wing position away from fastest action.

Match student with disability against a lower-ability student without disability.

Give student a peer to assist him or her during game.

Allow free substitution for student if he or she tires easily.

Give student's team extra player (12 versus 11 game).

Allow student to play only offense or defense if he or she has limited mobility.

Split the class and allow skilled students to play competitive, full-field games while allowing less skilled players (including student with disabilities) to play slower, less competitive games (half-field, six versus six, keep-away games, cooperative games).

Play lead-up soccer games.

Students who use wheelchairs (normal upper body strength and control)

Caution peers about wheelchair.

Have student play goalie (requires less mobility) and make rule that skilled students can not shoot from closer than 20 yards out.

Students who use wheelchairs (limited upper body strength and control)

Provide student with peer to assist him or her.

Allow student to use adapted equipment practiced during skills (e.g., ramps).

Allow student free shot at goal from close distance.

Students with visual impairments

Have peer guide student around field.

Have special zone for student marked with rope or cones where only he or she can play ball (make rule that ball should be played into zone every 2-3 minutes).

Have teammates give extra verbal cues to student to describe where he or she is, where teammates are, and where opponents are.

Use ball with bell.

Use brightly colored ball.

Place radio in goal.

Have teammates wear brightly colored pennies.

Allow student free shot from penalty line at least once during game.

Students with intellectual disabilities or autism

Provide student with peer to assist him or her.

Give student extra time to pass and shoot without being defended.

Give student occasional free shot at goal.

Softball

Throwing/Catching/Fielding

General

Use suspended balls.

Use Velcro balls and Velcro mitts.

Use larger or smaller balls.

Use playground balls, Nerf balls, or punch balls (large balloons).

Vary distance required to throw (have peers stand closer).

Throw balls slower as required.

Students who use wheelchairs (normal upper body strength and control)

Encourage student to find best way to throw (overhead versus sidearm).

Use soft balls (Nerf balls) for safety as needed.

Students who use wheelchairs (limited upper body strength and control)

Use soft balls (Nerf balls) for safety.

Have student push ball down ramp, and then have peer throw it rest of way.

Have student push ball held by peer, and then have peer throw it rest of way.

Have student push ball off lap, and then have peer throw it rest of way.

Have student hit ball off tee (or held by peer) with head, then have peer throw it rest of way.

Use legs and kick ball if student has more control over legs.

Students with visual impairments

Use soft balls (Nerf balls) for safety.

Use suspended ball.

Use verbal cues to help student stand facing correct direction.

Use verbal cues (tell student when ball is released for catching; tell student where to throw).

Put bells or beeper in ball.

Use physical assistance to instruct student.

Students with intellectual disabilities or autism

Use soft balls (Nerf balls) for safety.

Start with a balloon and gradually work toward faster-moving balls.

Use suspended balls.

Use physical assistance when teaching skill.

Encourage proper technique.

Batting

General

Use larger or smaller balls.

Use playground balls, Nerf balls, or punch balls (large balloons).

Use larger or smaller striking implements.

Use lighter striking implements.

Have student hit ball off tee.

Vary distance ball is pitched.

Students who use wheelchairs (normal upper body strength and control)

Encourage student to find best way to position chair for batting.

Students who use wheelchairs (limited upper body strength and control)

Use soft balls (Nerf balls) for safety.

Have student hit ball off tee with hand.

Strap small striking implement to hand for striking.

Have student push ball down ramp.

Have student push ball off lap.

Have student swing arm or use head to hit ball held by peer.

Have student kick ball if legs have more control than arms.

Students with visual impairments

Use verbal cues to tell student when ball is pitched.

Give student specific verbal feedback to tell student how close he or she was to hitting ball.

Use physical assistance to instruct and help student.

Put bells or beeper in ball.

Have student hit ball rolled across table.

Students with intellectual disabilities or autism

Use physical assistance when teaching skill.

Encourage proper technique.

Have student hit ball rolled across table.

Base Running

General

Vary distance to first base.

Vary width of base path.

Students who use wheelchairs (normal upper body strength and control)

Allow student to push wheelchair.

Students who use wheelchairs (limited upper body strength and control)

Have peer push chair while student tries to keep arms up.

Have peer push chair while peer tries to keep head up and look at first base.

Students with visual impairments

Use verbal cues to tell student where to run (first baseman).

Use physical assistance to instruct and help student.

Put bells or beeper at first base.

Put radio by first base.

Have rope between home and first to guide student's path.

Students with intellectual disabilities or autism

Use physical assistance as needed.

Encourage proper running technique.

Softball Game

General

Encourage students to develop modified rules that will be fair for everyone, including student with disabilities.

Establish special rules such as ground rule double when ball is hit to student with disabilities.

Give student extra strikes.

Allow student to hit ball off tee.

Allow pitcher to stand closer to player and pitch ball slower.

Allow student to use larger ball when it is his or her turn to bat.

Allow student to use lighter, larger bat (or even a racket) when batting.

Have student play outfield with peer assistant.

Have student play catcher (requires less mobility).

Place first base closer to home for student.

Give student a peer to assist him or her during game.

Allow student to only play offense or play every other inning if he or she tires easily.

Give student's team extra player (11 versus 10 game).

Split the class and allow skilled students to play competitive, regulation game while allowing less skilled players (including student with disabilities) to play slower, less competitive games with modified game (e.g., cooperative game).

Play lead-up softball games.

Students who use wheelchairs (normal upper body strength and control)

Caution peers about wheelchair.

Have student play catcher or first base (requires less mobility).

Students who use wheelchairs (limited upper body strength and control)

Provide student with peer to assist him or her.

Allow student to use adapted equipment practiced during skills (e.g., ramps).

Have player without a disability play regular depth on defense to give student fair chance to make it to first base.

Make different rules for scoring (if student hits ball a certain distance, he gets a single, double, triple, or home run).

Students with visual impairments

Have peer assist student in field.

Have teammates give extra verbal cues to student to describe where he or she is and where teammates are.

Use ball with bell or beeper and first base with beeper.

Place radio at first base.

Use brightly colored ball.

Make first base brightly colored.

Make different rules for scoring (if student hits ball a certain distance, he gets a single, double, triple, or home run).

Students with intellectual disabilities or autism

Provide student with peer to assist him or her.

Have student play catcher or outfield (less mobility and skill needed).

Volleyball

Setting/Passing

General

Use larger or smaller balls.

Use lighter and softer balls (Nerf balls, balloons, beach balls, volley trainers).

Vary distance requirements (stand closer to net).

Vary speed required (slow down the ball).

Lower the net.

Students who use wheelchairs (normal upper body strength and control)

Vary distance requirements (position closer to net).

Use lighter, softer balls (Nerf balls, balloons, beach balls, volley trainers).

Students who use wheelchairs (limited upper body strength and control)

Have student hit suspended ball.

Have student push ball held by peer, then have peer pick up ball and pass it to other teammates.

Have student push ball off lap tray, then have peer pick up ball and pass it to other teammates.

Have student push ball down ramp or across table, then have peer pick up ball and pass it to other teammates.

Have student use legs or head if student has better control with these body parts, then have peer pick up ball and pass it to other teammates.

Provide physical assistance as needed.

Allow student to touch ball, then have peer pick it up and pass it to other teammates.

Students with visual impairments

Use brightly colored balls.

Have peers tell student which direction to face and where to pass.

Put bells or beeper in ball.

Hold ball for student and let him or her hit it out of your hands.

Allow student to self-toss and then set ball.

Students with intellectual disabilities or autism

Allow students with limited coordination to toss ball rather than hit it.

Have peer assist student (with extra verbal and physical cues).

Encourage proper technique.

Bumping

General

Use larger or smaller balls.

Use lighter and softer balls (Nerf balls, balloons, beach balls, volley trainers).

Vary distance requirements (stand closer to net).

Vary speed required (slow down the ball).

Lower the net.

Students who use wheelchairs (normal upper body strength and control)

Encourage student to lean forward to bump or bump to side of chair.

Allow overhead passing to be used as substitute for bumping.

Students who use wheelchairs (limited upper body strength and control)

Have student hit suspended ball.

Have student push ball held by peer, then have peer pick up ball and bump it to other teammates.

Have student push ball off lap tray, then have peer pick up ball and bump it to other teammates.

Have student push ball down ramp or across table, then have peer pick up ball and bump it to other teammates.

Have student use legs or head if student has better control with these body parts, then have peer pick up ball and bump it to other teammates.

Provide physical assistance as needed.

Allow student to touch ball, then have peer pick it up and bump it to other teammates.

Students with visual impairments

Use brightly colored balls.

Have peers tell student which direction to face and where to bump ball.

Provide physical assistance as needed.

Put bells or beeper in ball.

Hold ball for student and let him or her bump it out of your hands.

Allow student to self-toss and then bump ball.

Students with intellectual disabilities or autism

Allow students with limited coordination to toss ball rather than bump ball.

Have peer assist student (with extra verbal and physical cues).

Encourage proper technique.

Serving

General

Use larger or smaller balls.

Use lighter and softer balls (Nerf balls, balloons, beach balls, volley trainers).

Vary distance requirements (stand closer to net).

Lower the net.

Students who use wheelchairs (normal upper body strength and control)

Encourage student to find best way to serve (overhand versus sidearm).

Students who use wheelchairs (limited upper body strength and control)

Have student hit suspended ball.

Have student push ball held by peer, then have peer pick up ball and serve it over net.

Have student push ball off lap tray, then have peer pick up ball and serve it over net.

Have student push ball down ramp or across table, then have peer pick up ball and serve it over net.

Have student use legs or head if student has better control with these body parts, then have peer pick up ball and serve it over net.

Provide physical assistance as needed.

Allow student to touch ball, then have peer pick it up and serve it over net.

Students with visual impairments

Use brightly colored balls.

Have peers tell student which direction to face and where to serve.

Provide physical assistance as needed.

Put bells or beeper in ball.

Put radio under net to help student locate net.

Students with intellectual disabilities or autism

Allow students with limited coordination to throw ball rather than serve it.

Have peer assist student (with extra verbal and physical cues).

Encourage proper technique.

Volleyball Game

General

Encourage students to develop modified rules that will be fair for everyone, including student with disabilities.

Set up special zone for student where only he or she can play ball.

Have student play back and outside positions for safety.

Allow student to throw ball rather than hit it.

Allow student to use different ball when it is his or her turn to dribble or shoot.

Make rule that student's team gets an extra hit.

Make rule that no student can block or interfere with student's pass.

Match student with disability against a lower-ability student without disability.

Give student a peer to assist him or her during game.

Allow free substitution for student if he or she tires easily.

Give student's team extra player (seven versus six game).

Split the class and allow skilled students to play competitive, regulation games while allowing less skilled players (including student with disabilities) to play slower, less competitive games (e.g., cooperative games).

Play lead-up games.

Students who use wheelchairs (normal upper body strength and control)

Caution peers about wheelchair.

Have student play back and side position only.

Students who use wheelchairs (limited upper body strength and control)

Provide student with peer to assist him or her.

Allow student to use adapted equipment practiced during skills (e.g., ramps).

Students with visual impairments

Have peer guide/assist student during game.

Mark floor with carpet squares to help student find position.

Have teammates give extra verbal cues to student to describe where he or she is, where teammates are, and where opponents are.

Use brightly colored ball.

Put brightly colored ribbons or streamers on net.

Use ball with bell.

Place radio under net.

Have teammates wear brightly colored pennies.

Allow student to hit ball held by peer.

Students with intellectual disabilities or autism

Provide student with peer to assist him or her.

Give student extra time to pass and shoot without being defended.

Allow student to hit ball held by peer.

INDIVIDUAL SPORTS

Tennis

Forehand

General

Use larger or smaller balls.

Use lighter and softer balls (Nerf balls, balloons, beach balls, volley trainers).

Use shorter, lighter rackets (racquetball racket, pantyhose racket).

Use rackets with larger heads.

Vary distance requirements (stand closer to net).

Vary speed required (slow down the ball).

Lower the net or do not use net.

Students who use wheelchairs (normal upper body strength and control)

Encourage student to find best position to hit forehand.

Have student hit ball off tee.

Encourage student to work on maneuvering wheelchair and then hitting ball.

Students who use wheelchairs (limited upper body strength and control)

Strap or Velcro racket or striking implement to student's hand.

Have student hit suspended ball.

Have student hit or push ball held by peer, then have peer pick up ball and hit over net.

Have student hit or push ball off lap tray, then have peer pick up ball and hit it over net.

Have student hit or push ball down ramp or across table, then have peer pick up ball and.

Have student hit it over net.

Have student use legs or head if student has better control with these body parts, then have peer pick up ball and hit it over net.

Provide physical assistance as needed.

Allow student to touch ball, then have peer pick it up and bump it to other teammates.

Students with visual impairments

Use brightly colored balls.

Have peers tell student which direction to face and where to hit ball.

Provide physical assistance as needed.

Put bells or beeper in ball.

Put radio by net for direction.

Hold ball for student and let him or her bump it out of your hands.

Allow student to self-toss and then hit ball.

Attach string to student and to ball so that student can quickly retrieve ball.

Students with intellectual disabilities or autism

Allow students with limited coordination to hit suspended ball.

Allow student with limited coordination to hit ball off tee.

Have peer assist student (with extra verbal and physical cues).

Encourage proper technique.

Backhand

General

Use larger or smaller balls.

Use lighter and softer balls (Nerf balls, balloons, beach balls, volley trainers).

Use shorter, lighter rackets (racquetball racket, pantyhose racket).

Use rackets with larger heads.

Vary distance requirements (stand closer to net).

Vary speed required (slow down the ball).

Lower the net or do not use net.

Students who use wheelchairs (normal upper body strength and control)

Encourage student to find best position to hit backhand.

Have student hit ball off tee.

Encourage student to work on maneuvering wheelchair and then hitting ball.

Students who use wheelchairs (limited upper body strength and control)

Have student hit suspended ball.

Have student hit or push ball held by peer, then have peer pick up ball and hit over net.

Have student hit or push ball off lap tray, then have peer pick up ball and hit it over net.

Have student hit or push ball down ramp or across table, then have peer pick up ball and hit it over net.

Have student use legs or head if student has better control with these body parts, then have peer pick up ball and hit it over net.

Provide physical assistance as needed.

Allow student to touch ball, then have peer pick it up and bump it to other teammates.

Students with visual impairments

Use brightly colored balls.

Have peers tell student which direction to face and where to hit ball.

Provide physical assistance as needed.

Put bells or beeper in ball.

Put radio by net for direction.

Hold ball for student and let him or her bump it out of your hands.

Allow student to self-toss and then hit ball.

Attach string to student and to ball so that student can quickly retrieve ball.

Students with intellectual disabilities or autism

Allow students with limited coordination to hit suspended ball.

Allow student with limited coordination to hit ball off tee.

Have peer assist student (with extra verbal and physical cues).

Encourage proper technique.

Serving

General

Use larger or smaller balls.

Use lighter and softer balls (Nerf balls, balloons, beach balls, volley trainers).

Use shorter, lighter rackets (racquetball racket, pantyhose racket).

Use rackets with larger heads.

Vary distance requirements (stand closer to net).

Lower the net or do not use net.

Students who use wheelchairs (normal upper body strength and control)

Encourage student to find best way to serve (overhand, sidearm).

Serve ball off tee or have ball tossed to person to serve.

Students who use wheelchairs (limited upper body strength and control)

Have student hit or push ball held by peer, then have peer pick up ball and hit over net.

Have student hit or push ball off lap tray, then have peer pick up ball and hit it over net.

Have student hit or push ball down ramp or across table, then have peer pick up ball and hit it over net.

Have student use legs or head if student has better control with these body parts, then have peer pick up ball and hit it over net.

Provide physical assistance as needed.

Allow student to touch ball, then have peer pick it up and bump it to other teammates.

Students with visual impairments

Use brightly colored balls.

Have peers tell student which direction to face and where to hit ball.

Provide physical assistance as needed.

Put bells or beeper in ball.

Put radio by net for direction.

Allow student to hit ball off tee.

Allow student to bounce ball then hit it.

Students with intellectual disabilities or autism

Allow students with limited coordination to hit ball off tee.

Toss the ball to student if this is easier for him or her.

Have peer assist student (with extra verbal and physical cues).

Encourage proper technique.

Tennis Game

General

Allow student to hit ball after two to three bounces.

Allow student to hit to doubles lines while opponent hits to singles line.

Match student with students without disabilities who have limited abilities.

Play lead-up games rather than regulation games.

Play game without net.

Play doubles and allow team with student to have extra player (three versus two).

Play modified or lead-up games.

Students who use wheelchairs (normal upper body strength and control)

Allow student to serve ball off tee or have ball tossed to person to serve.

Students who use wheelchairs (limited upper body strength and control)

Pair student with peer assistant.

Make special rule that if ball is hit a certain distance, it counts as over the net. Then, peer assistant can hit ball over net to opponent.

Allow student to use adapted equipment.

Students with visual impairments

Use brightly colored balls.

Have textured markers on court or guide wires so that student knows where he or she is on court.

Have peers tell student which direction to face and where to hit ball.

Provide physical assistance as needed.

Put bells or beeper in ball.

Put radio by net for direction.

Allow student to hit ball off tee for serving.

Allow student to bounce ball then hit it.

Students with intellectual disabilities or autism

Allow students with limited coordination to hit ball off tee for serving.

Toss the ball to student if this is easier for him when serving.

Have peer assist student.

Golf

Hitting Ball

General

Use larger balls.

Use lighter balls.

Use shorter, lighter clubs (junior clubs or children's plastic clubs).

Make club with a larger head.

Vary distance requirements (allow student to hit it shorter distance than peers).

Always put ball on tee.

Students who use wheelchairs (normal upper body strength and control)

Encourage student to find best way to hit ball.

Students who use wheelchairs (limited upper body strength and control)

Have student hit or push ball held by peer.

Have student hit or push ball off lap tray.

Have student hit or push ball down ramp or across table.

Have student use legs or head if student has better control with these body parts.

Provide physical assistance as needed.

Use switch that activates machine that hits ball off tee.

Students with visual impairments

Use brightly colored balls.

Have peers tell student which direction to face and which direction to hit ball.

Provide physical assistance as needed.

Put bells or beeper in ball.

Put radio out in field for target.

Students with intellectual disabilities or autism

Have peer assist student (with extra verbal and physical cues).

Encourage proper technique.

Archery

Shooting

General

Use shorter arrows.

Use lighter bows.

Use shorter, smaller, lighter bows.

Vary distance requirements (allow student to shoot a shorter distance than peers).

Make target larger.

Students who use wheelchairs (normal upper body strength and control)

Encourage student to find best way to shoot with bow.

Allow use of adapted release cuffs.

Use adapted archery bow.

Students who use wheelchairs (limited upper body strength and control)

Use crossbow with adapted trigger device.

Use adapted archery bow.

Shoot with physical assistance.

Students with visual impairments

Use brightly colored arrows and targets.

Have peers tell student which direction to face and which direction to shoot.

Provide physical assistance as needed.

Put bells or beeper in target.

Put radio in front of target.

Have target make sound if it is hit.

Use special auditory device for lining up shot.

Students with intellectual disabilities or autism

Use crossbow with adapted trigger device if strength is problem.

Use adapted archery bow if coordination is a problem.

Shoot with physical assistance.

Encourage proper technique.

For more information on the crossbow with adapted trigger, adapted archery bow, adapted release cuff, and other adaptations of archery to meet the needs of individuals with specific disabilities, see Adams and McCubbin (1991).

Badminton

Forehand

General

Use larger birdies.

Use lighter and softer birdies (Nerf balls, balloons).

Use shorter, lighter rackets (pantyhose racket).

Use rackets with larger heads.

Vary distance requirements (stand closer to net).

Vary speed required (slow down the birdie).

Lower the net or do not use net.

Have student practice with suspended birdie.

Students who use wheelchairs (normal upper body strength and control)

Encourage student to find best position to hit forehand.

Have student hit birdie off tee.

Encourage student to work on maneuvering wheelchair and then hitting birdie.

Students who use wheelchairs (limited upper body strength and control)

Strap racket to player's hand.

Have student hit or push birdie held by peer, then have peer pick up birdie and hit it over net.

Have student hit or push birdie off lap tray, then have peer pick up birdie and hit it over net.

Have student hit or push birdie down ramp or across table, then have peer pick up birdie and hit it over net.

Have student use legs or head if student has better control with these body parts, then have peer pick up birdie and hit it over net.

Provide physical assistance as needed.

Allow student to touch birdie, then have peer pick it up and bump it to other teammates.

Students with visual impairments

Use brightly colored birdies or balls.

Have peers tell student which direction to face and where to hit birdie.

Provide physical assistance as needed.

Put bells or beeper in birdie.

Put radio by net for direction.

Suspend birdie from string with Velcro so that birdie releases when hit.

Place birdie on tee.

Allow student to self-toss and then hit birdie.

Attach string to student and to birdie so that student can quickly retrieve birdie.

Students with intellectual disabilities or autism

Allow students with limited coordination to hit suspended birdie.

Allow student with limited coordination to hit birdie off tee.

Have peer assist student (with extra verbal and physical cues).

Encourage proper technique.

Serving

General

Use larger birdies.

Use lighter and softer birdies (Nerf balls, balloons).

Use shorter, lighter rackets (pantyhose racket).

Use rackets with larger heads.

Vary distance requirements (stand closer to net).

Lower the net or do not use net.

Students who use wheelchairs (normal upper body strength and control)

Encourage student to find best way to serve (overhand, sidearm).

Serve birdie off tee or have birdie tossed to person to serve.

Students who use wheelchairs (limited upper body strength and control)

Strap racket to player's hand.

Have student hit or push birdie held by peer, then have peer pick up birdie and hit it over net.

Have student hit or push birdie off lap tray, then have peer pick up birdie and hit it over net.

Have student hit or push birdie down ramp or across table, then have peer pick up birdie and hit it over net.

Have student use legs or head if student has better control with these body parts, then have peer pick up birdie and hit it over net.

Provide physical assistance as needed.

Allow student to touch birdie, then have peer pick it up and bump it to other teammates.

Students with visual impairments

Use brightly colored birdie or ball.

Have peers tell student which direction to face and where to hit birdie.

Provide physical assistance as needed.

Put bells or beeper in birdie.

Put radio by net for direction.

Allow student to hit birdie off tee.

Students with intellectual disabilities or autism

Allow students with limited coordination to hit birdie off tee.

Toss the birdie to student if this is easier for him or her.

Have peer assist student (with extra verbal and physical cues).

Encourage proper technique.

Badminton Game

General

Allow student to hit to wider court while opponent hits to narrower.

Match student with students without disabilities who have limited abilities.

Have students play lead-up games rather than regulation games.

Lower net or have students play game without net.

Have students play doubles and allow team with student to have extra player (three versus two).

Play modified or lead-up games.

Use balloon instead of birdie to slow down game.

Students who use wheelchairs (normal upper body strength and control)

Allow student to serve birdie off tee or have birdie tossed to person to serve.

Students who use wheelchairs (limited upper body strength and control)

Pair student with peer assistant.

Make special rule that if birdie is hit a certain distance, it counts as over the net. Then, peer assistant can hit birdie over net to opponent.

Allow student to use adapted equipment (e.g., shorter racket, lighter racket, balloon).

Students with visual impairments

Use brightly colored birdies.

Have textured markers on court or guide wires so that student knows where he or she is on court.

Have peers tell student which direction to face and where to hit birdie.

Provide physical assistance as needed.

Put bells or beeper in birdie.

Put radio by net for direction.

Allow student to hit birdie off tee for serving.

Use balloon instead of birdie to slow down game.

Students with intellectual disabilities or autism

Allow students with limited coordination to hit birdie off tee for serving.

Toss the birdie to student if this is easier for him when serving.

Have peer assist student.

For more information on unique adaptations of badminton to meet the needs of individuals with specific disabilities, see Adams and McCubbin (1991).

Dancing

General

Use colored markers or cones on floor for direction.

Use colored markers on hands and feet for left and right.

Have student practice small portions of dance and gradually add more steps.

Slow down music.

Students who use wheelchairs (normal upper body strength and control)

Substitute arm movement for leg movements.

Allow partner to push student's wheelchair as needed.

Students who use wheelchairs (limited upper body strength and control)

Substitute any controllable movement the student has for more traditional movements.

Allow peers to assist students in movements.

Allow students to push wheelchair.

Encourage student to maintain proper posture and to focus eyes on partner.

Students with visual impairments

Use brightly colored markers on floor.

Have partner wear brightly colored penny or shirt.

Have partner wear bells on wrist.

Have partner tell student which direction to face and where to move.

Have partner provide physical assistance as needed.

Students with intellectual disabilities or autism

Have peers assist student (with extra verbal and physical cues).

Encourage proper technique.

Facilitating Social Acceptance and Inclusion

by Martin E. Block and Iva Obrusnikova

Sam is a fourth grader at Lewis Elementary School. Although Sam loves physical education, he appears to be different from his peers because he has Asperger's syndrome, a disorder on the autism continuum. In spite of his brilliant skills in math and computers, Sam is obsessed with structure. He needs to stand next to the same peers, line up equipment in a certain way, and have teammates positioned properly around the ball before the game starts. He quickly becomes tremendously upset when things are changed. He listens to his physical education teacher carefully and follows directions without hesitation. However, if the teacher suddenly changes activities during the class, Sam explodes, throwing a nearby object or screaming. When overwhelmed by noise and confusion, he often bites himself or picks at his nails. In addition, Sam does not understand the social rules and often says or does inappropriate things. For example, when approached by an overweight classmate, Sam said, "I do not want to play on your team because you are too fat." His peers view Sam as odd. They initially tried to talk to and include him in physical education activities, but after several attempts his odd behaviors and social inappropriateness discouraged them. Worse, they have started to be intentionally cruel to him by making thoughtless comments. Sam's understanding of how to behave in society is muddled. This does not mean that Sam does not want to act more appropriately, to make friends, or be liked by his peers and teachers. Sam simply has trouble reading others' emotions, determining the social appropriateness of a situation, and dealing with change. Sam's behaviors make it hard for the teacher to meet his and other students' needs; she does not like seeing any of her students being left out and ostracized in her gymnasium. What can this physical education teacher do to get the class to understand Sam's challenges and stop the teasing? What can she do to encourage a few classmates to reach out and be friendly with Sam?

Keely is a 15-year-old girl with mixed spastic-athetoid cerebral palsy, and Talia is a 14-year-old girl with diplegic cerebral palsy. Keely and Talia have been good friends since preschool, and they are included in the same eighth-grade general physical education class at Greentown Middle School. Keely uses an electric wheelchair for mobility. Keely's movements are usually uncontrolled but tend to worsen with excitement or self-control. For example, it requires a great deal of effort for her to throw a ball to a peer or to shoot a ball at a lowered basket. Keely communicates by gaze, a few words, and facial expressions (usually grimaces when trying a skill). This results in others, particularly girls, underestimating her cognitive skills (she does not have any cognitive impairment) or making cruel comments. Because of her severe speech and motor limitations, Keely is assigned a teacher assistant who is helping her in many physical activities. Yet, Keely has always struggled to find friends and be an equal and contributing player on a team. In contrast, Talia has no problems communicating or controlling her movements. She uses crutches and sometimes a manual wheelchair for games such as basketball. Peer rejection is not as evident in Talia's case, but her sensitivity for Keely's troubles prevents her from participating in activities with other classmates. In addition, Talia's classmates often give her meaningless roles, such as being a goalie or retrieving balls. Thus, Keely and Talia do not have a wide circle of friends in school and tend to stay together most of the time. How can the general physical education teacher and teacher assistant promote more natural interactions between the students with and without a disability?

Students with disabilities should never be placed in general physical education solely for social development (NASPE, 1995). Yet, clearly one of the greatest benefits of inclusion is the opportunity for social acceptance and interactions between students with and without disabilities. Inclusion can promote such social factors as learning how to interact with peers, playing cooperatively, taking turns, dealing with anger, following directions, listening quietly, staying on task, and generally behaving appropriately. For some children (e.g., with behavior problems), social development is as important as motor and cognitive development and should be included in the child's IEP. In addition, peers without disabilities can learn that classmates who seem different on the outside might share similar interests, pleasures, problems, and concerns. Peers without disabilities can learn to be sensitive to, respectful of, and comfortable with differences and similarities with peers with disabilities. Finally, through appropriate interactions and contact, the opportunity for true acceptance, appreciation, and friendships between peers with and without disabilities becomes possible (Falvey & Rosenberg, 1995; Pearpoint, Forest, & O'Brien, 1996).

Simply placing a child with a disability into general physical education does not ensure appropriate and meaningful social interactions and acceptance. Sam, Keely, and Talia all experience difficulties in their relationship with peers. They rarely interact with their peers; and when they do, their social behavior does not elicit ongoing social interaction. Although not all children with disabilities have difficulties interacting with their peers, many children without disabilities require specific training in order to interact with their peers with disabilities in a positive and age-appropriate manner. Unfortunately, physical educators often unwittingly create barriers to social interactions and acceptance rather than facilitate it. What would happen if a physical educator did not tell peers that a child with behavioral problems might get angry when his equipment is touched? How would peers feel if a physical educator did not explain why a child with intellectual disabilities and a heart problem does not have to run the mile like everyone else in class? In fact, placing children with disabilities into general physical education without preparing children without disabilities can lead to feelings of confusion and resentment.

The purpose of this chapter is to discuss ways in which general physical educators can remove barriers to social acceptance and foster interactions between students with and without disabilities. The chapter focuses on the two major players who can facilitate the social acceptance and inclusion of students with disabilities: 1) the general physical educator and 2) classmates. Examples of three common problems in general physical education classes that hinder social inclusion and some possible solutions are given.

BEHAVIORS THAT FACILITATE SOCIAL INCLUSION

The general physical educator is perhaps the most important determinant in successful inclusion. General physical educators can either welcome students with disabilities or show disinterest. General physical educators can either view a student with disabilities as truly one of their students or as a visitor and someone else's burden. The attitude and commitment of the general physical educator will affect how classmates without disabilities accept students with disabilities. Although general physical educators might not always feel prepared to work with students who have disabilities, they should always help the student with disabilities feel welcome and a part of the group. The following are some suggestions on how to facilitate the social acceptance and inclusion of students with disabilities (see Table 9.1).

Have a Positive Attitude

It is very reasonable for general physical educators to feel nervous and even incompetent when working with children who have disabilities. Such feelings are quite common among general physical educators (Chandler & Greene, 1995; Janney, Snell, Beers, & Raynes, 1995; LaMaster, Gall, Kinchin, & Siedentop, 1998; Lieberman, Houston-Wilson, & Kozub, 2002; Lienert, Sherrill, & Myers, 2001). However, general educators have noted that these fears tend to be based on misconceptions, misunderstandings, and general inaccurate preconceptions about their ability to teach students with disabilities. For example, Janney and her colleagues (1995) interviewed both general and special education teachers who had gone from segregated to inclusive classes. A high school general physical education teacher who was interviewed in the study suggested the following to other general physical educators dealing with inclusion for the first time:

> Well, I just, I would go in with an open mind, don't be closed-minded. . . . I think what's on every teacher's mind is the fact that, oh no, this is double the workload and double the problems that you might have. And I think the best thing they can do is wait, and talk it over and see the situation, and at least try. There are always modifications you can make if something is not working out. (1995, p. 435)

Table 9.1.   Ways for teachers to facilitate social inclusion

- Have a positive attitude.
- Be the teacher for all students in your general education classes.
- Model appropriate behavior.
- Include the child in as many activities as possible.
- Individualize the curriculum and instruction.
- Reinforce positive interactions.
- Be knowledgeable about the child.

Although feelings of apprehensiveness and incompetence are common, general physical educators should commit themselves to giving inclusion their best shot by learning about the child with disabilities and experimenting with different ways to best include him or her into their general physical education program. There are plenty of resources in or around most school districts (e.g., special education teachers, therapists, adapted physical education specialists, other general physical educators) who can help general physical educators with the mechanics of how to safely and successfully include children with disabilities. But the first step is simply to be willing to try. General physical educators will be surprised how quickly they will become an expert on how to work with, motivate, and help particular students with disabilities in their general physical education program. In fact, many physical educators may find working with students who have disabilities to be more rewarding than working with students without disabilities. As another physical educator noted in Janney et al., "These kids seem to appreciate you a lot more . . . and that's a little pat on the back for the teacher" (1995, p. 435).

Janney et al. (1995) noted when teachers see trusted colleagues having success with inclusion, they are more likely to be open to change. There will always be general PE teachers who do not want to include students with disabilities. Finding the GPE teacher who is willing to work with students with disabilities is a good strategy.

Take Responsibility for Teaching All Students in Your Class

It is common for general physical educators to feel that a child with disabilities in their general physical education classes is not really one of their students. For example, some general physical educators have been heard to say, "I have 50 students in my third period physical education class plus Cassandra [the student with disabilities]. But Mrs. Jones [Cassandra's teacher assistant] works with Cassandra." General physical educators with this type of attitude often feel they are "hosting" a special visitor to

their general physical education class and are thus not responsible for the child's education. When the general physical educator perceives his or her role as a host, it becomes the responsibility of someone else (e.g., paraprofessional, APE specialist) to work with and teach this student (Giangreco, 1997). The general physical educator ends up having minimal contact with the student with disabilities.

Unfortunately, when the general physical educator chooses not to take responsibility for teaching the student with disabilities, major curricular and instructional decisions are left up to someone who is usually underqualified (e.g., paraprofessional, special education teacher).

It is important that general physical educators truly perceive themselves as the primary educator for all students who enter their gymnasium, including students with disabilities. Although support personnel might accompany a child with disabilities to general physical education, the general physical educator should make key decisions about what the child with disabilities is doing, how he or she is doing it, and with whom he or she is doing it. This also means personally spending time with each student in the class, including the student with disabilities. "If you are successful teaching students without disabilities, then you have the skills to be successful teaching students with disabilities" (Giangreco, 1997, p. 11).

Model Appropriate Behavior

Many children learn how to act around children with disabilities by modeling behavior of respected adults. One of the simplest things you can do is welcome children with disabilities and model friendly behavior through your actions and words (Giangreco, 1997). Greet and talk to the child with disabilities even if the child does not fully understand what you are saying. Pat the child with disabilities on the back, give high fives, choose the child first, and recognize the child during activities (e.g., "Good pushing your wheelchair, Billy!").

Include the Student in as Many Activities as Possible

Avoid excluding the child from activities whenever possible. Too often students with disabilities are placed in general physical education but not really included much of the time. Students with disabilities often spend a large portion of their time in general physical education away from their peers doing different activities. Time spent away from peers in general physical education inhibits learning and can lead to social isolation (Giangreco, 1997). For inclusion to be successful, it is critical that the student with disabilities be included in as many general physical education activities as possible (although his or her goals might be different from peers). Although modifications may be necessary to safely and fairly include the child, the child should be part of the larger group as much as possible. For example, a child with intellectual disabilities who cannot keep up with the fast warm-up routine of a fifth-grade class can be encouraged to focus on three or four key warm-up movements rather than all of the movements. Remember, "Where students spend their time, what they do, when, and with whom play major roles in defining affiliations and status within the classroom (and gymnasium)" (Giangreco, 1997, p. 13).

Individualize the Curriculum and Instruction

Related to attitudes is a commitment by general educators to change the curricula and how information is presented to account for individual differences (CAHPER, 1994; Sherrill, 2004). Interestingly, many general education texts include passages about individualization in general physical education classes (e.g., Graham, Holt-Hale, & Parker, 2004; Mosston & Ashworth, 2002; Pangrazi, 2007). Yet, dealing with diversity and individualizing requires a fundamental shift in philosophy and teaching style for many general physical educators.

The inclusion of students with disabilities and the realization that all students have individual needs can make general physical educators better teachers. As noted by Ginny Popiolek, an adapted physical educator in Maryland who specializes in helping general physical educators with inclusion,

> The best thing that has happened with inclusion is that we have all become better physical education teachers. With inclusion, our regular physical education staff was forced to use a larger array of teaching strategies and materials to accommodate students with disabilities. These teachers quickly found that individualizing instruction and creating a variety of accommodations helped all the students in the physical education classes. These teachers have become aware of the fact that all students learn differently and that adaptations create a positive atmosphere and facilitate development in all their students. (personal communication, 1994)

It is also important to realize that some students with disabilities will learn differently from their peers without disabilities. Again, this realization can be difficult for general physical educators who are used to homogenous groups. For example, students with severe attention-deficit/hyperactivity disorder may be so distracted that they get only half the number of turns as peers in general physical education. Yet, given the child's level of attending, this child may be benefiting from physical education to the best of his or her abilities. Similarly, a child with autism might benefit from physical education if he or she interacts with peers, demonstrates appropriate behavior, and follows directions given in a large-group setting. Expectations should be high but individualized to meet the unique learning as well as physical and motor needs of the student with disabilities.

Reinforce Positive Interactions

Encourage peers to befriend children with disabilities by being their partners, including them on their teams, and generally interacting with them during activities. When necessary, encourage peers to help the child with disabilities during physical education but have them avoid "mothering." This is particularly true for children with intellectual disabilities or autism who might not understand exactly what is going on. Do not tolerate teasing or negative interactions.

Be Knowledgeable About the Student

Although it is impossible to know everything about the child with disabilities, it is important to know medical and health information, how to communicate with the child, how to deal with behavior problems, and what activities the child really enjoys. This information can be obtained from the child's parents, special education teacher, therapists, and in some cases the child him- or herself (see Chapter 5). The key is to know as much as possible about the child so you can accommodate his or her unique needs and help peers understand why you are making certain modifications.

PREPARING CLASSMATES WITHOUT DISABILITIES FOR SOCIAL ACCEPTANCE AND INCLUSION

Peer acceptance can be the critical difference between successful and unsuccessful inclusion. Peer acceptance may lay the groundwork for successful inclusion of a peer with a disability and has the potential for playing a significant role throughout one's development (Odom, McConnell, & McEvoy, 1992). Without peer acceptance, the child with a disability is at a definite disadvantage, and rejection by peers can result in limited social learning opportunities. Peer rejection creates real barriers and inhibits the ability of the student with a disability to achieve independence, academic success, and his or her life goals. This can have powerful, far-reaching, long-term implications on the development of the individual with a disability.

Research suggests that many children without disabilities have positive attitudes toward including classmates with disabilities in physical education and sports activities (Block, 1995b; Block & Malloy, 1998; Block & Zeman, 1996; Obrusnikova et al., 2003; Verderber, Rizzo, & Sherrill, 2003). For example, Block and Malloy found that girls without disabilities ages 11-13 overwhelmingly accepted a child with a disability into their competitive, fast-pitch softball league. Furthermore, they were willing to allow modifications to make sure this peer was successful. Unfortunately, the initial response of many peers without disabilities may be negative just because they have no experience with peers who have disabilities. Some will be scared of students with disabilities, particularly students with physical disabilities. Others will immediately reject students with disabilities because they feel that these students will ruin their physical education program. Still others may be sympathetic toward students with disabilities and try to mother these students. Although none of these responses will facilitate successful inclusion, they are understandable given that most students without disabilities know very little about students with disabilities. Thus, an important part of the process of including students with disabilities is to prepare classmates.

Several authors have suggested ways in which teachers can help classmates without disabilities develop a more positive attitude toward students with disabilities (e.g., Auxter et al., 2005; Block & Brady, 1999; Clark, French, & Henderson, 1985, Getskow & Konczal, 1996; Lieberman & Houston-Wilson, 2002; Stainback & Stainback, 1985). However, research examining these disability awareness programs has been contradictory and inconsistent (Ellery & Rauschenbach, 2000; Lockhart, French, & Gench, 1998; Loovis & Loovis, 1997; Obrusnikova, Block, & Trussell, 2005). To illustrate, Ellery and Rauscherbach (2000) employed a structured disability awareness program (two 30-minute sessions), which included disability simulations (e.g., moving in a wheelchair or with a walker), video presentations, and lectures from an athlete with a physical disability. Surprisingly, they found a negative attitude shift after the program. Similarly, Lockhart et al. (1998) did not find any significant effect on attitudes among fifth-grade students without disabilities following either cognitive (lectures from experts and video presentations) or affective (simulation activities and discussions) em-

pathy training (ten 30-minute sessions). Several explanations for the lack of success of the two interventions can be offered. For example, the quality and structure of the interventions may have been inappropriate to change the attitude of the students without disability. Also, providing children without disabilities with knowledge of disabilities may have heightened student awareness of the differences. This may have led to a realization that including a peer with a disability can be a challenge and may negatively affect activities played in general physical education.

In contrast, Loovis and Loovis (1997) found a significantly positive effect on second- through sixth-grade females without disabilities (no effect on males) after a series of disability simulations (orientation and mobility when blindfolded, moving in a wheelchair, communicating with sign language). Likewise, Obrusnikova et al. (2005) found significantly positive effects on both males' and females' knowledge and general attitudes toward including students with disabilities in general physical education. The disability awareness program used in this study combined both the cognitive and affective component of disability awareness training. The key is to help classmates become more knowledgeable about disability in general to avoid myths and stereotypes, learn how to view peers with disabilities in a positive manner, and learn how to interact with peers with disabilities during general physical education (see Table 9.2).

Circle of Friends

A circle of friends is a systematic way of identifying and outlining all of the friends, acquaintances, and key people in one's life (Falvey & Rosenberg, 1995; Pearpoint et al., 1996). Most children without disabilities have an extensive network of friends. Some children with disabilities don't have any friends at all. The circle of friends process can help children without disabilities realize how important friends are in their life and how children who don't have

Table 9.2. Preparing classmates without disabilities for social acceptance and inclusion

- Teach about circle of friends.
- Host guest speakers with disabilities.
- Conduct disability role-plays.
- Discuss the concept of rules and handicapping.
- Lead a discussion on disabilities.
- Talk about famous people who have disabilities.
- Discuss the specific child who will be included.
- Explain how to interact with specific children.
- Provide ongoing information, encouragement, and support.

friends must feel. Through this process, children without disabilities often have a greater appreciation of the importance of accepting and befriending peers with disabilities.

The circle of friends process begins with a "social scan." This gives a picture of key people in a person's life. This also helps children without disabilities see very clearly who might be involved in certain activities and what circles need to be filled. The process involves each student in the class drawing four concentric circles (see Figure 9.1). Each child is told that they are in the center of the circles. Students are then prompted to fill in the people who are in each of the four circles. The first circle, *circle of intimacy*, lists the people most intimately connected to a student's life—those people the student could not imagine living without (e.g., parents, siblings, grandparents). The second circle, *circle of friendship*, lists each student's good friends. The third circle, *circle of participation*, lists people, organizations, and networks in which the student might be involved (e.g., sports teams, clubs, scouts)—people with whom the student participates. Finally, the fourth and outer circle, *circle of exchange*, lists people who are paid to provide services to the stu-

dent (e.g., teachers, medical professionals, barbers) (Falvey & Rosenberg, 1995; Pearpoint et al., 1996).

Once all students have finished their social scan, lead a discussion about the results, focusing on the circles of students with disabilities. Students will quickly see that students with disabilities have fewer names in their circle of friends and circle of participation, and more names in their circle of exchange. The process concludes with ways members of the class can help this have more friends and participate in more activities (Pearpoint et al., 1996).

To apply this process to general physical education, the general physical educator can ask students to draw and then fill in three circles: 1) who they play with and interact with during physical education on a daily basis, 2) who they play and interact with in class occasionally, and 3) who they never play or interact with. Students can learn through this process that they only interact with some children and not others, and that some children never really interact with anyone during physical education. Through discussion and prompting, the teacher can then help children realize that some children might be very lonely and isolated in physical education. Finally, the general physical educator can help chil-

You

Circle of Intimacy

Circle of Friendship

Circle of Participation

Circle of Exchange

Figure 9.1. Circle of friends. (From Pearpoint, J., Forest, M., & O'Brien, J. [1996]. MAPs, Circles of Friends, and PATH: Powerful tools to help build caring communities. In S. Stainback & W. Stainback [Eds.], *Inclusion: A guide for educators* [Figure 3, p. 75]. Baltimore: Paul H. Brookes Publishing Co.; adapted by permission.)

Questions from the Children's Attitude Toward Integrated Physical Education–Revised

Okay, let me tell you about **Mike.** *He is the same age as you, but he cannot walk. Mike likes playing the same games you do, but he does not do very well in the games. Even though Mike can move around, he is slower than you and tires easily. Mike can throw a ball but not very far. He can catch balls that are tossed straight to him, and he can hit a baseball off a tee, but he cannot shoot a basketball high enough to make basket. Because Mike's legs do not work well, he has difficulty kicking a ball.*

Let's get started. Listen to the following statement and think about Mike. Answer each with **yes, probably yes, probably no,** *or* **no.** *Remember, there are no right or wrong answers. Your answers will depend on your feelings and will probably be different from other kids in your class.*

		Yes	Probably yes	Probably no	No
1.	It would be okay having Mike come to my PE class.	____	____	____	____
2.	Because Mike cannot play sports very well, he would slow down the game for everyone else.	____	____	____	____
3.	If we were playing a team sport such as basketball, it would be okay having Mike on my team.	____	____	____	____
4.	PE would be fun if Mike were in my PE class.	____	____	____	____
5.	If Mike were in my PE class, I would talk to him and be his friend.	____	____	____	____
6.	If Mike were in my PE class, I would like to help him practice and play the games.	____	____	____	____
7.	Mike could hit a ball placed on a batting tee.	____	____	____	____
8.	Someone could tell Mike where to run when he hits the ball.	____	____	____	____
9.	The distance between home and first base could be shorter for Mike.	____	____	____	____
10.	Someone could help Mike when he plays in the field.	____	____	____	____
11.	If the ball was hit to Mike, the batter could only run as far as second base.	____	____	____	____

Figure 9.3. Questions from the Children's Attitude Toward Integrated Physical Education–Revised (CAIPE-R) Inventory. The Children's Attitude Toward Integrated Physical Education–Revised (CAIPE-R) was designed for children in fifth through twelfth grades. After reading the following vignette about a child with a disability, have students respond to the series of statements regarding how they feel about having this child in their PE class, and how they feel about specific modifications to a sport to facilitate inclusion. (From M.E. Block, 1995a, Developmental and validation of the Children's Attitudes Toward Integrated Physical Education–Revised [CAIPE-R] Inventory, *Adapted Physical Activity Quarterly, 12*[1]: 55, page 64–65 © by Human Kinetics Publishers, Inc. Adapted with permission from Human Kinetics [Champaign, IL].)

is okay or how to approach the child. For example, peers sometimes see a teacher assistant helping the child with disabilities and think that they are not supposed to interact with the child. Explain to peers that it is desirable to talk to and play with the child with disabilities. Also explain how important it is for this child to really feel like part of the class. Then explain how to talk to the child (if the child has unique communication techniques), how to include the child in activities (what simple modifications might work), and specific ways to befriend the child. For example, many elementary students love to learn basic sign language.

Similarly, it can be fun and challenging for peers to figure out the best way to modify various physical education activities to include peers with disabilities. Providing some suggestions on how to interact with classmates who have disabilities will help peers be more understanding and welcoming to these children. Note that these discussions may need to take place several times during the school year. For example, children may be very friendly and helpful to a child with intellectual disabilities in the beginning of the school year. However, after several months children may begin to ignore the child or forget that the child needs modifications to activi-

Table 9.4. Movies featuring disabilities

Name of movie	Year released	Director	Actor
Cognitive disability/Down syndrome			
I Am Sam	2001	Jessie Nelson	Sean Penn
The Other Sister	1999	Garry Marshall	Juliette Lewis
The Eighth Day (Le Huitième jour)	1997	Jaco van Dormael	Pascal Duquenne
Forrest Gump	1994	Robert Zemeckis	Tom Hanks
Autism			
Rain Man	1988	Barry Levinson	Dustin Hoffman
What's Eating Gilbert Grape	1993	Lasse Halström	Leonardo DiCaprio
The Boy Who Could Fly	1988	Nick Castle	Jay Underwood
Backstreet Dreams	1990	Rupert Hitzig & Jason O'Malley	John Vizzi
Miracle Run	2004	Gregg Champion	
Schizophrenia/mental illness			
A Beautiful Mind	2002	Ron Howard	Russell Crowe
Shine	1996	Scott Hicks	Geoffrey Rush
Benny and Joon	1993	Jeremiah S. Chechik	Mary Stuart Masterson
Cerebral palsy			
My Left Foot	1989	Jim Sheridan	Daniel Day-Lewis
Dwarfism			
Simon Birch	1998	Mark Johnson	Ian Michael Smith
Deafness			
Mr. Holland's Opus	1995	Stephen Herek	
Immortal Beloved	1994	Bernard Rose	Gary Oldman
Sound and Fury	2000	Josh Aronson	
Blindness			
Scent of a Woman	1992	Martin Brest	Al Pacino
Blink	1994	Michael Apted	Madeleine Stowe
At First Sight	1999	Irwin Winkler	Val Kilmer
The Miracle Worker	2000	Nadia Tass	Hallie-Kate Eisenberg

ties to participate successfully. In such cases, you may need to remind the group of the child's needs.

Provide Ongoing Information, Encouragement, and Support for Acceptance

Preparing peers for inclusion is important and should be ongoing. Too often students with disabilities are ignored in physical education because their classmates do not know how to interact or assist the student with a disability (Block & Brady, 1999). Provide ongoing encouragement to peers (both through modeling and direct suggestion) to talk to the student with disabilities, to provide feedback and positive reinforcement, and to ask the student if he or she needs assistance. The entire class should take responsibility for the special student, and students should be continuously prompted and reinforced for interacting with the student with disabilities. As classmates begin to feel more comfortable with the

student who has a disability, then interactions will become more spontaneous.

COMMON BARRIERS TO SOCIAL INCLUSION IN GENERAL PHYSICAL EDUCATION AND POSSIBLE SOLUTIONS

Unfortunately, the social aspects of inclusion are rarely addressed in general physical education. Simply placing a child with disabilities in general physical education will not ensure socialization. Furthermore, many physical educators unknowingly create situations that prevent the social development of students with disabilities. Four problems primarily prevent socialization in inclusive physical education: when teacher assistants try too hard, when usual activities are inappropriate, when peers serve only as tutors and not friends, and when students with disabilities are grouped together.

Problem #1: Teacher Assistants Trying Too Hard

Students with more severe disabilities often come to general physical education with a teacher assistant. These teaching assistants often know a lot about the student with disabilities but very little about physical education. Furthermore, these well-meaning teacher assistants feel compelled to assist the student as much as possible. Some students even consider their teacher assistants to be their closest friend. Although close ties between students with disabilities and teaching staff are not necessarily negative, these ties may prevent the students from learning appropriate social skills needed to make relationships with classmates. Unfortunately, teacher assistants who hover over a student with a disability unwittingly prevent interaction with peers without disabilities (Lisboa, 1997).

Similarly, peers often feel uncomfortable approaching the student with disabilities when a teacher assistant is working with the student. For example, at a throwing station a teacher assistant is instructing the student with a disability how to throw overhand. She also retrieves beanbags for this student to throw. Peers seeing this interaction may not want to interfere with the instruction that is taking place. The student also becomes very dependent on the teacher assistant in this activity.

Solution: Awareness Training for Teacher Assistants

Teacher assistants want to do what is best for their students with disabilities, and they want to be useful. Simply explaining that you want to encourage more interactions between the student with disabilities and his or her peers without disabilities is a good beginning. Explain how their presence could prevent important social interactions with peers. Show the teacher assistant how she can move away and help other students while still keeping an eye on the student with disabilities. In fact, a teacher assistant can be assigned a group of students that includes the student with disabilities.

Teacher assistants also can be given specific ideas how to promote interactions between peers with and without disabilities. For example, the teacher assistant can encourage peers to choose the child with disabilities as a partner. When a child needs assistance to retrieve balls or go to another station, the teacher assistant can encourage peers to help the child. When playing group games, the teacher assistant can encourage peers to help the child know where to stand and what to do. The teacher assistant may need to be in the general area for safety reasons, but she does not need to hover around the student with disabilities the entire period. By backing off, the student is given a greater opportunity for interaction with peers and a chance to become more independent.

Problem #2: Student Cannot Participate in the General Activity

In some cases students with disabilities cannot participate in a particular activity because of health or safety issues. Although it may be appropriate to have the child off to the side doing a more appropriate activity, such separation from peers encourages isolation and prevents social interactions. For example, it may be unsafe for a tenth grader with cerebral palsy who uses an electric wheelchair to play soccer with his peers or for a third grader with Down syndrome to participate in forward rolls during a tumbling unit. Yet, sitting off to the side and watching or playing by him- or herself is not an appropriate solution to the problem.

Solution: Utilize Peers without Disabilities

One relatively simple solution is to have peers rotate over to the student with a disability and participate with him or her in an alternative activity. Using the soccer example above, each player in the soccer game is given a number from 1 to 6. Because there are 30 students in the class, five players will have the number 1, five will have the number 2, and so on. At the start of the soccer game, players with the number 1 will be off to the side working with the student with cerebral palsy in an alternative activity. In keeping with the theme of soccer, students practice dribbling as quickly as they can through cones or pass a ball back and forth with a partner. The student with cerebral palsy practices maneuvering his wheelchair through the cones or pushing his ball off his lap tray to a partner. After about 3 minutes, the ones rotate in and the twos rotate out. Having peers at the alternative activity creates opportunities for social interactions.

Another way to promote more interactions with peers is to add more activities. For example, if a child with Down syndrome cannot do forward rolls due to the possibility of a neck injury, set up another area of the gym with mats for other tumbling activities such as log rolls and crab walks. Have all students rotate between all stations, except for the child with Down syndrome, who rotates only through the last two stations. With this setup, the child with Down syndrome is working on motor and fitness skills but also has an opportunity to interact with peers, to wait his turn, and to observe appropriate behavior.

Problem #3: Peers Are Tutors, But Not Friends

Using peers as tutors to facilitate inclusion has been promoted (e.g., Block, 1996; Wilson, Lieberman, Horton, & Kasser, 1997) because peers are a free, readily available source of support for students with disabilities who need extra attention or extra help. However, if peers only serve in the role of tutor, then there is an imbalance in the relationship. This imbalance promotes a feeling that students with disabilities always need help and are somehow less than students without disabilities. Such imbalanced relationships can lead to lower self-esteem in students with disabilities (Sherrill, 2004).

Solution: Utilize Reciprocal Rather than One-Way Peer Tutoring

While you still can use peers as tutors to help students with disabilities, create situations in which students with disabilities can serve as tutors. Known as the reciprocal style of teaching (Mosston & Ashworth, 2002) or classwide peer tutoring (Sherrill, 2004), the student with disabilities and a peer take turns serving as tutor and tutee. This works particularly well with students with mild disabilities such as learning disabilities or behavior problems. As tutee, the student with disabilities learns how to listen and accept feedback. As a tutor, the student with disabilities learns how to carefully observe others and to provide feedback in a nice way.

Furthermore, taking turns as tutor and tutee leads to more interactions and discussions between the two students. For example, a fourth grader who does not follow directions, is hyperactive, and can be belligerent is paired with a peer in a throwing activity. Students are given a score sheet with the components of the overhand throw. The student with the behavior problem starts as the tutor. She is encouraged by the tutee to watch her throw, paying particular attention to her stepping with the opposite foot. The tutor watches the throw and gives immediate feedback following a script written out by the teacher: "Good throw, you stepped with the opposite foot." After five throws, the students switch roles. The student with a behavior problem now gets to throw and receive feedback, but she has seen a model of how to stay on task, how to listen to feedback, and how to accept feedback properly.

Alternate Solution: Utilize Peers as Friends as Well as Tutors

Another solution to the imbalance of peer tutoring is to set up situations in which peers are simply friends. For example, a ninth grader with fetal alcohol syndrome has motor delays (about 3 years delayed compared to peers) as well as behavior problems (short attention span, impulsive, hyperactive, lies). In the past, this student has been assigned a peer to help him stay on task, follow directions, and stay with the group. However, the physical education teacher decides to have the entire class be this student's friend. All are assigned responsibility for helping the student stay on task and behave more appropriately in physical education. The class discusses this new model and their new roles as friends. For example, when students line up in squads for roll call and for warm-ups, peers in this student's squad call the student over to say hi and then remind him to line up. During warm-ups, peers in his squad remind when it is time to change to a new warm-up activity, and several peers try to be his partner during sit-ups. When the teacher is giving instructions, peers around the student provide gentle reminders to sit and listen quietly. During the basketball game, teammates guide the student on where to stand and who to pass to and warn him not to play too rough on defense. The other team, aware that the student is not as skilled, allows him a little more room to pass and to shoot, and they do not call traveling unless it is blatant. This more subtle approach to helping this student provides more dignity and promotes a more natural delivery of support. Furthermore, the student has a chance to interact with all his classmates rather than just one peer tutor.

Problem #4: Students With Disabilities Are Grouped Together

Despite the opportunities for social interaction, evidence has suggested that without adult intervention, students without disabilities tend to interact more frequently with their peers with disabilities in social situations (Sainato & Carta, 1992). Ellis, Wright, and Cronis (1996) found that when an entire self-contained special education class of 11 students was included in general physical education, they tended to maintain their group identity rather than interact with the rest of the class. In a similar study, Place and Hodge (2001) found that even three students with disabilities placed together in the same GPE class were significantly more likely to interact with each other than with peers without disabilities.

Solution: Teacher-Mediated Interaction

Recall from Chapter 2 that one of the basic premises of inclusion is the *principle of natural proportions* (placing only one or two students with disabilities into a GPE class of 20-25 students). Although special education teachers find it easier to bring a larger portion of the class (or even the entire class) to GPE, this creates a setting ripe for failure. If two or more students with disabilities absolutely have to be included in one class, then designing inclusive environments to facilitate the social behavior of children with disabilities, take into account the severity or level of disability of the child, and the number of socially competent peers available for interaction can be very helpful. Dividing the class into small groups with only one student with a disability in each group would create an environment conducive to social interactions between students with and without disabilities.

SUMMARY

Perhaps the greatest benefit to including students with disabilities into general physical education is the opportunity it creates for children with disabilities to interact with peers, make friends, and feel like a member of the group. Yet, such benefits will not occur if children with disabilities are simply placed in general physical education. The general physical education teacher and peers without disabilities have to welcome the child into general physical education by learning about the child, by trying to genuinely include the child in as many general physical education activities as possible, and by showing the child that he/she is welcome and a true member of the class.

Although it is never appropriate to include a child in general physical education just for socialization, social inclusion and acceptance is an important goal in any classroom. Quality physical education should promote motor, cognitive, and *social development*. This can be particularly important for students with disabilities.

CHAPTER 9 APPENDIX

Famous People with Disabilities

ATHLETES

Jim Abbott *(baseball)*	Physical disability (hand amputation)
Muhammad Ali *(boxing)*	Brain injury
Lance Armstrong *(cycling)*	Cancer
Larry Brown *(football)*	Hearing impairment
Harold Connelly *(track and field)*	Physical disability (left arm)
Tom Dempsey *(football)*	Physical disability (congenital foot deformity)
Jim Eisenreich *(baseball)*	Tourette syndrome
Sean Elliot *(basketball)*	Kidney disease
Pete Gray *(baseball)*	Physical disability (had one arm)
Nancy Hogshead *(swimming)*	Asthma
Catfish Hunter *(baseball)*	Diabetes, amyotrophic lateral sclerosis
Bruce Jenner *(track and field)*	Learning disability
Magic Johnson *(basketball)*	HIV
Jackie Joyner-Kersee *(track and field)*	Asthma
Tony Lazzeri *(baseball)*	Epilepsy
Greg Louganis *(diving)*	Asthma, HIV
Walter Payton *(football)*	Kidney disease
Wilma Rudolph *(track and field)*	Physical disability (birth defects and polio)
Ron Santo *(baseball)*	Diabetes, physical disability (leg amputation
O.J. Simpson *(football)*	Learning disability
Kenny Walker *(football)*	Deafness
Kristi Yamaguchi *(figure skating)*	Asthma

POLITICIANS

Winston Churchill	Learning disability
Robert Dole	Physical disability (right arm)
John F. Kennedy	Physical disability (back injury), Addison disease
Abraham Lincoln	Depression, Marfan syndrome (a connective tissue disorder)
George Patton	Learning disability
Ronald Reagan	Alzheimer's disease
Franklin D. Roosevelt	Physical disability
Woodrow Wilson	Learning disability

ACTORS

Chris Burke	Mental retardation (Down syndrome)
Cher	Dyslexia

(Cher uses a reading coach to learn television, movie, and commercial scripts.)

Tom Cruise	Dyslexia

(Cruise uses a reading coach to learn scripts.)

Sammy Davis, Jr.	Visual impairment
Walt Disney	Learning disability

(Disney did not learn how to read until he was 9. He drew pictures to help him remember what he was learning.)

Michael J. Fox	Parkinson disease
Annette Funicello	Multiple sclerosis
Danny Glover	Learning disability

(Glover was placed in a class for students with mental retardation until he was in high school, and he did not learn how to read or write until after he graduated from school.)

Whoopi Goldberg	Dyslexia

(Goldberg uses a reading coach to help her learn scripts.)

James Earl Jones	Communication disability (stuttering)

(Jones did not speak in school because he was so embarrassed. He learned to speak without stuttering by reading poetry. Poetry has a rhythm to it, and people who stutter often can sing or read poetry.)

Marlee Matlin	Deafness
Richard Pryor	Multiple sclerosis
Christopher Reeve	Quadriplegia

MUSICIANS

Beethoven	Deafness
Ray Charles	Blindness
Jacqueline du Pré	Multiple sclerosis

John Lennon	Learn
Freddie Mercury	
Itzhak Perlman	Phys
Stevie Wonder	

OTHER FAMOUS PEOPLE

Hans Christian Andersen *(writer)*	Learn
Agatha Christie *(writer)*	Learn
Thomas Edison *(inventor)*	
Albert Einstein *(physicist and Nobel laureate)*	Learn
Stephen Hawking *(physicist and writer)*	Amyo
Helen Keller *(writer)*	Deafness
Darci Kistler *(ballerina)*	

Sources: Appenzeller (1983); Getskow and Konczal (1996); Zygmunt, Larson, and Tilson (1994).

Making Inclusive Physical Education Safe

by Martin E. Block and Mel L. Horton

Not many things scare Mr. Strawberry. At 6 feet, 4 inches, and weighing 275 pounds, most people are a little scared of Mr. Strawberry, especially the kindergartners who meet him for the first time. Truthfully, Mr. Strawberry is a teddy bear who loves teaching physical education to elementary school children. He has been teaching elementary physical education for 10 years and is one of the few veteran teachers who really look forward to coming back to school each fall.

But Mr. Strawberry is not looking forward to returning to school this fall because of a little girl named Angel. Angel and her parents just moved to town. Over the summer, Mr. Strawberry received a call from the special education teacher at Perry Creek Elementary School, briefly explaining some of Angel's medical conditions. Angel is on a respirator for oxygen. She is fed via a feeding tube. She uses a wheelchair for mobility, but she needs someone to push it for her. Due to severe scoliosis and frequent hip dislocations, several different straps and wedges on her wheelchair help her stay in the correct position. Angel is also considered deaf and blind. She wears hearing aids, which allow her to hear sounds. She wears very thick glasses, which help her identify large images and people directly in front of her. She is nonverbal and has intellectual disabilities, so it is difficult for her to communicate and to understand what others want.

Mr. Strawberry was told that Angel would attend general physical education with the support of a full-time nurse. Separate programming was not an option, at least not for the first few months of school, to determine if Angel would be successful in general physical education. Reports from her previous school said that Angel successfully attended general physical education.

Mr. Strawberry wants to do what is best for Angel, but is scared that she might have a medical crisis in the gymnasium. He is also unclear about how to ensure the safety of someone who seems so fragile in a gymnasium where balls and kids are constantly flying around.

Mr. Strawberry has a plan for getting the kids out of the gym when there is a fire drill, and he has a basic first aid kit for cuts and scrapes. But a more extensive emergency plan seems to be needed for Angel. Yes, despite his size, Mr. Strawberry is definitely scared of Angel and all of the challenges that she presents. What should Mr. Strawberry do?

Gallahue and Cleland-Donnelly noted that "the very nature of physical education classes, which take place in the gymnasium, swimming pool, or playground, exposes the teacher to greater liability for accidents and injuries than any other area of the school curriculum" (2003, p. 397). Safety issues in physical education are compounded when children with disabilities are included in general physical education programs. There are three major safety concerns for students with disabilities who are included in general physical education. First, safety is a problem for students with disabilities who do not have the same level of speed, strength, stamina, balance, or coordination as their peers without disabilities. In addition, many students with disabilities have cognitive and perceptual impairments that can add to their confusion and inability to react to situations as quickly as their peers. Such differences can easily lead to injuries. For example, in a dodging/fleeing activity, a child with cerebral palsy who is very unstable in standing could easily be knocked down. Similarly, a child who has intellectual disabilities may not know that he or she is standing too close to the batter during a softball game. The student could be in danger of getting hit by the ball or the bat.

Second, safety is an issue for children who have medical conditions that can lead to emergency complications. For example, many with asthma at times require emergency medical attention (Butterfield, 1993). Similarly, changes in diet and exercise patterns can have severe consequences for children who have diabetes (Petray, Freesemann, & Lavay, 1997). Of even greater concern are children with disabilities who are medically dependent for life support, such as tracheostomies for children who need oxygen for breathing, gastrostomy tubes for children with feeding problems, shunts for children with hydrocephalus, and colostomies and ileostomies for children with bowel and bladder problems. Children with such severe medical conditions used to be in hospital and special schools; however, a greater number of these children are being placed in general school settings (Graff, Ault, Guess, Taylor, & Thompson, 1990; Prendergast, 1995; Troher, 1992). In fact, the Supreme Court of the United States ruled that public schools must provide a wide array of medical care for children with disabilities in public school settings, including general physical education (Biskupic, 1999).

Third, including students with disabilities in general physical education poses dangers to students without disabilities. For example, a student who uses a wheelchair may be involved in a game of tag. During the excitement of the game a child without a disability could easily run into the child's wheelchair. Similarly, a child with crutches could accidentally hit or trip another student during a soccer game, or a child with an artificial arm could accidentally bump into and hurt a peer during movement exploration activities.

Safety certainly should be a priority in physical education for students with and without disabilities, and there are some cases in which children with disabilities cannot safely be included in general physical education. However, safety concerns should not be used as a blanket excuse to separate all students with disabilities into separate physical education classes. As noted in Chapters 1 and 2, placements need to be made on a case-by-case basis. Only when the setting is deemed unsafe or inappropriate after attempts at making it safe and appropriate through supplementary aids and supports can the student be placed in a separate setting (Block, 1996; IDEA 2004, 20 U.S.C. § 1412[a][5][A]; *Oberti v. Board of Education*, 1992).

The purpose of this chapter is to share strategies that can be used to make general physical education settings and activities safe for all students. First, liability and negligence are discussed. This is followed by a brief discussion of six key aspects of making inclusive settings safe: 1) the student with disabilities, 2) the general environment, 3) the equipment, 4) class organization, 5) content, and 6) emergency procedures. It is understood that some students in some activities and environments may not be able to participate safely and should receive physical education in an alternative setting. This process allows general physical educators to make more objective decisions about which children need alternative programs or placements. However, this process allows most students with disabilities, including those with severe disabilities, to be safely accommodated within general physical education.

A PRIMER ON LEGAL LIABILITY

Liability

From a legal standpoint, legal or *tort liability* refers to someone being at fault, this "fault" leading to or causing an injury or death, and that "someone" being legally responsible for the injury or death (Appenzeller & Appenzeller, 1980; Black, 1990; Gallahue & Cleland-Donnelly, 2003). With regard to physical education, a student can hold a physical education teacher liable (at fault) for injuries received during physical education class. For example, a child with a visual impairment is knocked down during a dodging and fleeing game. Her parents sue the physical education teacher for their child's injuries. Although the parents have the right to hold the physical education teacher liable for their daughter's injuries, the court must show that the cause of the child's injuries was the physical education teacher's "negligence."

Negligence

Fault that results in personal injury is also known as *negligence* (Appenzeller, 1983; Dougherty, 1987). Negligence is defined as failure on the part of the physical education teacher to act in a manner that is judged to be reasonable, careful, and prudent for someone with that level of training or status (Dougherty, 1987; Gallahue & Cleland-Donnelly, 2003; Gray, 1995). This is also known as the "prudent or reasonable person principle" (Dougherty, 1987). That is, would another reasonably prudent physical education teacher placed in that same situation have done the same thing to ensure the safety of the child who was injured? A physical educator who places children in unnecessarily risky situations or who does not provide proper supervision of activities may be considered negligent. Appenzeller (1983), Dougherty (1987), Gallahue and Cleland-Donnelly (2003), and Pangrazi (2007) noted that negligence must be proven in a court of law and the following four factors must be shown if negligence is to be established:

1. *Duty:* It must be determined that the defendant (i.e., the physical education teacher) had a re-

sponsibility to provide for the safety and welfare of the plaintiff (i.e., the student). If the injured party is a student in the defendant's physical education class, then established duty is a foregone conclusion. It is important to note that the licensed physical education teacher has the duty to provide for the safety and welfare of all students who enter his or her physical education program including children with disabilities, even when the child with a disability is accompanied by a teacher assistant, volunteer, or peer tutor. In fact, the licensed physical education teacher is responsible for the safety of the teacher assistant, volunteer, and peer tutors who enter the physical education setting as well.

2. *Breach of duty:* It must be shown that the defendant failed to provide the standard or service that could be reasonably expected of a professional under similar circumstances. A duty can be breached by "nonfeasance" or "act of omission," failure to do something that a prudent physical educator should have done such as providing alternative instruction to students who are deaf; "malfeasance" or "act of commission," doing something that a prudent physical educator should not have been doing such as allowing a child with Down syndrome who tested positive for atlanto-axial instability (problem in the neck that can lead to paralysis if pressure is placed on the neck) to do forward and backward rolls with the other children; or "misfeasance," following proper procedures but not to the required standard of conduct expected by a prudent physical education teacher such as supervising children in a game of tag but having too small a space and too many children moving at once, causing a child with low vision to collide with another child.

3. *Foreseeability:* It must be shown that the physical education teacher could have been able to predict the likelihood of an accident or injury occurring due to the specific circumstance or situation. For example, could the physical education teacher have foreseen that a third-grade peer tutor did not have the strength or control to safely push a child in a wheelchair down a steep hill? Could the physical education teacher have foreseen that a child prone to asthma attacks might have an asthma attack when running the mile on a hot June day?

5. *Damage:* Damage refers to actual injury or loss. The plaintiff has to prove damage to receive compensation from the defendant. Real damages could be things such as medical expenses, rehabilitation, psychological stress, and time away from school. Compensation for damages then could be in the form of medical expenses, compensation for medical discomfort, psychological counseling, home tutoring, and even a legal restraint on the physical education teacher.

6. *Proximate cause:* If a breach of duty has been established, then the plaintiff must prove that there was a reasonable relationship between the defendant's breach of duty and the student's injury. In other words, was it the physical education teacher's specific breach of duty that led to the damage incurred by the student? If, for example, a child with intellectual disabilities who was properly supervised and instructed got hurt due to "an act of God" (e.g., the child trips over his own feet and breaks an ankle while working at a basketball station), then the physical education teacher is not necessarily liable. As noted by Appenzeller,

> The fact that an accident occurs does not necessarily mean the teacher or coach is negligent or liable for damages. It must be proved that the injury is reasonably connected with negligence . . . No court has held a defendant liable where there was substantial evidence that the defendant acted with prudence and caution in the performance of his duties. (1983, p. 183)

When an Injury to a Student Is Not Negligence

A physical education teacher could be found not negligent in relation to an injury incurred by a student during physical education class under the following circumstances: contributory negligence, act of God, and proximate cause (Appenzeller, 1983; Dougherty, 1987; Gallahue & Donnelly, 2003; Pangrazi, 2007).

1. *Contributory negligence:* This refers to the plaintiff (i.e., the student) being held partially or wholly responsible for the injury he or she received. Note that a court will take into consideration a student's age, physical capabilities (both mental and physical), and training before it rules. In other words, the defense tries to prove that the activity and equipment were familiar to the student, that the student received training in the activity or with the equipment, and that the injured student did not follow proper safety procedures that would be expected of other students his age and with his capabilities. For example, a 16-year-old child who uses a wheelchair, has no intellectual impairments, and has been in the same school in the same gymnasium for 3 years wheels his chair into the wall while playing basketball and suffers a broken leg and a concus-

sion. The court could reasonably rule that this child was old enough and capable enough to move his wheelchair safely within the confines of the gymnasium and that running into the wall was at least partially the student's own fault. In some states the concept of "comparative negligence" is used, which means that fault for a given situation is portioned out based on the information presented to the court (e.g., physical education teacher is 30% at fault while the student is 70% at fault). In such cases, the student can still receive compensation for damages but at a prorated basis.

2. *Proximate cause:* As noted previously, this suggests that the injury was not caused by the negligence of the physical education teacher. There must be a close relationship between the breach of duty by the teacher and the resulting injury to the student. For example, a teacher sets up five stations for children to work on their physical fitness. The teacher would normally move around the room supervising the various stations but not directly assisting any of the children (they all could do all of the fitness activities independently). However, at one point during class, a therapist comes into the gym to ask the physical education teacher a "quick question." While the physical education teacher is talking to this therapist, a child who uses crutches but has excellent upper body strength strains to do one more pull-up. With her last effort, she slips off the bar and hits the back of her head on a mat on the floor. This causes the child to have a concussion and bruised spinal cord. Even if the physical education teacher was watching this child as he normally would, the child still could have fallen and hurt herself. Therefore, while it could be argued that the physical education teacher was not providing proper supervision, this lack of supervision was not the proximate cause of this child's injury.

4. *Act of God:* This suggests that the injury occurred due to an event that was completely unexpected or could not be foreseen. In other words, something happened that caused an accident that was beyond the reasonable control of the teacher. For example, while playing outside a sudden gust of wind knocks down a child who has muscular dystrophy, causing him to break several bones. To prove an "act of God," the defense must show that the accident still would have occurred even though reasonable action had been taken.

In summary, teachers who act responsibly, with common sense, and with an aim to create the safest possible setting while still allowing children to be actively involved in movement and fitness activities should not be scared of liability and negligence. Always ask yourself, what would a prudent physical educator do in this situation? Also, think of worst-case scenarios in an attempt to foresee potential safety concerns. It is important to learn as much as you can about each child so you can anticipate any possible problems, provide proper supervision and instruction, make sure equipment is in proper working order, and provide activities and progressions that are appropriate for each child's abilities.

LEGAL ISSUES SPECIFIC TO STUDENTS WITH DISABILITIES

Many students with disabilities have visible impairments that present an immediate concern to the physical educator (e.g., students who use wheelchairs or students who are blind). Others have hidden disabilities (e.g., seizure disorder, asthma, diabetes, HIV/AIDS). Hidden disabilities are particularly dangerous because special educators and parents often forget to inform physical education staff about conditions that can result in injury. Being unaware of a student's health/medical problems can lead to participation in unsafe activities in unsafe ways and possible lawsuits. Ultimately, you as the physical educator are responsible for the safety of all the students you serve (Aufsesser, 2003; Cotton, 1994; Dougherty, 1987).

The first step is to simply identify children with health problems and/or specific disabilities by carefully reviewing the medical records of all the students you serve (Pangrazi, 2007). An easier way is to review the emergency cards on file in the main office. These cards usually highlight children with special health problems such as asthma, diabetes, allergies, and medications taken, among others. In addition, you can ask the school nurse or each classroom teacher to identify students with special health problems or disabilities.

Once you have identified students with health problems and/or disabilities, examine their medical records and cumulative folders, both of which should be available in the main office. If for some reason, detailed records are outdated or not available, then contact the child's parents to obtain more information. Another relatively simple way to obtain information about children with special health problems or disabilities is to send home a checklist for parents and/or a physician to fill out (see Figure 10.1). Some school districts require such forms to be filled out before a child with a disability can participate in physical education (Fairfax County Public Schools, 1994). Detailed information on each child with special health problems or disabilities can then be stored

Physical Education Information Form

I. **General information** (to be filled out by parent/guardian)

Child's name: _____ Date of birth: _____

Parent/guardian: _____ Telephone: _____

II. **Medical information** (to be filled out by parent/guardian and/or doctor)

A. **Nature of disability** (If your child does not have a disability, skip to B.)

What type of disability(ies) does the child have: _____

_____

_____

Please describe in more detail the characteristics of the child's disability(ies): _____

_____

_____

Is there anything I should be aware of in physical education? _____

_____

_____

B. **Specific health conditions** (If your child does not have any health conditions, skip to C.)

Asthma _____ yes _____ no

If you answered yes, is there an inhaler at school? _____ yes _____ no

If you answered yes, where is it located? _____

Bee sting allergies _____ yes _____ no

If you answered yes, is there a bee sting kit at school? _____ yes _____ no

If you answered yes, where is it located? _____

Diabetes _____ yes _____ no

If you answered yes, does your child take insulin? _____ yes _____ no

If you answered yes, where is it located? _____

Heart problems _____ yes _____ no

If you answered yes, please explain in more detail.

_____

_____

Other health conditions

Are there any other health conditions we should be aware of?

_____

_____

_____

_____

(continued)

Figure 10.1. Physical education information form. (*Sources:* Fairfax County Public Schools, 1994; Kelly & Wessel, 1986; Markos & Jenkins, 1994.)

Figure 10.1. *(continued)*

C. Medications

Does your child take any medications? _____ yes _____ no

If you answered yes, what are the names of the medications, and what are they used for?

_____

_____

_____

_____

When are the medications administered? _____

_____

_____

_____

Do they have any effects on physical/motor performance? _____

_____

_____

Are there any specific concerns regarding medications that I should be aware of in physical education including any activities

that the child should not do? _____

_____

_____

III. PE activities that may be inappropriate (to be filled out by parent, physical therapist, and/or doctor)
Some activities can be dangerous for children with particular disabilities. Please place an X next to any activity that you have concerns about and explain why, along with any accommodations that would allow the student to participate safely in the activity.

ELEMENTARY SCHOOL (K–5)

Locomotor skills	**Manipulative skills**	**Body management**	**Fitness**
Running	Throwing	Twisting	Continuous running
Jumping	Catching	Turning	Sprinting
Galloping	Striking	Stretching	Stretching
Hopping	Kicking		Push-ups/pull-ups
Skipping	Dribbling (with feet)		Sit-ups
Bouncing			Rope climbing
			Aerobic dance
			Weight lifting
			Stationary bike

Tumbling	**Games**	**Water activities**
Balance beam	Chasing/fleeing	Getting wet
Log roll	Dodging	Standing in water
Forward roll	Tag	Floating
Backward roll	Racing	Basic strokes
Head/hand stand	Team sports	Lap swimming
Vaulting	Skating	Diving
Pyramids	Jumping rope	
Rope climbing		

MIDDLE/HIGH SCHOOL

Team sports	**Individual sports**	**Gymnastics**	**Dance**
Basketball	Golf	Rings	Aerobic
Softball	Tennis	High bar	Square
Volleyball	Archery	Parallel bars	Folk
Soccer	Bowling	Vault	Modern
Flag football	Badminton	Floor exercise	
Floor hockey	Wrestling		
Lacrosse			

Comments on activities that you have concerns about for this student:

_____

_____

_____

_____

_____

_____

_____

_____

_____

_____

_____

_____

_____

_____

_____

Name(s) of person(s) who filled out this form and their relationship to the child:

_____

_____

_____

_____

Signature: _____ Date: _____

Signature: _____ Date: _____

Signature: _____ Date: _____

Signature: _____ Date: _____

in a database and updated yearly. A database allows you to sort children based on necessary precautions (e.g., having an inhaler or other medicine available, not doing strenuous exercise in the fall during heavy pollen season).

Although this may seem like a tremendous task, it is critical that you know as much as possible about each child with special health concerns or disabilities in order to ensure safe participation in general physical education. Physical activity can lower blood sugar in children with diabetes, which can cause a hypoglycemic reaction (Petray, Freesemann, & Lavay, 1997; Schwartz, 1999). Many children with spina bifida have shunts to drain fluid from their brains, and most physicians recommend some restrictions in physical education activities (French, Keele, Silliman-French, 1997). Children with exercise-induced asthma are particularly sensitive to continuous exercise (Butterfield, 1993). A physical educator who is not aware of these and other conditions could put a child into dangerous situations.

Another way to get this and other information is to participate in the individualized education program (IEP) meeting. All critical team members including parents attend this meeting and share information about the child with disabilities. This meeting also is a great place to educate IEP team members about your program and what you know about the child. You can share information such as the child's fitness level, gross motor skills, perceptual motor abilities, skills in specific activities, and general motivation and behavior during physical education. Once team members begin to understand your program, the unique aspect of the physical education environment, and the gross motor/fitness skills of the student, they can provide more specific suggestions to make your program safe.

Having updated medical and health information is imperative. You also need to know about each child's physical fitness level, body and space awareness, balance, eye-hand coordination, and other motor abilities and how these might impact safe participation in physical education. For example, if a child has problems with eye-hand coordination, you should plan accommodations during dodging, catching, rebounding, and striking activities, such as using foam balls. Similarly, you could allow children who have balance problems, including children who use walkers or canes, to move in a special zone so that they will not get bumped or knocked down during chasing and fleeing activities. Figure 10.2 provides a list of questions regarding a child's fitness level and gross motor abilities.

Finally, you need to find out about each child's communication skills and behavior problems. Again, you can get much of this information at the IEP meeting by listening to and talking to parents, general and special education teachers, therapists, and teacher assistants. For example, the general and special educator can note behaviors that could create safety problems (e.g., aggressive behaviors, tendency to run away), and the speech therapist can note how much verbal information the child understands. Figure 10.3 provides questions to guide you when meeting with these professionals.

CREATING A SAFE TEACHING ENVIRONMENT

Making the general physical education environment safe for students without disabilities is very similar to best practices in making physical education safe for all students.

Space

First and foremost, the general physical educator should consider the amount of teaching space available. The area in which students will be working should allow for movements that are free from restrictions (Graham, Holt-Hale, & Parker, 2004). This is particularly true for students with intellectual disabilities or learning disabilities who may not be very aware of their personal space. For example, if a student with intellectual disabilities is working on striking with a bat, there should be enough space to freely swing the bat without harming peers. If a child who uses a wheelchair is involved in a warm-up activity such as a chasing/fleeing type game, extra space may be needed to ensure safety. An example from an actual case involved a 16-year-old student with quadriplegia (Aufsesser, 2003). This student (who used an electric wheelchair) was playing basketball in a mainstreamed physical education class. One of the students without disabilities was hurt when he ran into the wheelchair. As a result, the student using the wheelchair was removed from the general physical education class. This error in lack of safety precautions relative to spatial relations created an unfortunate, yet preventable, circumstance for all those involved.

Boundaries and Equipment Set Up

The teaching environment should have boundaries that separate activity and hazardous areas. You may need to highlight boundaries for children with low vision, perceptual motor concerns, or attention-deficit/hyperactivity disorder (ADHD). Students with visual impairments might benefit from brightly colored cones or tape. Peers can provide extra physical assistance and verbal cues to students with autism,

Safety Inventory

Child's name: _____   Date of birth: _____

Person filling out this form: _____

Relationship to child: _____

Does the child have specific problems in space awareness?   ____ yes ____ no

Activities that might be affected _____

Possible solutions/modifications _____

Does the child have specific problems with body awareness?   ____ yes ____ no

Activities that might be affected _____

Possible solutions/modifications _____

Does the child have specific problems with upper body strength?   ____ yes ____ no

Activities that might be affected _____

Possible solutions/modifications _____

Does the child have specific problems with lower body strength?   ____ yes ____ no

Activities that might be affected _____

Possible solutions/modifications _____

Does the child have specific problems with endurance?   ____ yes ____ no

Activities that might be affected _____

Possible solutions/modifications _____

Does the child have specific problems with flexibility?   ____ yes ____ no

Activities that might be affected _____

Possible solutions/modifications _____

Does the child have specific problems with speed?   ____ yes ____ no

Activities that might be affected _____

Possible solutions/modifications _____

Does the child have specific problems with eye-hand coordination?   ____ yes ____ no

Activities that might be affected _____

Possible solutions/modifications _____

Does the child have specific problems with balance?   ____ yes ____ no

Activities that might be affected _____

Possible solutions/modifications _____

Figure 10.2.   Safety inventory.

Communication, Behaviors, and Reinforcement Inventory

Child's name: _____   Date of birth: _____

Person filling out this form: _____

Relationship to child: _____

Communication skills

1. Does the child understand simple verbal directions?   ____ yes ____ no

2. If no, do you have suggestions to facilitate communication? _____
    _____
    _____

3. Can the child convey his or her wishes and/or needs?   ____ yes ____ no

4. If no, do you have any suggestions regarding how I might know what the student wants or needs?
    _____
    _____

Behaviors

1. Does the child understand simple rules of games?   ____ yes ____ no

2. If no, do you have suggestions to help the student play safely? _____
    _____

3. How does the child handle conflicts, such as being on the losing team?
    _____
    _____

4. Is the child ever aggressive?   ____ yes ____ no

5. If yes, what do you do when this happens? _____
    _____

6. Does the child have a hard time paying attention and staying on task?   ____ yes ____ no

7. If yes, what do you do when this happens? _____
    _____

Reinforcers

1. What activities, objects, and/or people does the child like?
    _____
    _____

2. What activities, objects, and/or people does the child dislike?
    _____
    _____

Figure 10.3.   Communication, behaviors, and reinforcement inventory.

visual impairments, or intellectual disabilities who may not be aware of safe boundaries.

Working space should be organized to ensure safe participation. One of the easiest yet most effective safety measures is to keep extraneous equipment out of the activity area. Large equipment such as volleyball standards and gymnastics equipment should be placed off to the side of the activity area. Smaller equipment to be used that day should be kept out of the way until needed. Although this may be a little inconvenient, it will make the environment much safer for all children.

Unique Environment Considerations

Some students present unique concerns in terms of creating a safe environment. For example, it is necessary to familiarize students who have visual impairments with the surroundings. This includes identifying where equipment is set up, where boundaries are, and where extraneous equipment such as chairs, tables, water fountain, steps, and ramps are. Similarly, it will be necessary for students who use walkers or wheelchairs to have an uncluttered environment through which to move (Auxter, Pyfer, & Huettig, 2004). As noted, extraneous equipment should be off to the side until needed. Finally, for students with asthma or other respiratory disorders, the teaching environment should be well ventilated and the temperature set at a comfortable level. In addition, the gym should be as dust-free as possible. Request that duct work and support beams be cleaned annually. Finally, you may need to allow students who are sensitive to pollen to stay inside during days when the pollen count is high.

Adapted Equipment

Equipment should accommodate the unique movement needs of each student. This can be accomplished by varying the size, weight, and texture of catching and throwing objects, striking implements, and other manipulative equipment. For example, a catching station should have balls ranging in size from small to large, light to heavy, and foam to rubber. At a striking station, balloons may be more appropriate for children with limited object control skills; beep balls would assist children who are blind. In addition, peers need to be sensitive to the motor skills of classmates with disabilities by varying such components as speed, distance, and force. For example, when tossing a ball to a partner with intellectual disabilities and limited catching skills, students should use light force and stand closer to the catcher.

When adapting equipment, it also is important to consider the developmental level of the student with disabilities. Just as it would be unsafe for kindergartners to practice striking using regulation-size tennis rackets, it would be unsafe for a student with Down syndrome who has small hands to use a regulation size softball bat when striking. Instead, they should strike with their hand and then progress to small, light foam paddles. Grips of such implements may also need to be altered for some children. If you are not sure how the child is supposed to use special equipment, whether special equipment is fitted properly, or whether special equipment is in good repair, consult with the child's physical/occupational therapist or special education teacher or parent (CAHPER, 1994).

Teaching How to Use Equipment Properly

Perhaps the greatest concern for students with disabilities, particularly students with intellectual disabilities and emotional disturbances, is teaching safe and appropriate use of equipment. For example, some children with intellectual disabilities may not be aware of safe ways to use physical education equipment such as looking around before swinging a golf club or a racket. Children with behavior problems may exhibit inappropriate behavior with equipment such as using improper force when throwing balls to peers. Children with ADHD may be so impulsive with equipment that they do not take the time to think of the consequences of their actions. Similarly, a child with autism who sees a brightly colored cage ball may run and try to jump on the ball, not realizing that his forceful action is going to cause the ball to slide across the gym floor, resulting in the student falling and banging his chin on the floor. In all of the above cases, it is important to teach these students how to use equipment safely.

SAFE TEACHING TECHNIQUES

Quality physical education presumes that general techniques regarding safety are common practice among physical educators. Teachers have a responsibility for providing appropriate instruction, proper supervision, and conducting activities in a safe manner (Nichols, 2001; Pangrazi, 2007).

Establish Safety Rules

The first safe teaching technique is to establish and review safety rules with the class. While you do not need to have hundreds of safety rules and regulations, it is important to establish a few critical safety rules such as establishing stop/start signals, maintaining good personal space, adhering to set boundaries, avoiding equipment that is off limits, and encouraging safe use of equipment. These rules should be posted in a visible place and reviewed frequently with all students. Focus special attention on students with intellectual disabilities, ADHD, or emotional disturbances who may tend to forget or ignore these rules. In addition, frequently remind students without disabilities to move cautiously around students who use wheelchairs, walkers, or who are blind.

Supervision

Because physical educators are legally responsible for everything that goes on in the physical education setting, it is imperative that they observe all that is going on in the class, particularly when students with disabilities are included. Observing the entire class involves establishing a position such as the "back-to-the-wall" technique and scanning, which allows you to see all students at all times (Graham et al., 2003). Halsey (2005) noted that the level of supervision provided to a specific child depends on that child's ability to understand the dangers of the activity, judge his or her skill level as it relates to the activity, and follow the established safety procedures related to the activity. This is particularly important for children with intellectual disabilities or autism. For example, a child with autism can participate in a golf unit in high school, but extra supervision is needed to help this student understand the dangers of swinging golf clubs. In such a situation, a peer, community volunteer, or even teacher assistant could be used to ensure the safe participation of this student in this activity.

Also, always be aware of children who have impulsive tendencies, children who can be aggressive, and children who wander away. When possible, place these students close to you. If this is not possible, utilize peers, community volunteers, or teacher assistants. When opting to utilize peers or aides, provide them specific precautions and outline their responsibilities in assisting the child.

Delivery of Instructional Cues

Proper instruction is an important part of creating a safe physical education program (Halsey, 2005). The delivery of instructional cues should be provided in such a manner that everyone understands directions and safety cues. Do not assume that all students in your class understand verbal cues. For example, children who have hearing impairments may need visual aids such as demonstrations or pictures to understand complex directions. Children with intellectual disabilities, autism, or children who are blind may need physical assistance. Even children with relatively mild disabilities such as specific learning disabilities, may benefit from extra demonstrations. If students do not understand directions and safety cues, there is a greater chance of injury.

Another factor in the delivery of instructional cues involves positioning children. Children with visual impairments who have some residual vision might benefit from demonstrations if they are positioned at the front of the class. Similarly, children with hearing impairments should be positioned so that they can read lips and have a better vantage point for picking up visual cues. Finally, children with ADHD, emotional disturbances, or autism should be positioned away from antagonizing peers, extraneous equipment, and markings on the floor. Children who are prone to physically attacking peers (e.g., biting, hitting, scratching) should be positioned close to you.

Warm-Up

One of the most important teaching techniques in preparing students for physical activity is a warm-up activity. For students with disabilities, this is particularly important. For example, a student with cerebral palsy needs to stretch hamstrings and groin muscles prior to walking with a walker during a movement exploration activity. Similarly, children with autism often need to experience repetition in warm-ups before they can be expected to participate in new activities.

While most students with disabilities can participate in the same warm-up activities as their peers, some students might need special warm-up activities. For example, the student with cerebral palsy might need to work on special leg stretches designed by the physical therapist and carried out by a teacher assistant while peers work on different stretches. Similarly, children with limited strength can be allowed to do modified sit-ups and push-ups, and children with asthma can be allowed to alternate between walking and running laps. Such individualization can be implemented with minimal disruption to your regular program.

Activities

It is important to plan activities that are progressive in nature (Halsey, 2005). When activities are progressive, injuries can be avoided (CAHPER, 1994; Pangrazi, 2007). To illustrate, consider a student with low muscle tone who is working on hand-stands. This student could receive a serious injury because he or she is not ready to support total body weight on his or her hands. Instead, there should be various levels of weight transfer at this station that eventually lead to a handstand. This student may simply need to work on transferring weight from feet to hands before focusing on an actual handstand.

Many unsafe practices can be avoided with care-ful planning that allows for the foreseeability of ac-cidents (Gray, 1995; Grosse, 1990; Pangrazi, 2007). For example, extra precautions should be taken from the start when planning high-risk activities such as gymnastics, aquatics, or the rope climb. To illus-trate, during an aquatics session, the teacher can ar-range for peers to assist students who use walkers and might need extra help walking around the pool area. At the same time, a student with a seizure dis-order may need a "buddy" in case the student has a seizure while in the water. In tumbling or gymnas-tics, students with ADHD, autism, or intellectual disabilities may not be aware of the inherent risks of using the equipment without supervision. A child might run over and try to swing on the uneven bars or try to climb on the rope unsupervised. When you have children with impulsive behaviors, you should constantly review safety rules with them, assign peers to assist in preventing them from inappropri-ate use of the equipment, and in extreme cases as-sign a teacher assistant to the student. In all cases, each student's unique characteristics must be con-sidered (CAHPER, 1994).

Attitude

Safe teaching techniques include having a positive attitude toward teaching children with disabilities. This involves serving as a role model for students without disabilities on how to interact with, assist, and befriend students with disabilities. Peers can be a tremendous resource in terms of making the envi-ronment safe, but peers will not know what to do unless you show them by example. While safety should be of utmost concern, care should be taken to not be overly protective. All students should be allowed certain experiences without the hindrance of exorbitant safety concerns (CAHPER, 1994). For ex-ample, children who use wheelchairs often are ex-cluded from team sports such as basketball and soc-cer. While participation in such activities can pose a risk to the student in the wheelchair as well as peers, with proper modifications and careful review of safety rules, many of these children can participate safely in team sports. An excellent way to illustrate

how modifications to team sports might work is to invite an athlete from the community who partici-pates in wheelchair sports such as wheelchair bas-ketball to come speak to students.

CONTENT

One of the biggest misconceptions with inclusion is that students with disabilities have to follow the same content at the same level as their peers with-out disabilities. Actually, all students should be pre-sented with physical activities that are individual-ized to meet their unique needs. In some cases these needs can be met by following the general curricu-lum with simple modifications; in other cases an al-ternative curriculum will need to be followed. In ei-ther case, forcing a child with or without a disability to participate in an activity that he or she is not physically, mentally, and/or emotionally ready for can lead to injury. Therefore, it is important to de-termine if the content that you present is appropri-ate for the student's abilities and, if not appropriate, determine what adjustments (or alternatives) will be needed to ensure safe participation in physical education.

SPECIFIC DISABILITIES AND SAFE ACTIVITIES

It is important to remember that physical activity is often recommended in treating a variety of condi-tions. Because the benefits of exercise are numerous, worries about safety issues should not be a reason to keep students with disabilities from participating in general physical education. To illustrate, an increased awareness of diabetes and new ways to manage it in children have resulted in increased participation in physical activity (Schwartz, 1999). The implications of this for the safety-conscious physical educator in-clude allowing a student to check blood glucose lev-els, recognizing changes in a student's behavior that could be related to changes in blood glucose, creat-ing an action plan in the event of a hypoglycemic or hyperglycemic episode, and providing access to a fast-acting form of glucose by taping it to a clipboard when participating in outdoor activities. Such solu-tions can assist a child with diabetes in participating safely in a variety of activities that require any type of energy output. Table 10.1 provides a list of com-mon chronic diseases and disabilities with recom-mended activities deemed safe and essential (Durs-tine et al., 2000). The job of the physical educator is to encourage physical activity and participation in sports for all students, with safety for all as the utmost concern.

Table 10.1. Safe activities for specific conditions

Disease/disability	Recommended safe activities
Bronchial asthma	Aquatics, intermittent with long warm-ups
Cerebral palsy	Aquatics, with proper flotation devices
Cystic fibrosis	Jogging, swimming, walking, selected games
Muscular dystrophies	Swimming, calisthenics, wheelchair sports
Obesity	Walking, recreational games, swimming, biking
Rheumatoid arthritis	Swimming, calisthenics, cycling, water aerobics
HIV/AIDS	Any activity; use universal precautions

From Durstine et al. "Physical activity for the chronically ill and disabled." *Sports Medicine* 2000 30(3): 207–219 (Table IV page 212); adapted by permission.

Emergency Procedures

Make sure you have an emergency plan in place and that all staff are familiar with and have practiced this plan in the unlikely event of an injury (Clements, 2000; Halsey, 2005; see Table 10.2). First and foremost, you should know CPR and first aid (Halsey, 2005; Hawkins, 2005; Pangrazi, 2007). In addition, familiarize yourself with universal precautions for handling blood (Bailey, 2005; Brown & Richter, 1994). Rubber gloves, gauze, and other essentials should be placed into a first aid kit and readily available. Also, fill an ice cooler with ice and bags each morning. The school nurse and the child's parents can help formulate special emergency procedures. For example, there may be a special way to handle a student who has a particular type of seizure disorder. If your school does not have a school nurse, have a plan in place for emergencies such as contacting a rescue squad or doctor's office that is close to the school.

Have emergency cards on all students. In addition, notations can be made on your roll book to signify students who have medical problems such as asthma, diabetes, seizures, and allergies. For example, a child who is stung by a bee might be allergic to bee stings. By noting this allergy on an emergency card or in your roll book, you will know right away to immediately contact the nurse for assistance. Similarly, you may be more sensitive to a child who you know has asthma and is wheezing after a tag activity.

You will need to establish special emergency plans for some children with health problems or disabilities such as a plan for removing children who are in wheelchairs from the gymnasium in the event of a fire or other emergency. Children with health problems may need to bring emergency materials to

Table 10.2. Emergency procedures—action plan

Preparation

1. Identify kinds of injuries, emergencies, and health incidents that might occur.
2. Learn emergency care for each of these incidents.
3. Create an incident surveillance system to track all incidents for a particular student, for the facility, or for the program.
4. Examine medical information and talk to parents and other professionals for clues to possible medical situations for particular students with disabilities.

Plan

1. Create a written emergency action plan.
2. The plan should include, but not be limited to, the identification of the injured person, recognition of injury or medical need, initiation of first aid, and the obtaining of professional help.
3. Detailed protocols for seeking assistance and talking with medical personnel should be posted in appropriate places.

Learn and rehearse

1. Each employee and classmates knows his or her role in the emergency plan.
2. First aid, rescue, and emergency equipment are adequate, routinely checked, and ready for use.
3. Staff members know how to use all equipment.
4. The system has been created with input from community emergency medical crews.
5. The plan is rehearsed with the staff and with community emergency medical crews. Approximate times required to reach a facility are determined by each of these agencies.
6. Rehearsals are conducted periodically and whenever new staff are employed.
7. Records of all practice and those involved are prepared and retained.

Follow-up

1. Follow-up procedures for seriously injured persons exist and are used.
2. Parents are notified in a uniform fashion.
3. A means of working with the media exists and is used.
4. The entire system is known by all, rehearsed often, and periodically monitored for flaws.
5. Legal counsel and insurance representatives are invited to review the entire system.

From Clement, A. (2000, March). *Emergency action plans.* Paper presented at the American Alliance for Health, Physical Education, Recreation and Dance, Orlando, FL.

physical education in the event of an emergency. For example, children who are prone to asthma attacks should bring an inhaler with them to physical education, and orange juice and insulin should be available for children with diabetes. While you may not feel comfortable with medical procedures such as giving insulin, you should have these materials available when qualified personnel arrive. Finally, notify the office in the event of a medical emergency or injury, and complete a student accident report immediately (see Pangrazi, 2007).

SUMMARY

Safety is the most important part of any quality physical education programming. Physical educators should follow safety procedures and conduct safe physical education programs for all children who enter their gymnasium. Inclusion of children with disabilities heightens awareness of safety issues, but rarely does it result in major changes to physical education programs. However, there are some things that should be examined to ensure the safety of children with disabilities in general physical education. When children with disabilities are included in general physical education, find out as much as possible about the child, including medical and health information, motor and fitness skills, and learning and behavioral characteristics. Carefully examine the physical education environment as well as the equipment that you use to make sure it safely meets the needs of students with disabilities. Critique your classroom management techniques, teaching practices, and content that you plan on presenting to the class to ensure that they match the learning style and individualized goals of students with disabilities. Finally, have an emergency plan in place, including special plans for children with unique health concerns. Safety concerns should be addressed, and necessary modifications, including the use of support personnel, should be implemented. However, safety should not be the sole reason for excluding students with disabilities from general physical education.

Accommodating Students with Behavior Challenges

by Martin E. Block, Ron French, and Lisa Silliman-French

Mrs. McCray has had her share of students with behavior problems. She was always able to handle them until she met James and Mike Jones, twins who have severe behavior problems. Both repeated kindergarten and third grade and were much older than their seventh-grade peers. Both were suspended multiple times in elementary and middle school, mostly for fighting and vandalism. In addition, both have had run-ins with the law, James for stealing a car and taking it for a ride and Mike for trying to steal CDs and clothes from a local Wal-Mart. James and Mike have been labeled as emotionally disturbed, with a secondary diagnosis of attention-deficit/hyperactivity disorder (ADHD). Both are taking medication for their ADHD.

Last year in sixth grade, it did not take long for the boys to begin to cause problems in Mrs. McCray's sixth-grade physical education class. First, neither boy brought his gym uniform for the first 2 weeks of school, so they both had to sit out and watch. Rather than just sit, they constantly talked to each other or yelled and teased their peers. Mrs. McCray tried to ignore this behavior, but the boys became louder and more aggressive. Mrs. McCray then warned the boys that they would have to go to the office if they continued to disrupt her class; this did not seem to help. She eventually sent the boys to the office, but they returned the next day unfazed. Once the boys remembered to bring their uniforms, they continued to bully their peers by yelling at them and pushing them. Mrs. McCray put the boys in time out and again threatened to send them to the office. This resulted in a fair amount of cursing and posturing at Mrs. McCray. Mrs. McCray was not one to be intimidated by a couple of middle school boys and again sent them to the office. The next day they were back and doing their best to disrupt the class, threaten classmates, and taunt Mrs. McCray.

Mrs. McCray had a sneaking suspicion that something was going on with Mike and James that might be contributing to their acting out. Perhaps someone at home or at school was triggering these bullying behaviors. Perhaps the boys were embarrassed by their limited fitness (both boys were pretty overweight) or motor skills. Perhaps the boys had never learned how to appropriately make friends and socialize with peers. Whatever the cause, Mrs. McCray felt that traditional behavior management techniques such as time-out, being sent to the office, and suspension were not effective and did not address the root of the boys' problem. Mrs. McCray, in a quest to understand these boys and develop and implement a behavior program, arranged to meet with the special education teacher.

The importance of physical educators effectively and efficiently managing student behaviors and improving performance and learning is obvious. Without these abilities, instruction and learning are difficult. A chaotic class results in physical educators spending more time dealing with inappropriate behavior and less time on instruction and student practice. Because of this, teachers consistently mention behavior management as an area in which they need more training (Maag, 2001). This is particularly true when general physical educators teach in an inclusive environment. More and more students who exhibit inappropriate behaviors are being placed in general physical education settings. These include students with emotional or behavioral disorders, traumatic brain injuries, ADHD, or autism spectrum disorder. While not all students with these diagnoses will necessarily demonstrate behavior problems, they do tend to display behaviors that can make teaching physical education difficult (see Table 11.1). As a result, physical educators are facing a higher level of disruption that can negatively influence the learning environment for all students (Smith & Rivera, 1995).

Table 11.1. Common disabilities and related behaviors that can affect learning

- *Attention-deficit/hyperactivity/disorder (ADHD)* is made up of three subtypes. First subtype is Predominantly Inattentive. Students have difficulty sustaining physical or motor tasks and often appear to be daydreaming or not listening. The second subtype is Predominantly Hyperactive-Impulsive, in which students demonstrate the inability to stay on their attendance spot, are not able to wait for their turn, or blurt out answers or questions when the physical educator is giving instructions. The third subtype is the Combined Type. In all three types students have chronic problems in internally regulating their attention, impulses, and activity level.

- *Autism spectrum disorder (pervasive developmental disorder)* is a disability noted by problems with social interacting, language used in social interaction, play skills, repetition, or stereotyped patterns of behavior. Common characteristics of students with this disorder include making inappropriate sounds, making inappropriate gestures, having inappropriate affect (e.g., laughing when no one else is laughing), being withdrawn, being anxious in new and different situations, and running away.

- *Emotional (behavioral) disorder* is a condition involving one or more of the following behaviors over a long period of time, which must adversely affect educational performance: (a) inability to learn, which cannot be explained by intellectual, sensory, or health factors; (b) inability to build or maintain satisfactory interpersonal relationships; and (c) demonstrating inappropriate behavior or feelings, such as a general pervasive mood of unhappiness or depression or a tendency to develop physical symptoms or fears. Common characteristics for students with this disorder vary widely based on the specific type of emotional disability, ranging from juvenile delinquency, depression, obsessive-compulsive disorder, eating disorders, and bipolar disorders.

- *Intellectual disabilities* refers to substantial limitations in personal capabilities manifested as significantly subaverage intellectual functioning occurring with significant deficits in adaptive behavior (e.g., self-help skills, communication, working, academics). Common characteristics of students with intellectual disabilities vary based on the specific cause and level of functioning. For example, many students with fetal alcohol syndrome are impulsive and hyperactive, while students with Down syndrome tend to have trouble understanding and following complex directions.

- *Traumatic brain injury* refers to a permanent damage caused by concussion, contusion, or hemorrhage. In many cases this condition may cause severe impairments in perception, emotion, cognition, and motor function. Again, common characteristics vary widely based on the extent and location of the brain injury.

HISTORY OF APPROACHES

Unfortunately, new physical educators may lack the ability to manage students' behaviors in such heterogeneous classes. Even veteran physical educators who employ a variety of techniques to manage student behavior may need to go beyond traditional behavioral techniques. Physical educators are being asked to move toward positive approaches that teach students new self-management skills. There are numerous approaches to managing student behavior, but the psychodynamic approach and behavior modification are most widely used in educational settings. With the *psychodynamic approach*, the focus

is on the psychotherapeutic reasons why the behavior is or is not being demonstrated (Walker, Shea, & Bauer, 2003). It is assumed in this approach that most behavior problems are a result of an unconscious motivation (i.e., power, attention). Through a series of questions, such as the following, the teacher helps the student determine the unconscious motivation that has evoked the behavior.

- Do you want to show me that I can make you jog?

- Do you want me to pay more attention to you?

- Do you want to perform the activity alone?

This approach fell out of favor but has had a rebirth because of its ability to "humanize the behavior management process by improving communication between teachers and students" (Kaplan & Carter, 1995, p.11). Further, in a school environment, the student's well being and ability to learn are connected (Zionts, Zionts, & Simpson, 2002). Techniques such as the talking bench, reality therapy, and self-talk are just some techniques used within this approach (Lavay, French, & Henderson, 2006).

In *behavior modification* the focus is on what in the environment is causing the behavior to occur or not occur. Physical educators who use this approach are generally manipulating the events that occur just before the behavior is exhibited in hopes to reduce or eliminate the behavior. The approach is based on an *ABC* paradigm, in which a stimulus or antecedent (A), precedes the behavior (B), which is followed by a positive and/or negative consequence (C) that results in an increase or decrease of the behavior (Lavay, French, & Henderson, 2006). The focus is on carefully analyzing the antecedents and consequences that surround the behavior as well as examining the behavior itself to determine what might be responsible for producing it. Physical educators who use this approach manipulate A and/or C to increase or decrease B. That is, changing the environment (A) prevents inappropriate behaviors, and adding reinforcement [positive consequences] (C) to increase behaviors or mild forms of punishment [negative consequences] (C) to decrease behaviors. Clearly the focus is on preventing the occurrence of inappropriate behaviors. Only when this fails are interventions instituted; likewise, they are removed as soon as appropriate. This is particularly true when unnatural consequences, such as overcorrection, must be used.

The behavior modification approach has been the most widely used in both general and adapted physical education environments. This is clearly reflected by the amount of information about elementary (Hastie & Martin, 2006; Pangrazi, 2007), secondary (Darst & Pangrazi, 2006), and adapted physical education (Seaman, DePauw, Morton, & Omoto, 2003) that is focused on behavior modification. It is interesting to note that the same findings (i.e., wide use of behavior management) have been reported in an Asian country (Hsu, 2001). The trend is to use behavior modification along with other approaches, particularly the psychodynamic approach. For instance, Janney and Snell stated that there is "a movement away from traditional behavior practices and toward behavior interventions grounded in person-centered values" (2000, p. 2). These values are

1. To develop respect and trust between students, teachers, staff, and parents

2. To provide suitable opportunities for students, whenever appropriate, to interact with their peers not only in the school, but the community environment

3. To focus on prevention or the reduction of situations that could involve more than what would be considered a normal amount of failure and increase the success rate to a level that would be considered normal

4. To focus on the instruction of communication and social interaction skills

5. To emphasize the development of individualized and positive behavioral support where the "one size fits all approach" is eliminated

The result has been the development of a new approach known as *positive behavior support* (PBS) (Crone & Horner, 2003; Jackson & Panyan, 2001; Janney & Snell, 2000). PBS combines some behavior modification techniques (e.g., analyzing what might be causing a behavior and creating a plan to prevent the behavior from occurring) with the psychodynamic approach (e.g., determining why a child displays a behavior, teaching more appropriate ways to interact with the environment and self-manage his or her behavior). Lavay, French, and Henderson (2006) developed a model to illustrate the infusion or overlapping of traditional behavior modification with the psychodynamic approach within physical activity environments. Hellison (2003) also developed and effectively applied a physical education-based behavior model to develop responsible students, including students who have been labeled at risk. Incorporated into Hellison's model are five components of responsibility which range from irresponsibility (Level 0) to caring (Level 4). This system has been modified by adapted physical educators working with students who have cognitive disabilities to include the use of portable display boards (Alexander, Lavay, & Lawrence, 2005). Their hierarchy system also has five levels. Levels I and II focus on human decency, and Levels III through V on self-development. Hellison's (2003) specific levels are as follows:

- Level O, Irresponsibility: involves blaming others, talking back, or fighting

- Level I, Self-control: involves controlling temper, waiting turn, not speaking at the same time as the teacher

- Level II, Involvement: includes cleaning up, playing with others, putting away equipment, and attempting new activities

- Level III, Self-responsibility: involves returning physical education equipment without being asked, going immediately to attendance spot before the tardy bell, learning new skills outside of class

- Level IV, Caring: includes help other students learn a skill and asking other students who are friends or are not friends to join an activity

- Level V: Application of Levels I through IV outside of the class environment

It should be noted that the last level of both the Hewett (1968; Hewett & Taylor, 1980) and the Hellison systems are the same. They emphasize generalizing what has been learned to the home and the community. It is important to note that the levels are meant to be guidelines and are to be adjusted to specific teaching situations. It is not a cookbook approach in which "one size fits all." Although this model is based on the psychodynamic approach, it also uses techniques such as time-out and the Premack principle, which are integral components of the traditional behavior modification approach. The Premack principle recommends making a high-frequency behavior contingent on completing a low-frequency behavior. For instance, a student does not like to participate in the warm-up jogging activity (low frequency). He does love to play tetherball (high frequency). If the student jogs during the warm-ups for a week, he earns the privilege to play 5 minutes of tetherball.

This chapter provides physical educators with basic information about managing student behavior, specifically using PBS. The chapter begins with a detailed description of the key components of PBS, along with information on how to conduct a functional behavioral analysis and create a PBS plan. This is followed by strategies to reinforce appropriate behaviors or decrease inappropriate behaviors. The chapter concludes with basic consideration for an effective and efficient PBS-focused program.

A POSITIVE APPROACH TO BEHAVIOR MANAGEMENT

The PBS approach is designed to determine what within the specific school and/or home environment is causing a behavior problem to occur, and then to teach the student appropriate skills that prevent the behavior from occurring (e.g., how to communicate), reinforce appropriate behaviors such as when the student deals appropriately with conflict (e.g., when the student uses his words rather than hitting when he is finished with an activity), and change the environment to reduce situations that might trigger the behavior and thus prevent the behavior from occurring (e.g., change the time of day or change who the child works with in physical education). PBS has been recommended as the most effective, most appropriate, and most ethical behavioral model for children with challenging behaviors (Crone & Horner, 2003; Janney & Snell, 2000).

PBS emphasizes collaborative problem solving, prevention through effective educational programs, teaching students more appropriate alternative behaviors, and supporting the student through systematic planning rather than trial and error. The use of reinforcement to strengthen behaviors and negative consequences to reduce behaviors play a smaller part than in more traditional behavioral management approaches (Jackson & Panyan, 2001; Janney & Snell, 2000).

Goals of PBS include helping students develop new communication, social, and self-control skills; form more positive relationships with classmates, teachers, and community members; and take more active roles in their classrooms, schools, and communities. The success of PBS is judged not only by whether a target behavior has been reduced but also by whether students have learned new skills and ways to control their behaviors so that their lifestyle has been improved (Crone & Horner, 2003; Janney & Snell, 2000).

As the name suggests, the heart of the model is the provision of positive behavioral supports that prevent students from displaying unwanted behavior and teach them new, more appropriate behaviors. These supports include IEP accommodations (e.g., place to calm down, additional adult supervision during transitions, extending time for completing tasks), curricular adaptations (e.g., simplified curriculum or one that emphasizes functional skills), instruction in social skills or self-management techniques, changes to the classroom environment (e.g., preferential seating, a quiet place to study or read), scheduling changes (e.g., placement in classes with particular peers, placement in heterogeneous classes, alternating between easy and difficult subjects or courses), more assistance in doing an assignment or task, and support of peer buddies, partners, or tutors (Crone & Horner, 2003; Janney & Snell, 2000). Another important aspect of PBS is the recognition that

all behaviors serve a purpose. These purposes include social-communication functions such as getting attention, escape or avoidance, or getting something tangible, and sensory function such as self-regulation and play or entertainment (Jackson & Panyan, 2001; Janney & Snell, 2000).

The following outlines the key components of the PBS model: 1) identifying a behavior, 2) examining antecedents for possible causes, 3) exploring the consequences, 4) examining possible functions of behavior, and 5) considering ways to teach appropriate behaviors and prevent and respond to the behavior (see Table 11.2). It is important that each step in the PBS model be followed in order to develop the most appropriate and effective plan possible. See Figure 11.1 for a Functional Behavior Assessment.

Table 11.2. Creating a behavior plan

1. *Identify the behavior in objective, measurable terms.*
   a. Describe what the student is doing.
   b. Describe how the student is acting.
   c. Record the behavior.

2. *Examine antecedents for possible causes.*
   a. When does behavior usually occur?
   b. Where does behavior usually occur?
   c. What is usually happening when behavior occurs?

3. *Examine possible functions of behavior.*
   a. Does the student want attention?
   b. Does the student want to be involved?
   c. Is the student angry?
   d. Is the student frustrated?
   e. Is the student in pain or discomfort?
   f. Does the student need help with something?
   g. Other possible reasons

4. *Explore the consequences.*
   a. What happened when the behavior occurred?
   b. When did the consequences take place (immediate/delayed)?
   c. How did the student react to the consequences?

5. *Consider simple alternatives that might prevent/reduce the behavior*
   a. Move student.
   b. Rearrange the environment.
   c. Change the activity.
   d. Give the student a partner.
   e. Regroup the class.

6. *Create the behavior plan.*
   a. Clearly state targeted behavior on measurable terms.
   b. Outline procedures for increasing appropriate behaviors.
   c. Outline procedures for preventing/reducing the behavior.
   d. Outline consequences for dealing with the behavior if it occurs.

Functional Behavior Assessment

Student: _____   School: _____

Disability: _____   Evaluator(s): _____

Today's date: _____   Student's date of birth: _____

This functional behavior assessment is being conducted because (check all that apply):

_____ Student exhibits persistent behavior problem(s) that impedes the learning of peers.

_____ Traditional supports/interventions/consequences have not been effective.

_____ Assessment is in response to disciplinary actions by school personnel.

_____ Alternative services or programs are being considered.

I.   Analyze the situation.

1.   What is/are the student's problem behavior(s)? (Write in measurable terms.)

_____

_____

2.   Describe the behavior in detail (frequency, duration, and level of intensity [distracting, disturbing, or destructive]).

_____

_____

3.   What are the student's strengths (e.g., interests, skill level, support systems)?

_____

_____

4.   What seems to trigger the student's behavior(s)?

Who? _____

What? _____

Where? _____

When? _____

Other? _____

5.   What other factors at home or at school appear to adversely influence the student's behaviors?

_____

_____

6.   What happens to the student immediately after he or she engages in the problem behavior(s)?

_____

_____

_____

(continued)

Figure 11.1.   Functional behavior assessment. (From Albemarle County Public Schools. [n.d.]. *Functional behavior assessment form 80.01.* Charlottesville, VA: Author; adapted by permission.)

Figure 11.1. *(continued)*

7. **Why might the student be acting this way** (e.g., attention, escape/avoidance, getting something, self-regulation)?

    a. What might he or she get by behaving this way?

    _____

    _____

    _____

    b. What might he or she be avoiding by behaving this way?

    _____

    _____

    _____

    _____

II. **Develop a hypothesis statement.**

Use this format: When (antecedent event, see Item 4) happens in (specific setting), he or she does (problem behavior, see Item 1) in order to (perceived function, see Item 7).

_____

_____

_____

_____

III. **Develop a plan.**

What teaching strategies would you use to teach the student more appropriate, functional behaviors?

_____

_____

_____

_____

What prevention strategies would you use to keep the student from displaying the targeted behavior?

_____

_____

_____

_____

In the event the student displays the targeted behavior at a high intensity, how would you respond?

_____

_____

_____

_____

_____

Identify the Behavior

Identifying the target behavior(s) seems a simple task. However, all too often physical educators have trouble specifying exactly what behavior is bothersome. Some examples of unhelpful identification and helpful identification of behaviors are the following:

Unhelpful identification	Helpful identification
"He is always in my face."	"Every day, when Bill enters the gym, he comes directly to me and wants to know what exactly we will be doing in class."
"He is constantly in motion."	"Reggie cannot stay on his attendance spot on the bench when his team is at bat or while I am explaining an activity for more than 20 consecutive seconds."
"She is destroying my gym."	"Alyssa will come to class and immediately begin to move the equipment at each station in the class for the obstacle course lesson."
"The devil sent this student to torture me."	"Bruno is the class bully. He is skilled at pushing and hitting students in class on a daily basis. The students complain about him, and I am afraid to recognize that it is occurring more often than I observe."

Certainly conveying emotions is very important, but even more important to determining a behavior plan is the student's actual behavior. The physical educator, with help from other professionals, needs to carefully examine what the student is doing and document the behaviors in measurable, objective terms.

Being able to measure the behavior will allow physical educators to chart progress. There are three common ways to measure behaviors in physical education. First, in *event recording*, the physical educator records the number of times a behavior is exhibited in a given period of time. For example, a teacher might record how many times a student inappropriately touches other students during a 30-minute class period. Second, in *duration recording*, a physical educator records how long a behavior is exhibited during a given period of time. For example, a teacher might record how long a student makes inappropriate sounds during physical education. Third, in *interval recording*, a physical educator divides the class period into intervals and records when the behavior occurs during that interval. For instance, a physical educator records every minute if a student is on or off-task. If the student is off-task when the teacher observes the student at the end of a 1-minute interval, then she notes it on a piece of paper. At the end of the class, she can tally how many intervals (see Figure 11.2).

The type of recording mechanism used should be based on the nature of the behavior. Behaviors

---

Event recording: How many times does the student talk back in 30 minutes?

Day	Tally count per day	Total
Day 1	1 1 1 1 1 1 1 1 1 1 1 1 1 1 1 1 1 1 1 1	20
Day 2	1 1 1 1 1 1 1 1 1 1 1 1 1 1 1 1	16
Day 3	1 1 1 1 1 1 1 1 1 1 1 1 1 1 1 1 1	17
Day 4	1 1 1 1 1 1 1 1 1 1 1 1 1 1 1 1 1 1	18

Average: 17.75 occurrences

Duration recording: How long does the student choose to pout in the corner of the gym?

Day	Duration of each episode of pouting			Total time pouting
Day 1	2:00	4:00	1:00	7:00 minutes
Day 2	3:00	3:30		6:30 minutes
Day 3	2:00			2:00 minutes
Day 4	5:00	1:30		6:30 minutes

Average: 5:30 minutes per 30-minute class

Interval recording: How much is the student touching other students?

Day	30 minutes, broken into 2-minute intervals	Number of incidences in interval
Day 1	y n y y y n y n y n n y n y y	9/15
Day 2	n n y y y y n y y y y n n n y y	9/15
Day 3	y y n n n y y n n n n n n y y	6/15

Average # of intervals per 30 minutes: 8/15

Figure 11.2. Ways to measure behavior in general physical education: Example for a student off task.

that occur frequently but for short duration (e.g., touching peers) should be recorded using event recording. Behaviors that do not occur frequently but last a long time (e.g., crying) should be measured using duration recording. And behaviors that occur so frequently that it is too difficult to count specific instances (e.g., tics) should be measured using interval recording. Later, the physical educator can again use this information to determine if the behavior intervention used was effective (i.e., reduction in targeted behavior).

Examine Antecedents for Possible Causes

Once the behavior has been identified, defined, and measured, the next step in the process is to examine what environmental factors might be causing the behavior. Many times something in the environment might trigger the behavior. For example, having to sit and wait while the teacher takes roll might cause a student with ADHD to get antsy and misbehave. Similarly, a student with autism who does not like loud noises might yell and try to scratch and bite his teacher assistant just before the music used for warm-ups is played. In both cases, something in the environment seems to be causing the behavior. Through careful analysis of antecedents surrounding the behavior, the physical educator might be able to detect what is causing the student's inappropriate behaviors. Things to examine can be divided into four categories.

1. Who is present when the behavior occurs? In other words, are particular adults or peers in the environment triggering the behavior?

2. When does the behavior usually occur?

3. Where does the behavior usually occur?

4. What is usually happening when the behavior occurs ?

Although the cause of all behaviors cannot be determined by analyzing the antecedents in the environment, such an analysis may reveal why the student is displaying certain inappropriate behaviors.

Examine the Consequences

What happens to the student after he or she displays a behavior is known as a consequence, and determining the effects of the consequence can be as important as analyzing antecedents and functions. Consequences may be the reason the student is displaying the behavior in the first place. For example,

a student does not want to participate in physical education during a particular unit so he displays noncompliant behavior and talks back to the teacher, resulting in time-out during physical education. This is what the student wanted all along! Consequences can make the behavior stronger or weaker, depending on how the student reacts to the consequences. Things to examine related to a consequence include asking three questions:

1. What happened immediately after the behavior occurred? For example, a student who has been known to be mean to other students pulled another student's hair that resulted in the student crying. This made the mean student laugh. Even being verbally reprimanded by the teacher and then sent to time-out was not enough of a deterrent compared to the reinforcement of hearing the girl cry.

2. When was the consequence presented—immediately or delayed? If a consequence is delayed for too long, the student might forget why he/she is receiving the consequence in the first place.

3. How did the student react to the consequence? Did the student happily gallop off to time-out, or did the student curse and yell at the physical educator? Did the student apologize to the peer whom he pushed, or did he fold his arms and choose to go to time-out? Again, how the student reacts to the consequence that results from the behavior may provide insight as to why the student displayed the behavior in the first place and what consequences will and will not work in the future (see Figure 11.3).

Examine Possible Functions of Behavior

Once the environment has been analyzed for possible causes of the behavior, the next step is to examine why the student might be displaying the behavior. That is, what does the student want or what does the student hope to accomplish by displaying the inappropriate behavior? Rarely does a student display inappropriate behavior without a goal in mind, even if the student does not really understand the goal. For example, a student with autism might suddenly strike out at his teacher assistant or peer for no apparent reason. However, a close examination of antecedents and some guess work by the general and adapted physical educator reveals that the student is avoiding playing with balloons. Perhaps the student is afraid of the sound of balloons when they pop or of the way they feel. But for whatever reason, the student clearly gets agitated when bal-

Behavioral Observation Data Sheet

Student's name: _____

Person filling out this form: _____

Date: _____ Student's age: _____

Behavior: How is the student acting? Describe in measurable terms.

Examine antecedents: What in the environment might be causing inappropriate behaviors?

When does the behavior usually occur? _____

_____

_____

_____

Where does the behavior usually occur? _____

_____

_____

_____

What is usually happening when the behavior occurs? _____

_____

_____

_____

Who is in the environment when the behavior occurs? _____

_____

_____

_____

Examine function: What might the student be trying to communicate?

_____ Does the student want attention?

_____ Does the student want to tell you something?

_____ Does the student want a particular piece of equipment?

_____ Does the student want to be with a particular friend?

_____ Does the student not want to do the activity?

_____ Does the student need to go to the bathroom?

(continued)

Figure 11.3. Behavioral observation data sheet.

Figure 11.3. *(continued)*

_____ Does the student want to escape the situation?

_____ Is the student angry?

_____ Is the student frustrated?

_____ Is the student in pain or discomfort?

_____ Does the student need help with something?

_____ Other possible reasons: _____

_____

Examine selected negative consequences: Check the selected negative consequences, and explain how the student reacted to them.

Consequence	Reaction
_____ Received angry look	_____
_____ Teacher moved closer to student	_____
_____ Received verbal warning	_____
_____ Received verbal reprimand	_____
_____ Told to tell peer he or she was sorry	_____
_____ Told to clean up mess	_____
_____ Lost equipment privileges	_____
_____ Changed partner or group	_____
_____ Given a time-out	_____
_____ Received physical assistance	_____
_____ Was physically restrained	_____
_____ Was sent to principal	_____
_____ Other	_____

Suggestions for plan: _____

_____

_____

_____

_____

_____

loons are mentioned or introduced. Scratching and screaming is how this student communicates his fear of balloons. With this information, the behavior plan might include having the student do a different activity at the other end of the gymnasium when peers are playing with balloons. Other possible functional causes of behavior include the following: attempting to gain attention; wanting to be involved; anger against a student, teacher, or situation; frustration; pain or discomfort; needing help with something; needing to go to the bathroom; and/or not liking the peers he or she has been assigned. As with antecedents, it may not be possible to fully understand why a student is displaying particular behaviors. However, such a functional analysis in many cases will help the physical educator begin to see why some students do what they do.

Consider Ways to Teach Appropriate Behaviors and Prevent and Respond to the Behavior

With information about the behavior, antecedents, possible functional causes, and results of consequences, the physical educator and other team members are ready to discuss ways to teach more appropriate behaviors and respond to the behavior if it does occur. These strategies should be based on the previous analyses of what might trigger the behavior (antecedents), reactions to the behavior (consequences), and the function or purpose of the behavior. The following reviews several strategies that can be used to prevent and respond to unwanted behaviors and teach more appropriate behaviors and self-management skills.

Preventing Behaviors

Some behaviors can be prevented by *adding support* such as increasing the number of people (e.g., peers), adding new places to the student's schedule (e.g., going outside for a walk a few times during the day), or changing activities (e.g., adding some highly reinforcing physical activities such as shooting baskets or riding a scooter board). Other behaviors can be prevented by *avoiding antecedents* known to trigger the behavior such as changing who the student sits next to, what activities are presented, or when activities are presented. For instance, a student with autism has trouble transitioning from his classroom to the gymnasium. His behaviors have escalated (he often hits peers or his teacher when walking down the hall to the gym) ever since the physical educator started doing a different activity for warm-ups each day. The special educator suggested that the physical educator have the students do the same thing every day upon entering the gym. This simple change has helped this student feel more confident when he comes to the gym. Although he still displays inappropriate behaviors at times during physical education, the transition from the classroom to the gym is no longer a problem. Other simple changes that might work immediately with some students include moving the student closer to you or away from particular peers, rearranging the environment such as not putting out equipment until you are ready to use it, changing the activity from competition to cooperation (at least making this a choice for some students), having a special colored ball or mark on the floor for the student that he knows is his, or giving the student a partner. See Table 11.3 for more suggestions.

Teaching New Behaviors

It also is important to teach new, alternative skills as well as social and self-management skills that allow the student to interact with his environment in more appropriate, functional ways. Strategies for teaching alternative, more appropriate skills might include modeling (demonstrating the appropriate behavior), prompting and shaping (reinforcing attempts at or approximations of the behavior), behavioral rehearsal (repeated practice of the appropriate behavior), and incidental learning (highlighting and reinforcing the behavior when it occurs naturally) (Janney & Snell, 2000). Strategies for teaching social and self-management skills include student checklists, picture schedules, self-reinforcement and self-talk, problem solving, and anger control and relaxation training (Janney & Snell, 2000).

Responding Strategies

Students should be reinforced when they demonstrate appropriate behaviors, recently learned behaviors, or appropriate self-management skills (see later section in this chapter on responding strategies to increase appropriate behaviors). If a student displays unwanted behavior, then the teacher and others around the student must respond in a manner that does not reinforce the student for displaying the behavior (e.g., not chasing after a student who runs away to get attention). Proper responding can lead to immediate reduction in the duration and intensity of the unwanted behavior (e.g., student only runs a few feet before he realizes that no one is chasing after him) and ultimately to extinction of the unwanted behavior. Positive responding strategies include nonreinforcement (not responding in a way that allows behavior to work/achieve its purpose) and redirection (redirecting student to alternative

Table 11.3. Techniques for preventing behavior problems

1. *Determine cause of behavior* (try and determine what might be causing the unwanted behavior, then try to rearrange the environment or the situation to prevent the behavior from reoccurring)

2. *Tune into your class* (be aware of what is going on; pay particular attention to students who have a history of problem behavior)

3. *Set the right pace* (lesson should run so there is a smooth flow from activity to activity; have a comfortable pace—one that is not too fast or too slow)

4. *Manage time efficiently* (reduce non-teaching time to prevent misbehavior that occurs when students are bored or waiting)

5. *Encourage clarification of instructions* (make sure students understand instructions by repeating instructions, asking students to repeat instructions back to you, or giving some students extra cues or help from peers)

6. *Set realistic goals* (set goals or help students set goals that are realistic for them that are both achievable and challenging; students get bored if activities are too easy and frustrated if they are too hard)

7. *Make sure students are appropriately placed* (some students cannot handle large classes or classes that are very competitive. Either try and place the student in a smaller or less competitive class or separate the class into smaller groups with some playing competitive activities and others cooperative activities)

8. *Involve the entire group* (organize the class to encourage maximum, active participation – avoid waiting in line, elimination games, and sharing equipment)

9. *Hold students accountable for what is taught* (make sure students know what they are supposed to be working on and what is expected of them, then hold them accountable for their performance)

10. *Keep the class attentive* (use creative techniques to keep students' attention such as unique equipment, novel games, and having high school or college athletes come and help teach an activity)

11. *Keep the students motivated* (be aware of the motivational level of the class and individual students—note that it is better to stop an activity when students are still enjoying it rather than wait until they become bored)

12. *Be assertive but gentle* (face problems immediately, do not ignore them; be direct yet calm when dealing with students who display behavior problems)

13. *Use humor* (use humor to reduce tension and defuse stressful situations)

14. *Appeal to your students' values* (appeal to students' sense of fairness, their commitment to the group's code of behavior, and to the positive relationship you have and want to continue to have with them)

15. *Generate enthusiasm* (show your students genuine enthusiasm about physical activity and about how you care about their success by cheering, clapping hands, and generally having a good time)

16. *Know your stuff* (students respect and want to learn from teachers who are competent in the skills and activities being taught. Make sure you are prepared for your lessons, and get experts in the community to help you with units you do not feel comfortable with)

17. *Take responsibility for managing behavior* (try to deal with students' behavior problems in the gymnasium rather than always sending students to the principal)

18. *Establish a consistent behavior management plan* (develop your plan for physical education with plan used in other parts of the building by other professionals)

19. *Use proximity control* (students will be less likely to misbehave if you stand closer to them)

20. *Take an interest in your students* (students are more willing to cooperate with a teacher who shows interest in them by discussing their interests, asking about their weekend, noting their achievements, etc.)

21. *Be a good role model* (since many students imitate their teacher, model appropriate dress, talk, and conduct including showing self-control in heated discussions when you get angry or a student gets angry at you)

22. *Redirect disruptive behavior* (try and redirect disruptive or dangerous situations into more productive tasks)

23. *Provide vigorous activities* (help students release their anger and frustration through vigorous activity such as sprints, volleyball spiking, hitting a softball, or aerobics)

24. *Befriend a disliked student* (a teacher who befriends a disliked student often helps other students accept him/her)

25. *Use nonverbal cues* (teach and then use simple gestures such as finger to the lips, the time-out sign, or simply giving direct eye contact to deal with minor disruptions)

26. *Establish class rules early* (establish and review class rules and consequences from the first day of class; post the rules in a conspicuous place, and review the rules often)

27. *Grade fairly* (establish clear and fair criteria for grades; explain the grading system on the first day of class and keep careful records of progress for calculating grades)

28. *Avoid nagging* (continually nagging can make students anxious or may cause them to "tune out" the teacher —give one warning or reminder, then give a negative consequence)

29. *Develop an appropriate physical environment* (create an environment that promotes enthusiasm, learning, and participation; make sure the environment is as comfortable as possible; ensure that students have enough space for a given activity; try and limit auditory and visual distractions in the environment)

30. *Place a large laminated poster* at the entrance and exit doors to the class that can easily be touched by the students. At the top of the poster place a happy face, in the center a neutral face, and at the bottom a frowning face. As the students come into class have the students "tap in" and "tap out" of class touching the picture that best describes their present state of mind. This will give the physical educator an idea of how a specific student or the general class is feeling.

From Henderson, H.L., & French, R. W. (1993). *Creative approaches to managing student behavior* (2nd ed.). Park City, UT: Family Development Resources; adapted by permission.

behavior and then reinforcing alternative behavior). Punitive strategies to reduce a behavior include corrections, restitutions, verbal reprimands, removal of privileges or rewards, and time out (Janney & Snell, 2000). Other, more punitive responding strategies are discussed under the heading *punishment*.

Create the Behavior Plan

If simple solutions do not work, then a behavior plan will need to be developed following the PBS model. The behavior plan should include a clear statement of the targeted behavior written in measurable terms, information about the student's background and current living circumstances that might be related to the behavior, description of what might be triggering the behavior (antecedents), information about things that may be reinforcing the behavior (analysis of current consequences), functional analysis of why the student might be displaying the unwanted behaviors, specific procedures for preventing and/or reducing the behavior, specific procedures for teaching appropriate behaviors, and specific procedures for responding if the unwanted behavior does occur. The appendix at the end of this chapter presents an example of a completed behavior plan. It may be appropriate for a variety of team members to participate in the development of the final plan.

PROCEDURES TO MAINTAIN OR STRENGTHEN A BEHAVIOR

Many techniques within the PBS approach are based on the principles of operant conditioning. In operant conditioning, a systematic application of consequences is presented following a behavior in order to strengthen, maintain, or weaken a behavior. When something is presented or taken away that increases the likelihood that the behavior will be repeated, it is known as *reinforcement*. When something is presented or taken away that decreases the likelihood that the behavior will be repeated, it is known as *punishment*. Note that the term punishment is used here as a technical descriptor for several common behavior techniques used in public schools such as time out, taking away equipment from a child, or giving a child a stern look. We do not advocate any type of punishment that demeans or causes any physical or emotional harm to the student.

Reinforcement

Reinforcement refers to consequences of behavior that increase the future rate of that behavior. Reinforcement can be positive, negative, or non-reinforcement.

Positive reinforcement involves the presentation of something following a particular response that has the effect of maintaining or increasing that response. For example, allowing students to ride scooter boards (positive reinforcer) after completing their warm-ups without complaining (targeted response) may increase the likelihood that the students will do their warm-ups without complaining. Because positive reinforcement is easier, more appropriate, and more effective in physical education than negative reinforcement, the following discussion focuses on the many different forms of positive

reinforcement. (Negative reinforcement is discussed later in this chapter.)

The key is to begin at the most natural level of reinforcement and move along the continuum until a reinforcer works (see Table 11.4). Also, note that a "one size fits all" approach when selecting a reinforcer generally is ineffective. There are individual differences among students as to what acts as a reinforcer. Furthermore, a student will respond better when he or she has a variety of reinforcers to choose from (reinforcement menu) and a reinforcer that may be effective for a student in one situation may not be in another. Student observations, a reinforcement survey (Figure 11.4), and talking to other teachers and the student's parents can be used to help determine which reinforcers will be most effective.

Intrinsic Reinforcement

Intrinsic reinforcement occurs when the activity itself is reinforcing. The goal is to have all students functioning at this level, with desire and interest in the activities in the physical education class. This permits them to perform and learn at their capacity. For example, a student does not need external motivation or reinforcement to happily join his or her peers when a parachute activity is about to begin. Playing with a parachute is reinforcing in and of itself.

Social Praise

"Make ample use of praise. When you see good behavior, acknowledge it. This can be done verbally; of course it doesn't have to be. A nod, a smile or a

Table 11.4.   Guidelines for using reinforcement

1. Make sure the student is performing the target behavior before you provide reinforcement.

2. Reinforce the behavior immediately after it occurs.

3. Be specific in your praise. For example, tell the student "good swinging your leg when you hop" rather than "good job."

4. When students are first learning to perform a skill or display a behavior appropriately, make sure you reinforce that skill or behavior every time it is done correctly.

5. After a skill or behavior has been learned, then you, the physical educator, need only reinforce that skill or behavior periodically.

6. If social praise is effective in maintaining or increasing a behavior, do not use other rewards. Only use more tangible rewards when social praise is not effective.

7. If a tangible reinforcer has to be introduced, pair it with social praise and then gradually fade away the use of the tangible reinforcer.

8. Make sure that what you are using as a reward for the student is truly reinforcing. Each student might find different things rewarding.

From Henderson, H.L., & French, R. W. (1993). *Creative approaches to managing student behavior* (2nd ed.). Park City, UT: Family Development Resources; adapted by permission.

Reinforcement Survey

For each activity, please mark an *X* in the column that most explains your feelings.

	Like very much	Like	Dislike
Do you like juice?	_____	_____	_____
Do you like fruit?	_____	_____	_____
Do you like candy?	_____	_____	_____
Do you like sports equipment of your own?	_____	_____	_____
Do you like to rollerblade?	_____	_____	_____
Do you like soccer?	_____	_____	_____
Do you like basketball?	_____	_____	_____
Do you like football?	_____	_____	_____
Do you like softball?	_____	_____	_____
Do you like recess?	_____	_____	_____
Do you like to be a squad leader?	_____	_____	_____
Do you like to demonstrate a skill?	_____	_____	_____
Do you like to play in groups?	_____	_____	_____
Do you like activities that you can do alone?	_____	_____	_____
Do you like your teacher to ask you for help?	_____	_____	_____
Do you like to win at relays and games?	_____	_____	_____
Do you like certificates and awards?	_____	_____	_____
Do you like to help other students?	_____	_____	_____
Do you like to play music during class?	_____	_____	_____
Would you like to talk to a sports star?	_____	_____	_____

Please answer the following questions:

What is your favorite activity at home? _____

_____

What is your least favorite activity at home? _____

_____

What is your favorite activity at school? _____

_____

What is your least favorite activity at school? _____

_____

What is your favorite activity in physical education? _____

_____

What is your least favorite activity in physical education? _____

_____

Figure 11.4. Reinforcement survey. (*Source:* Walker, Shea, & Bauer, 2003.)

'thumbs up' will reinforce behavior" (Churchword, 2001, p. 6). Communicate to the student that you are pleased with some aspect of his or her performance or behavior. Social reinforcement is the most common and easiest form of reinforcement used in physical education, and it can be quite effective. Although the use of social praise can by overly used, it generally is not used enough with students who are learning to behave or master a new task. Some types of social praise are gestures (i.e., look of pleasure, a grin), statements (i.e., "better," "excellent," "terrific"), or a pat on the shoulder or back. Another type of social recognition is public posting. This technique involves posting in public view (i.e., physical education bulletin board) names of student who have mastered an individual challenge.

Physical Activity

This involves using a favorite physical activity as a reward for demonstrating an appropriate behavior. Physical activity is an excellent type of reward that is highly appropriate in physical education (Lavay, French, & Henderson, 2006). Using physical activity as a positive reinforcer is beneficial to the student and the program (Armstrong, Rosengard, Condon, Sallis, & Bernal, 1993). In fact, physical activity itself may be a behavioral intervention. After an in-depth review of the literature, Sallis and Owen (1999) concluded that there is a positive relationship between exercise and emotional health, particularly in reducing depression and anxiety. Some other benefits include no extra cost to the physical education budget, the availability of many types of equipment and games, and the potential of physical activity to improve the student's level of physical fitness and motor skills (Lavay, 1984).

Sensory Stimuli

Sensory stimuli involves presenting auditory, visual, or kinesthetic sensations as reinforcement for appropriate behaviors. This technique is particularly effective with students who have autism. For example, allowing a student with autism to swing (vestibular stimulation) after he or she completes a warm-up routine can be very reinforcing. Music is also very reinforcing. While riding a stationary bike or walking on a treadmill, music can be played or stopped contingent on the student staying within his or her target heart range zone. Providing sensory stimuli as reinforcement can be disguised to be very functional for older students. For example, wearing a headset and listening to music (auditory stimulation) or going for a brisk walk or jog (kinesthetic/vestibular stimulation) is performed daily by millions of people in the United States.

Tangibles

Tangibles are given to a student to reinforce a behavior. A variety of tangibles are appropriate to use in physical education settings, including objects and edibles. Objects used in physical education include stickers, stamps, certificates, award ribbons, patches, trophies, and plaques. Edibles should only be used if the student is not motivated by other methods. When using tangible rewards, make sure they are age appropriate and similar to rewards that are used in a typical environment. For example, giving a doll to a 16-year-old female is not age appropriate and only makes this student look unusual in the eyes of her peers. A better solution is giving this student a magazine such as *Seventeen*.

Other Methods to Increase Appropriate Behaviors

Group Contingencies

Group contingencies refer to the presentation of a reinforcer to a group of students based on the group's following an appropriate set of rules. This technique may be more effective with older students who seek and desire peer approval. For example, if all the students sit quietly in their squad while the teacher takes roll, then the squad gets to choose one warm-up activity. Each squad member exerts peer pressure to control the behavior of the other squad members. This technique has proven to be very successful in the physical education environment, and, in certain instances, it is superior to individual reinforcement technique in managing behavior.

Group contingencies can be categorized into three basic types (Kauffman, Mostert, Trent, & Hallahan, 1998). First, there is the dependent group contingency in which a target student must earn the desired reinforcer for the entire squad. To assure that undue peer pressure is not placed on the student, the teacher must be certain the target student is capable of earning the reinforcement. For example, if the group can get Billy (a student with Down syndrome who often refuses to walk or run on the track) to run one lap, then the group gets to play a game of soccer. Second is an independent group contingency in which a squad goal is stated, and students work individually to earn the desired reinforcer. This eliminates the competitiveness of other group contingencies. For example, everyone in the squad has to complete their own prescribed number of push-ups and sit-ups. When everyone in the squad completes their sit-ups, the squad gets to shoot baskets for a few minutes. Third is an interdependent contingency. In this type of group contingency, the desired reinforcer is dependent on the behavior of the entire squad or class. This is the most commonly used and the most effective group contingency method. Note that if one student constantly ruins the chances of the entire group to earn the desired reinforcer, an individual behavior management technique may need to be implemented within the group contingency procedure.

The Good Behavior Game (Vogler & French, 1983) is an example of an interdependent group contingency. The physical educator places the students in various squads and explains that they will earn 10 minutes of free time if the squad members follow the class rules. Each squad begins with 10 points. If a squad at the end of the class or week has retained 8 or more points, free time will be awarded. Those squads that have fewer than 8 points remaining continue with the class activity. It is possible that all squads can win because they are not competing against each other. It must be clear that free play means the selection by students from a menu of activities that focus on daily or weekly instructional goals and objectives of the teacher.

Token Economies

Token economies are effective to modify the behavior of individuals as well as groups. Tokens are symbolic rewards used as temporary substitutes for more substantial reinforcers. Tokens may take the form of checkmarks, points, poker chips, colored strips of paper, or play money tokens that have a predetermined value and are earned for performing specific behaviors. An advantage of a token system is that the symbolic rewards can be presented immediately following the demonstration of the appropriate behavior or task with minimal interference in the ongoing activity. In addition, it can easily be added to contracts. It has been reported that paraprofessionals could assist in providing the tokens as well as student peers.

Contracts

Contracts are written agreements between at least the physical educator and the student regarding improvement in behavior or task performance (see Figure 11.5). Many authorities consider contracts the most sophisticated behavior management technique. In addition, contracts are very adaptable to a variety of behaviors and situations. There are three basic types of contracts. First, there is the physical educator-controlled contract in which the educator determines the target behavior and the reinforcers (see Figure 11.6). This type of contract is commonly referred to as a *proclamation*. Second, there is the student-controlled contract where the student determines the task and the reinforcer (see Figure 11.7). Third, there is a mutual contract where both the physical educator and the student determine the

---

This is an agreement between Shawn Jackino and his physical education teacher. This contract begins on September 1, 2007, and will be reviewed daily by the physical education teacher.

I, Shawn Jackino, agree to discuss my behavior with the physical education teacher each day immediately after class. At that time, we will determine whether I earned a point in each of four categories: 1) class attendance, 2) class participation, 3) appropriate interaction with peers, and 4) use of appropriate language. A maximum of four points per day can be earned. A weekly behavior chart will be used to keep track of my points. Once I have earned enough points, I can choose from the reinforcement menu I have developed with my physical education teacher (shown below).

Shawn Jackino, Student	Date
George McCall, General Physical Education Teacher	Date
Jennifer E. Austin, Licensed School Psychologist	Date

Reinforcement menu — Points needed

	Points needed
Free time with peer (e.g., shooting baskets)	10
Opportunity to be teacher's aide	10
Opportunity to choose class activity	10
Opportunity to lead daily stretching activities	5
Sports drink	5

Figure 11.5.   Token economy contract.

Billy will pay attention in physical education this week. He will earn the right to choose the class activity from four choices on Monday.

_____   _____
Billy Smith, Student   Date

_____   _____
John Matthews, General Physical Educator   Date

Figure 11.6.   Teacher-controlled contract.

terms of the contract together (see Figure 11.8). Perhaps the most appealing feature of the latter two contracts is that they remove the onus of responsibility from the educator's shoulders (see Table 11.5).

Prompts

Prompts are cues that help the student identify target behaviors. There are three major types of prompts. First are *visual prompts* such as markings on the gymnasium floor or posters on the wall. Second are *auditory prompts* such as a whistle or verbal directions. The third type of prompt is *physical guidance* in which the physical educator may hold the student's hand or put his or her hand on the student's shoulder when walking from activity to activity (see Chapter 6 for more detail on prompts). Prompts can help students who are hesitant to perform a skill. Prompts also aid in the student being successful. For example, using prompts with a student with intellectual disabilities to hold a bat and hit a ball off a

tee may make the student more willing to try the activity because he knows he will be successful.

Shaping

Shaping refers to the development of a new behavior by reinforcing a series of behaviors that are gradually and progressively similar to the desired new behaviors. This is also referred to as *reinforcing successive approximations.* For example, the targeted goal for a student is to come into the gym and go directly to his squad. However, this student tends to run directly to the equipment and start playing until the physical educator literally pulls him away and takes him to his squad. Rather than waiting for the student to display the complete targeted behavior, the physical educator may reinforce this student when he comes in, runs over to the equipment but does not touch it, then goes and sits down in his squad. Reinforcing successive approximations rather than waiting until the student has mastered the skill will

My physical education contract for success:

I, Jeramias Williams, promise to

* Follow teacher directions
* Participate in all physical education activities without arguing 4 of 5 days per week
* Get dressed for physical education and do all activities Monday through Thursday
* Not fight with other students
* Not curse in class

If I do all of the above, I will be rewarded by

* Not having to get dressed for physical education on Fridays
* Passing physical education

_____   _____
Jeramias Williams, Student   Date

_____   _____
Clarence Thompson, General Physical Educator   Date

_____   _____
Sallie H. Swisher, Licensed School Psychologist   Date

Figure 11.7.   Student-controlled contract.

> Michelle will dress for class for the next 15 class periods. After Michelle reaches the 15th class period, Coach Morales will reward Michelle with a shirt with a logo of her favorite soccer team.
>
> _____   _____
> Michelle Roberson, Student   Date
>
> _____   _____
> Anthony Morales, Coach   Date

Figure 11.8. Mutual contract.

more likely result in the student eventually achieving mastery.

Chaining

Chaining is a procedure of identifying a series of steps needed to perform a specific target behavior and taking the student through the steps. In this procedure each step might be taught separately, and then the separate responses are linked together. There are two types of chaining: backward and forward chaining. *Backward chaining* involves teaching the steps to perform a target behavior in the reverse order it would normally occur. For example, in backward chaining a student would work on the follow-through in the overhand throw first, and then working backward would work on releasing the ball, then trunk rotation, then extending his arm backward, and finally side orientation. Typically in backward chaining the physical educator assists the student through all of the steps of the movement except the last step. Then the physical educator assists with all components except the last two, and so forth. Backward chaining provides more errorless learning. In contrast, *forward chaining* involves teaching the steps to perform a target behavior in the order that it normally occurs.

Table 11.5. General guidelines in designing and implementing contracts

1. Read and explain the conditions of the contract aloud with the student.
2. Make sure the contract is fair for all persons.
3. Design the contract in a positive manner.
4. Design the contract in small approximations that leads to the target behavior or skill.
5. Allow for frequent reinforcement that is given immediately following successful achievement.
6. Be consistent and systematic in using a contract.
7. Whenever possible, all persons concerned should sign and receive a copy of the contract.
8. Renegotiate contract if it is not effective.
9. Start the contract as soon as possible after signing.

Source: Jansma and French (1994).

Negative Reinforcement

Negative reinforcement refers to taking something away to maintain or increase a behavior. Negative reinforcement is a less commonly used method of behavior management (Henderson & French, 1989). There are two major procedures involved in negative reinforcement. The first is *avoidance procedure.* For example, the physical educator may state that all students who run a mile in less that 10 minutes will not be required to run the mile the next day. Since most students do not want to run the mile a second day, they will attempt to run the mile in less than 10 minutes. The second is the *escape procedure.* Using this procedure, a group of students in a gymnastic class are preparing for a school demonstration. The presentation is the next day and the physical educator tells the students that everyone must know their routines perfectly. He states that during this class the students will repeat the routines until they do them without error before he will allow them to take a break.

There should be some caution when using negative reinforcement. Some students have encountered considerable negative reinforcement situations in their lives and have developed considerable resistance to it by adopting a belligerent attitude that sometimes leads to an escalation of punishers. Thus, negative reinforcement can set a negative tone for the student and the physical educator (Rizzo & Zabel, 1988). However, negative reinforcement can be used positively. For example, a student with intellectual disabilities who is overweight does not want to dress out for physical education when the class is doing the mile run. He is a slow runner, and he knows he cannot run the entire way. The physical educator realizes that the student will not participate if she makes him run the entire mile. She decides to tell the student that he only needs to run as far as he can and then walk the rest of the way (takes away the threat of having to run a mile). The student feels less threatened, dresses out for physical education, and runs farther and faster than he ever did before.

Nonreinforcement refers to not responding to a student's displaying a particular behavior, especially when the intent of the behavior is to get the teacher's attention. An example of nonreinforcement is the use of silence. Sometimes silence (5–10 seconds) by the physical educator who remains calm and does not react to the student's behaviors is enough to get the message to the student that his or her behavior is not appropriate (Janney & Snell, 2000).

PROCEDURES TO REDUCE OR ELIMINATE BEHAVIORS

When reinforcement alone is ineffective in developing, maintaining, or increasing the demonstration of an appropriate behavior or task performance, the physical educator may be required to use techniques that decrease the problem behavior. There are two main techniques that a physical educator can use to reduce or eliminate behaviors: differential reinforcement and punishment. These techniques should be carefully implemented and consequences should be as natural, as logical, and as educationally appropriate as possible (Janney & Snell, 2000).

Differential Reinforcement

There are three general differential reinforcement strategies: differential reinforcement of low rates of behavior (DRL), differential reinforcement of other behaviors (DRO), and differential reinforcement of incompatible behaviors (DRI) (Alberto & Troutman, 1990).

Differential Reinforcement of Low Rates of Behavior (DRL)

This procedure uses a specific schedule of reinforcement to decrease the rate of a problem behavior that may be tolerable or even desirable at low rates but inappropriate when it occurs too often or too rapidly. Examples include a student who talks to his friends through the entire class or a student not performing her warm-up activities.

There are two types of DRL reinforcement delivery schedules based on the frequency, intensity, and duration of the problem behavior. First there is DRL in which the total number of inappropriate responses that occur during the entire class is compared with a preset criterion. A reinforcer is given if the occurrences of the problem behavior are at or below the predetermined criterion. For example, a physical educator is frustrated because it seems so much time is wasted during one of his classes. He believes the problem is transitioning between activities. The teacher records that it takes the students 12 minutes to transition between activities; the actual class time is 50 minutes (almost 20% of the class was transition time). The teacher decided to develop a behavior management program to reduce this time to 4 minutes, so that during the entire class, if the transition time was reduced to 8 minutes or less (predetermined criteria), the entire class would earn a reinforcement.

Second is interval DRL which involves dividing the class period into an activity or time interval where the behavior is occurring across numerous intervals. This approach could be used if the problem occurs during various times in the class period and it is believed that reinforcement will be effective only if it is awarded at various times during the class rather than waiting to the end of the class. For example, there could be time periods after each activity within a lesson (i.e., dressing out, roll taking, instruction, warm-up, activity, cool-down, closure). At the completion of each activity, the student is given a reward if the number of inappropriate responses in a specified period of time was less than or equal to a prescribed limit. As the problem behavior dissipates, the number of activities in which appropriate behavior is awarded increases until the student is on a class DRL delivery schedule. The procedure is then gradually removed until traditional reinforcement is provided as with the other students in class.

Differential Reinforcement of Other Behaviors (DRO)

This differential reinforcement strategy involves a reinforcer being delivered contingent on the target behavior not being demonstrated for a specific period of time. For example, Hayden continually talks during all activities. The physical educator can verbally reinforce Hayden every 5 minutes if he is listening and participating in all activities. Whereas DRL is used to reinforce a gradual reduction of a problem behavior, DRO is only used to reinforce zero occurrences of the behavior. There are at least two variations of DRO that are similar to those variations in the DRL procedure. In the first, reinforcement is contingent on the nonoccurrence of behavior for a specified time period. In the second, reinforcement is contingent on the nonoccurrence of a behavior within a time period that has been divided into smaller intervals (Alberto & Troutman, 1990).

Differential Reinforcement of an Incompatible Behavior (DRI)

In this procedure, a behavior is reinforced that is incompatible with the inappropriate behavior. For example, a student receives reinforcement for standing on his spot or for being quiet in line, which is incompatible with standing in the wrong spot or being disruptive in line. Similarly students are reinforced for clapping their hands to the music, which is incompatible with inappropriate hand waving behavior. This procedure has been reported to be quite effective in reducing aggressive behavior and other inappropriate behaviors (Goldstein, 1995).

Punishment

As noted, punishment is defined as the presentation of an aversive event or consequence immediately following a behavior that leads to a decrease in the occurrence of that behavior. If punishment is used appropriately, it can make positive differences. For instance, at the beginning of class Frank goes to the playground equipment rather than lining up with his class. As a consequence, Frank's teacher has Frank walk to and from the locker room to his class squad five consecutive times (*overcorrection*). The next class, Frank walks directly to his squad. The teacher then rewards him for the appropriate behavior by patting him on the back and verbally praising him. Generally, though, based on the published research of Kohn (1998), punishment generally undermines the prosocial values that physical educators are attempting to teach (Deci, Koestner, & Ryan, 2001).

Punishment also can be abusive, leading to withdrawal, anger, frustration, and even further misbehavior. Therefore, punishment should *only* be used when positive techniques have not been effective. When punishment is used, it is important to remember that it is easy to focus on decreasing or eliminating an inappropriate behavior and forgetting the importance of teaching positive, alternative behaviors. This involves behavior pairs, targeting both the behavior to increase and the behavior to decrease. For example, Frank was reinforced for walking directly to his squad. It is important to get approval from the student's parents and special education teacher before implementing any type of program that includes punishment.

If it is determined that punishments must be used, it is important that certain guidelines be followed (see Table 11.6). Again, if punishment must

Table 11.6. Guidelines for the use of punishment

1. Always talk to the student privately first to determine the cause of misbehavior.

2. Establish classroom rules so students know beforehand what the punishable behaviors are and what their consequences will be.

3. Post the rules in the gym and go over them with the students.

4. Send a list of the rules of unacceptable behaviors and consequences home to the parents so they know what is expected of their child.

5. Provide models of acceptable behavior so students know appropriate ways of behaving.

6. Do not allow a student to exhibit an inappropriate behavior for too long a period of time so that it increases in intensity before you attempt to intervene. Punishment must occur immediately after the behavior is first observed. Afterward, it is important that you provide opportunities for the student to behave appropriately and to receive positive reinforcement for this appropriate behavior.

7. Distinguish between intentional and unintentional disruptions. Do not treat students who make accidental mistakes the same way as those who misbehave on purpose. For instance, a student who accidentally throws a ball that hits another person should be treated differently that a student who throws a ball with the intention of hitting someone. Make the punishment suit the behavior.

8. Do not lose control over your own emotions. The problem will only become worse if both the student and the teacher have lost control.

9. Avoid confrontations with the student, especially in front of peers. Secondary level students, in particular, tend to function as a member of a group and are quite protective of each other. By confronting one student, you may lose respect of the other students as well.

10. Avoid the use of sarcasm. Some teachers use sarcasm to chastise or demean a student in an attempt to control behavior. Using words as weapons of control can alienate all students in the class. Many times the teacher unconsciously slips into using this technique or considers it a form of joking to get the point across. Sarcasm is generally not considered funny by the students, and could negatively affect their self-image and status with their peers. It is not a recommended way to manage behaviors.

11. Be consistent in your use of punishment. What is wrong today must be wrong tomorrow, and the consequences must be the same.

12. Be fair. Behavior that is wrong for Tommy to exhibit must also be wrong for Mary to exhibit.

13. When a student does misbehave, make sure that in your reprimand you specify that it is the behavior, NOT the student, of which you disapprove. For example, do not say, "You are a bad person, and I will not tolerate you in my class," but rather, "That behavior is inappropriate, and I will not tolerate that behavior in this class."

14. Avoid touching a student when you are angry. Physical restraint, however, may be appropriate with aggressive, self-destructive, or dangerous behaviors when the teacher is unable to successfully use a more gradual, positive approach due the possibility that the student may cause harm to himself or to others. When using physical restraint, hold the student firmly but not roughly, to give the student a sense of protection – not punishment. The preferred technique is for the teacher to stand behind the student and hold the student's wrists with the student's arms crossed over his or her chest.

15. Never hit a student. Hitting is totally inappropriate for a teacher. There are too many negative side effects of hitting a student for it ever to be an approved management technique. In addition to all of the negative repercussions of hitting a student, there is an issue of legal liability.

From Henderson, H.L., & French, R. W. (1993). *Creative approaches to managing student behavior* (2nd ed.). Park City, Utah: Family Development Resources; adapted by permission.

be used, use the mildest form possible, making sure it is a natural punishment and paired with teaching appropriate behaviors. There are six basic types of punishments that are appropriate in public school settings: silent look, verbal reprimand, extinction, time-out, overcorrection, and response cost.

Silent Look

As a mild punisher, a silent look by the physical educator when a student exhibits an inappropriate behavior can sometimes be effective. This gesture may stop the reoccurrence of the behavior. For example, a student is talking while the teacher is trying to give directions. The teacher stops giving directions and glares at the student. The student then realizes he is disturbing the teacher and stops talking.

Verbal Reprimand

Verbal reprimands are used widely and, in many cases, effectively in physical education. The key is to always address the behavior problem of the student, not the student him- or herself. The verbal reprimand must target a specific behavior. The following illustrates appropriate ways to use verbal reprimands: "Do not bounce the ball when I am talking." or "You are not standing in the circle as I requested you to do." Examples of inappropriate uses of the technique include "You can't do anything right!" or "Can't you control yourself and act your age!" Henderson and French (1993) listed numerous verbal reprimands in which the student, not the behavior, is the focus.

Extinction

There are students whose main goal is to upset, frustrate, or anger teachers and others. These students are reinforced in two ways. First, they receive attention from the teacher or other students. Second, they get revenge. One way to reduce or eliminate this type of behavior is to use an extinction procedure (Lavay, French, & Henderson, 2006). In this method, the physical educator eliminates or extinguishes maladaptive behaviors by simply ignoring them. Extinction is the most effective way to permanently remove an inappropriate response and is most effective, as other punishers, when combined with positive reinforcement. Extinction can be difficult to implement, as it takes a great deal of self-control on the part of the physical educator and peers (see Table 11.7).

Time-Out

This technique involves the removal of the student from positive reinforcement for a fixed period of time. There are different thoughts on the length of the time-out period. Some authorities suggest it should be no longer than 2 or 3 minutes. Others believe the student should stay in time-out for the equivalent of 1 minute for each year of his or her age. There are three general forms of time-out (Lavay, French, & Henderson, 2006). First is the *observational time-out* in which the student is removed from the activity but allowed to view the activity. Second is the *seclusion time-out* in which the student is required to sit or stand in a corner within the physical education environment but cannot see students participating in the activity from which he or she was removed. Third is the *exclusionary time-out* in which the student must leave the environment to a setting that is supervised and not more reinforcing than the environment that he or she must leave. Time-out is simple to implement in a short amount of time and has been shown to be effective in decreasing many undesirable student behaviors. The major disadvantage is that the student is not participating in the activities. Some students who want to avoid participating in physical education find time-out reinforcing.

Overcorrection

Overcorrection is designed to reduce the inappropriate side effects of intense punishment. There are two basic types of overcorrection. First, *restitution overcorrection* refers to the student restoring the environment. For example, if a student put his chewing gum on top of his locker, he would be required to clean his gum off his locker plus all of the gum that others have put on their lockers. Second, *positive practice overcorrection* refers to the technique in which a student is required to repeatedly practice a positive behavior in the correct manner. For example, suppose the physical educator sees a student running in the locker room. In positive over-

Table 11.7. Guidelines when using an extinction procedure

A. Generally combine with other methods such as strategies related to differential reinforcement.

B. Be consistent, and do not occasionally reinforce the problem behavior.

C. Practice not responding to the misbehavior.

D. Be aware of what is termed "extinction bursts." After the extinction procedure is initiated, the inappropriate behavior may occur more often, more vigorously, or for longer periods of time by the student in an effort to gain attention. Eventually the extinction burst will fade and the problem behavior gradually diminishes.

E. Do not give eye contact, verbal cues, verbal contact, or physical contact.

F. Some form of punishment may be the procedure of choice if the problem behavior intensifies over a long period of time.

correction, the student may be required to walk correctly at the required speed for 10 consecutive times.

An advantage to using this technique is that overcorrection reduces the undesired behavior faster, more completely, and for a longer time than other punishment techniques, such as time-out. Although an effective technique to reduce more extreme behavior problems, the physical educator must be aware of a number of disadvantages associated with using overcorrection. It is difficult and time-consuming to implement. Additional staff members usually are required to ensure that the corrective procedure is correctly implemented. Finally, informed consent from parents needs to be obtained as in the use of most techniques used to eliminate or reduce severe behavior.

Response Cost

This procedure refers to the removal from a student of a specific quantity of reinforcement that has been previously earned such as minutes of time to perform an activity, loss of equipment, or points taken away from a grade. This system of punishment is used in most traditional sports. For instance, if a player inappropriately hits another player in football, the penalty will cost the team valuable yardage or even possibly possession of the ball as in basketball. In using this type of punishment, the physical educator must consider the following: magnitude of the cost in relation to the problem behavior exhibited, provision of opportunities to regain the lost privilege or points when the appropriate behavior has replaced

the inappropriate behavior, and ensuring the student understands the rules for the removal of the reinforcing event (Jansma & French, 1994).

LEVELING SYSTEMS

Many behavior management techniques have been incorporated into a leveling system. In a *leveling system*, students are placed on one of a series of clearly defined steps based on present level of performance. These steps involve increasing student responsibility and privileges as the level of performance and learning improves. Moving up a step is contingent on reaching specific, observable goals and objectives based on accompanying criteria. As students move up the steps, additional rewards can be earned. The criteria and rewards in most cases are part of a complementary behavior management system such as a token economy or a contract. Generally at the lower steps, the teacher is in control. As the student progresses up the steps, the control is slowly shifted to more student independence and self-responsibility. When a student is successful in reaching this step, the student generally is given an opportunity to be placed in a more inclusive environment.

For instance, Terrance is an eighth-grade student who has been classified as having a behavioral disorder. His special education teacher developed a leveling system that was approved as part of his formal behavioral intervention plan. Further, this plan was developed in partnership with the itinerant adapted physical educator who provides services with some

Table 11.8. Illustration of the use of the leveling system

Level	Behavior and conditions	Reinforcer
LEVEL I	Walk 20 minutes twice a day daily for 10 consecutive school days without verbally abusing or physically contacting the other two students.	Can participate in the adapted physical education class once a week
LEVEL II	Participate in the adapted physical education class once a week for 5 weeks without verbally abusing or inappropriately physically contacting another student. If inappropriate behavior is exhibited, Terrance will be placed back into Level I environment.	Can participate in the adapted physical education class twice a week
LEVEL III	Same as Level II but twice a week	Can participate in the adapted physical education class twice a week and general physical education class once a week
LEVEL IV	Participate in both the adapted and general physical education classes for 4 weeks without verbally or inappropriately physically contacting other students in class. If an inappropriate behavior is exhibited, Terrance will be placed back to Level II.	Can participate in the adapted physical education class twice a week and general physical education class once a week
LEVEL V	Same as Level IV but twice a week in general physical education.	Can fully participate in the general physical education class three days a week which is the physical education requirement for his age-related peers. No adapted physical education services provided.
LEVEL VI	Participates only in general physical education program. If Terrance is verbally abusive or inappropriately physically contacts other students, Terrance will be placed back to Level II.	

other students in this class twice per week along with the general physical educator. Presently the only physical activity that Terrance is allowed to do is walk laps on the school track for 20 minutes, twice per day, with two other students in his special education class under the supervision of the paraprofessional. Table 11.8 shows Terrance's leveling system.

Two leveling systems have been used in inclusive physical education environments. The first was implemented more than 30 years ago by French (1973). This leveling system was modified from one developed by Hewett (1968) and Hewett and Taylor (1980) for use in a classroom for students with behavior disorders. Two underlying principles guide this system. The first is based on the basic principles of effective learning: knowing the level of learning of a student, knowing the appropriate conditions of learning, and knowing the appropriate consequences. The second relates to the levels of learning. The hierarchy of learning ranges from the lower levels of attending and responding to actually mastering and using what was learned in class outside the school environment and to the family and community. This type of leveling system was effectively applied by Zachofsky (1974) with students with learning disabilities in a physical education environment. The focus of the second leveling system is to use the physical education environment as a medium to develop self-responsible individuals, including students identified as at risk.

SOME FINAL THOUGHTS ON ADDRESSING BEHAVIOR PROBLEMS

The previous sections presented a great deal of information on how to understand and help students who display behavior problems in general physical education using the PBS model. The following provides some final points related to the application of the PBS model that should be considered when working with students with behavioral problems.

Plan on Teaching Appropriate Behaviors

The management of behavior problems should be treated in the same way as the management of instructional problems. For example, if a student makes an error in performing a motor task, a correction procedure is implemented and the student is provided more practice and review. If the problem is not corrected, the physical educator re-diagnoses the problem and rearranges the practice session.

However, when an inappropriate behavior occurs, the student typically is given a reminder of the disregarded rule or expected behavior and administered a penalty for exhibiting the inappropriate behavior. Appropriate behavior must be taught.

Communicating with Students

Communication is vital to develop positive interactions with students that lead to trust and acceptance. In physical education programs in which there is a great deal of communication, students are more likely to do what teachers ask of them. Just talking to or listening to students will help. Some authorities have suggested that physical educators should interact in some way with each student in class during each class period. This could include verbal or nonverbal communication. In large classes, this may take two class periods. One technique that is useful is meeting students at the door when they are entering or leaving the gym. Another technique is to stand near students during the daily activity and provide feedback. For instance, if students are jogging, position yourself in one corner of the gym so you can provide a friendly look, a high-five, or word of encouragement as they pass by. Table 11.9 presents techniques to consider when communicating with students.

Communicating with Parents

Parents should be kept abreast of how well the student is doing in all school settings including physical education. This is particularly true for students who have a history of displaying inappropriate behaviors. Communication with parents can be by telephone, e-mail, or notes. Communication should include times when the student has displayed appropriate behaviors as well as times the student has had problems. Also, contact parents and other team members if you notice changes in the student's behavior. Sometimes you will learn that the student's medication is being changed or there are changes in the home situation. For example, a student may be starting a new medication to combat a seizure disorder, and the medication may be affecting his or her coordination and stamina in physical education. Similarly, a student who seems very depressed and does not want to dress out for physical education might be dealing with his or her parents' divorce.

The key is to view parents as allies in developing the most appropriate behavior management program. Remember that many parents have had very poor experiences throughout their education career, leading to negative attitudes toward their child's

Table 11.9. Techniques to consider when communicating with students

1. Focus on behaviors, not on the student. Do not say "that behavior problem student"; say "the student with a behavior problem."

2. Listen to the student as long as the student is not using the opportunity to control the physical educator. For example, a primary-grade student during an elementary physical education class kept coming up to the teacher and holding her hand. The physical educator, in attempt to manage and instruct the class of 28 students, kept asking the student to go back to his spot or station. This behavior continued throughout the class period. After school, the physical educator went to the classroom teacher to see if this behavior also occurred in the classroom. The physical educator was informed that the night before the young student had upset his father and the father had forced the student to sleep alone outside the home that night. It would have been better if the physical educator was informed of this information earlier.

3. Understand your feelings toward the student. With heterogeneity in the levels of behavior and learning of students, teachers must modify traditional teaching styles. If a student has a cognitive deficiency, techniques must be implemented to ensure the student understands the instructions. If this does not occur, the teacher may become constantly frustrated because this student is continually in the wrong place and talking to other students to figure out what he is supposed to do in class.

4. Accentuate students' strengths. With large classes it seems that it is a constant chore just to "put out fires." Focusing on a student's appropriate behavior and learning and not just their deficiencies may decrease many of the problems that are being exhibited in class. Students who are never reinforced may not be supportive of this environment.

5. Respect students' legitimate opinions. When a student provides his or her opinion, reinforce that you support students' opinions when they are honest and not negative. Many times these opinions can improve instruction. Sometimes a student states that it is too cold out, that he or she is bored of the activity, or that he or she never gets to play a certain position during a game; the student may not be the only one to feel this way. Maybe the physical educator should be listening and making the appropriate modifications, not ignoring.

6. Assist in developing positive peer relationships.

Source: Pangrazi (2004).

teachers. This negative attitude needs to be changed in order to earn their support for your program. Some ways to communicate with parents include

- Using school newsletters or e-mail to explain the class rules and consequences

- Developing behavioral awards that are sent home

- Posting pictures of the students who had a significant behavioral improvement in the gymnasium or on a bulletin board (parents can see the displayed pictures when they visit the school)

- Having conferences or meetings

- Having a family play day

Communicating with Administrators

Developing positive relationships with administrators is extremely beneficial. Talk to the administrators about how they would like you to deal with behaviors. Often, administrators do not want physical educators to send students with problem behaviors to the office too frequently but instead to deal with these issues in class. However, you cannot ignore serious problems. A good rule before interacting with the administrator is to document student misbehavior, particularly safety and legal problems. Try not to focus on teacher inconvenience. In addition, do not walk into the administrator's office with a problem; be prepared to share your thoughts on possible solutions. This demonstrates to the administrator that the issue has been well thought out. Remember that most administrators have years of experience and could be excellent mentors.

Establish Class Rules

Having rules, consequences, and a clear class structure will prevent many students (including students with disabilities) from displaying inappropriate behaviors. In developing the class rules by yourself or with your students, always consider cultural diversity. Class rules for all students should be clearly defined and established early in the school year. The consequences do not have to be entirely negative. There should also be positive consequences for following the rules, such as a popcorn party for all students who have followed the class rules. These activities should reflect the goals and objectives within the class unit or theme. Rules and consequences could be laminated and posted on various walls, on a clipboard, on a fence, on a chair, or on large cones or equipment carts (Seaman, DePauw, Morton, & Omoto, 2003). In addition, most physical educators review the rules with the class at the beginning of school and occasionally during the school year. Some will ask students to repeat the rules either verbally or in a written quiz in order to determine their understanding. Others send the rules home in a written format for parents to review, sign, and send back. It is generally recommended to not have more than eight rules. Some of the traditional rules and consequences used in physical education can be found in Table 11.10.

Consistency in Enforcing Rules

In addition to establishing class rules and consequences, it is critical that these rules and consequences be consistently enforced. If students perceive

Table 11.10. Traditional rules and consequences used in physical education

Rules for physical education

Raise your hand	Listen to instructions
Be quiet when others talk	Enter and exit the room quietly
Remain on your spot	Show respect to your classmates/teachers
Practice assigned task	Take care of equipment
Follow directions	Throw chewing gum away before class

Consequences used in physical education

For following the rules	*For not following the rules*
Free play at end of period or week	First warning
Choice of activity (e.g., parachute)	Second warning
Game at end of class	Three-minute time out
Choice of music during activity	Letter home to parents (negative)
Stickers or stamps	Send back to classroom teacher
Letter home to parents (positive)	Send to principal

that some students can get away with misbehavior while others cannot, then students will become confused and angry. This does not mean that you cannot establish some alternative rules and consequences for students with disabilities. Just make it clear to all the students why such an alternative is necessary. For example, a student with intellectual disabilities often tries to talk to peers when the teacher is giving instructions. Rather than timing the student out, peers have been instructed to gently and quietly tell the student not to talk while the teacher is talking. Later, peers talk to the student on the way to a station or at other times when it is appropriate.

Utilize a Team Approach

For problem behaviors to be modified, collaboration between faculty, staff, parents, and the community may be required. Include as many team members as possible in the diagnosis of the problem and development of a plan. This should include a consensus on how the plan will be implemented and who is responsible for each part of the plan. For example, a teacher assistant might not be needed to accompany a student with an emotional disability to physical education every day, but she may be asked to be available in emergencies. Similarly, in large high schools that have several vice principals, the team should decide which assistant principal is in charge of behavior problems for particular students.

Generalization

When possible select behaviors and activities to teach that can by generalized—that is, behaviors that occur in different environments such as the home or the community. In addition, activities that are taught are periodically checked to make sure they are maintained. For instance, it is not an effective use of time to teach a skill such as bowling a ball in the gymnasium and then not make sure it is maintained over time and in different settings. Waiting until the next year when the unit will be taught again will only lead to regression of skill performance.

Schoolwide and Communitywide Behavior Programs

Who would have thought 25 years ago there would be security cameras on buses, drug-sniffing dogs in the schools, metal detectors at the entrances of school, and teachers carrying walkie-talkies to be able to call for immediate assistance? Today, because of the serious behavior problems that are occurring throughout schools, teachers are working together to develop schoolwide behavior programs (Zionts, Zionts, & Simpson, 2002). Behavior management plans that are developed independently by one teacher and implemented in only one setting are rarely effective for dealing with students with behavior problems. Many schoolwide programs have expanded to include parents as active partners. And in some small towns, there is communitywide involvement including storekeepers, police, fire fighters, and park and recreation staff. Physical educators teaching students with disabilities must become an integral part of the schoolwide behavior management system. A schoolwide system should be infused into the more comprehensive programs used in settings with students with disabilities, such as leveling systems. This will enable students reaching the upper steps of the leveling system to transition into more fully included settings if they have practiced and learned to effectively function in the schoolwide program.

Teaching Social Responsibility through Physical Education

It is important that all students in class learn to respect and value others. For some students, this must be taught through knowledge and experiences. Physical educators may want to reanalyze the games and activities they use, focusing on rewarding points for appropriate behaviors and respecting/including peers instead of rewarding in the traditional manner by the number of runs scored or baskets made. One system that infuses this concept into traditional physical educator's games and activities is referred to as points modification (Davis & French, 1986). For example, in traditional relay races, the team that finishes first receives the most points, and then the second place earns points, and so on. Points can be added to each team not only for placing but also for demonstrating appropriate behaviors. For instance, a physical educator can add points to the teams that are participating cooperatively (e.g., not starting a game until a classmate gets back from the bathroom, staying in line, and not yelling at another player). This will increase group cooperation (i.e., respect for others). Another example in a physical education class is a third grade student, Jodie, with poor motor skills who does not seem to belong to any subgroup in class. Most students in class would generally consider her a loner. Jodie also demonstrates some inappropriate behaviors, but most of the time she does seem to want to belong. The physical educator is just beginning a kickball unit and decides to incorporate the points modification approach. She decides that when Jodie is one of the players who touch the ball when her team is in the field, her team automatically earns a point. This modification encourages peers to include Jodie more as a team member in the game.

Another approach that is supported by Hellison (2003) is class meetings to solve intra- and interpersonal problems that may affect the valuing of self or others. This approach is designed to develop social relationships and to teach students how to resolve conflicts within a physical education environment. Janney and Snell (2000) identified eight basic steps for educators (including physical educators) to follow in this class problem-solving process: 1) identify specific behavioral problem, 2) gather necessary information, 3) brainstorm possible solutions, 4) evaluate the agreed solutions, 5) select the best solution, 6) develop a place of action, 7) implement the plan, and 8) evaluate the plan.

Know the Laws

Physical educators must know federal, as well as, state and local policies and laws related to discipline. For instance, based on Section 504 of the Rehabilitation Act of 1973 (PL 93-112) and its amendments (PL 105-220) and the Individuals with Disabilities Education Improvement Act (IDEA) of 2004, different procedures are used for students with and without disabilities related to discipline. Specifically related to improving discipline for students with disabilities, it is now stated in IDEA 2004 that schools are required to conduct functional behavioral assessments and

provide behavioral services to students who are disciplined beyond 10 days. Further, schools are required to continue providing services that enable students who are disciplined to participate in the general curriculum and to meet their IEP goals. For example, under most circumstances a student with a disability cannot be expelled from school unless a trained and knowledgeable group of persons first determine whether the student's misconduct is related to his/her disabling condition. This is commonly termed manifestation determination. There are two key concepts physical educators need to know:

1. *Understand the term "disciplinary action."* Within 10 days after the date disciplinary action is taken against a student with a disability, the school district must conduct a review of the relationship between the student's disability and the behavior that is the subject of the disciplinary action. This stipulation is for students who do not carry weapons or illegal drugs to school. The 504 or IEP committee may determine that the student's behavior was or was not a manifestation of the student's disability, based on the evaluation and diagnostic results, observations of the student, review of the appropriateness of the student's IEP and placement.

If it is determined that the student's disability did not impair his or her ability to understand the impact and consequences of the behavior subject to the disciplinary action, the student can be disciplined in the same manner as students without disabilities. If the student is suspended or expelled though, the district must continue to provide the student a free appropriate public education to decrease the possibility of educational regression. These laws do not require this provision for students without disabilities who were suspended or expelled for the same inappropriate behavior.

If the behavior is determined to be a manifestation of the student's disability, the student cannot be disciplined for the behavior. Instead, the district must attempt to remediate the deficiency in the student's 504 plan or IEP and/or its implementation. This could mean the 504 plan or IEP team may need to develop or revise a behavioral intervention plan. There are some exceptions. A student with a disability may be placed in an alternative education setting, determined by the 504 or IEP committee, for the same amount of time a student without a disability would be subjected to, but for no more than 45 days if the student carries a weapon to school or school function or knowingly possesses or uses illegal drugs or sells or solicits the sale of a controlled substance while in school or at a school function. In addition, if school officials believe that a student with a disability is substantially likely to injure him or herself or others in the student's general placement, they can ask an impartial hearing officer to order the student be removed to an interim alternative educational setting for a period of up to 45 days. It is important to note that if the student is identified under IDEA 2004, he/she is protected from zero tolerance rules (cannot expel a student with a disability who is served under IDEA 2004). However, this does not apply to a student who receives Section 504 protection (can expel a student served under a 504 plan).

2. *Behavior intervention plan* (BIP): This plan contains strategies to address specific behaviors exhibited by a student that interferes with his or her performance or with the learning of others. This plan must include strategies, consequences (rewards and punishers) and educational supports to increase the student's performance and learning. This plan is designed by a student's IEP committee, which includes a student's general education teacher in the development of the BIP. The BIP must be developed for any student who has committed a drug or weapon offense, and the IEP committee must meet no later than 10 days after the offense to develop a functional behavior assessment plan review and modify an existing BIP for the student. For example, Sam is a ninth grader who just began attending high school. His IEP committee (which includes a general physical educator) determined that Sam has emotional disturbances, exhibiting behaviors that negatively affect his education performance. Although he has the capacity to understand school rules, he will not follow them. Specifically, Sam has frequent unexcused tardiness, uses inappropriate language, verbally interrupts, and does not complete assignments. He appears to respond well to responsibility and opportunities to participate in activities that set him apart from the rest of the class. Various behavior management techniques have been implemented. Some have been a little effective (e.g., parent conference, loss of privileges) and others not effective (e.g., detention, suspension). The IEP team decided to develop and implement a BIP to accompany Sam's IEP.

Using Physical Restraint

Some students demonstrate aggressive or violent behavior to a point where it is referred to as a "crisis." Teachers and specialists who deal with such students need to be trained in crisis management techniques that often include some form of personal restraint. Crisis management is not an intervention. When students hurt themselves or others, the behavior needs to be stopped immediately. The purpose of a crisis management plan is to protect the student from harming him- or herself as well as others, and help the student calm down and deescalate the prob-

lem (Janney & Snell, 2000). The crisis plan should be developed and practiced by all school members who are in contact with the student. With this plan, there is a better chance for human dignity and recovery for the student in crisis and for safety for all involved. Janney and Snell (2000) outlined five steps that are useful in managing a behavioral crisis:

1. *Ignore* the behavior problem when possible.

2. *Protect* the individual or others from physical consequences of behavior.

3. *Momentarily restrain* the individual during problem behavior.

4. *Remove* anyone that is in danger from the area where the crisis is occurring.

5. *Introduce cues* that evoke nonproblem behavior.

Physical restraint may be needed within an overall crisis management plan for some students who lose total emotional and physical control. These students "feel totally and absolutely helpless," and "physical restraint is not only necessary but an act of kindness" (Walker, Shea, & Bauer, 2003, p. 229). Specific procedures should be used to protect the student and the teacher. Physical educators must be trained to use the appropriate restraint techniques. In addition, restraint techniques should not be used without written, parental permission, and they must be supported by the school administrators as a part of the school district's policy. If you do not have experience with crisis management techniques, it is highly recommended that you attend a district-approved restraint program. This may also protect you. Teachers who try to restrain a student without knowing the appropriate techniques sometimes find themselves in lawsuits in which parents claim that the educator caused physical harm to their child.

Behavior and Motor and Physical Assessment

In some cases students have the skills but will not exhibit acceptable behaviors. In such cases, it may make sense to use reinforcement techniques. For example, Sarah, a 10-year-old student with a learning disability, was required to throw a softball as far as she could as part of norm-referenced test. This student's first attempt was lackluster. The physical educator, Mr. Brown, told Sarah if she gave 100% effort and threw the ball as far as she could, he would give her a dollar. Sarah's next throw traveled more than 75 feet! In another case, Robert, another 10-year-old with a learning disability, was asked to perform as many curl-ups as he could. Robert performed only two. Mr. Brown felt this was way below Robert's ability, but he could not get Robert to do more. After discussing the situation with another teacher, Mr. Brown decided to try an experiment. Mr. Brown told Robert that if he performed as many curl-ups as he could really do, he would earn nachos with his lunch, something Mr. Brown knew Robert loved. Robert performed 61 curl-ups! Although the use of money and food are not often recommended, in these cases they seemed to do the trick—at least for the short term.

Other reinforcement techniques do not require the use of food or money. For example, Emily, a teenager with a profound intellectual disability could or would not throw a ball underhand or perform a curl-up as part of an assessment. Ms. Hunter tried to use numerous reinforcers to get her to respond, but she would not attempt either activity. She decided to use a technique termed *positive practice* that involves physically taking the student through the motor pattern numerous times. For the ball test item, Ms. Hunter actually put her hand over Emily's and moved her arm through the correct motion saying, "Good, you are throwing the ball!" Similarly, in the curl-up activity, Ms. Hunter held Emily's arms while she was lying on her back with knees bent, and Ms. Hunter gently pulled the girl up to a sit-up position, saying, "Good, you are doing a curl-up." This was done 10 times in a row. In both cases, after positive practice with just a verbal cue, Ms. Hunter was able to fade the extra support so Emily began to perform the task on her own.

Begin with Simple Techniques

Once the teacher knows the possible causes and reasons for a student's inappropriate behavior, the teacher should begin with the simplest technique. Some techniques could be just using cues, prompts, or social praise. This may be all that is required to put the student on task. Simple cues or prompts may help some students re-focus on the task at hand. Simple hand signals can be used to cue and prompt children. For example,

- One hand over head means the student immediately goes to his or her spot,

- Two hands overhead means freeze,

- Two hands overhead and locked together means stop,

- Two hands over mouth means quiet,

- A clicker or whistle means go.

Verbal statements can also be used. For example,

- One, two, three, clap.

- Eyes on me.

Another simple technique is *name-dropping*. Name-dropping involves saying a student's name when that student is off-task. For instance, when speaking to the class say, "You can see, Bill, we are still working on our throwing skills." Sometimes just hearing one's name helps a student to get back on task. If cues and prompts are not effective, use praise when the student is demonstrating the appropriate behavior.

CONCLUSIONS

Some physical educators feel frustration, isolation, and lack of understanding when teaching students with severe behavior or learning disabilities. For general physical educators to be effective with these students, at least four major factors must be considered. First, the physical educator has to set the tone for the entire class by demonstrating a caring yet firm affect. The physical educator must be a good communicator with all the students, be consistent, have good rapport, be sensitive and understanding yet firm, and have a fair code of conduct. If a physical educator is unorganized and lacks consistent and fair behavior management skills, then he or she will become angry, depressed, and feel helpless. In turn, students will react with fear and hostility.

Second, physical educators have to learn as much as possible about students with disabilities who are in their classes before they can plan appropriate behavior management programs. What reinforces each student? When does the student display particular behaviors? What seems to set the student off? What might the student be trying to accomplish by displaying inappropriate behaviors? How does the student react to consequences? Answers to these and other questions will aid the physical educator in developing a behavior program that matches each student's unique abilities and needs.

Third, preservice and in-service training is the initial step in helping general physical educators meet their professional responsibilities for educating students with behavior problems who are included in their classes. Today, more and more teacher preparation programs are requiring their physical education majors to take a course on the topic of behavior management or have infused this type of information across numerous courses. When these services are provided, two factors must continually be considered: change is a slow, difficult, and gradual process and should not be expected in a one-shot in-service program, and continued support and follow-up is necessary after initial training.

Fourth, think about your own philosophies, values, and goals before you attempt to develop your behavior management plan for your students. Consider a 10-step plan that may assist you in areas in which you as an educator may need improvement (Lavay, French, & Henderson, 2006):

Step 1: Examine your philosophy of teaching and behavior management.

Step 2: Based on your philosophy, establish your teaching and behavior management goals.

Step 3: Evaluate the effectiveness of your current teaching practices.

Step 4: Implement the changes you have determined need to be made and analyze the results.

Step 5: Decide what remaining problems you need to deal with.

Step 6: Examine the problem behavior, and then make an earnest attempt to determine its cause.

Step 7: Design an intervention to change the problem behavior.

Step 8: Implement the intervention, and then evaluate its effectiveness.

Step 9: Repeat steps 6 through 8 for the other behaviors you listed.

Step 10: Repeat the entire process at least annually.

CHAPTER 11 APPENDIX

Sample Functional Behavior Plan

The following pages contain a completed functional behavior plan for Jordan, a fourth grader with challenging behavior.

Functional Behavior Plan

Name: Jordan Johnston   Grade: Fourth grade   Examiner: M. Block

School: Crestview Elementary   Date: September 20, 2006

Describe the targeted behavior.

The targeted behavior consists of three parts: noncompliance, disruptiveness, and aggression. The behavior begins as noncompliance when Jordan runs away from a situation and turns into disruptive behavior when he destroys property. Finally, the behavior escalates into aggression when Jordan tries to physically attack the instructor.

What is the student's quality of life?

1. Jordan lives at home with his mother, who is 3 months pregnant. Occasionally, there is a live-in boyfriend. Jordan does not know his father or have any access to him. He attends a full-day special-needs preschool from 8:00 to 2:00 P.M. Following school, Jordan stays with a baby sitter for 2 hours. Jordan does not have any interaction with other children outside of the school environment. His classroom is the only preschool class in the elementary school, so he does not have the opportunity to interact with same-age peers without disabilities. Jordan's class goes on a field trip once per week. Jordan's mother indicated that away from school they do not go out much because his behavior is too bad.
2. Jordan is essentially nonverbal. He can pronounce five words (lunch, no, yes, dog, and bad). Typically, Jordan communicates using gestures and sounds. He has excellent receptive language abilities. Jordan understands and can follow teacher directions.
3. Jordan learns best verbally. Jordan has some motor planning difficulty, so in the gross motor environment, he has a hard time copying movement; therefore, I provide verbal directions when explaining a skill. Jordan does not respond to visual instruction or visual attempts to reinforce. Jordan works best when given frequent breaks between tasks, especially with nonpreferred activities. Rewards for work completion have been effective from time to time.

Observe the behavior.

1. Jordan receives individual instruction by the adapted physical education specialist in the cafeteria when other students are not present.
2. The behavior occurs during gross motor skill practice in a station format.
3. The behavior may occur when a demand is placed on Jordan, during transitions, and when Jordan does not earn his reward for doing work.

Describe the behavior.

1. Jordan's inappropriate behavior occurs in two stages. It begins with running away from the situation and culminates with hitting, biting, spitting, or destruction of property. The individual outbursts of behavior last about 30 seconds before the teacher can intervene. In a 20-minute session, the behavior can occur at least five times.
2. The intensity of the behavior increases with each succession. The first one or two episodes are mild, and Jordan can be redirected. Jordan tends to increase the intensity of his outbursts until he is out of control and cannot calm himself down.

Describe the result of the behavior.

1. Immediately following the onset of the behavior, I run after Jordan to stop him from going into restricted areas and to maintain his safety. Following the behavior outburst, Jordan is redirected back to his work.
2. If Jordan does complete the assigned task, he can choose to be rolled up in the gymnastic mat or to take a ride on a scooter board. If his behaviors prevent him from completing his work, then he does not earn the reward.
3. The consequences occur immediately. Jordan is reminded that he will not be able to earn his reward immediately after his outburst.
4. Jordan's inappropriate behavior increases as a result of not earning the reward and not being allowed to get what he wants.

Develop a hypothesis.

1. Jordan's behavior probably occurs for two reasons. First, the behavior is attention getting. Jordan craves and seeks attention, especially verbal attention. Unfortunately, he does not care whether the attention is negative or positive. Second, the behavior is a means of escaping an activity in which he does not want to participate. He knows that the teacher's time with him is limited, so if he behaves inappropriately for 15 minutes, there is less time for work.
2. The overall purpose of the behavior is to get out of doing work.
3. No particular antecedents have been identified. His inappropriate behavior occurs across multiple environments and with various staff members.
4. The consequence of not being rewarded causes the behavior to escalate to a point in which Jordan cannot calm himself down or be redirected without direct adult intervention.

Conduct a functional analysis.

1. Attention: Jordan's behavior allows him to receive a lot of individual attention from the teacher that he would not otherwise receive.
2. Escape/Avoidance: The behavior allows Jordan to escape the work he is expected to perform. He enjoys movement play but not structured movement

activities. By behaving inappropriately, he avoids doing any work.

3. Getting something: Jordan does not behave inappropriately in order to get something. He does not receive anything from his behavior with the exception of attention.

4. Self-regulation: Jordan's behavior is disruptive and violent and does not provide self-regulation. Jordan is not a student that needs to perform self-stimulating behavior in order to regulate himself.

5. Play: The observed behavior does not occur for play reasons. The behavior starts out as attention getting, then turns into anger.

Plan the behavior program.

1. Prevention: First, because the behavior begins as running away, Jordan could be moved to a smaller room. Instead of using the cafeteria with wide open spaces, a smaller tutoring room could be used. Second, removing all nonessential equipment from the teaching environment may provide less of a distraction. Third, adding another adult and a peer without a disability may provide more interaction and attention.

2. Teaching: First, use the adult and peer helper to model desirable behavior and reinforce appropriate behavior. Second, review a Social Story (Gray, 1994) before the activity to describe the activity and appropriate behavior for activity. Third, create an activity with clear expectations with starting and stopping times. Fourth, before the activity, have Jordan practice appropriate behavior. Use verbal praise for demonstrating the appropriate behavior. Fifth, use a picture schedule to provide a clear understanding of when Jordan will earn his reward for completing work (e.g., first throw the ball 10 times, then roll up in mat). Sixth, provide a clearly defined area that is blocked off so that Jordan has a harder time running away.

3. Responding:
   a. When Jordan tries to run away, run alongside him and pretend that running was a planned activity, and turn it into a positive form of redirection. Remain quiet; use only gestures, prompts, and visual cues to respond. Jordan loves verbal feedback, so eliminating the verbal feedback may decrease the escalation.
   b. When Jordan tries to hit or kick, sit behind him and hold his hands for 1 minute without talking to him, then redirect him to the task.
   c. Remind Jordan of his reward when he completes his work.
   d. If Jordan tries to destroy pieces of equipment, provide a different piece of equipment to him.

Including Students with Disabilities in General Aquatics Programs

by Martin E. Block and Philip Conatser

Laura's parents want Laura to participate in the 6-week aquatics program for all sixth graders at Raintree Middle School. Laura loves the water, and she and her parents swim every evening in the summer at the public swimming pool. They realize that Laura needs help in the pool, but they have seen how much Laura loves the water. But the aquatics instructors at Raintree Middle are not allowing Laura to participate in the swim program. They say that there are issues with safety and supervision and that they do not have the experience or the adapted equipment needed to help Laura be successful in the program. They also say that they have a very specific aquatics curriculum that includes teaching all of the children basic swimming and survival strokes, and there is no way that Laura could ever learn any of these strokes.

Laura has athetoid cerebral palsy with involvement in all four of her limbs. She cannot walk and needs someone to push her wheelchair. She can say some words, and she understands most things said to her. There is no doubt that Laura's participation in the general middle school aquatics program creates many challenges. But is there a way that Laura could safely and successfully participate in this program? What types of supports, accommodations, and adapted equipment could perhaps change the minds of the instructors? Would it be reasonable for Laura to work on different skills in the water that are more appropriate for her?

Aquatics have long been recognized as a means of developing physical and motor fitness, social skills, and self-esteem in individuals with disabilities (Bull et al., 1985; Christies, 1985; Daniels, 1954; Grosse, 1996; Newman, 1997; Sherrill, 2004; Skinner & Thompson, 1983). Aquatic activities such as swimming provide a form of exercise that is relaxing, socially acceptable, and in the mainstream of society (Broach & Dattilo, 1996; Koury, 1996; Lepore, Gayle, & Stevens, 1998; Morris, 1999). Swimming can be a fun way to improve cardiorespiratory endurance, muscle strength, motor coordination, flexibility, postural stability, and enhance overall physical fitness, locomotor, and object-control skills without putting undue pressure on joints ("Aquatic Sports," 1993; Grosse, 1995, 1996; Horvat & Fobus, 1989; Hutzler, Chacham, Bergman, & Szeinberg, 1997; Reid, 1979). Aquatic activities often increase normal muscle tone through proprioception and sensory stimulation and decrease pain and stereotypic behaviors (Geis, 1975; Horvat, Forbus, & Van Kirk, 1987; Hurley & Turner, 1991; Koury, 1996; Langendorfer, 1986).

Traditionally, swim programs for individuals with disabilities were provided in segregated programs (Conatser et al., 2000; Conatser, Block, & Gansneder, 2002). Also, many aquatic organizations mistakenly believed federal laws mandating equality and inclusion did not apply to them (Berry, 1990; Conatser et al., 2002; Osinski, 1993). In fact, many aquatics programs around the United States continue to offer separate swimming programs for individuals with disabilities (Conatser, 2003; Conatser et al., 2000, 2002). As a result, individuals with disabilities are twice as likely to not participate in aquatics programs (Clair, 2005). However, there is a trend to include individuals with disabilities in community recreation and school-based swim programs (Conatser & Block, 2001; Conatser, 2003). Over time the impact of federal laws, such as the Individuals with Disabilities Education Act (IDEA) and Americans with Disabilities Act (ADA), have heightened awareness among parents and advocacy groups, leading to more inclusive swimming opportunities for individuals with disabilities (Christies, 1985; Grosse, 1995, 1996; Langendorfer, 1990). Today, many individuals with disabilities and their parents are opting for participation in general aquatics programs (American Red Cross, 1992a, 1992b; Bryant & Graham, 1993). This has forced aquatic instructors to rethink their instructional strategies, teaching methods, and use of equipment (Conatser et al., 2000; Osinski, 1993). Conatser et al. (2002) found that increased training improved instructors' attitudes and confidence resulting in students with disabilities being included in general aquatics programs.

The purpose of this chapter is to present information on how to safely and meaningfully include students with disabilities into general swim programs. The chapter focuses on three areas: planning for a general aquatics program that includes students with disabilities, specific instructional and equipment modifications that can be used to facilitate the inclusion of students with disabilities into general aquatics programs, and safety considerations unique to inclusive aquatics programs. Assessment, a critical part of the process, is embedded within each of these key areas.

PLANNING FOR AN INCLUSIVE AQUATICS PROGRAM

As noted in Chapter 4, planning is a multi-step approach that is designed in large part to determine what to teach a student with a disability, how well these unique goals and objectives fit into general physical education, how to teach these goals and objectives, and who should teach these goals and objectives. The following applies the model outlined in Chapter 4 to planning for a student with a disability who will be included in a general aquatics class.

Determining What to Teach

The first step in the planning process is to determine what to teach the students in aquatics. Aquatics goals for students with disabilities can vary from simply tolerating the water to mastering complex strokes. In addition, social and behavioral goals such as interacting with peers, exhibiting appropriate social behaviors, displaying more awareness of peers and surroundings, and improving self-confidence can be embedded within the aquatics venue. Carter, Dolan, and LeConey (1994) grouped goals for students with disabilities who participate in aquatics programs as therapeutic goals, adapted/specialized goals, and mainstream/integrative goals (see Table 12.1). For most students, a combination of therapeutic, adapted, and integrative goals will be most appropriate. For example, Laura might be working on improving ambulation and standing balance (therapeutic), learning how to float on her back and develop a modified back stroke (adapted), and improving her awareness of and trust in peers (integrative). These broad goals can then be written into short-term instructional IEP objectives based on assessment/present level of performance information (see Figure 12.1).

In addition to specific goals selected, the team approach must from the beginning guide the entire aquatics program and keep focused on the specific skills they want the student to master. Assessment information that can help guide this process includes the student's physical, cognitive, and social/emotional strengths and weaknesses; capabilities as they relate to the amount of time the student realistically has to learn to swim; parent and student interests; and what other goals are already in place in the IEP (e.g., motor, language, social) that can be embedded within the aquatics setting (Conatser & Block, 2002).

Table 12.1.   Aquatics goals for students with disabilities

Therapeutic goals
- Improve range of motion
- Improve strength of trunk and/or extremities
- Improve sitting or standing balance
- Reduce muscle contractions
- Improve ambulation
- Improve cardiovascular endurance
- Improve respiratory function
- Improve cognitive functioning, such as problem solving
- Improve posture
- Improve body awareness
- Improve perceptual and spatial awareness

Adapted/specialized goals
- Develop and improve swim skills
- Develop and improve water and personal safety skills
- Improve self-care skills related to swimming, such as dressing
- Improve independence like water entry/exit and ambulation
- Increase social interaction skills
- Improve self-concept

Mainstream/inclusive goals
- Develop age-appropriate social interaction skills
- Develop fitness and physical well-being
- Develop community resource awareness and access
- Create awareness by the community-at-large of swimming abilities of person with disabilities
- Develop friendships among swimmers with and without disabilities

Reprinted from *Designing Instructional Swim Programs for Individuals with Disabilities* (1994), with permission from the American Association for Physical Activity and Recreation (AAPAR/AAHPERD), 1900 Association Drive, Reston, VA 20191, USA.

Long-term goal 1: Laura will improve her ability to stand and walk in the water.

Present level of performance: Laura can stand in 4 feet of water without support for about 10 seconds. She tends to lean back too far, and she does not use any righting or balance responses to keep herself from falling. She can take about three steps in 4 feet of water before she loses her balance. Again, she does not use righting or balance responses to keep herself from falling.

Short-term instructional objectives:
1. Laura will stand in 4 feet of water for 1 minute independently and without any support in three of four trials.
2. Laura will walk in 4 feet of water for 10 feet independently and without any support in three of four trials.

Long-term goal 2: Laura will develop the ability to float and swim on her back.

Present level of performance: Laura lies on her back in the water with a neck flotation device for about 15 seconds before she seems to panic and tries to turn over. She needs to work on extending her arms out to the side and relaxing. When attempting to propel herself, Laura will move her arms, but she does not do a good job of coordinating the left and right side of her body. This causes her to angle off to the side. She also panics after three or four arm strokes and tries to turn over. For Laura to stay on her back is important for several reasons: on her front she drinks the pool's water and cannot breathe; also, being on her back allows for better propulsion through the water.

Short-term instructional objectives:
1. Laura will float on her back independently for 3 minutes while wearing a neck support flotation device without turning for three of four trials.
2. Laura will swim on her back in 4 feet of water using her arms simultaneously to move independently while wearing a neck support flotation device so that she travels a distance of 10 feet for three of four trials.

Long-term goal 3: Laura will improve her awareness of and trust in peers (refer to individualized education program objectives).

Figure 12.1. Sample long-term goals and short-term instructional objectives for Laura, a sixth-grader with cerebral palsy.

Analyzing the General Aquatics Curriculum

Once the team determines long-term goals, evaluates the student on these goals, and then develops short-term instructional objectives, the next step is to determine if the student's individual program matches the general aquatics program. This requires a careful analysis/assessment of the general aquatics program, including an analysis of both the activities that will be presented during the unit and the general format of each class (see Table 12.2).

Instructors could organize a quick and easy-to-read reference that lists the students' objectives, activities and instructional arrangements, and modifi-

cations to instructors' activities and instructional arrangements to accommodate the student with disabilities (see Figure 12.2).

Determining How to Teach Students with Disabilities in General Aquatics Programs

The next step in the planning process is to determine how to teach targeted goals and objectives within the inclusive setting. This includes modifications to the curriculum, instructional modifications, and the use of adapted aquatic equipment.

Table 12.2. Quick modification reference list for lesson plan

Skills	Modifications match general program	Laura's goals
Water entry: dives from side of pool	Partial match	Sits and rolls in with assistance
Water adjustment: rotary breathing	Match	Rotary breathing
Buoyancy and breath control: supine float for 10 minutes	Partial match	Supine floats for 3 minutes without assistance
Locomotion/strokes: front crawl	Partial match	Moves through water with personal flotation device (PFD)
Personal safety: treads water for 5 min.	No match	Walks/moves in shoulder deep water
Game: water tag	Partial match	Uses PFD to be "unfreezer"

Locker room: Change into physical education uniform (approximately 10 minutes)

Laura's teacher assistant or other personnel will help her change into her swimsuit. This is a good time to help Laura work on her self-help skills. Consider allowing her to enter the locker room a few minutes earlier to work on these skills.

Squads/attendance: Students stand in squads in water while attendance is taken (2 minutes)

Good place to work on Laura's objective of standing independently. Also, this is a good place for Laura to show regard and awareness of peers (encourage peers in front and behind Laura to talk to her).

Warm-ups: Students led by instructor in several warm-up activities in the water (10 minutes)

Aquatics instructor and teacher assistant will need to help Laura get into the pool. This is a good time to work on standing and walking balance with Laura's teacher assistant. Also, encourage peers around Laura to say hi to her, and encourage Laura to regard her peers.

Skill focus: Work on specific swim strokes as prescribed each day by instructor (20 minutes)

Laura should work on her walking in the water, floating on her back, and doing her modified back stroke. She will need her neck flotation device for floating and the back stroke. She should be around peers without disabilities as much as safely possible. Encourage peers around Laura to say hi to her, and encourage Laura to regard her peers.

Cool down: Work on relaxing and safety skills (5 minutes)

This is a good place to work on slow movements for all of Laura's extremities to help her relax. Also, this is a good place to work on stand-ing balance. If the class is going to work on rescue techniques (e.g., throwing a rescue line), then Laura could hold onto the rope and help secure the line. Aquatics instructor and teacher assistant will need to help Laura get out of the pool.

Locker room: Shower, grooming, put on street clothes (approximately 10 minutes)

This is a good place to work on dressing and grooming skills. Have Laura stay an extra 10 minutes with teacher assistant to work on these skills.

Travel: bus, vans, or walking (approximately 15 minutes)

This is a good time to work on friendships and fun interactive activities. Laura could play all types of sitting games such as card games or Tic-Tac-Toe with assistance. Although Laura takes longer to dress, other students are equally slow. Therefore, have faster dressers do an activity while waiting.

Figure 12.2.   General daily lesson plans for sixth-grade aquatics work, with notes about Laura.

Curricular Modifications

At this point, you determine which of three curricular modifications can be employed to help students with disabilities work on their objectives within the general aquatics setting. If a student has similar objectives as are found in the general aquatics curriculum but at a different level, then *multilevel curricular selection* is appropriate. Multilevel curricular selection involves all students (including the student with disabilities) working on the same objectives but at different levels of ability. For example, all children in the class might be learning how to float on their backs. However, the student with disabilities needs a flotation device or assistance from a TA or is expected to float for a shorter period of time. Another way to individualize the same objectives for all children is the use of extended skill stations. Children all go the same station to work on the same skill. However, each student works on the skill at his or her own level of ability. For example, all students at a station work on the back crawl kick. But each student works on this same component in one of the following ways:

1. Holds onto kickboard with personal flotation device and tries to kick

2. Holds onto kickboard with personal flotation device and kicks using good form

3. Holds onto kickboard without personal flotation device and kicks using good form for 5 yards

4. Holds onto kickboard and kicks using good form for 25 yards

5. Without kickboard, kicks using good form for 5 yards

6. Kick for 25 yards

7. Incorporates arms and legs when kicking

Another multilevel curricular selection technique that can be used in the water is cooperative learning. Cooperative learning involves a group of students with different abilities working together to accomplish a team goal (Johnson & Johnson, 1989). For example, the aquatics instructor sets a team goal of continuous treading for 10 minutes. Because every person in this beginning-level team of five can only tread water for 1-3 minutes, each person will have to take a turn to achieve the team goal. Jonathan goes first and treads water for 1:30. When he says he needs to stop, Jamisha takes over and treads water for 2:30. When she gets tired, Jo (a girl with cerebral palsy) takes her turn and treads water with the aid of floaties around her arms for 1:30. Next comes Felipé who treads water for 2:00, and finally Kara (the strongest swimmer in the group) who treads water for 3:00. The team works together to accomplish a goal that none could do independently.

Yet another way to use multilevel curricular selection is to teach by invitation (Mosston & Ashworth, 2002). In this technique, the teacher invites but does not demand that students perform gradually more difficult movements. By allowing students some choices, children who are delayed can still participate successfully with the group. For example, a teacher asks the students to try and swim across the pool using an elementary backstroke. The next lap, the teacher invites children to either continue the elementary backstroke or try any other stroke. This allows the student who does not feel comfortable with or cannot accomplish the regular back crawl to still be successful.

Many children with significant disabilities will have IEP objectives that are different from objectives in the general aquatics curriculum. In such cases, the student can still be included in the general aquatics program. However, this student will work on unique aquatics objectives while other students work on their general aquatics objectives. For example, a general seventh-grade aquatics class is working on increasing endurance in selected strokes (swimming 50 yards or more with any stroke). Included in this class is William, a student with Duchenne muscular dystrophy. William is in the pool primarily to relax his muscles, practice standing (which he cannot do on land), and to enjoy the water and his peers. William is at the end of the pool working on standing and stretching with the aid of his physical therapist. When a peer swims by him, he needs to move (walk) so that he does not interfere with this student. In addition, William is able to see the large clock at the end of the pool, and he calls out lap times to two students who are using the same lanes as him. In this way, William is part of the group and has an opportunity to interact and help his peers.

Cooperative learning can also allow you to overlap two different curricular areas. In this form of cooperative learning, the student with disabilities helps the team by working on his or her own objectives. For example, students are placed in groups of five, with each group working on different objectives. The group goal is to get 50 points, and each member of the team can get 10 points for meeting their own, unique objective as follows:

• Student 1: Elementary backstroke for 160 yards

• Student 2: Sculling on back 30 yards

• Student 3: Back crawl 50 yards

• Student 4: Diving off diving board

• Student 5 (William): Walking 5 yards in the pool

Yet another way to overlap curricular areas is to give the student with a disability a special job within the activity that matches his or her objectives. For example, William can be the permanent "unfreezer" in a game of water freeze tag. When a student gets tagged and is frozen, William has to walk over to the student and unfreeze him or her by tapping on the back. Thus, students work on their swimming and William works on walking in a fun, interactive way.

In very unique cases, a student with a disability might not be allowed to swim. This student still can be part of the group through curricular overlapping. For example an eleventh grader is just returning from school after a year of rehabilitation following a car accident. Because of decubitus ulcers (pressure or body sores from lying or sitting down too long), his doctor has recommended that he not swim. In order to work on his goal of continuing to improve upper body range of motion as well as grasping and releasing, this student throws sponges into the pool with the help of his nurse-assistant; the other students retrieve the sponges, taking them across the pool using whatever stroke they want. The student gets to interact with peers and work on his unique goals.

Sometimes it is impossible to overlap two different curricular areas. In such cases, the student with disabilities might work on *alternative activities* either in the water or on the pool deck. To make this alternative activity inclusive, the teacher can rotate peers without disabilities into this alternative activity. For example, the aquatics instructor might have two stations set up. One station is lap swimming, and the other is treading water. At the treading water station the student with disabilities is working on stretching on his back with the help of his adapted physical education instructor. By having the students without disabilities in the same area as the student with disabilities, there are more opportunities for interactions between students with and without disabilities. Similarly, a student might not be allowed to swim, so she is on the pool deck working on bowling. Peers who have finished their laps and are resting can help set up pins and take turns bowling too.

Instructional Modifications

Chapter 6 reviews several different instructional modifications that should be considered when including students with disabilities into general physical education. These modifications, with some slight adaptation, are relevant when including students with disabilities into general aquatics programs. For example, the class format (whole group, small groups, stations, peer buddies) can have a profound impact on the how well students with disabilities follow directions and behave in the pool. Similarly, the level of methodology (verbal cues, demonstrations, physical prompts) will affect how well a student with cognitive or sensory disabilities will understand instructions. Table 12.3 highlights some points within each of these categories as they relate to aquatics.

Equipment and Task Modifications

Equipment and task modifications can make a big difference in the success of a child with disabilities in a general aquatics program (Conatser & Block, 2002; Coelho & Fielitz, 2003). The addition of personal flotation devices, kickboards, mats, and other equipment allows a student with disabilities to participate in the same activities as their peers (Stopka, 2001a). For example, allowing a child to use arm floaties for safety and for confidence may allow a child with severe intellectual disabilities to feel comfortable swimming a length of the pool independently. In addition, pool toys can be used as motivators for students (Stopka, 2001c). For example, a child with autism is initially fearful of the pool. This student can be encouraged to stand in the shallow end of the pool for 1–2 minutes while he hits a balloon in the air using his hand.

Many different types of equipment modifications can be used. The key is to find out the student's strengths and weaknesses before determining what equipment might be necessary (Stopka, 2001b). For example, a child with good endurance and strength who has a visual impairment might need equipment that cues her to her location in the pool and warn when she is getting close to the end of the pool. Similarly, a student who is working on walking in the pool can use the side rail for balance. Table 12.4 presents various types of impairments along with suggested equipment and task modifications. Table 12.5 presents other considerations regarding equipment and the pool environment.

Prepare General Aquatics Instructor

Most experts support the notion that the aquatics instructor is a key factor to a successful inclusive swim program (Conatser et al., 2000; Reid, 1979; Weiss, & Karper, 1980). Unfortunately, many aquatic instructors have limited training and experience teaching students with disabilities (American Red Cross, 1992b; Conatser et al., 2000, 2002). Insufficient training of aquatic staff and aquatic instructors who lack experience and specific instruction in conducting integrated aquatic programs are major

Table 12.3. Accommodations to how information is presented

Instructional factor	General considerations	Modifications for Laura
Teaching style	Command, problem-solving, discover	Use command
Teaching methodology	Verbal cues, demos., physical assist	Verbal, pictures, physical assistance
Student's communication	Verbal, sign, pictures, interpreter	Verbal, pictures
Starting/stopping signals	Whistle, hand signals, physical assist	Verbal
Time of day	Morning, before lunch, afternoon	Morning—she often sleeps in p.m.
Duration	Student on task	Short, many tasks
Order of learning	What is the best order of learning	Likes routine, start with familiar activity first
Size/nature of group	Small/large group	Small group if possible
Group instruction	Station/whole class/peer tutoring	Peer tutoring utilizing TA
Instructional setting	Indoor or outdoor pool	Indoor with warm water
Eliminating distractions	Equipment, lighting, people	Laura likes to play with flotation devices
Providing structure	Organization of instruction	N/A
Level of difficulty	Complexity or instruction	Simple, skill need to be broken down, have a peer or a TA assist
Level of motivation	Use extra reinforcers if needed	Needs extra verbal reinforcement; loves hugs in the water

Table 12.4. Sample task/equipment modifications

Students with limited strength

- Use Velcro (e.g., on a glove and on a bat).
- Provide equipment of different sizes, weight, length, shapes, and texture.
- Offer flotation devices if student does not have enough strength to keep himself afloat.
- Use switches.

Students with limited speed or endurance

- Create special zones in tag games or make game area smaller.
- Shorten distances for swimming.
- Allow more rest periods for some students.
- In relay or tag games, have typical students put constraints on their ability (e.g., swim using only one side of their body).
- In relay races or tag games, have typical students perform a more difficult skill (butterfly stroke) or slower stroke (breaststroke).

Students with limited balance or coordination

- Provide physical assistance.
- Use different types of flotation devices that are more or less buoyant.
- Use several flotation devices at once.
- Use different water levels (waist deep, chest deep, shoulder deep).
- Allow student to hold on to lane dividers or edge of pool when doing activities.

Table 12.5. Preparing equipment and the pool environment for inclusion

- Send checklists home the day before swimming to remind parents to send a towel, swim suit, and, if needed, plastic pants, ear plugs, and goggles. Remember, some students with disabilities will need to wear plastic pants or eye protection because of bladder inconsistency or hypersensitive eyes.
- Instructors should only be in 80-degree water temperature for 5 hours at a time and in 90-degree water temperature for 3 hours at a time.
- Provide towels.
- Make sure personal flotation devices (Type I, II, or III) fit the student properly (i.e., straps should not leave impression on skin more than few minutes after release) and do not impede the student's swimming mechanics.
- Keep swimming/lap pool water temperature at 76–78 degrees; for water aerobics keep at 85–87 degrees, and therapy pools at 90–94 degrees. Most students with disabilities will prefer warmer water because of circulation problems, lack of intense exertion, and/or respiratory problems. The one exception is students with multiple sclerosis who usually prefer cooler water.
- The air temperature in the pool area and changing room should be 3 degrees above that of the water temperature.
- If the water temperature is unpleasant and uncontrollable, keep the swim session short.
- Post visible signs indicating where the changing room is and where to enter and exit the pool. Further, place students' names on lockers for easy identification.
- Use slip-resistant surfaces in high-traffic areas.
- Develop and implement regular inspection and maintenance schedules for all equipment.

reasons why these types of programs fail (Conatser et al., 2002; Lepore, Gayle, & Stevens, 1998; Priest, 1979). In addition, lack of training and experience leads to unfavorable beliefs and lower confidence in working with individuals with disabilities in general swim programs (Conatser et al., 2001). Therefore, a big part of making an inclusive swimming program successful is the training, experience, and beliefs of the aquatics instructor (Conatser et al., 2000, 2001, 2002; Lepore et al., 1998).

The most important thing to help general aquatics instructors feel more comfortable with an inclusive aquatics program is to arm them with information. Aquatics instructors need information about the student with disabilities, what the student should be working on, who (if anyone) will be available for support, what they can expect regarding behaviors, how to communicate with the student, adapted equipment needs, and inclusion strategies (Conatser & Block, 2002)

For example, Jamal, a child with autism is going to be included in a general aquatics class. The aquatics instructor is apprehensive about communicating with this student and has concerns about safety in the locker room and in the pool. The team invites the aquatics instructor to three short (15-minute) introductory training sessions during the week of in-services before the school year starts (the art teacher,

physical educator, and music teacher are part of this training as well). Team members first explain to the aquatics instructor that Jamal's teacher assistant will be assisting Jamal with aquatics on Monday and Friday; his physical therapist will be assisting on Wednesday. Team members are careful to explain to the aquatics instructor that he is still responsible for helping decide what to teach Jamal, helping reinforce Jamal, deciding what equipment Jamal might need to be successful, devising safety plans, and encouraging interactions between Jamal his classmates. Team members then share a short video that shows how they present information to Jamal using a picture schedule. They note that they will create a picture schedule for the aquatics instructor and show him how to use it. Finally, they talk about Jamal's behaviors and how to deal with them.

The more information an aquatics instructor has, the more competent he or she will feel about working with students with disabilities (Conatser et al., 2001). However, overwhelming the aquatics instructor with reams and reams of paper will not work. Face-to-face meetings over a period of several days with a variety of team members is the best way to present information (Conatser, 2004). In addition, demonstrating and then physically assisting the aquatics instructor in working, communicating, lifting, and transferring a student with disabilities will help instructors feel more confident (Conatser, 2001). Finally, providing ongoing support is critical for the success of the student and the comfort level of the aquatics instructor (Conatser, 2004). Team members should be prepared to visit with and help the aquatics instructor and the student with disabilities several times during the first part of the unit to make sure the aquatics instructor is teaching correctly and feels comfortable with the student (see Chapter 4 for more information on training general physical educators for inclusion).

Prepare Students without Disabilities

Without a doubt, students without disabilities will notice differences in appearance and/or behavior of students with disabilities who are included in their general aquatics program. As noted in Chapter 9, helping students without disabilities accept, interact with, and befriend peers with disabilities can go a long way in making the aquatics experience successful for the student with disabilities. Students without disabilities could benefit from knowing why the student with a disability looks and behaves the way he or she does, why he or she is in their class, and what they can do to help this student and make his or her experience as positive as possible. This information can be provided through a relatively informal, 10-minute chat with the classmates before the child joins the class. Figure 12.3 presents an outline of this type of discussion for a student with autism who was included in a seventh-grade aquatics class.

Other activities that can help classmates accept peers with disabilities include the following: talk about students with disabilities in general and how swimming can be an important fitness and leisure activity for them, role-play various types of disabilities in the water such as trying to swim with your eyes closed or with your legs tied together, invite guest speakers with disabilities to your class who have used swimming to help them in some way (e.g., a person with intellectual disabilities who has won gold medals in swimming at Special Olympics), show videos of elite swimmers with disabilities such as highlights from the Paralympics, talk specifically about the student who will be coming to the class (focus on abilities rather than just disabilities) and ways to support the student in the pool and locker room. Simply do whatever you can to help peers without disabilities feel comfortable with the stu-

---

Jerry is 12 years old, and he just transferred here from a special school for students with autism. He is in Mr. Johnson's homeroom, so some of you may see him in the morning. Has anyone seen or met Jerry yet? Why does Jerry look and act the way he does?

Jerry has autism. Has anyone heard of that term before or know anyone who has autism? Autism basically affects the way Jerry learns and deals with his environment. For example, Jerry does not like loud noises. He gets really upset when the fire alarm sounds or when the bell rings between classes. Jerry also does not like change. He may have a difficult time at first in the aquatics unit because he was used to going to the gym and playing basketball. It will take him a few days to adjust to the new setting and new routine. Jerry also does not talk very well, nor does he understand a lot of what you say. You can still talk to him, just talk slow and use short sentences. Jerry does best when you show him what you want. Finally, Jerry gets confused easily and doesn't always know what to do. His way of coping with this is to withdraw; sometimes he makes strange sounds or does strange things with his arms and hands. Jerry will not harm you, and he really likes being around kids his own age. Does anyone have any questions?

Jerry is the same age as you, and his parents and teachers thought that Jerry would enjoy swimming and would benefit from being around other students his age. His parents in particular were hoping that some of you would help Jerry and try to be his friend. Do some of you think you can help Jerry and try and be his friend?

Even though Jerry comes to aquatics with Mrs. Kelly, his teacher assistant, we need everyone to watch out for Jerry. Mrs. Kelly and I are here to help Jerry, but it would be great if you would help him, too. What are some things you think you can do to help Jerry? Sometimes he does not know where he is supposed to go, so you can tell him or show him where to go. If he seems confused about what he is supposed to do, you can repeat my directions but in a simpler way. If he begins to get anxious and make strange sounds and movements, simply go up to him and tell him to stop. This usually works. Remember to go up to him whenever you can and talk to him, be his friend, include him in activities and conversations, and try to make him feel comfortable and part of the group. If you ever have any questions, just ask me or Mrs. Kelly.

Figure 12.3. Sample discussion to help prepare peers without disabilities.

Including Students in General Aquatics Programs

dent with disabilities and willing to help and befriend this student.

Prepare Support Personnel

Many students with severe disabilities attend aquatics class with a teacher assistant or other support person (e.g., peer tutor, community volunteer). These support persons are committed to helping the students with disabilities, yet they often have no formal training or experience working with students with disabilities in aquatics. Thus, these support persons typically have no idea what they should be doing. Obviously, such a situation prevents the students from learning targeted objectives and can be dangerous, depending on the activity. For example, a student with cerebral palsy may need help getting into the pool, and she might do best with a particular flotation device and certain types of physical assistance. Clearly, training of support personnel is a critical part of the inclusion process.

Training of support persons for assisting a student with disabilities in aquatics should be an ongoing responsibility of all team members. This training should focus on both general information about their role as a support person, specific information about the student they will be working with, and how they will facilitate the integration of the stu-

dent into the general aquatics program (Conatser, 2004). Table 12.6 presents specific suggestions regarding information to present to support staff. Note how much information the aquatics instructor can (and should) contribute to the training of the support personnel.

OTHER CONSIDERATIONS FOR INCLUSION IN AQUATICS

Lifting, Transferring, and Positioning

It is beyond the scope of this chapter to detail all of the various ways to lift, transfer, and position students with disabilities in the pool environment. Readers are referred to Lepore et al. (1998) and Carter et al. (1994) for more information on lifting and transferring in aquatics. Still, there are some general things to consider when lifting, transferring, and positioning students with physical disabilities in the pool area. Pool lifts, portable or stationary ramps, railing systems or two- to four-man lifts are all appropriate ways for students with disabilities to enter and exit the water. The exact type of lift will depend on the student's abilities and disabilities. Consult the

Table 12.6. Preparing support personnel for aquatics

Information	Team member who can provide info
General information (perhaps in the form of a brochure or handout) regarding their role as a support person and what is expected of them	Aquatics instructor, APE specialist
Information regarding the philosophy of the aquatics program and the general goals that this student might work on during aquatics (i.e., opportunities to interact with typical peers, improved social behavior, improved communication skills, improved independence in a variety of functional skills)	Aquatics instructor, APE specialist, special education teacher
Resources and key personnel who they can go to with questions or if they need help (e.g., go to the aquatics instructor or adapted physical educator if they have questions about modifying specific aquatics activities, go to the physical therapist if they have specific questions about positioning or contraindicated activities)	APE specialist, special education teacher, physical therapist (PT)
Detailed description of student including IEP objectives related to aquatics, medical/health concerns, unique behaviors, likes and dislikes, who special friends are.	APE specialist, special education teacher, parents
Specific information regarding safety/emergency procedures for the pool area (e.g., what to do if a student has a seizure or an asthma attack; make sure particular students warm-up properly)	Aquatics instructor, APE specialist, nurse, parents
Specific information regarding what typically happens in aquatics including daily routines, rules and regulations, typical teaching procedures, measurement and record keeping procedures.	Aquatics instructor, APE specialist
General suggestions for modifying activities and use of adapted equipment	Aquatics instructor, APE specialist, PT
Alternative activities when general aquatics activities are deemed inappropriate (e.g., when kids are working on diving, student can work on entering and exiting the pool with assistance)	Aquatics instructor, APE specialist
Suggestions for facilitating interactions with typical peers	APE specialist, special education teacher, parents

Table 12.7.　Considerations for lifting students

- Student's weight (heavier students may need two people or a mechanical lift)
- If student has seizures, what are the triggers?
- If student has primitive reflexes, are they stimulated by vestibular movement or tactile pressure?
- Does the student have any joint deformities or limited range of motion requiring unusual grip placement?
- Is student's motor control and strength limited?
- Always bend from the legs when picking up a student (do not bend at the waist); never lift and twist at the same time.
- Lift the student completely out of his or her chair before turning; turn by walking using your feet rather than twisting using your back.
- Make sure wheelchair brakes are locked and/or electric wheelchair is turned off.
- Make sure student's straps are off and out of the way before lifting begins, and make sure straps are reattached when returning student to the chair.
- Have a mat or comfortable place for the student to lay or sit.

student's physical therapist, adapted physical education teacher, or adapted aquatics instructor for the most appropriate ways to lift and transfer a student. Inappropriate techniques can frighten or injure the student or the instructor. Table 12.7 provides general guidelines for lifting and transferring in the pool.

Safety Considerations

The aquatic environment possesses many serious hazards (Almquist, 2001; Sawyer, 2001). Because constantly wet floors increase the danger of falling and being submerged under water any extended length of time could cause brain damage, aquatic instructors need to be constantly on guard. "Pool hazards exist in any aquatics programs, but are a greater risk for some individuals with disabilities. The person's

Table 12.8.　Safety guidelines and considerations for aquatics

- Always obtain signed parent's/guardian's permission report, which should include student's personal and medical characteristics.
- Have a signed eligibility report by a licensed physician. The report should include type of impairment, precautions, restrictions, and recommendations.
- Before the student comes to the pool, make sure all necessary paperwork is properly processed.
- Keep effective incident report documents.
- Use only lifeguards, instructors, and aquatics administrators with sufficient supervisory skills and current credentials and certifications appropriate to their area of responsibility.
- Conduct on-site in-services for aquatics staff regularly and include knowledge of specific students with disabilities that will be using the facility and specific problems that might be associated with that population (Conatser, 2004).
    - *Lifeguards*: Lifeguard Training, CPR, Standard First Aid, and on-site in-service
    - *Aquatics instructors*: Water Safety Instructor certification, lifeguard training, CPR training, standard first aid training, on-site in-service
    - *Aquatics administrators*: Water Safety Instructor certification or Lifeguard Training Instructor, CPR training, standard first aid training, pool operator training or additional experience/training, good personal attributes and management skills
- Never under any circumstances leave individuals with disabilities unattended in or around a pool.
- The instructor/student ratio for testing should be 1 to 3 with severe disabilities and 4 to 6 with mild disabilities. Factors that can influence this ratio are the students' age and their physical, cognitive, and social skills. In addition, the instructor or teacher assistant's competence, confidence, and attitude toward inclusion will contribute to the size and ratio of the class.
- Be aware of and clearly post pool's emergency plan, first aid equipment, rescue equipment, and phone.

- Before entering the pool area, all rules should be explained clearly to the student. Rules need to be explained at the student's level (e.g., pictures, demonstration, sign-language).
    - Rules often include no diving, running, horseplay, climbing on benches or railing, etc. All rules should be posted in clearly defined spaces (e.g., locker room, pool entrances/exits, around the deck).
- Try to keep the floors of all decks, ramps, and changing areas dry and free of objects.
- Store unused equipment that could become a hazard around the pool.
- Glass or breakable items should be prohibited in the aquatic area.
- Scum gutters collect the pool's unwanted bacteria and items, so encourage swimmers to avoid them.
- Keep environmental noise to a minimum around the pool.
- Wheelchairs should be locked or turned off if electric and stored out of the way when not in use.
- Clearly mark varying water depths in the pool, steps, slides, diving areas, ramps, and lifts.
- Clearly mark rules and safety procedures for pool equipment and paraphernalia.
- During cold weather allow students ample time to dry completely before exiting the facility.
- Make provision if the pool is outside, (sun-screen, shade, clothing, etc.).
- Know your local weather conditions and have alternative plans if needed.
- Develop, use and maintain a comprehensive reevaluation plan of every aspect of your facility (i.e., equipment, personal, instruction, and safety).
- Always shower after being in the pool and use plenty of lotion for yourself and the student's skin and wash hair with a pH-balanced shampoo.
- To avoid "swimmer's ear," use rubbing alcohol on a cotton swab to clean the ear.

vision, balance, sense of direction, concept of space, perception of space and distance, and muscular control should all be considered." (Red Cross, 1992a). For example, a teacher assistant was helping Josh (a student with autism) dress in the locker room. The teacher assistant turned his back on Josh for a second, and Josh, now fully dressed, ran out of the locker room and jumped into the pool!

Most aquatics instructors are already very aware of safety issues for their general education students. However, they have to be even more aware of potential risks, safety precautions, and emergency techniques when students with disabilities are included in their general aquatics classes. Readers are encouraged to review Chapter 10 carefully. In addition, Table 12.8 provides some other safety guidelines with specific reference to aquatics.

In some cases it may be contraindicated for students with disabilities to participate in swimming programs. Some situations in which a student with or without a disability should not be allowed in the pool include contact precautions (e.g., bacterial infections), open or oozing wounds, conjunctivitis (pink eye), ringworm, lice, menses without protection. Other students with disabilities, while allowed in the pool, have medical equipment that may require special precautions. Talk with the student's physician, physical therapist, parent, or other knowledgeable person about any precautions. Some examples include staples or stitches, nasogastric, PEG or any indwelling tube, bowel and bladder incontinence, tracheotomies, fluctuating blood pressure, healing wounds that are uncovered, limited respiratory function, cardiac insufficiencies, and seizures.

Some students with disabilities (e.g., cerebral palsy, spinal injury, traumatic brain injury, multiple sclerosis, spina bifida) have problems feeling pressure or pain, and/or adjusting to extreme hot or cold water. Extra caution needs to be given to cuts, bruises, scrapes, and overexertion in hot water or prolonged periods in cold water. The body can lose or gain temperature 10 times faster than in air.

Practical Steps to Comply with the Americans with Disabilities Act of 1990

- Ask the special education teacher, APE teacher, teacher assistant, medical professionals, parents, or the student with a disability what modification would improve the facility's accessibility as required by the Americans with Disabilities Act of 1990 (Osinski, 1993). Maintain open collaboration between all individuals involved with continued reevaluation and monitoring of the environment. Remember that different disabilities require different modifications.

- Review current programs and protocols and see if these policies or practices are discriminatory.

- Use in-service training to facilitate a positive inclusive program.

- Review safety considerations and emergency procedures to ensure that individuals with disabilities can take part safely and are warned of the inherent risks of the activity.

SUMMARY

Aquatics programs are beneficial to people with disabilities in many ways. Because of federal laws and advocacy groups, more people with disabilities are participating in inclusive swim programs. Therefore, instructors need to stay abreast of current trends and techniques. The methods and examples given throughout this chapter will help facilitate a successful inclusive aquatics program. Inclusion strategies help aquatics instructors individualize instruction that benefits all students.

CHAPTER 13

Including Students with Disabilities in General Community Recreation Programs

Meghan is a 6-year-old girl who wants to play softball just like her big sister. However, Meghan has spina bifida, a congenital condition that has left her paralyzed from the waist down. She uses a wheelchair and is very skilled in her wheelchair. Meghan also has become very skilled at throwing, catching, and hitting a ball off of a tee with the help of her big sister. There is a Little League T-ball league in her community; there also is a Challenger Baseball league (just for children with disabilities) in her community. Which program should Meghan choose? Can the regular Little League T-ball league refuse to allow Meghan to play because she uses a wheelchair?

Randy is an 18-year-old boy who attends Southern Curry High School. Randy is a popular student at Southern who helps at the concession stand at football games in the fall, attends every home boys and girls basketball game in the winter, and is the manager of the boys baseball team in the spring. Randy loves sports, and he would love to develop the skills needed to participate in a lifetime leisure sport. However, Randy has intellectual disabilities, and he has a very difficult time understanding rules and strategies of most team sports. He also has some difficulties with eye-hand co-ordination, especially trying to hit a moving ball or catching a moving ball. He is in good physical shape and can walk pretty much forever (he is often seen walking to and from town even though he lives 5 miles from the nearest shopping center). Randy's parents are willing to help Randy find a sport or physical activity that Randy enjoys and can do for the rest of his life. What would be a good community-based lifetime leisure sport for Randy?

Many children such as Meghan want to play little league sports in the community. Others such as Randy reach an age when participation in community recreation is more appropriate than school physical education. There are many reasons why children with disabilities should participate in extracurricular recreational pursuits (see Schleien, et al., 1995; Schleien, Ray, & Green, 1997; and Smith et al., 2005, for more detailed review of studies).

1. Participation in leisure activities is related to increases in skills in other curricular areas. For example, research shows that problem-solving skills, personal-social behavior, gross and fine motor skills, and even reading comprehension and mathematics improve when students participate in leisure skills (Voeltz & Apffel, 1981; Wehman & Schleien, 1981). It has been suggested that students with disabilities are more receptive to instruction in these areas when participating in an enjoyable leisure activity (Wehman & Schleien, 1981).

2. An increase in appropriate play and leisure skills leads to decreases in inappropriate behavior. It is thought that unstructured "down time" may lead to boredom, which in turn can lead to students with disabilities engaging in self-stimulatory behaviors, excess behaviors (e.g., overeating), acting out behaviors, and even self-injurious behaviors. However, constructive use of leisure time has been shown to decrease such negative behaviors when implemented as part of a positive behavioral support program (Gaylord-Ross, 1980; Meyer & Evans, 1989; Schleien, Kiernan, & Wehman, 1981).

3. Constructive use of leisure time also is related to success in living in the community. Again,

down time leads to boredom and dissatisfaction with one's placement in the community. Parents often report that they are unhappy how their child uses his or her leisure time when living in an independent or supported community living arrangement, noting that their child seems to need constant supervision and cannot "entertain him or herself" (Katz & Yekutiel, 1974). Teaching students with disabilities to fill their leisure time with appropriate, active recreation pursuits can help them feel more positive about their lives in the community and also reduce the need for such supervision (Schleien, Ray, & Green, 1997).

4. Finally, having a repertoire of enjoyable leisure activities is essential for quality of life (Sylvester, Voelkl, & Ellis, 2001). For many people the most satisfying and enjoyable part of the day is recreation time, including after-school clubs or athletic programs, on the weekends playing tennis or golf or going hiking with friends, or in the evening relaxing, working out, or taking the dog for a walk. People who do not have enjoyable leisure activities to fill their free time (whether with or without disabilities) are more likely to become bored, lonely, and depressed (Schleien et al., 1995). Thus, it is important to teach students with disabilities appropriate recreation and leisure skills so they can use their leisure time in a satisfying, fulfilling way.

Unfortunately, there are several reasons why there are few opportunities for students with disabilities to participate in active community recreation programs. The following highlights some of these problems:

1. Students with disabilities often lack the physical and/or cognitive skills needed to participate in regular community sports programs (Schleien, et al., 1995; Smith et al., 2005). For example, while Meghan is very skilled in moving her wheelchair, the wheelchair itself may make it difficult for her to play a sport like youth soccer. First, the game is played on the grass, and it is difficult to move a wheelchair on the grass. Second, many parents and coaches may feel that a wheelchair is unsafe in an environment like competitive soccer. And Randy, with all his love and enthusiasm for sports, does not have the motor skills, speed, or understanding of sports such as basketball or soccer to be successful.

2. There tends to be an emphasis on specialized leisure programs and environments. Many communities offer regular sports programs for very skilled athletes and special sports programs for individuals with disabilities (e.g., Special Olympics). Unfortunately, communities rarely offer something in between that allows less skilled individuals without disabilities and individuals with disabilities to par-

ticipate together (Schleien et al., 1995). In other words, if one cannot play regular five-on-five basketball at a high level but does not want to be in a wheelchair league, then there may be no other options to play basketball in the community.

3. Recreation activities that are age-appropriate tend to be passive. This is particularly true for older students with severe disabilities. For example, a preschooler with a severe disability can play with a stuffed animal or color with crayons. However, such activities are inappropriate for high school students with disabilities. But popular recreation activities for older students with disabilities, such as playing simple card games, watching TV, listening to the radio, or looking through magazines do not promote physical activity.

4. Physical education programs—particularly middle and high school programs—often emphasize non-lifetime sports such as football, soccer, and basketball. These sports require a high level of skill to be successful in community-based programs, and they are not readily available for young adults in most communities. Sports that would be more beneficial to students with disabilities across the lifespan include bowling, tennis, golf, hiking, and weight training.

5. Special education teachers are not familiar with or not comfortable with more active recreation programs. Most special educators do not have training in active recreation and sports programs. For example, most special educators feel uncomfortable trying to teach students with disabilities the skills necessary to play basketball or golf. As a result, most special education teachers do not offer such active recreation and sports programs unless they have an interest or skill in one of these recreation or sports activities.

6. Participation in community recreation and sports programs require money, transportation, and specialized equipment (Rimmer, Rubin, & Braddock, 2000). For example, purchasing golf clubs, getting to the golf course, and then paying for green fees can be very expensive, especially for an adult with a disability who is making minimum wage. In addition, participants with disabilities may not have the necessary support groups (e.g., peers, parents, co-workers) who are interested in participating in active community recreation and sports programs (Davis & Sherrill, 2004; Krueger, DiRocco, & Felix, 2000).

Given the importance of recreation and leisure in the lives of individuals with disabilities coupled with the problems with access to community recreation programs, the purpose of this chapter is to discuss ways to make community recreation and sport programs available to students with disabilities. The first part of this chapter reviews the Americans with Disabilities Act (ADA) of 1990 with specific examples of how the law provides access to recreation programs for individuals with disabilities. The second part of this chapter outlines a model for creating and implementing a community-based recreation program for individuals with disabilities. And finally, the chapter concludes with a review of several community sports programs that have been designed for individuals with disabilities.

LAWS REGARDING PARTICIPATION IN COMMUNITY SPORTS PROGRAMS

On July 26, 1990, President George H.W. Bush signed into law the Americans with Disabilities Act (ADA; PL 101-336), arguably the most extensive civil rights legislation since the Civil Rights Act of 1964. ADA was designed to prevent people with disabilities from being treated differently solely because of their disability and eliminate the discrimination of individuals with disabilities from participating in all aspects of life that most of us consider basic rights of being an American (Imber & Van Geel, 2001; U.S. Department of Justice, 2001, 2002). The law protects individuals with disabilities in a wide range of public and private services such as education, transportation, housing, employment, and recreation (Carpenter, 2000; Epstein, McGovern, & Moon, 1994; Fried, 2005; Sullivan, Lantz, & Zirkel, 2000). Although not specified in the Act, sports and recreation activities and facilities are covered under ADA (Block, 1995).

It is important to note that ADA was not designed to be an affirmative action program. There are no quotas stating that a certain amount of one's employees or club members must have disability. Rather, it assures equality of opportunity and full participation. As such, the law prohibits persons with disabilities from being excluded from jobs, services, activities, or benefits based solely on their disability (Stein, 1993; U.S. Department of Justice, 2002). For example, it would be a violation of the ADA to tell a child with intellectual disabilities that he could not play Little League Baseball.

Who Is Protected?

The ADA does not identify specific disabilities. Rather, the ADA provides the following general description of who is covered: an otherwise qualified individual who 1) has a physical or mental impairment that substantially limits one or more of the major life activities of the individual (i.e., seeing, hearing, speaking, walking, breathing, performing manual tasks, learning, caring for oneself, and working), 2) has a record of such an impairment (e.g., a person who is recovering from cancer, mental illness, or an alcohol problem), or 3) is regarded as having such an impairment (e.g., limits major life activities as the result of negative attitudes of others toward the disabilities such as severe burns, HIV/AIDS, epilepsy, facial abnormalities, or alcoholism) (U.S. Department of Justice, 2001, 2002). Individuals with minor conditions that can be corrected, for example with glasses or hearing aids, are generally not covered in the act. Similarly, conditions that affect a person for a short period of time (e.g., sprain, broken limb, or the flu) are not considered "disabling conditions" under this act (U.S. Department of Justice, 2002).

ADA regulations are waived for an individual who is a direct threat to the health or safety of others that cannot be alleviated by appropriate modifications or aids (Appenzeller, 2000, 2005; Block, 1995; Imber & Van Geel, 2001). Three criteria must be met before one can exclude a person based on health and/or safety factors: 1) the threat must be real, 2) the threat should be based on objective and unbiased information, and 3) attempts must be made to reduce or eliminate the risk (Appenzeller, 2000, 2005). For example, a community soccer league would not have to accept a player with severe autism who has a well-documented history of unpredictable, violent behavior when placed in a group setting. However, the league would have to accept a player with HIV/AIDS whom a doctor has determined not to be dangerous to others if those around this individual take universal precautions when handling blood.

Note that a student with a disability cannot be denied participation in an activity because someone feels the activity is too dangerous for that student. It is the right of all Americans to choose activities including those that involve a certain level of risk (Block, 1995). While recreation program staff can tell a student about the risks involved in a particular activity, in the end it is the student's decision (with consult from the student's parents and physician) whether or not to participate in a recreation program (Block, 2005).

The ADA is divided into five major titles: Employment, Public Service, Public Accommodations, Telecommunications, and Other Provisions (U.S. Department of Justice, 2001, 2002). Title III—Public Accommodations—includes recreation. According to Title III, it is illegal to discriminate against a person with disabilities by denying them full and equal enjoyment of goods, services, facilities, privileges, advantages, or accommodations that are available to the general public. This includes hotels, restaurants, banks, business offices, convention centers, retail stores, libraries, schools, and recreation facilities. For example, a county recreation program must make sure that all facilities it uses are accessible to individuals who use wheelchairs. Similarly, a local basketball league must make sure it does not have any policies or practices that discriminate against individuals with disabilities.

Reasonable Accommodation and Undue Hardship

Two important parts of the ADA are reasonable accommodations and undue hardships. The ADA defines a reasonable accommodation as an adaptation to a program, facility, or workplace that allows an individual with a disability to participate in the program or service or perform a job. Accommodations also may consist of changes in policies, practices, or services and the use of auxiliary aids (Carpenter, 2000; Imber & Van Geel, 2001). Examples of reasonable accommodations include qualified interpreters for the deaf in a community soccer league, bowling guide rails at a local bowling alley, and flotation devices at a community swimming pool. Reasonable accommodations also can include making a facility more accessible, adding more staff, and providing extra staff training. Note that these accommodations should not fundamentally alter the nature of the activity, give the participant with a disability an unfair advantage, or cause undue hardship to the recreation program (Block, 1995; Paciorek & Jones, 2001; Stein, 2005).

Undue hardship refers to actions that are considered significantly difficult, costly, extensive, substantial, disruptive, or that fundamentally alter the nature of the program. Factors to be considered include the following: nature and cost of the accommodation, overall financial resources of the facility including number of persons employed, and type of operation of covered entity, including the composition, structure, and function of work force (U.S. Department of Justice, 2002). For example, it may be an undue hardship (significantly expensive, fundamentally alter the activity) for a golf course to make all its sand traps and greens accessible to people who use wheelchairs. It would be reasonable (known as "readily achievable" according to ADA) to allow this golfer to use a regular golf cart to get around the course and facilities, allow the golfer to hit from the golf cart, allow the golfer some rule modifications such as free lift from the sand trap, and allow the golfer to use a special golf cart that does not damage the greens. Determining what is an undue hardship

or what fundamentally alters the nature of a game can be very tricky. This concept was the heart of *Casey Martin v. the PGA*. Casey Martin argued that riding a golf cart would not fundamentally alter the game of golf, while the PGA felt that walking was fundamental to competitive golf and would give Casey an advantage. The Supreme Court ruled in favor of Casey Martin (Lane, 2001; Paciorek & Jones, 2001).

What Must Recreation Programs Do to Meet the Mandate of ADA?

The following sections, modified from Block (1995) highlight key things community recreation programs must do to meet the mandate of ADA.

Opportunity to Participate

Publicly or privately controlled recreation facilities that are open to the general public must provide people with disabilities the opportunity to participate in their general recreation programs that have no other criteria (e.g., no skill criteria). For example, a local soccer league accepts all soccer players who live in the county, meet an age level criteria, and pay the entrance fee. This soccer league could not deny a child who is blind the chance to participate in this league. In addition, the league would have to allow reasonable accommodations (e.g., allowing the child's dad to assist him during practices and during the game). Even recreation programs that have special skill criteria (e.g., travel soccer team) must provide an opportunity for individuals with disabilities to try out or qualify for a place on the team.

Even if a specialized recreation program is offered in a particular community or by a particular agency, the community recreation program still must provide opportunity for an individual with a disability to participate in their regular programs. For example, a community might offer Special Olympics soccer. Nevertheless, an individual with intellectual disabilities may choose to participate in the community-based soccer program rather than Special Olympics.

Facilities

Publicly or privately owned recreation programs that are open to the general public must make facilities accessible to individuals with disabilities if such accommodations are readily achievable and do not cause an undue hardship (Fried, 2005; Paciorek & Jones, 2001). In most cases, reasonable accommodations mean that a portion of existing facilities needs to be made accessible. For example, it would be reasonable to have one "handicap accessible" stall in the bathroom rather than changing all the stalls. Similarly, one or two soccer fields in a multi-field complex should be accessible to individuals who use wheelchairs (see Fried, 2005, for simple, inexpensive ways to modify facilities to meet the mandate of the ADA). Note that any structure built after 1993 must be fully accessible to individuals with disabilities. ADA regulations contain a wide range of relatively moderate measures that may be taken to remove barriers including installing ramps, making curb cuts, repositioning shelves, rearranging tables, repositioning telephones, adding Braille markings on doorways and elevators, and creating designated parking spaces (Fried, 2005; U.S. Department of Justice, 2002).

Transportation

Publicly or privately sponsored programs that are open to the general public must make transportation and telecommunications available to individuals with disabilities if such services are provided to individuals without disabilities. Vehicles with a seating capacity of 16 passengers or less do not necessarily have to be accessible for individuals with disabilities, but at least one vehicle within the fleet must be accessible. All vehicles with a seating capacity in excess of 16 passengers must be accessible (U.S. Department of Justice, 2002). Again, reasonable accommodations for a smaller recreation program with one bus might be as simple as hiring a special lift bus for a participant who uses a wheelchair rather than making expensive alterations to their bus.

IMPLEMENTATION PROCESS FOR INCLUSIVE, COMMUNITY-BASED RECREATION PROGRAMS

Chapter 4 outlines a systematic process for developing and implementing an inclusive physical education program for children with disabilities. A similar model was suggested by Wagner and her colleagues (1994) (see Table 13.1). The following section details the key steps and components of this model.

Step 1: Initial Contact and Registration Process

Assessing the Student's Interests

The first step in the process is identifying the recreational activity and then assisting the student and/or the student's parents in signing up for the program. Wagner et al. (1994) suggested that the first

Table 13.1. Implementation process for inclusive recreation

Step 1: Initial contact, data gathering, and registration process
Step 2: Accommodations
Step 3: Training
Step 4: Participation
Step 5: Follow-up
Step 6: Evaluation
Step 7: Documentation of progress

From Wagner, G., Wetherald, L., & Wilson, B. (1994). A model for making county and municipal recreation department programs inclusive. In M.S. Moon (Ed.), *Making school and community recreation fun for everyone: Places and ways to integrate* (pp. 182). Baltimore: Paul H. Brookes Publishing Co.; adapted by permission.

component of this step is to assess the student's interests in various community-based recreation programs. When possible, simply ask the student what types of recreation programs he or she enjoys. For example, one student might talk at length about basketball, while another student might express an interest in hiking, roller blading, or weight lifting. Figure 13.1 provides an example of a leisure interest survey that can be used to determine a student's leisure interests (Schleien, Green, & Ray, 1997).

When a student cannot clearly articulate his or her interests, various recreation activities can be presented to the student. The student then could be observed participating in the activity to gauge his or her reaction and interest when participating in these activities.

For example, a physical education teacher is trying to decide what community-based recreation activities might be of interest to a student who has autism who is moving from middle to high school. This physical educator knows from reports from the middle school physical educator and other members of the student's IEP team (including the student's parents) that the student does not like being in crowds or in places where there are loud noises. The student also likes routines and repetitive activities. However, even with this knowledge, the IEP team does not know what recreation activities are available in the community or what recreation activities might be of interest to the student. The high school physical educator decides to spend the first several weeks of the semester assisting the student in sampling various appropriate recreation activities in the community. This includes taking the student to the tennis courts to try to hit tennis balls off a tee or with a gentle toss, to an open field to hit golf balls (similar to hitting balls at a driving range), to shoot baskets on the playground (student could shoot baskets by himself or with a roommate in the driveway of his group home), riding a stationary bike and weight lifting in the school's weight room (similar to a weight room available in the community), and hiking through the woods that surround the school

Leisure Activity Selection Checklist

Date: _____

Name: _____

Age: _____ Sex: _____ Telephone: _____

Address: _____

Activity	Currently do	Interested in	Activity	Currently do	Interested in
Team sports			**Individual sports** (continued)		
Bowling	___	___	Archery	___	___
Softball	___	___	Swimming	___	___
Basketball	___	___	Golf	___	___
Soccer	___	___	Badminton	___	___
Tee ball	___	___	Horseback riding	___	___
Football	___	___	Fishing	___	___
Hockey	___	___	Bike riding	___	___
Other (specify) _____	___	___	Walking	___	___
Music			Other (specify) _____	___	___
Singing	___	___	**Arts and crafts**		
Playing instruments	___	___	Painting	___	___
Attending concerts			Knitting	___	___
Other (specify) _____	___	___	Crocheting	___	___
Dance			Latch hook	___	___
Folk	___	___	Ceramics	___	___
Modern	___	___	Other (specify) _____	___	___
Square	___	___	**Table games**		
Aerobic	___	___	Cards	___	___
Tap	___	___	Checkers	___	___
Ballet	___	___	Chess	___	___
Jazz	___	___	Dominoes	___	___
Other (specify) _____	___	___	Scrabble	___	___
Individual sports			Puzzles	___	___
Gymnastics	___	___	Billiards	___	___
Jogging/running	___	___	Table tennis	___	___
Tennis	___	___	Other (specify) _____	___	___

Figure 13.1. Leisure interest survey. (From Schleien, S.J., Ray, M.T., & Green F.P. [1997]. Community recreation and people with disabilities: Strategies for inclusion [2nd ed., pp. 224–225]. Baltimore: Paul H. Brookes Publishing Co., adapted by permission.)

Activity	Currently do	Interested in
Outdoor leisure/social		
Hiking	_____	_____
Gardening	_____	_____
Camping	_____	_____
Barbeques/picnics	_____	_____
Skiing	_____	_____
Canoeing	_____	_____
Other (specify) _____	_____	_____
Day trips		
Historical	_____	_____
Cultural	_____	_____
Sporting	_____	_____
Shopping/restaurants	_____	_____
Other (specify) _____	_____	_____
Social clubs		
Scouts	_____	_____
Photography	_____	_____
Travel	_____	_____
Gourmet cooking	_____	_____
Card playing	_____	_____
Other (specify) _____	_____	_____

My leisure experiences usually are:

_____ Physical	_____ Individual	_____ Structured
_____ Active	_____ Planned	_____ Expensive
_____ Mental	_____ Social	_____ Nonstructured
_____ Passive	_____ Long term	_____ Spontaneous
_____ Inexpensive		

With whom do you usually engage in leisure experiences?

_____ Alone	_____ A friend(s)
_____ Family member(s)	

During what time of day do you participate in leisure activities?

_____ Morning	_____ Afternoon
_____ Evening	

Do any of the following prevent you from participating in leisure activities?

_____ Financial difficulties	_____ Lack of transportation
_____ Facility not accessible	_____ No one to participate with
_____ Geographic location	_____ Disability/lack of skill
_____ No motivation	_____ Child care problems
_____ Other (specify) _____	

_____

Please check any special needs or considerations that may affect your participation.

_____ Physical

_____ Mental

_____ Social

_____ Other (specify) _____

_____

Would you be interested in serving as a member of a community leisure advisory board on recreation for people with disabilities?   _____ yes   _____ no

Would you attend an open organizational meeting to assist us in planning leisure services for people with disabilities in your community?   _____ yes   _____ no

(similar to hiking trails available in the community). Some activities were never even considered because of this student's unique characteristics. These included bowling (environment tends to be very loud), Special Olympics sports (all sports, even individual sports, are practiced and competed with many other participants), skating and swimming (not available in the community), and basketball, soccer, softball, and volleyball (too unpredictable and too many participants).

Assessing Parent Interests

In addition to the student's interests, it also is important to determine parents' recreation interests. Parents tend to have the greatest influence on the type of recreation activities their children participate in as well as whether their children participate in segregated or inclusive recreation programs (Modell & Imwold, 1998). Parents also can promote recreation programming for their child as well as advocate for recreation programs in their community (Heyne & Schleien, 1997). Therefore, determining parents' recreational interests is an important part of the process.

Other Factors to Consider

In addition to student and parent interests, choosing an activity also depends on what recreation activities are popular with similar age peers without disabilities and what recreation activities are readily available in the community. For example, it does not make sense to teach a student to play golf if his parents, siblings, and peers have no interest in golf. Similarly, it does not make sense to teach a student how to roller skate if no one in the community roller skates. And finally, it does not make sense to teach a student to ice skate or snow ski if such activities are not available in the community (see Chapter 4 for more detail on selecting an activity).

Still, an activity that is readily available in the community may be inappropriate for a particular student. For example, even though soccer is popular and readily available in a particular community, and even though a student loves soccer, soccer may be beyond the abilities of a child with severe cerebral palsy. Or, even though a child expresses an interest in playing golf in the community, the IEP team may decide that the cost of golf is too expensive when compared with how much this student makes in his part-time job and how much he receives in Supplemental Security Income (SSI). However, the IEP team should be careful when dismissing recreation programs that are available in the community. Although the student with cerebral palsy cannot play soccer in the community, he may enjoy and get exercise benefits from kicking a ball around with his friends at his group home or with his parents after school. While golfing at a golf course is expensive, hitting plastic golf balls in the backyard is very inexpensive yet enjoyable for a particular student and his peers. The IEP team should think creatively how a student who really loves a particular recreation activity can participate in that activity. See Figure 13.2 for factors to consider when selecting a recreation activity (Schleien, Meyer, Heyne, & Brandt, 1995).

Step 2: Identify a Suitable Program

With an appropriate recreation activity selected, the next step is to identify suitable programs in the community. The key to finding a suitable recreation program is to determine the student's abilities in the targeted recreation activity, the student's interest in participating in an inclusive program or a special program, how flexible the community program is regarding accepting and perhaps modifying the program to include a student with a disability, and cost (how expensive) and transportation (how far) factors related to the program (see Figure 13.2 [Schleien, Meyer, & Heyne, 1995] and Part I-A of Figure 13.3).

Finding suitable recreation programs will most likely be easier in larger communities. Many larger communities will offer a variety of programs at many different levels ranging from high-level teams that compete nationally to recreation leagues where participants play for fun. In addition, these communities may offer different levels of Special Olympics softball for people with intellectual disabilities (from highly competitive, integrated team play to individual skill competitions), beep baseball for people with visual impairments, and Challenger Baseball for children with varying disabilities. In such communities it would be easy to find a match for a student with almost any type of disability who really wants to play softball. Smaller communities, however, may only offer fairly high-level softball team play with no lower-level recreation softball programs or special softball/baseball programs. This makes finding a suitable program more challenging.

One solution is to create lower-level recreation programs or special programs in smaller communities in order to provide the necessary program for students with disabilities. For example, three rural counties can come together to create the first Tri-County Softball League (TCSL). The TCSL is designed for people interested in playing recreation softball with a focus on having fun rather than winning and losing. Each county by itself does not have enough interest to create a recreation league. However, by pooling all interested participants across the three counties, a six-team league is created. Because this is a recreation program, the teams accept players

Leisure Activity Selection Checklist

Participant: _____   Date: _____

Completed by: _____

For each activity, circle *yes* or *no* for each criterion. Tally the number of *yes* responses for each of these subsections and record them on the appropriate line. Tally the overall score for each activity. Activities that receive a score of 11–14 points are generally considered appropriate for instruction.

Lifestyle: Select activities that are socially valid and will facilitate typical play and leisure behaviors, as well as provide opportunities for increasingly complex interactions.

	Activity 1	Activity 2	Activity 3
1. *Age appropriateness:* Is this activity something a peer without disability would enjoy during free time?	yes no	yes no	yes no
2. *Attraction:* Is this activity likely to promote the interest of others who frequently are found in the participant's leisure-time environments?	yes no	yes no	yes no
3. *Environment flexibility:* Can this activity be used in a variety of potential leisure-time situations on an individual and group basis?	yes no	yes no	yes no
4. *Degree of supervision:* Can the activity be used under varying degrees of caregiver supervision without major modifications?	yes no	yes no	yes no
5. *Longitudinal application:* Is the activity appropriate for both an adolescent and an adult?	yes no	yes no	yes no

Individualization: Issues related to logistical and physical demands of leisure activities on current and future environments and free-time situations

	Activity 1	Activity 2	Activity 3
1. *Skill level flexibility:* Can the activity be adapted for low- to high-entry skill levels without major modifications?	yes no	yes no	yes no
2. *Prosthetic capabilities:* Can the activity be adapted to various disabilities?	yes no	yes no	yes no
3. *Reinforcement power:* Is the activity sufficiently novel or stimulating to maintain interest?	yes no	yes no	yes no
4. *Preference:* Is the participant likely to prefer and enjoy the activity?	yes no	yes no	yes no

Environmental: Challenges and accommodations to leisure activities related specifically to the individual so that he or she can be successful in current or future free-time situations

	Activity 1	Activity 2	Activity 3
1. *Availability:* Is the activity available (or can it easily be made so) across the participant's leisure environments?	yes no	yes no	yes no
2. *Durability:* Is the activity likely to last without need for major repair or replacement of parts for at least a year?	yes no	yes no	yes no
3. *Safety:* Is the activity safe (i.e., would not pose a serious threat to harm the participant, others, or the environment if abused or used inappropriately)?	yes no	yes no	yes no
4. *Noxiousness:* Is the activity not likely to be overly noxious (noisy, space consuming, distracting) to others in the participant's leisure environments?	yes no	yes no	yes no
5. *Expense:* Is the cost of the activity reasonable?	yes no	yes no	yes no

Scores

	Activity 1	Activity 2	Activity 3
1. Lifestyle	_____	_____	_____
2. Individualization	_____	_____	_____
3. Environmental	_____	_____	_____
TOTAL ACTIVITY SCORES	_____	_____	_____

A Teacher's Guide to Including Students with Disabilities in General Physical Education, Third Edition,
by Martin E. Block. Copyright © 2007 by Paul H. Brookes Publishing Co., Inc. All rights reserved.

Figure 13.2. Leisure activity selection checklist. (From Schleien, S.J., Meyer, L.H., Heyne, L.A., & Brandt, B.B. [1995]. Lifelong leisure and lifestyles for persons with developmental disabilities [p. 245]. Baltimore: Paul H. Brookes Publishing Co.; adapted by permission.)

I. **SKILL SELECTION CONSIDERATIONS/FACILITY DESCRIPTION**

   A. **Appropriateness of leisure skill facility**
1. Is skill or facility selected appropriate for individuals without disabilities of the same chronological age?
2. Has the individual with disabilities previously acquired any skills related to the activity?
3. If the particular responses would be difficult to perform, are material/procedural adaptations available to enhance participation?
4. Does the individual with disabilities have access to the facility or materials (e.g., distance from home, transportation concerns)?
5. Is the cost prohibitive? Are there other resources to help pay for the cost of the facility (e.g., reduced fee, waived fee, sponsorship)?
6. Has the individual with disabilities expressed interest in this particular activity?

   B. **Description of leisure skills: environmental inventory/discrepancy analysis**
1. See Figure A13.1 in the appendix at the end of this chapter.

   C. **Description of leisure facility or environment**
1. Provide a general description of leisure facility or environment.
2. Conditions under which the participant will be required to participate and interact (who else will be there, noise level, other distractions, etc.)?
3. Provide a diagram of facility or environment.

   D. **Description of social environment**
1. What social interactions with peers, supervisors, and others are required in the immediate environment?
2. What is the typical dress for the environment?

II. **ANALYSIS OF COMPONENT SKILLS AND ADAPTATIONS FOR FULL/PARTIAL PARTICIPATION**

   A. **List of required equipment and materials**
1. Provide a detailed listing (and description, as needed) of all the equipment and materials that a person may come in contact with in the environment.

   B. **Physical considerations: gross motor, fine motor, fitness**
Describe each motor response using the following as a guideline:
1. Number and complexity of coordinated movement patterns?
2. What strength is required to perform the activity or to manipulate materials?
3. What body positions and flexibility are required to perform the activity?
4. What speed is required to perform the activity?
5. What levels of endurance are required to perform the activity?
6. What are the minimal health conditions necessary to participate in the activity?

   C. **Perceptual considerations: visual, auditory, body awareness**
1. What visual skills (including discrimination) are needed in the environment and in the activity?
2. What auditory skills (including discrimination) are needed in the environment and in the activity?
3. What body awareness skills are needed in the environment and in the activity?

   D. **Interpersonal interaction considerations: exchange between participants**
1. What typical types of interactions occur in the environment (e.g., turn taking, cooperating, unstructured)?
2. What optional interactions might you expect (e.g., getting a drink)?
3. What are the language requirements in the environment? (List typical nouns, verbs, cues, and statements used in activity.)

   E. **Functional academics: reading, writing, math/scoring, time telling**
1. What reading skills are needed? Can they be bypassed with modifications?
2. What writing skills are needed? Can they be bypassed with modifications?
3. What math skills are needed? Can they be bypassed with modifications?
4. What time telling skills are needed? Can they be bypassed with modifications?

   F. **Decisions/judgments necessary for successful participation**
1. What time and situation judgments may have to be made by the person with a disability to successfully participate in the leisure activity?

   G. **Specific adaptations/adjustments needed for partial participation**
When making suggestions for adaptations, keep the following in mind:
1. Whenever possible, activities should not be altered to make the individual stand out.
2. Whenever possible, adaptations should be considered temporary.
3. Adaptations should be made on an individual basis (as opposed to making modifications for the entire group when only one person needs modification).

III. **ANALYSIS OF SUPPORTIVE SKILLS**

   A. **Preparation prior to participation in leisure activity**
1. Can the student prepare him- or herself for participation (e.g., choose appropriate clothes; eat appropriately; bring correct amount of money; bring ID card, towel, and lock)? If not, who will assist student in preparation?

   B. **Transportation**
1. What mode of transportation will be used?
2. Does the student have the mobility skills needed to independently use this type of transportation? If not, who will assist student?

   C. **Informed consent**
1. Has the student and/or parent/guardian signed consent form for participation in program?
2. Does student have insurance?

Figure 13.3.   Outline for developing a community-referenced leisure skill inventory. (From Certo, N.J., Schleien, S.J., & Hunter, D. [1983]. An ecological assessment inventory to facilitate community recreation participation by severely disabled individuals. *Therapeutic Recreation Journal, 17*[3], 29-38.)

of all abilities (including players with disabilities), and the league is willing to be flexible in rules (e.g., allowing players to hit a ball off a tee) to ensure the success and fun of all participants.

Observe Community Programs

With a recreation program identified, the next component in Step 1 is to observe the community program. This observation can be conducted by staff at the student's school or by the student's parents. Whenever possible, the student should observe the program to further validate his or her interest in the particular program. For example, tee-ball is targeted for a bright 6-year-old girl with cerebral palsy (she uses crutches to aid her when she walks). She loves to play catch with her dad and older sister, and she loves to hit a ball off a tee. However, when she goes with her dad and sister to watch a tee-ball game, she quickly realizes that there is a lot of standing and waiting. She observes that most children only get two or three turns to hit a ball off a tee during the entire game (she gets to hit 20–30 balls off a tee in 15 minutes when playing with her dad and sister in her backyard). She also observes that most children never get to touch the ball, let alone throw it during the game (again, playing with her dad and sister she gets lots of turns to throw). So, after watching tee-ball a few times she decides that she does not want to play. Instead, she expresses interest in wheelchair tennis. She has seen wheelchair tennis when watching the Paralympics on TV, and she thinks she could really enjoy that sport. She also saw how some wheelchair tennis players practiced and played with able-bodied peers, and one girl even played on her high school tennis team. She decides that she would like to check out what tennis programs are available in her community.

Discuss Client with Staff

After observing the program, the next component in Step 1 is to discuss the student with the staff of the recreation program. It would be unfair to the staff and to the student to simply have the student show up the first day to the program without giving the staff a "heads up" and some training. At this step in the process, you simply want to inform the staff of the recreation program that a student with a disability is interested in participating in the program. Then, after providing some general information about the student and his or her disabilities, allow the staff to ask questions. The staff may need several days to generate questions about the student.

For example, a 14-year-old student who uses a wheelchair may want to join a local health club. The student's parents arrange a meeting with one of the managers of the health club to introduce and discuss the student's abilities and needs. When asked if she

had any questions, the manager simply said no. However, after talking to other managers of the club, she e-mailed the student's mom with several questions.

Help Register the Participant

The last component of Step 1 is to help register the participant for the program. When appropriate, the participant should register him- or herself. However, even participants who can register themselves may need help reading over the registration materials and contracts. For example, health clubs are notorious for getting people to sign up for upgraded or lengthy contracts. The participant may benefit from help in navigating the various options offered by the health club (full club membership versus the weight and cardio rooms) and the length of the contract ($300 for a 1-year membership when paid up front versus $20 per month for a 3-year contract). This may be a place to negotiate a reduced fee for participants with low income. For example, a student with autism plans on going to driving range and hitting a bucket of golf balls twice each week (the driving range is an easy bus ride from his parent's house). It costs $5 for a bucket of balls, which totals $40 per month. The student's mother explains that while this is not much for most people, this is a significant expense for this student (he does not have a job, he is not yet eligible for SSI, and his mom is a single parent who does not have a lot of extra money). The driving range is pretty quiet between 3:00 and 4:00 (the time when this student plans on going to the range), and the manager realizes that this student will be a consistent client throughout the year. He is willing to reduce the cost to $2.50 per bucket.

Step 2: Data Gathering

The next step in the process is to prepare the student and his or her parents for participation in the program. This step involves sitting down with the family and discussing the student's participation in the program. This is a chance for the student and his or her parents to ask questions about participation. Table 13.2 presents several questions that parents/students might ask regarding participation in community recreation programs.

Step 3: Accommodations

Step 3 focuses on determining specific accommodations the student needs to successfully and safely participate in the community recreation program. Hopefully, potential accommodations were discussed with the manager or leader of the recreation program earlier in the process. For example, it would not make sense at this point in the process to spring the idea of not allowing defensive players to steal the

Table 13.2. Questions parents ask about community recreation programs

What children and/or adults participate in this program (e.g., novice, recreation level, competitive, very skilled)?

Where is the program located?

How much will the program cost?

What equipment or clothing will I need?

What transportation will be provided to the program, or do parents provide transportation?

When and how many times per week does the program take place?

Are any of the student's friends or classmates participating in this program?

What safety precautions and emergency plans are in place in the event the student has a medical problem (see Chapter 10)?

How did the staff at the program react to having a student with a disability in the program?

How will the staff and other participants be prepared for this student?

What accommodations are anticipated to allow for the student's safe, successful, and meaningful participation in the program?

ball from a child with intellectual disabilities and allowing him free shots in a basketball game. What if the league commissioner says these types of accommodations would fundamentally alter the game? Therefore, while specific accommodations are created at this point in the process, a preliminary discussion of accommodations needs to be discussed earlier in the process.

Determining specific accommodations to a recreational program should follow a systematic process. Certo, Schleien, and Hunter (1983) created a model for analyzing the various aspects of a recreation program in order to determine the need for specific accommodations (see Figure 13.3). The focus of this model starts with an ecological inventory with a discrepancy analysis (see Figure 4.8 in Chapter 4 and Figure A13.1 in the appendix at the end of this chapter). This allows the physical educator and the community recreation provider an opportunity to analyze all the steps of the program and then determine specific accommodations a student needs to be successful. For example, there are several important activities related to the subenvironment of "driving range shop" (see Figure 13.4).

While this student can do many of the activities in the subenvironment independently, the ones that require communication and waiting require some accommodations. With the help of this student's speech therapist and special education teacher, it is decided that relatively simple accommodations (including having the counter worker do some simple prompting, substituting a written note for speaking) can help this student become independent in this subenvironment.

Other areas that should be carefully analyzed to determine the need for any accommodations include gross and fine motor skills (types and complexity of coordinated movements), fitness requirements (minimal strength, endurance, and flexibility required to participate in the activity), perceptual requirements (any visual, auditory, or body awareness skills that are needed for the activity), interpersonal skills and appropriate behavior/etiquette (turn taking, typical interactions, language requirements), functional academics (any reading, writing, math, or time telling skills needed for the activity), financial assistance (cost of program, equipment, and transportation), and transportation (how will student get to and from recreation program) (Certo et al., 1983) (see Figure 13.3 for more detail).

Step 4: Training

Training staff is the last step before the student is included in the community recreation program. This is a critical yet often-missing step in the process. Without proper training, staff who take the student to the recreation program as well as the staff who work at the recreation program will not be able to facilitate meaningful inclusion. In addition, training prevents the staff from making assumptions about the participant based on the participant's label (Fink, 2001). For example, a 16-year-old girl with Down syndrome's recreation program involves going to a local health club to lift weights and walk on a treadmill. The program has been carefully planned with several modifications to help the student be successful. Unfortunately, no one has prepared the teacher assistant who will take the student to this health club. The assistant struggles to figure out how to help this student independently check in to the health club and change in the locker room, so she ends up doing much more for the student than is necessary. Staff at the health club assume that strenuous activities are probably dangerous for people "like her" and choose to restrict the student from using the elliptical trainer or using the free weights and only allowing this girl to walk slowly on the treadmill. The teacher assistant does not know how to help the student use the weight machines, so the student does not do any weight lifting. As a result, this student rides a sta-

Subenvironment: Driving range clubhouse

Name: __Bart Atkins__   Date of birth: __March 26, 1989__

Evaluator: __Martin Block__   Date: __September 7, 2006__

Activities	Assistance currently needed	Accommodations
1. Opens door to club house	I	None needed
2. Walks to counter	I	None needed
3. Waits turn (if necessary)	V	Counter worker knows to tell person to wait
4. Asks counter worker for a medium bucket of balls to hit	V	A child has a card that says he wants to hit a medium bucket of balls
5. Waits for response by counter worker	I	None needed
6. Takes money out of wallet	V	Cue by counter worker
7. Gives counter worker money for bucket	I	None needed
8. Waits for change (if necessary)	V	Cue by counter worker
9. Waits for bucket	V	Cue by counter worker
10. Takes bucket and thanks counter worker	I	None needed
11. Takes bucket and walks to door	I	None needed
12. Opens door and walks out of club house	I	None needed

Figure 13.4.   Sample of ecological inventory for hitting a bucket of golf balls. (*Key:* I, independent; V, verbal cues or reminder; P, physical assistance.)

tionary bike (something she does not like to do) and then sits in the health club café, drinking a cola and eating a bagel.

Clearly, training is a critical final step but it does not have to be a particularly difficult step. The person accompanying the student to the recreation facility should be trained on the following information: the goal of the program, the student's particular abilities/needs, any medical or behavioral issues and programs, how to teach skills (e.g., verbal cues versus demonstrations versus physical assistance as well as how to teach specific parts of a motor skill or how to use equipment), how to collect data, and how and who to ask for help. This training should be a collaborative effort conducted by the special education teacher (behaviors, how to teach the student in general), therapists (communication, physical considerations and contraindications, safety), and the physical educator (how to teach specific sport skills, rules of the game, social etiquette of the game).

Training the staff at the recreation facility (e.g., league commissioners, coaches, staff at recreation centers) should include the following information: goals of the program (why is this student in your recreation program), background on the student's abilities/disabilities and how these have been accommodated, medical/health problems and emergency plans (if needed), student's social and behavioral skills and problems, what behaviors you might see from the student and what tends to set the student off, and how the staff at the recreation program can prevent behavioral problems, importance of facilitating social interactions between the student and other participants and how such interactions

can be facilitated, and how they can help the student be successful in the program.

Step 5: Participation

The student is now ready to be included in the recreation program. All the pre-planning involved in Steps 1–4 has increased the odds that the student will have a successful experience in the program. However, things do not always go smoothly, especially the first few sessions. First, the student may be apprehensive of the new facility, new people, and new expectations (even adults without disabilities get a little anxious when starting a new recreation program). However, with time, support, and successful experiences, most students settle into a routine and enjoy the program. Second, the staff (both those who assist the student and those associated with the recreation program) need time to learn about the student and how best to help the student have a successful experience. Again, time and continued support from the IEP team (parents, teachers, therapists) will help the staff successfully include the student into the program.

An important part of this step is to collect ongoing data to determine how well the student is doing in the program. How does the student seem to be enjoying him- or herself? How are the student's behaviors? Is the student interacting with peers? How successful is the student in the program? How are coaches and recreation staff feeling about the student's inclusion? Any anticipated adjustments to the program to make the student more successful?

These questions can be answered with simple checklists created by the student's IEP team.

For financial and transportation reasons, it will be difficult to take a student to community recreation programs more than once per week. Nevertheless, the student needs a great deal of practice if he or she is going to acquire key skills needed to be successful in the community recreation program. Creating a simulated environment back at school can help the student acquire these key skills. Although not the same as practicing at the community recreation facility, practicing key parts of the activity in a simulated setting such as the school gymnasium can help the student be more successful when the student actually goes to the community facility. For example, the physical educator can set up a driving range on a grassy area behind the school, a bowling alley in the gymnasium, and a health club in the school's weight room. Key motor skills such as placing the ball on the tee and then hitting the ball, walking up to the foul line and rolling the ball, and properly using weight lifting equipment can be practiced and mastered in these simulated settings. Whenever possible, this simulated setting should mirror the community-based setting as much as possible. For example, the bowling setting in the gymnasium should include chairs to sit on to wait one's turn, a place to retrieve the ball from the ball return, a second lane next to the student's lane (with other students bowling), and a foul line. This way skills learned in the practice sessions in the simulated settings will have the greatest opportunity to transfer to the community-based setting.

Step 6: Follow-Up

The student has now begun to participate in the program. Hopefully, the pre-participation process has created a setting that has allowed the student to have a meaningful and successful community recreation experience. To be sure everything is going as planned, it is important to follow up with the staff who are implementing the program, the student, and the staff at the community recreation facility. This can be an e-mail or telephone call, or it can involve a face-to-face meeting. The important point is to not assume that the program is being implemented as planned and the student is successful. So many things (anticipated and unanticipated) can derail a well-planned community recreation program. For example, a student who initially expressed interest in working out at a health club finds the targeted club too busy and noisy at the times he planned on working out. As a result, the student does not work out at the club as planned. Or, a golfer from the community (retired person) who said he would be a golfing buddy to a student with a disability (play 9 holes of golf once per week) suddenly is too busy to play more than once per month. Without the support of this buddy (transportation, helping the student check in at the club house, help the student on the golf course), this student is unable to play golf.

Follow-up discussions or meetings can lead to solutions and get the student's recreation program back on track. These follow-up discussions can include discussions of the student's success and how the student feels about the program, problems that have arisen and potential solutions to any problems, or adjustments to the program to make it even more successful. Again, these discussions can be as simple as a telephone call or e-mail. However, a visit to observe the student participating in the activity at the recreation facility is the best way to truly find out how the student is doing. And as noted, these discussions should include the staff or volunteers implementing the program, the student, and the staff at the community recreation program.

Step 7: Evaluation

Toward the end of the program, it is important to conduct a formal evaluation of the program. This allows the staff who implemented the program, the student (when appropriate), and the staff at the community recreation program to reflect on what went well in the program, what did not go so well in the program, and recommendations to improve the program for the next time they implement a similar program for this student or other students with disabilities. This evaluation can be a written survey with open-ended questions, a more detailed written survey with several yes/no questions about the program, or a face-to-face interview. Figure 13.5 provides an example of a simple participant satisfaction survey that can be administered to a student with a disability after completion of the program.

It is important that this step is completed in order to get a fair evaluation of the program and to make improvements for future programming. Too often, community recreation programs are implemented, but no one takes the time to conduct an end-of-program analysis. The staff and the student may know whether the program was successful, but without a formal evaluation, no one may know why the program was or was not a success. For example, a student indicates on the Participant Satisfaction Survey that she does not plan to play youth soccer in the spring. Clearly something about the program must have had a negative effect on this student. But

Participant Satisfaction Survey

Name: _____

Support staff: _____

Name of activity: _____ Date: _____

1. Was the recreation facilitator helpful in finding activities in which you were interested? ____ yes ____ no

2. Did you get a chance to express your preferences before activities were identified for you? ____ yes ____ no

3. Did you enjoy the activity/program in which you participated? ____ yes ____ no

4. Was the recreation facilitator helpful in assisting you to participate in the activity to your fullest ability? ____ yes ____ no

5. Did you make any new friends while participating in the program? ____ yes ____ no

6. Did you develop any new interests as a result of participating in the program? ____ yes ____ no

7. Were the other participants and program staff/volunteers friendly and helpful? ____ yes ____ no

8. Will you continue to participate in this activity or another similar one? ____ yes ____ no

9. Would you like more support in participating in this or another similar activity? ____ yes ____ no

Recommendations/comments: _____

_____

_____

_____

_____

_____

_____

Figure 13.5. Participant satisfaction survey. (From Moon, M.S., Stierer, C.L., Brown, P.J., Hart, D., Komissar, C., & Friedlander, R. [1994]. Strategies for successful inclusion in recreation programs. In M.S. Moon [Ed.], *Making school and community recreation fun for everyone: Places and ways to integrate* (pp. 33–53). Baltimore: Paul H. Brookes Publishing Co.; reprinted by permission.)

the staff that helped implement the program as well as the program staff (the coach) did not sense any problems. However, after answering questions on a post-participation survey, they realized that the child really did not interact with peers that much. In fact, they now recall that interactions with peers—while pretty good at the beginning of the program—were almost nonexistent at the last few games. By looking at the student's satisfaction with the program as well as helping the staff analyze the program, the team was able to pinpoint what went wrong toward the end of the program. They now realize that the discussion they presented to the other players on the team at the beginning of the soccer season (who the child was, how to interact with her, the importance of making her feel a part of the team) needed to be repeated halfway through the season.

Step 8: Documentation of Progress

This final step in the process involves sending a report home to the student's parents as well as to other team members who may not have had first-hand experience with the community program. Parents will want to know if their child was successful in the program, what specific skills the student acquired as a result of the program, if the student is now more independent with the activity, and what is recommended for future community recreation pursuits. Similarly, other staff members who may have helped design the program but who did not participate in the implementation of the program will want to know if the program was successful and what adjustments might need to be made in the future for this student or for other students with disabilities.

Name: __Lakeisha Jefferson__   Activity: __Softball__

Support: __Ron Carter (community volunteer)__   Date: __5/31/06__

Staff person: __Kari Johnston, CAPE (APE specialist)__

Lakeisha has been playing softball with a local softball team of 12- and 13-year-olds for the past 8 weeks. Lakeisha was really excited to join the team, and she has made some very good progress during the season. Below is a description of her progress in the key softball skills we targeted for her this season. In addition, there is a description of her improvement in social skills and behaviors during the season. Ron Carter (a volunteer from The University of Virginia who has helped Lakeisha during the season) did a great job assisting her while still allowing Lakeisha to become more independent as the season progressed.

Object control skills

Lakeisha has worked on the two-hand strike and the catch during the season. Activities used to help Lakeisha included practicing with a peer, receiving direct physical assistance on how to hold the bat and how to position herself to catch, and using a lighter bat and hitting off a tee (she was allowed to hit off a tee during games after trying to hit three tossed pitches). The following describes Lakeisha's progress this season. Note that O indicates <u>not observed in at least three of four trials</u> and 1 indicates <u>observed in at least three of four trials.</u>

	2/27/06	5/25/06
Two-hand strike		
1. Dominant hand grips bat above nondominant hand	O	1
2. Nondominant side of body faces the tosser	O	1
3. Hip and spine rotation	O	O
4. Weight is transferred by stepping with front foot	O	1
5. Hits ball off tee consistently	1	1
6. Hits pitched ball (tossed from 5' away) consistently	O	O
Catch		
1. Preparation phase where elbows are flexed and hands are in front of body	O	1
2. Arms extend in preparation for ball contact	O	1
3. Ball is caught and controlled by hands/mitt only	O	O
4. Elbows bend to absorb force	O	O
5. Catches softball when tossed from 5' away directly to her	1	1
6. Catches softball when tossed from 10' away directly to her	O	1
7. Catches softball when tossed from 15' away directly to her	O	O

Behaviors/interaction with peers

Important goals included helping Lakeisha learn how to wait her turn, follow directions, and generally get along with peers. We have helped Lakeisha work on these goals by reminding her of appropriate behaviors, praising her for appropriate behaviors, preparing her for situations when she will have to wait her turn or interact with peers, and removing her from the group and allowing her to sit down for a few minutes in order to help her calm down. The following describes Lakeisha's progress during the season:

	2/27/06	5/25/06
1. Waits turn for up to 30 seconds without getting out of line	O	1
2. Follows verbal directions after first verbal cue	O	O
3. Follows demonstrations after first demonstration	O	1
4. Attends to peers for 30 seconds in partner activities	O	O
5. Plays in the games with assistance but without crying, hitting, or running away.	O	1

We are pleased with Lakeisha's progress, and we anticipate seeing similar progress if she chooses to play softball again next year. She seemed to enjoy both practices and the games (practices more than games, as she gets a little bored with all of the waiting in the games), and she seemed to enjoy the interactions with her teammates. Her teammates really did a nice job of befriending Lakeisha and really trying to make her a part of the team.

_____   _____
Kari Johnston, CAPE (APE specialist)   Parent signature

Figure 13.6. Sample progress report.

Figure 13.6 provides a sample of a progress report for a 12-year-old girl with autism who participated in an after-school softball program. This type of progress report provides the key information that Lakeisha's parents and the other members of the IEP team need to understand how well she did in this program. The program described was an intramural/interscholastic program offered to all girls at all the middle schools in the school district. The APE specialist thought this girl would benefit from the sport's setting, which provided many opportunities to improve her motor skills, interact with peers, and practice appropriate behaviors. The IEP team agreed with the idea, but they realized the girl would need support to be successful due to her limited motor skills and her behaviors. The APE specialist contacted the local university's volunteer program, which matches students from the university with various community needs. The university recommended a junior who was a physical education major looking to volunteer for Special Olympics or some similar program. After receiving training from the APE specialist and working with Lakeisha during APE a few times, Ron was on his own, assisting Lakeisha during all practices (once each week) and during all games (once each week).

SPECIAL COMMUNITY-BASED SPORTS PROGRAMS FOR STUDENTS WITH DISABILITIES

The ideal is to have students with disabilities participate in general community recreation and sports programs. However, there are circumstances in which special sports program might be more appealing to students with disabilities. For example, even with modifications some students with disabilities just do not have the skill level to compete with athletes without disabilities. Also, some students with disabilities (and their parents) may want their child to have a more successful experience, and special sports programs tend to be more accommodating. Finally, some athletes just feel more comfortable and seek a sense of camaraderie with peers who have similar abilities. For those students with disabilities interested in special sports programs, there are several special sports programs designed for individuals with disabilities. The first two—Challenger Baseball and VIP Soccer—are designed for children with a variety of disabilities. The other sports associations discussed are for children and adults with specific disabilities.

Challenger Division of Little League of America

Little League of America offers a special baseball program for boys and girls ages 5–21 with disabilities. The Challenger Baseball program is offered in many localities throughout the United States where Little League Baseball is played. The Challenger division differs from traditional Little League Baseball in that it is not a competitive program. Teams play against each other, but there are no winners and los-

ers. Rather, the goal of games is for active participation, to learn about baseball, and to have fun.

There are several modifications in Challenger Baseball. First, each player is assigned a "buddy" to assist the player during the game. This buddy can be a parent, sibling, or volunteer. Second, Challenger players do not pitch, although a player is assigned to field the pitcher's mound. Third, players are given six swings and the option of hitting off a tee. Fourth, all team members (which can be up to 15-20 players) get to bat when their team is up. In addition, all team members play in the field at least half of the game. Finally, games are limited to four innings (Little League of America, 2006).

AYSO VIP Program

The AYSO VIP Program provides a quality soccer experience for children and adults whose physical or mental disabilities make it difficult to successfully participate on mainstream teams. VIP (very important players) carries the philosophy "everybody plays." Program goals include players have fun, understand the fundamentals of the game, learn teamwork and fair play, increase positive self-esteem, become more physically fit, and meet and become comfortable with new people. The program is very much like regular soccer with the following key modifications:

- Buddies assist players on the field in playing the game.

- Teams can have as few as five players.

- Teams may be co-ed.

- Teams are balanced with players rated by size and physical ability.

- Older and younger players form their own divisions when numbers allow.

- Teams play on smaller fields, but the field is part of the regular soccer league field.

- Players wear uniforms similar to what other players in the league wear.

- Rules are relaxed (e.g., no offside calls, latitude on throw-ins, no side changes at half-time).

- Buddies assist as necessary, but are faded away when possible (Lavay & Semark, 2001).

Special Olympics

Special Olympics is an international organization dedicated to empowering individuals with intellectual disabilities to become physically fit, productive, and respected members of society through sports training and competition. Special Olympics offers children and adults with intellectual disabilities year-round training and competition in 26 Olympic-type summer and winter sports (see Table 13.3). There is no charge to participate in Special Olympics (Special Olympics, 2005). Special Olympics also offers two unique programs: 1) the Motor Activities Training Program (MATP) for individuals with severe limitations who do not yet possess the physical and/or behavioral skills necessary to participate in official Special Olympics Sports, and 2) Unified Sports, which brings together athletes with and without intellectual disabilities to train and compete together on the same teams.

Special Olympics serves nearly 2 million people with intellectual disabilities in 200 programs in more than 150 countries. To be eligible to participate in Special Olympics, you must be at least 8 years old and identified by an agency or professional as having one of the following conditions: intellectual disabilities, cognitive delays as measured by formal assessment, or significant learning or vocational problems due to cognitive delay that require or have required specially designed instruction (Special Olympics, 2005).

Special Olympics sports programs follow the same rules as regular Olympics sports programs. However, there are accommodations that make Special Olympics different. First, athletes compete among those of equal abilities through the "10% rule." Athletes are pre-tested on their individual or team skill level. Results of these pre-tests are used to "heat" athletes or teams against athletes or teams of similar abilities. For example, 10 athletes all have been pre-tested on the 50-meter dash with scores (in seconds) as follows: 8, 9, 10, 11, 13, 14, 15, 20, 22, 24. Three heats would be created with heat #1 consisting of the four athletes with times of 8, 9, 10 and 11 seconds; heat #2 consisting of three athletes with times of 13, 14, and 15 seconds; and heat #3 consisting of 20, 22, 24 seconds. Each heat is competed as a separate competition so that the person who finishes first in heat #1 would get gold medal, the person who wins heat #2 would get a gold medal, and the person who wins heat #3 would get a gold medal. This way everyone, no matter how skilled, has a reasonable chance of getting a medal in his or her heat.

As noted, no fees are charged to athletes to train or compete in any Special Olympics program. While this may seem like a small thing, Special Olympics is one of the only sports programs that does not charge fees to its athletes. In addition to no fees, Special Olympics provides awards to all participants. Even if a child does not come in first or even second or third, the athlete receives a ribbon for finishing in the top eight or for participating in the event.

Special Olympics also conducts a random draw for advancement to higher levels of competition. To advance from a local competition to a state competition, a local program randomly selects athletes rather than picking the best athletes. Similarly, advancing from state level to national or international competition is done randomly, with all athletes who received a gold medal at the state level eligible to be randomly selected to compete at the national or international level (Special Olympics, 2005).

United States Association for Blind Athletes

The mission of the United States Association of Blind Athletes (USABA) is to increase the number and quality of sport opportunities for Americans who are blind or have visual impairments. This is achieved by providing athletes and coaches infor-

Table 13.3. Special Olympics sports

Alpine skiing	Bocce	Figure skating	Power lifting	Softball	Volleyball
Aquatics	Bowling	Floor hockey	Roller skating	Speed skating	
Athletics	Cross-country skiing	Football (soccer)	Sailing	Table tennis	
Badminton	Cycling	Golf	Snowboarding	Team handball	
Basketball	Equestrian	Gymnastics	Snowshoeing	Tennis	

Table 13.4. Classification of the United States Association of Blind Athletes

Class	Definition
Class B1	*From* no light perception in either eye *to* light perception but inability to recognize the shape of a hand at any distance or in any direction.
Class B2	*From* ability to recognize the shape of a hand *to* visual acuity of 20/600 and/or a visual field of less than 5 degrees in the best eye with the best practical eye correction.
Class B3	*From* visual acuity of greater than 20/600 *to* visual acuity of 20/200 and/or a visual field of less than 20 degrees and more than 5 degrees in the best eye with the best practical eye correction.
Class B4	*From* visual acuity of greater than 20/200 *to* visual acuity of 20/70 and a visual field larger than 20 degrees in the best eye with the best practical eye correction.

From United States Association of Blind Athletes (USABA). (n.d.). *IBSA visual classifications.* Retrieved October 16, 2006, from http://www.usaba.org/Pages/sportsinformation/visualclassifications.html; reprinted by permission.

mation on programs, support, and sports training and competition programs at the state and national levels, and representation at the international levels. One important value stressed by USABA, the opportunity to demonstrate through sports the abilities of people who are blind and visually impaired (USABA, 2005).

Since its founding in 1976, the USABA has reached more than 100,000 blind individuals. Sports under USABA include bowling, cycling, goal ball, golf, gymnastics, judo, outdoor recreation, power lifting, skiing, swimming, and wrestling.

The organization has emerged as more than just a world-class trainer of athletes with visual impairments; it has become a champion of the abilities of Americans who are legally blind. Although an athlete may be blind, he or she has the ability to compete alongside his or her sighted peers. In fact, USABA athletes have competed in the regular Olympics. Marla Runyan qualified for the 2000 Olympic Team in the 1,500-meter race event and made the finals. She also finished as the top American in the Boston and New York Marathons (USABA, 2005).

One unique aspect of sports for the blind is the use of athlete classification based on each athlete's functional visual abilities and limitations. These four classifications are designed to make competition as equitable as possible (see Table 13.4).

Wheelchair Sports, USA

Wheelchair Sports, USA, was founded in 1956 as the National Wheelchair Athletic Association. Its mission was to serve athletes with disabilities—mostly World War II veterans—who wanted to participate in sports other than basketball. Wheelchair basketball was popular at U.S. veterans hospitals in the 1950s. During these early days, many wheelchair basketball players saw participation in individual wheelchair sports as supplementary training for their primary interest in basketball. However, the Wheelchair Sports, USA, programs appealed to even greater numbers of athletes with disabilities be-

cause it was able to incorporate women and quadriplegics (those with paralysis in upper as well as lower extremities), two populations that basketball could not reasonably accommodate at that time (Wheelchair Sports, USA, 2005). Since the early 1970s additional efforts have been undertaken to organize Wheelchair Sports, USA, programs on local and regional levels throughout the United States. Today, Wheelchair Sports, USA, is organized geographically into 14 regional associations, each responsible for developing local wheelchair sports programs and for conducting qualifying meets for the National Wheelchair Games.

Europe's first organized wheelchair sports program was introduced in 1948 by well-known neurosurgeon, Dr. Ludwig Guttman, founder of the Spinal Injury Center in Stoke-Mandeville, England. The first Stoke-Mandeville Games included only a handful of participants (26), and few events (shot put, javelin, club throw, and archery), but growth in both the number of events and participants came quickly. In 1952, a team from the Netherlands was invited to compete with the British team. This was the first International Stoke-Mandeville Games, an event that has been held annually ever since.

Wheelchair Sports, USA, sports programs currently include archery, table tennis, shooting, swimming, and weight lifting (wheelchair basketball and winter sports are run by a different organization). Wheelchair Sports, USA, has expanded its offerings to junior athletes, which make up 30% of the total membership. Regional associations conduct annual local competitions for youths ages 5–18. The WSUSA Junior National Championships, the organization's largest annual event, was first held in July 1984. This event provided the first national program of competitions for junior athletes.

The National Disability Sports Alliance (NDSA)

The National Disability Sports Alliance (NDSA) is the national coordinating body for competitive

Table 13.5. National Disability Sports Alliance athlete classification system

Wheelchair classifications	Definitions
Class 1	Severe involvement in all four limbs (usually spasticity). Limited trunk control. Unable to grasp a softball. Poor functional strength in upper extremities often requiring power wheelchair.
Class 2	Severe to moderate quadriplegia (usually athetoid). Normally able to propel a wheelchair slowly with arms or by pushing with feet. Poor functional strength and severe control problems in upper extremities.
Class 3	Moderate quadriplegia (often diplegia or severe spastic hemiplegia), fair functional strength and moderate control problems in upper extremities and torso. Propels wheelchair independently.
Class 4	Lower limbs have moderate to severe involvement. Good functional strength and minimal control problems in upper extremities and torso. Uses wheelchair well.

Ambulatory classifications	Definitions
Class 5	Good functional strength and minimal control problems in upper extremities (usually spasticity). May walk with or without assistive devices for ambulation.
Class 6	Moderate to severe quadriplegia (usually athetoid). Ambulates without walking aids. Less coordination. Balance problems when running and throwing. Has greater upper extremity involvement.
Class 7	Moderate to minimal hemiplegia. Good functioning ability in non-affected side. Walks/runs with noticeable limp.
Class 8	Minimally affected. May have coordination problems. Able to run and jump freely. Has good balance.

Source: National Disability Sports Alliance (2005)

sports for individuals with cerebral palsy, traumatic brain injuries, and survivors of stroke. NDSA was originally formed as the United States Cerebral Palsy Athletic Association (USCPAA) in 1987. NDSA also provides programming for conditions such as muscular dystrophy and multiple sclerosis. As the national coordinating body for cerebral palsy sports, NDSA creates rules and policies, conducts national championships in 10 sports, provides information on safety and sports medicine, and selects the athletes to represent the United States in international competition. NDSA is affiliated with the Paralympics and is one of only seven disabled sports organizations recognized as a member of the U.S. Olympic Committee (NDSA, 2005; Paciorek & Jones, 2001).

USCPAA offers local, national, and international training and competitive opportunities in the following sports: basketball, bocce, bowling, cycling, equestrian, indoor wheelchair soccer, power lifting, soccer, swimming, track and field, youth, and developmental sports. Sports follow the rules of regular Olympic sports with modification as needed to ensure the athletes' success. Most modifications are needed for athletes who use wheelchairs. The most notable modifications focus on the athletic classification system used by NDSA. This classification system is a subjective process utilizing a series of functional tests to classify athletes into eight cate-

gories ranging from severe (class 1) to minimal dysfunction (class 8) (NDSA, 2005; Paciorek & Jones, 2001). There are four wheelchair (class 1–4) and four ambulatory (class 5–8) categories (see Table 13.5).

SUMMARY

Community sports and recreation programs are such an important part of growing up in America, and participation in these programs can teach students so much more than the skills of the game. Because of this, one important goal of all physical education programs is to help students acquire the skills and behaviors needed to be successful in community sport and recreation programs. Most students without disabilities will acquire these skills and have many different community sport and recreation opportunities readily available to them. Unfortunately, this is not the case with students with disabilities. Students with disabilities often do not have the requisite skills, knowledge, or behaviors needed to be successful even with entry-level recreation and sport programs. Also, students with disabilities often need extra support to be successful in community sport and recreation programs. As a result, students with disabilities often never have the chance to participate in and gain the benefits from community sports and recreation programs. One way to help students with disabilities move into community sports and recreation programs is to carefully plan and support students in acquiring the skills to be successful in these programs.

When skills are beyond a student's abilities, accommodations can be implemented to the program to allow the student to participate successfully. And when accommodations to regular sports cannot be achieved, special community sports and recreation programs should be explored. The important point is that community sports and recreation can be such a wonderful experience, and students with disabilities should be given every opportunity to participate in these programs.

CHAPTER 13 APPENDIX

Sample Community-Referenced Leisure Skill Inventory

I. SKILL SELECTION CONSIDERATIONS/ FACILITY DESCRIPTION

Adaptive Skiing, Wintergreen Resort

A. Appropriateness of leisure skill facility

1. *Is skill or facility selected appropriate for individuals without disabilities of the same chronological age?* Yes. Skiing is a great workout and tons of fun for all ages and ability levels (with or without disabilities). Skiing can also be a wonderful self-confidence builder for an individual with a disability. This activity can also be a wonderful social outlet.

2. *Has the individual with disabilities previously acquired any skills related to the activity?* Yes. Maura is able to stand, walk, and jog on her own.

3. *If the particular skills would be difficult to perform, are material/procedural adaptations available to enhance participation?* Yes. Wintergreen has adapted equipment to help any individual be successful on the slopes. Wintergreen also provides at least one trained volunteer per student.

4. *Does the individual with disabilities have access to the facility or materials (distance from home, transportation concerns)?* Yes. Maura's family has a house at Wintergreen Resort, so she is able to come to Wintergreen for 2 weeks over Christmas break and on most weekends throughout the skiing season. However, this is obviously not possible for all individuals with disabilities. Individuals who need transportation can contact Wintergreen and find out if any volunteer drivers live in their vicinity.

5. *Is the cost prohibitive? Are there other resources to help pay for the cost of the facility (e.g., reduced fee, waived fee, sponsorship)?* Wintergreen provides ski instruction, a lift ticket, and adapted or regular equipment from 10 A.M. to 4 P.M. for $75, or $40 for 1 P.M. to 4 P.M. An individual who does not need instruction and can ski independently may obtain half-price tickets and rental equipment. Skiing is an extremely expensive sport, but Wintergreen will help those with disabilities in need of financial help.

6. *Has the individual with disabilities expressed interest in this particular activity?* Yes. Maura loves the thrill of skiing. She is only 14 years old, but she has already made it clear that she wants to ski for the rest of her life. She has Down syndrome and cannot compete with her peers in most other physical activities, but on the slopes with the appropriate equipment and support, she is probably a better skier than 60% of her peers.

B. Description of leisure skills: environmental inventory and discrepancy analysis

Wintergreen Adapted Skiing (WAS)
Student's name: Maura McDonald
Student's birth date: 1/26/92
Teacher: Harmony Craft
Environment: APE Skiing
Dates of unit: Skiing season
Suggested assistant: Any WAS volunteer or employee
See Figure A13.1 for an environmental inventory and discrepancy analysis.

Subenvironment	What are the steps of the activity that a person without disabilities uses?	What assistance does the student with disabilities currently need?	What adaptations or levels of assistance might help this student?
Parking lot/entrance	Get out of car.	I	Usually her mom, dad, or sibling accompanies her.
	Walk from car to the Wintergreen Adapted Skiing (WAS) house.	I	Usually her mom, dad, or sibling accompanies her
	Open WAS house door and enter building.	I	Usually her mom, dad, or sibling accompanies her.
WAS building	Find a seat so that she is not in the way of others (the building is extremely small).	V	Remind Maura to sit down and wait for someone to help her with her equipment.
	Check to make sure she has all of her ski clothes (i.e., pants, gloves, hat, jacket).	V	WAS volunteer will remind Maura if she forgets to check something.
	Begin putting on ski clothing.	PP	WAS volunteer will assist Maura with clothing.
	Check to make sure that all clothing is on properly (i.e., gloves tucked under jacket, hat not blocking vision, socks pulled up and put under/over ski pants).	PP	WAS volunteer will double check everything to make sure that nothing is uncomfortable and that Maura will be warm/cool enough, depending on the weather for the day.
	Get prepared to go outside (e.g., put on helmet, goggles, ski boots).	PP	WAS volunteer will check to make sure that the helmet fits properly, goggles are not too tight/loose, and ski boots are buckled and snug/loose enough so that they can be functional but not painful.
On ski slope directly outside of WAS building	Stand up and depart from building.	I/PP	Maura is good at walking in her ski boots, but it is important that someone, usually the WAS volunteer, is close by in case she loses her balance.
	Open door to deck of building.	I/PP	Someone may have to help Maura open the door.
	Walk down steps to the slope.	I/PP	Someone will need to make sure that Maura is not going to trip and fall while going down the steps.
	Walk on the slope to where her equipment will be waiting for her.	V/PP	Maura will receive the verbal cue of "heel to toe," which is how she is supposed to walk in her ski boots on the snow. A WAS volunteer will need to be nearby Maura, in case she loses her balance.
	Put skis on.	V/PP	WAS instructor will tell Maura, "Put your toe in the binding first and then step down hard to smash the bug!" Maura knows what this means, but someone will still have to physically guide the boot to the correct placement in the binding. Sometimes several tries may be necessary.
On ski slopes	Begin skiing down the slope.	I/V	WAS instructor will remind Maura to make her "pizza pie" with the skis and slowly begin down the hill.
	Ski down the slope.	I/V	Maura is a capable skier on the two beginner slopes, but she does like to follow the WAS instructor. The WAS instructor often skis backwards, making large turns across the slope, verbally cuing Maura to push out with her right ski to make a good left turn and vice versa. When Maura goes on an intermediate slope, she becomes very timid and forgets the skills that she knows so well. Often, when Maura makes this transition, she needs a lot of coaching and encouragement to overcome her fear.

Figure A13.1. Sample environmental inventory and discrepancy analysis for adapted skiing for Maura. (*Key:* I, independent; V, verbal cues or reminder; PP, partial physical assistance; P+, physical assistance [student tries to help]; P, physical assistance [student is passive]).

Subenvironment	What are the steps of the activity that a person without disabilities uses?	What assistance does the student with disabilities currently need?	What adaptations or levels of assistance might help this student?
	After falling, getting up and/or putting her skis back on (if they have come off), and begin going down the hill again.	V/P+/P	The most important thing for Maura to do when she falls is to place her skis perpendicular (across) to the slope. Putting skis on when on the hill is much more difficult than when they are on a flat surface. The WAS instructor will gather anything that Maura may have lost in the fall (e.g., gloves, skis) and will say to Maura, "Put your skis <u>across</u> the hill." Then the WAS instructor will stand downhill from Maura, help her stand up and put on her skis again (with same verbal cues as before when putting on skis). Sometimes Maura may be extremely helpful in this entire process and sometimes she is dead weight and has to be physically picked up and manipulated by the instructor.
	Stop at the bottom of the hill.	V/PP	WAS instructor will give Maura verbal cue to "make a big pizza pie and turn across the hill (or open space below the lift) to stop."
Ski lift	Get in ski lift line.	P+	Maura does not have poles, so it is hard for her to move on flat ground. She is pulled by her instructor to the line but does try to help by trying to move her feet/skis forward.
	Get on lift.	V/PP	Give Maura verbal cues: "Wait at the cones (line); then go forward when the chair passes in front of you; stop at the next set of cones (line); look behind you and watch your chair come toward you; and sit down when the chair gets to you, just like you would sit down on a normal chair." Even with these cues, Maura will need someone beside her telling her when to stop/go and helping her move forward.
	Ride on lift.	V	WAS instructor will give Maura verbal cues: "Lean back while we put the bar down and try to put your feet on the foot rest."
	Prepare to get off the lift.	V	WAS instructor will tell Maura, "Lean back, move skis off of foot rests, put bar up, and point ski tips upward."
	Get off lift.	I/V/PP	WAS instructor will tell Maura, "Make large pizza pie with your skis, put skis down on snow, lean forward and stand up, let the hill take you down, then keep your pizza pie until you come to a stop, and turn to the left or right to stop." Maura is capable of doing all of this by herself but likes to have the safety of the instructor by her side. (Sometimes the instructor has to help Maura stand up when exiting the lift.)
Ending the skiing day	Go down slope to WAS house.	I/V	WAS instructor will say, "Keep pizza pie, make good turns (push out with right ski to turn left and push out with left ski to turn right), make sure to follow me."
	Get to WAS house.	I/V	WAS instructor will remind Maura, "Remember to stop in front of the WAS house. Turn across the hill by the stairs, remember to start turning before you get there—it is okay to stop early."

(continued)

Figure A13.1. *(continued)*

Subenvironment	What are the steps of the activity that a person without disabilities uses?	What assistance does the student with disabilities currently need?	What adaptations or levels of assistance might help this student?
Ending the skiing day (continued)	Walk up the stairs, open the door, and enter the WAS house.	I/PP	Have someone near Maura to make sure that she does not lose her balance and to help her open the door.
	Take off ski equipment and clothing (e.g., gloves, hat, helmet, boots, jacket)	I/V/PP	WAS instructor will ask Maura, "What do you need to take off now that we are inside?" Someone can help her take off her ski equipment and clothing, but she usually can do it by herself.
Exit/parking lot	Put regular shoes back on, open door, leave WAS house, and walk to parking lot.	I/PP	Maura may need help with her shoes. At this point someone from her family will be at the WAS house to walk with her out to the car.
	Get in car and drive home.	I	Maura can walk with her family member and ride home with them.

C. **Description of leisure/facility environments**
   1. *General description of leisure environment:* Wintergreen Ski Resort is located at an altitude of 4,000 feet on the eastern slope of the Blue Ridge Mountains and has beautiful views of the local scenery. The resort's main attraction in the winter is skiing and snowboarding, but there are also snowtubing, banquet halls, restaurants, bars, and an exercise and spa center. At other times in the year, the resort has the attractions of a golf course, horseback riding, tennis, mountain biking, outdoor swimming pools, hiking trails, and youth outdoor camps. The mountain has five beginner slopes, four intermediate slopes, six expert slopes, and a total of four lifts. The lift that provides transportation for the majority of the beginner slopes at Wintergreen, often the most crowded area of the mountain, is only a few years old and runs at a high speed while holding six people per chair.
   2. *Conditions under which the participant will be required to participate and interact (who else will be there, noise level, other distractions)?* At times, especially around the holidays and on weekends, the ski slopes can be extremely crowded, with many individuals who know how to ski and many who do not know how to ski. Thus, there may be skiers/snowboarders of all ages and sizes flying down the mountain completely out of control. On a busy day, the mountain probably houses at least 1,000 people, most of whom will be on the beginner slopes. Another huge obstacle at Wintergreen are the snow blowers, which are strategically placed on many slopes and make a horribly loud noise while shooting manmade snow in the faces of any skier passing by. These snow blowers cause skiers' vision to be temporarily blurred, and at worst can completely blind a skier for several seconds, until he/she moves through the blower's area. Maura seems to do fine with all of these obstacles. She is completely bundled up (face covered and eyes protected by goggles) in preparation for the snow blowers, and her WAS instructor always watches out for her safety in the crowds.
   3. *A diagram of facility or environment is usually included in a community-referenced leisure skill inventory.*

D. **Description of social environment**
   1. *What social interactions with peers, supervisors, and others are required in the immediate environment?* Maura will interact with multiple WAS volunteers, other students of all ages and

various disabilities, lift attendants, people in lift lines and on the lifts, and any individual on the slope whom she may run into or who may run into her (hopefully neither will occur). Overall, Maura has to be okay with having many people around her at all times, which she seems to enjoy.

2. *What is the typical dress for the environment?* The typical dress for skiing is a long underwear top and bottom, followed by multiple layers of fleeces, sweatshirts, and more long underwear. It is important to have many layers so that if a person gets too hot he or she can just remove a layer. If possible, it is best to not wear cotton (especially on the layer directly against the skin) because cotton absorbs a person's sweat and becomes damp. The final layer on both the top and bottom should be something waterproof or water resistant because it is important not to get wet. If a person's underlayers become wet, the person can quickly become cold, which if not taken care of can quickly lead to hypothermia. Additional dress requirements include warm gloves or mittens (preferably waterproof or water resistant), warm socks that can be pulled up onto the shins, a warm hat, a helmet, and goggles/sunglasses. Other optional dress includes scarves, facemasks, vests, and any other warm clothing that an individual prefers.

II. ANALYSIS OF COMPONENT SKILLS AND ADAPTATIONS FOR FULL/PARTIAL PARTICIPATION

A. **List of required equipment and materials**
   1. *What equipment and materials might a person come in contact with in the environment? Provide a detailed listing (and description as needed).*
      a. Snow
      b. Skis, boots, poles, snowboards
      c. Adapted ski equipment
         i. *Bi-ski:* A sit-down form of ski that has two large skis stabilizing the "chair" portion of the ski
         ii. *Mono-ski:* A sit-down form of ski that has one large ski stabilizing the chair portion of the ski
         iii. *Outriggers:* Ski poles that have tips of skis attached at the bottom, used so that a person with poor balance (or a person who has lost part of a leg) can ski with more stability (used with regular skis as well as with sit-down skis)
         iv. *Ski-bra:* A device that holds the tips of skis together
         v. *Tail pipe:* A device that goes behind the boots in ski bindings and functions to keep the skis from wandering too far apart in the back.
      d. Snow blowers—machines that shoot manmade snow onto the ski slopes
      e. Ski lifts

B. **Physical considerations: manipulatory, motoric, health**
   Describe each motor response:
   1. *Number and complexity of coordinated movement patterns?* 1: skiing (very complex)—includes balance, coordination, strength, and body weight transition
   2. *What strength is required to perform the activity/manipulate materials?* Lower body strength is extremely important in making turns, stopping, and overall just supporting the body. The quadriceps muscles are constantly being used because the proper position for skiing is with knees bent and the body leaning downhill. This position can be extremely tiring on the quadriceps and butt muscles. The calf muscles are also used often because when making a turn on skis, it is important to put pressure on the foot (ball of the foot) on the opposite ski of whatever direction the turn is going. This process is initiated by flexing the calf muscle. Also, when an individual falls, it takes a lot of lower and upper body strength to get back up.
   3. *What body positions and flexibility are required to perform the activity?* Stretches: Stretching is not commonly done, but stretching the calf muscles, the quadriceps, the back, and the hamstrings before and after skiing will save a person from muscle soreness and/or possible injuries. The main position for skiing is a semi-squat, which constantly works the quadriceps, calves, and butt muscles.

4. *What speed is required to perform the activity?* Speed is arbitrary. As long as skiers have control, they can go as slow or as fast as their hearts desire.

5. *What levels of endurance are required to perform the activity?* A high level of muscular endurance and low level of cardiovascular endurance are needed.

6. *What are the minimal health conditions necessary to participate in the activity?* A skier must be healthy with no chance of having a seizure and no atlantoaxial instability.

C. **Perceptual considerations: visual, auditory, body awareness**

1. *What visual skills (including discrimination) are needed in the environment and in the activity?* It is definitely important to have good vision when skiing, but if vision is a problem, it can be worked around. Vision is important so that an individual can avoid obstacles, such as trees; snow blowers; ski lift poles; and the most important obstacle, the many other people on the slopes. However, even a blind person can ski with the help of a WAS instructor. As long as an individual has someone with him or her, telling him or her about the surroundings and which way to turn, the individual can ski.

2. *What auditory skills (including discrimination) are needed in the environment and in the activity?* Auditory skills are not necessary when skiing. However, it is extremely helpful to know if someone is coming, either by hearing the noise of snow moving or by hearing him or her yell.

3. *What body awareness skills are needed in the environment and in the activity?* An individual needs to know where he or she is in relation to other people on the slopes and always needs to know that he or she is responsible for not running into someone downhill from him or her. Again, however, this can be supplemented by a WAS instructor informing the individual of his or her location in relation to others.

D. **Interpersonal interaction considerations: exchange between participants**

1. *What are the typical types of interactions that occur in the environment (e.g., turn taking, cooperating, unstruc-*

tured)? It is important to wait one's turn in the lift line. WAS skiers and instructors do get to cut in the public line but still have to wait their turn at the ski school. It is important to sometimes wait to take one's turn because one can see that someone is coming into the space that you were going to turn into.

2. *What optional interactions might you expect (e.g., getting a drink)?* Maura might get cold and want to go the cafeteria to get some hot chocolate (which she loves). This can be an excellent form of motivation. She may be thirsty for some water or hungry for a snack. Maura may be too hot or too cold, in which case we would go back to the WAS house and rethink the clothing situation.

3. *What are the language requirements in the environment (list typical nouns, verbs, cues, and statements used in the activity)?* "Turn right/left," "Push out with your right/left ski," "Put pressure on your right/left foot," "Bend your knees," "Try to lean forward," "Make your pizza pie bigger/smaller," "Turn across the hill and stop," "Look behind you," "Sit down when the lift gets here," "Stop now," "Smash the bug," "Toe in the binding and step straight back with all your weight," "One more good run and then we will go in to get some chocolate," "Follow me," "You lead, I'm going to follow," "Try to speed up/slow down," "Watch out for the person on your right/left," "Lean back-I'm putting the bar down/up," "Put your ski tips up, and make your pizza pie-get ready to get off," "And up"

E. **Functional academics: reading, writing, math/scoring, time telling**

1. *What reading skills are needed? Can they be bypassed with modifications?* No reading skills are needed, as long as the skier can read the color code of green being the easiest slopes, blue being intermediate, and black being the hardest. In Maura's case, she is always with someone telling her where to go.

2. *What writing skills are needed? Can they be bypassed with modifications?* None

3. *What math skills are needed? Can they be bypassed with modifications?*

The only math skill needed is the ability to have basic money skills. Maura always has someone with her who takes care of money.

4. *What time telling skills are needed?* None, except if a person is supposed to meet someone else at a specific time. Again, Maura always has someone doing this for her.

F. **What decisions/judgments are necessary for successful participation?**

1. *What time and situation judgments may have to be made by the person with a disability to successfully participate in the leisure activity?* It is important for a person with a disability to make sure that he or she has contacted WAS about what day he or she will be coming. If WAS is not contacted in advance, WAS most likely will not have anyone available to work with the individual for the day.

G. **What specific adaptations/adjustments are needed for partial participation?**

1. *When making suggestions for adaptations,* keep the following in mind:
   - *Whenever possible, activities should not be altered to make the individual stand out.*
   - *Whenever possible, adaptations should be considered temporary.*
   - *Adaptations should be made on an individual basis (as opposed to modifications for the entire group when only one person needs modification).*

The only modifications for Maura are the following:
   - *Maura is placed with a WAS instructor who has a jacket identifying him or herself as such.*

   - *Maura does not use poles, but many other able skiers also do not use poles.*
   - *Maura has a ski-bra keeping the tips of her skis together and a tail pipe keeping the backs of her skis from drifting too far apart.*

III. **ANALYSIS OF SUPPORTIVE SKILLS**

A. **Leisure preparation prior to participation in leisure activity**

1. *Can the student prepare him/herself for participation? If not, who will assist the student in preparation?* Maura receives help from her family when choosing what clothes and money to bring for the day and what to eat for breakfast. Once Maura is at the WAS house, the instructors make sure that she is dressed appropriately for the day and that she stops skiing if she is cold, hungry, or tired.

B. **Transportation**

1. *What mode of transportation will be used?* Maura's family will bring her to and from the WAS house.

2. *Does the student have the mobility skills needed to independently use this type of transportation? If not, who will assist student?* Yes, she will be with her family.

C. **Informed consent**

1. *Has the student and/or parent/guardian signed consent form for participation in program?* Yes, when a student participates with WAS, his or her parents must sign a consent form. If he or she is over 18, then he or she must sign the consent.

2. *Does student have insurance?* Maura is currently covered by her parents' insurance coverage.

CHAPTER 14

Multicultural Education and Diversity Issues

by Ana Palla-Kane and Martin E. Block

Tamika is an 11-year-old African American girl with multiple disabilities. She comes from a poor family and lives with her grandmother and three siblings. She has been included in a general elementary school since preschool. Jessica, Tamika's adapted physical education (APE) specialist, thought it would be good to videotape Tamika before defining her goals and accurately measuring her progress. Jessica sent a letter home to request guardian authorization. Weeks passed by, but no letter was returned. Jessica decided to call Tamika's grandmother. In that conversation, the grandmother said that she did not want any videotape made of Tamika but refused to give a reason via telephone. So Jessica set up a time in which she could meet with Tamika's grandmother at her home. While driving to the grandmother's house, Jessica became concerned about how the interactions would go. She knew that the grandmother was an older African American woman who was the guardian of four grandchildren. In contrast, Jessica was white, young, and well educated.

Jessica arrived at their very simple home. Tamika's grandmother opened the door, invited Jessica in, and offered her coffee; in that moment, all of Jessica's concerns disappeared and she was glad she came. Jessica and the grandmother spoke for more than an hour. The grandmother explained that in the past, people had videotaped Tamika and used her images inappropriately, and she did not want it to happen again. She was not against Jessica or the school; she just did not want them videotape her granddaughter. She was very supportive and grateful for all that Jessica and the school had provided her granddaughter, and she asked Jessica to use other ways to assess Tamika. As Jessica said good-bye, she was happy and very satisfied. She was able to fully understand and respect Tamika and her family and to establish goals and assessment tools that most suited the family's wishes and needs.

Mario is a sixth-grade Hispanic student with intellectual disabilities. His family has recently arrived in the United States from Peru and is facing difficulties with his placement in the general public school. He attended a special school in Lima, and the U.S. regulations, IEPs, and placements are very confusing to them. Their English proficiency is low, which makes communicating with teachers and specialists even more difficult. Mario receives APE services, but Mr. Taylor, Mario's APE specialist, has had problems with Mario from the beginning of the school year. Mario often refuses to participate in both APE and general physical education, and he does not like to change into his physical education uniform in the locker room with other students. Mario also seems unmotivated, but Mr. Taylor wonders if Mario simply is confused as to what to do because of his language barrier (Mario does not speak any English). Mr. Taylor wrote a note home to Mario's parents, but he never received a response. Mr. Taylor found out later that Mario's parents could barely read English and probably were unable to read his note. In an attempt to communicate with Mario's parents during the IEP meeting, Mr. Taylor and the special education team brought in an interpreter. Mario's mother came to the meeting and said that when Mario is not at school, he stays home watching TV or playing with his siblings. She could not understand why he is refusing to participate in adapted physical education. She also did not know if he had physical education back in Lima. Even though she seemed to be very interested in learning how Mario was doing in school, she didn't provide information that could help Mr. Taylor. After the meeting, Mr. Taylor was confused and frustrated. He did not know how to define Mario's IEP goals and was very concerned about the school year.

Fatima is a 14-year-old girl whose parents are from Saudia Arabia. She has been in the United States from birth, but her parents continue to practice traditional Islam, including having all girls and women in the family wear clothing that covers their entire body, neck, and head. Fatima has never had a problem with the way she dresses, and her friends have never ridiculed or teased her about the clothes she wears to school. Fatima actually is very popular at her middle school and participates in a variety of school-related activities, including band and student council. She is getting ready to move to high school in the fall, and she is worried about dressing out for physical education. In middle school, dressing out was optional. However, at high school all students have to dress out. Her religion does not allow her to dress in front of others (even other girls), and she is not allowed to show her legs or arms or head or neck when in public. Should Fatima be allowed to wear clothing to cover her body while in physical education, or should she be forced to dress out like everyone else in physical education?

Racial, economic, cultural, religious, language, and educational differences are present in almost all interactions that teachers have with students, parents, and colleagues. Our society is becoming more and more diverse. One third of the student population in the United States are minority students; this number may approach as much as one half by 2020 (Patrick & Reinhartz, 1999). The numbers of minority students are even greater in special education, with more than 50% of students with disabilities coming from backgrounds considered "other than white" (U.S. Department of Education, 2004b; see Table 14.1). This diversity contributes to the challenge of teaching children with disabilities and requires educators to take drastic steps in making education multicultural, not only curricula and learning resources but also instructional techniques and strategies (Chepyator-Thomson, 1994).

Adapted and general physical educators are expected to teach a wide range of learners with disabilities (Sutherland & Hodge, 2001). Unfortunately, re-

search in adapted and general physical education has not considered the impact of multiculturalism on attitudes toward people with disabilities. A lot of attention has focused on including students with disabilities in general physical education based on their disabilities and level of performance. However, no attention has been given to inclusion strategies to accommodate students with disabilities that come from different backgrounds or represent a minority.

The purpose of this chapter is to highlight and discuss the most common issues that adapted and general physical education teachers deal with when teaching students with disabilities from culturally diverse backgrounds. We start with a review of multicultural education and why multicultural awareness is important. This is followed by a look inside the culture of the most prevalent, diverse groups of students in the public school in the United States (e.g., African Americans, Asian Americans, Hispanics, impoverished, English as a second language). The chapter concludes with an examination of how people with disabilities have been treated in American society, as disability itself is considered as a minority group. Misunderstanding, stereotyping, prejudice, and discrimination toward students with disabilities still persists in our society. We invite you to look to your own background, professional experiences, and views of disability. Overall, teachers are not aware of the impact of their culture and their biases toward students from minority groups, and the majority of teachers are white, female, and from a Christian background (Lynch & Hanson, 2004; Zamora-Duran & Artiles, 1997). By approaching inclusion from a multicultural education perspective, we expand our view and our abilities to offer quality education and physical education for all students.

WHAT IS MULTICULTURAL EDUCATION?

A multicultural approach is essential, considering the diversity of American schools and their students. A multicultural perspective and culturally re-

Table 14.1. Racial/ethnic composition of students with disabilities, ages 6–21, served under IDEA, as of 2003

State	American Indian/ Alaskan	Asian/ Pacific Islander	Black (Not Hispanic)	Hispanic	White (Not Hispanic)
U.S. AND OUTLYING AREAS					
Number	91,236	129,391	1,253,492	1,054,196	3,590,032
(percentage)	(1.49)	(2.11)	(20.49)	(17.23)	(58.68)
50 STATES, D.C., P.R.					
Number	91,318	125,325	1,252,251	1,053,856	3,589,966
(percentage)	(1.51)	(2.08)	(20.79)	(16.71)	(59.55)

Reprinted from U.S. Department of Education, Office of Special Education Programs (OSEP), Data Analysis System (DANS). (2004b). *Report of children with disabilities receiving special education under Part B of the Individuals with Disabilities Education Act.* Data updated as of July 30, 2005. Retrieved November 6, 2006, from https://www.ideadata.org/tables28th%5Car_1-16.htm

sponsive instruction are needed to meet the needs of children of varied backgrounds and cultures (Sparks, 1994). It is important to embrace diversity and to perpetuate the notion that all students have the right to educational equity and access to educational programs. Banks and Banks (2004) defined multicultural education as an idea or concept, an educational reform movement, and a process:

> Multicultural education incorporates the idea that all students—regardless of their gender or social class and their ethnic, racial or cultural characteristics—should have an equal opportunity to learn in school. Another important idea in multicultural education is that some students, because of these characteristics, have a better chance to learn in schools as they are currently structure than do students who belong to other groups or have different cultural characteristics. (p. 3)

> Multicultural education is also a reform movement that is trying to change the schools and other educational institutions so that students from all socioclass, gender, racial, language, and cultural groups will have an equal opportunity to learn. (p. 4)

> Multicultural education is also a process whose goals will never be fully realized. Educational equality, like liberty and justice, is an ideal which human beings work but never fully attain. Racism, sexism, and discrimination against people with disabilities will exist to some extent no matter how we work to eliminate [these] problems. (p. 4)

Adams, Bell, and Griffin (1997) explained that learning about diversity and social justice enables teachers and students to become conscious of their operating worldview and able to critically examine alternative ways of understanding the world and social relations. In multicultural education and education for social justice, there is the expectation that individuals learn to critique current social relations and to envision more just and inclusive possibilities for social life, including educational settings.

Teaching in a multicultural society and implementing equality and social justice principles is not an easy task. There is an overrepresentation of minority children in special education (Trent, Artiles, Fitchett-Bazemore, McDaniel, & Coleman-Sorrell, 2002). For example, African Americans make up about 15% of the public school population, yet about 20% are identified as having a disability, according to data from the 2000–2001 school year (U.S. Department of Education, Office of Special Education Programs [OSEP], 2001). In certain categories, the numbers are striking. African Americans make up nearly 34% of those identified with intellectual disability and 27% of those identified with an emotional disturbance (OSEP, 2001). African American students are far more likely to spend their time in more restrictive placements than their Caucasian peers (OSEP, 2001). Moreover, there is a huge achievement gap between Caucasian and African American and Hispanic students (Berlak, 2001; Haycock, 2001; Trent et al., 2002, Viadero, 2000) as well as a disproportionality in discipline (Osher, Woodruff, & Sims, 2002; Skiba, Michael, Nardo, & Peterson, 2002; Townsend, 2000). Although there are no specific data regarding participation and overrepresentation of minority students in APE, it is expected that this tendency is reflected among students with disabilities receiving APE services. When biases, stereotypes, stigmas, racism, and discrimination are present in education, they strongly affect teachers' expectations of students from minority cultures (Hall, 2003).

One of the challenges is to make schools more efficient in working with children, families, and the community. Educators need to recognize the diversity in the classrooms and create more suitable educational environments if they expect all children to do well at school (Verre, McLughlin, & Webb-Johnson, 2003). A multicultural education approach is needed to guarantee the success of students with disabilities in general or adapted physical education as well.

Multicultural Education in General and Adapted Physical Education

Multicultural education strategies and practices are considered essential in physical education (Boyce, 1996; Butt & Pahnos, 1995; Chepyator-Thomson, 1994; Harrison & Worthy, 2001; Hodge, 1997; Hutchinson, 1995; Kahan, 2003; King, 1994; McCollum, Civlier & Holt, 2004; Sparks, 1994; Sutherland & Hodge, 2001; Sutliff, 1996; Sutliff & Perry, 2000; Wessinger, 1994; Williamson, 1993). However, there is a lack of research in multicultural education as it relates to physical education, and there are virtually no resources concerning multiculturalism and diversity as it relates to adapted physical education. Studies and articles in multicultural education and physical education focus mainly on incorporating games and dances of different countries and cultures into the physical education curriculum. While including such activities into physical education is a good start, it is a far cry from truly embracing a multicultural education approach.

Sparks advocated for a culturally sensitive pedagogy in physical education, stating, "Teachers have a moral responsibility to be culturally responsive or to design curricular programs that are responsive to the educational needs of learners from diverse cultural backgrounds" (1994, p. 35). In our view, multicultural education is designed to meet the needs of a socially diverse, changing, global society by promoting the understanding and appreciation of the principles of social diversity and cultural pluralism. "Multicultural education is designed to empower all teachers and students to become knowledgeable, caring, and active citizens in a deeply troubled and ethnically polarized nation and world" (Banks & Banks, 2004, p.7).

In order to effectively integrate multicultural education, general and adapted physical educators need to 1) develop the knowledge and skills to be able to promote social justice and equality for all people (e.g., students, their families, colleagues); 2) foster positive attitudes toward diverse groups among students; and 3) promote an environment in which students can be successful. A lack of successful physical activity experiences in school can contribute to a lack of interest in physical education and sports among adolescence and adulthood (Beveridge & Scruggs, 2000). As teachers attempt to become more responsive to the demographics of a changing world, they must understand the effect of culture on the ongoing development of children's attitudes and values. Our values are determined by our culture, which influences our behavior and our decisions (Sparks, 1994).

A multicultural education context in physical education is important to ensure students' achievement. Although there is agreement on the relevance of diversity in education, issues such as race and culture often make people uncomfortable. Teachers and students have a variety of feelings, experiences, and awareness with these issues (Adams et al., 1997). There is a need to create opportunities for teachers to express their views and share their personal experiences about diversity because fear, distrust, anger, denial, guilt, ignorance, and naiveté can prevent teachers from truly becoming multicultural (Adams et al., 1997).

> Integration of multicultural concepts within a physical education (or adapted physical education programs) is more than an introduction of different cultural games; it is the acquisition of informed social attitudes through the creation of a knowledge base that conveys the desirability and value of diversity. For multicultural instructional units that foster well-informed, nonprejudicial attitudes to be developed and promoted in teaching practices, teachers at all levels must gain an understanding and appreciation of diversity. Culturally responsive pedagogy in physical education would help eliminate discriminatory practices and promote multicultural understanding. Physical education, because of its strength in social orientation, can lead in this process. (Chepyator-Thomson, 1994, p. 32)

Wessinger (1994) also defended the idea of a multicultural education as one that fosters cultural pluralism and equal opportunity for all in physical education. She pointed out a list of knowledge, attitudes, and skills needed to address ethnicity in general and adapted physical education classes:

1. *Knowledge*

   Understanding prejudice, stereotyping, and discrimination, and the definitions of ethnicity and culture

   Learning about different cultures

   Recognizing diversity and pluralism as strengths

   Learning how various cultures contribute to pluralistic society

   Discovering one's own roots, as well as others' in community

2. *Attitudes*

   Appreciating the value of cultural diversity, and human rights

   Accepting one's own differences

   Appreciating others' experiences

   Being prepared to take action on behalf of others

3. *Skills*

   Cooperating, sharing, and the human relations skills of self-awareness

   Interpersonal communication

   Group process, problem solving, and decision making

   Seeing from different perspectives

It is extremely important that both adapted and general physical educators purposely structure physical education and create teaching strategies that promote high levels of active participation across diverse groups (Beveridge & Scruggs, 2000). Banks and Banks (2004), Beveridge and Scruggs (2000), Butt and Pahnos (1995), and Sparks (1994) identified several strategies to build a culturally responsive and multicultural physical education program.

Constantly Develop Your Relationships and Build Trust

- Create ways to show that you are interested and that you want to establish a relationship with your students, their parents, and your colleagues.

- Create a practice where you acknowledge your students, their family, your colleagues and yourself. It is important that you recognize and be proud of your own achievement.

- Let students know that their efforts are valued and will be rewarded.

- Learn the names of your students and how to pronounce them. If necessary, use nametags in the beginning. Students will have fun in creating nametags. Ask your students how they want to be called: African American, Black, African, Hispanic, Latino, Asian, Asian American, or something else.

- Include games that reflect the culture of your students.

- Share your accomplishments with your colleagues; it will give you the opportunity to share what is working in your teaching and contribute to them.

- Use a collaborative approach with your IEP team and colleagues. As you face a problem with your students, share with your colleagues and be open to contribute to them when they need your help. Being open to others' contributions and support will allow you to not feel alone in these circumstances.

- Be in communication every time you are facing a challenging situation. Avoid hiding what is happening and hoping that everything will be fine.

Expand Your Cultural Knowledge and Become Culturally Literate

- Learn about your students' backgrounds (e.g., language they speak, characteristics of culture and country they come from, traditions, interaction styles, or social values). A lot of this information cannot be found in books; ask your students and their parents. Each one has a unique culture, and you will never get to a point where you know enough.

- Learn about your own background and share with your students.

- Observe students in settings outside of school. Get to know their families. Make home visits. Talk to parents on the phone.

- Learn a few words from the vocabulary of your non–English-speaking students.

- Ask your students and their parents about typical and cultural parties/events, and participate.

- Read about cultures and share information with class during discussions or by creating bulletin boards with cultural information. You can identify favorite sports and physical activities in different cultures; select a list of athletes, gather their pictures, and share them with the class.

- Identify cultures present in your class and assign students to do research about physical activities and sports in that culture, country or region. You can start with the city that you are in and expand to other parts of the world.

- Introduce new units of instruction through games or activities that provide cultural and historical perspectives.

- Travel to different places and areas within your community, your state, country, or even internationally. As you experience life in different communities and lifestyles, you will start appreciating the differences in the way that people approach life. You can find completely different cultures even in a small town. Search for them and have fun even if you feel uncomfortable. Everything new tends to be uncomfortable at first.

- Participate in activities with people from different groups and ages. You will be able to expand your ability to share yourself and to understand about other groups' cultures and routines. Be open to personally experience and participate in different sports and games that are not part of American culture.

Create New and Transform Current Methodological Approaches

- Learn about different learning styles of children from different cultures (e.g., organization level; visual, tactile or auditory style; working alone rather than in groups).

- Vary your instructional approach. Use visual learning (e.g., instructor's or student's demonstrations, visual displays, or films); tactile learning (e.g., reciprocal peer instruction and feedback by physically assisting each other, or instructor physically assisting and guiding student through movement); auditory learning (e.g., develop good listening skills; use sounds as cues for activities, changes, or to guide activity/skill rhythm).

- Do not assume that a student from a different culture has particular academic or athletic interests. Encourage broad participation and ask students about their preferences.

- Use music in your activities. It can give you an opportunity to share your music preferences and to ask students to bring music from their cultures. Be aware of appropriate language.

- Learn individual student needs. Remember that assessment tools are traditional and norm-referenced, and that using a functional or ecological approach (see Chapter 5, Assessment to Facilitate Successful Inclusion) can support you to have more adequate assessment tools effective for your diverse group of students.

- Provide in your lessons culturally relevant student-centered activities and cooperative opportunities. Use more cooperative activities and games, placing less emphasis on competition.

- Create classes where you can have students working on different activities in different groups. Creating stations might be a good idea to accommodate students who prefer to work alone or to whom you need to emphasize a skill.

- Ask students what their preferences are. Always consider your students' knowledge by allowing them to contribute in the activities.

- Have a variety of activities. It will allow your students to choose.

- Give yourself time to implement new strategies. It is okay if a new strategy did not work as you expected. Give yourself and your students time to get used to a new methodology. It is common that students have resistance to new activities in the beginning.

- Teach personal and social responsibility skills. Practice them during classes. For example, teach students to use integrity principles (e.g., keeping their word regarding agreements they made to follow the rules, be on time, and be honest regarding issues that might come up). Create a community of respect (e.g., speaking when given the opportunity, respecting others, thanking and offering help, understanding and respecting differences, speaking when they are disappointed or upset). These principles are important and easy to implement.

- Create a structure where students can be in communication with you regarding any issue that might come up. If during the class there is not enough time, ask them to come to your class later or to write a letter to you.

- Review the instructional resources, curriculum, support materials, and activities with each new class.

- Ensure that materials, equipment, and teaching strategies include perspectives from different cultural and ethnic groups. Do not assume that a student knows how to use certain pieces of equipment.

- Remember that physical education and sports have a rich heritage that has evolved from cultures throughout the world. Use these resources and highlight different racial or ethnic contributions or the unique contributions made by women.

- Use reward systems to encourage and promote full participation. Negotiate with students what they would like to have as a reward (e.g., give students an opportunity to choose activities; use favorite physical education activity, equipment, or game as reward given at end of class; or create stickers, cards or medals with students' names and goals achieved).

- Increase physical activity time and opportunities and provide developmentally and age-appropriate activities and equipment.

Use Activities that Promote Critical Thinking and that Give Students the Opportunity to Express Their Views

- Offer a variety of activities and variations within each activity so that students can choose. By providing variety and choice in your curriculum, you promote recognition of your students' diverse cultures, promote decision-making, and respect students' individuality. You might have classrooms where it is not possible to offer different activities, so try to vary levels of intensity, equipment, and rules in the same activity. Make sure students participate in the creation process.

- Promote discussion about games and activities before they start. Discuss rules and create new rules with students.

- Have students develop mental images or verbalize physical skills as they are taught. Ask them to create variations of the skill and play with it.

- Have students teach other students. As they give instruction and feedback, they also learn and process the components of skills learned.

- Use problem-solving approaches. Avoid giving "the answer" on how to execute basic or complex skills. Let students come up with options and experience them. Change rules or basic forms of equipment (e.g., move or lower basketball goals, play with balls of different sizes and shapes). A football might be completely different for some students. Explore the use of a football in other sports. Create games with elementary school students where they can use their imagination and use metaphors when performing basic skills (e.g., ford a river, crawl through a cave, climb a small hill, walk like a bear).

Provide Effective Feedback and Instruction

- Give concrete and specific feedback. In teaching a physical skill, focus on the specific qualities of the skill or activity being taught.

- Give feedback that is positive, specifically corrective, and of equal quality for all students regardless of race or ethnicity.

- Emphasize that performance of skills is individual, and discourage comparison of any nature. Avoid comparing a current class with classes that you have taught in the past. Remember that you are teaching a class of students with different body types and shapes, height and weight, past experiences in activities, families and cultures, etc. Even if they all come from similar backgrounds, each student has his own uniqueness. So, avoid generalizing and comparing your students.

- Avoid stereotypical, racist, or gender-biased language such as "throwing like a girl," "sit like a Indian," and "you guys." Avoid assertions such as "This is the way it should be," "This is the right and only way to do it," and "You should do it like. . . ." Be open and flexible in your teaching. All techniques of basic skills were made up in a certain way to suit the American culture. Do not assume that students coming from other cultures have had experience with basic activities. Students from South America, Asia, or Africa might never had experience with baseball, softball, American football, or lacrosse skills or rules.

- Keep in mind that teachers also communicate things in nonverbal ways. Be aware of negative body language.

Create Positive Relationships with Your Students' Parents and Families

- Build relationships with your students' parents and families.

- Communicate with parents or guardians to acknowledge students' successes. Do not wait until students are having difficulties to communicate with parents.

- Be in communication with parents and ask about students' strengths, weaknesses, and family activities and interests, and use them to plan your activities. For your students with disabilities, make sure that parents fully participate in the creation of your student's IEP goals and objectives. Create a structure where you can frequently be in communication with parents (phone, letters, e-mail, or meetings). For ESL parents, avoid communication by phone; use letters or meet in person. Use an interpreter as needed (e.g., family members can be interpreters).

- Be partners with parents because you share common objectives for your students' success.

- Get to know the siblings of your students with disabilities. They can be great support during classes, after school, and helping their brothers

and sisters with "PE homework" (you might ask the student to practice activities at home, or to start creating an active routine with activities). They can help you to define what is important to their brothers and sisters based on their life experience.

Distinguish and Recognize Your Prejudices and Biases

Teachers have control of the classroom and will choose whether to implement a culturally responsive approach. Teachers can build sensitivity to diversity in numerous ways. However, they must first face their own biases, stereotypes, prejudices, and behaviors before helping children recognize and address their own (Butt & Pahnos, 1995; see Table 14.2).

Teachers can directly influence how students are treated in their classrooms. Although teachers try to be fair to all students, there is evidence that teachers differentiate among them (Hutchinson, 1995). To recognize and eliminate stereotypes, teachers must acknowledge that they exist. To eradicate this, teachers must look closely at the ways in which they encourage or discourage certain groups (e.g., girls, children with disabilities, African Americans, Asian, Hispanics and others) during physical education classes. It is important for teachers to reflect on their own behaviors and how these behaviors influence their teaching strategies (Hutchinson, 1995). Table 14.3 presents an exercise on behaviors that indicate differentiation among students. Also, by observing the interactions among students, teachers can determine how to structure lesson plans and include activities that promote cooperation and interaction among and between diverse groups (Hutchinson, 1995).

Table 14.2.   Bias awareness exercise

It is important to know yourself and what are the assumptions that you "automatically" make about a student. Be honest with yourself when answering the following questions.

> What are my expectations toward my students?
> Am I challenging one student more than the other?
> What are the assumptions that I am making?
> What can I do to include all students?

Always consider that you might have some biases and pre-existing ideas toward your students and their families that come from your education, upbringing, values, and past experiences.

It is not about "you" discriminating against your students; in our society, "white, male, American, Christian, rich" students have more privileges than other groups. By recognizing your views about students with disabilities who come from certain backgrounds, you will start to be aware of those views and have the ability to change your views.

Biases are not bad, but they limit your relationships with your students and their achievements as well as their parents.

Table 14.3. Exercise on reactions to children from diverse backgrounds

I often avoid students based on their gender, race, ethnicity, level of disability, or performance.

I ignore comments or proper behaviors by minority students.

I usually call on majority students and students with better level of performance in class.

I praise minority students (e.g., girls, children with disabilities) on effort, but I praise majority students on physical performance.

I interrupt or do not give minority students a chance to speak.

I use patronizing and impatient tones with minority students.

I provide limited feedback and guidance.

I attribute success of minority students to luck rather than to hard work.

I stand closer to and assume more of an attentive posture with majority students.

I use stereotypical examples in ways that reinforce negative attitudes.

I group students by minority groups, gender, and disability.

I keep the class gender segregated.

Source: Hutchinson (1995).

DISABILITY AND DIVERSITY

People with disabilities are the largest minority group in America (nearly 50 million). However, not until the Rehabilitation Act of 1973 (PL 93-112) were those with disabilities considered a class of people. Typically, their rights and privileges are associated with their cultural and/or gender group (Bryan, 1999).

An examination of Census 2000 data on the population of noninstitutionalized people with disabilities (age 5 and older) by race shows that African Americans and American Indians shared the highest disability rate (24%). Asian Americans had the lowest disability rate (17%); Hispanics had 21%. Table 14.1 shows the number and percentage of students with disabilities by racial ethnic groups served in 2004 under the Individuals with Disabilities Education Act (IDEA) Amendments of 1997 (PL 105-17). People with disabilities who are members of a racial minority group must be considered from two perspectives when considering cultural diversity (Bryan, 1999). Multicultural education helps educators within the special education team (including APE specialist) become more responsive and sensitive to the needs of students with disabilities from culturally diverse backgrounds.

Professionals often ignore diversity and cultural characteristics, and individuals with disabilities may end up not receiving appropriate services. The combination of disability and ethnicity, race, and/or cultural background often results in a double form of discrimination. Individuals with disabilities who are members of minority ethnic, racial, or cultural groups frequently experience more discrimination disproportionately than their Caucasian counterparts (Bryan, 1999).

Reality dictates that in any society one group will become dominant. Therefore, that group's standards, values, belief system, and morals will often become the dominant culture. This fact is neither good nor bad, simply a fact of how society has been organized. However, the extent to which the dominant culture extends itself to include or exclude other belief systems, values, and standards as a significant part of overall society causes the dominant group's motives and actions to be considered oppressive or inclusive (Banks, 1999).

Euro-American culture has been the dominant culture in America for several hundred years and its domination has been so encompassing that practically all other cultures have been suppressed, assimilated, or eliminated. Wehrly explained how immigrants were induced to adopt a pattern of determined Euro-American values:

> For a time, it was thought that the United States would become a melting pot of all the cultures brought by the immigrants and an idealized blended national culture would emerge. As more and more immigrants came to United States in the late 19th and early 20th centuries, the white European men in power became concerned about the different values and behaviors brought by immigrants, and so the norm was changed from the melting pot to that of assimilation. Cultural assimilation, as practiced in United States, is the expectation by the people in power that all immigrants and all people outside the dominant group will give up their ethnic and cultural values and will adopt the values and norms of the dominant society—the white, male Euro-Americans. (1995, p. 12)

Many discriminatory acts have been ruled unconstitutional and have been replaced by humane and empowering laws such as the Civil Rights Act, the American with Disabilities Act of 1990 (PL 101-336), and IDEA. During the past 20 years those with professional as well as personal concerns regarding education, employment, counseling, and other health and social issues, such as rehabilitation, human relations, and human resource development, began to pay close attention to the issues of cultural diversity in the population with disabilities.

PEOPLE WITH DISABILITIES FROM CULTURALLY DIVERSE BACKGROUNDS

Because children from diverse backgrounds are overrepresented in special education, it is important that general and adapted physical educators be familiar with these culturally diverse minority groups. The first part of this section examines race and ethnic background as it contributes to diversity. This information is meant to be an introduction to specific racial and ethnic groups; it is important to seek out more specific information from the student's parents, the school, and community agencies. It is also important to note that the information in this section provides generalities common to people within each racial and ethnic group. By no means should this list of commonalities imply that all people who come from these groups will demonstrate all of these commonalities. Each child should be viewed as an individual whose racial and ethnic heritage only partially defines him or her. The discussion of race and ethnicity is followed by a discussion of noncultural factors known to contribute to diversity in the public schools. This section includes information on gender, English as a second language, religion, poverty, and refugees. These noncultural factors often coexist with racial and ethnic factors.

Race and Ethnicity

American Indian/Alaskans

American Indian/Alaskans represented 1.49% of students (91,236) ages 6–21 served under IDEA (OSEP, 2004b). The census bureau uses the term "American Indian and Alaska Native," which refers to people whose ancestors were any of the original inhabitants of North America, Central America, and South America and who maintain tribal affiliation or community attachment. Small, but fast growing, the Native American population growth is expected to outpace Hispanic growth during the next 5 years (11.2%). The Native American population is young (37% are between the ages of 5 and 24). A large portion of Native American households (47.1%) earn less than $25,000 annually. The lower middle class is also a large portion of this community (Wellner, 2002).

Native American children have been found to be more rejected, depressed, and withdrawn than Anglo children (Sutliff, 1996). Adapted and general physical education teachers must educate themselves about unique cultural characteristics of this group when working with Native American students. "Without proper information, cultural incompatibilities can lead to misjudgments" (Sutliff, 1996). A letter written by a father of a Native American student to his teacher expresses stereotypes and misjudgments often experienced by these children:

> He is not culturally "disadvantaged" but he is culturally different! I want my child to succeed in school and in life. I don't want him to be a dropout or juvenile delinquent or to end up on drugs or alcohol

because of discrimination. I want him to be proud of his rich heritage and culture, and I would like him to develop the necessary capabilities to adapt to, and succeed in, both cultures. But I need your help. What you say and what you do in the classroom, what you teach and how you teach it will have a significant effect on the potential success or failure of my child. All I ask is that you work with me, not against me, to help educate my child in the best way. My son, Wind Wolf, is not an empty glass coming to your class to be filled. He is a full basket coming into a different environment and society to share. Please let him share his knowledge, heritage, and culture with you and his peers. (Lake, 1990, pp. 51–52)

African Americans or Blacks and Africans

The African American population is projected to grow faster than the white population, at a rate that falls between that for Asian Americans and Hispanics. Four in ten African Americans are younger than age 24. In fact, those ages 5–24 make up more than one third of all African Americans. It is estimated that by 2007 there will be almost 40 million African Americans in the United States, representing a growth of 11.6% since 2000 (Wellner, 2002).

African American households earn less than the average and are overrepresented among the lowest income groups. However, 44.6% of African American households earn between $25,000 and $74,999; 42.9% earn less than $25,000. Fifty-seven percent of African Americans have less than a high school education or are high school graduates; 22% have some college education, and 21% have an associate's, bachelor's, or graduate degree. African Americans are less likely to live in a married-couple household (31%) than the general population (52%). African American woman are far more likely to be single parents; 19% of households consist of an unmarried woman with children younger than 18 (Wellner, 2002). In 2004, 1,253,492 students ages 6–21 were served under IDEA (OSEP, 2004b).

Asian and Pacific Islanders

> The experience of being treated as foreigners, exotics, outsiders, hordes, dangerous, those kind of images that are recycled in American media . . . perpetuate some kind of basis for people of different backgrounds to come together. (Meadows, 2005, p. 40)

> When I was in high school, I went to a small Catholic school and we took a field trip to Virginia. . . . Our bus stopped for lunch and there was a diner with two signs. One said "Whites Only" and the other said "For Colored." For a moment, I didn't know where I fit. My classmates linked their arms with mine and walked me through the whites-only door. You don't know how people are going to accept you. You wonder, what are you really entitled to? (Meadows, 2005, p. 30)

In the face of language barriers, cultural adjustments, and government and societal oppression, Asian Americans appear to have done quite well in America (Meadows, 2005). The myth of universal affluence and intelligence among Asian Americans, however, has not stopped society from classifying them as minorities. They are seen as smart, wealthy, and successful—on the surface, a positive perception. The belief that Asian Americans can succeed on their own diminishes the notion that some could benefit from programs ranging from Medicaid to affirmative action (Meadows, 2005).

The census defines Asians as people who have origins in any of the original peoples of the Far East, Southeast Asia, or Indian subcontinent. It also includes some people of Hispanic origin who may be of any race. By 2007, the number of Asian Americans is expected to soar by 27%, a faster rate than other groups. The two biggest groups are from China and the Philippines. Teachers need to be sensitive to the culture of each Asian student. Asian Americans represent nearly 25 countries with completely different cultural backgrounds, races, religious beliefs, and languages. In 2004, 129,391 Asian American students ages 6–21 were served under IDEA (OSEP, 2004b). Depending when the family immigrated, language could be an issue. Also, many Asian Americans follow religions other than traditional Christian religions, so activities revolving around Christmas and Easter may be foreign to Asian Americans. On a positive note, Asian Americans tend to have a strong sense of family and of education, and Asian American parents of children with disabilities will tend to be very supportive of any educational programs offered their children.

Hispanics or Latinos

Since the 1960s, the United States witnessed an accelerated demographic transformation as the Latino community has surged past African Americans to become the nation's largest minority group. Latino immigrants from Mexico, Puerto Rico, Cuba, Central America, and South America continue to arrive daily. The Hispanic/Latino community, which now totals about 40 million, has brought subtle and overt changes to American society, influencing education, political life, business, and mass media. It is important to recognize the vast cultural, geographic, historic, racial, and ethnic differences among various Latino groups. Latinos or Hispanics can be of any race. Nearly half of Hispanics (47.9%) identify themselves as white, and 42.2% identify themselves as some other race. Married couples make up a solid majority of the Hispanic households, and a larger share than the American population as a whole (Wellner, 2002).

In 2004, slightly more than 1 million Hispanics were being served under IDEA. McCollum and Holt (2004) noted that language is the biggest obstacle for educators and therapists who work with Hispanic children with disabilities. Many Hispanic immigrants to the United States use Spanish as their first language and are "limited English proficient" (LEP) (see Tables 14.4 and 14.5).

White Americans

The census defines "white" as people who have origins in any of the original peoples of Europe, the Middle East, or North Africa. Three quarters (75.1%) of the U.S. population identified themselves as "white alone." However, the white population is expected to grow by less than 2% between 2002 and 2007. Approximately 30.4% of whites are between the ages of 35 and 54, and 26.2% are between the ages of 5 and 24. Whites are more likely to have higher household incomes than the population as a whole (their median income is $44,517). In 2004, 3,590,032 white students age 6–21 were served under IDEA (OSEP, 2004b).

Noncultural Factors

Gender

Physical educators tend to have very specific stereotypes about boys and girls. Beveridge and Scruggs (2000) argued that boys and girls are influenced into behaving according to specific social and cultural roles, and that parental and cultural expectations for physical activity and sport engagement are usually higher for boys than for girls. Limitations are imposed on girls when physical educators do not recognize that they may be treating their female students differently than their male students. In a case study, Palla and Block (2004) found that the APE specialists expressed bias based on a student's gender. One teacher said, "The other day I felt frustrated with one of my students, he was being so stubborn, and crying . . . so I left him alone in the class. I hope he learned a lesson." When the teacher was asked if he would have left a girl alone, the teacher smiled, expressed embarrassment, and said, "I would not. I can see that I am hard on him and that the fact that he is a boy probably influenced my reaction . . . but I am not sure."

Hutchinson (1995) reminded that we cannot forget gender discrimination and inequalities in our classrooms, in physical education programs, and in sports. She approaches gender discrimination in physical education as a socially constructed issue, noting that perpetuating gender differences helps to continue inequalities in instruction, participation, and opportunities for girls. Several central misconceptions about women's and girls' participation in sport and physical activity can influence the way teachers treat and plan for girls with disabilities. For example, some teachers

> Consider ... certain activities inappropriate for girls, such as vigorous and competitive sports that are believed to make women develop masculine traits and are potentially harmful to women's ability to have children. (Hutchinson, 1995)

These conceptions and stereotypes support the view of women as weak and fragile. Physical education curriculum and experiences must be implemented in ways that convey equitable messages about sport and physical activity for girls and boys. Gender stereotyping and sex segregation in PE continue to perpetuate stereotypic views of woman (Hutchinson, 1995).

English as a Second Language

Imagine preparing to attend an IEP meeting knowing that everyone you meet with will be speaking Chinese. How would you feel? How well do you think you will understand what is being said, and how well do you think the others will understand what you are saying? This is how parents and students who have LEP or speak English as a second language (ESL) feel when they step into an American school.

The Virginia Department of Education (2005), like many states, uses the definition of LEP found in the No Child Left Behind Act of 2001 (PL 107-110) (see Table 14.4). Enrollment of LEP students across the country has grown. For example, in Virginia the numbers of LEP students has grown from just over 19,000 in 1994 to 67,000 in 2004. These numbers are no doubt higher in states that attract a high number of immigrants such as New York, California, Texas, and Arizona. Although Spanish is the predominant language of most LEP students, more than 120 different languages were spoken by LEP students in Virginia in 2002 (Virginia Department of Education, 2005).

Lynch and Hanson (2004) pointed out that language is the primary means of access to understanding, relationships, and services. Whenever someone is speaking in a language other than the majority language (English in the United States), they are putting more effort into their communication. These difficulties in communication often lead to frustration. Even if family members speak and understand English, the language used in typical IEP meetings by school personnel and specialists is often highly technical. When family members do not speak English, they must rely on interpreters who do not always provide accurate information. Unfortunately, interpreters may lack the language abilities or tech-

Table 14.4. Definition of students with limited English proficiency (LEP)

An LEP student is classified as one:

A. who is age 3 through 21;

B. who is enrolled or preparing to enroll in an elementary or secondary school;

C. (i) who was not born in the United States or whose native language is a language other than English; and who comes from an environment where a language other than English is dominant.

OR

(ii) (I) who is Native American or Alaska Native, or native resident of outlying areas; and

(II) who comes from an environment where a language other than English has had a significant impact on the individual's level of English language proficiency.

OR

(iii) who is migratory, whose native language is a language other than English, and who comes from an environment where a language other than English is dominant.

AND

D. whose difficulties speaking, reading, writing, or understanding English language may be sufficient to deny the individual—

(i) the ability to meet the State's proficient level of achievement on State assessments described in section 1111(b)(3)

(ii) the ability to achieve successfully in classrooms where the language of instruction is English; or

(iii) the opportunity to participate fully in society.

Reprinted from No Child Left Behind Act of 2001, PL 107-110, Title IX, Part A, Section 9101(25).

nical expertise to translate special education jargon accurately, and more than likely some languages do not have adequate translations. Many times, younger or extended family members are asked to interpret, and their own concerns may shape the information being transmitted (Lynch & Hanson, 2004). For example, a daughter may be hesitant to tell her parents that their son (her brother) has been diagnosed with intellectual disabilities or may have to be placed in a special school for children with disabilities away from their neighborhood school.

Being able to understand and being understood by others is critical in situations like IEP meetings where interpersonal relationships and interactions are important. This includes both verbal and nonverbal means of communication. Some nonverbal gestures that seem subtle and innocuous may be offensive. Both sending and understanding messages are prerequisites to effective interpersonal interactions. Because language and culture are so closely tied together, communicating with families from different cultural backgrounds is very complex (Lynch & Hanson, 2004).

Working with students and their families who have limited English skills can be particularly challenging for both general and adapted physical educators. Information presented in Table 14.5 provides strategies for general and adapted physical educators

when teaching students with LEP. Table 14.6 provides a listing of commonly used words in PE in English and Spanish.

Religion

With more immigration from around the world, our schools are becoming more religiously diverse. Today it is not uncommon to teach children whose religious affiliations vary from Islam to Hindu to Buddhism. Such religious diversity should not only be tolerated but also embraced. However, the United States and, in turn, public schools were founded under a Judeo-Christian belief system, and the majority of students in the public schools continue to be Christian (Lynch & Hanson, 2004). For the physical education teacher, challenges include issues with dressing out for students who for religious reasons are forbidden from showing their legs in public (Muslim and Hindu), challenges with boys and girls participating in physical activity together (Muslim), and challenges with dietary rules such as month-long fasting (Muslim) (Kahan, 2003). In addition, many physical educators incorporate popular Christian (e.g., Christmas, Easter) and pseudo-Christian (Halloween) holidays into their physical education programs. Such practices may be disrespectful of religious beliefs. The important point is

Table 14.5. Strategies for teaching students with limited English proficiency

Use computer software for English/Spanish translation for instructional aids, cognitive assessments, parent info, individualized education program (IEP) forms, authorization for assessment.

Learn basic words to use during adapted physical education classes.

Invite peers to support students during class.

Call students by their correct names.

Learn to read the student. Body language, gestures, and facial expressions can often communicate intent and feelings better than verbal language.

Minimize the use of verbal language and rely on demonstrations, gestures, and body language for communication.

Post the physical education rules in Spanish as well as in English.

Use commands for addressing an individual student and the verb form of locomotor, nonlocomotor, and manipulative skills (as well as enunciation).

Use instructional strategies that foster social interactions (e.g., peer teaching, cooperative learning).

Use a buddy system (e.g., pair the student with limited English proficiency with a student who understands some of the language or is bilingual).

Use instructional aids (e.g., pictures, key words for the day in Spanish, directional arrows).

Use visual demonstrations along with verbal explanations of learning task.

Include activities that have a Hispanic origin (e.g., Mexican hat dance, La cucaracha with lummi sticks) when relevant to lesson objectives.

When using music for starting and stopping activity, play music that is in Spanish or Latin rhythms.

Give physical education word cues to the Spanish teacher to teach the students with limited English proficiency before they come to class.

For more effective classroom management and communication, learn some basic words in Spanish.

Source: McCollum, Civalier, and Holt (2004).

Table 14.6. Commonly used words in physical education and their Spanish translation

Word type	English	Spanish	Pronunciation
Commands	Walk	Camina	Kah me nah
	Run	Corre	Kor ray
	Look	Mira	Me rah
	Quiet	Silencio	See lain see owe
	Stop	Para	Pah rah
	Ready	Listo	Lee stow
	Go	Ve	Bay
	Behave	Pórtate bien	Pore tah tay bee in
	Be careful	Cuidado	Kwee dah doe
	Come here	Ven aquí	Been a key
	Sit down	Siéntate	See in tah tay
	Stand up	Levántate	Lay bon tah tay
	No pushing	No empujes	No aim poo hays
Locomotor skills	Walk	Caminar	Kah me nar
	Run	Correr	Kor rare
	Hop	Brincar en un pie	Breen kar in oon pee aye
	Skip	Brincar	Breen kar
	Jump	Saltar	Sall tar
	Gallop	Galopar	Ga low par
	Leap	Saltar	Sall tar
	Slide	Deslizar	Day slee sar
Nonlocomotor skills	Turn	Voltear	Bowl tee ar
	Twist	Torcer	Tore sair
	Bend	Doblar	Doe blar
	Curl	Enroscar	In roe skar
	Swing	Meser	May sair
	Stretch	Extender	Ex tain dair
	Push	Empujar	Aim poo har
	Pull	Alar	Ah lar
	Spin	Dar vueltas	Dar bwell tass
	Balance	Balancear	Bah lon see ar
Manipulative skills	Throw	Lanzar	Lon sar
	Catch	Agarrar	A gah rrar
	Kick/Punt	Puntapié	Poon tah pee aye
	Dribble (with feet)	Regatear	Ray gah tee ar
	Dribble (with hand)	Rebotar	Ray bow tar
	Volley	Volear	Bow lee ar
	Strike (golf)	Golpear	Goal pee ar
	Strike (bat)	Batear	Bah tee ar

From McCollum, S., Civalier, A., & Holt, A. (2004). Equitable learning for Spanish speaking students in elementary physical education. *Strategies, 17*(6), 21–23; reprinted by permission.

that physical educators should be aware of children who come from religious backgrounds different from theirs and different from the community norm and allow these children to honor their religious practices as these practices relate to physical education participation. This might include allowing children who are fasting for the month of Ramadan to be excused from overly vigorous activity, allowing excused absences for students who are observing important holidays for their faith (e.g., Yom Kippur and Rosh Hashanah for Jewish students), creating private dressing areas in the locker room and relaxing showering rules for students whose religion pro-

hibits public nudity (Muslim, Hindu), and having flexible dress codes for students such as allowing Muslim girls to wear a long-sleeve shirt and loose sweats under her physical education uniform as well as a *hijab* to cover her head, neck and ears (Kahan, 2003).

Disability Linked to Poverty

Living in poverty means that one has the minimum or less than the minimum required for basic survival, including housing, clothing, food, transportation, and access to quality health care. The United

States government calculates poverty based on a formula that combines annual income, overall family size, and number of related children under 18 years (U.S. Census Bureau, 2004; see Table 14.7). For example, the threshold for a single person younger than age 65 to be considered as "living in poverty" is $9,573, while the threshold for a family of four that includes two related children younger than the age of 18 is less than $18,660. Based on this definition, in 2003 12.5% of the population (35.9 million Americans) lived in poverty. Among these, 12.9 million are children (U.S. Census Bureau, 2004). The National Center for Children in Poverty (2005) suggested that an additional 27 million children live in low-income families.

Families living in poverty tend to

1. Be headed by a single parent, typically a mother

2. Have at least one wage earner whose wages are insufficient to move the family out of poverty

3. Live in the central or core area of a city

4. Live in the South

5. Be white in terms of absolute numbers, although a considerably larger percentage of Latino and African American families are poor compared with the percentage of white families

6. Be undereducated, with the best-educated parent completing less than high school (Hanson & Lynch, 2004)

In 2000, 17.6% (8.7 million) of people with disabilities were defined as living in poverty, compared with 10.6% of the general population. Approximately 25% of children with disabilities in America live in poverty (Census, 2000). Low-income families are almost 50% more likely to have a child with a disability compared with higher income families. Compared with higher income single mothers, low-income single mothers are more likely to be disabled (29% versus 17%) and have considerably higher rates of severe disability (17% versus 5%) (Lee & Oh, 2002). This data is not surprising given that children who live in poverty are more likely to be subjected to factors related to disability, including low birth weight, chronic health problems, limited access to health care, inadequate nutrition, and trauma (Hanson & Lynch, 2004). In addition, children who grow up in poverty are more likely to be abused, have lower quality health care, be exposed to various environmental toxins, and have parents who abuse drugs (Lawrence, Chau, & Lennon, 2004). Finally, there appears to be a relationship between growing up in poverty and various child outcomes, including teenage pregnancy, low academic achievement and learning disabilities, juvenile delinquency, and

Table 14.7. Poverty thresholds for 2003 by size of family and number of related children younger than age 18

Size of family unit	Weighted average thresholds (in dollars)	Related children younger than age 18								
		0	1	2	3	4	5	6	7	8+
One person (unrelated individual)	9,393									
Younger than 65 years	9,573	9,573								
65 years and older	8,825	8,825								
Two persons	12,015									
Householder younger than 65 years	12,384	12,321	12,682							
Householder 65 years and older	11,133	11,122	12,634							
Three persons	14,680	14,393	14,810	14,824						
Four persons	18,810	18,979	19,289	18,660	18,725					
Five persons	22,245	22,887	23,220	22,509	21,959	21,623				
Six persons	25,122	26,324	26,429	25,884	25,362	24,586	24,126			
Seven persons	28,544	30,289	30,479	29,827	29,372	28,526	27,538	26,454		
Eight persons	31,589	33,876	34,175	33,560	33,021	32,256	31,286	30,275	30,019	
Nine persons or more	37,656	40,751	40,948	40,404	39,947	39,196	38,163	37,229	36,998	35,572

Source: U.S. Census Bureau (2004).

social-emotional difficulties (e.g., conduct disorder, anxiety, depression) (see Hanson & Lynch, 2004, for a review of these studies).

Clearly, poverty is an issue in the lives of many children with and without disabilities in the United States. What are the implications for general and adapted physical educators? First and foremost, physical educators can have a more empathetic understanding of what it must be like to grow up in poverty. Most children are going home to a nice house and a warm meal. These children will watch television, play on the Internet, have parental and peer support to help with homework, and participate in community sports teams. These children will wear different clothes to school every day and have no problem buying clothes, school supplies, and athletic equipment. In contrast, children who grow up in poverty may not have a house to live in and may not know where their next meal will come from. These children likely will not have regular access to a television or a computer, will not have parental or peer support to help with homework, and will not have opportunities to play community sports programs. These children may have to wear the same clothes several days in a row during the week, and they will have a difficult time purchasing basic school supplies, let alone luxury items such as soccer shoes or a lacrosse stick. Just being aware of these facts and understanding the challenges children in poverty face on a daily basis may help you understand and more compassionately deal with some of the physical, emotional, and cognitive problems these children bring with them to the gymnasium. This new awareness might include finding some extra clothes for a child who wears the same clothes to school every day, creating general rules for your physical education classes that encourage interacting with everyone in class and discourage teasing and isolating children, and giving away extra physical education equipment that you might have received for free or that you planned on discarding anyway.

Physical educators should also understand the issues that face the child's family and try to support and help the families as much as possible. This does not necessarily mean giving things to parents, although finding a used pair of soccer shoes or a used lacrosse stick will surely be welcomed. A large part of supporting families who live in poverty is to help parents feel that they can have a big impact on their child's education and welfare. This includes helping parents understand that they can provide stimulating and supportive environments (both scholastically and athletically) for the child, that they can and should have the same academic, behavioral, and athletic expectations as other parents, and that they can help their child (Hanson & Lynch, 2004). For ex-

ample, you might send a jump rope along with a note home to a child's parents saying that you have been working on teaching Samantha (a second-grade girl with mild mental retardation) how to jump rope. In your note you can say that Samantha has learned how to jump rope, but she still needs lots of practice to become more consistent. You then can ask the parents if they would use the rope you provided to encourage Samantha to jump rope at home. They can keep the rope as long as they want, as long as they practice with Samantha.

Lewis (2001) suggested several things that all schools can do to help children who live in poverty and/or who come from diverse backgrounds:

1. Help parents understand how children's social and learning abilities develop.

2. Increase the emphasis on cognitive skills, especially the development of early literacy.

3. Make sure transitions between grades and between schools are as seamless and smooth as possible for children and parents.

4. Gather data on evaluation of children's academic progress and achievement. Provide remedial support early, and check for biases that could prematurely label children.

5. Set academic success (including success in physical education) for all students as the school's mission. Provide no opportunity to use excuses for underachievement.

6. Include everyone—teachers, parents, and students—in setting and carrying out this mission.

7. Cultivate a philosophy within the school of respecting and cultivating family cultural values and traditions.

8. Make sure students and families are aware of community-based services that are available.

9. Provide support for creating professional learning environments for teachers (in-services).

10. Oppose both retention and social promotion: The goal must be to ensure all students are meeting, at the minimum, grade-level standards, no matter what it takes.

11. Use the diversity of students, their families, and neighborhoods/communities to make the curriculum relevant to students.

12. Adopt fair discipline policies and apply them consistently.

13. Publicize progress.

Refugees

The refugee student is an individual who is outside his/her country and is unable or unwilling to return to that country because of well-founded fear that she/he will be persecuted because of race, religion, nationality, political opinion, or membership in a particular social group. This does not include persons displaced by natural disasters or persons who, although displaced, have not crossed an international border or persons commonly known as "economic migrants," whose primary reason for flight has been a desire for personal betterment rather than persecution. (Virginia Department of Education, 2005)

There are 9 million stateless people in every corner of the globe. In 2002, the United States accepted the largest number of refugees for resettlement, with 26,800 people emigrating mostly from Somalia, Angola, Bosnia-Herzegovina, Vietnam, China, Mexico, Colombia, Haiti, and India (UNHCR, 2003).

Refugee children are usually enrolled in school as soon as possible after arrival. Many are enrolled in school without speaking any English and often experience a drastic culture shock. Newly arriving students are generally placed in a grade on the basis of age and previous academic study. Children speaking little English may be placed initially in a lower grade. Students with no English or poor English skills tend to be placed into ESL but included in art, music, and physical education classes. Some children may need 2–5 years to adjust fully to life in the new community (Center for Applied Linguistics, Cultural Orientation Resource Center, 1996).

Teachers often refer refugee students for APE, because cultural and language problems often make these children seem delayed when compared with their American peers. Some of the students may come from completely different cultures, in which being instructed to be physically active was not part of their lifestyle. Be aware of the child's needs and be sensitive to cultural differences when choosing assessment tools and deciding upon goals and placement. Running laps, using the locker room, use of appropriate clothing and shoes, and engaging in physical activity with certain equipment might be completely unfamiliar for a lot of refugee children. Detailed planning might be needed. Understanding class rules in physical education as well as basic instruction will be a challenge for ESL refugee students. Initially, students might be confused and refuse to participate in physical education. Written tests and health education classes bring an extra challenge. Also, seek support from local refugee agencies in your community to learn more about the student's background and ways to accommodate the student in your program (Palla & Block, 2004).

DISABILITY AS A MINORITY GROUP

Membership in the world of disability has no boundaries. Anyone, regardless of race, gender, ethnicity, socioeconomic status, or age is subject to become a member at any time in his or her life. Equity of inclusion notwithstanding, people with disabilities make up the largest open-class group in the world (Bryan, 1999).

As the population of America has increased, the rate of disabilities has also increased. There were 50 million people with some type of long-lasting condition or disability living in the United States in 2000. This represented 19% of the 257 million ages 5 and older who were not living in prisons, nursing homes, and other institutions, or nearly one person in five (U.S. Census Bureau, 2000).

Gaining equal access to the benefits and opportunities in our society has long been a challenge of people with disabilities. Historically, people with disabilities have faced serious and persistent forms of discrimination, segregation, exclusion, and sometimes elimination. People with disabilities have struggled to establish their place in society and secure their basic civil rights.

The passage of the ADA was the result of the efforts of a cross-disability coalition that took root in the early 1970s. The ADA asserts the equality of people with disabilities and opens the door to the benefits and responsibilities of full participation in society (Adams et al., 1997). The IDEA Amendments of 1997 require that special education, including physical education, is made available to all students with disabilities (Sutherland & Hodge, 2001).

Data from the U.S. Department of Education (2003) show that 6,726,193 children between ages 3 and 21 have been served under IDEA. Table 14.8 shows placement of children with disabilities (ages 6–21) in different educational environments. The majority of children are served in general education schools with different amounts of time in the general education classroom.

IDEA, along with the inclusion movement, has given students with disabilities new opportunities. Today more and more students with disabilities are included in general education settings. Unfortunately, people with disabilities are still generally viewed unfavorably in society. The cultural and societal system of oppression against people with disabilities can be defined as *ableism*.

What Is Ableism?

People with disabilities are often viewed as inadequate to meet expected social and economic roles.

Table 14.8. Number of students ages 6–21 served under IDEA, Part B, in 2004, by educational environment

Locations	Outside Regular Class			Public Separ Facil	Private Separ Facil	Public Resid Facil	Private Resid Facil	Home Hosp Envir	Total
	< 21%	21%–60%	> 60%						
U.S. AND OUTLYING AREAS	3,191,458	1,612,692	1,071,743	108,626	73,257	18,414	17,779	26,419	6,120,388
50 STATES, D.C. & P.R.	3,130,759	1,599,356	1,061,943	107,859	73,049	18,400	17,762	26,248	6,035,376

Facil = Facility; Resid = Residential; Separ = Separate; Hosp = Hospital; Envir = Environment

Reprinted from U.S. Department of Education, Office of Special Education Programs (OSEP), Data Analysis System (DANS). (2004a). *Part B, Individuals with Disabilities Education Act implementation of FAPE requirements.* Data updated as of July 30, 2005. Retrieved October 18, 2006, from http://www.ideadata.org/tables28th/ar_2-2.htm

The term *ableism* is used to describe the exclusionary policies and attitudes of institutions, groups, and individuals against those with mental, emotional, or physical disabilities. Ableism could be said to be perpetuated by the media, both public and private, and reflects our society's deeply rooted beliefs about human health, beauty, and the value of human life (Rauscher & McClintock, 1997).

Because many do not know how to deal with people with disabilities, they try to avoid contact with or even talking about people with disabilities. One reason for this avoidance is fear to be around someone who is so different from oneself (Henderson & Bryan, 1997). Also, lack of knowledge can lead to lack of interest, ignoring, concern, anxiety, and/or withdrawal. People without disabilities have mixed feelings when they encounter a person with disabilities (Sherrill, 2004). As a result of unanswered questions and unexpressed concerns or fears, people without disabilities begin to create their own assumptions and rationalizations, which are often used to comfort, protect, and justify themselves.

One of the many roots of ableism is the fear of becoming disabled. Disability reminds us of the fragility of life and confronts us with questions about our own mortality. Yet, disability remains a normal part of human experience. Every racial, ethnic, and religious group includes people with disabilities. In fact, everyone who lives long enough will have some form of disability.

Prejudice and discrimination against people with disabilities have been perpetuated through language. Using language to talk about disability, the experience of being disabled, and people who have disabilities is sometimes difficult and has gone through many changes. Terms once used to describe people with disabilities in the 19th and 20th centuries have fallen into disfavor (e.g., *crippled, deformed, deaf and dumb, insane, idiot*). Terms acceptable just a few years ago, such as *retardation, handicap*, or *mental illness*, have been replaced with terms such as *developmental disability* and *emotional disability*. The increased use of people-first language (e.g., *a person with a disability*) encourages viewing people who have disabilities as people first and disabled second. These different uses of language reflect the different perspectives held by people with disabilities and the evolution of thinking about disabilities. The terms *people with disabilities* and *disabled people* are most commonly used by the disability rights movement (Rauscher & McClintock, 1997).

Images of People with Disabilities in the Media

The media is one the most powerful ways to perpetuate stereotypes of people with disabilities. A stereotype is a generalization about a person or group of persons. Stereotypes can lead to unfair discrimination and persecution when the stereotype is unfavorable. Assumptions, biases, and preconceived notions toward a group, a person, or a situation can lead to exclusion and segregation (Banks & Banks, 2004).

When we meet a person with a disability, we often do not see the unique characteristics, abilities, talents, and capacities of that person. Instead, we tend to focus on the person's disability and what it means for them and for society. Depending on the circumstance or the type of disability, we might have different views and interpretations. As we start to identify the societal and culturally determined stereotypes toward people with disabilities, we can identify which ones interfere in our relationship with the person or student. For example, if as a teacher we see the student as a victim or someone that needs help, it might limit our view of what the student can accomplish. In turn, this stereotype might determine how much we challenge the student in physical education.

The culturally and socially predetermined stereotypes toward people with disabilities may impact each one of us. The image of people with disabilities in the media is often as people to be feared, pitied, and avoided. Persons with disabilities often are characterized as victims who possess undesirable social skills and personal qualities. When depictions of disability are present, they usually are accompanied by circumstances with some sort of stress, trauma, overcompensation, character flaw, or bizarre behavior tendencies (Donaldson, 1981).

Lester and Ross (2003), in their book *Images that Injure: Pictorial Stereotypes in the Media*, reported negative stereotypes of different groups in the United States, including people with disabilities. They stated that stereotypes of people with disabilities fit a pattern that is represented in the media and reflected in social interactions. Nelson (2003) listed six major stereotypes of people with disabilities in our society: a victim, a hero, a threat, someone unable to adjust, one to be cared for, and as one who should not have survived (see Table 14.9). Negative stereotypes can influence educators' views, attitudes, and behaviors and can affect how they plan and teach their classes. For example, teachers may choose infantile toys, activities, or music because they see these students as childlike. Most of the stereotypes of people with disabilities show that the disability is the central focus of a person's life. However, having a disability does not in any way limit people from having meaningful and valuable lives or from contributing to their families, work, and communities.

Altering the Image of People with Disabilities

In the past 30 years, attitudes toward minorities have shifted. Attitudes toward those with disabilities, however, still need some major shifts. New images seem to be developing, but many of the negative attitudes of the past that viewed people with disabilities as invisible or unworthy of notice remain. The impact of the image and stereotypes of people with disabilities in television and movies cannot be overestimated. In our world where the information superhighway is taking a central role in people's lives, there is also a vast promise of what this powerful force can do to alter attitudes toward people with disabilities (Lester & Ross, 2003).

As adapted and general physical education teachers and coaches, we live in a culture in which people with disabilities have been defined by stereotypes and labels. Although labels of disabilities are important for administrative and funding purposes, they can lead to negative stereotyping of students and tend to focus attention on students' disabilities rather than their abilities. It is crucial to understand students' abilities and functioning level when planning for successful and meaningful physical education curriculum (Sutherland & Hodge, 2001). It is

Table 14.9. Pattern of stereotypes in the media toward people with disabilities

The Victim

People with disabilities are seen as childlike, incompetent, needing total care, nonproductive, and a drain on taxpayers. This image of people with disabilities as a victim, a cripple, and confined in a wheelchair is kept alive by shows like telethons and fund-raising campaigns, where pity is used by featuring stories to get money. In these cases, they are rarely seen as those who manage to live happy and productive lives despite having a disability. Their accomplishments are rarely pointed out.

The Hero

The word "supercrip" describes this stereotype. The common inspiring story is of someone who faces the trauma of a disability and, through courage and stamina, rises above it or surrenders heroically. It shows the person with a disability as a hero when succeeding in college, business, relationship, or sports. It diminishes the much-needed attention to access, transportation, jobs, and housing issues, and for the movement to improve the status of all those with disabilities. This stereotype perpetuates the view that a lot of ordinary people with disabilities feel like failures if they have not done something extraordinary.

A Threat

People with disabilities look as if they were evil and warped. They are a threat and represent evil characters in the movies, whose presence implies danger. This stereotype is frequently represented in portrayals of villains whose evil is exemplified by some obvious physical limitations such as the lack or addition of a limb, a hook for a hand, a black patch over the eye, a hunchback, or a facial deformation. These representations play on and reinforce subtle and deeply held fears and prejudices. "These attitudes have been nurtured by Hollywood portrayals and carry over into attitudes toward others with similar limitations in real life" (Nelson, 2003, p. 178).

The One Unable to Adjust

This is the image of a person with disabilities who ended up maladjusted, unable to handle the trauma of his or her problem, and bitter and full of self-pity. The message is that people with disabilities need a friend or family member to set the "pitiable person" straight. The message is often "just buck up and take control of your life." It perpetuates the idea that the person without the disability is the one that understands the problem better than the one with the disability. It implies that people with disabilities are helpless and do not really understand their situations, and are unable to make sound judgments themselves.

The One to Be Cared For

People with disabilities are seen as a burden. This is one consistent representation of a person with disabilities as the frail person who needs to be cared for, a burden on family and society. As a "dramatic device" (Nelson, 2003, p. 179), the depiction shows the noble intent and generosity of those who furnish the care, which makes the person with a disability little more than a prop, not a human capable of interacting with others to the profit of both.

The One Who Should Not Have Survived

One of the most cruel stereotypes of people with disabilities comes under the heading of the better-off dead syndrome. "This comes from the attitude that those with a serious disability would really be better off if they hadn't survived. It echoes the belief that anyone with a serious physical impairment cannot live a fulfilling and happy life and, therefore, might as well not be alive" (Nelson, 2003, p. 180). This stereotype perpetuates the fear and aversion some people feel for people with disabilities. It frightens and reminds people of their own mortality and vulnerability.

Source: Nelson (2003).

our job to create strategies and generate conversations (in IEP meetings, with our colleagues, with parents, your classroom, friends, and your own family) that minimize the restrictive and oppressive views of people with disabilities. Speaking effectively about people with disabilities can transform the environment in your class, then in your school, and perhaps throughout your community.

A significant segment of people with all types of disabilities have reclaimed and redefined the terms *disability* and *disabled* in a positive way. They reject the notion that being disabled is an inherently negative experience, or in any way descriptive of something broken or abnormal. From this perspective, *disability* is a positive term. Proponents of this perspective take pride in the differences in their bodies and minds and strive to make others aware of their experiences and accomplishments. Many people with disabilities take part in an ongoing struggle against the oppressive social, economic, and environmental forces that limit their ability to achieve their full potential (Rauscher & McClintock, 1997). Adapted and general physical education teachers coming from this perspective can empower their students with disabilities and their families toward accomplishing goals and maximizing the positive view of disability inside their communities.

Teachers' Attitudes Toward Teaching Students with Disabilities

Block, Griebenauw, and Brodeur (2004) reviewed research examining attitudes of physical educators and coaches toward working with children with disabilities in general physical education and sport settings (Block & Rizzo, 1995; Conatser, Block, & Lapore, 2000; Kozub & Porreta, 1998; Rizzo, Bishop, & Tobar, 1997; Rizzo & Vispoel, 1991; Theodorakis, Bagiatis, & Goudas, 1995). Attitudes of teachers and coaches toward students with disabilities varied, based on the number of students with disabilities in the classroom and the individual student's personal characteristics and disability label. For example, research has shown that physical educators have more favorable attitudes toward children with learning disabilities compared with children with mental retardation. And physical educators had more favorable attitudes toward people with mild to moderate disabilities than people with severe disabilities. Two factors found to have a positive impact on physical educators' attitudes toward individuals with disabilities were training and experience. Teachers and coaches who had received training in adapted physical education or special education, who had positive experiences working with students with disabilities, and/or who perceived themselves to be competent when working with students with disabilities had more favorable attitudes toward students with disabilities compared with physical educators who had no extra training, less experience, and/or had lower perceived competence.

Related to this idea of positive experience influencing attitudes toward students with disabilities is the *contact theory* (Sherrill, 2004). When interactions between teachers or coaches and students with disabilities are frequent, pleasant, and meaningful, the interactions produce positive attitudes (Sherrill, 2004). In other words, the more positive interactions and experiences an adapted or general physical educator has with students with disabilities, the more likely this teacher will have a positive attitude toward students with disabilities.

Increasing Diversity Proficiency in Adapted Physical Education Specialists

Federal legislation suggests that "efforts within special education must focus on bringing a larger number of minorities into the profession in order to provide appropriate practitioner knowledge, role models, and sufficient manpower to address the clearly changing demography of special education" (IDEA, 1997, p. 40). There is a need to find creative ways to increase the proportion of African Americans and other ethnic and culturally diverse graduate students in the APE profession (Webb & Hodge, 2003).

The number of African Americans in both general and adapted physical education teacher education programs is small. Today the majority of general and adapted physical educators are Caucasian. Less than 5% of all physical education professionals are persons of color, and an even smaller percentage choose APE as part of their major (Webb & Hodge, 2003). Webb and Hodge (2003) evaluated the factors that influence career choices of African American students. They found that participants who chose APE as a profession 1) enjoyed working with individuals with disabilities and 2) had satisfying practical experiences with individuals with disabilities. The ones who did not chose APE as a profession said that they 1) did not have interest in APE and 2) had no professional preparation in the area of APE. These data do not indicate whether the lack of such preliminary exposure was due to the choice of the undergraduate students or if this type of exposure was absent in the participants' current professional preparation programs.

The most obvious solution is to make sure undergraduate students from ethnic and culturally diverse backgrounds are provided with early exposure to APE coursework, including positive practical experiences with people with disabilities. The effectiveness of APE services relies on teachers' successful interactions with students, parents, and team members. More than any time in the history of education in the United States, students, parents, and team members are likely to come from different backgrounds (e.g., different race, ethnicity, culture, religion, socioeconomic status, educational levels, etc.). As a result, today's physical education classes include a large number of students who more than likely look different from the physical education teacher and different from many of their peers. Some students may look different but share a common language or religion. Some may look the same but speak a different language or have a different cultural heritage. Consequently, there is a need for multicultural education resources, training, and support for both general and adapted physical education teachers.

CONCLUSIONS

Physical educators are only human, and no doubt have stereotypes and prejudices based on how people look, dress, act, and speak. It is time for each of us to start looking closely at these stereotypes and views. Because we live with a diverse group of people, including our students, we must be conscious of our own prejudices and limitations when dealing with people from diverse backgrounds (including people with disabilities). We often see our students through stereotyped views and labels, and these views limit what is possible for our students with and without disabilities and our fulfillment as teachers. It will require a daily effort and willingness to look at yourself; to ask for help; to work in collaboration; and to stand for equality in your classroom, in your school, and in your communities.

References

Academy for Certification of Vision Rehabilitation and Education Professionals (ACVREP). (2005). *Scope of practice for orientation and mobility specialists.* Retrieved June 22, 2005, from http://www.acvrep.org/Orientation_Mobility.htm

Adams, M., Bell, L.A., & Griffin, P. (1997). *Teaching for diversity and social justice. A sourcebook.* New York: Routledge.

Adams, R., & McCubbin, J. (1991). *Games, sports and exercises for the physically disabled* (4th ed.). Philadelphia: Lea & Febiger.

Albemarle County Public Schools. [n.d.]. *Functional behavior assessment form 80.01.* Charlottesville, VA: Author.

Alberto, P.A., & Troutman, A.C. (2005). *Applied behavior analysis for teachers* (7th ed.). Columbus, OH: Merrill.

Alexander, S., Lavay, B., & Lawrence, B. (2005). *The trifold display board: A practical and portable behavior management tool.* Unpublished manuscript, Santa Ana Unified School District, CA.

Almquist, S. (2001). The emergency plan. *Strategies, 14*(5), 30–32.

American Association on Mental Retardation. (1992). *Mental retardation: Definition, classification, and systems of supports* (9th ed.). Washington, DC: Author.

American Occupational Therapy Association (AOTA). (2005). *What is occupational therapy?* Retrieved June 22, 2005, from http://www.aota.org/featured/area6/index.asp

American Physical Therapy Association (APTA). (2005). *APTA background sheet 2005: The physical therapist.* Retrieved June 22, 2005, from http://www.apta.org

American Red Cross. (1992a). *American Red Cross swimming and diving.* St. Louis: Mosby-Year Book.

American Red Cross. (1992b). *Water safety instructors manual.* St. Louis: Mosby-Year Book.

American Speech-Language-Hearing Association. (2005). *Fact sheet: Speech-language pathology.* Retrieved June 22, 2005, from http://www.asha.org/public/slp.htm

American Therapeutic Recreation Association (ATRA). (2005). *Frequently asked questions about therapeutic recreation.* Retrieved June 22, 2005, from http://www.atra-tr.org/aboutfaq.htm

American Youth Soccer Organization (AYSO). (1998). *Everyone plays: VIP program guide.* Hawthorne, CA: Author.

Americans with Disabilities Act of 1990 (ADA), PL 101-336, 42 U.S.C. § 12101 *et seq.*

Appenzeller, H. (1983). *The right to participate.* Charlottesville, VA: Miche.

Appenzeller, H., & Appenzeller, T. (1980). *Sports and the courts.* Charlottesville, VA: Miche.

Appenzeller, T. (2000). *Youth sport and the law: A guide to legal issues.* Durham, NC: Carolina Academic Press.

Appenzeller, T. (2005). Youth sports and the law. In H. Appenzeller (Ed.), *Risk management in sports: Issues and strategies* (2nd ed., pp. 131–142). Durham, NC: Carolina Academic Press.

Arbogast, G., & Lavay, B. (1986). Combining students with different ability levels in games and sports. *Physical Educator, 44,* 255–259.

Armstrong, C.A., Rosengard, P.F., Condon, S.A., Sallis, J.F., & Bernal, R.F. (1993). *Self management program: Level 2.* San Diego: San Diego University Foundation.

Arnold, J.B., & Dodge, H.W. (1994). Room for all. *The American School Board Journal,* 22–26.

Assistance to States for the Education of Children with Disabilities, 34 C.F.R. § 300 (2006).

Aufsesser, P.M. (1991). Mainstreaming and the least restrictive environment. How do they differ? *Palaestra, 7*(2), 31–34.

Aufsesser, P.M. (2003, Winter). Liability considerations for placement of students with disabilities in general physical education classes. *Palaestra, 19*(1), 40–43, 58.

Auxter, D., Pyfer, J., & Huettig, C. (2004). *Principles and methods of adapted physical education* (9th ed.). New York: McGraw-Hill.

Auxter, D., Pyfer, J., & Huettig, C. (2005). *Principles and methods of adapted physical education and recreation* (10th ed.). Madison, WI: WCB McGraw-Hill.

Bailey, T.R. (2005). Blood borne pathogens. In H. Appenzeller (Ed.), *Risk management in sport: Issues and strategies* (2nd ed., pp. 175–180). Durham, NC: Carolina Academic Press.

Banks, J.A. (1999). *An introduction to multicultural education.* Boston: Allyn & Bacon.

Banks, J.A., & Banks, C.A.M. (2004). *Multicultural education: Issues and perspectives* (5th ed.). York, PA: John Wiley & Sons, Inc.

Bateman, B.D. (1998–2000). *Better IEPs* (3rd ed.). Longmont, CO: Sopris West.

Bateman, B.D., & Chard, D.J. (1995). *Legal demands*

and constraints on placement decisions. In J.M. Kauffman, J.W. Lloyd, D.P. Hallahan, & T.A. Astuto (Eds.), *Issues in educational placement* (pp. 285–316). Mahwah, NJ: Lawrence Erlbaum Associates.

Bateman, B.D., & Herr, C.M. (2003). *Writing measurable IEP goals and objectives.* Verona, WI: IEP Resources.

Beirne-Smith, M., Patton, J.R., & Ittenbach, R. (1994). *Mental retardation* (4th ed.). Upper Saddle River, NJ: Prentice Hall.

Berlak, H. (2001). Race and the achievement gap. *Rethinking Schools, 15*(4), pp. 10–11.

Berry, W.D. (1990). Contemporary trends in aquatics. *Journal of Physical Education, Recreation and Dance, 60*(5), 35.

Beveridge, S., & Scruggs, P. (2000). TLC for better PE: Girls in elementary physical education. *Journal of Physical Education, Recreation and Dance, 71*(8), 22–27.

Biskupic, J. (1999, March 4). Disabled pupils win right to medical aid. *The Washington Post,* pp. A01.

Black, H.C. (1990). *Black's law dictionary* (6th ed.). St. Paul, MN: West.

Blinde, E.M., & McCallister, S.G. (1998). Listening to the voices of students with physical disabilities. *Journal of Physical Education, Recreation and Dance, 69*(6), 64–68.

Block, M.E. (1992). What is appropriate physical education for students with profound disabilities? *Adapted Physical Activity Quarterly, 9,* 197–213.

Block, M.E. (1994). Why all students with disabilities should be included in regular physical education. *Palaestra, 10*(3), 17–24.

Block, M.E. (1995a). Development and validation of Children's Attitudes Toward Integrated Physical Education, Revised (CAIPE-R) Inventory. *Adapted Physical Activity Quarterly, 12,* 60–77.

Block, M.E. (1995b). Using task sheets to facilitate peer tutoring of students with disabilities. *Strategies, 8*(7), 9–11.

Block, M.E. (1996). Modifying instruction to facilitate the inclusion of students with disabilities in regular physical education. *Strategies, 9*(4), 9–12.

Block, M.E. (1999). Did we jump on the wrong bandwagon? Problems with inclusion in physical education. *Palaestra, 15*(3), 30–38.

Block, M.E. (2005). The preparticipation physical examination. In H. Appenzeller (Ed.), *Risk management in sport: Issues and strategies* (2nd ed., pp. 191–210). Durham, NC: Carolina Academic Press.

Block, M.E., & Block, V.E. (1999). Functional v. developmental motor assessment for students with severe disabilities. In P. Jansma (Ed.), *The psychomotor domain and the seriously handicapped* (4th ed., pp. 89–100). Lanham, MD: University Press of America.

Block, M.E., & Brady, W. (1999). Welcoming students with disabilities into regular physical education. *Teaching Elementary Physical Education, 10*(1), 30–32.

Block, M.E., & Burke, K. (1999). Are your students receiving appropriate physical education? *Teaching Exceptional Students, 31*(3), 18–23.

Block, M.E., & Conatser, P. (1999). Consultation in adapted physical education. *Adapted Physical Activity Quarterly, 16,* 9–26.

Block, M., & Garcia, C. (1995). *A position statement on inclusion in physical education.* Reston, VA: National Association of Sport and Physical Education (NASPE).

Block, M.E., Griebenauw, L., & Brodeur, S. (2004). Psychological factors and disability: effects of physical activity and sport. In M. Weiss (Ed.), *Developmental sport and exercise psychology: A lifespan perspective* (pp. 429–455). Morgantown, WV: Fitness Information Technology, Inc.

Block, M.E., & Krebs, P.L. (1992). An alternative to the continuum of the least restrictive environments: A continuum of support to regular physical education. *Adapted Physical Activity Quarterly, 9,* 97–113.

Block, M.E., & Malloy, M. (1998). Attitudes of girls towards including a child with severe disabilities in a regular fast-pitch softball league. *Mental Retardation, 36,* 137–144.

Block, M.E., Oberweiser, B., & Bain, M. (1995). Utilizing classwide peer tutoring to facilitate inclusion of students with disabilities in regular physical education. *Physical Educator, 52*(1), 47–56.

Block, M.E., & Obrusnikova, I. (in press). A research review on inclusion of students with disabilities in general physical education. *Adapted Physical Activity Quarterly.*

Block, M.E., & Provis, S. (1992, October). *Effects of ball size on throwing patterns in children with Down syndrome.* Paper presented at the North American Federation of Adapted Physical Activity Symposium, Montreal, Canada.

Block, M.E., Provis, S., & Nelson, E. (1994). Accommodating students with special needs in regular physical education: Extending traditional skill stations. *Palaestra, 10*(1), 32–35.

Block, M.E., & Rizzo, T.L. (1995). Attitudes and attributes of GPE teachers associated with teaching individuals with severe and profound disabilities. *Journal of The Association for Persons with Severe Handicaps, 20,* 80–87.

Block, M.E., & Vogler, E.W. (1994). Including children with disabilities in regular physical education: The research base. *Journal of Physical Education, Recreation, and Dance, 65*(1), 40–44.

Block, M.E., & Zeman, R. (1996). Including students with disabilities into regular physical education: Effects on nondisabled children. *Adapted Physical Activity Quarterly, 13,* 38–49.

Bondy, A., & Frost, L. (2001). *A picture's worth: PECS and other visual communication strategies in autism.* Bethesda, MD: Woodbine House.

Boyce, B.A. (1996). Dealing with student diversity through the case-study approach. *Journal of Physical Education, Recreation and Dance, 67*(5), 46–50.

Brasher, B., & Holbrook, M.C. (1996). Early intervention and special education. In M.C. Holbrook (Ed.), *Children with visual impairments: A parent's guide* (pp. 175–204). Bethesda, MD: Woodbine House.

Bricker, D. (1995). The challenge of inclusion. *Journal of Early Intervention, 19,* 179–194.

Broach, E., & Dattilo, J. (1996). Aquatic therapy: Making waves in therapeutic recreation. *Parks & Recreation, 31*(7), 38–43.

Brown v. Board of Educ., 347 U.S. 483 (1954).

Brown, J.D., & Richter, J. (1994). How to handle blood & body fluid spills. *Strategies, 7*(7), 23–25.

Brown, L. (1994, December). *Including students with significant intellectual disabilities in regular education.* Paper presented at the annual conference of The Association for Persons with Severe Handicaps, Atlanta, GA.

Brown, L., Branston, M.B., Hamre-Nietupski, S., Pumpian, I., Certo, N., & Gruenewald, L. (1979). A strategy for developing chronological-age-appropriate and functional curricular content for severely handicapped adolescents and young adults. *The Journal of Special Education, 13,* 81–90.

Brown, L., Long, E., Udvari-Solner, A., Schwarz, P., VanDeventer, P., Ahlgren, C., Johnson, F., Gruenewald, L., & Jorgensen, J. (1989). Should students with severe intellectual disabilities be based in regular or in special education classrooms in home schools? *Journal of The Association for Persons with Severe Handicaps, 14,* 8–12.

Brown, L., Schwarz, P., Udvari-Solner, A., Kampschroer-Frattura, E., Johnson, F., Jorgensen, J., & Gruenewald, L. (1991). How much time should students with severe intellectual disabilities spend in regular education classrooms or elsewhere? *Journal of The Association for Persons with Severe Handicaps, 16,* 39–47.

Bruininks, R.H. (1978). *Bruininks-Oseretsky Test of Motor Proficiency: Examiner's manual.* Circle Pines, MN: American Guidance Service.

Bryan, W.V. (1999). *Multicultural aspects of disabilities: A guide to understanding and assisting minorities in the rehabilitation process.* Springfield, IL: Charles C Thomas.

Bryant, M.D., & Graham, A.M. (1993). *Implementing early intervention from research to effective practice.* New York: The Guilford Press.

Bull, E., Haldorsen, J., Kahrs, N., Mathiesen, G., Mogensen, I., Torheim, A., & Uldal, M. (1985). *In the pool: Swimming instruction for the disabled.* Oslo, Norway: Ungdoms-Og Idrettsavdelingen.

Burgeson, C.R., Wechsler, H., Brener, N.D., Young, J.C., & Spain, C.G. (2001). Physical education and activity: Results for the school health policies and programs study 2000. *Journal of School Health, 71,* 279–293.

Butt, K.L., & Pahnos, M.L. (1995). Why we need a multicultural focus in our schools. *Journal of Physical Education, Recreation and Dance, 66*(1), 48–53.

Butterfield, S.A. (1993). Exercise-induced asthma: A manageable problem. *Journal of Physical Education, Recreation, and Dance, 64,* 15–18.

Canadian Association of Health, Physical Education, and Recreation (CAHPER). (1994). *Moving to inclusion: Introductory binder.* Gloucester, Ontario, Canada: Author.

Carpenter, L.J. (2000). *Legal concepts in sport: A primer* (2nd ed.). Reston, VA: American Alliance of Active Lifestyles and Fitness (AAALF).

Carter, M.J., Dolan, M.A., & LeConey, S.P. (1994). *Designing instructional swim programs for individuals with disabilities.* Reston, VA: AALR/American Association of Health, Physical Education, Recreation, and Dance (AAHPERD).

Center for Applied Linguistics, Cultural Orientation Resource Center. (1996). *Welcome to the United States: A guidebook for refugees.* Available on line at http://www.culturalorientation.net/welcome/index.htm

Certo, N.J., Schleien, S.J., & Hunter, D. (1983). An ecological assessment inventory to facilitate community recreation participation by severely disabled individuals. *Therapeutic Recreation Journal, 17*(3), 29–38.

Chadsey-Rusch, J. (1990). Social interactions of secondary-aged students with severe handicaps: Implications for facilitating the transition from school to work. *Journal of The Association for Persons with Severe Handicaps, 15,* 69–78.

Chandler, J.P., & Greene, J.L. (1995). A statewide survey of adapted physical education service delivery and teacher in-service training. *Adapted Physical Activity Quarterly, 12,* 262–274.

Chaves, I.M. (1977). Historical overview of special education in the United States. In P. Bates, T.L. West, & R.B. Schmerl (Eds.), *Mainstreaming: Problems, potentials, and perspectives* (pp. 25–41). Minneapolis: National Support Systems Project.

Chepyator-Thomson, J. (1994). Multicultural education. Culturally responsive teaching. *Journal of Physical Education, Recreation and Dance, 65*(9), 31–32.

Christies, I. (1985). Aquatics for the handicapped: A review of literature. *Physical Educator, 42*(1), 24–33.

Churchword, B. (2001). *Eleven techniques for better classroom discipline.* Retrieved August 12, 2005, from http://www.honorlevel.com/techniques.html

Civil Rights Act of 1964, PL 88-352, 20 U.S.C. §§ 241 et seq.

Clair, S. (2005, May/June). Universal thinking: Just how accessible is your facility? *Recreational Management,* 22–27.

Clark, G., French, R., & Henderson, H. (1985). Teaching techniques that develop positive attitudes. *Palaestra, 5*(3), 14–17.

Clements, A. (March, 2000). *Emergency action plans.* Paper presented at the American Alliance for Health, Physical Education, Recreation, and Dance, Orlando, FL.

Coelho, J., & Fielitz, F. (2003). Making waves in your aquatic program. *Strategies, 17*(2), 29–31.

Conatser, P. (2003). Current issues in adapted aquatics 2003. *National Aquatics Newsletter, 8*(1), 16–17.

Conatser, P. (2004, May 1). Aquatic supervision for individuals with disabilities. *Adapted Physical Education, 6*(5). Retrieved from http://www.pelinks4u.org/sections/adapted/adapted.htm

Conatser, P., & Block, M.E. (2001). Factors that improve aquatic instructors' beliefs toward inclusion. *Therapeutic Recreation Journal, 35*(2), 170–184.

Conatser, P., & Block, M.E. (2002). Adapted aquatics and inclusion. *Journal of Physical Education, Recreation and Dance, 73*(5), 31–34.

Conatser, P., Block, M.E., & Gansneder, B. (2002). Aquatic instructors' beliefs toward inclusion: The theory of planned behavior. *Adapted Physical Activity Quarterly, 19,* 172–187.

Conatser, P.K., Block, M.E., & Lapore, M. (2000). Aquatic instructors' attitudes toward teaching students with disabilities. *Adapted Physical Activity Quarterly, 17,* 173–183.

Condon, M.E., York, R., Heal, L.W., & Fortschneider, J. (1986). Acceptance of severely handicapped students by nonhandicapped peers. *Journal of The Association for Persons with Severe Handicaps, 11,* 216–219.

Cotton, D. (1994). Students acting as teachers: Who is liable? *Strategies, 8,* 23–25.

Council for Exceptional Children. (1975). What is mainstreaming? *Exceptional Children, 42,* 174.

Council for Exceptional Children. (1999). *IEP team guide.* Reston, VA: Author.

Council on Physical Education for Children (COPEC). (1992). *Developmental appropriate physical education practices for children.* Reston, VA: National Association of Sport and Physical Education.

Council on Physical Education for Children (COPEC). (2000). *Appropriate practices for elementary school physical education: A position statement of the National Association of Sport and Physical Education.* Reston, VA: National Association of Sport and Physical Education.

Council on Physical Education for Children (COPEC). (2001). *Appropriate practices for middle school physical education: A position statement of the National Association of Sport and Physical Education.* Reston, VA: National Association of Sport and Physical Education.

Council on Physical Education for Children (COPEC). (2004). *Appropriate practices for high school physical education: A position statement of the National Association of Sport and Physical Education.* Reston, VA: National Association of Sport and Physical Education.

Covey, S.R. (1989). *The 7 habits of highly effective people.* New York: Fireside/Simon & Schuster.

Craig, S.E., Haggart, A.G., & Hull, K.M. (1999). Integrating therapies into the educational setting. Strategies for supporting children with severe disabilities. *Physical Disabilities: Education and Related Services, 17,* 91–110.

Crone, D.A., & Horner, R.H. (2003). *Building positive behavior support systems in schools: Functional behavior assessment.* New York: Guilford Press.

Daniels, S.A. (1954). *Adapted physical education.* New York: Harper & Brothers.

Darst, P.W., & Pangrazi, R.P. (2006). *Dynamic physical education for secondary school students* (5th ed.). San Francisco: Pearson and Benjamin Cummings.

Davis, R., & French, R. (1986). Managing student behaviors in physical education through a positive modified scoring system. *Directive Teacher, 8*(1), 15.

Davis, R.W., & Sherrill, C. (2004). Sports recreation and competition: Socialization, instruction, and transition. In C. Sherrill (Ed.), *Adapted physical activity, recreation, and sport* (6th ed., pp. 413–440). New York: McGraw-Hill.

Davis, W.E., & Burton, A.W. (1991). Ecological task analysis: Translating movement behavior theory into practice. *Adapted Physical Activity Quarterly, 8,* 154–177.

Deci, E.L., Koestner, R., & Ryan, R.M. (2001). Extrinsic rewards and intrinsic motivation in education: Reconsidered once again. *Review of Educational Research, 71,* 1–27.

DePaepe, J.L. (1984). Mainstreaming malpractice. *Physical Educator, 41,* 51–56.

DePaepe, J. (1985). The influence of three least restrictive environments on the content, motor-ALT and performance of moderately mentally retarded students. *Journal of Teaching in Physical Education, 5,* 34–41.

Donaldson, J. (1981). The visibility and image of handicapped people on television. *Exceptional Children, 47*(6), 413–416.

Dougherty, A.M. (1995). *Case studies in human service consultation.* Albany, NY: Brooks/Cole.

Dougherty, N.J. (1987). Legal responsibility for safety in physical education and sport. In N.J. Dougherty (Ed.), *Principles of safety in physical education and sport* (pp. 15–22). Reston, VA: American Association of Health, Physical Education, Recreation, and Dance (AAHPERD).

Downing, J.E. (1996). *Including students with severe and multiple disabilities in typical classrooms.* Baltimore: Paul H. Brookes Publishing Co.

Downing, J.E. (2002). *Including students with severe and multiple disabilities in typical classrooms: Practical strategies for teachers* (2nd ed.). Baltimore: Paul H. Brookes Publishing Co.

Doyle, M.B. (2002). *The paraprofessional's guide to the inclusive classroom: Working as a team* (2nd ed.). Baltimore: Paul H. Brookes Publishing Co.

DuBow, S. (1989). Into the turbulent mainstream: A legal perspective on the weight given to the least restrictive environment in placement decisions for deaf children. *Journal of Law and Education, 18,* 215–228.

Dunn, J. (1997). *Special physical education* (7th ed.). Madison, WI: Brown & Benchmark.

Dunn, L.M. (1968). Special education for the mildly retarded: Is much of it justifiable? *Exceptional Children, 35,* 5–22.

Durstine, J.L., Painter, P., Franklin, B.A., Morgan, D., Pitetti, K.H., & Roberts, S.O. (2000). Physical activity for the chronically ill and disabled. *Sports Medicine, 30*(3), 207–219.

Education for All Handicapped Children Act of 1975, PL 94-142, 20 U.S.C. §§ 1400 *et seq.*

Education of the Handicapped Act Amendments of 1983, PL 98-199, 20 U.S.C. §§ 1400 *et seq.,* 97 Stat. 1357.

Education of the Handicapped Act Amendments of 1986, PL 99-457, 20 U.S.C. §§ 1400 *et seq.*

Eichstaedt, C.B., & Lavay, B.W. (1992). *Physical activity for individuals with mental retardation.* Champaign, IL: Human Kinetics.

Elementary and Secondary Education Act of 1965, PL 89-10, 20 U.S.C. §§ 241 *et seq.*

Ellery, P.J., & Rauschenbach, J. (2000). Impact of disability awareness activities on nondisabled student attitudes toward integrated physical education with students who use wheelchairs [Abstract]. *Research Quarterly for Exercise and Sport, 71,* A106.

Ellis, D.N., Wright, M., & Cronis, T.G. (1996). A description of the instructional and social interactions of students with mental retardation in regular physical education settings. *Education and Training in Mental Retardation and Developmental Disabilities, 31,* 235–241.

Ellmo, W., & Graser, J. (1995). *Adapted adventure activities.* Dubuque, IA: Kendall/Hunt.

Epstein, R.S., McGovern, J., & Moon, M.S. (1994). The impact of federal legislation on recreation programs. In M.S. Moon (Ed.), *Making school and community recreation fun for everyone: Places and ways to integrate* (pp. 87–96). Baltimore: Paul H. Brookes Publishing Co.

Etzel-Wise, D., & Mears, B. (2004). Adapted physical education and therapeutic recreation in schools. *Intervention in School and Clinic, 39*, 223–232.

Fairfax County Public Schools (1994). *Fairfax County Public Schools: Physician referral form-physical education.* Fairfax, VA: Author.

Falvey, M.A., Forest, M., Pearpoint, J., & Rosenberg, R.L. (1997.) *All my life's a circle: Using the tools. Circles, MAPs, & PATH.* Toronto: Inclusion Press.

Falvey, M.A., & Rosenberg, R.L. (1995). Developing and fostering friendships. In M.A. Falvey (Ed.), *Inclusive and heterogeneous schooling* (pp. 267–284). Baltimore: Paul H. Brookes Publishing Co.

Federal Register. (1977, August 23). *Education of Handicapped Children: Implementation of Part B of the Education of the Handicapped Act,* Vol. 42, No. 163, Part II, 42474–42518.

Federal Register. (1992, September 29). *P.L. 101-476, Individuals with Disabilities Education Act.*

Ferguson, D.L. (1995). The real challenge of inclusion: Confessions of a "rabid inclusionist." *Phi Delta Kappan, 77*(4), 281–306.

Fink, D.B. (2001). Carlton plays tee-ball: A case study in inclusive recreation. *Parks and Recreation, 36*(8), 54–58.

Fluegelman, A. (1976). *New games book.* New York: Doubleday & Company.

Fluegelman, A. (1981). *More new games! And playful ideas from the New Games Foundation.* New York: Dolphin Books/Doubleday.

Forest, M., & Lusthaus, E. (1989). Promoting educational equality for all students: Circles and maps. In S. Stainback, W. Stainback, & M. Forest (Eds.), *Educating all students in the mainstream of regular education* (pp. 43–58). Baltimore: Paul H. Brookes Publishing Co.

French, R. (1973). *Behavioral modification: Its role in the instruction of physical education for the educationally handicapped* (pp. 57–58). Conference on techniques and methods for handicapped children and youth, Los Angeles.

French, R., Keele, M., & Silliman-French, L. (1997). Students with shunts: Program considerations. *Journal of Physical Education, Recreation, and Dance, 68*(1), 54–56.

Fried, G.B. (2005). ADA and sport facilities. In H. Appenzeller (Ed.), *Risk management in sport: Issues and strategies* (2nd ed., pp. 289–302). Durham, NC: Carolina Academic Press.

Gabbard, C. (2004). *Lifelong motor development* (4th ed.). San Francisco: Benjamin Cummings.

Gagen, L., & Getchell, N. (2004). Combining theory and practice in the gymnasium: Constraints within an ecological perspective. *Journal of Physical Education, Recreation and Dance, 75*, 25–30.

Gallahue, D.L., & Cleland-Donnelly, F.C. (2003). *Developmental physical education for all children* (4th ed.). Champaign, IL: Human Kinetics.

Gallahue, D.L., & Ozmun, J.C. (2006). *Understanding motor development: Infants, children, adolescents, adults* (6th ed.). New York: McGraw-Hill.

Gaylord-Ross, R. (1980). A decision model for the treatment of aberrant behavior in applied settings. In W. Sailor, B. Wilcox, & L. Brown (Eds.), *Methods of instruction for severely handicapped students* (pp. 135–158). Baltimore: Paul H. Brookes Publishing Co.

Geis, G.C. (1975). Therapeutic aquatics program for quadriplegia. *American Corrective Therapy Journal, 29*(5), 155–157.

Getskow, V., & Konczal, D. (1996). *Kids with special needs.* Santa Barbara, CA: The Learning Works, Inc.

Giangreco, M.F. (1997). *Quick-guides to inclusion.* Baltimore: Paul H. Brookes Publishing Co.

Giangreco, M.F., & Putnam, J.W. (1991). Supporting the education of students with severe disabilities in regular education environments. In M.H. Meyer, C.A. Peck, & L. Brown (Eds.), *Critical issues in the lives of people with severe disabilities* (pp. 245–270). Baltimore: Paul H. Brookes Publishing Co.

Givner, C.C., & Haager, D. (1995). Strategies for effective collaboration. In M.A. Falvey (Ed.), *Inclusive and heterogeneous schooling: Assessment, curriculum, and instruction* (pp. 41–57). Baltimore: Paul H. Brookes Publishing Co.

Goldstein, L.S. (1995). *Understanding and managing students' classroom behavior.* New York: John Wiley & Sons.

Goodwin, D.L. (2001). The meaning of help in PE: Perceptions of students with physical disabilities. *Adapted Physical Activity Quarterly, 18*, 289–303.

Goodwin, D.L., & Watkinson, E.J. (2000). Inclusive physical education from the perspective of students with physical disabilities. *Adapted Physical Activity Quarterly, 17*, 144–160.

Graff, J.C., Ault, M.M., Guess, D., Taylor, M., & Thompson, B. (1990). *Health care for students with disabilities.* Baltimore: Paul H. Brookes Publishing Co.

Graham, G., Holt-Hale, S., & Parker, M. (2004). *Children moving: A reflective approach to teaching physical education* (6th ed.). Boston: McGraw-Hill.

Gray, C. (1994). *The new Social Story book.* Arlington, TX: Future Horizons.

Gray, G.R. (1995). Safety tips from the expert witness. *Journal of Physical Education, Recreation, and Dance, 66*(1), 18–21.

Grineski, S. (1996). *Cooperative learning in physical education.* Champaign, IL: Human Kinetics.

Grosse, S.J. (1990). How safe are your mainstreamed students? *Strategies, 4*(2), 11–13.

Grosse, S. (1991). Is the mainstream always a better place to be? *Palaestra, 7*(2), 40–49.

Grosse, S. (1995). Try a water aerobics course. *Strategies, 9*(3),18–21.

Grosse, S. (1996). Aquatics for individuals with disabilities: Challenges for the 21st century. *International Council for Health, Physical Education, Recreation, Sport, and Dance, 33*(1), 27–29.

Gutkin, T.B. & Curtis, M.J. (1982). School-based consultation: Theory and techniques. In C.R. Reynolds & T.B. Gutkin (Eds.), *The handbook of school psychology* (pp. 796–828). New York: John Wiley & Sons.

Halsey, J.J. (2005). Risk management for physical educators. In H. Appenzeller (Ed.), *Risk management in sport: Issues and strategies* (2nd ed., pp. 151–163). Durham, NC: Carolina Academic Press.

Hanft, B.E., & Place, P.A. (1996). *The consulting therapist.* San Antonio: Therapy Skill Builders.

Hanson, M.J., & Lynch, E.W. (2004). *Understanding families: Approaches to diversity, disability, and risk.* Baltimore: Paul H. Brookes Publishing Co.

Harrison, L., & Worthy, T. (2001). "Just like all the

rest": Developing awareness of stereotypical thinking in physical education. *Journal of Physical Education, Recreation and Dance, 72*(9), 20–24.

Hastad, D.N., & Lacky, A.C. (1998). *Measurement and evaluation in physical education and exercise science* (3rd ed.). Boston: Allyn & Bacon.

Hastie, P.A., & Martin, E.H. (2006). *Teaching elementary physical education: Strategies for the classroom teacher.* San Francisco: Benjamin Cummings.

Hawkins, J.D. (2005). Emergency medical preparedness. In H. Appenzeller (Ed.), *Risk management in sport: Issues and strategies* (2nd ed., pp. 235–239). Durham, NC: Carolina Academic Press.

Haycock, K. (2001). Helping all students achieve: Closing the achievement gap. *Educational Leadership, 58*(6). Retrieved June 19, 2006, from http://ascd.org/readingroom/edlead/0103/haycock.html

Hazzard, A. (1983). Children's experience with, knowledge of, and attitude toward disabled persons. *Journal of Special Education, 17*(2), 131–139.

Heikinaro-Johansson, P., Sherrill, C., French, R., & Huuhka, H. (1995). Adapted physical education consultant service model to facilitate integration. *Adapted Physical Activity Quarterly, 12*, 12–33.

Hellison, D.R. (2003). *Teaching responsibility through physical activity* (2nd ed.). Champaign, IL: Human Kinetics.

Helmstetter, E. (1989). Curriculum for school-age students: The ecological model. In F. Brown & D.H. Lehr (Eds.), *Persons with profound disabilities: Issues and practices* (pp. 239–264). Baltimore: Paul H. Brookes Publishing Co.

Henderson, G.. & Bryan, W.V. (1997). *Psychological aspects of disability.* Springfield, IL: Charles C Thomas.

Henderson, H., & French, R. (1989). Negative reinforcement or punishment? *Journal of Physical Education, Recreation and Dance, 60*(5), 4.

Henderson, H.L., & French, R.W. (1993). *Creative approaches to managing student behavior* (2nd ed.). Park City, UT: Family Development Resources.

Herkowitz, J. (1978). Developmental task analysis: The design of movement experiences and evaluation of motor development status. In M. Ridenour (Ed.), *Motor development: Issues and applications* (pp. 139–164). Princeton, NJ: Princeton Book Co.

Heron, T.E., & Harris, K.C. (1993). *The educational consultant: Helping professionals, parents, and mainstreamed students* (3rd ed.). Austin, TX: PRO-ED.

Hewett, F.M. (1968). *The emotionally disturbed student in the classroom.* Boston: Allyn & Bacon.

Hewett, F.M., & Taylor, F.D. (1980). *The emotionally disturbed student in the classroom* (2nd ed.). Boston: Allyn & Bacon.

Heyne, L., & Schleien, S.J. (1997). Teaming up with parents to support inclusive recreation. *Parks and Recreation, 32*(5), 76–81.

Hodge, S.R. (1997). Mentoring: perspectives of physical education graduate students from diverse cultural backgrounds. *Physical Educator, 54*(4), 181–195.

Hollis, J., & Gallegos, E. (1993). Inclusion: What is the extent of a school district's duty to accommodate students with disabilities in the regular classroom? *Legal Digest, 9*(9), 1–8, 17.

Horton, M. (2001). Utilizing paraprofessionals in the general physical education setting. *Teaching Elementary Physical Education, 12*(6), 22–25.

Horton, M., Wilson, S., & Gagnon, D. (2003). Collaboration: A key component for successful inclusion in general physical education. *Teaching Elementary Physical Education, 14*(3), 13–17.

Horvat, M., Block, M.E., & Kelly, L. (in press). *Assessment in adapted physical education.* Champaign, IL: Human Kinetics.

Horvat, M.A., & Forbus, W.R. (1989). *Using the aquatic environment for teaching handicapped children* (2nd ed.). Kearney, NE: Educational Systems Associates.

Horvat, M.A., Forbus, W.R., & Van Kirk, L. (1987). *Teacher and parent guide for the physical development of mentally handicapped in the aquatic environment.* Athens: The University of Georgia, Department of Physical Education.

Houston-Wilson, C., Dunn, J.M., van der Mars, H., & McCubbin, J. (1997). The effects of peer tutors on the motor performance in integrated physical education classes. *Adapted Physical Activity Quarterly, 14*, 298–313.

Houston-Wilson, C., Lieberman, L. Horton, M., & Kasser, S. (1997). Peer tutoring: A plan for instructing students of all abilities. *Journal of Physical Education, Recreation, and Dance, 68*(6), 39–44.

Hsu, Y-F. (2001). Behavior management techniques used by secondary school general physical educators in Taiwan. Unpublished thesis, Texas Woman's University, Denton.

Hurley, R., & Turner, C. (1991). Neurology and aquatic therapy. *Clinical Management: The Magazine of the American Physical Therapy Association, 11*(1), 26–29.

Hutchinson, G.E. (1995). Gender-fair teaching in physical education. *Journal of Physical Education, Recreation and Dance, 66*(1), 42–47.

Hutzler, Y., Chacham, A., Bergman, U., & Szeinberg, A. (1997). Effects of exercise on respiration in children with cerebral palsy. *Palaestra, 13*(4), 20–24.

Hutzler, Y., Fliess, O., Chacham, A., & van den Auweele, Y. (2002). Perspectives of children with physical disabilities on inclusion and empowerment: Supporting and limiting factors. *Adapted Physical Activity Quarterly, 19*, 300–317.

Imber, M., & Van Geel, T. (2001). *A teacher's guide to education law* (2nd ed.). Mahwah, NJ: Lawrence Erlbaum Associates.

Improving America's Schools Act of 1994, PL 103-382, 20 U.S.C. §§ 630 *et seq.*

Individuals with Disabilities Education Act Amendments of 1997 (IDEA), PL 105-17, 20 U.S.C. 1400 *et seq.*

Individuals with Disabilities Education Act (IDEA) of 1990, U.S.C., Title 20, §§ 1400 *et seq.*

Individuals with Disabilities Education Improvement Act (IDEA) of 2004, 20 U.S.C. §§ 1400 *et seq.*

Jackson, L., & Panyan, M.V. (2001). *Positive behavioral support in the classroom: Principles and practices.* Baltimore: Paul H. Brookes Publishing Co.

Janney, R., & Snell, M. (2000). *Teachers' guides to inclusive practices series: Behavioral support.* Baltimore: Paul H. Brookes Publishing Co.

Janney, R.F., Snell, M.E., Beers, M.K., & Raynes, M. (1995). Integrating students with moderate and severe disabilities into general education classes. *Exceptional Children, 61*, 425–439.

Jansma, P., & Decker, J. (1992). *Project LRE/PE: Least*

restrictive environment usage in physical education. Washington, DC: Department of Education, Office of Special Education.

Jansma, P., & French, R. (1994). *Special physical education.* Upper Saddle River, NJ: Prentice-Hall.

Johnson, D.W., & Johnson, R.T. (1989). *Learning together and alone: Cooperation, competition, and individualization* (5th ed.). Needham Heights, MA: Allyn & Bacon.

Johnson, D.W., & Johnson, R.T. (1999). *Learning together and alone: Cooperation, competition, and individualization* (7th ed.). Needham Heights, MA: Allyn & Bacon.

Johnston, T., & Wayda, V.K. (1994). Are you an effective communicator? *Strategies, 7*(5), 9–13.

Kahan, D. (2003). Islam and physical activity: Implications for American sport and physical educators. *Journal of Physical Education, Recreation and Dance, 74*(3), 48–54.

Kaplan, J.S., & Carter, J. (1995). *Beyond behavior modification* (3rd ed.). Austin, TX: PRO-ED.

Karagiannis, A., Stainback, W., & Stainback, S. (1996). Rationale for inclusive schooling. In S. Stainback & W. Stainback (Eds.), *Inclusion: A guide for educators* (pp. 3–16). Baltimore: Paul H. Brookes Publishing Co.

Kasser, S.L. (1995). *Inclusive games.* Champaign, IL: Human Kinetics.

Kasser, S.L., & Lytle, R.K. (2005). *Inclusive physical activity: A lifetime of opportunities.* Champaign, IL: Human Kinetics.

Katz, S., & Yekutiel, E. (1974). Leisure time problems of mentally retarded graduates of training programs. *Mental Retardation, 12,* 54–57.

Kauffman, J.M. (1993). How we might achieve the radical reform of special education. *Exceptional Children, 60,* 294–309.

Kauffman, J.M., Mostert, M.P., Trent, S.C., & Hallahan, D.P. (1998). *Managing classroom behavior* (2nd ed.). Boston: Allyn & Bacon.

Katz, S., & Yekutiel, E. (1974). Leisure time problems of mentally retarded graduates of training programs. *Mental Retardation, 12,* 54–57.

Kelly, L.E. (1991). National standards for adapted physical education. *Advocate, 20*(1), 2–3

Kelly, L.E. (1995). *Adapted physical education national standards.* Champaign, IL: Human Kinetics.

Kelly, L.E. (1998). National certification in adapted physical education. *Virginia Journal of Physical Education, Recreation and Dance, 20*(1), 21–22.

Kelly, L.E., & Gansneder, B.M. (1998). Preparation and job demographics of adapted physical educators in the United States. *Adapted Physical Activity Quarterly, 15,* 141–154.

Kelly, L.E., & Melograno, V.J. (2004). *Developing the physical education curriculum: An achievement-based approach.* Champaign, IL: Human Kinetics.

Kelly, L., & Wessel, J.A. (1986). *Achievement-based curriculum development in physical education.* Philadelphia: Lea & Febiger.

Kelly, L.E., et al. (1991). *Achievement-based curriculum: Teaching manual.* Charlottesville: The University of Virginia.

King, S.E. (1994). Winning the race against racism. *Journal of Physical Education, Recreation and Dance, 65*(9), 69–74.

Kirchner, G., & Fishburne, G.J. (1998). *Physical education for elementary school children* (10th ed.). Boston: WC Brown/McGraw Hill.

Kline, F.M., Silver, L.B., & Russell, S.C. (Eds.). (2001). *The educator's guide to medical issues in the classroom.* Baltimore: Paul H. Brookes Publishing Co.

Kohn, A. (1998). *What to look for in the classroom.* San Francisco: Jossey-Bass.

Koury, J. M. (1996). *Aquatic therapy programming: Guidelines for orthopedic rehabilitation.* Champaign, IL: Human Kinetics.

Kowalski, E.M. (2000). Rhythm and dance. In J.P. Winnick, *Adapted physical education and sport* (3rd ed., pp. 341–352). Champaign, IL: Human Kinetics.

Kozub, F.M. (2001). Adapted physical activity programming within the family: The family systems theory. *Palaestra, 17*(3), 30–38.

Kozub, F.M., & Porreta, D.L. (1998). Interscholastic coaches' attitudes toward integration of adolescents with disabilities. *Adapted Physical Activity Quarterly, 15,* 328–344.

Kraus, R.G., & Curtis, J.E. (1986). *Creative management: In recreation, parks and leisure services* (4th ed.). St. Louis: Time Mirror/Mosby.

Krebs, P.L., & Block, M.E. (1992). Transition of students with disabilities into community recreation: The role of the adapted physical educator. *Adapted Physical Activity Quarterly, 9,* 305–315.

Krueger, D.L., DiRocco, P., & Felix, M. (2000). Obstacles adapted physical education specialists encounter when developing transition plans. *Adapted Physical Activity Quarterly, 17,* 222–236.

Kurpius, D.J., & Rozecki, T.G. (1993). Strategies for improving interpersonal communication. In J.E. Zins, T.R. Kratochwill, & S.N. Elliott (Eds.), *Handbook of consultation services for children* (pp. 137–158). San Francisco: Jossey-Bass.

Lake, E. (1990). An Indian father's plea. *Teacher, 2*(1), 49–52.

LaMaster, K., Gall, K., Kinchin, G., & Siedentop, D. (1998). Inclusion practices of effective elementary specialists. *Adapted Physical Activity Quarterly, 15,* 64–81.

Lane, C. (2001, March 30). Disabled pro golfer wins right to use cart. *Washington Post,* A01.

Langendorfer, S. J. (1986). Aquatics for the young child: Facts and myths. *The Journal of Physical Education, Recreation and Dance, 57*(6), 61–66.

Langendorfer, S.J. (1990). Contemporary trends in infant/preschool aquatics: Into the 1990s and beyond. *The Journal of Physical Education, Recreation and Dance, 60*(5), 36–39.

Latest shape of the nation to be released. (2001, Fall). *NASPE News, 58*(5), 1.

Lavay, B. (1984). Physical activity as a reinforcer in physical education. *Adapted Physical Activity Quarterly, 1,* 315–321.

Lavay, B., & DePaepe, J. (1987). The harbinger helper: Why mainstreaming in physical education doesn't always work. *Journal of Health, Physical Education, Recreation, and Dance, 58*(7), 98–103.

Lavay, B., French, R., & Henderson, H. (2006). *Positive behavior management strategies for physical educators (2nd ed.).* Champaign, IL: Human Kinetics.

Lavay, B., & Semark, C. (2001). Everyone plays: Including special needs children in youth sports programs. *Palaestra, 17*(4), 40–43.

Lawrence, S., Chau, M., & Lennon, M.C. (2004). *Depression, substance abuse, and domestic violence.* New York: National Center for Children in Poverty, Columbia University.

Lee S., Sills, M., & Oh, G. (2002). *Disabilities among children and mothers in low-income families. Research-in-Brief.* Washington, DC: Institute for Women's Policy Research. Retrieved August 8, 2005, from http://www.iwpr.org/pdf/d449.pdf

Lepore, M. (2000). Aquatics. In J.P. Winnick, *Adapted physical education and sport* (3rd ed., pp. 391–408). Champaign, IL: Human Kinetics.

Lepore, M., Gayle, G.W., & Stevens, S.F. (1998). *Adapted aquatics programming: A professional guide.* Champaign, IL: Human Kinetics.

Lester, P.M., & Ross, S.D. (2003). *Images that injure. Pictorial stereotypes in the media.* Westport, CT: Greenwood Publishing Group, Inc.

Lewis, A. (2001). *Add it up: Using research to improve education for low-income and minority students.* Washington, DC: Poverty and Race Research Action Council.

Lewis, R.B., & Doorlag, D.H. (1991). *Teaching special students in the mainstream* (3rd ed.). New York: Macmillan.

Lieberman, L.J., Dunn, J.M., van der Mars, H., & McCubbin, J. (2000). Peer tutors' effects on activity levels of deaf students in inclusive elementary physical education. *Adapted Physical Activity Quarterly, 17,* 20–39.

Lieberman, L., & Houston-Wilson, C. (2002). *Strategies for inclusion: A handbook for physical educators.* Champaign, IL: Human Kinetics.

Lieberman, L.J., Houston-Wilson, C., & Kozub, F.M. (2002). Perceived barriers to including students with visual impairments in general physical education. *Adapted Physical Activity Quarterly, 19,* 364–377.

Lieberman, L.J., Newcomer, J., McCubbin, J., & Dalrymple, N. (1997). The effects of cross-aged peer tutors on the academic learning time of students with disabilities in inclusive elementary physical education classes. *Brazilian International Journal of Adapted Physical Education Research, 4*(1), 15–32.

Lienert, C., Sherrrill, C., & Myers, B. (2001). Physical educators' concerns about integrating children with disabilities: A cross-cultural comparison. *Adapted Physical Activity Quarterly, 18,* 1–17.

Lipsky, D.K., & Gartner, A. (1987). *Beyond separate education: Quality education for all.* Baltimore: Paul H. Brookes Publishing Co.

Lipsky, D.K., & Gartner, A. (1998). *Inclusion and school reform: Transforming America's classrooms.* Baltimore: Paul H. Brookes Publishing Co.

Lipton, D. (1994, April). *The full inclusion court cases: 1989–1994.* Paper presented at the Wingspread Conference, Racine, WI.

Lisboa, F.L.F. (1997). Interaction and social acceptance of children with autism in physical education. *Brazilian International Journal of Adapted Physical Education Research, 4,* 1–14.

Little League of America (2006). *Challenger Division.* Retrieved March 29, 2006, from http://www.littleleague.org/divisions/challenger.asp

Lockhart, R.C., French, R., & Gench, B. (1998). Influence of empathy training to modify attitudes of normal children in physical education toward peers

with physical disabilities. *Clinical Kinesiology, 52,* 35–41.

Loovis, E.M., & Loovis, C.L. (1997). A disability awareness unit in physical education and attitudes of elementary school students. *Perceptual and Motor Skills, 84,* 768–770.

Luckasson, R., Coulter, D.L., Polloway, E.A., Reiss, S., Schalock, R.L., Snell, M.E., et al. (1992). *Mental retardation: Definition, classification, and systems of supports* (9th ed). Washington, DC: American Association on Mental Retardation.

Lynch, E.W., & Hanson, M.J. (Eds.). (2004). *Developing cross-cultural competence: A guide for working with children and their families* (3rd ed.). Baltimore: Paul H. Brookes Publishing Co.

Maag, J.W. (2001). Reward by punishment: Reflections on the misuse of positive reinforcement in schools. *Exceptional Children, 67*(2), 173–186.

MacDonald, C., & Block, M.E. (2005). Self-advocacy in physical education for students with physical disabilities. *Journal of Physical Education, Recreation and Dance, 76*(4), 45–48.

Madden, N.M., & Slavin, R.E., (1983). Mainstreaming students with mild handicaps: Academic and social outcomes. *Reviews of Educational Research, 53,* 519–569.

Maeda, J., Murata, N.M., & Hodge, S.R. (1998). Physical educators' perception of inclusion: A Hawaii school district perspective. *Clinical Kinesiology, 51,* 80–85.

Maloney, M. (1994). Courts are redefining LRE requirements under the IDEA. *Inclusive Education Programs, 1*(1), 1–2.

Margolis, H., & Fiorelli, J. (1987, Winter). Getting past anger in consulting relationships. *Organization Development Journal,* 44–48.

Margolis, H., & McCabe, P.P. (1988). Overcoming resistance to a new remedial program. *The Clearing House, 62*(3), 131–134.

Markos & Jenkins. (1994). *Medical information form: Broadus Woods Elementary School.* Earlysville, VA: Author.

McCollum, S., Civalier, A., & Holt, A. (2004). Equitable learning for Spanish speaking students in elementary physical education. *Strategies, 17*(6), 21–23.

McCollum, S., Elliott, S., Burke, S., Civalier, A., & Pruitt, W. (2005). PEP up your P.E. program: Writing and implementing a PEP grant. *Teaching Elementary Physical Education, 16*(4), 44–52.

McCubbin, J., Jansma, P., & Houston-Wilson, C. (1993). The role of the adapted (special) physical educator: Implications for educating persons with serious disabilities. In P. Jansma (Ed.), *Psychomotor domain training and serious disabilities* (4th ed., pp. 29–40). Lanham, MD: University Press of America.

Meadows, A.J. (2005). To be Asian in America. *Diversity Inc, 4*(3), 28–47.

Meyer, L.H., & Evans, I.M. (1989). *Nonaversive intervention for behavior problems: A manual for home and community.* Baltimore: Paul H. Brookes Publishing Co.

Mills versus Board of Education of District of Columbia, 348 F. Supp. 866 (D.D.C 1972).

Minner, S.H., & Knutson, R. (1982). Mainstreaming handicapped students into physical education: Initial considerations and needs. *Physical Educator, 39,* 13–15.

Mizen, D.W., & Linton, N. (1983). Guess who's coming to P.E.: Six steps to more effective mainstreaming. *Journal of Health, Physical Education, Recreation, and Dance, 54*(8), 63–65.

Modell, S.J., & Imwold, C.H. (1998). Parental attitudes toward inclusive recreation and leisure: A qualitative analysis. *Parks and Recreation, 33*(5), 88–93.

Moon, M.S., Stierer, C.L., Brown, P.J., Hart, D., Komissar, C., & Friedlander, R. (1994). Strategies for successful inclusion in recreation programs. In M.S. Moon (Ed.), *Making school and community recreation fun for everyone: Places and ways to integrate* (pp. 33–53). Baltimore: Paul H. Brookes Publishing Co.

Morreau, L.E., & Eichstaedt, C.B. (1983). Least restrictive programming and placement in physical education. *American Corrective Therapy Journal, 37*(1), 7–17.

Morris, B. (1999). I just want to be a normal kid at summer camp. *Palaestra, 15*(2), 26–28.

Morris, G.S.D., & Stiehl, J. (1999). *Changing kids' games* (2nd ed.). Champaign, IL: Human Kinetics.

Mosston, M., & Ashworth, S. (2002). *Teaching physical education* (5th ed.). Upper Saddle River, NJ: Pearson Benjamin Cummings.

Murata, N.M., Hodge, S.R., & Little, J.R. (2000). Students' attitudes, experiences, and perspectives on their peers with disabilities. *Clinical Kinesiology, 54,* 59–66.

Murata, N.M., & Jansma, P. (1997). Influence of support personnel on students with and without disabilities in general physical education. *Clinical Kinesiology, 51,* 37–46.

National Association for Sport and Physical Education (NASPE). (1992). *Outcomes of quality physical education programs.* Reston, VA: American Association of Health, Physical Education, Recreation, and Dance (AAHPERD).

National Association for Sport and Physical Education (NASPE). (1995a). *Including students with disabilities in physical education.* Reston, VA: Author.

National Association for Sport and Physical Education (NASPE). (1995b). *Moving into the future: National standards for physical education. A guide to content and assessment.* St. Louis: Mosby-Year Book.

National Association for Sport and Physical Education (NASPE). (2004). *Moving into the future: National standards for physical education* (2nd ed.). Reston, VA: Author.

National Association of State Directors of Special Education. (1991). Physical education and sports: The unfulfilled promise for students with disabilities. *Liaison Bulletin, 17*(6), 1–10.

National Consortium on Physical Education and Recreation for Individuals with Disabilities (NCPERID). (1995). *Adapted physical education national standards.* Champaign, IL: Human Kinetics.

National Consortium on Physical Education and Recreation for Individuals with Disabilities (NCPERID). (2006). *Adapted physical education national standards* (2nd ed.). Champaign, IL: Human Kinetics.

National Disability Sports Alliance. (2005). *About us.* Retrieved July 12, 2005, from http://www.ndsaonline.org/purpose.htm

Nelson, J.A. (2003). The invisible cultural group: images of disability. In P.M. Lester & S.D. Ross (Eds.), *Images that injure: Pictorial stereotypes in the media* (pp.175–184). Westport, CT: Greenwood Publishing Group, Inc.

Newman, J. (1997). *Swimming for children with physical sensory impairments.* Springfield, IL: Charles C Thomas.

Nichols, B. (2001). *Moving & learning: The elementary physical education experience* (3rd ed.). Madison, WI: WCB McGraw-Hill.

Nirje, B. (1969). The normalization principle and its human management implications. In R.B. Kugel & W. Wolfensberger (Eds.), *Changing patterns in residential services for the mentally retarded* (pp. 179–195). Washington, DC: Government Printing Office.

No Child Left Behind Act of 2001, PL 107-110, 115 Stat. 1425, 20 U.S.C. §§ 6301 *et seq.*

Oberti v. Board of Education of the Borough of Clementon School District, 995 F.2d 1204 83 Ed.Law Rep. 1009 (3rd Cir. 1993).

O'Brien, J., Forest, M., Snow, J., & Hasburg, D. (1989). *Action for inclusion.* Toronto, Ontario, Canada: Frontier College Press.

Obrusnikova, I., Block, M.E., & Trussell, J.E., III. (2005). *Effects of a disability awareness program on students without disabilities in general physical education.* Manuscript in preparation.

Obrusnikova, I., Block, M.E., & Válková, H. (2003). Impact of inclusion in GPE on students without disabilities. *Adapted Physical Activity Quarterly, 20,* 230–245.

Odom, S.I., McConnell, S.R., & McEvoy, M.A. (1992). Peer-related social competence and its significance for young children with disabilities. In S.I. Odom, S.R. McConnell, & M.A. McEvoy (Eds.), *Social competence of young children with disabilities: Nature, development and intervention* (pp. 3–35). Baltimore: Paul H. Brookes Publishing Co.

Orlick, T. (1978). *The cooperative sports and games book.* New York: Pantheon Press.

Orlick, T. (1982). *The second cooperative sports and games book.* New York: Pantheon Press.

Orelove, F.P., Sobsey, D., & Silberman, R.K. (Eds.). (2004). *Educating children with multiple disabilities: A collaborative approach* (4th ed.). Baltimore: Paul H. Brookes Publishing Co.

Osborne, A.G. (1996). *Legal issues in special education.* Boston: Allyn & Bacon.

Osher, D., Woodruff, D., Sims, A.E. (2002). Schools make a difference: The overrepresentation of African American youth in special education and the juvenile justice system. In D.J. Losen & G. Orfield (Eds.), *Racial inequity in special education.* Cambridge, MA: The Civil Rights Project at Harvard University and Harvard Education Press.

Osinski, A. (1993). Modifying public swimming pools to comply with provisions of The American with Disabilities Act. *Palaestra, 9*(1), 13–18.

Paciorek, M.J., & Jones, J.A. (2001). *Disability sport and recreation resources (3rd ed.).* Traverse City, MI: Cooper Publishing Group.

Paige, R. (2003). *No child left behind: A toolkit for teachers.* Washington, DC: U.S. Department of Education.

Palla, A., & Block, M. (2004, October 28–30). *Impact of multiculturalism and diversity on adapted phys-*

ical educator's teaching: A case study (abstract p. 57). Poster session presented at North American Federation of Adapted Physical Activity (NAFAPA), Thunder Bay, Canada.

PARC (Pennsylvania Association for Retarded Citizens) v. Commonwealth of Pennsylvania, Civil Action No. 71–42, 3–Judge Court (E.D. Pa., 1971).

Pangrazi, R.P. (2004). *Dynamic physical education for elementary school children* (14th ed.). San Francisco: Pearson Benjamin Cummings.

Pangrazi, R.P. (2007). *Dynamic physical education for elementary school children* (15th ed.). San Francisco: Pearson Benjamin Cummings.

Patrick, D., & Reinhartz, J. (1999). The role of collaboration in teacher preparation to meet the needs of diversity. *Education, 119,* 388–399.

Pearpoint, J., Forest, M., & O'Brien, J. (1996). MAPs, Circle of Friends, and PATH: Powerful tools to help build caring communities. In S. Stainback & W. Stainback (Eds.), *Inclusion: A guide for educators* (pp. 67–86). Baltimore: Paul H. Brookes Publishing Co.

Peck, C.A., Donaldson, J., & Pezzoli, M. (1990). Some benefits nonhandicapped adolescents perceive for themselves from their social relationships with peers who have severe handicaps. *Journal of The Association for Persons with Severe Handicaps, 15,* 211–230.

Pedron, N.A., & Evans, S.B. (1990). Modifying classroom teachers' acceptance of the consulting teacher model. *Journal of Educational and Psychological Consultation, 1,* 189–200.

Pennell, R.L. (2001). Self-determination and self-advocacy. *Journal of Disability Policy Studies, 11*(4), 223.

Petray, C., Freesemann, K., & Lavay, B. (1997). Understanding students with diabetes: Implications for the physical education professional. *Journal of Physical Education, Recreation, and Dance, 68*(1), 57–64.

Place, K., & Hodge, S.R. (2001). Social inclusion of students with physical disabilities in GPE: A behavioral analysis. *Adapted Physical Activity Quarterly, 18,* 389–404.

Prendergast, D.E. (1995). Preparing for children who are medically fragile in educational programs. *Teaching Exceptional Children, 27*(2), 37–41.

Price, L.A., Wolensky, D., & Mulligan, R. (2002). Self-determination in action in the classroom. *Remedial and Special Education, 23,* 109–116.

Priest, L. (1979). Integrating the disabled into aquatics programs. *Journal of Physical Education and Recreation, 50*(2), 57–59.

Rainforth, B., York, J., & Macdonald, C. (1992). *Collaborative teams for students with severe disabilities: Integrating therapy and educational services.* Baltimore: Paul H. Brookes Publishing Co.

Rainforth, B., & York-Barr, J. (1997). *Collaborative teams for students with severe disabilities: Integrating therapy and educational services* (2nd ed.). Baltimore: Paul H. Brookes Publishing Co.

Rauscher, L., & McClintock, M. (1997). Ableism curriculum design. In M. Adams, L.A. Bell, & P. Griffin (Eds.), *Teaching for diversity and social justice: a source book.* New York: Routledge.

Rehabilitation Act Amendments of 1998, PL 105-220, 29 U.S.C. §§ 701 *et seq.*

Rehabilitation Act of 1973, PL 93-112, 29 U.S.C. §§ 701 *et seq.*

Reid, G. (1979). Mainstreaming in physical education. *McGill Journal of Education, 14,* 367–377.

Rimmer, J.H., Rubin, S.S., & Braddock, D. (2000). Barriers to exercise in African American women with physical disabilities. *Archives of Physical Medicine and Rehabilitation, 81,* 182–187.

Rizzo, J.V., & Zabel, R.H. (1988). *Educating children and adolescents with behavior disorders: An integrative approach.* Boston: Allyn & Bacon.

Rizzo, T.L., Bishop, P., & Tobar, D. (1997). Teaching students with mild disabilities: What affect attitudes of future physical educators. *Adapted Physical Activity Quarterly, 12,* 205–216.

Rizzo, T.L., & Vispoel, W.P. (1991). GPE teachers' attributes and attitudes toward teaching students with handicaps. *Adapted Physical Activity Quarterly, 8,* 4–11.

Rizzo, T.L. & Vispoel, W.P. (1992). Changing attitudes about teaching students with handicaps. *Adapted Physical Activity Quarterly, 9,* 54–63.

Rohnke, K. (1977). *Cowtails and cobras: A guide to ropes courses, initiative games, and other adventure activities.* Hamilton, MA: Project Adventure.

Rohnke, K. (1989). *Cowtails and cobras II: A guide to games, initiatives courses, and adventure curriculum.* Dubuque, IA: Kendall/Hunt.

Rohnke, K., & Butler, S. (1995). *Quicksilver: Adventure games, initiative problems, trust activities, and a guide to effective leadership.* Dubuque, IA: Kendall/Hunt.

Sailor, W., Gee, K., & Karasoff, P. (1993). Full inclusion and school restructuring. In M.E. Snell (Ed.), *Instruction of students with severe disabilities* (4th ed., pp. 1–30). New York: Merrill.

Sainato, D.M., & Carta, J.J. (1992). Classroom influences on the development of social competence in young children with disabilities. In S.I. Odom, S.R. McConnell, & M.A. McEvoy (Eds.), *Social competence of young children with disabilities: Nature, development and intervention* (pp. 93–109). Baltimore: Paul H. Brookes Publishing Co.

Sallis, J.F., & Owen, N. (1999). *Physical activity and behavioral medicine.* Thousand Oaks, CA: Sage.

Santomier, J. (1985). Physical educators, attitudes and the mainstream: Suggestions for teacher trainers. *Adapted Physical Activity Quarterly, 2,* 328–337.

Savner, J.L., & Myles, B.S. (2000). *Making visual supports work in the home and community: Strategies for individuals with autism and Asperger syndrome.* Shawnee Mission, KS: Autism Asperger Publishing Co.

Sawyer, T.H. (2001). Planning for emergencies in aquatics. *Journal of Physical Education, Recreation and Dance, 72*(3), 12–13.

Schleien, S.J., Kiernan, J., & Wehman, P. (1981). Evaluation of an age-appropriate leisure skills program for moderately retarded adults. *Education and Training of the Mentally Retarded, 16*(1), 13–19.

Schleien, S.J., Meyer, L.H., Heyne, L.A., & Brandt, B.B. (1995). *Lifelong leisure and lifestyles for persons with developmental disabilities.* Baltimore: Paul H. Brookes Publishing Co.

Schleien, S.J., Ray, M.T., & Green, F.P. (1997). *Community recreation and people with disabilities* (2nd ed.). Baltimore: Paul H. Brookes Publishing Co.

Schnorr, R.F. (1990). "Peter? He comes and goes . . ." First graders' perspective on a part-time mainstreamed student. *Journal of the Association for Persons with Severe Handicaps, 15,* 231–240.

Schwartz, S. (1999, August). Actions for coaches and physical education teachers. *Diabetes Management at School.* Retrieved from http://www.diabetes123.com/d_0q_500.htm

Seaman, J.A., & DePauw, K.P. (1989). *The new adapted physical education: A developmental approach.* Mountain View, CA: Mayfield.

Seaman, J.A., DePauw, K.P., Morton, K.B., & Omoto, K. (2003). *Making connections: From theory to practice in adapted physical education.* Scottsdale, AZ: Holcomb Hathaway.

Section 504 of the Rehabilitation Act of 1973, 29 U.S.C. § 794.

Semmel, M.I., Gottlieb, J., & Robinson, N.M. (1979). Mainstreaming: Perspectives on educating handicapped children in the public school. *Review of Research in Education, 7,* 223–279.

Sherrill, C. (2004). *Adapted physical activity, recreation, and sport: Crossdisciplinary and lifespan* (6th ed.). New York: McGraw-Hill.

Siedentop, D. (2004). *Introduction to physical education, fitness, and sport* (5th ed.). New York: McGraw-Hill.

Siedentop, D., Hastie, P. A., & van der Mars, H. (2004). *Complete guide to sport education.* Champaign, IL: Human Kinetics.

Siedentop, D., & Rushall, B.S. (1972). *The development and control of behavior in sport and physical education.* Philadelphia: Lea & Febiger.

Sigmon, S. (1983). The history and future of educational segregation. *Journal for Special Educators, 19,* 1–13.

Skiba, R.J., Michael, R.S., Nardo, A.C., & Peterson, R.L. (2002). The color of discipline: Sources of racial and gender disproportionality in school punishment. *The Urban Review, 34*(4).

Skinner, A.T., & Thompson, A.M. (Eds.). (1983). *Duffield's exercises in water* (3rd ed.). London: Bailliere Tindall.

Slininger, D., Sherrill, C., & Jankowski, C.M. (2000). Children's attitudes toward peers with severe disabilities: Revisiting contact theory. *Adapted Physical Activity Quarterly, 17,* 176–196.

Smith, D.D., & Rivera, D.P. (1995). Discipline in special education and general education settings. *Focus on Exceptional Children, 27*(5), 1–14.

Smith, R.W., Austin, D.R., Kennedy, D.W., Lee, Y., & Hutchison, P. (2005). *Inclusive and special recreation: Opportunities for persons with disabilities* (5th ed.). New York: McGraw-Hill.

Snell, M.E. (1988). Gartner and Lipsky's "Beyond special education: Toward a quality system for all students." Messages for TASH. *Journal of The Association for Persons with Severe Handicaps, 13,* 137–140.

Snell, M.E. (1991). Schools are for all kids: The importance of integration for students with severe disabilities and their peers. In J.W. Lloyd, N.N. Singh, & A.C. Repp (Eds.), *The regular education initiative: Alternative perspectives on concepts, issues, and models* (pp. 133–148). Sycamore, IL: Sycamore.

Snell, M.E., & Brown F. (2000). Development and implementation of educational programs. In M.E. Snell & F. Brown (Eds.), *Instruction of students with se-*
vere disabilities (5th ed., pp. 115–172). Upper Saddle River, NJ: Merrill, Prentice Hall.

Snell, M.E., & Drake, G.P. (1994). Replacing cascades with supported education. *The Journal of Special Education, 27,* 393–409.

Snell, M.E., & Eichner, S.J. (1989). Integration for students with profound disabilities. In F. Brown & D.H. Lehr (Eds.), *Persons with profound disabilities: Issues and practices* (pp. 109–138). Baltimore: Paul H. Brookes Publishing Co.

Snell, M.E., & Janney, R. (2005). *Teachers' guides to inclusive practices series: Collaborative teaming* (2nd ed.). Baltimore: Paul H. Brookes Publishing Co.

Sparks, W.G., III. (1994). Culturally responsive pedagogy: A framework for addressing multicultural issues. *Journal of Physical Education, Recreation and Dance, 65*(9), 33–36, 61.

Special Olympics, Inc. (2005). *About us.* Retrieved July 11, 2005, from http://www.specialolympics.org/Special+Olympics+Public+Website/English/About_Us/default.htm

Stainback, S., & Stainback, W. (1985). *Integration of students with severe handicaps into regular schools.* Reston, VA: Council for Exceptional Children.

Stainback, S., & Stainback, W. (1987). Educating all students in regular education. *TASH Newsletter, 13*(4), 1, 7.

Stainback, S., & Stainback, W. (1990). Inclusive schooling. In W. Stainback & S. Stainback (Eds.), *Support networks for inclusive schooling* (pp. 3–24). Baltimore: Paul H. Brookes Publishing Co.

Stainback, W., & Stainback, S. (1991). A rationale for integration and restructuring: A synopsis. In J.W. Lloyd, N.N. Singh, & A.C. Repp (Eds.), *The regular education initiative: Alternative perspectives on concepts, issues, and models* (pp. 225–239). Sycamore, IL: Sycamore.

Stainback, W., Stainback, S., & Bunch, G. (1989). A rationale for the merger of regular and special education. In W. Stainback, S. Stainback, & M. Forest (Eds.), *Educating all students in the mainstream of regular education* (pp. 15–28). Baltimore: Paul H. Brookes Publishing Co.

Stein, J.U. (1993). The Americans with Disabilities Act: Implications for recreation and leisure. In S.J. Grosse (Ed.), *Leisure opportunities for individuals with disabilities: Legal Issues* (pp. 1–11). Reston, VA: American Association of Health, Physical Education, Recreation, and Dance (AAHPERD).

Stein, J.U. (2005). Accommodating individuals with disabilities in regular sports programs. In H. Appenzeller (Ed.), *Risk management in sports: Issues and strategies* (2nd ed., pp. 389–398). Durham, NC: Carolina Academic Press.

Stopka, C. (2001a). Equipment to enhance an adapted aquatic program: Part 1. *Palaestra, 17*(1), 36–42.

Stopka, C. (2001b). Equipment to enhance an adapted aquatic program: Part 2. *Palaestra, 17*(2), 40–43.

Stopka, C. (2001c). Equipment to enhance an adapted aquatic program: Part 3. *Palaestra, 17*(3), 39–42.

Sullivan, K.A., Lantz, P.J., & Zirkel, P.A. (2000). Leveling the playing field or leveling the players? Section 504, the Americans with Disabilities Act, and Interscholastic sports. *The Journal of Special Education, 33,* 258–267.

Sutherland, S. (1999). Special Olympics' unified sports,

partners club, and sports partnership models. In P. Jansma (Ed.), *The psychomotor domain and serious disabilities* (5th ed., pp. 333–340). Lanham, MD: University Press of America.

Sutherland, S.L., & Hodge, S.R. (2001). Inclusion of a diverse population. *Teaching Elementary Physical Education, 12*(2), 18–21.

Sutliff, M. (1996). Multicultural education for Native American students in physical education. *The Physical Educator, 53,* 157–163.

Sutliff, M., & Perry, J. (2000). Multiculturalism: Developing connections in elementary physical education. *Strategies, 13*(5), 33–36.

Sylvester, C., Voelkl, J.E., & Ellis, G.D. (2001). *Therapeutic recreation programming: Theory and practice.* State College, PA: Venture Publishing, Inc.

Taylor, S.J. (1988). Caught in the continuum: A critical analysis of the principle of the least restrictive environment. *Journal of The Association for Persons with Severe Handicaps, 13,* 41–53.

Temple, V.A., & Walkley, J.W. (1999). Academic learning time—physical education (ALT-PE) of students with mild intellectual disabilities in regular Victorian schools. *Adapted Physical Activity Quarterly, 16,* 64–74.

Theodorakis, Y., Bagiatis, K., & Goudas, M. (1995). Attitudes toward teaching individuals with disabilities: Application of the planned behavior theory. *Adapted Physical Activity Quarterly, 12,* 151–160.

Townsend, B. (2000). The disproportionate discipline of African American learners: Reducing school suspensions and expulsions. *Exceptional Children, 66*(3).

Trent, S.C., Artiles, A.J., Fitchett-Bazemore, K., McDaniel, L., & Coleman-Sorrell, A. (2002). Addressing theory, ethics, power, and privilege in inclusion research and practice. *Teacher Education and Special Education, 25*(1), 11–22.

Tripp, A., French, R., & Sherrill, C. (1995). Contact theory and attitudes of children in physical education programs towards peers with disabilities. *Adapted Physical Activity Quarterly, 12,* 323–332.

Troher, K. (1992, March 1). Handle with care: Fragile kids fit into normal classes. *Chicago Tribune,* Section 18, pp. 3.

Turnbull, H.R. (1990). *Free appropriate public education: The law and children with disabilities* (3rd ed.). Denver, CO: Love.

Udvari-Solner, A., Causton-Theoharis, J., & York-Barr, J. (2004). Developing adaptations to promote participation in inclusive environments. In F.P. Orelove, D. Sobsey, & R.K. Silberman (Eds.), *Educating children with multiple disabilities: A collaborative approach* (4th ed., pp. 151–192). Baltimore: Paul H. Brookes Publishing Co.

Ulrich, D.A. (1985, August). *Current assessment practices in adapted physical education: Implications for future training and research activities.* Paper presented at the annual meeting of the National Consortium on physical education and recreation for the handicapped, New Carollton, MD.

United Nations High Commissioner for Refugees. (2003, September). *Refugees by numbers.* Retrieved from http://www.unhcr.ch/cgi-bin/texis/vtx/basics/opendoc.pdf?tbl=BASICS&id=3c149b007

United States Association for Blind Athletes (USABA).

(2005). *About us.* Retrieved June 9, 2005, from http://www.usaba.org/pages/about.html

United States Association for Blind Athletes (USABA). (n.d.). ISBA visual classification. Retrieved June 9, 2005, from http://www.usaba.org/Pages/visualclassifications.html

U.S. Census Bureau. (2003). *Disability status: 2000.* Retrieved August 8, 2005, from http://www.census.gov/prod/2003pubs/c2kbr-17.pdf

U.S. Census Bureau. (2004). *Poverty thresholds 2003.* Retrieved August 8, 2005, from http://www.census.gov/hhes/poverty/threshld/thresh03.html

U.S. Department of Education, Office of Special Education Programs, Data Analysis System (DANS). (2001). *Table AA15.* Retrieved January 11, 2006, from http://www.ideadata.org/AnnualTables.asp

U.S. Department of Education, Office of Special Education Programs, Data Analysis System (DANS). (2004a). *Part B, Individuals with Disabilities Education Act implementation of FAPE requirements.* Data updated as of July 30, 2005. Retrieved October 18, 2006, from http://www.ideadata.org/tables28th/ar_2-2.htm

U.S. Department of Education, Office of Special Education Programs, Data Analysis System (DANS). (2004b). *Report of children with disabilities receiving special education under Part B of the Individuals with Disabilities Education Act.* Data updated as of July 30, 2005. Retrieved November 6, 2006, from https://www.ideadata.org/tables28th%5Car_1-16.htm

U.S. Department of Health and Human Services (US-DHHS). (1996). *Physical activity and health: Persons with disabilities. A report of the Surgeon General.* Atlanta, GA: Author.

U.S. Department of Health and Human Services (US-DHHS). (2000). *Healthy People 2010: Understanding and improving health* (2nd ed.). Washington, DC: U.S. Government Printing Office.

U.S. Department of Justice. (2001). *A guide to disability rights.* Retrieved July 25, 2002, from http://www.usdoj.gov/crt/ada/cguide/htm

U.S. Department of Justice. (2002). *Americans with Disabilities Act: Questions and answers.* Retrieved July 25, 2002, from http://usdoj.gov/crt/ada/qandaeng.htm

Vandercook, T., & York, J. (1990). A team approach to program development and support. In W. Stainback & S. Stainback (Eds.), *Support networks for inclusive schooling: Interdependent integrated education* (pp. 95–122). Baltimore: Paul H. Brookes Publishing Co.

Vandercook, T., York, J., & Forest, M. (1989). The McGill action planning system (MAPS): A strategy for building the vision. *Journal of The Association for Persons with Severe Handicaps, 14,* 205–215.

Verre, J., McLughlin, M., & Webb-Johnson, G. (2003). *Addressing disproportionate representation in special education: A NERRC invitational forum.* Retrieved from http://www.wested.org/nerrc

Viadero, D. (2000). Lags in minority achievement defy traditional explanation. *Education Week, 19*(28), 1, 18–19, 21–22.

Virginia Department of Education. (2005). *English as a second language.* Retrieved August 3, 2005, from http://www.doe.virginia.gov/VDOE/Instruction/ESL/

Voeltz, L.M. (1980). Children's attitudes toward handicapped peers. *American Journal of Mental Deficiency, 84*(5), 455–464

Voeltz, L.M. (1982). Effects of structured interactions with severely handicapped peers on children's attitudes. *American Journal of Mental Deficiency, 86,* 380–390.

Voeltz, L.M., & Apffel, J.A. (1981). Leisure activities curricular components for severely handicapped youth. Why and how? *Viewpoints in Teaching and Learning, 57,* 82–93.

Voeltz, L.M., Wuerch, B.B., & Bockhaut, C.H. (1992). Social validation of leisure activities training with severely handicapped youth. *Journal of The Association for the Severely Handicapped, 7*(4), 3–13.

Vogler, E.W., Koranda, P., & Romance, T. (2000). Including a child with severe cerebral palsy in physical education: A case study. *Adapted Physical Activity Quarterly, 9,* 316–329.

Vogler, E.W., van der Mars, H., Cusimano, B., & Darst, P. (1998). Analysis of student/teacher behaviours in junior high physical education classes including children with mild disability. *Journal of Sport Pedagogy, 4*(2), 43–57.

Wagner, G., Wetherald, L., & Wilson, B. (1994). A model for making county and municipal recreation department programs inclusive. In M.S. Moon (Ed.), *Making school and community recreation fun for everyone: Places and ways to integrate* (pp. 181–192). Baltimore: Paul H. Brookes Publishing Co.

Walker, J.E., Shea, T.M., & Bauer, A.M. (2003). *Behavior management* (8th ed.). New York: Prentice Hall.

Wang, M.C., & Baker, E.T. (1986). Mainstreamed programs: Design features and effects. *The Journal of Special Education, 19,* 503–521.

Wang, M.C., Reynolds, M.C., & Walberg, H.J., (1987). Rethinking special education. *Journal of Learning Disabilities, 20,* 290–293.

Webb, D., & Hodge, S.R. (2003). Factors that influence career choice of African American students to enter the adapted physical education profession. *The Physical Educator. 60*(3), 134–149.

Webster, G.E. (1987). Influence of peer tutors upon academic learning time-physical education of mentally handicapped students. *Journal of Teaching in Physical Education, 6,* 393–403.

Wehman, P., & Schleien, S. (1981). *Leisure programs for handicapped persons: Adaptations, techniques, and curriculum.* Austin, TX: PRO-ED.

Wehrly, B. (1995). *Pathways to multicultural counseling competence: A developmental journey.* Pacific Grove, CA: Brooks/Cole Thomson Learning.

Weiss, R., & Karper, W.B. (1980). Teaching the handicapped child in the regular physical education class. *Journal of Physical Education and Recreation, 51,* 22–35, 77.

Wellner, A.S. (2002). Diversity in America: A portrait of our melting pot, with projections for the black, Hispanic, Asian, white and Native American populations to the year 2007. *Supplement American Demographics.* Retrieved June 19, 2006, from http://extranet.mapinfo.com/common/library/diversity.pdf

Wenzel, K.C. (2000). *What is therapeutic recreation?* Retrieved June 22, 2005, from http://www.nrpa.org/content/default.aspx?documentId=955

Wessel, J.A., & Kelly, L. (1986). *Achievement-based curriculum development in physical education.* Philadelphia: Lea & Febiger.

Wessel, J.A., & Zittel, L.L. (1995). *Smart Start: Preschool movement curriculum designed for children of all abilities* (p. 271). Austin, TX: PRO-ED.

Wessinger, N.P. (1994). Celebrating our differences: Fostering ethnicity in homogeneous settings. *Journal of Physical Education, Recreation and Dance, 65*(9), 62–68.

West, J.F., Idol, L., & Cannon, G.S. (1989). *Collaboration in the schools: An in-service and pre-service curriculum for teachers, support staff, and administrators.* Austin, TX: PRO-ED.

Wheelchair Sports, USA. (2005). *About.* Retrieved June 9, 2005, from http://www.wsusa.org/about.htm

Wilder, L.K., Dyches, T.T., Obiakor, F.E., & Algozzine, B. (2004). Multicultural perspectives on teaching students with autism. *Focus on Autism and other Developmental Disabilities, 19*(2), 105–114.

Will, M.C. (1986). Educating children with learning problems: A shared responsibility. *Exceptional Children, 52,* 411–416.

Williams, N.F. (1992). The physical education hall of shame. *Journal of Physical Education, Recreation, and Dance, 63*(6), 57–60.

Williams, N.F. (1994). The physical education hall of shame: Part II. *Journal of Physical Education, Recreation, and Dance, 65*(2), 17–20.

Williams, N.F. (1996). The physical education hall of shame: Part III: Inappropriate teaching practices. *Journal of Physical Education, Recreation, and Dance, 67*(8), 45–48.

Williamson, K.M. (1993). Is your inequity showing? Ideas and strategies for creating a more equitable learning environment. *Journal of Physical Education, Recreation and Dance, 64*(8), 15–23.

Wilson, C., Lieberman, L., Horton, M., & Kasser, S. (1997). Peer tutoring: A plan for instructing students of all abilities. *Journal of Physical Education, Recreation and Dance, 68*(6), 39–44.

Winnick, J.P. (2000a). An introduction to adapted physical education. In J.P. Winnick (Ed.), *Adapted physical education and sport* (3rd ed., pp. 3–18). Champaign, IL: Human Kinetics.

Winnick, J.P. (2000b). Program organization and management. In J.P. Winnick (Ed.), *Adapted physical education and sport* (3rd ed., pp. 19–32). Champaign, IL: Human Kinetics.

Winnick, J.P. (2005). Program organization and management. In J.P. Winnick (Ed.), *Adapted physical education and sport* (4th ed., pp. 21–38). Champaign, IL: Human Kinetics.

Wolfensberger, W. (1972). *The principle of normalization in human services.* Toronto, Ontario, Canada: National Institute on Mental Retardation.

Woodruff, G., & McGonigel, M.J. (1988). Early intervention team approaches: The transdisciplinary model. In J.B. Jordan, J.J. Gallagher, P.L. Hutinger, & M.B. Karnes (Eds.), *Early childhood special education: Birth to three* (pp. 163–182). Reston, VA: Council for Exceptional Children.

Wright, P.W.D., & Wright, P.D. (2004). *Wrightslaw on line.* Retrieved August 15, 2005, from http://www.wrightslaw.com/nclb/info/myths.realities.napas.htm

Wright, P.W.D., Wright, P.D., & Heath, S.W. (2004).

Wrightslaw: No child left behind. VA, Hartfield: Harbor House Law Press.

York, J., Giangreco, M.F., Vandercook, T., & Macdonald, C. (1992). Integrating support personnel in the inclusive classroom. In S. Stainback & W. Stainback (Eds.), *Curriculum considerations in inclusive classrooms: Facilitating learning for all students* (pp. 101–116). Baltimore: Paul H. Brookes Publishing Co.

York, J., Vandercook, T., Macdonald, C., Heise-Neff, C., & Caughey, E. (1992). Feedback about integrating middle-school education students with severe disabilities in general education classes. *Exceptional Children, 58*(3), 244–258.

Zachofsky, D. (1974). *The effects of extrinsic reinforcement upon motor performance of learning disabled children on a selected motor task.* Unpublished master's thesis, State University of New York College at Brockport.

Zamora-Duran, G., & Artiles, A.J. (1997). Disproportionate representation: Current issues and future directions. In A.J. Artiles & G. Zamora-Duran (Eds.), *Reducing disproportionate representation of culturally diverse students in special and gifted education* (pp. 1–6). Reston, VA: The Council for Exceptional Children.

Zionts, P., Zionts, L., & Simpson, R.L. (2002). *Emotional and behavioral problems: A handbook for understanding and handling students.* Thousand Oaks, CA: Corwin.

Zygmunt, L., Larson, M.S., & Tilson, G.P., Jr. (1994). Disability awareness training and social networking. In M.S. Moon (Ed.), *Making school and community recreation fun for everyone: Places and ways to integrate* (pp. 209–226). Baltimore: Paul H. Brookes Publishing Co.

Resources

GROUPS ON SPECIFIC DISABILITIES

Amputees

American Amputee Soccer Association
1022 Creekside Drive, Wilmington, DE 19804
Phone: 302-683-0997
http://www.ampsoccer.org
E-mail: rgh@ampsoccer.org

Amputee Coalition of America
900 East Hill Avenue, Suite 285, Knoxville, TN
37915
Phone: 865-525-4512
Fax: 865-525-7917
http://amputee-coalition.org
E-mail: membership@amputee-coalition.org

Amputee Resource Foundation of America, Inc.
2324 Wildwood Trail, Minnetonka, MN 55305
http://www.amputeeresource.org
E-mail: info@amputeeresource.org

Amputee Treatment Center
8388 Lewiston Road, Batavia, NY 14020
Phone: 585-343-4154
Fax: 585-343-8101
http://amputee-center.com
E-mail: mlove011@rochester.rr.com

International Child Amputee Network
I-Can, Post Office Box 514, Abilene, TX 79604
Phone: 325-675-6434
http://www.child-amputee.net
E-mail: jbaughn@child-amputee.net

Attention-Deficit/ Hyperactivity Disorder

Attention Deficit Disorder Association
Post Office Box 543, Pottstown, PA 19464
Phone: 484-945-2101
Fax: 610-970-7520
http://www.add.org
E-mail: mail@add.org

Children and Adults with Attention-Deficit/
Hyperactivity Disorder
8181 Professional Place, Suite 201, Landover, MD
20785
Phone: 800-233-4050; 301-306-7070
Fax: 301-306-7090
http://www.chadd.org
E-mail: webmaster@chadd.org

National Resource Center on AD/HD
8181 Professional Place, Suite 150, Landover, MD
20785
Phone: 800-233-4050
http://www.help4adhd.org

Autism, Asperger Syndrome, Fragile X Syndrome, Hyperlexia

American Hyperlexia Association
195 West Spangler, Suite B, Elmhurst, IL 60126
Phone: 630-415-2212
Fax: 630-530-5909
http://www.hyperlexia.org
E-mail: president@hyperlexia.org

Autism Initiatives
7 Chesterfield Road, Crosby, Liverpool, L23 9XL
United Kingdom
Phone: +44 (0)151 330 9500
Fax: +44 (0)151 330 9501
http://www.autisminitiatives.org
E-mail: headoffice@autisminitiatives.org

Autism Research Institute
4182 Adams Avenue, San Diego, CA 92116
Phone: 619-281-7165
Fax: 619-563-6840
http://www.autismwebsite.com
E-mail: media@autismresearchinstitute.com

Autism Society of America
7910 Woodmont Avenue, Suite 300, Bethesda, MD
20814
Phone: 301-657-0881; 800-3AUTISM
Fax: 301-657-0869
http://www.autism-society.org
E-mail: editor@autism-society.org

The Cambridge Center for Behavioral Studies
336 Baker Avenue, Concord, MA 07142
Phone: 978-369-2227
Fax: 978-369-8584
http://www.behavior.org
E-mail: harshbarger@behavior.org

Cure Autism Now
5455 Wilshire Boulevard, Suite 2250, Los Angeles,
    CA 90036
Phone: 888-8-AUTISM; 888-828-8476
Fax: 323-549-0547
http://www.cureautismnow.org
E-mail: tmacdonald@cureautismnow.org

Fragile X Research Foundation
45 Pleasant Street, Newburyport, MA 01950
Phone: 978-462-1866
Fax: 978-463-9985
http://www.fraxa.org
E-mail: kclapp@fraxa.org

National Autistic Society
393 City Road, London, EC1V 1NG United
    Kingdom
Phone: +44 (0)20 7833 2299
Fax: +44 (0)20 7833 9666
http://www.nas.org.uk
E-mail: nas@nas.org.uk

The National Fragile X Foundation
Post Office Box 190488, San Francisco, CA 94199
Phone: 800-688-8765
Fax: 925-938-9315
http://www.fragilex.org
E-mail: NATLFX@FragileX.org

Blind and Visual Impairments

American Council of the Blind
1155 15th Street NW, Suite 1004, Washington, DC
    20005
Phone: 800-424-8666; 202-467-5081
Fax: 202-467-5085
http://www.acb.org
E-mail: info@acb.org

American Foundation for the Blind
11 Penn Plaza, Suite 300, New York, NY 10001
Phone: 800-AFB-LINE (232-5632); 212-502-7600
http://www.afb.org
E-mail: afbinfo@afb.net

Canadian National Institute for the Blind
1929 Bayview Avenue, Toronto, Ontario M4G 3E8,
    Canada
Phone: 416-486-2500
Fax: 416-480-7677
http://www.cnib.ca
E-mail: webmaster@cnib.ca

National Federation of the Blind
1800 Johnson Street, Baltimore, MD 21230
Phone: 410-659-9314
Fax: 410-685-5653
http://www.nfb.org
E-mail: imagine@nfb.org

Cerebral Palsy

American Cerebral Palsy Information (4MyChild)
Post Office Box 251688, West Bloomfield, MI
    48325
Phone: 800-4MYCHILD; 800-469-2445
http://www.cerebralpalsy.org
E-mail: help@4mychild.org

Scope (About cerebral palsy)
6 Market Road, London, N7 9PW United Kingdom
Phone: +44 (0)808 800 3333
http://www.scope.org.uk
E-mail: cphelpline@scope.org.uk

United Cerebral Palsy Associations
UCPA National, 1660 L Street NW, Suite 700,
    Washington, DC 20036
Phone: 800-872-5827; 202-776-0406
Fax: 202-776-0414
http://www.ucp.org
E-mail: webmaster@ucp.org

Cerebral Palsy/Brain Injury

American Academy for Cerebral Palsy and
    Developmental Medicine
555 East Wells Street, Suite 1100, Milwaukee, WI
    53202
Phone: 414-918-3014
http://www.aacpdm.org/index
E-mail: Raymond@aaos.org

Centre for Neuro Skills
2658 Mt. Vernon Avenue, Bakersfield, CA 93306
Phone: 800-922-4994; 661-872-3408
Fax: 661-872-5150
http://www.neuroskills.com
E-mail: bakersfield@neuroskills.com

Neurologic Disabilities Support Project
3901 Rainbow Boulevard, Kansas City, KS 66160
Phone: 913-588-5943
Fax: 913-588-5942
http://guest1.altec.org/ndsp/NDSPautism/
    NDSPHome.html
E-mail: jtyler@kumc.edu

Deaf and Hearing Impairments

American Speech-Language-Hearing Association
10801 Rockville Pike, Rockville, MD 20852
Phone: 800-498-2071; 301-571-0457
Fax: 301-571-0457
http://www.asha.org
E-mail: actioncenter@asha.org

National Association of the Deaf
8630 Fenton Street, Suite 820, Silver Spring, MD
    20910
Phone: 301-587-1788; 301-587-1789
Fax: 301-587-1791
http://www.nad.org
E-mail: NADinfo@nad.org

National Institute on Deafness and Other
    Communication Disorders
31 Center Drive, MSC 2320, Bethesda, MD 20892
Phone: 301-496-7243; 301-402-0252
Fax: 301-402-0018
http://www.nidcd.nih.gov
E-mail: nidcdinfo@nidcd.nih.gov

RNID (Changing the world for deaf and hard of
    hearing people)
19-23 Featherstone Street, London, EC1Y 8SL
    United Kingdom
Phone: +44 (0)20 7296 8000; +44 (0)20 7296 8001
Fax: +44 (0)20 7296 8199
http://www.rnid.org.uk
E-mail: informationline@rnid.org.uk

Deaf-Blind

American Association of the Deaf-Blind
8630 Fenton Street, Suite 121, Silver Spring, MD
    20910
Phone: 301-495-4402
Fax: 301-495-4404
http://www.aadb.org
E-mail: AADB-Info@aadb.org

The Deafblind Association
616 Riversdale Road, Camberwell, Victoria 3124,
    Australia
Phone: +61 (0)3 9882 7055
Fax: +61 (0)3 9882 9210
http://www.dba.asn.au
E-mail: info@dba.asn.au

Helen Keller National Center
141 Middle Neck Road, Sands Point, NY 11050
Phone: 516-944-8900
Fax: 516-944-7302
http://www.hknc.org
E-mail: HKNCinfo@hknc.org

Developmental Disabilities

Developmental Delay Resources
5801 Beacon Street, Pittsburgh, PA 15217
Phone: 800-497-0944
Fax: 412-422-1374
http://www.devdelay.org
E-mail: devdelay@mindspring.com

Developmental Disabilities Resource Center
1117 West 8th Avenue, Suite 300, Lakewood, CO
    80215
Phone: 303-233-3363
Fax: 303-233-4622
http://www.ddrcco.com
E-mail: aguess@ddrcco.com

Florida Developmental Disabilities Council, Inc.
124 Marriot Drive, Suite 203, Tallahassee, FL
    32301
Phone: 850-488-4180
Fax: 850-922-6702
http://fddc.org
E-mail: fddc@fddc.org

Down Syndrome

Association for Children with Down Syndrome
4 Fern Place, Plainview, NY 11803
Phone: 516-993-4700
Fax: 516-933-9524
http://www.acds.org
E-mail: info@acds.org

The Down Syndrome International
The Sarah Duffen Centre, Belmont Street,
    Southsea, PO5 1NA United Kingdom
Phone: +44 (0)23 9289 3898
Fax: +44 (0)23 9289 3899
http://www.down-syndrome-int.org
E-mail: enquiries@down-syndrome-int.org

National Association for Down Syndrome
Post Office Box 206, Wilmette, IL 60091
Phone: 630-325-9112
http://www.nads.org
E-mail: webmaster@nads.org

National Down Syndrome Congress
1370 Center Drive, Suite 102, Atlanta, GA 30338
Phone: 800-232-6732; 770-604-9500
Fax: 770-604-9898
http://www.ndsccenter.org
E-mail: info@ndsccenter.org

National Down Syndrome Society
666 Broadway, New York, NY 10012
Phone: 212-460-9330; 800-221-4602
Fax: 212-979-2873
http://www.ndss.org
E-mail: info@ndss.org

Dwarfism

Association for People of Short Stature in Sweden
Magnus Edman, International Correspondent
Dynäs 120 870 33, Docksta, Sweden
Phone: +46 613-410-85
http://www.fkv.se
E-mail: magnusedman@swipnet.se

Association of Little People of Czech Republic
    (Palecek)
Kroftova 1/329 150 00, Praha 5, Czech Republic
Phone : +420 257 325 770
http://www.palecek.nebesa.cz
E-mail: palecek@nebesa.cz

Crecer, Asociación Nacional Para Problemos de
    Crecimiento
Cuartel de Artilleria, 12, bajo E-30002 Murcia,
    Spain
Phone: +34 968 34 62 18
Fax: +34 968 34 62 02
http://www.crecimiento.org
E-mail: crecer@crecimiento.org

Dutch Organization of Little People
Belangenvereniging Van Kleine Mensen
Wevelaan 75, Utrecht 3571, The Netherlands
Post Office Box 2776, 3500 GT Utrecht, The
    Netherlands
Phone: +31 (0)3027 11198
Fax: +31 (0)3027 11198
http://www.bvkm.nl
E-mail: info@bvkm.nl

Little People of America
5289 Northeast Elam Young Parkway, Suite F-100,
    Hillsboro, OR 97124
Phone: 888-LPA-2001; 503-846-1562
Fax: 503-846-1590
http://www.lpaonline.org
E-mail: info@lpaonline.org

The Quebec Association of Persons of Short
    Stature
(L'Association québecoise des personnes de petite
    taille)
2177, rue Masson, Suite 205, Montreal, Québec,
    H2H 1B1 Canada
Phone: 514-521-9671
Fax: 514-521-3369
http://www.aqppt.org
E-mail: info@aqppt.org

Fetal Alcohol Syndrome/Effects

FASlink (Fetal Alcohol Disorders Society)
2445 Old Lakeshore Road, Bright's Grove, Ontario,
    N0N 1C0 Canada
Phone: 519-869-8026
http://www.faslink.org
E-mail: info@faslink.org

Fetal Alcohol Syndrome Consultation, Education
    and Training Services
Post Office Box 83175, Portland, OR 97283
Phone: 503-621-1271
Fax: 503-621-1271
http://www.fascets.org
E-mail: dmalbin@fascets.org

National Organization on Fetal Alcohol Syndrome
900 17th Street, NW, Suite 910, Washington, DC
    20006
Phone: 800-66NOFAS; 202-785-4585
Fax: 202-466-6456
http://www.nofas.org
E-mail: mitchell@nofas.org

Hydrocephalus and Spina Bifida

Association for Spina Bifida and Hydrocephalus
42 Park Road, Peterborough, PE1 2UQ United
    Kingdom
Phone: +44 (0)1733 555988
Fax: +44 (0)1733 555985
http://www.asbah.org
E-mail: info@asbah.org

Hydrocephalus Association
870 Market Street, Suite 705, San Francisco, CA
  94102
Phone: 888-598-3789; 415-732-7040
Fax: 415-732-7044
http://www.hydroassoc.org
E-mail: info@hydroassoc.org

International Federation for Spina Bifida and
  Hydrocephalus
Cellebroersstraat 16 B-1000, Brussels, Belgium
Phone: +32 (0)2 502 0413
Fax: +32 (0)2 502 1129
http://www.ifglobal.org
E-mail: info@ifglobal.org

Society for Research into Hydrocephalus and Spina
  Bifida
Gagle Brook House, Chesterton, Bicester,
  Oxfordshire, OX26 1UF United Kingdom
http://www.srhsb.org
E-mail: hsec@srhsb.org

Spina Bifida and Hydrocephalus Association of
  Canada
#977-167 Lombard Avenue, Winnipeg, Manitoba,
  R3B 0V3 Canada
Phone: 204-925-3650
Fax: 204-925-3654
http://www.sbhac.ca
E-mail: spinab@mts.net

Spina Bifida and Hydrocephalus Association of
  South Australia Inc.
68 Day Terrace, West Croydon, South Australia
  50007, Australia
Phone: +61 (0)88366-5900
Fax: +61 (0)88366-5901
http://www.spinabifida.asn.au
E-mail: info@spinabifida.asn.au

The Spina Bifida Association of America
4590 MacArthur Boulevard NW, Suite 250,
  Washington, DC 20007-4226
Phone: 800-621-3141; 202-944-3285
Fax: 202-944-3295
http://www.sbaa.org
E-mail: sbaa@sbaa.org

Language/Speech Disorders

American Speech-Language-Hearing Association
10801 Rockville Pike, Rockville, MD 20852
Voice: 800-498-2071; 888-321-ASHA
TTY: 301-571-0457
Fax: 301-571-0457
http://www.asha.org
E-mail: actioncenter@asha.org

National Aphasia Association
7 Dey Street, Suite 600, New York, NY 10007
Phone: 800-922-4622
http://www.aphasia.org
E-mail: responsecenter@aphasia.org

Learning Disabilities

The Center for Learning Differences, Inc.
6 Highland Avenue, Great Neck, NY 11021
Phone: 516-773-4737
http://www.centerforlearningdifferences.org

Council for Learning Disabilities
Post Office Box 4014, Leesburg, VA 20177
Phone: 571-258-1010
Fax: 571-258-1011
https://www.cldinternational.org

The Dyslexia Institution
Park House, Wick Road, Egham, Surrey, TW20
  OHH United Kingdom
Phone: +44 (0)1784 222300
Fax: +44 (0)1784 222333
http://www.dyslexiaaction.org.uk
E-mail: info@dyslexia-inst.org.uk

The International Dyslexia Association
Chester Building, Suite 382, 8600 LaSalle Road,
  Baltimore, MD 21286
Phone: 410-296-0232
Messages: 800-ABCD123 (800-222-2123)
Fax: 410-321-5069
http://www.interdys.org
E-mail: rhott@interdys.org

Learning Disabilities Association of America
4156 Library Road, Pittsburgh, PA 15234
Phone: 412-334-1515
Fax: 412-344-0224
http://www.ldaamerica.org
E-mail: info@LDAAmerica.org

National Center for Learning Disabilities
381 Park Avenue South, Suite 1401, New York,
    NY 10016
Phone: 888-575-7373; 212-545-7510
Fax: 212-545-9665
http://www.ncld.org
E-mail: help@ncld.org

Mental Retardation

American Association on Mental Retardation
444 North Capitol Street NW, Suite 846,
    Washington, DC 20001
Phone: 800-424-3688; 202-387-1968
Fax: 202-387-2193
http://www.aamr.org
E-mail: anam@aamr.org

The Arc of the United States
1010 Wayne Avenue, Suite 650, Silver Spring, MD
    20910
Phone: 301-565-3842
Fax: 301-565-5342; 301-565-3843
http://www.thearc.org
E-mail: info@thearc.org

Mental Disability Rights International
1156 15th Street NW, Suite 1001, Washington, DC
    20005
Phone: 202-296-0800
Fax: 202-728-3053
http://www.mdri.org
E-mail: mdri@mdri.org

Muscular Dystrophy

Muscular Dystrophy Association
3300 East Sunrise Drive, Tucson, AZ 85718
Phone: 800-FIGHT-MD (800-344-4863)
http://www.mdausa.org
E-mail: mda@mdausa.org

Muscular Dystrophy Association of Australia
Post Office Box 2200, North Melbourne, 3051
    Australia
Phone: +61 3 9320 9555, 800 656 MDA
Fax: +61 3 9320 9595
http://www.mda.org.au
E-mail: info@mda.org.au

Muscular Dystrophy Association of Canada
2345 Yonge Street, Suite 900, Toronto, Ontario,
    M4P 2E5 Canada
Phone: 866-MUSCLE-8
Fax: 416-488-7523
http://www.muscle.ca
E-mail: info@muscle.ca

Muscular Dystrophy Campaign
7-11 Prescott Place, London, SW4 6BS United
    Kingdom
Phone: +44 (0)20 7720 8055
Fax: +44 (0)20 7498 0670
http://www.muscular-dystrophy.org
E-mail: info@muscular-dystrophy.org

Muscular Dystrophy Family Foundation
3951 North Meridian Street, Suite 100,
    Indianapolis, IN 46208
Phone: 800-544-1213; 317-923-MDFF
Fax: 317-923-6334
http://www.mdff.org

Paralysis and Spinal Cord Injury

American Paraplegia Society
75-25 Astoria Boulevard, Jackson Heights, NY
    11370
Phone: 718-803-3782
Fax: 718-803-0414
http://www.apssci.org
E-mail: aps@unitedspinal.org

American Spinal Injury Association
2020 Peachtree Road NW, Atlanta, GA 30309
Phone: 404-355-9772
Fax: 404-355-1826
http://www.asia-spinalinjury.org
E-mail: pat_duncan@shepherd.org

Christopher Reeve Foundation
636 Morris Turnpike, Suite 3A, Short Hills, NJ
    07078
Phone: 800-225-0292
http://www.christopherreeve.org
E-mail: info@paralysis.org

Foundation for Spinal Cord Injury Prevention, Care
    & Cure
11230 White Lake Road, Fenton, MI 48430
Phone: 800-342-0330
Fax: 810-714-0354
http://www.fscip.org
E-mail: info@fscip.org

The National Spinal Cord Injury Association
6701 Democracy Boulevard, Suite 300-9, Bethesda,
    MD 20817
Phone: 800-962-9629; 301-214-4006
Fax: 301-990-0445
http://www.spinalcord.org
E-mail: info@spinalcord.org

Rett Syndrome

International Rett Syndrome Association
9121 Piscataway Road, #2B, Clinton, MD 20735
Phone: 800-818-RETT; 301-856-3334
Fax: 301-856-3336
http://www.rettsyndrome.org
E-mail: admin@rettsyndrome.org

Rett Syndrome Association UK
113 Friern Barnet Road, London, N11 3EU United
   Kingdom
Phone: +44 (0)20 8361 5161
Fax: +44 (0)20 8368 6123
http://www.rettsyndrome.org.uk
E-mail: info@rettsyndrome.org.uk

Rett Syndrome Research Foundation
4600 Devitt Drive, Cincinnati, OH 45246
Phone: 513-874-3020
Fax: 513-874-2520
http://www.rsrf.org
E-mail: craig@rsrf.org

Seizure Disorders

American Epilepsy Society
342 North Main Street, West Hartford, CT 06117
http://www.aesnet.org
E-mail: sberry@aesnet.org

Epilepsy Action
New Anstey House Gate Way Drive, Yeadon,
   Leeds, LS19 17XY United Kingdom
Phone: +44 (0)113 210 8800
Fax: +44 (0)113 391 0300
http://www.epilepsy.org.uk
E-mail: epilepsy@epilepsy.org.uk

Epilepsy Foundation of America
4351 Garden City Drive, Landover, MD 20785
Phone: 800-332-1000
http://www.epilepsyfoundation.org
E-mail: webmaster@efa.org

Tourette Syndrome

The National Tourette Syndrome Association
42-40 Bell Boulevard, Bayside, NY 11361
Phone: 718-224-2999
Fax: 718-279-9596
http://tsa-usa.org
E-mail: tracy.flynn@tsa-usa.org

Tourette Syndrome Foundation of Canada
194 Jarvis Street, #206, Toronto, Ontario, N5B 2B7
   Canada
Phone: 800-361-3120; 416-861-8398
Fax: 416-861-2472
http://www.tourette.ca
E-mail: tsfc@tourette.ca

Tourette Syndrome (UK) Association
Post Office Box 26149, Dunfermline, KY12 7YU
   United Kingdom
Phone: +44 (0)1383 629600
Fax: +44 (0)1383 629609
http://www.tsa.org.uk
E-mail: enquiries@tsa.org.uk

PROFESSIONAL ASSOCIATIONS FOR PHYSICAL EDUCATORS

Adapted Physical Activity Council
American Alliance for Health, Physical Education,
   Recreation and Dance
1900 Association Drive, Reston, VA 20191
Phone: 800-213-7193; 703-476-3430
Fax: 703-476-9527
http://www.aahperd.org
E-mail: aaalf@aahperd.org

Adapted Physical Education National Standards
E224 Park Center, SUNY Cortland, Box 2000,
   Cortland, NY 13045
Phone: 888-APENS-Exam; 607-753-4969
http://www.cortland.edu/apens/
E-mail: apens@cortland.edu

American College of Sports Medicine
Post Office Box 1440, Indianapolis, IN 46206
Phone: 317-637-9200
Fax: 317-634-7817
http://www.acsm.org
E-mail: membership@acsm.org

American Dance Therapy Association
2000 Century Plaza, Suite 108, 10632 Little
   Patuxent Parkway, Columbia, MD 21044
Phone: 410-997-4040
Fax: 410-997-4048
http://www.adta.org
E-mail: info@adta.org

American Kinesiotherapy Association
Post Office Box 1390, Hines, IL 60141
Phone: 800-296-2582
http://www.akta.org
E-mail: ccbkt@aol.com

American Occupational Therapy Association
4720 Montgomery Lane, Post Office Box 31220,
  Bethesda, MD 20824
Phone: 800-377-8555; 301-652-2682
Fax: 301-652-7711
http://www.aota.org
E-mail: helpdesk@aota.org

American Physical Therapy Association
111 North Fairfax Street, Alexandria, VA 22314
Phone: 800-999-2782
Fax: 703-684-7343
http://www.apta.org
E-mail: svcctr@apta.org

American Psychological Association
750 First Street NE, Washington, DC 20002
Phone: 800-374-2721; 202-336-5500
Fax: 202-336-5997
http://www.apa.org
E-mail: mis@apa.org

American Therapeutic Recreation Association
1414 Prince Street, Suite 204, Alexandria, VA
  22314
Phone: 703-683-9420
Fax: 703-683-9431
http://www.atra-tr.org
E-mail: membership@atra-tr.org

Canadian Association for Health, Physical
  Education, Recreation and Dance
301-2197 Riverside Drive, Ottawa, Ontario, K1H
  7X3 Canada
Phone: 800-663-8708; 613-523-1348
Fax: 613-523-1206
http://www.cahperd.ca
E-mail: info@cahperd.ca

Canadian Fitness and Lifestyle Research Institute
201-185 Somerset Street West, Ottawa, Ontario,
  K2P 0J2 Canada
Phone: 613-233-5528
Fax: 613-233-5536
http://www.cflri.ca
E-mail: info@cflri.ca

Council for Exceptional Children
1110 North Glebe Road, Suite 300, Arlington, VA
  22201
Phone: 866-915-5000; 703-620-3660
Fax: 703-264-9494
http://www.cec.sped.org
E-mail: service@cec.sped.org

National Association of State Directors of Special
  Education
1800 Diagonal Road, Suite 320, Alexandria, VA
  22314
Phone: 703-519-3800
Fax: 703-519-7008
http://www.nasdse.org

National Consortium for Physical Education and
  Recreation for Individuals with Disabilities
University of Wisconsin–La Crosse, Department of
  Exercise and Sport Science, 131 Mitchell Hall,
  La Crosse, WI 54601
Phone: 608-785-5415
http://www.uwlax.edu/sah/ncperid
E-mail: tymeson.gart@uwlax.edu

National Dissemination Center for Children with
  Disabilities
Post Office Box 1492, Washington, DC 20013
Phone: 800-695-0285
Fax: 202-884-8441
http://www.nichcy.org
E-mail: nichcy@aed.org

National Rehabilitation Association
633 South Washington Street, Alexandria, VA
  22314
Phone: 703-836-0850
Fax: 703-836-0848
http://www.nationalrehab.org
E-mail: info@nationalrehab.org

National Rehabilitation Information Center
4200 Forbes Boulevard, Suite 202, Lanham, MD
  20706
Phone: 800-346-2742
Fax: 301-459-4263
http://www.naric.com
E-mail: naricinfo@heitechservices.com

National Therapeutic Recreation Society
22377 Belmont Ridge Road, Ashburn, VA 20148
Phone: 703-858-0784
Fax: 703-858-0794
http://www.nrpa.org
E-mail: dvaira@nrpa.org

Rehabilitation International, USA
25 East 21st Street, New York, NY 10010
Phone: 212-420-1500
Fax: 212-505-0871
http://www.riglobal.org
E-mail: RI@riglobal.org

SPORTS AND RECREATION ORGANIZATIONS FOR PEOPLE WITH DISABILITIES

Active Living Alliance for Canadians with a Disability
Alliance de Vie Active pour les Canadiens/Canadiennes ayant un handicap
720 Belfast Road, Suite 104, Ottawa, Ontario, K1G 0Z5 Canada
Phone: 800-771-0663; 613-244-0052
Fax: 613-244-4857
http://www.ala.ca
E-mail: info@ala.ca

Adaptive Sports Center
Post Office Box 1639, Crested Butte, CO 81224
Phone: 866-349-2296; 970-349-2296
Fax: 970-349-4950
http://www.adaptivesports.org
E-mail: info@adaptivesports.org

Australian Deaf Sports Federation
Level 3/340 Albert Street, East Melbourne, Victoria, 3002 Australia
Phone: +61 (03) 9473 1191
Fax: +61 (03) 9473 1122
http://www.deafsports.org.au
E-mail: john.hook@deafsports.org.au

Canadian Amputee Sports Association
399 Pre-den-Haut Street, Memranmcook, New Brunswick, E4K 1K5 Canada
Phone: 506-758-3096
Fax: 506-851-2599
http://www.interlog.com/~ampsport/index.html
E-mail: quybel@rogers.com

Canadian Paraplegic Association Ontario
520 Sutherland Drive, Toronto, Ontario, M4G 3V9 Canada
Phone: 416-422-5644
Fax: 416-422-5943
http://www.canparaplegic.org
E-mail: info@canparaplegic.org

Canadian Wheelchair Sports Association
#108-2255 St. Laurent Boulevard, Ottawa, Ontario, K1G 4K3 Canada
Phone: 613-523-0004
Fax: 613-523-0419
http://www.cwsa.ca
E-mail: info@cwsa.ca

Cerebral Palsy International Sport & Recreation Association
Post Office Box 16, 6666 ZG, Heterren, The Netherlands
Phone: +31 26 47 22 593
Fax: +31 26 47 23 914
http://www.cpisra.org
E-mail: contact@cpisra.org

Cerebral Palsy Sports Association of British Columbia
6235A 136 Street, Surrey, British Columbia, V3X 1H3 Canada
Phone: 877-711-3111; 604-599-5240
Fax: 604-599-5241
http://www.cpsports.com
E-mail: sportinfo@telus.net

Disabled Sports USA
451 Hungerford Drive, Suite 100, Rockville, MD 20850
Phone: 301-217-0960
Fax: 301-217-0968
http://www.dsusa.org
E-mail: information@dsusa.org

Dwarf Athletic Association of America
418 Willow Way, Lewisville, TX 75077
Phone: 972-317-8299
Fax: 972-966-0184
http://www.daaa.org
E-mail: Daaa@flash.net

International Blind Sport Association
c/o Da Pieve Via Luigi Vaccari, 2 I-41100, Modena, Italy
Phone: +39 059 223543
Fax: +39 059 223543
http://www.ibsa.es
E-mail: silvia.aldini@libero.it

International Committee of Sports for the Deaf
528 Trail Avenue, Frederick, MD 21701
Fax: 301-620-2990
http://www.deaflympics.com
E-mail: info@ciss.org

International Paralympic Committee
Adenauerallee 212-214, Bonn, 53113 Germany
Phone: +49-228-2097-200
Fax: +49-228-2097-209
http://www.paralympic.org
E-mail: info@paralympic.org

Leisure Education for Exceptional People
929 North 4th Street, Mankato, MN 56001
Phone: 507-387-5122
Fax: 507-387-1676
http://www.mankatoleep.org
E-mail: leep@hickorytech.net

National Disability Sports Alliance
25 West Independence Way, Kingston, RI 02881
Phone: 401-792-7130
Fax: 401-792-7132
http://www.ndsaonline.org
E-mail: info@ndsaonline.org

National Sports Center for the Disabled
Post Office Box 1290, Winter Park, CO 80482
Phone: 970-726-1540; 303-293-5711
Fax: 303-293-5448
http://www.nscd.org
E-mail: info@nscd.org

Special Olympics International
1133 19th Street NW, Washington, DC 20036
Phone: 202-628-3630
Fax: 202-824-0200
http://www.specialolympics.org
E-mail: info@specialolympics.org

United States Association of Blind Athletes
33 North Institute Street, Colorado Springs, CO
    80903
Phone: 719-630-0422
Fax: 719-630-0616
http://www.usaba.org
E-mail: mlucas@usaba.org

USA Deaf Sports Federation
102 North Krohn Place, Sioux Falls, SD 57103
Phone: 605-367-5761; 605-367-5760
Fax: 605-997-6625
http://www.usdeafsports.org
E-mail: HomeOffice@usdeafsports.org

Wheelchair Sports, USA
Post Office Box 5366, Kendall Park, NJ 08824
Phone: 733-422-4546
Fax: 733-422-4546
http://www.wsusa.org
E-mail: wsusa@aol.com

Wheelchair Sports Worldwide
Olympic Village, Guttmann Road, Aylesbury
    Bucks, HP21 9PP United Kingdom
Phone: +44 (0) 01296 436179
Fax: +44 (0) 01296 436484
http://www.wsw.org.uk
E-mail: info@wsw.org.uk

ORGANIZATION BY SPORTS

Archery

Wheelchair Archers, USA
6020 Pioneer Park Place, Langley, WA 98260
Phone: 360-321-5979
Fax: 206-546-4609
E-mail: bowcoach@whidbeyisland.com

Billiards

National Wheelchair Billiards Association
4345 Beverly Street, Suite D, Colorado Springs, CO
    80918
Phone: 719-264-8300
Fax: 719-264-0900
E-mail: steve@bca-pool.com

Boccia

International Boccia Committee
http://www.bocciainternational.com
E-mail: peter.pearse@ntlworld.com

Bowling

American Blind Bowling Association
1735 Blair Road SW, Roanoke, VA 24015
Phone: 540-982-3838
E-mail: abbapres@aol.com

American Wheelchair Bowling Association
Post Office Box 69, Clover, VA 24534
Phone: 434-454-2268
Fax: 434-454-6276
http://www.awba.org
E-mail: bowlawba@aol.com

Canadian Deaf Bowling Association
350-1367 West Broadway, Vancouver, British
    Columbia, V6H 4A9 Canada
http://www.cdba.ca

Independent Disabled Tenpin Bowlers of the
    Australian Capital Territory
Post Office Box 1738, Tuggeranong, Australian
    Capital Territory, 2901 Australia
Phone: +61 (02)62922426
Fax: +61 (02)62922280
E-mail: mecooke@austarmetro.com.au

United States Deaf Bowling Federation
8071 Cherrystone Avenue, Panorama City, CA
91402
Phone: 818-785-1478
Fax : 818-785-1478
http://hometown.aol.com/kchodak/myhomepage/
profile.html
E-mail: kchodal@aol.com

Equestrian/Horseback Riding

Federation of Riding for the Disabled International
Post Office Box 886, Werribee, Victoria, 3030
Australia
Phone: +61 3 9731 7282
Fax: +61 3 9731 7395
http://www.frdi.net
E-mail: frdi@rda.org.au

National Center for Equine Facilitated Therapy
5001 Woodside Road, Woodside, CA 94062
Phone: 650-851-2271
Fax: 650-851-3480
http://www.nceft.com
E-mail: rosi@nceft.com

North American Riding for the Handicapped
Association
Post Office Box 33150, Denver, CO 80233
Phone: 800-369-RIDE (800-369-7433)
FAX: 303-252-4610
http://narha.org
E-mail: narha@narha.org

Fencing

Association of Wheelchair Fencing in Germany
Schluesselwiesen 35 D-70186, Stuttgart, Germany
Phone: +49 711 470 83 25
Fax: +49 711 470 8325
http://www.rollstuhlfechten.de
E-mail: fechten@rollstuhlsport.de

Espada Fencing Club (United Kingdom)
Phone: +44 (0)7811 238195
http://www.espadafencing.co.uk
E-mail: info@espadafencing.co.uk

International Wheelchair Fencing Committee
http://www.iwfencing.com
E-mail: iwfencing@iwfencing.com

Japan Wheelchair Fencing Association
23 Shimogamo-Takagicho, Sakyoku, Kyoto, Japan
606-0864
Phone: +81 75 781 1676
Fax: +81 75 781 1676
http://www.jwfa.gr.jp
E-mail: jwfa@jwfa.gr.jp

The Louisville Fencing Center
1401 West Muhammad Ali Boulevard, Louisville,
KY 40203
Phone: 502-504-5004
http://www.louisvillefencing.org
E-mail: I.stawicki@insightbb.com

Goalball

Goalball New Zealand
http://goalball-nz.org
E-mail: goalball@paradise.net.nz

Minnesota Goalball
3457 Zenith Avenue North, Robbinsdale, MN
55422
Phone: 763-587-4963
Fax: 763-529-9124
http://www.mngoalball.org
E-mail: info@mngoalball.org

Golf

Association of Disabled American Golfers
Post Office Box 280649, Lakewood, CO 80228
Phone: 303-922-5228
Fax: 303-969-0447
E-mail: adag@usga.org

Australian Blind Golfers Association
http://www.blindgolf.org.au
E-mail: info@blindgolf.org.au

Canadian Deaf Golf Association
9707 105th Street, #801, Edmonton, Alberta, T5K
2Y4, Canada
http://www.cdga.net
E-mail: jrose641@golden.net

Deaf Golf Association
http://www.deafgolf.com
E-mail: rhsark@aol.com

Handcycling

Handcycling Association UK
4 Monty Place, Fenton, Stoke on Trent, ST4 3RQ
  United Kingdom
Phone: +44 (0)1782 593647
http://www.handcyclinguk.org.uk
E-mail: masbury@ukonline.co.uk

Handcycling Australia
Phone: +61 (0)8 9443 4833
Fax: +61 (0)8 9443 4252
http://www.handcycling.org.au
E-mail: gary@wheelchairsportswa.org.au

United States Handcycling
Post Office Box 3538, Evergreen, CO 80439
Phone: 303-459-4159
http://www.ushf.org
E-mail: info@ushf.org

Quad Rugby

International Wheelchair Rugby Federation
http://www.iwrf.com

United States Quad Rugby Association
5861 White Cypress Drive, Lake Worth, FL 33467
Phone: 561-964-1712
Fax: 888-453-0773
http://www.quadrugby.com
E-mail: dragonsedge@juno.com

Racquetball

National Wheelchair Racquetball Association
c/o American Amateur Racquetball Association,
  815 North Weber, Colorado Springs, CO 80903
Phone: 719-636-5396

Road Racing

International Wheelchair Road Racers Club, Inc.
30 Myano Lane, Stamford, CT 06902
Phone: 203-967-2231

Oita International Wheelchair Marathon
  Organizing Committee
1393 Kamegawa, Beppu, Oita, 874-0011 Japan
http://www.wheelchair-marathon.com
E-mail: info@wheelchair-marathon.com

Shooting

The National Rifle Association
Disabled Shooting Services
11250 Waples Mill Road, Fairfax, VA 22030
Phone: 877-NRA-2000
https://www.nrahq.org/compete/disabled.asp
E-mail: Membership@nrahq.org

National Wheelchair Shooting Federation
11250 Waples Mill Road, Fairfax, VA 22030
Phone: 703-267-3941
Fax: 703-267-3941

Sledge Hockey

New England Bruins Sled Hockey
255 Pine Point Road, Scarborough, ME 04074
http://www.SledHockey.org
E-mail: info@sledhockey.org

U.S. Sled Hockey Association
2236 East 46th Street, Davenport, IA 52807
Phone: 563-344-9064
http://www.usahockey.com/ussha
E-mail: TQCSHA@aol.com

Soccer

American Amputee Soccer Association
http://www.ampsoccer.org
E-mail: rgh@ampsoccer.org

Softball/Baseball

Little League International Baseball and Softball
539 US Route 15 Highway, Post Office Box 3485,
  Williamsport, PA 17701
Phone: 570-326-1921
Fax: 570-326-1074
http://www.littleleague.org
E-mail: ckester@littleleague.org

The National Beep Baseball Association
5568 Boulder Crest Street, Columbus, OH 43235
Phone: 614-442-1444
http://www.nbba.org
E-mail: secretary@nbba.org

National Softball Association for Deaf
Post Office Box 3363, Frederick, MD 21705
http://www.nsad.org
E-mail: sport_information@nsad.org

National Wheelchair Softball Association
6000 West Floyd Avenue, #110, Denver, CO 80227
Phone: 773-779-7470
http://www.wheelchairsoftball.org
E-mail: nwsainfo@yahoo.com

Swimming/Aquatics

Handicapped Scuba Association International
1104 El Prado, San Clemente, CA 92672
Phone: 949-498-4540
Fax: 949-498-6128
http://www.hsascuba.com
E-mail: hsa@hsascuba.com

United States Aquatic Association of the Deaf
2211 South Road, Baltimore, MD 21209
Phone: 410-664-3727
http://members.tripod.com/USAAD
E-mail: USAADeaf@yahoo.com

Table Tennis

American Wheelchair Table Tennis Association
23 Park Street, Port Chester, NY 10573
Phone: 914-937-3932
E-mail: johnsonjennifer@yahoo.com

Tennis

National Capital Wheelchair Tennis Association
http://www.magma.ca/~ncwta
E-mail: ncwta@magma.ca

USA Wheelchair Tennis
United States Tennis Association
70 West Red Oak Lane, White Plains, NY 10604
Phone: 914-696-7000
http://www.usta.com/usatenniswheelchair/custo
  m.sps
E-mail: volk@USTA.com

Wheelchair Tennis Federation
International Tennis Federation
Bank Lane, Roehampton, London, SW15 5XZ
  United Kingdom
Phone: +44 (0)20 8878 6464
Fax: +44 (0)20 8392 4741
http://www.itftennis.com/wheelchair
E-mail: wheelchairtennis@itftennis.com

Volleyball

Deaf Volleyball Canada
http://home.interhop.net/igowans
E-mail: mpersi@bconnex.net

Sitting Volleyball Australia
16 Station Street, Kogarah, New South Wales 2217,
  Australia
http://www.sittingvolleyball.org.au
E-mail: eaglectc@tpg.com.au

USA Volleyball Disabled Division
715 South Circle Drive, Colorado Springs, CO
  80910
Phone: 719-228-6800
Fax: 719-228-6899
http://www.usavolleyball.org/disabled
E-mail: postmaster@usav.org

Waterskiing

American Disabled Water Skiers
2681 Cove Circle, Atlanta, GA 30319
Phone: 779-452-3562
E-mail: bfurbish@mindspring.com

British Disabled Water Ski Association
Heron Lake Hythe End Road, Wraybury,
  Middlesex, TW 19 6HW United Kingdom
Phone: +44 (0)1784 483664
Fax: +44 (0)1784 482747
http://www.bdwsa.org.uk
E-mail: info@bdwsa.org.uk

International Water Ski Federation Disabled
  Council
http://www.iwsf.com/disabled/report1.htm

Water Sports

Access to Sailing
6475 East Pacific Coast Highway, Long Beach, CA
  90803
Phone: 562-433-0561
http://www.accesstosailing.org/home.html
E-mail: info@accesstosailing.org

Chesapeake Region Accessible Boating
Post Office Box 6564, Annapolis, MD 21404
http://crab-sailing.org

Weightlifting/Powerlifting

The British Weightlifting Association for The Disabled
Stoke Mandeville Stadium, Guttmann Road, Stoke Mandeville, Buckinghamshire, HP21 9PP United Kingdom
Phone: +44 (0)1296 395995
Fax: +44 (0)1296 424171
http://www.wheelpower.org.uk/sports/ dyncat.cfm?catid=16970
E-mail: sjosullivan@btinternet.com

International Paralympic Committee Powerlifting
Elzenstraat 12, Brugge 8000 Belgium
Phone: +32-50-310126
Fax: +32-50-311805
http://www.paralympic.org/release/Summer_Sport s/Powerlifting
E-mail: wautermatens@polifting.org

United States Cerebral Palsy Athletic Association
25 West Independence Way, Kingston, RI 02881
Phone: 401-874-7465
Fax: 401-874-7468
http://www.uscpaa.org
E-mail: uscpaa@mail.bbsnet.com

U.S. Wheelchair Weightlifting Federation
39 Michael Place, Levittown, PA 19057
Phone: 215-945-1964

Wheelchair Basketball

Canadian Wheelchair Basketball Association
2211 Riverside Drive, Suite B2, Ottawa, Ontario, K1H 7X5 Canada
Phone: 613-260-1296
Fax: 613-260-1456
http://www.cwba.ca
E-mail: cwba@cwba.ca

Great Britain Wheelchair Basketball Association
Technology Center, Suite B, Epinal Way, Loughborough, Leiscestershire, LE11 3GE United Kingdom
Phone: +44 (0)1509 631671
Fax: +44 (0)1509 631672
http://www.gbwba.org.uk
E-mail: c.bethel@gbwba.org.uk

International Wheelchair Basketball Federation
http://www.iwbf.org
E-mail: iwbf@optusnet.com.au

National Wheelchair Basketball Association
6165 Lehman Drive, Suite 101, Colorado Springs, CO 80918
Phone: 719-266-4082
Fax: 719-266-4876
http://www.nwba.org
E-mail: toddhatfield@nwba.org

Wheelchair Football

The Universal Wheelchair Football Association
9555 Plainfield Road, Cincinnati, OH 45236
Phone: 513-792-8625
Fax: 513-792-8624
E-mail: john.kraimer@uc.edu

Wheelchair Hockey

Australian Electric Wheelchair Hockey Association
Post Office Box 490, South Hurstville, New South Wales, 2221 Australia
Phone: +61 2 9580 8351
http://www.auselectricwheelchairhockey.com
E-mail: president@auselectricwheelchairhockey.com

Canadian Electric Wheelchair Hockey Association
Phone: 416-757-8544
http://www.geocities.com/cewha
E-mail: daube@whitecapcanada.com

U.S. Electric Wheelchair Hockey Association
7216 39th Avenue North, Minneapolis, MN 55427
Phone: 763-535-4736
http://www.powerhockey.com
E-mail: info@powerhockey.com

Winter Sports

Disabled Sports USA
451 Hungerford Drive, Suite 100, Rockville, MD 20850
Phone: 301-217-0960
Fax: 301-217-0968
http://www.dsusa.org
E-mail: information@dsusa.org

Disabled WinterSport Australia
15 Beverly Street, Merimbula, New South Wales, 2548 Australia
Phone: +61 (02) 6495 2082
Fax: +61 (02) 6495 2034
http://www.disabledwintersport.com.au
E-mail: finsko@biqpond.net.au

Sitski
504 Brett Place, South Plainfield, NJ 07080
Phone: 908-313-5590
Fax: 908-668-1634
http://www.sitski.com
E-mail: sitski@sitski.com; sitskitom@hotmail.com

The Skating Association for the Blind and
   Handicapped
1200 East and West Road, West Seneca, NY 14222
Phone: 716-675-7222
http://www.sabahinc.org
E-mail: sabah@sabahinc.org

United States Deaf Ski & Snowboard Association
1772 Saddle Hill Drive, Logan, UT 84321
Phone: 435-752-2702
http://www.usdssa.org
E-mail: USDSSA_Secretary@usdssa.org

U.S. Disabled Ski Team
1500 Kearns Boulevard, Box 100, Park City, UT
   84060
Phone: 435-649-3613
Fax: 435-649-3613
http://www.ussa.org
E-mail: info@ussa.org

ADAPTIVE EQUIPMENT FOR SPORTS AND RECREATION

Adapted Physical Education/Sports Equipment

Flaghouse, Inc.
601 Flaghouse Drive, Hasbrouck Heights, NJ 07604
Phone: 800-793-7900
Fax: 800-793-7922
http://www.flaghouse.com
E-mail: feedback@flaghouse.com

Gym Closet
Post Office Box 549, Temperance, MI 48182
Phone: 800-445-8873
Fax: 810-997-4866
http://www.gymcloset.com
E-mail: email@gymcloset.com

Gopher Sport
220 24th Avenue NW, Post Office Box 998,
   Owatonna, MN 55060
Phone: 800-533-0446
Fax: 800-451-4855
http://www.gophersport.com
E-mail: email@gophersport.com

S & S Worldwide
75 Mill Street, Colchester, CT 06415
Phone: 800-288-9941
Fax: 800-566-6678
http://www.ssww.com
E-mail: service@ssww.com

Sportime
3155 Northwoods Parkway, Norcross, GA 30071
Phone: 800-283-5700
Fax: 800-845-1535
http://sportime.com
E-mail: catalog.request@sportime.com

US Games
Post Office Box 7726, Dallas, TX 75209
Phone: 800-327-0484
Fax: 800-899-0149
http://www.us-games.com
E-mail: feedusq@sportsupplygroup.com

Bibs

Event Promotion Supply
11420 East 51st Avenue, Denver, CO 80239
Phone: 303-317-1717
Fax: 303-371-9149
http://www.eps-doublet.com
E-mail: allisont@eps-doublet.com

Reliable Racing Supply, Inc.
643 Upper Glen Street, Queensbury, NY 12804
Phone: 800-274-6815
Fax: 800-585-4443
http://www.reliableracing.com
E-mail: customerservice@reliableracing.com

Bi Skis

Mountain Man
720 Front Street, Bozeman, MT 59715
Phone: 406-587-0310
Fax: 406-585-5513
E-mail: darvinv@avicom.net

Spokes'n Motion
2225 South Jason Street, Denver, CO 80223
Phone: 303-922-0605
Fax: 303-922-7943
http://www.spokesnmotion.com
E-mail: info@spokesnmotion.com

Handcycles

American Wheel Sports
721 North Taft Hill, Fort Collins, CO 80521
Phone: 800-800-5828; 303-221-4290

Angletech
318 North Highway 67, Post Office Box 1893,
    Woodland Park, CO 80866
Phone: 719-687-7475
http://www.angletechcycles.com
E-mail: angletech@att.net

Freedom Factory
1943 Karen Circle, Cookeville, TN 38506
Phone: 931-520-4898
Fax: 931-520-4864
http://www.freedomfactory.org
E-mail: info@freedomfactory.org

Lightning Handcycles
360 Sepulveda Boulevard, Suite 1005, El Segundo,
    CA 90245
Phone: 888-426-3292
Fax: 310-335-1543
http://www.handcycle.com
E-mail: information@handcycle.com

Sportaid
78 Bay Creek Road, Loganville, GA 30052
Phone: 800-743-7203
Fax: 770-554-5944
http://www.sportaid.com
E-mail: Stuff@sportaid.com

Hockey/Klondike Sleds

Spokes 'n Motion Bi Ski
2225 South Platte River Drive, West Denver, CO
    80223
Phone: 303-922-0605
Fax: 303-922-7943
http://www.spokesnmotion.com
E-mail: info@spokesnmotion.com

Mono-Skis

Freedom Factory
1943 Karen Circle, Cookeville, TN 38506
Phone: 931-520-4898
Fax: 931-520-4864
http://www.freedomfactory.org
E-mail: info@freedomfactory.org

Grove Innovations, Inc.
120 West Church, Box 185, Centre Hall, PA 16828
Phone: 814-364-2677
Fax: 814-364-2760
E-mail: willinnovate@hotmail.com

Nordic Sit-Ski

Jackson XC
153 Main Street, Jackson, NH 03846
Phone: 603-383-9355
http://www.jacksonxc.org/Good_stuff_4_sale.htm
E-mail: info@jacksonxc.org

Outriggers

LaCome, Inc.
Post Office Box 1026, Questa, NM 87556
Phone: 505-586-0356

Radventures, Inc.
20755 Southwest 238th Place, Sherwood, OR
    97140
Phone: 971-219-4897
Fax: 503-628-0517
http://www.yetti-radventures.com
E-mail: RADYETTI@aol.com

Shadow Rehabilitation Equipment Association
8030 South Willow Street, Unit 4, Manchester,
    NH 03103
Phone: 603-645-5200

Ski Doctor: Shockshaft
609 Munroe Street, Sacramento, CA 95825
Phone: 916-488-5398

Spokes'n Motion
2225 South Jason Street, Denver, CO 80223
Phone: 303-922-0605
Fax: 303-922-7943
http://www.spokesnmotion.com
E-mail: info@spokesnmotion.com

Tennis Wheelchairs

SpinLife
1108 City Park Avenue, Columbus, OH 43206
Phone: 614-449-8123
Fax: 888-873-6543
http://www.spinlife.com
E-mail: customerservice@spinlife.com

Sportaid
78 Bay Creek Road, Loganville, GA 30052
Phone: 800-743-7203
Fax: 770-554-5944
http://www.sportaid.com
E-mail: Stuff@sportaid.com

Tip Retention, Ski Bras

SKI-EZE Products International, Inc.
85 Woodmere Road, Bridgeport, CT 06610
Phone: 203-372-2223
Fax: 203-372-7175
http://www.ski-eze.com

Index

Page numbers followed by *f* and *t* indicate figures and tables, respectively.